REAL ESTATE FINANCE AND INVESTMENTS

RISKS AND OPPORTUNITIES

Peter Linneman, PhD
Bruce Kirsch, REFAI®
Edition 5.2

REAL ESTATE FINANCE AND INVESTMENTS:
RISKS AND OPPORTUNITIES
EDITION 5.2

Copyright © 2018-2022 by Dr. Peter Linneman

Authors: Dr. Peter Linneman and Bruce Kirsch, REFAI®

Editor: Deborah C. Moy

Contributors: Lou Dimitrov, Minzhou Jin,
Mukund Krishnaswami, Matthew R Larriva, CFA,
Deborah C. Moy

Assistant Editing Team: Christopher Braatz, Robyn Choo,
Erez Cohen, Anoop Dave, Manning Feng, James Forman,
Michael Franzese, Michael Givner, Robert Greco,
Jason Gruenbaum, Karren Henderson, Avivah Hotimsky,
Jared Joella, Jeremiah Kane, Jared Karpf, Chresten Knaff,
Adam Leslie, Douglas Linneman, Bharat Nagaswami,
Jared Prushansky, Joshua Schwartz, Brendan Stone,
Adi Weinstein, Eugene Wong, Yucheng Tina Xu, Laura Yablon

Project Coordinator: Douglas Linneman

Cover Art: Frances Wan, Eugene Wong

ARGUS Chapter courtesy of: Altus Group
John Lim, Katie Foley

ISBN: 978-1-7923-7713-6

Linneman Associates
The Victory Building
1001 Chestnut Street, Suite 101
Philadelphia, PA 19107
www.linnemanassociates.com

Table of Contents

PREFACE   I

ABOUT THE AUTHOR: PETER LINNEMAN, PhD | ACKNOWLEDGEMENTS   II

ABOUT THE AUTHOR: BRUCE KIRSCH, REFAI® | ACKNOWLEDGEMENTS   IV

ABOUT THE EDITOR: DEBORAH C. MOY | ACKNOWLEDGEMENTS   VI

TESTIMONIALS   VIII

PERMISSIONS TO RE-PRINT   XII

CHAPTER	TITLE	PAGE
1	INTRODUCTION: RISKS AND OPPORTUNITIES	1
2	WHAT IS REAL ESTATE AND WHO OWNS IT?	16
3	INTERNATIONAL REAL ESTATE INVESTING	36
4	THE FUNDAMENTALS OF COMMERCIAL LEASES	45
5	PROPERTY-LEVEL PRO FORMA ANALYSIS	55
6	FINANCIAL MODELING	84
7	REAL ESTATE DUE DILIGENCE ANALYSIS	98
8	ANALYZING METROPOLITAN LONG-TERM GROWTH PATTERNS	104
9	THE USE AND SELECTION OF CAP RATES	120
Chapter 9 Supplement A	"A Disconnect in Real Estate Pricing?" *Wharton Real Estate Review*, Spring 2004, Peter Linneman	134
Chapter 9 Supplement B	"The Equitization of Real Estate" *Wharton Real Estate Review*, Fall 2006, Peter Linneman	140
Chapter 9 Supplement C	"If Interest Rates Determine Cap Rates, Where Is the Evidence?" *The Linneman Letter*, Fall 2020 Vol. 20, Issue 3	153
Chapter 9 Supplement D	"What Determines Cap Rates?" *The Linneman Letter*, Summer 2015 Vol. 15, Issue 2	163
10	DEVELOPMENT PRO FORMA ANALYSIS	165
11	DEVELOPMENT FEASIBILITY ANALYSIS	178
12	REAL ESTATE COMPANY ANALYSIS	194

CHAPTER	TITLE	PAGE
13	DISTRESSED REAL ESTATE LOAN AND BANKRUPTCY BASICS	206
14	SHOULD YOU BORROW?	211
15	THE USE OF DEBT AND MORTGAGES	225
16	SOURCES OF LONG- AND SHORT-TERM DEBT	238
17	GROUND LEASES AS A SOURCE OF FINANCE	249
18	REAL ESTATE OWNER EXIT STRATEGIES	256
19	REAL ESTATE PRIVATE EQUITY FUNDS	266
20	INVESTMENT RETURN PROFILES	279
21	REITs AND LIQUID REAL ESTATE	298
22	THE FORCES CHANGING THE REAL ESTATE INDUSTRY FOREVER	309
23	CORPORATE REAL ESTATE DECISION MAKING	320
24	SOME OBSERVATIONS ON REAL ESTATE ENTREPRENEURSHIP	334
25	REAL ESTATE CYCLES	344
26	THERE ARE A LOT OF RIGHT WAYS TO DO IT	359
Prerequisite I	THE BASICS OF DISCOUNTED CASH FLOW & NET PRESENT VALUE ANALYSES	364
Prerequisite II	INTERNAL RATE OF RETURN	378
Prerequisite III	AMORTIZATION FUNDAMENTALS	384
Supplemental I	THE RETURN CHARACTERISTICS OF COMMERCIAL REAL ESTATE	397
Supplemental IA	"The Return Volatility of Publicly- and Privately-Owned Real Estate" *Wharton Real Estate Review*, Fall 2004, Peter Linneman	404
Supplemental II	CMBS CASE STUDY	412
Supplemental III	CAREERS IN REAL ESTATE	419
Supplemental IV	ARGUS Enterprise by ARGUS Software	423
Supplemental V	CASES	441
INDEX		462

PREFACE

This textbook explores the key concepts of real estate finance and investment strategy. It is not a formulaic analysis of numbers that yield "the answer" to any and all real estate investment decisions. Instead, this book is designed to help you understand that there is no singular or simplistic answer to any real estate finance problem. Rather, real estate finance is fundamentally driven by judgment and experience, with an eye to the numbers. The goal of this book is to help you embark upon the long and unending road of building your judgment.

The chapters in the text assume that you have a mastery of the foundational material in the Prerequisite chapters, including loan amortization, discounted cash flows, net present value, and IRR. Before you start, be absolutely certain that you are comfortable with the materials in these Prerequisite chapters. The Supplemental chapters provide interesting information, but are not essential for you to master the chapters in the text.

The formulas and templates found in the chapters and in the Online Companion will help you assemble and organize information. However, mastering these tools is merely the beginning — not the end — of real estate finance. This book focuses on what to do after you have mastered the basic financial tools. Just as knowing how to use a hammer and saw is not the same as building a wonderful building that will last the ages, knowing how to build a financial model and calculating the internal rate of return is not the same as making a profitable real estate investment. And no one would ever fly on a plane which has only been modeled. Judgment comes one mistake at a time, and better to make some of those mistakes in the classroom than "in real life."

Please note that throughout the text, for the purpose of conveying concepts in a more digestible manner, we assume that loans and loan debt service reflect interest-only loans, unless otherwise specified.

Additionally, please take note of the Online Companion icons in each chapter, as they provide you with valuable hands-on exercises and point you to additional audio content that will enrich your learning experience. You can access the Online Companion here: Textbook.GetREFM.com/toc/.

We hope you enjoy the book.

Peter Linneman, PhD   Bruce Kirsch, REFAI®

ABOUT THE AUTHOR: PETER LINNEMAN, PhD

Dr. Peter Linneman is the Emeritus Albert Sussman Professor of Real Estate and Public Policy at the Wharton School of Business, the University of Pennsylvania. For over 40 years he has been one of the nation's top real estate scholars, publishing over 100 papers on topics including real estate capital markets, public real estate companies, corporate real estate, real estate private equity funds, urban markets, and homeownership. His writings, lectures and advice to major real estate players have established him as one of the most influential thought leaders in the real estate industry.

He was the founding co-editor of the *Wharton Real Estate Review*, and from 1985-1998 served as the Director of Wharton's prestigious Samuel Zell and Robert Lurie Real Estate Center. In addition, he was the founding Chairman of Wharton's Real Estate Department. His courses on real estate research and real estate development were popular with Wharton students for over two decades.

As the Founding Principal of Linneman Associates, he has served for over 40 years as a consultant to numerous leading real estate companies and investors around the world. *The Linneman Letter* is one of the most respected economic and real estate market research publications in the industry. Among his many assignments as a corporate board member was serving as Chairman of Rockefeller Center Properties REIT, leading the successful foreclosure and sale of Rockefeller Center in 1995. He has served as a director of over 20 public and private corporations. He was Vice Chairman of American Realty and a Senior Managing Director of Equity Group Investments, and is founder and CEO of the American Land Fund, KL Realty and AOZA. He has been named one of the "25 Most Influential People in Real Estate" by *Realtor Magazine*, "One of the 100 Most Powerful People in New York Real Estate" by the *New York Observer*, and one of the "Most Influential People in Real Estate" by *Commercial Property Executive*. He also is the recipient of Wharton's Zell-Lurie Real Estate Center's Lifetime Achievement Award and received PREA's prestigious Graaskamp's Award for Lifetime Achievement in Real Estate Research. His rare combination of scholarly discipline and industry experience makes him a popular speaker.

Raised in Lima, Ohio, he graduated from Ashland University, before receiving both his Masters and Doctorate degrees in Economics from the University of Chicago. Married for well over 48 years, he remains physically active. He and his wife Kathy share their lives with their beloved god-daughters and their children, an assortment of nieces and nephews, and the wonderful children in their *Save A Mind, Elimu charity* program.

DR. LINNEMAN'S ACKNOWLEDGEMENTS

Too often we fail to acknowledge the people who shape our lives. As such, I must acknowledge some special people who have impacted my life. Anything I have achieved is attributable to Lucille G. Ford. Lucille is a great teacher, mentor, and lifelong friend, who literally changed my life. Without her love, friendship, and generosity, neither my career nor this book, would exist. Tom Shockney is another lifelong friend and source of amazement, admiration, and fun.

At the University of Chicago, I was deeply influenced and assisted by many rigorous and creative scholars, most notably Gary Becker, George Stigler, George Tolley, Jim Heckman, Theodore W. Schultz, and Milton Friedman. John Abowd was a terrific friend, study mate and colleague. During my many years at Wharton, I was blessed with a wise, wonderful, and loving mentor of irreplaceable value in Anita Summers. In addition, Tom Dunfee, Joe Gyourko, Jeremy Siegel, and Susan Wachter found ways to stimulate and challenge me, while Russell Palmer gave me the opportunity to create and lead Wharton's real estate program.

My thought process was unalterably changed by my many friends in the real estate industry over the past 40 years. I continually learn from their creativity, drive, and ingenuity. While it is impossible to identify all of these influences, Dean Adler, Claude Ballard, Peter Bedford, Albert Behler, Marshall Bennett, Chaim Katzman, Christine Kwak, Ira Lubert, David Marshall, Debbie Moy, Albert Ratner, Shelly Seevak, A. Alfred Taubman, Ron Terwilliger, Bill Tucker, Samuel Zell, and Michael von Zitzewitz merit special thanks. In spite of their many lessons, I marvel at how little I know, and relish the fact that so much remains to be learned.

I apologize to the roughly 4,000 students who suffered in my classes over the years, and hope that they have forgiven my ignorance and impatience.

I was blessed to have worked with Anoop Dave and Jared Prushansky on the first edition of this book. If you find this book is useful, they deserve all of the credit. Christopher Braatz, Robyn Choo, Erez Cohen, Manning Feng, James Forman, Michael Francese, Michael Givner, Robert Greco, Jason Gruenbaum, Avivah Hotimsky, Jared Joella, Jeremiah Kane, Jared Karpf, Chresten Knaff, Adam Leslie, Bharat Nagaswami, Joshua Schwartz, Brendan Stone, Adi Weinstein, Eugene Wong, Laura Yablon and Tina Xu all provided assistance on subsequent editions of this book, as has my brother Douglas Linneman. Thank you to Debbie Moy, a former student and longtime colleague and friend, who has worked tirelessly editing this edition.

My former student, Bruce Kirsch, has not only diligently edited and improved previous editions but has contributed mightily to enhance this edition as my co-author. In addition, Bruce has created an online interview series to accompany the book, which is available at the Linneman Associates website, www.linnemanassociates.com.

Thank you also to John Lim and Katie Foley of ARGUS Software, Inc. for the ARGUS chapter.

In closing, I must thank Felicitas Abel, Lisa Anderson, Mercy Angaine, Kelley Brasfield, Kathy Oberkircher, Jessica Pretzell, Celina Richters, and Leslie Albrecht for being wonderful, loving, and supportive "daughters."

Never least, but too often last in my focus, is my soul mate Kathy, who for over five decades has suffered my wanderlust, impatience, and narcissism. My greatest piece of life and career advice is to marry a saint!

ABOUT THE AUTHOR: BRUCE KIRSCH, REFAI®

Bruce Kirsch, REFAI® is the founder and CEO of Real Estate Financial Modeling, LLC (GetREFM.com). Mr. Kirsch has trained thousands of university real estate students and industry professionals in Excel-based financial modeling for commercial real estate transactions. In addition, REFM's self-study products, Excel-based modeling templates and its Valuate® investment analysis software are used by more than 250,000 professionals.

Along with Peter Linneman, Mr. Kirsch is the co-author of the acclaimed **Real Estate Finance and Investments Certification Program (REFAI®)** (GetREFM.com/refai/), a rigorous self-study credential program tied to this textbook. The REFAI program is available to universities, corporations and individuals.

Mr. Kirsch's firm has assisted with modeling for the raising of billions of dollars of equity and debt for individual property acquisitions and developments, as well as for major mixed-use projects and private equity funds. Mr. Kirsch has also maintained a blog on real estate financial modeling, *Model for Success*, authoring more than 500 posts.

Mr. Kirsch began his real estate career at CB Richard Ellis, where he marketed highrise New York City office buildings for re-development in the Midtown Manhattan Investment Properties Institutional Group. After CBRE, Mr. Kirsch was recruited to lead acquisitions at Metropolis Development Company, and later joined The Clarett Group, a programmatic development partner of Prudential Global Investment Management.

While at The Clarett Group, Mr. Kirsch was responsible for making development site acquisition recommendations for office, condominium, and multi-family investment opportunities in the greater Washington, D.C. metropolitan area. In addition, Mr. Kirsch had significant day-to-day project management responsibilities for the entitlement, financing and marketing of the company's existing D.C.-area development portfolio.

Mr. Kirsch holds an MBA in Real Estate from The Wharton School of the University of Pennsylvania, where he was a student of Dr. Linneman's and was awarded the Benjamin Franklin Kahn/Washington Real Estate Investment Trust Award for academic excellence. Prior to Wharton, Mr. Kirsch performed quantitative equity research on the technology sector at The Capital Group Companies. Mr. Kirsch served as an Adjunct Faculty member in real estate finance at Georgetown University School of Continuing Studies. Mr. Kirsch graduated with a BA in Communication from Stanford University.

MR. KIRSCH'S ACKNOWLEDGEMENTS

I owe so much to so many who have helped me selflessly along the way. First and foremost, I am grateful for my wife Elizabeth's unwavering partnership, encouragement and support of my career and life since the day we met. I am blessed to have ended up with such a strong, intelligent and caring best friend.

I am obliged to Peter Linneman for bringing his prodigious talent and work ethic to bear on the field of commercial real estate finance and investments. As one of his former graduate students, I am incredibly fortunate to have benefited firsthand from Peter's singular capacity and passion for teaching complex concepts in an elegant manner. I continue to be humbled by Peter's intellect and his generosity in allowing me to contribute to his legacy, and am inspired by his continued thirst for knowledge about real estate.

I owe a special thank you to Charles "Chuck" Schilke, who saw promise in my teaching abilities and allowed me to instruct as faculty at Georgetown University. In addition, Chuck introduced me to Bulkeley "Bucky" Banks, an REFM colleague of many years, who impressed me with his brilliance and perseverance, and taught me that keeping a sense of humor is paramount to success. Thank you to Bucky for assisting in the shaping of the textbook Online Companion and for authoring REFAI® testing content.

I am ever grateful for Doug Linneman's support and trust in me in pitching in as a quasi-team member of Linneman Associates on the textbook front, and allowing me to help him drive the Linneman Associates mission forward. Doug is an inspiration on the organizational and marketing front.

A huge thank you to Debbie Moy, who has elevated this textbook significantly through her incredible laser focus and deep grasp of the world of real estate finance and investments. She has also been eagle-eyed yet kind in her enforcement of grammatical rules, for which I now have a higher regard. Amazing job!

Thank you to all of my Wharton School and University of Pennsylvania real estate professors and lecturers, including Joseph Gyourko, Robert Inman, Asuka Nakahara, Georgette Chapman Phillips, and Witold Rybczynski, among others. I am also appreciative of how Janice Leberman and Ron Smith of the Zell-Lurie Center helped me so many times as I was trying to break into real estate. And I am thankful for Kenneth Balin, who served as my mentor through the Center and taught me many lessons about the real estate business.

Thank you also to my Wharton MBA real estate course classmates and to my colleagues and mentors from the Washington, D.C. real estate world, for your patience and generosity in helping me learn about the real estate business.

Last but not least, I am also blessed to have had the support of my parents and brother and extended family in my pursuits. The examples you have set in your own lives and careers continue to inspire and drive me daily. Thank you.

And to my children, I wish you an education and career filled with all the great challenges, colleagues and adventure that I have been so lucky to have. As you have re-taught me, when we fall, we get right back up and try again.

ABOUT THE EDITOR: DEBORAH C. MOY

Deborah Moy is a Principal of Linneman Associates, where she is the Managing Editor of *The Linneman Letter*, the highly regarded quarterly publication focusing on commercial real estate and macroeconomic analysis. *The Linneman Letter* covers the office, industrial, multifamily, retail, hotel, and senior housing sectors across more than 40 metropolitan areas. Ms. Moy also oversees Linneman Associates' strategic consulting projects including investment strategy, portfolio analysis, industry white papers, and market research.

She has co-authored several articles published in the Wharton Real Estate Review. She received a 2011 Outstanding Paper Award from the Emerald Literati Network as a co-author of "Responsibility for and performance of corporate real estate functions," published in the *Journal of Corporate Real Estate* (Vol. 12 No. 1, 2010).

Ms. Moy previously worked at Lehman Brothers in its Real Estate Investment Banking Division in New York, primarily working with clients issuing corporate and mortgage debt. Prior to that, she was with Prudential Real Estate Investors (PREI) in its Research division, responsible for the Northeast Region of the U.S. She also worked in Sales and Acquisitions and Asset Management at PREI.

Ms. Moy received her Bachelor of Arts degree in Economics from Rutgers University and is a member of the Phi Beta Kappa Honor Society. She also holds a Master of Business Administration in finance and real estate from the Wharton School of Business, the University of Pennsylvania. She is currently a board member and treasurer of Chinese Service Center USA, a cultural and education-based non-profit, and previously served as co-principal of Bergen Chinese School. She also enjoys volunteering in her community through the Girls Scouts and her church. She is married and resides in Northern New Jersey with her husband and two daughters.

MS. MOY'S ACKNOWLEDGEMENTS

I am indebted to Peter Linneman, who as my professor, mentor, and business partner, has been a guiding presence in my career. I am grateful for his insights, encouragement, and trust and am thrilled to have been a part of edition 5.2 of Risks and Opportunities.

Much appreciation also goes to Bruce Kirsch, with whom I have spent countless hours commiserating on everything from the meticulous dissection of real estate finance to the most mundane rules of grammar and punctuation.

Looking back, I am also thankful to have had the guidance of my academic advisors, Professor/Dean James Hughes (urban planning) and the late Professor Michael Taussig (economics) at Rutgers, as well as real estate finance Professor Joe Gyourko at Wharton.

A special and fond shout-out goes to those who guided me through my years in corporate America: Mike Miles, Barry Ziering, Bill Anderson, Paul Bordogna, Avis Tsuya, Sheri Nixon, Bob Lieber, and Rob Heller.

Much appreciation to my long-time business partner Mukund Krishnaswami and trusted collaborator Christine Kwak, both of whom exemplify enduring entrepreneurial spirit; and to my current and former Linneman colleagues Doug Linneman, Jocelyn Cassidy, Kathy Linneman, Karren Henderson, Christine Burk, Christopher Sylvan, and our many student interns for keeping the wheels greased in our small but far-reaching operation. A heartfelt acknowledgement in memory of Ronen Katz, analyst extraordinaire, who accomplished so much but left us too soon.

And finally, profound gratitude to my family: my parents for teaching me the importance of giving back to the community, being kind, and the value of a dollar; my grandparents for their entrepreneurial spirit and strong work ethic, and for making courageous life choices; my sisters who supported and watched over me and forged paths before me to make mine easier; to my husband for his humor, love, and patience in supporting my entrepreneurial endeavors; and to my girls, who keep me grounded and whom I hope will one day find their passions and to pursue their own fulfilling life paths, both personal and professional. Keep learning every day!

TESTIMONIALS

Peter's book brings a much-needed blend of theory and practice to the analysis of real estate finance and investment. Too often this field is presented as little more than algebra, with students assembling rows and columns of numbers, but having no idea what they mean.

Samuel Zell
Chairman of Equity Office Properties and Equity Residential Properties
Chairman of Group Investments

Linneman's text provides the best investment analysis of real estate that I have seen. The book is comprehensive, clearly written, and the examples are both relevant and well presented. For students, professors, and young professionals desiring a thorough grounding in real estate finance and investment analysis, this text will provide a compelling and satisfying answer.

Dr. Joe Gyourko
Martin Bucksbaum Professor of Real Estate and Finance
Wharton School of Business, University of Pennsylvania

As a real estate practitioner and academic, I have found Dr. Linneman's textbook to be the best one for real estate finance and investments. He successfully synthesizes theoretical perspectives with the practical world in a succinct manner. The book covers commercial real estate from both a micro and macro view, including a robust analysis of real estate cycles and the Great Recession. The book is the most prominent real estate finance and investments textbook in the marketplace today and is currently used by several industry employers.

Mark K. Bhasin, CFA, FRM, CAIA, CMT, ERP, PRM, LEED Green Associate, WELL AP
Basis Investment Group, LLC
Adjunct Professor, New York University Stern School of Business

---

There is just no other textbook in the same league.

Dr. David Nickerson
Rogers School of Management, Ryerson University

TESTIMONIALS

I started using Peter Linneman's text with his first edition. The text has proven itself with helping me teach the basics of real estate investment. In fact, I had an outside professional speak to the class who exclaimed that the text was given to all of his agents. He said that it was definitely used in the market, and that it prepares students well for a career in real estate.

Sarah K. Bryant, Ph.D.
Professor of Finance, Shippensburg University of PA

Peter Linneman's book offers a great blend of theoretical concepts and practical applications. I particularly enjoy the way important concepts are emphasized with examples and empirical findings. The book makes it easy for me to explain how I believe the world should work, and how it actually does. It also offers ways to analyze and explain any differences, all with flawless presentation and clear and concise writing.

Andrey Pavlov
Professor of Finance, Beedie School of Business, Simon Fraser University

Linneman's text stimulates real analysis, as opposed to just number-crunching. It takes students above and beyond the mechanics of entering data into a spreadsheet and challenges them to think logically and economically about the unique aspects of the commercial real estate market. The combination of the text, the supplemental material and the pre-requisite sections provides a complete package for students at all levels.

Andrea J. Heuson
Professor of Finance, University of Miami

The 5th edition of the text, as expanded and reconfigured, serves as a more comprehensive source where information flows more logically than ever before. I say congratulations. This may well be the best textbook ever written concerning the subject of Real Estate Finance and Investment Analysis."

Mark Munizzo
Adjunct Professor, Roosevelt University Chicago

TESTIMONIALS

I've now had an opportunity to use Peter's textbook for teaching graduate level courses in Real Estate Private Equity and Real Estate Structured Finance. In both cases, the book served as an excellent primer on general real estate concepts, in addition to providing in depth analysis of such topics as asset valuation, deal structuring and real estate capital market considerations. The supplemental articles provided great context for discussing the lessons of class, giving the students a much more complete perspective on our industry and its unique challenges.

Thomas Burton
Alex. Brown Realty, Inc.
Adjunct Professor, University of Maryland

Our industry is dynamic, rapidly changing and in need of sound fundamental instruction. Dr. Linneman understands and articulates how sound real estate theory and application collide to make us profitable professionals. His text provides the "must know," tremendous insight into the "should know" and the occasional "glad I know now." A must use (and apply) for any real estate professional.

Daniel Thomas
Partner, St. John Properties, Inc.
Adjunct Professor, University of Baltimore

The Linneman book takes a common-sense approach and is an ideal tool for the student interested in building a career in real estate investment and finance.

Richard Powers
Managing Member, Grand Street Investments, LLC
Lecturer, Yale College

It resolves the tension between the "tower" and "street" perspectives as well as any treatment of real estate investment to date. Moreover, it offers any reader — advanced or neophyte — an indispensable guide to enlightened analysis.

George A. Overstreet
Professor, McIntire School of Commerce, University of Virginia

TESTIMONIALS

I think the new edition of Dr. Linneman's book is an excellent textbook...in commercial real estate investment and finance. It is concise (no-nonsense), easy to read, merging seamlessly the industry practice with academic discipline in a logical way. I found the real-world examples and cases refreshing.

Peng (Peter) Liu
Associate Professor of Real Estate and Finance, Cornell University

I enjoy using this book because it is straightforward and not afraid to tackle nuances that are often ignored, such as problems with using cap rates to evaluate hotel investments. The structure also allows you to teach at multiple levels within the same class. Topics are covered succinctly in a nuts-and-bolts manner, but there are supplemental chapters that bring more complex analyses within the context of historic events and current markets.

Glenn Williamson
Amber Real Estate LLC
Adjunct Professor, Georgetown University

This book offers students a rare glimpse into the tools and decision making of real estate finance. Its straightforward exposition allows one to grasp the challenges facing real estate investors, and provides them with an excellent foundation upon which to build their careers. This book will be required reading for new real estate professionals for many years to come.

Dean Adler
Principal, Lubert-Adler Real Estate Funds

The text is an excellent reference material for real estate and land development students and those interested in the finance side of real estate development and investment. Each chapter in your text is clear and user friendly. Case studies and tables, charts and data sets are easily understood for their contextual intent.

Tony Graham
Associate Professor, North Carolina State University

PERMISSIONS TO RE-PRINT

- Chapter 3: "International Real Estate Investing" adapted and revised with permission from the *Wharton Real Estate Review*.

- Chapter 8: "Forecasting 2020 U.S. Country and MSA Populations" adapted and revised with permission from Albert Saiz and the *Wharton Real Estate Review.*

- Chapter 8: "Where Will US Population Growth Occur: A Glimpse at 2020 and 2030" adapted and revised with permission from Linneman Associates and *The Linneman Letter.*

- Chapter 8: "Regional Growth Variability" adapted and revised with permission from Deborah Moy and the *Wharton Real Estate Review*.

- Chapter 8: "MSA Alpha-Beta Analysis Revisited" adapted and revised with permission from Lou Dimitrov and *The Linneman Letter.*

- Chapter 9 Supplement A: "A Disconnect in Real Estate Pricing?" adapted and revised with permission from the *Wharton Real Estate Review*.

- Chapter 9 Supplement B: "The Equitization of Real Estate" reprinted with permission from the Wharton Real Estate Review.

- Chapter 9 Supplement C: "If Interest Rates Determine Cap Rates, Where Is the Evidence?" reprinted with permission from Matthew R Larriva, CFA and *The Linneman Letter.*

- Chapter 9: "How We Got to the Credit Crisis" adapted and revised with permission from Linneman Associates.

- Chapter 9: "The Capital Markets Disarray" adapted and revised with permission from the *Wharton Real Estate Review.*

- Chapter 11: "Construction Costs" adapted and revised with permission from Linneman Associates.

- Chapter 20: "Revisiting Return Profiles of Real Estate Investment Vehicles" reprinted with permission from Linneman Associates.

- Chapter 20: "Understanding the Return Profiles of Real Estate Investment Vehicles" reprinted with permission from Deborah Moy and the *Wharton Real Estate Review* and *The Linneman Letter.*

- Chapter 22: "The Forces Changing the Real Estate Industry Forever" reprinted with permission from the Wharton Real Estate Center.

PERMISSIONS TO RE-PRINT

- Chapter 22: "The Forces Changing the Real Estate Industry Forever; 5 Years Later" reprinted with permission from the *Wharton Real Estate Review*.

- Chapter 23: "A New Look at the Homeownership Decisions" adapted and revised with permission from the *Housing Finance Review*.

- Chapter 23: Evaluating the Decision to Own Corporate Real Estate reprinted with permission from the *Wharton Real Estate Review*.

- Chapter 24: "Some Observations on Real Estate Entrepreneurship" adapted and revised with permission from the *Wharton Real Estate Review*.

- Supplemental IA: "The Return Volatility of Publicly- and Privately-Owned Real Estate" reprinted with permission from the *Wharton Real Estate Review*.

Chapter 1
Introduction: Risks and Opportunities

"Saying 'no' is as important as saying 'yes,' only tougher."
- Dr. Peter Linneman

Before you dive in, please note that the chapters in the text assume that you have a mastery of the foundational material in the three Prerequisite chapters, which start on page 364. Before you start with this chapter, please be certain that you are comfortable with the discounted cash flow, net present value, IRR, and loan amortization materials covered in the Prerequisites.

To hear spoken definitions of the book's **bolded key terms**, launch Amazon Alexa and say **"Alexa, open Commercial Real Estate Glossary."**

RISK AND OPPORTUNITY – THAT'S WHAT IT'S ALL ABOUT

Real estate investment is all about risk and opportunity. There is never an opportunity without risks, and the greater the perceived risks, the larger the perceived opportunity must be to justify investment. The value of a property reflects the assessments of the associated risks and opportunities. What is the property worth if everything goes according to plan? More importantly, what can go wrong; what do you do when it does; and how does that impact the property value? Identifying the relevant risks and answering such questions dominates the analysis of both equity investors and lenders. While spreadsheets and math will be required, these tools cannot make judgments about risks and opportunities any more than a hammer or saw can decide what type of building to build. There are many "wrong answers," but there is no single "right answer," as different investors and lenders have different operating skills and risk profiles. Sadly, "the right decision" is never 100% clear at the time a decision must be made, so if you are seeking "the right decision," look elsewhere.

It is critical to understand that equity owners, once they have fulfilled their financial obligations to their lenders, receive the upside (financial reward) of their investment. Lenders, on the other hand, have a contractual ceiling on the return they can receive from lending on a property (interest and timely return of principal), though the return from interest can be large.

In this chapter, we draw the distinction between equity investing and lending (debt) to clarify that both sides are critical to real estate investing. Throughout this textbook, we look primarily through the lens of equity investors. Nonetheless, in many cases, when we use the terms "investor" and "investment," they can potentially apply to both equity investors and lenders.

Suppose you are faced with the opportunity to be a financial stakeholder in the acquisition of an office building, Felicitas Tower, leased to the U.S. government for 10 years. Based on your analysis, you estimate that net cash flow will be about $3 million each year of the lease. How do you assess what the property is worth? If you have a financial background, you will immediately turn to **discounted cash flow analysis (DCF)**. You select a residual capitalization rate to determine a potential terminal (sale) value in year 10 based on expected cash flow. Then you select a discount rate with which you discount each year's expected net cash flow (including the terminal value) to the present. That "present value" is the estimated value of the property today. Given that this is a 10-year lease to the U.S. government, the risk-free 10-year Treasury rate might seem like an appropriate discount rate, but how does the risk of investing in this building differ from that of a 10-year Treasury bond? Would you rather own the Treasury note or Felicitas Tower, assuming your annual cash flow projections for both investments were the same? Will your cash flow estimates prove to be accurate? What happens when the current lease expires in 10 years? And what discount rate should you use?

Always utilize a risk and opportunity framework relative to other investments in addressing such questions. Potential upside needs to compensate for the reality of risks. What risks and opportunities are unique to Felicitas Tower versus your investment alternatives? If you become a financial stakeholder in Felicitas Tower, are you emotionally and operationally situated to deal with unexpected challenges?

THE RISKS

Unexpected and even unimaginable outcomes can (and will) occur while a financial stakeholder in real estate. Planes crash into the mall courtyard two days before Christmas, seemingly great credit tenants like Lehman Brothers, Arthur Andersen, and Enron disintegrate overnight, energy prices double in a year, and sometimes these all happen at once.

Operating Expenses

You could experience an unexpected increase in operating costs which would decrease the building's net cash flows below your expectations. Utilities, property taxes, maintenance, salaries, insurance, and numerous other costs are likely to fluctuate throughout the life of the lease. Although specific contractual lease terms may alleviate some of this risk, you may be unable to pass all operating cost risk to the tenant. No matter how carefully you analyze these costs, I promise you that your forecasts will be wrong. But "wrong" does not necessarily render your analysis meaningless. It just means that you must understand the actual outcomes are not as certain as they appear to be on your beautiful and beloved spreadsheet.

Vacancy

As a financial stakeholder, your cash flows are directly dependent on the U.S. government performing on the lease (i.e., making their rent payments in full and on time). There may be intricate wording in the lease — a thick and detailed document — which provides the government with relief from its lease obligation under certain obscure circumstances. If the government is the sole tenant and ceases to pay rent, you will receive no income as an equity investor. If you are the lender, you will receive no **debt service** payment for weeks, months, and perhaps even years. How fast can brokers re-lease the space if the government is able to get out of the lease and decides to leave? Will ownership be able to obtain equal or better terms from a new tenant? Will the new tenant require the landlord to remodel or reconfigure the space?

Pandemic

The world was reminded in 2020 that life can change drastically when a deadly virus ravages the globe at light speed. Many property owners, equity investors and lenders were financial victims of the COVID-19 pandemic. The crisis reminded all involved in real estate of the potential fragility of expected rent streams, especially those coming from retail, office, and apartment tenants. For example, The Cheesecake Factory, a national restaurant chain, notified the landlords of its nearly 300 U.S. locations that the company would not be making April 2020 rent payments. Additionally, residential landlords were legally forbidden by the Centers of Disease Control and Prevention from evicting their tenants for non-payment of rent beginning in September 2020. With extensions, this moratorium was in effect for an entire year!

Natural Disaster

Although it may seem remote, there is a chance that a natural disaster may substantially damage the building. In such a case, depending on the lease, you could face significantly reduced income streams, or no income at all. In addition, ownership will have to spend time and money to renovate the property. For this reason, it is particularly important to know whether the space is, for example, in a hurricane-prone area or a flood zone. Since property and casualty insurance can reduce the impacts of disasters, you must also evaluate the property's insurance coverage. In some events, insurance may be cost-prohibitive.

Leasing

What happens at the end of 10 years? If you hold a U.S. Treasury note you get your money back with certainty. With building ownership, you must either extend the government's lease or find another tenant. If the government does not renew, ownership receives no income until they successfully re-lease the building, and the lender will simultaneously suffer the consequences of no debt service payments.

Liquidity

Liquidity refers to the ease with which one can convert an asset to cash. The building is far less liquid than a government bond. You can sell Treasury bonds in minutes for a small fee, while selling the building may cost you 3% in fees and take 6-8 months. What if you need capital in a hurry? How quickly do you think you could sell the building? What will the real estate market look like when you are ready to sell? All too often, when you are under pressure to sell, it is because there is a shortage of interested capital. Thus, you run the risk that your attempt to sell will occur in a distressed market.

This is far from a complete listing of the risks associated with investing in a building either with equity or debt, yet you can see that the risk is greater for owning the property than for a 10-year U.S. Treasury note. Consequently, the potential reward must be commensurate with this higher risk.

THE OPPORTUNITIES

While there is no cash flow upside in holding a U.S. Treasury note for 10 years, there may be opportunities to enhance the cash flow from the building, further protecting the lender's debt service and augmenting ownership returns.

Operating Expenses

Ownership may be able to leverage and exploit their management expertise to lower the cost of operating the property, thereby increasing cash flows. There may also be potential operating cost synergies between this property and other real estate owned by the equity holders.

Terminal Value

The value of the building at the end of the lease may appreciate due to economic growth or general inflation, allowing you to sell the property for a considerable profit. Alternatively, you may be able to re-lease the property to the government or another tenant for more favorable terms at the end of the initial lease.

Rental Growth

The lease may provide mechanisms to increase total rental payments over the term of occupancy. Instead of $3 million per year for 10 years, the lease may call for 3% annual rental rate increases. Such contractual cash flow increases need to be factored into your analysis.

Although there are many additional opportunities for increasing the realized return, you can see that the opportunity is greater for owning Felicitas Tower than holding a U.S. Treasury note for 10 years.

Since the property has both greater potential upside and downside than the 10-year Treasury note, you need to adjust the discount rate accordingly. Conceptually the "right" discount rate to use is always the rate which is reflective of the risk of the anticipated cash flows. How many basis points ("bps"; 100 basis points equal 1 percentage point) you must add to the 10-year Treasury rate is based upon your assessment of the likelihood of the property's risks. But there is no magical website or formula that will tell you the "right" discount rate for an office property leased to the U.S. government for 10 years. If, as the equity owner, you think the risks are minimal and you are certain you will never sell the building, then you do not require a much higher discount rate than the Treasury rate to offset the added risks of owning the building. By using a low discount rate, you will impute a higher value and submit a higher bid, increasing your opportunity to acquire the property. Of course, you also increase the risk of overpaying for the building if unexpected negative events occur. Are you right for using the lower discount rate and offering a higher bid? Only time will tell.

On the other hand, you may demand significant compensation for the additional risks of the property. In this case, you will use a notably higher discount rate and offer a lower price for the building, running the risk of losing the building to a competing bidder. Is this the wise move? Again, only time will provide the answer. Figure 1.1 displays how various discount rates drastically alter the value of an existing commercial property, Kuo Office, with an assumed 6% annual income growth rate. There is more than a 40% difference between the sum of the property's nominal expected total cash flows and the property's present value when cash flows are discounted at 12% annually. The former case reflects a perception of zero risk (i.e., a 0% discount rate), while the latter reflects perception of significant risk.

FIGURE 1.1

Present Value of Kuo Office Property at Various Constant Annual Discount Rates							
		Year 1	Year 2	Year 3	Year 4	Year 5	Year 6
Annual Rental Income		3,000,000	3,180,000	3,370,800	3,573,048	3,787,431	4,014,677
Sale Value	Total	0	0	0	0	0	36,497,061
Total Cash Flow	$57,423,017	3,000,000	3,180,000	3,370,800	3,573,048	3,787,431	40,511,738
"Long-hand" Present Value				Present Value of Cash Flows			
	Present Value	Year 1	Year 2	Year 3	Year 4	Year 5	Year 6
Discounted at 0.00%	$57,423,017	3,000,000	3,180,000	3,370,800	3,573,048	3,787,431	40,511,738
Discounted at 3.00%	$49,364,457	2,912,621	2,997,455	3,084,760	3,174,607	3,267,071	33,927,943
Discounted at 8.00%	$38,913,190	2,777,778	2,726,337	2,675,850	2,626,297	2,577,662	25,529,267
Discounted at 12.00%	$32,557,251	2,678,571	2,535,077	2,399,269	2,270,737	2,149,090	20,524,507
PV-calculated Present Value				Present Value of Cash Flows			
	Present Value	Year 1	Year 2	Year 3	Year 4	Year 5	Year 6
Discounted at 0.00%	$57,423,017	3,000,000	3,180,000	3,370,800	3,573,048	3,787,431	40,511,738
Discounted at 3.00%	$49,364,457	2,912,621	2,997,455	3,084,760	3,174,607	3,267,071	33,927,943
Discounted at 8.00%	$38,913,190	2,777,778	2,726,337	2,675,850	2,626,297	2,577,662	25,529,267
Discounted at 12.00%	$32,557,251	2,678,571	2,535,077	2,399,269	2,270,737	2,149,090	20,524,507
NPV-calculated Present Value							
	Present Value						
Discounted at 0.00%	$57,423,017						
Discounted at 3.00%	$49,364,457						
Discounted at 8.00%	$38,913,190						
Discounted at 12.00%	$32,557,251						

Online Companion Hands On: Go to Textbook.GetREFM.com/toc/ and select the link for the Online Companion to Chapter 1. Scroll down to the Excel Figures section and download the Excel file and open it. Take note of the Assumptions provided at the top of the Figure 1.1 tab, formatted in **bold blue** font. The convention of formatting assumptions this way will be observed throughout the Online Companion.

Enter 3,000,000 in cell E15 for the Year 1 **Annual Rental Income** amount. Then grow the rental income on a compounded basis for Years 2-6, calculating the Year 2+ values as: (prior year value) * (1 + **Annual Rental Income Growth** rate). Next calculate the Year 6 **Sale Value** by dividing the Year 6 **Annual Rental Income** by the **Terminal Value Sale Capitalization Rate** assumption provided. Finally, sum the **Annual Rental Income** and **Sale Value** lines to calculate the **Total Cash Flow** line, and fill in the **Total** of the **Total Cash Flow** line in cell C17.

There are three calculation methods for solving for the **Present Value** of Kuo Office Property. Naturally, all produce the same results. Instructions on how to apply the methods in Excel are below.

First is the **"long-hand"** discounted cash flow method. In this method, you will solve for the present value of the cash flow stream at the various annual discount rates by dividing each year's nominal amount by: (1 + **Discount Rate**) ^ (**Current Year #**). For example, to calculate Year 1's value Discounted at 3%, in cell E22, type: =E17/(1+$E6)^(1). The dollar sign before the row coordinate anchors the reference, allowing you to copy and paste this formula horizontally across the projection period without the discount rate reference changing. Apply this method to all periods in all four rows. Then sum the present values for each "Discounted at x%" row in column C.

Second is the **PV function**-based method. In this method, you will solve for the present value using Excel's PV function. As an example, to use this function, in cell E28, type the following: =-PV($E5,E27,,E17) [note that there are 2 commas before E17, by design]. The three elements of the function provided from left to right within the parentheses are the **Discount Rate**, the **Number of Periods** (years), and the **Future Value**. Excel will return the PV as a negative value unless you put the negative sign at the front of the formula. Repeat this for all periods in all four rows. Then sum the present values for each row in column C.

Last is the **NPV function**-based method. In this method, you will use Excel's **NPV function**, which should be applied to the Years 1-6 values of the Total Cash Flow line. As an example, to apply this function, in cell C38, type the following: =NPV(E7,E17:J17). Repeat this for all rows.

All three of these methods can also be applied using the financial calculator of your choice. The latter two methods will require the use of the Time Value of Money functions.

Going back to the Felicitas Tower investment opportunity, how would your analysis change if the tenant was a start-up company instead of the U.S. government, even if all of the financial terms of the lease were the same? What additional risk and opportunities are associated with this tenancy? To start, you need to assess tenant credit risk. Will the tenant pay on time? Will the tenant default on the lease? If so, will you be able to re-lease the property for similar terms? How long will it take you to re-lease the space? What costs do you incur when re-leasing the space? You must measure the discount rate based on your assessment of these additional risks as the U.S. government is clearly a better credit tenant. How many basis points should you add? Only you can decide. As you gain experience and expertise, you will become better at assessing these risks and opportunities. As this occurs, you will become more accurate in your assessment of value.

WHERE YOU SHOULD FOCUS YOUR ANALYSIS

Now that you know how to think about selecting a discount rate and realize that there is no magical valuation website, what should you spend time trying to calculate: the future cash flows or the discount rate you apply to those cash flows? The answer is, of course, both. But at the margin, focus on understanding the expected future cash flows. You need to know what can happen at the property and understand how the property generates its cash streams. After all, how can you analyze the risks if you do not understand the business? Carefully exploring future cash flows is nothing more than trying to understand the business and its risks. Therefore, choose your discount rate wisely, but do not obsess over its selection.

Understanding expected future cash flows provides insight into why you may fail to meet your projections. This will force you to focus on a game plan if the property cash flows do not meet your expectations. You should focus primarily on the downside, because if the property does better than expected, trust me, you will be able to cope with it. Even more important than your cash flow projections, and certainly more important than the discount rate selection, is understanding why things may fail to go according to plan and what will happen when this occurs. This, and being able to say "no" to most opportunities is what makes a great real estate investor.

MARKET RESEARCH

One of the most important elements of underwriting (assessing) the purchase, sale, or development of a property is to carefully analyze the market's supply and demand balance. These supply and demand conditions provide the backbone for assumptions about future rents, operating costs and associated recoveries, marketing costs, the time required to lease vacant space, the vacancy rate, and ancillary income opportunities.

Focusing first on supply, it is essential that you conduct a detailed evaluation of properties in the marketplace. What are their strengths and weaknesses? How are they priced? Are they experiencing increasing vacancy? Are their tenants satisfied? Why? Are major leases about to expire at these properties? Have new tenants entered the market? Which tenants have become too large (or too small) for their current space? What ancillary income are owners achieving? What design features and amenity packages at these premises do tenants value most and least? What marketing techniques are attracting customers? What leasing commissions are they paying brokers? What are their typical tenant improvements (TI) and concession packages? Can these properties be expanded or easily modified to meet additional demand?

In addition, you must carefully check what new properties and property expansions are underway, as well as what building permits have been granted and are soon to be granted. Talk to local brokers and bankers to assess who has tentative plans for new properties in the market. Are major competitive property renovations or repositioning projects anticipated? Which of these projects are most likely to come to fruition, and which are probably pipe dreams? While doing this homework, never forget that talk is cheap, but bricks and mortar are very expensive.

When investigating a property site, aerial photography can help identify other sites which are available for competitive product, as well as provide a perspective on local land use patterns. For larger projects, you may want to tour the area by helicopter to better understand traffic flows and development patterns. Google Earth and Google Maps are also cost-effective resources for getting a bird's eye view of the surrounding area. Study the past 30-40 years of local development to see in what directions development is going and at what speed. Figures 1.2 through 1.6 display the development patterns of the rapidly growing Las Vegas metropolitan area over 40 years. You need to understand the local zoning ordinances and politics to assess whether new product is easily brought online, and if so, potentially where and by whom. Carefully assess planned traffic and infrastructure improvements, as well as where the utility backbone extends. Assess whether state or local tax incentives are available to you, your competitors, or key tenants.

FIGURE 1.2

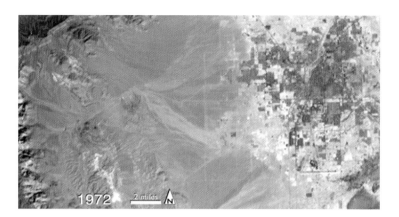

FIGURE 1.3

FIGURE 1.4

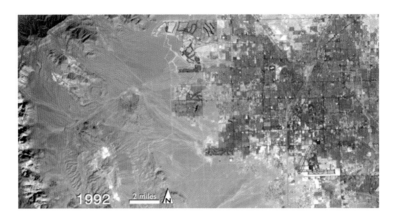

FIGURE 1.5

FIGURE 1.6

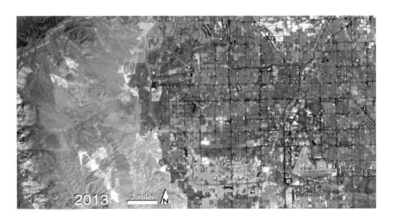

Turning to market demand, do you have a major tenant "in your pocket" that can fill vacant space? Has a major competitor of your tenant, such as Walmart, recently moved into the area? If not, can they easily do so? Where and when? What adjustments can you make at reasonable cost to the property to attract tenants? What design and amenities can you use to effectively market your property? How do the location, signage, and ingress and egress aspects of your property compare with others? How do the operating costs, design and technological capacities of your property compare to competitive properties? Can you increase rents and remain competitively priced?

In addition, you should study the fundamentals of local, regional, and national growth. To this end, you can utilize research publications such as *The Linneman Letter* and Rosen Consulting Group analyses to evaluate if, and why, the area will grow, and how it is affected by national and international economic forces. Taken together, these analyses will enable you to better assess the risks to the property. Who are the major local employers? Are they growing? What major challenges do they face in their businesses? What type of space do these tenants use? Ask brokers about unhappy tenants looking to relocate. Can their business support the increases in rental costs you project and remain competitive in their industry?

Always extensively drive and walk your market. Understand who lives in the area, and whether the market is moving up, down, or sideways. The cars in the neighborhood generally provide an excellent predictor of the residents' economic status. In addition, you may purchase a more detailed local market study, but be wary of people selling "the next big thing," as supply frequently has been put in place over the years in anticipation of "next big things" that never happened. Evaluate why projects have failed in your market, as well as why they have succeeded. Ask yourself whether you can provide tenants something better, cheaper, or faster than your competition. If you can, your property will probably succeed over the long term.

Read all available market reports and analysis of competitors. The advent of publicly-traded real estate firms has greatly increased the quality and quantity of such information, as some of your competitors may be public companies. Just remember that such information is often conflicting or merely promoting faddish ideas (e.g., Dotcom mania in the late 1990s) and is never a substitute for informed judgment.

The best way to understand a particular market is to devote your career to a specific product type and geography. Your goal is to get to the point where literally nothing happens in your market without your knowing about it well before it occurs. Obtaining market knowledge is not glamorous, but it pays handsome returns for the diligent. Remember that there is no shortcut to understanding a market. Becoming a real estate professional entails building a knowledge base and acquiring the expertise to answer the many questions we have raised rather than just "assuming" answers. I am frequently asked, "Is it alright to assume…?" I invariably respond by saying, "You can assume whatever you want, but you will ultimately be judged on the accuracy and defensibility of your assumptions."

PERSONAL DECISION

Your investment decision ultimately depends upon who you are, how much risk you are willing and able to take, what expertise and cost synergies you bring to the deal, and your investment goals and experiences. Figures 1.7 through 1.10 provide examples of how personal choices and perspectives can drive real estate investment decisions. Each graph displays the probability distributions of expected financial returns for four distinct real estate investments. Each of these hypothetical opportunities has, in retrospect after exiting the investment, an expected IRR (average annual return) to equity of 15%. That is, the "pro forma" (projected) numbers for each of these investments are the same, namely a 15% average annual return. However, the investments are vastly different in terms of the likelihood of the projected numbers occurring. Consider the unique risk and return profiles of these four investment opportunities, reflected in the different simulated probability distributions of their respective returns. Depending on your expertise, balance sheet, risk preference, experience, and deal flow, these 15%-return deals may or may not appeal to you.

Opportunity 1 (Figure 1.7) is the acquisition of Henderson Office Park, a fully-leased property with a large number of high-quality tenants and lease expirations occurring smoothly over a 20-year horizon. This investment offers a 15% expected average annual return, with a relatively symmetric chance that the property will perform above and below expectations. The vast majority of the expected return outcomes for investment in this property are very close to the expected return. Finally, this investment opportunity offers relatively little chance of losing invested capital.

FIGURE 1.7

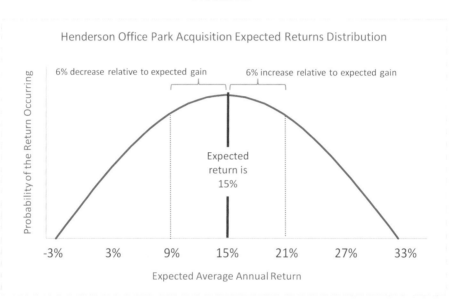

Opportunity 2 (Figure 1.8) is the acquisition of Jessica Distribution Center, a built-to-suit logistics property 100% occupied by a single tenant with a long-term lease. The tenant has low credit quality but is growing fast. The investment opportunity, which also has an expected 15% average annual return, offers three potential return outcomes. In Scenario 1, the tenant goes out of business, and no one else wants to lease the space. In Scenario 2, the tenant goes out of business, and you re-lease the space, though at less favorable terms. In Scenario 3, the tenant prospers and renews their lease, allowing you to avoid additional lease-up costs. While the overall expected return is 15%, the return distribution offers a substantial chance that you will lose money. However, Opportunity 2 offers greater potential upside than Opportunity 1, with about a one-third chance of returning greater than 30% (the right-most curve in Figure 1.8). In contrast, Opportunity 1 has a significantly lower chance of generating a return in excess of 30%.

FIGURE 1.8

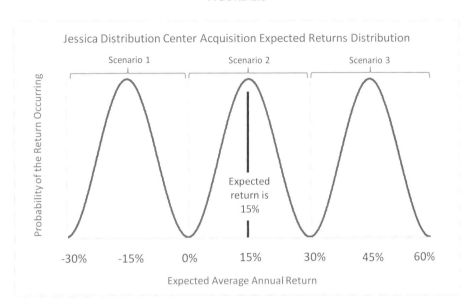

Opportunity 3 (Figure 1.9) is the ground-up development of Celina Gardens Apartments, also offering an expected 15% average annual return. The property is in a "frontier" location with relatively little operating history for your product. Since there is little information that you can use to determine the expected returns, the project seems to offer a relatively uniform opportunity of success and failure. In this case, the opportunity offers greater chances of both substantial success and failure than either Opportunity 1 or 2, with less chance for mediocre performance.

FIGURE 1.9

Opportunity 4 (Figure 1.10) is the ground-up development of Leslie Center, a complicated and expensive major mixed-use project that you hope will revolutionize the market. The opportunity, which also has an expected average annual return of 15%, presents two very distinct outcomes. Under Scenario 1, the market rejects the product, causing you to lose a lot of money, while under Scenario 2, the market loves the product, making it a huge success. If it succeeds, Leslie Center makes significantly more money than the other properties.

FIGURE 1.10

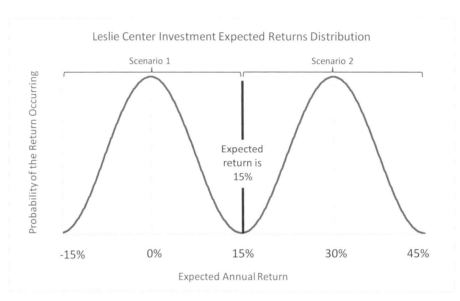

Which one of these pro forma "15%-return" investments is best for you? Note that these investments look the same based on pro forma IRRs but offer radically different real estate and investment propositions. Which, if any, of these investments you make depends on who you are, your investment goals, and your operating expertise. What is right for you will often be wrong for another investor. Never think that the numbers can make investment decisions for you. A mastery of "the numbers" is important but merely the starting point for investment analysis. You must learn how to do the numbers but understand that it is just (barely) the beginning.

RISK PARAMETERIZATION

What differentiates these four investment return distributions is not the average annual expected return but their risk profiles around the expected return. Normally, financial economists frame investment risk through statistical analysis methods. Specifically, they look at the standard deviation of the asset's return as well as the covariance between returns for the asset and returns of a broader set of investable instruments. While these concepts are appropriate, they are of little assistance to you in evaluating any specific real estate investment. Why? First, summarizing an investment's risk by its standard deviation and covariance of expected returns assumes that the returns have a Gaussian Normal Distribution. However, as is obvious in our four examples, most real estate deals do not have Normal return distributions, and therefore, the standard deviations and covariances are not sufficient to fully summarize the investment risks. This problem is exacerbated for properties with return distributions that are non-continuous, asymmetric, and highly skewed.

An additional difficulty of utilizing the standard deviation and covariance of returns to summarize risk is that it is almost always impossible to calculate these statistics for most real estate investments. Unlike stocks and bonds, a typical real estate investment lacks the return history with which to parameterize or estimate either the standard deviation or the covariance. The problem, in this case, is not a conceptual one but a practical one.

A further challenge is that the expected return, the distribution of positive returns, and the covariance of returns with other assets can change quickly and dramatically. For example, in the early 1990s and 2007-2009, the expected returns for all assets plummeted simultaneously due to soaring risk premiums relative to government bonds. As a result, even assets with historically low covariances suddenly experienced near-perfect covariance with the market. Assets experienced plunging expected returns and much larger left-side tails (i.e., downside risk) in terms of return outcomes. In short, risk is not a fixed concept but rather an ever-changing reality.

As a result, while the notions of standard deviation and covariance as measures of risk are useful intuitions to bear in mind, as a real estate investor, you must rely on less statistically based analyses of risk. This includes addressing questions to determine what makes the property succeed or fail. Can it weather a downturn in the economy? What if a tenant leaves? What happens if interest rates rise? This is how you attempt to measure the risk of the investment. Never forget that your brain is an extraordinarily sophisticated computer as well as a great synthesizer of information. As your experience and knowledge grow, this truly portable computer becomes increasingly sophisticated in calculating risk.

Bearing this in mind, real estate returns tend to have a comparatively low correlation with stocks and bonds because real estate's relatively fixed income streams are driven by contractual lease obligations. As a result, when the economy does well, real estate responds with a lag, as leases expire and renew based on their specific calendars. The converse is also true. Similarly, real estate is partially a fixed-income investment and, like a bond, is somewhat sensitive to interest rates. However, unlike most bonds, the cash streams and residual values of real estate tend to rise with inflation. Therefore, real estate tends to have a low correlation with bonds, but never forget that when capital seeks extreme safety, all asset classes become very highly correlated.

It is also important to remember that if you are in the real estate business, you are in the business of taking risks. It is your expertise and core competency. As such, you may want diversification, but that is a luxury afforded primarily to passive investors. As a real estate professional, you seek to exploit your expertise, even though it may not keep you as diversified as you would like. For example, if you have $2 million in available capital, and the typical project in which you specialize requires $2 million to execute, you will not have enough money to both execute the project and diversify your portfolio. Does this fly in the face of portfolio theory? As an investment matter, yes. But it is consistent with the exploitation of your competitive advantage. That is, leverage your core competency, and in doing so, maximize your profits.

There is generally a conflict between the desire to diversify your portfolio and exploiting your expertise. You cannot do all the deals you evaluate, even if they are attractive on a risk-return basis. You do not have enough capital, labor, or resources available. Therefore, you strive to determine which deals deserve a "no," not only because they may have negative net present values but also because they do not most effectively utilize your skills and meet your investment objectives.

The spectrum of real estate investment profiles, examples of transactions, general targeted returns, and leverage levels employed are displayed in Figure 1.11.

FIGURE 1.11

	The Real Estate Risk Spectrum			
	Less Risk ⟵	More Risk ⟶		
		Investment Profile		
	Core	Core-Plus	Value-Add	Opportunistic
Sample Transaction	Acquisition of a well-occupied, stable cash-flowing office or apartment building in an established sub-market.	Acquisition of Core-type property that needs some relatively minor enhancement; sub-market can be secondary.	Significant value enhancement needed through operating, re-leasing or re-development.	Re-positioning of ailing properties; Ground-up development; Emerging market investments; Buying entire companies with owned operating assets.
Target Levered IRR	7-9%	9-12%	12-16%	16%+
Leverage Employed	0-30%	> 30% <= 60%	> 60% <= 70%	> 70%

CLOSING THOUGHT

Becoming a successful real estate investor comes very slowly. It is a process of making decisions, dealing with the consequences, and hopefully learning from the experience. If you go into business as a real estate entrepreneur, you will start your career making relatively small investments because the capital available to you will be limited due to your lack of sophistication and experience. As you develop your expertise, become more sophisticated and better at managing risks, and learn how to generate returns even when things go wrong, you will find that you will attract a larger investor base and have the ability to take on larger and more complex deals. Real estate investing is a career rather than a one-time event; a marathon, not a sprint. Thus, if you want to be a successful real estate professional, patience and learning when to say "no" will be your greatest allies.

 Online Companion Audio Interview: To hear a conversation about this chapter's content, go to the Online Companion and select the link for Chapter 1. Scroll down to the Audio Interview section and listen.

Chapter 2
What is Real Estate and Who Owns It?

"Overnight success almost always took 10-25 years."
- Dr. Peter Linneman

To hear spoken definitions of the book's **bolded key terms**, launch Amazon Alexa and say **"Alexa, open Commercial Real Estate Glossary."**

REAL ESTATE IS ABOUT SPACE

Before you can begin to analyze real estate investments, you must gain an understanding of space. How big is the Empire State Building? How big is your home, apartment, or the local mall? Figure 2.1 lists typical square footages for several property types.

FIGURE 2.1

Sizes of Various Properties	
Type of Property	Square Feet*
Urban Studio Apartment	500
Suburban 1-Bedroom Garden Apartment	650 - 850
Suburban 2-Bedroom Garden Apartment	900 - 1,100
One Floor of Large Highrise	15,000 - 20,000
Strip Retail Center	125,000 - 200,000
Regional Mall	750,000 - 1,250,000
One Acre	43,560
Football Field including endzones (160' x 360')	57,600

* Square footages are illustrative of average areas. Individual properties (except for an acre and football fields) will vary.

You have been involved with real estate your entire life. Every building and piece of land is owned by someone, with properties such as parks and national forests owned by governments. Other properties are owned by churches and not-for-profit organizations. The office building, hotel, warehouse, and empty building you walked past today are generally owned by for-profit owners.

You should become aware of the different classifications of properties, their design features, and what makes a high performing and functional building. Walk around with an inquisitive eye and think about how your dorm complex works, whether the supermarket has a well-designed floor plan, where the mall developer wanted people to congregate, and how auto and foot traffic flow at the retail center where you get your dry cleaning done.

LAND

Land is perhaps the most basic type of real estate. **Greenfield** land is undeveloped land, such as a farm or pasture (Figure 2.2). **Infill** land is primarily in urban areas, is generally vacant or undeveloped, and is surrounded by developed parcels of land. Often, an infill location has already been developed but is currently vacant. **Brownfield** sites are parcels of land that had an industrial use and may be environmentally impaired (Figure 2.3).

Be cautious before developing land, as you would rather have land not generating income than the extra cost of a non-productive building on top of the land. People often use surface parking lots to generate some revenue while land awaits development. Similarly, cattle graze, and flea markets and Christmas markets operate on vacant land to generate some cash flow to offset the carrying costs (insurance and property taxes) of vacant land.

The size and location of a parcel of land are important in determining its "developability." A common phenomenon in urban areas is that at an earlier point in history, someone refused to sell their property and large buildings were built on either side of the parcel, so nothing functional can be built on the parcel unless one of the adjacent buildings is demolished.

Land is a component of all other property types, each of which leverages the land as its base. There are two basic business models for property development: development of an income-producing property, such as a retail plaza, or development of units, such as single-family houses that are sold to individual end-users. In the second case, the land is subdivided into individual **tax lots** separated by **property lines** (increasing its overall value), and **titles** to the lots are transferred to the buyers. In the case of an operating property, like a retail plaza, multiple tenants lease suites and have no ownership claim to the land.

While operating properties share many common characteristics, such as deriving income from tenants leasing space, each property type has its own unique design and operational traits.

FIGURE 2.2

Greenfield land

FIGURE 2.3

Brownfield site

RETAIL PROPERTIES

Retail properties come in many different forms and sizes, each intended to maximize sales from individual consumers. Retail properties serve the public by providing points of purchase for physical goods and places to receive services, such as an oil change for your car. The formula to success for a physical goods retailer is to be conveniently located and accessible to shoppers (and their cars), have the right product in stock at the right time, display it in an attractive manner, and price it to sell, all while removing barriers that could deter the consumer from making their intended purchase.

Physical goods retailers everywhere have been challenged by the advent of online shopping, with online retailers competing aggressively on price, without the added financial burden associated with brick and mortar stores. Square footage for warehouse space is generally less expensive to rent than that for retail, aiding the economics of online retailers in their pursuit to divert sales from physical outlets. Physical goods retailers have also been under sales pressure due to the convenience of online shoppers not having to travel any further than their computer or smart phone. This is especially attractive to consumers when it is 15 degrees or miserably rainy outside, and their purchases show up at their doorstep or office within a few days or hours.

A common type of retail property is a **strip retail center (strip center)**, which may be **anchored** or **unanchored**. Having an **anchor** means the center has one or more large retail stores, such as Walmart, Publix, or Safeway that attracts customers to the center (Figure 2.4). Unanchored strips lack such large retail stores and are combinations of small **in-line** stores, ranging from 600-10,000 square feet each (e.g., nail salons, UPS stores) and low- to mid-priced stores (e.g., restaurants, clothing boutiques, pet grooming salons), which total to 10,000-200,000 square feet, excluding any parking area. Strip centers tend to be located on major local artery roads, with good ingress and egress. Although a center may be well-located, if you are unable to enter or exit the center easily, or you can only enter from a single entrance or direction, its value will be reduced due to its inaccessibility.

Anchored strip centers tend to be larger than unanchored centers because the anchors require a lot of space and are complemented by smaller tenants. You frequently find supermarkets at anchored strips. Anchor supermarkets typically run 30,000-70,000 square feet, either in the shape of a rectangle or an L. The anchor supermarket will generally have signage visible near the entrance of the center. Anchored centers are generally 50,000-300,000 square feet. **Stand-alone centers** have a single store such as Walmart, Target, or Kmart with no other stores. Often strip centers have **outparcels**, with tenants such as fast food restaurants or a local bank branch located separately and apart from the strip and close to the street. These outparcels may be managed and owned independently from the rest of the center.

FIGURE 2.4

Strip retail center with Whole Foods anchor

Community retail centers are generally 150,000-350,000 square feet. These centers have several anchors, such as a supermarket and a drugstore, as well as several specialty stores such as Foot Locker and smaller in-line stores. Restaurants will generally be part of the center as well. Community retail centers can be laid out as a single center or as two or three contiguous strip centers. These centers are located on local artery roads with excellent ingress and egress, near interstate highway exits (Figure 2.5).

FIGURE 2.5

Community retail center

A **power center** has 3-5 major "big box" retailers such as a Walmart, Home Depot, Fresh Foods, or Staples, but few in-line stores. Big box retailers generally are 30,000-200,000 square feet each. The center may also contain outparcels (Figure 2.6). There are also individually-owned downtown shops. A major problem with such properties is that each shop is interested in maximizing their profit, rather than maximizing the profits for the entire retail environment. In contrast, a multi-tenant shopping center attempts to maximize the entire shopping experience through complementary tenancy, design, shared amenities, and **common area maintenance (CAM).** The cost of CAM is typically reimbursed, at least in part, by the tenants, as uniform upkeep of shared landscaping, sidewalks and parking areas benefits all tenants. As a result, multi-tenant shopping centers are generally a more productive retail format in terms of sales than downtown shops, as they are able to create and exploit positive externalities.

Power center aerial view

Regional malls run 400,000-2,000,000 square feet (more than 30 football fields!) and usually have 2-6 anchor stores. These anchors are typically department stores such as Nordstrom and Macy's, as well as big boxes like Barnes & Noble. Mall anchors are generally 60,000-120,000 square feet and may extend one or more levels. The mall is populated with in-line stores between the anchors. The strategy is that the anchors draw customers to the center, while the complementary in-line stores of 600-12,000 square feet create a rich retailing environment (Figures 2.7 and 2.8).

Common areas in malls are often large and elaborate, and mall owners bear the financial cost of maintaining them to a high standard, even in the face of in-line shops or an anchor vacating and leaving their space dark. High vacancy in malls is especially financially challenging for landlords to remain profitable because aggregate CAM cost reimbursements from tenants will decline as they vacate the property.

FIGURE 2.7

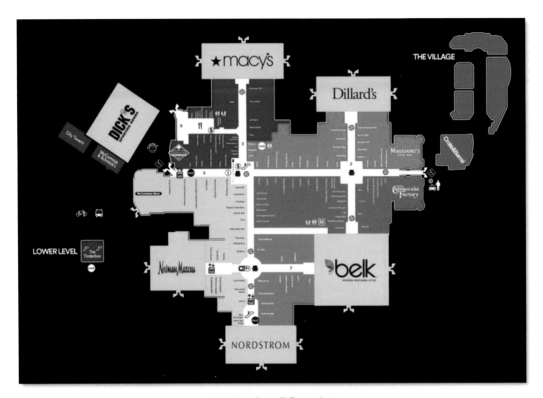

Regional mall floorplan

FIGURE 2.8

Regional mall interior

WAREHOUSE AND INDUSTRIAL PROPERTIES

Warehouse properties are used for storage of raw materials and finished goods. These are generally simple physical structures, but they may have demanding specifications in terms of floor slope, dust in the air, cooling, humidity, ceiling height, and loading dock design. Key design issues are **clear height** for ceilings and the ease of entry and exit of the property. Clear height is the lowest vertical space which exists without any obstruction such as lights or support beams. A clear height of 30 feet is preferred by large tenants who utilize forklifts to move boxes and pallets. Such properties also increasingly require **superflat floors**, which have strict transverse and longitudinal tolerances. In contrast, e-commerce warehouse space is configured to optimize the picking, sorting, and packing of individual items for shipping.

Industrial properties serve the manufacturing and assembly of finished goods. **Heavy manufacturing** facilities are generally special purpose properties that can be thought of more as pieces of equipment rather than real estate (but for the location dimension). For example, if you own a Kraft cheese manufacturing facility, you will not have an easy alternative use for the property without substantial renovation.

Light assembly space combines warehouse, product assembly, and office space, and may be multi-tenanted. Usually, they are fairly simple structures that allow easy reconfiguration. These facilities are generally designed along warehouse principles, with **dropped ceilings** used for the office component to hide mechanical elements and reduce sound echo. Light assembly structures will have some parking in front of the building to service the office space. If it is easily convertible, the structure is referred to as a **flex building** (Figure 2.9). A common construction technique for flex buildings is a concrete slab structure that tilts up to finish the building. Such properties do very well in a strong market because of their flexibility, but in a down market, they suffer because there is no shortage of superior office or warehouse space.

FIGURE 2.9

Light assembly/office flex building

Bulk warehouses are very large buildings that range from 50,000-1,000,000 square feet. These expansive structures are located near major transportation hubs for ease of truck access. Warehouse users focus on cubic square footage, as stacking height is critical. The buildings are typically simple rectangular designs and face the challenges of efficiently processing large volumes of trucks in and out of the property. Warehouse sites must be able to accommodate multiple trucks entering and exiting the building loading docks and allow them to conveniently off-load regardless of truck height and size (Figure 2.10).

FIGURE 2.10

Warehouse interior

OFFICE PROPERTIES

Office space serves commercial and medical tenants in both urban and suburban markets. **Central business district (CBD)** office space is usually located in a city's central corridor, is **highrise** in form (10 or more stories), and has a "Main & Main" orientation related to the transportation network, as well as historic and government nodes (Figure 2.11). Office space is loosely classified as either Class A, B, or C, but there is no definitive "grading" system. It is akin to judging who is tall and who is short; it is a matter of context. Someone who is short for the NBA may be quite tall relative to the general population. Similarly, an A building in Birmingham may be a B building in New York City. Be careful when reading reports indicating how much space is Class A, as classification discrepancies frequently exist.

Office buildings in Europe tend to be smaller, shorter, and narrower than buildings found in the U.S. This is for both regulatory and historical reasons. European highrises also generally have small floorplates, often only 4,000-10,000 square feet per floor. In Europe, a property's location plays a larger role in determining whether it is Class A than its design, age, or amenities.

A **Class A** CBD office property is relatively new and well located, has modern HVAC (heating, ventilation, air conditioning) and electrical systems, and benefits from quality architecture. A so-called "trophy building" would be among the top 2-3% of the Class A properties, basically the best of the best. **Class B** space is less well located, smaller, older, has fewer modern amenities, and is of simpler design. **Class C** space comprises the remainder of the properties.

During a real estate market downturn, Class A buildings are generally more resilient and tend to remain better leased, as tenants move up from lesser-quality buildings when rents fall (a.k.a., "flight to quality"). Class B and C properties tend to perform best in strong markets, by focusing on price-sensitive tenants.

Class A CBD highrises in cities such as Chicago, Philadelphia, and New York typically have floorplates running 15,000-25,000 square feet, with 4-8 corner offices per floor. The **chevron** (V-shaped) corner design provides eight or more corners by notching an otherwise rectangular building. Among the challenges facing highrises are efficient vertical transportation and life safety (especially fire). In addition, highrises have faced increased security issues since the 9/11 attacks.

FIGURE 2.11

CBD office highrises

Suburban office buildings are relatively unique to the U.S. Class A suburban properties tend to be new **midrise** structures (5-9 stories) of 80,000-400,000 square feet, with 8,000-14,000-square foot floorplates (Figure 2.12). Class B and C spaces are older and are not as well located. Suburban office parks provide a campus-like assemblage of office buildings, with the buildings sharing common amenities.

The business model for office properties is to lease space to tenants, typically on a long-term basis (5+ years). **Subleasing** of unused leased space by the tenants is sometimes forbidden by the landlord as this space competes with the absorption of any other **direct vacant space** in the building available through the landlord. However, there has been a sub-lease business model in CBD and select suburban markets for a very long time. In such cases, the tenant leases out individual desks and offices within their suite on a reserved or unreserved short-term basis (as short as a day) at a rent high enough to produce a profit to the tenant after their own rent and labor costs. This sub-lease model has most recently manifested in what is known as "creative office" or "shared" or "co-working" space, where significant portions of the suite are dedicated to attractive, comfortable common areas that double as zones for socializing, eating, and collaborating, as well as working individually. Typical tenants of these creative office spaces are sole proprietors, small- to medium-size businesses, and groups or divisions from large companies.

Some medical office properties are set up legally as **condominiums**, wherein each suite is individually owned (generally by the tenant of the space). This makes sense for a doctor who wants to open and sustain a local practice at the same address for an entire career. Non-medical commercial condominiums also exist but are more the exception than the rule in western countries.

FIGURE 2.12

Suburban office building with chevron corners

MULTIFAMILY

Many types of multifamily property exist, including urban highrise (Figure 2.13), midrise (often infill properties), suburban garden apartments, and small properties. The primary problem with small properties is that a single unleased unit is a large portion of the property. For example, if you own a 2-unit building, you either have 0%, 50%, or 100% occupancy. Smaller properties tend to be owned by "Mom and Pop" operations with a "do it yourself" mentality. These properties often generate a lot of headaches to tenants due to the lack of expertise on the part of the landlords.

FIGURE 2.13

Urban highrise multifamily

Suburban garden apartments began in the 1960s and 1970s, as young renters moved to the suburbs. Garden apartments are typically 3-4-story wood structures, with 50-400 units, without elevators, and with surface parking (Figure 2.14). The preferred units are on the top floor because of the vaulted ceilings, or the bottom floor because you do not have to walk up stairs. The middle units tend to be the least desirable because you do not get vaulted ceilings, yet you must walk up stairs, and there is greater potential for noisy neighbors both above and below you.

FIGURE 2.14

Suburban garden apartments

Midrise apartments are 5-9 stories, steel framed, and tend to be an urban infill product. These properties have 30-110 units and are elevator serviced (Figure 2.15). In a few markets, you find multifamily highrises which tend to be professionally operated and encompass increased security features. Outside of the U.S., multifamily tends to be a less important economic property category because housing is often provided either by the government or corporations (for their workers). In addition, rent controls protect renters from rent increases and eviction, effectively transferring aspects of ownership to the tenants. Japan is an exception, with an active rental and investment multifamily market.

FIGURE 2.15

Midrise apartments

There are many specialized products within multifamily, such as student housing, age-restricted (55+) communities, retirement communities, and assisted living, each with its own nuances and unique operational characteristics.

HOTELS

There are many types of hotels. The **full service** category includes urban CBD and resort properties, which may carry the flag of a high-price point operator such as a Four Seasons or Mandarin, or a mid-price point operator like Marriott. Most full service hotels provide room service, restaurants, banquet space, convention services, and food and beverage services. Full service hotels may also provide spas and limited retail (Figures 2.16 and 2.17).

Limited service urban hotels are usually boutique properties. The distinguishing feature for these hotels is that they are smaller and do not offer amenities such as room service, restaurants, banquet service, or convention space. This limits overhead and tends to stabilize operating income. The major difficulty with limited service hotels is effective marketing.

The hotel business is an operating business which also involves design and location components. Success hinges on the property's "flag" (brand) and how well that property is operated. In the U.S., hotels are not generally leased, although in Europe they are frequently leased. In the U.S. the owner either operates the hotel or hires a management company. The typical management contract requires the owner to pay the operator a fixed fee plus a percentage of gross revenues, as well as a fee for business generated by the operator's central reservation system. As a result, if the hotel does poorly, the landlord suffers financially. On the other hand, the manager (operator) does adequately even if the hotel is doing poorly. Hotel businesses are heavy fixed-cost operations, and while location and design are important, value is created through superior operation.

Another class is **extended stay hotels**, which have larger rooms, small kitchens, and provide limited services. These are designed for people staying a week or more, and attempt to make guests feel like they are at home.

Hotels face organized competition in the form of AirBnB and similar online short-term rental platforms, which provide room-night supply to the market. While the rooms offered through such platforms are typically heterogeneous and these room nights are not yet recognized as supply in traditional market studies, hotel owners and operators are keeping a close eye on the proliferation of these lodging alternatives. Marriott even launched its own home-sharing offering as a separate business division in 2019.

FIGURE 2.16

Urban CBD full service hotel

FIGURE 2.17

Resort full service hotel

SELF-STORAGE

Self-storage properties are located in both urban and suburban areas. Their simple design reflects the commoditized nature of the product. Secure, individually partitioned storage units come in various dimensions and are either in **climate-controlled** (Figure 2.18) or **non-climate controlled** structures. The former are more expensive to build, operate and rent. Some self-storage properties offer both types of units. The unique characteristic of self-storage is that while the leases are typically month-to-month, it is very sticky in terms of tenant retention. People do not typically move their secondary belongings and keepsakes to save a few dollars. This means that a newly developed property does not acquire tenants by pulling renters from existing properties, but rather by demand growth or by being located in an underserved area.

FIGURE 2.18

Self-storage facility

SINGLE-FAMILY RENTAL HOME COMMUNITIES

While a long-standing asset class in the overall housing space, single-family rental home communities ("SFR") have received increased institutional investment in the years since the 2009 financial crisis. These clusters of professionally managed homes take the form of both single-family detached houses as well as attached townhomes and comprise around 10% of the U.S. housing stock. Whether acquired one at time, as a pre-existing portfolio, or purposefully built for rent as a new contiguous set of homes, these communities are mostly found in suburban and rural areas.

REAL ESTATE IS MANY DIFFERENT INDUSTRIES

Different property types serve very different users, and require specialized leases, marketing, design and engineering. This is why real estate professionals are increasingly specializing in a particular property type. Just because you are very good at marketing multifamily units to 24-year-olds does not mean you are good at marketing a CBD office building to corporate America. When you are marketing a bulk warehouse facility, you must know the major manufacturing companies and understand how they operate, while for retail properties, you not only must know who the hot tenants are but also have the clout to convince them that your property is right for them.

GROSS VERSUS NET LEASABLE SQUARE FOOTAGE

It is generally not possible to lease every square foot of a building. Elevator shafts, mechanical space, lobbies, stairwells, and hallways cannot be leased. As a result, there is a distinction between the **gross square footage (GSF)** of a property and its **net leasable square footage (LSF)**, also referred to as **rentable square footage (RSF)**. The gross square footage refers to the total area of a building, usually measured from inner wall to inner wall, with no deductions for obstructions or non-leasable space. In contrast, net leasable area refers to the floor area that can be leased (Figure 2.19).

Efficient building design attempts to minimize the **loss factor**, that is, the difference between gross and net leasable footage. Buildings with enormous lobbies, such as those often found in corporate headquarters, have large loss factors. Similarly, tall buildings with small floorplates have large loss factors as the elevator banks, stairwells, and support columns eat up a larger portion of the space on every floor. Faulty design will haunt a property, as once built, a large loss factor (i.e., a low economic **efficiency**) is difficult to solve.

FIGURE 2.19

Relative proportions of square footages

A similar concept applies to land. How much of the land is economically usable? For example, half of the property may be swampland or environmentally protected, and land is needed for things such as roads, sidewalks, and retention ponds, thus limiting the economic use of the property.

A property's **floor area ratio (FAR)** is the ratio of a building's above-grade gross floor area (both vertically and horizontally) to the area of the lot upon which the building is constructed. Outside of the United States, some countries use the term **FSI (Floor Space Index)** instead of FAR. You will encounter this concept when analyzing zoning density restrictions. If the lot is 10,000 square feet and the FAR is 1.00, you have the right to build a structure with one floor that is 10,000 square feet, or a two-story structure with 5,000 square feet per floor, etc. Stated differently, with a FAR of 1.0, the total gross square footage of the building cannot exceed the size of the lot. Figures 2.20 and 2.21 illustrate this concept. Of course, each floor does not have to be the same size, as long as the gross square footage does not exceed the lot size multiplied by the allowed FAR.

FAR limits are generally accompanied by height and **setback restrictions**. For example, in addition to a maximum FAR of 1.5, there may be a maximum allowable building height of 100 feet, and the building must be set back at least 40 feet from the outer edge of the property boundary. In many continental European countries, there are also restrictions that dictate that every employee working in the property must have access to natural light. Architects and designers work to maximize a property's economic potential subject to these and many other restrictions.

FIGURE 2.20

Examples of How FAR Can Impact Building Individual Floor Dimensions					
Assumed lot size: 10,000 SF Assumed design: no projections or setbacks at any floor					
Building Height	1 Floor	2 Floors	3 Floors	4 Floors	5 Floors
Square Feet per Floor when:					
FAR = 1.0 (Max. building size = 10,000 GSF)	10,000 GSF	5,000 GSF	3,333 GSF	2,500 GSF	2,000 GSF
FAR = 2.0 (Max. building size = 20,000 GSF)	20,000 GSF	10,000 GSF	6,667 GSF	5,000 GSF	4,000 GSF
FAR = 3.0 (Max. building size = 30,000 GSF)	30,000 GSF	15,000 GSF	10,000 GSF	7,500 GSF	6,000 GSF

FIGURE 2.21

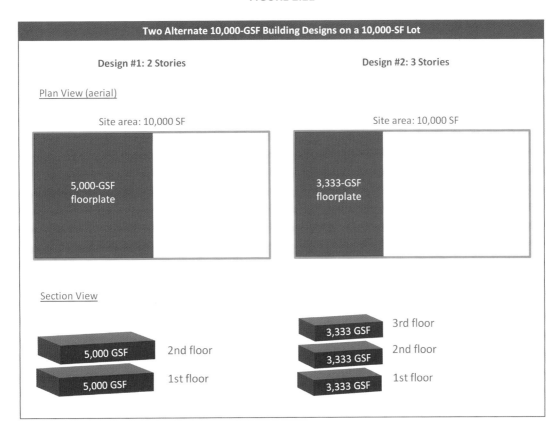

Two Alternate 10,000-GSF Building Designs on a 10,000-SF Lot

Design #1: 2 Stories   Design #2: 3 Stories

Plan View (aerial)

Site area: 10,000 SF   Site area: 10,000 SF

5,000-GSF floorplate   3,333-GSF floorplate

Section View

5,000 GSF — 2nd floor
5,000 GSF — 1st floor

3,333 GSF — 3rd floor
3,333 GSF — 2nd floor
3,333 GSF — 1st floor

OCCUPANCY AND VACANCY

Another critical distinction is between economically- and physically-occupied space. **Economic occupancy** refers to space that is currently generating rent. Not all space generating rent may be physically occupied. For example, a firm may lease space in a building in anticipation of future expansion, leaving it vacant for a period. Or a tenant may have vacated the property but continues to pay rent in accordance with their lease.

Physical occupancy refers to space that is physically occupied, regardless of whether it generates rent. A tenant in bankruptcy may not be paying rent, even though it still occupies the space, or the tenant may occupy the space but not currently pay rent due to lease concessions or so-called "free rent."

Figure 2.22 displays estimates of physical and economic vacancy rates for U.S. office space in two historically soft market periods. The high economic vacancy rates experienced in 1990 were the result of lease concessions, where 1-2 years of free rent were given to tenants in order to lock them into 4-5-year leases. Thus, while physical occupancy was about 82%, economic occupancy was much lower (55-70%). In contrast, the physical vacancy rate in 2002 was similar to the 1990 rate, but 2002 tenants were still paying rent on about one-third of the vacant space. While landlords received rent on this vacant space, they faced leasing competition from tenants attempting to sublease their empty space.

FIGURE 2.22

U.S. Office Vacancy in Two Soft Markets		
	1990	2002
Physical Vacancy	18%	16%
Economic Vacancy	30-45%	10-11%
Notes	High Free Rent	Rent paid on 1/3 of vacant space

STACKING PLAN

Tracking vacancy and lease expirations for a property are essential to effective **asset management**. Figure 2.23 displays Brasfield Tower's **stacking plan**, which is a visual representation of the building's leases. The stacking plan notes tenant names, locations and square footages leased, lease expiration dates, and current rental rates. This information provides the foundation for the landlord's leasing strategy.

At the point of acquisition, this 84,000-leasable square foot building had about 14,000 square feet vacant, for an approximate 17% vacancy rate. Most of this vacancy is from a single tenant that previously occupied 12,000 square feet on floors 9 and 10. Why did this firm leave the property? Were they having financial difficulty? Were they unhappy with the property services? Was their space too small or too large? Were rents too high? Could management have been better prepared in dealing with their exit? If they left because their industry, technology, is in trouble, then perhaps BHUMI and Gross Tech, which are in the same industry, may also experience premature vacancies.

Often a firm may leave because their space was inadequate. In this case, management must evaluate whether the building needs to be upgraded or marketed to a different tenant base. For example, the building might need better Internet connection speed to remain competitive.

FIGURE 2.23

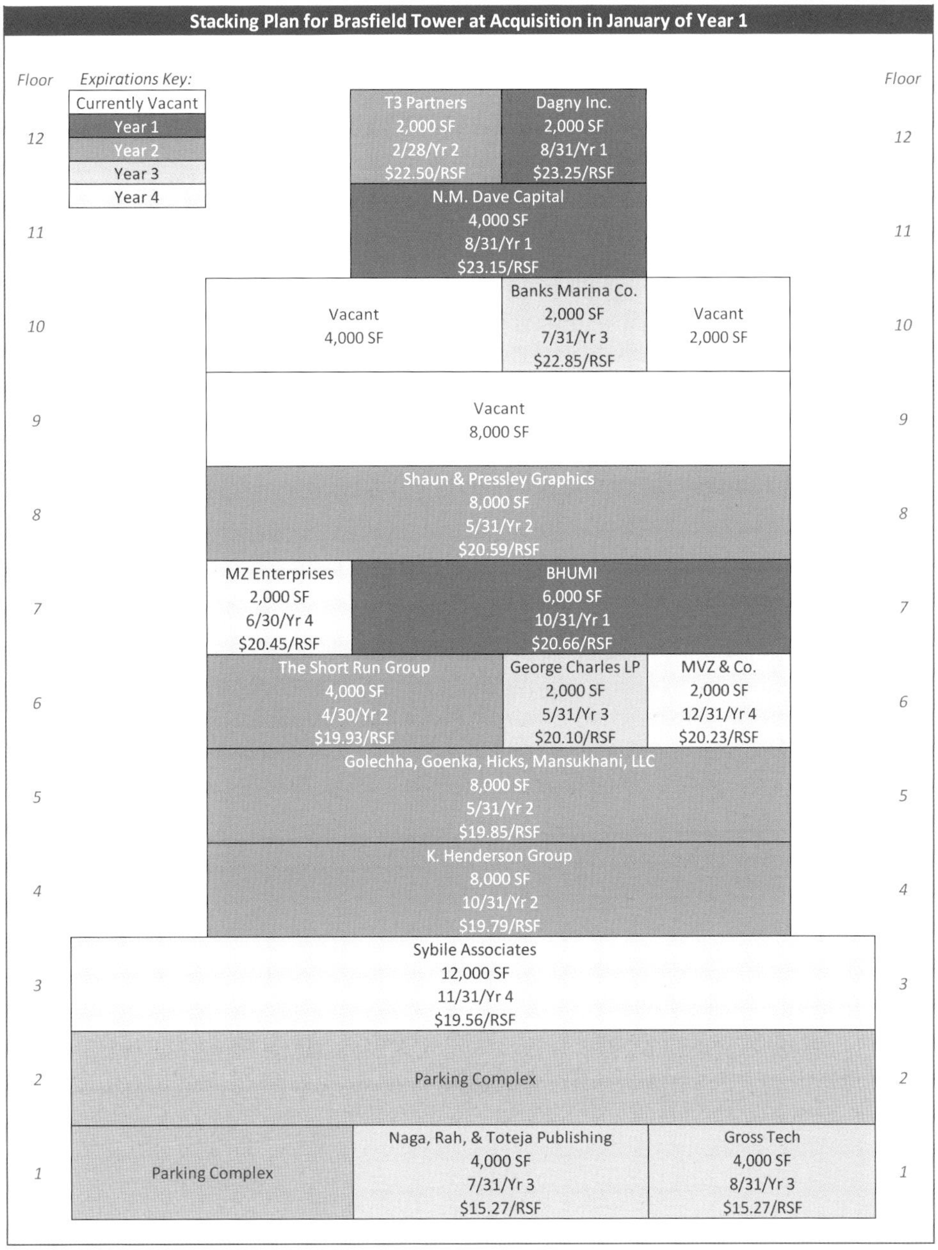

Stacking Plan for Brasfield Tower at Acquisition in January of Year 1

Floor						Floor
	Expirations Key:					
	Currently Vacant		T3 Partners	Dagny Inc.		
12	Year 1		2,000 SF	2,000 SF		12
	Year 2		2/28/Yr 2	8/31/Yr 1		
	Year 3		$22.50/RSF	$23.25/RSF		
	Year 4		N.M. Dave Capital			
11			4,000 SF			11
			8/31/Yr 1			
			$23.15/RSF			
				Banks Marina Co.		
10		Vacant		2,000 SF	Vacant	10
		4,000 SF		7/31/Yr 3	2,000 SF	
				$22.85/RSF		
9			Vacant			9
			8,000 SF			
8			Shaun & Pressley Graphics			8
			8,000 SF			
			5/31/Yr 2			
			$20.59/RSF			
		MZ Enterprises		BHUMI		
7		2,000 SF		6,000 SF		7
		6/30/Yr 4		10/31/Yr 1		
		$20.45/RSF		$20.66/RSF		
		The Short Run Group		George Charles LP	MVZ & Co.	
6		4,000 SF		2,000 SF	2,000 SF	6
		4/30/Yr 2		5/31/Yr 3	12/31/Yr 4	
		$19.93/RSF		$20.10/RSF	$20.23/RSF	
		Golechha, Goenka, Hicks, Mansukhani, LLC				
5		8,000 SF				5
		5/31/Yr 2				
		$19.85/RSF				
		K. Henderson Group				
4		8,000 SF				4
		10/31/Yr 2				
		$19.79/RSF				
		Sybile Associates				
3		12,000 SF				3
		11/31/Yr 4				
		$19.56/RSF				
2			Parking Complex			2
			Naga, Rah, & Toteja Publishing	Gross Tech		
1	Parking Complex		4,000 SF	4,000 SF		1
			7/31/Yr 3	8/31/Yr 3		
			$15.27/RSF	$15.27/RSF		

Online Companion Hands On: Go to the Online Companion and select the link for Chapter 2. Scroll down to the Excel Figures section and download the Excel file and open it. On the Figure 2.23 tab, in the table provided, fill in the Annual Lease Expiration schedule table for Brasfield Tower to show the SF Expiring, % Total SF, and Cumulative % SF for Years 1 through 4.

WHO OWNS U.S. COMMERCIAL REAL ESTATE?

Excluding corporate-, non-profit-, and government-owned buildings, as well as single-family and owner-occupied residences, the aggregate value of U.S. commercial real estate is approximately $4 trillion. There are both privately-owned and publicly-owned (both traded and untraded) entities that are real estate debt and equity stakeholders. The market is roughly 65% privately owned and 35% publicly owned. Of the roughly $2.5 trillion which is privately owned, 25% is equity and 75% is debt. Of the $1.5 trillion that is publicly owned, about 28% is equity and 72% is debt.

Equity owners include individual investors big and small, as well as private equity firms, which taken together represent about 40% of all privately-owned, income-producing real estate. The balance of real estate equity owners includes Real Estate Investment Trusts (REITs) (26%), pension funds (17%), foreign investors (9%), and life insurance companies, private financial institutions, and public untraded funds (collectively 8%). Debt players include banks, savings and loans, and mutual savings banks (collectively 61%); commercial mortgage-backed securities (13%); life insurance companies (14%); REITs (9%); and pension funds, governmental credit agencies, and public untraded funds (collectively 3%).

The U.S. commercial real estate market and the population it serves is massive, with a diverse set of equity and debt players, each with a specific risk profile and investment objective.

CLOSING THOUGHT

Properties come in an infinite variety of designs, shapes, and sizes. Study carefully what drives a property's success by examining buildings that generate high rents and have consistently high occupancy. Buildings are economic entities that are enhanced by well-conceived design and efficient operations. Whenever you pass or enter a property, ask yourself these questions: "Does it work?" "Why not?" "How could it function better?" "Why hasn't anyone done it?" A thorough understanding of space and tenant preferences is the foundation of becoming a great real estate investor.

Online Companion Audio Interview: To hear a conversation about this chapter's content, go to the Online Companion and select the link for Chapter 2. Scroll down to the Audio Interview section and listen.

Chapter 3
International Real Estate Investing

"You don't have to go far from home to lose a lot of money."
- Dr. Peter Linneman

GREAT POTENTIAL IS ONLY THAT

As a freshman college football player, I was impressed when I read in a press guide that I possessed "great potential." In my naïveté, I thought that this meant I would be a top-notch college player. However, as I read the press guide more closely, I realized that the word "potential" did not appear in the descriptions of the really talented players. "Potential" was just the press guide's way of saying, "He doesn't really have enough talent to play, but we're too polite to tell him." This memory comes back to me as I consider the "great potential" of investing in international real estate.

The attractions of international real estate investing are both obvious and alluring. Perhaps as much as 60% of investment-quality real estate lies outside the U.S. Non-U.S. real estate is occupied by a globalizing tenant base and is financed by capital sources that are increasingly international and integrated. In addition, the prevalence of large, passive owners such as banks, insurance companies, corporate real estate users, and government entities outside the U.S. makes these markets appear ripe for U.S.-style entrepreneurial real estate investors and operators.

In spite of these attractions, many efforts to create truly global property investment portfolios have fallen short. Notable disasters include JMB Realty Corporation's acquisition of Randsworth Trust (U.K.), Mitsubishi Estate's acquisition of Rockefeller Center, Chinese purchases in the 2010s, and the early attempts at expansion of Paris-based Rodamco, which eventually merged with Unibail and then Westfield via Unibail. In analyzing why such disasters have occurred, a number of problems with international real estate investment become apparent.

A major problem is that most non-U.S. property markets are not "markets" in any meaningful sense of the word. In most, properties rarely trade; information is scarce, distorted, and self-serving; many properties are overtly manipulated by (often corrupt) governments; there are only a limited number of capital sources; and the rules of the game frequently change, often in mid-play. The result is many locales with high degrees of uncertainty and inefficiency.

At first blush, these inefficiencies may appear attractive to "smart" operators, who see an opportunity to realize abnormal returns. On closer inspection, however, these inefficiencies can reduce property values and severely limit exit options. When market inefficiencies create excessively high property values, it is hard to harvest one's profits, as exit is difficult due to market illiquidity. In fact, many markets are so inefficient that no reliable exit options exist. The inability of investors to short (bet against) the market in order to pressure property values downward, when property values are excessively high, means that markets can remain out of balance for prolonged periods. Even entering inefficient markets opportunistically during periods when property values are below long term economic levels is risky, as property values may remain depressed regardless of improved operational fundamentals. These risks are particularly severe for outsiders entering markets that possess little in the way of legitimate legal infrastructure.

THE CAPITAL SHORTAGE MYTH

It is commonly believed that non-U.S. real estate markets generally experience shortages of capital. In fact, major international markets such as London, Paris, Frankfurt, Madrid, Milan, Zurich, and Amsterdam are no different from New York City, Chicago, or Los Angeles from a capital sourcing perspective. Specifically, there is too little capital available a few years out of every decade, too much capital 2-3 years out of every 10 years, and the majority of the time the supply and demand for real estate capital are roughly in balance. This is hardly surprising, as all major markets possess substantial financial institutions and participants with a relatively high level of financial sophistication.

The fact that major international markets in developed countries are generally in capital supply balance presents a problem for outsiders looking to enter, as such investors must possess either a significant value-added operating ability or access to "hidden" deals to realize above-average returns. Unfortunately, an outsider rarely has access to "hidden" deals, which are generally parceled out to favored insiders with longstanding relationships with the country's major financial institutions. In fact, one of the keys to their global successes is that players like Blackstone, Brookfield and Starwood have slowly become "locals". In addition, it is difficult for new entrants to add substantial economic value to a property in ways that are not also available to top-quality domestic operators. A notable exception is when a major U.S.-based tenant expands into a non-U.S. market and the operator's established relationship with this tenant provides significant value-added ability.

When there is too much capital in major markets, outsiders can buy – even in many relatively closed markets. The best evidence of this phenomenon are the inflated prices that have been paid over the years in numerous markets by oil money and thieving potentates laundering money. Frequently, the smartest locals have sold their prized assets to such outsiders, often repurchasing these assets when the overpaying buyers are squeezed during periods of capital shortages.

Well-developed local infrastructure and information networks are essential to exploiting opportunities created by capital shortages. In periods when there is too little capital in real estate markets, it is usually the smart locals — not outsiders — who are the first to spot the best opportunities. Generally, only as a long-depressed market exhibits some upward momentum do outsiders enter, frequently too late to realize the best investment opportunities. A notable exception is that some major U.S. private equity funds have successfully utilized their networks to invest in major markets experiencing temporary capital market shortages.

THE LAND OF THE RISING SUN

Supporting the overhead associated with maintaining an international operational and investment infrastructure (especially when markets are not experiencing capital shortages) is a paramount challenge for non-domestic investors. This is why most fund investments have been transacted through local partners and only in the largest and most liquid markets, where internal organizations can be justifiably supported. In this regard, Japan presents a particular challenge. The cost of establishing a Tokyo office is extremely high, while the transaction velocity can be low. Japan, particularly Tokyo, is a unique situation where real estate is very expensive by global standards. As a result, just as only Japanese investors are willing to invest in Japanese government bonds that effectively pay 0% (and even negative) interest, only Japanese capital sources have generally been willing to invest significantly in Japanese properties.

Japan is a wealthy, high-income country with a large and diverse property pool and lots of domestic capital. Real estate yields available in Japan are generally too low for most global investors to justify substantial investments given the lack of transparency, illiquidity and stagnancy of the economy. With 2-4% cap rates, even a billion dollars of investment does not go very far in terms of creating a substantial operating base.

A RISKY WORLD

Real estate capital is almost always scarce in places where there is high political risk, high economic risk, and an absence of markets with meaningful exit opportunities. Extreme examples are Afghanistan, Sierra Leone, and Zimbabwe.

While these areas offer potential high returns, they also pose serious risks. For example, although South Korea experienced a strong rebound from its economic collapse in the late 1990s, considerable risk existed in its real estate markets for many years. Risks included the elimination of many of the weak subsidiaries of the major *chaebols* (the large, typically family-owned business conglomerates). At the bottom of the market, many *chaebols* attempted to sell secondary properties at high cap rates (low prices) on 5-year sale-leaseback terms. The buildings offered were generally new but located in secondary locations and were occupied by the weakest subsidiaries of the *chaebols*. Even at those yields, pricing generally remained unattractive. Savvy investors in 2001 realized that even if South Korea continued its rebound, and the subsidiary tenants were to survive, the investing equity parties would be capped at a 12-15% return (before taking into account currency risk), as the tenants executed their repurchase options in year 5. Such deals meant that if the economy were to flounder and the weak subsidiary failed, the property (and many others) would remain vacant for some time. In this case, the cash flow would disappear, the repurchase option would not be exercised, and the owner would be stuck with a building in a secondary location with no obvious tenants. This is an arduous and challenging process in the most transparent and stable markets, and a nightmare elsewhere.

In a similar vein, at various times, markets like Thailand, Indonesia, and Malaysia have all experienced shortages of real estate capital. However, these shortages reflected the multitude of risks presented by these economies. Vast amounts of empty (often partially completed) speculative properties can take many years to absorb. Even when occupied, these properties may not generate sufficient cash flows to justify their construction costs until the next up-cycle. In addition, the business climates in these countries are non-transparent. While the legal infrastructure has improved, it will be a long time before they achieve an effectively functioning real estate market.

THE OLD SOVIET EMPIRE

The former Soviet Union offers a number of intriguing opportunities for global real estate investors. Unfortunately, the heart of the former Soviet Union, Russia, remains an undesirable location for global real estate investors. It is a country where people believe that the road to riches lies in stealing from others rather than by adding value. As a result, newly arrived international investors are viewed as prime opportunities for exploitation via fraudulent contracts, self-dealings, government expropriation, and other nefarious acts. The near-term prospects for the Russian economy are always murky while the Russian political and judicial systems show only the faintest signs of a liberal democracy. As a result, Russia remains an investment target only for those who are both politically connected and have deep pockets — as well as strong stomachs.

In contrast, Poland and the Czech Republic have undergone dramatic economic reforms, and are now modern economies. They have integrated into mainstream Europe. However, these are relatively small economies. As a result, it is difficult to establish the critical mass of local operations necessary to justify the costs associated with researching the markets, mastering legal and tax structures, etc. Nevertheless, global tenants are in these countries and demanding global quality space, presenting the opportunity for global real estate operators to leverage their relationships with these tenants.

Development risks in many countries are compounded by the fact that the political infrastructure is less transparent than in the U.S. Further, the depth of demand in many developing markets is thin. This phenomenon is often ignored by investors and was vividly displayed in Warsaw in the mid-1990s. Developers were attracted by the very high rents being paid by a very small number of international tenants. These developers calculated that at these rents, they could build to western European standards and achieve substantial returns. Unfortunately, as these properties came on-line, developers often discovered that there were only few tenants willing to pay such rents. Stated differently, developers developed Mercedes quality properties for what ended up being a market of Chevy consumers.

Integrating the economies of Eastern Europe into Western Europe offered the attractive investment bet that Eastern Europe would see notably lower initial yields post integration. The bet was that cap rates would fall by more than the decline in rents, yielding attractive returns, particularly where leverage was available. And as these countries successfully became part of an integrated European economy, Warsaw, Prague, and Budapest now price at cap rates similar to those found in leading Western European.

SOUTH OF THE BORDER

Latin America is a very fragmented region, under the shadow of inflation, populist politics, narco-economies, corruption, and the return of military dictators. The fear of inflation is analogous to the fear of the Great Depression held by many retired Americans. That is, real estate is viewed as a unique asset which provides substantial protection against inflation. In Latin America, this attitude generates real estate prices higher than what is justified simply based on supply and demand, as many wealthy local investors are willing to pay a premium for the inflation protection offered by real estate. For example, local investors frequently purchase condominium interests in commercial properties or fund new development at returns well below those demanded by international investors.

In Argentina, Brazil, and Chile, there are properties yielding 7-12% U.S-equivalent IRRs. However, it is difficult to generate returns on equity above these levels due to the absence of long-term debt, a condition that is the outgrowth of political and economic uncertainty combined with a history of runaway inflation in these economies. As a result, most global real estate operators find the risks too high relative to the returns on equity that can be found elsewhere.

THE UNITED STATES OF EUROPE

Most major cities in Western Europe generally have an excess supply of real estate capital. This is the result of the low returns on government debt and equity that remain acceptable to European — particularly French, German, and Italian — banks, insurance companies, and "Mom and Pop" investors. These low returns have fed capital into European real estate as a favored investment class even at very low yields. This is reflected by the homogeneity of returns in major urban property markets, where high-quality properties trade at sub-4% initial yields even though the lease structures, growth prospects, asset liquidity, and tenant quality are very different. Perhaps the most interesting example of this phenomenon is seen in Paris, where top-quality office properties trade at 2-4% initial yields. This is despite the fact that standard leases in Paris are 9 years, indexed to the CPI for construction costs, can be broken by the tenants every third year, and give the tenant an absolute right of occupancy at the end of year 9. This lease structure means that if market rents fall, tenants will break their leases every third year, producing returns less than 4-5%. Alternatively, if rents rise substantially over the term of the lease, tenants will remain in place and rents will rise only 1-2% annually. Active investors in Paris fantasize that they will receive big rent bumps at the end of the lease, however, this seems to be somewhat wishful thinking, as France remains a fundamentally socialist country. Thus, it is doubtful that landlords would be allowed to triple a tenant's rental rate upon lease expiration, even if market rents tripled over the term of the lease.

A difficult question facing real estate investment in Western Europe is how the "local hero" problem will be resolved. European countries have long protected their banks, telecommunication companies, automobile companies, airlines, power companies, etc. to safeguard jobs and hence gain votes. The result is that there are too many carmakers, electronics firms, major telecoms, banks, etc. — the local heroes — in major cities. Ultimately every country will not have a major bank, a major electronics company, a major automobile company, etc. In fact, many of these local heroes will be eliminated by global competition, while others will be forced to consolidate. As a result, while some cities will see enormous demand growth for headquarters offices, much of the space currently occupied by these non-competitive local heroes will be vacated. A similar phenomenon took place in the U.S. when the banking, telecommunications, and electrical supply sectors, etc. moved, shrank, or disappeared from many cities, while rapidly expanding in others.

The local hero problem is exacerbated by political pressures to stop "globalization." Europeans are generally reluctant to move within their own country, much less across international borders. It is difficult enough to move from Cleveland to Dallas, but many times more difficult to move from Copenhagen to Madrid, which involves a change in language, business cultures, governmental structures, tax systems, and legal protections. Instead, premium pricing for real estate cash flows driven by the availability of capital keeps properties globally expensive. If European financial institutions are required to achieve higher returns on equity at lower risk, the adverse reverberations on property prices will be felt throughout European property markets.

INDIA

With a population of nearly 1.4 billion growing 1% a year, and a relatively stable, democratic government, India is a market with seemingly endless rewards. But as enticing as the Indian market appears at first glance, it is fraught with corruption and a lack of transparency. It has been the ultimate insider's market, where outsiders are sheep to be shorn. It generally lacks a verifiable long-term track record of international investment, as the Indian investment market was opened to international parties only in 2005. The lack of multiple property cycles over which patterns can be observed is also a major deterrent for global players.

As with most markets around the world, opacity and reliability of data are major issues when investing in India. The Indian government has recognized this, and in the short span of time since foreign direct investment was legalized there, regulations intended to improve real estate market transparency have been put in place. In addition, the most recent implementation of the Real Estate Regulatory Act (RERA), the Goods and Services Tax (GST) and banking sector reform have all created a more positive environment for large companies and international investors alike.

Publicly traded REITs were approved in India in 2014 and launched in 2019 via a Blackstone sponsored joint venture. There are currently three REITs, with presumably more to follow. The formation of REITs is expected to expand quality real estate investment opportunities.

In 2016, India established a landmark Insolvency and Bankruptcy Act designed to reform the decades-old system of debt recovery. The Act established supposedly strict timelines for the bankruptcy process, limited the ability of company owners and developers (promoters) to bid on their own assets, and established separate tribunals to oversee the process. But the early years have not been smooth and some key aspects of the Act were suspended during Covid. However, it is hopefully a critical first step toward attracting long-term, stable, foreign capital that has historically stayed away from India due to a lack of confidence in its legal system.

CHINA

Similar to India, mainland China is revered for its population size and pace of growth. Unlike India, China is a communist country and becoming even more so. All land is owned by the government. Prior to the late 1990s, when the housing sector was privatized, housing was allocated to individuals through the "work unit" system as a benefit associated with a person's job. As China transitioned to a more market-centered economy, there was an enormous housing construction boom that has been characterized from time-to-time as a for-sale residential property bubble. In some rural areas, land was taken from farmers and entire city-sized highrise developments were completed, though many sat partially or totally empty due to lack of resident demand. These became known as "ghost cities."

Local governments benefited greatly from taxing land leases in their jurisdictions, and property taxes on those now private properties are key to keeping local government coffers filled. As such, there is an incentive for governments to keep housing prices high.

A few U.S.-based platforms have invested in China since the early 2000s, setting up offices and joint ventures there to capitalize on the high growth opportunities across all the major property types. The largest risks related to being an international investor in Chinese real estate is the legal system and the potential for the rules to change unexpectedly in a detrimental way. China is also known for corruption and bribery as well as human rights and child labor abuses.

In 2021, the Chinese development company, Evergrande, presented a massive credit issue, representing some $400 billion of maturing debt. But it is useful to put this in perspective relative to world GDP and global wealth. Even if this debt is a 100% write off (it was at the time selling for around $0.90 on the dollar), it is only 0.5% of world GDP and 0.1% of global wealth. Of course, it is more notable for China, where this debt primarily resides, at 2.7% of its GDP and 0.5% of its wealth. And that is if it is a complete loss (which is very unlikely). As such, a global cataclysmic event is unlikely, even when the roughly $3.5 trillion of debt of other Chinese developers is included in the analysis. For example, even if the entire $4 trillion of Chinese developer debt is worthless, it would represent only 1% of global wealth and 5% of wealth in China. Big, but not such awful numbers.

BRAZIL

As the largest economy in South America and one of the world's biggest democracies, Brazilian real estate has attracted some U.S. investors. For U.S. investors, Brazil is a bit "less foreign" than many other countries since it is in the West and flying there does not involve crossing several time zones. However, its political and economic frameworks can be breathtaking for western economy investors.

While turbulently democratic today, Brazil was under military rule as recently as the mid-1980s, and in 2017, its President was impeached and removed from office for fiscal manipulation. This political crisis was magnified by the successor President being accused of bribery as part of a comprehensive and government-led corruption crackdown. This political turmoil arose during Brazil's GDP contraction of more than 7% from 2014-2016. Brazil's ongoing economic constraints, corruption and political instability are regularly on display.

Crisis spells opportunity for some global real estate investors, whose strategies in Brazil have included lending in a tight national credit market and acquiring distressed properties, with a plan to turn them around as economic and political stability improves.

NON-U.S. INVESTORS ARE NOT DUMB

It is often assumed by Americans that non-U.S. firms are not as smart or savvy as U.S. real estate operators. While in many countries, local real estate operators are not as adept at sophisticated financial analysis and at the slicing, dicing, and re-slicing of real estate cash flows, this is more than offset by the fact that they are intelligent, well-educated, and know the rules by which local real estate markets operate. The knowledge of how these local markets work is much more important than it is in the U.S. or U.K., as the rules of the game and of transactions are much less predictable and transparent. Not unlike the "old days" in the U.S., local operators generally have a cozy relationship with a friendly local financial institution. In fact, in many cases these operators *are* the major local banks and insurance companies acting directly as real estate investors. They may not be as nimble or as customer-friendly as the more entrepreneurial global real estate operators, but tenants in most countries are dominated by large, governmentally-influenced institutions, making it difficult for entrepreneurial global real estate operators to achieve the necessary prestige and clout as outsiders.

LOCAL PARTNERS

One of the most difficult questions faced when deciding to enter a local real estate market is whether to use a local partner. Local partners bring a wealth of knowledge and expertise. In addition, they know the rules of the game and the major players, as well as which properties have historically been duds (and why). However, these partners generally operate within a different institutional framework from major U.S. real estate operators. They are generally more reliant on governmental and institutional contacts and inside deals, and less reliant on detailed financial analysis and carefully conceived exit strategies so cherished by their global partners.

Particularly in less developed markets, a strong local partner is attractive because of extensive contacts and their ability to "make it happen." This ability, however, often recoils on the international investor when the local partners turn their attention to "making it happen." All too often, international investors find that their local partners use their powers to restrike their partnership, and that there is little that can be done to stop them.

In many markets, particularly less developed economies, the strength of local partners can change very quickly. Perhaps the best example is that for years the Suharto family was the ultimate local partner in Indonesia. Yet overnight, they became a liability. Even in more developed and stable economies, this problem exists due to the large economic role played by governments.

The alternative to a local partner is to purchase or build a deep local infrastructure. This allows the international investor to control their culture and incentive structures but requires a much greater commitment of capital and managerial effort. Few real estate investment companies can afford to put in place the necessary infrastructure before they have a business. As a result, most global real estate investors choose to use a local partner initially, building their own infrastructure as they generate a sufficient level of business.

CURRENCY RISK

An important issue facing every international real estate investor is currency risk. It is possible that even if the real estate investment performs superbly in terms of local currency, a sufficiently large adverse currency movement can destroy the investment's dollar performance. This risk is not unique to real estate investments and has been addressed by global corporations for many years. There are several ways that such corporations have historically dealt with currency risks. First, they usually hedge the risks, at least in major currencies, associated with the investment transactions. That is, once a transaction is entered, a **currency hedge** is used to protect against adverse currency movements prior to closing. Such hedges are usually of short duration and hence, relatively cheap. However, in countries with thin currency markets, this risk cannot be efficiently hedged, and currency swings between signing and closing are often a contingency for which they may break a deal.

Hedging cash flows associated with the ongoing operation of the properties and the residual value of the asset is much more difficult. This is because even in relatively thick currency markets, it is difficult and expensive to hedge long-term currency exposures. Some companies use dynamic hedging models that combine a rolling series of short-term hedges. These models provide adequate hedging coverage on short-term investments, but for longer periods, their hedging capability greatly diminishes, and the expense rises substantially.

An alternative is to underwrite currency erosions that are expected to occur during the investment lifetime process. In the long run, expected changes in currency rates are theoretically equal to the difference between expected inflation rates between the two countries. For example, the dollar could be expected to strengthen to the extent that the U.S. expected inflation rate is less than that of the target country. Investors may use the difference in long-term bond rates, adjusted for differences in credit quality, payment mechanics, and liquidity to proxy the differential inflation rates expected by the market. This simple model, while theoretically sound, performs far from perfect. Even then, it is undermined by the fact that inflationary expectations will deviate from actual outcomes. A number of developing countries often quote rents, either legally or de facto, in U.S. dollars or Euros in order to offset the volatility and illiquidity of their currency, which greatly reduces the currency risk. However, it does not completely eliminate it because the residual value and the rent renewal cash flows are not in dollars.

Another common currency risk management technique is the use of local currency debt to partially match the currency exposures of assets and liabilities, thus notably reducing cash flow volatility. Further, to the extent that real estate investors intend to keep their money at work in the country to grow their business, currency risk is greatly reduced because the returns are made and reinvested in local currency. Thus, even if the currency falls versus the dollar, it still purchases the same amount of new assets and services in the target country. This is the reason why many international corporations do little other than hedge their purchase transactions, leaving their cash flows unhedged, while leveraging in local currency. For most long-term real estate investors, this is probably the most efficient long-term strategy.

All of these currency risk management approaches for long-term cash flows are seriously limited. Therefore, the committed international real estate investor must simply accept that currency risks are inherent to cross-border investing, and those risks must be tolerated to achieve the performance and diversification advantages of international investing. While some investors may conclude that currency and other risks unique to international investing outweigh the potential returns, other investors view currency risks as yet another reason to opportunistically enter non-U.S. markets.

CLOSING THOUGHT

Will a successful large-scale global real estate investment company ultimately evolve? Despite the perils, the answer is "yes," for the simple reasons that both the tenant base and capital markets are continually globalizing. It makes sense that banks, automobile companies, electronic companies, accounting firms, and law firms will turn to global space providers. In addition, global capital sources will gravitate to the most efficient real estate firms pulling them into new markets. Further, just as the demise of local banks in the U.S. radically changed the nature of the U.S. real estate market, the demise of local hero banks and life insurance companies will create a demand for global real estate operators who can best service customers and yield the highest returns. As the home of the globalization process, U.S. real estate companies are among the leaders of this process, and many American firms have demonstrated that globalized real estate investment is more than just an idea with potential.

 Online Companion Audio Interview: To hear a conversation about this chapter's content, go to the Online Companion and select the link for Chapter 3. Scroll down to the Audio Interview section and listen.

Chapter 4
The Fundamentals of Commercial Leases

"Analyze first; then leap."
- Dr. Peter Linneman

An essential dimension of real estate finance is understanding leases. With the exception of hotels and multifamily properties, the pro formas (income projection models) we discuss are to a large degree driven by the terms of existing leases. Real estate is a business, and lease terms dictate how specific aspects of that business must be conducted. If you as the current owner, or the property's previous owners, agreed to specific lease terms, those terms dictate the property's planned performance through the life of the lease(s). This is true even if the current market would dictate very different lease terms.

The general rationale behind lease negotiations is that the landlord (the **lessor**) provides the space (the "premises") to the tenant (the **lessee**) in exchange for rental payments sufficient to yield an adequate return on the real estate. In addition, the tenant should pay all operating and maintenance costs associated with their premises, as those are their costs of conducting business. This simple rationale is complicated by the fact that in weak market conditions, landlords often compromise in order to attract and retain tenants. Reality is also complicated by the fact that most properties have operating and maintenance costs associated with the common areas of the property (lobbies, elevators, stairwells, roofs, parking decks, etc.). Are these common costs part of the individual tenants' costs of doing business? "Yes," as these costs maintain the tenant's general operating environment and vary based on property occupancy **(variable expenses)**. But also "no," to the degree that many of these common costs exist whether the tenant is in the building or not **(fixed expenses)**. Prevailing market conditions will dictate how these common costs are allocated between the landlord and tenants, as well as any **cost recoveries** or **reimbursements** of operating expenses specific to each tenant's space.

What are the significant aspects of leases, and the reasoning and negotiations that create lease terms? We will primarily focus our discussion on retail leases, as shopping centers and regional mall leases most vividly demonstrate many of the issues that you need to consider. The relevant issues for retail leases tend to be more extensive than for non-retail properties. However, each property type has its own lease nuances.

To understand the rationale of key lease terms, assume that you own a 1 million-square foot regional mall and are negotiating a lease with a potential tenant for 5,000 square feet. What are some of the most important terms you need to address? Bear in mind that the space being leased is only a small part of a large retail property.

ECONOMIC TERMS

Rent

Students invariably suggest the rental rate is the most important lease term. Of course, rent is important as it determines how much money you will collect from the tenant, and to a large extent dictates your revenue stream from that space for the length of the lease. Rent is comprised of three components: **base rent; base rent escalations**; and **percentage rent**. Base rent is the initial rent for the space, while the rent escalation specifies how, if at all, this rent changes during the life of the lease. This escalation may be based upon inflation measures, for example, with base rent growing each year proportionate to changes in the Consumer Price Index. Alternatively, it may grow at specified dollar or percentage increments over the lease, or there may be no rent escalations in the lease at all.

The third component is percentage rent, also known as **overage**, which is unique to retail rents. Percentage rent is a form of **additional rent** that specifies the percentage of the tenant's gross sales revenue that the landlord receives in addition to the base rent and escalations. For instance, the lease may specify that the landlord receives 2% of store revenues in excess of sales of $300 per square foot, monitored monthly. Why is percentage rent used in retail but not in other types of properties? Because the landlord controls store mix and the overall retail environment, and a good store mix and retailing environment can increase tenant sales. In contrast, the productivity of office and warehouse tenants is rarely impacted by their neighbors. In addition, since store sales are relatively easily monitored, it is easy to assess the sales productivity of the space.

Percentage rent helps to align retail tenant interests with those of the landlord. If the landlord has no economic incentive to enhance the tenants' sales, the landlord will primarily focus on leasing the space to whomever will pay the highest base rent. If, on the other hand, the tenant rewards the landlord for their superior sales which result from an enhanced tenant mix, the landlord will focus more on creating a tenant mix that maximizes total center sales. The landlord will attempt to create the optimal mix of tenants by avoiding redundant stores, optimizing the location of tenants, and signing leases with complementary stores. For example, a good tenant mix might position tenants like Bostonian, Brooks Brothers, and Troudeau in proximity to each other, as people who shop at one of these stores are likely to shop at the others. Another synergistic combination would be a Gap near a Victoria's Secret and a Lady Foot Locker store. The goal is to generate positive externalities across stores, which the landlord shares with tenants via percentage rents. Percentage rents typically represent 5-10% of a tenant's total rent payment.

Marketing Budget

Shopping centers can be very complicated in their execution as they are operating businesses. For example, centers generally charge anchors a low base rent, while in-line stores, which are the smaller stores located between the anchors, pay notably higher base rents plus percentage rent. Historically, landlords often gave away space to department stores and, to a much lesser extent, supermarkets, even though their stores cost as much as $100 per square foot to build. In return, these anchor stores advertise (including your center's location) and draw customers to the center. Your center's design and tenant mix attempt to channel that traffic to the in-line stores, whose rents are your primary sources of revenue.

Leases will generally require that each tenant pay a share of the center's marketing budget. For example, you will hold promotional days at your center, sponsor a local youth organization, advertise in local newspapers, etc., and each lease will specify how much of these marketing expenses are paid by each tenant.

Utilities, Insurance, and Property Taxes

Another key lease item is the treatment of utility charges. There are two general components of utility costs. The first is the utility expense you as the landlord pay for the **common areas** of the property, including lighting the walkway in front of the stores, water in the public bathrooms, air conditioning for the hallways, etc. These common areas are amenities of the center that benefit all tenants. While the expenses associated with **common area maintenance (CAM)** are not specific to any tenant, they are a critical part of a store's operating environment. You will negotiate how much of these CAM expenses will be passed through to each tenant.

The second component of utility costs relates to expenses that are specific to each tenant's space. In older properties there may not be meters that gauge each tenant's utility usage, but rather only a single "master" meter for the entire property. For such properties you attempt to determine the appropriate allocation of the property's expense for each tenant, with each lease detailing the allocation of these expenses. Modern buildings are metered individually to gauge each tenant's usage of water, electricity, gas, etc. Leases in modern buildings generally specify that each tenant is responsible for their own metered utility bills.

Property tax and casualty insurance payments paid by the landlord are part of the cost of the property's operation. Tenants are usually allocated their pro rata share of these expenses based on their share of the property's rentable square footage. However, there are frequently **expense caps** specified in the lease that limit the extent to which these items can rise during any single year or over the term of the lease. These caps may be negotiated for any component of operating costs, including utilities, property taxes, and insurance.

Expenses for these items are sometimes passed on only to the extent that they exceed levels at the time the lease is signed (the lease's **base year**). The base year expense amount is known as the **expense stop**. For example, the property tax at the time the lease was signed is $1 per square foot per year, and the lease specifies that only increases in property taxes above the $1 per square foot expense stop are passed through to the tenant, up to a maximum of $0.10 per square foot per year, and not to exceed an increase of $1 per square foot over the 15-year term of the lease. These base year designations, recoveries, and caps are determined by market conditions at the time the lease is negotiated, as well as the risk-sharing preferences of the landlord and tenant.

HVAC – Heating, Ventilation and Air Conditioning

In order to save money, a landlord in Phoenix will attempt to limit air conditioning usage, while a landlord in Buffalo will try to turn down the heat. In addition, tenants have different temperature preferences and usage patterns. As a result, you will negotiate when, and how much, HVAC you need to provide to each tenant and to the common areas, as well as who pays these expenses. In newer buildings, tenants are generally able to control the HVAC in their space. Like individual metering, this makes usage patterns and expense allocation much easier, as the lease generally states that the tenant is responsible for their own HVAC usage. However, you still must specify the policy for common areas. In older properties, the lease will specify when heat or air conditioning must be provided (for example, starting at 8 AM on weekdays).

Security and Property Maintenance

The lease will specify the type of security provided at the property, and who pays for this security. This is also true of property maintenance, including the common areas and grounds. For example, how often are the grounds and buildings cleaned? How often are windows washed? Who selects the cleaners? Who is responsible for building maintenance? Are security cameras provided in parking areas? Are employees escorted to their cars after hours by security personnel? These, and many similar terms should be addressed in each lease.

Tenant Improvements

Tenant improvements (TIs) include those items necessary to make a tenant's space fully operational. Commonly, the landlord provides the tenant with "as is" space. For a new building, this will be base ("raw") space, while for existing buildings, it will be the space as left by the last tenant. However, the tenant may want new fixtures, carpeting, a kitchen for restaurants, shelving, etc. to run the business. Who pays for these tenant improvements on the space? It depends on the market. In a weak leasing market, the landlord may have to provide the tenant with much of the necessary funding for their TIs in the form of a **TI allowance**, which is typically quoted in dollars per square foot.

The parties will not only negotiate over who pays for the TIs and how much will be paid, but also who is responsible for completing the work, who the contractor will be, who has rights to the improvements after the lease expires, who pays for the removal of any TIs after the lease expires, etc. Remember that after the lease expires, the space returns to the landlord, irrespective of which party paid for the TIs. Therefore, the landlord has a significant interest in who does the work, how it is done, and what the quality of the space is. Again, the market will dictate which party has the negotiating power in resolving these matters.

Why would a landlord pay for improvements made to a tenant's space? First, consider the case of a new building under construction. Rather than paying to paint, install lighting fixtures, erect divider walls, etc. that the tenant may not want, you will say to a tenant (who has the alternative of leasing fully completed space in another property), "Why don't I just give you the money to finish the space as you want, instead of me putting money into finishing the space in a way you may not want?" In this way, you attempt to turn your unfinished space from a negative to a positive. In turn, owners of finished (but vacant) space frequently have to offer TI allowances in order to attract tenants who do not like the current finish of the space.

A second reason landlords provide TIs is that weak markets force you to offer discounted economics to attract tenants. Why not just reduce rents rather than providing TI dollars up front? After all, aren't you indifferent between offering $35 a foot in TIs up front versus reducing rents over the term of the lease by an equivalent present value? Not really. While tenants may be indifferent between TIs and equivalent NPV rent concessions up to the point where the TIs exceed their desired improvements, TI expenditures go into your building, while rent concessions walk out your door. As a result, if you must give concessions, you would rather give TI concessions in order to keep the money in the building, as you hope that these improvements will have some value to future tenants if the current tenant leaves the space.

TI costs can run as much as the equivalent of 1-2 years of rent, especially in weak markets with substantial amounts of new empty space coming on the market.

Free Rent

Free rent or **rent abatement** occurs when no rent is paid during the first weeks, months, or years of the lease term. In a weak market, you may prefer to give a period of free rent, rather than discount rents over the term of the lease by an equivalent NPV amount. This is done to protect the property value by keeping rents closer to typical rental rates for when you plan to sell or refinance the property in future years.

Capital Costs

Leases often specify that the tenant is responsible for all or part of common area capital costs, including items such as the repair and maintenance or replacement of the HVAC system, elevators, parking decks, and structural components. This may take the form of a requirement that the tenant pays capital costs as they occur, or that they annually reimburse the landlord for such costs on an amortized basis. Alternatively, the lease may specify that the property be returned at the end of the lease "in commercially acceptable condition" or in its "original condition." The typical lease in London, for example, requires tenants to pay all capital costs as they occur and return the space to its original condition at the tenants' expense.

Net Rent

Net rent refers to the rent after all operating costs are paid. The term **triple net lease** (often abbreviated as "NNN") generally refers to situations where the tenant pays all operating (and frequently capital) costs, including insurance, utilities, and property taxes in addition to the contractual base rent and escalation payments to the landlord. **Net leases** shift the risk of increases in such costs from the landlord to the tenant, altering the ownership risk of the property.

Net effective rent is used somewhat ambiguously in the commercial real estate industry. Generally stated, it is annual rent, net of: unrecovered maintenance and operating costs (property taxes, insurance, utilities, etc.), the amortized value of free rent, the amortized value of leasing commissions, and the amortized value of TIs. For example, a gross rent of $30 per square foot per year, with a $5 per square foot per year cost recovery on $10 per square foot per year of maintenance and operating costs, yields a net annual rent of $25 per square foot. If one year of free rent was provided on a 10-year lease, this amounts to amortized free rent of $3 per square foot per year ($30 per square foot / 10 years). If $40 per square foot in TIs are provided on this 10-year lease, this amounts to amortized TIs of $4 per square foot per year. If the leasing commissions are 2% of the face value of the 10-year lease, they are $6 per square foot ($30 * 10 * 2%), which amortizes to $0.60 per square foot per year. Thus, in this example the landlord's net effective rent is $17.40 per square foot per year ($30 + $5 − $10 − $3 − $4 − $0.60) as summarized in Figure 4.1.

FIGURE 4.1

Annual Net Effective Rent PSF Calculation	
Gross Rent	$30.00
Cost Recoveries	5.00
Maintenance and Operating Costs	(10.00)
Amortized Free Rent	(3.00)
Amortized Tenant Improvement	(4.00)
Amortized Leasing Commissions	(0.60)
Annual Net Effective Rent	$17.40 PSF

Online Companion Hands On: Go to the Online Companion and select the link for Chapter 4. Scroll down to the Excel Figures section and download the Excel file and open it to the Exercise tab. Using the Assumptions provided at the top of the tab, fill out the remaining 9 years of the 10-year projection of the above example, and calculate the NPV of the cash flow at a 10% discount rate. What is the value of the lease to the landlord when calculated on this basis? What would the NPV be if instead of rent growing at 2% a year, it was flat for Years 1 through 5, bumped up $4.00 PSF in Year 6 and then remained constant?

Note that this approach to net effective rent ignores the time value of money, as TIs, free rent, and leasing commissions are all up-front costs, while rents are received in the future. However, since this term is not the basis of valuation or lending calculations, but rather a simple summary statistic, there is no harm in this simplification.

NON-ECONOMIC TERMS

Thus far, we have discussed lease terms which are primarily concerned with payments made by the tenants. These monetary components are generally viewed by students as the most important terms of a lease. But never forget that the tenant is just a small part (0.5% in our example) of a larger whole. By effectively organizing your space, the center can be worth more than the sum of its parts. In a way, shopping centers are like a sports team. You could have an NBA team made up of just high scoring shooting guards, but the team would be unsuccessful without good defenders, passers, and rebounders. Below are some of the most important lease issues that you must consider, particularly for retail centers. In fact, they can be far more important aspects of retail leases than the monetary issues we have discussed, because if they are not correctly contracted, they can destroy your retail environment.

Signage

One of the most important terms of a retail lease is the location, size, and design of each tenant's signage. If you have no restrictions on signage, each tenant will only be interested in maximizing his or her visibility. For example, a small tenant that sells products geared towards young men might put a huge sign of a naked woman in front of the store absent signage restrictions in the lease. Such a sign might attract young men to that tenant, but is such signage optimal for your overall retail environment? Only if every store in your center is geared towards young men! But usually, the bulk of your stores are geared towards children and young and middle-aged women, who will find such signage offensive. Therefore, the lease will carefully regulate the size, location, format, content, colors, and other details of each tenant's signage.

Going Dark

What happens if an anchor tenant, who pays little rent, decides to close their store with a lease in effect for 15 more years? For example, the tenant could decide to stop operating in your center and move to a competing center, while still making their minimal lease payments to you. This prevents a potential competitor from moving into their vacated space.

If the lease does not protect against such behavior (known as **going dark**) and it occurs, you will have dramatically reduced traffic at your property, destroying the performance of your in-line tenants, who are your primary sources of rental income. Therefore, you will try to negotiate terms that prevent a tenant from continuing to pay rent but not operating a store in their space. You will try to assure that the anchor operates until the lease expires or until you are able to more productively rent the space.

Walmart, the largest retailer and grocer in America, presents landlords with a particular dilemma. Since Walmart draws shoppers to their stores, you want them in your center, right? Not so fast. Walmart is also the largest tenant of dark space in America, time and again going dark in older stores with low-rent long-term leases, in order to move a mile down the road into a larger store. Walmart continues to pay rent on the old store, but the fact that it is not operating destroys your in-line tenants, and hence the center's profitability. So why not simply prohibit them from going dark? Leverage, or more accurately, the lack of leverage. The reality is that Walmart may not sign such a lease. If you insist upon this clause, they might go down the road and sign a long-term lease without a go-dark provision at a competitive center, drawing customers from your center. Hopefully, you are beginning to understand the importance of negotiating leverage, especially when you do not have any. The industry has evolved into being damned if you sign Walmart to a long-term lease or being damned if you don't. Fun business, isn't it? This is further complicated by the risk that online retail erodes the economic viability of your tenants.

Hours and Days of Operation

The lease will specify when the store and center must, or can, be open. If you do not do this, tenants will operate only when they want, and without standardized hours of operations, customers may not experience a rich shopping environment. For this reason, all stores in the mall open and close around the same time, even though not all retailers may like this restriction. For example, certain restaurants may only want to be open at night, but your center needs food available at all hours of operations.

Why do you limit when stores can be open? If a store decides to operate very late at night (i.e., in the early morning), it may create security issues. Therefore, you may decide to restrict the permitted hours of operation to "shopping hours."

Length of Lease

You need to specify how long the lease will run. Remember that a long-term lease will impact your revenue and operations for many years. If you sign a long-term lease in a hot market, you will receive a relatively high rent for years. On the other hand, you could suffer for years if you sign a long-term lease at low rents due to a current excess-supply environment.

Tenants usually want a very short-term lease with a lot of extension options. With that structure, the tenant can walk if business does not go well, a better location arises, or market rents fall. On the other hand, if they want to remain, they have the option to stay at the location. Depending on the economic environment, landlords usually prefer the security of a long-term lease, but remember that today's "red hot" retailer may be tomorrow's dud.

Expansion Rights

Larger tenants, particularly in office and warehouse properties, want the option to satisfy growth at the same location. Therefore, landlords often sell the **expansion rights/option** to additional future space near or adjacent to the tenant's current location. In the meantime, the landlord can lease that space to another tenant. The problem is the temporary tenant will have to leave if the option is exercised. As a result, you may have a problem leasing space that is optioned. Frequently you rent option space to short-term users, such as political campaign offices. Juggling option space is an art which can yield unexpected revenues.

Usage Restrictions

You do not want to sign a tenant to occupy space as a woman's clothing store and find out the tenant decides to run a slaughterhouse from the space. That is not the retail environment you envisioned! Therefore, the lease must be extremely precise in describing the kind of business activities the tenant can, and cannot, conduct in the space.

Sublet Rights

Assume that a woman's clothing store has a lease with 15 years to run. Can they sublease their space to another retailer? If the tenant subleases space to a lesser-quality store or to a computer repair shop, it can greatly reduce the productivity of your center. Therefore, the lease will specify sublet rights, including whether the landlord has the right to approve all sublease activity.

Location Assignment

If you are a retail tenant in a strip shopping center, where do you want to be located within the center? Close to the anchor tenant might be best for your sales. Close to the street might give you more visibility for people driving or walking by the property. The importance of where tenants are located within a property is not unique to retail. In an apartment building, you want a higher floor for a better view, less ground noise, and (if on the top floor) no neighbors stomping around overhead.

There are unique location dynamics in regional malls that shape mall design. First, you have to understand that there is a tradeoff between land costs and building additional floors for all types of buildings. The incremental hard construction costs of an additional floor generally increase disproportionately more than the cost of the floor directly beneath it. That is, a three-story building will be more than three times as expensive to build as a one-story building. This is because you need more concrete, more steel, more support structures to handle three floors rather than one. How many floors there are in a building will partially depend on the cost of land. If it costs more to build higher, and land costs are low, you will spread the structure over more land. If land costs are high, such as in Manhattan, you would rather incur the additional costs of building higher in order to spread the cost of the land over more floors. You will use engineers to help analyze this trade off.

Human nature also determines the design of the exterior and interior of a mall. Roughly 90% of the products sold in a regional mall are purchased on impulse. Therefore, you want to maximize the retail stimuli to which a shopper is exposed, as the more stimuli, the more shoppers will tend to spend. Assume your mall is one story. Shoppers will park their cars, walk through your mall, and then walk back through the mall to return to their cars. On the way back, buyers will generally walk faster and shop less than on their initial walk through the mall, because they are seeing "old" stimuli. You will realize lower sales productivity from impulse shoppers on their way out, as they are exposed to fewer "new" impulses.

To "solve" this problem you could build a two-story mall. With two stories, you are providing additional retail stimuli, as people can walk back through the second floor experiencing entirely new impulse shopping stimuli. If the second floor generates enough impulse buying, you can generate enough rent to justify the additional costs of building a second floor. However, you must contend with the fact that most people would rather go down a flight of stairs (unless that flight leads down to a basement) than up a flight of stairs. Why? That is for psychologists to determine, but for you, it is just an unfortunate fact of life. Therefore, few tenants reliant on impulse shopping want to occupy space on the second floor, as fewer shoppers will make it to the second story (even with elevators and escalators).

Then why do you see so many two-story regional malls? In some cases, it was an ill-informed development decision. This second-story space was surely leased in the financial models for these centers, and justified the cost paid for the development. But retail reality does not conform to your ill-conceived pro forma. As a result, there are a lot of centers with vacant second floors.

In other cases, it is because clever design addressed the problem. For example, if people will not go up a floor or down into a basement, you need to make them think they are on the main floor even though they are on the second floor. Alfred Taubman figured out a way to make people believe they are on the main floor when they enter a mall. To construct a building you have to dig a hole for the foundation. Instead of paying to haul away the dirt from the excavation, he decided to build an embankment with it. As customers drive onto this elevated surface and enter what looks like the first story of a one-story mall, they are actually entering the second floor of a two-story mall. When shoppers enter on the second floor, whether they shop on that floor first or not, they will eventually go downstairs to shop on the first floor because they know it is not the basement. Then for the return trip, they go back upstairs and walk to their car. This return trip generates new impulses, and hence purchases. With the addition of shoppers that enter on the second floor and are willing to go down the stairs, you are able to generate sufficient productivity for tenants on both floors, particularly if the majority of the shoppers enter on the second floor. This design, which can also be executed by exploiting a natural elevation difference, reduces some of the biases of floor location in a multi-floor mall. Another design solution is to locate "destination," rather than "impulse," stores on the second floor. Examples include food, theatres, bars, doctor's offices, and spas.

Interior design, including corridor width, common areas, and amenities also are important. For instance, if the corridor is too narrow and becomes overly crowded, people will not shop. On the other hand, if the corridor is too wide, the mall appears empty. Think about a comedy club, where you do not want to be the only one there and feel obligated to laugh, but you also do not want people crowded on top of you. Therefore, regional mall developers seek an optimal corridor design to enhance the shopping experience, boost tenants' revenues, and create more desirable retail space.

Detailed Description of the Space

In addition to identifying the location, the lease will include a detailed description of the space to be leased. Further, you must specify what is included in "the space." Is the carpet included? What about the light fixtures, the counter, wiring, windows, shelving, etc.? Do these physical elements stay when a tenant leaves? Do they have to be removed? The lease describes these details.

Tenant Mix

Percentage rents encourage you to create an exciting shopping environment. Some tenants refuse to lease if other similar stores are in the center, as they want complementary stores, but not direct competition. Therefore, you will have to negotiate the terms under which you can lease space to competitors. Many conflicts arise as a result of these **non-compete clauses**. For example, if you signed a lease with a woman's clothing store that states you cannot lease space in the center to another "top quality woman's clothing store," is Burlington Coat Factory a top-quality woman's clothing store? They sell clothing for women, but does that make Burlington Coat Factory a "top quality woman's clothing store"? Or does the lease clause prohibiting the presence of a second florist in the center prohibit Walmart from selling poinsettias and Christmas trees during the Christmas season?

In other cases, a tenant will lease only if other tenants remain in the center. As a result of these **co-tenancy clauses**, a center could lose several tenants if one key tenant goes under, goes dark, or refuses to renew their lease. On the other hand, the landlord may prohibit the tenant from opening other stores within a certain distance. These **radius restrictions** protect the landlord from the tenant potentially cannibalizing sales at the center. For instance, if an anchor grocery store tenant was not subject to a radius restriction, they could open a new store across the street at a competing center. This would no doubt lower sales for your in-line tenants, reduce your percentage rents, and could even cause in-line tenants to go out of business. That is why landlords seek a radius restriction, particularly for anchor tenants.

Parking

Tenants are concerned with the amount, location, and maintenance of parking. If there are not enough spaces to service the customers, the stores will lose business. As a result, you will lose percentage rent and/or have tenants vacate the space. In addition, tenants will also want sufficient parking close to their location. If customers cannot park within proximity to their destination, they may not visit the location. The lease may also specify the layout of the parking lot, which may inhibit the redevelopment of the center for several years. In addition, maintenance and lighting of parking lots is of critical importance to tenants.

Recourse and Security Deposit

Who exactly from the tenant side is responsible under the terms of the lease? Is it a new division of a high credit company? If so, and the new division ceases to operate, you are stuck with no tenant and no payment **recourse** to the high credit parent. This issue of recourse frequently arises in office leases. For example, Coca Cola U.S. is a very high credit tenant, but the tenant who leases from you in Moscow is Coca Cola Russia. If they cannot establish a profitable business in Russia, Coca Cola Russia will fold, and you cannot look to Coca Cola U.S. for rent payment. Therefore, you will try to get both the subsidiary and the parent as signatories to the lease. Not surprisingly, the tenant will generally try to keep the parent off the lease.

You will want the individual entrepreneurs and partners of the tenant to be on the lease in addition to their firm. Thus, if the firm goes bankrupt, you can look to these individuals for continued rental payment. Law firms, consulting firms, and accounting firms often must sign the lease as individual partners if they want to get the space they desire.

Alternative forms of landlord protection are to require that the tenant puts up a **security deposit** or **letter of credit**, which is only available to you as recourse if the tenant fails to perform on the lease. A problem frequently arises when the tenant goes bankrupt, and you attempt to lay claim to the security deposit or draw upon the letter of credit, as the bankruptcy court may rule that these are corporate assets that must be used to satisfy the claims of the most senior lenders. But what about the rights specified in your lease? Unfortunately, they are generally trumped by bankruptcy law.

CLOSING THOUGHT

We have just scratched the surface concerning the numerous terms that are critical to leases, most of which are non-monetary in nature. Remember that real estate is a business, and smart operation is what generates profits over the long term. You must understand the underlying business to successfully negotiate effective leases, even in difficult markets, that protect your interests under various scenarios that may never occur. You also begin to appreciate why leases are so thick.

 Online Companion Audio Interview: To hear a conversation about this chapter's content, go to the Online Companion and select the link for Chapter 4. Scroll down to the Audio Interview section and listen.

Chapter 5
Property-Level Pro Forma Analysis

"Run the numbers carefully but understand why these numbers will not occur."
- Dr. Peter Linneman

LEASE-BY-LEASE ANALYSIS

For office, retail, and industrial properties, tenant leases provide detailed information about expected cash flows for years to come. For multifamily properties, this visibility is generally limited to 12 months due to the typical year-long lease term. Although the tremendous detail provided in office, retail, and industrial leases enhances the likelihood of the accuracy of your multi-year future cash flow projections, the task of reading and analyzing numerous commercial leases is laborious and tedious. Each lease contains different economic terms, often written by different landlords, drafted in different market and tax environments, and structured to reflect each tenant's and owner's needs at the time the lease was negotiated. Fortunately, software programs such as *Argus* assist the arduous task of creating financial models lease by lease.

Although you use software to assemble and organize lease information into beautiful rows and columns on a pro forma spreadsheet, only you can think about the property's risks and opportunities. For example, what happens when a lease expires? Is the space leasable? To what credit quality tenant? What rent and rent bumps will you receive for the space? What tenant concessions will be required? For how long? How long will it take to lease vacant space? How much of the building will never be leased?

To systematically analyze a property, you enter key lease information for each tenant and effectively create fictional tenants for any vacant space that exists today and that you expect in the future. A thorough understanding of the market, product, and tenants is critical for this analysis. If you are too optimistic, you will forecast results that cannot realistically occur, resulting in severe return shortfalls versus your pro forma. But if you are unduly conservative, you will undervalue the property, causing you to be outbid, sell too cheaply, or never do a deal.

LINE ITEM ANALYSIS

With the help of sophisticated property software packages, such as *Argus*, you can create detailed financial pro formas for multi-tenant commercial properties. What is the appropriate time frame to analyze? Pro formas are usually presented on an annual basis, but depending on your investment and information needs, a shorter time interval (quarters or months) may be in order. As an investor, you will need to know in great detail when the property generates cash, because you will have monthly operating expenses and debt service payments. Small changes in the timing of cash flows may force you to miss payments, causing headaches with employees, vendors, and lenders.

Typically, a detailed monthly pro forma analysis is carried out for 5-7 years. Little value is gained by carrying out the analysis for 50 years, as accuracy rapidly diminishes. In addition, if you have 500 columns in your financial model, you will probably lose "bifocal points," as your spreadsheet will be very difficult to read. And if your target user (be it your loan officer, asset or portfolio manager, potential investor, or professor) is unable to read your entries, he or she may not bother to analyze, let alone approve, your deal. There is no gain from making a spreadsheet too complex to effectively utilize, as in the end it is just simple mathematics. If a major event is about to occur, such as a key tenant vacating the building in the 8th year, or a tax abatement expiring in the 10th year, then it is prudent to carry out the pro forma analysis a year or two beyond such an event. Otherwise, keep your financial model detailed, but simple enough to be useful. Bad analysis will generate useless results. You need to make informed and realistic, not capricious, assumptions about likely market outcomes. In the balance of this chapter, we walk through the individual line items of a retail property operating cash flow projection as well as the calculation of after-tax cash flow to equity.

OPERATING INCOME

Gross Potential Rental Revenue

To calculate rental income, you start with the revenue you would receive if the building's leasable space was 100% occupied. This is the **gross potential rental revenue (GPR)**. Gross potential rental revenue is calculated as the base rent multiplied by the property's total leasable square feet. For instance, assume you are the owner of Kathy Center, a 300,000-leasable square foot strip shopping center in Bethesda, Maryland, which you purchased for $48.5 million. The average base rent you charge to current tenants is approximately $15 per leasable square foot per year. Thus, your annual gross potential rental revenue is $4.5 million ($15 per square foot * 300,000 total leasable square feet), as summarized in Figure 5.1.

FIGURE 5.1

Kathy Center	
Gross Potential Rental Revenue Calculation	
Total Leasable Square Feet	300,000
Average Annual Base Rent PSF	$15.00
Gross Potential Rental Revenue	$4,500,000

Our use of average base rent is a simplification, as you will charge tenants different rents for their space. Thus, the precise calculation of gross potential rental revenue is a complex lease-by-lease calculation and only provides an estimation of the rent you will receive on any vacant space. Based on your existing leases and your expectations for future leasing, Figure 5.2 displays your estimates of the gross potential rental revenue from Kathy Center for the next five years.

FIGURE 5.2

Kathy Center Cash Flow Statement					
	Year 1	Year 2	Year 3	Year 4	Year 5
OPERATING INCOME					
Rental Income:					
Gross Potential Rental Revenue	4,500,000	4,590,000	4,816,287	4,924,653	4,957,649

Online Companion Hands On: Find the blank formatted Excel version of this Figure in Chapter 5 of the Online Companion and note the Assumptions for **Base Rent Year Over Year Growth** at the top of the tab. (continued on next page)

Key in the <u>Year 1</u> value of 4,500,000, and then calculate the subsequent year values as: (prior year **Gross Potential Rental Revenue** * (1 + current year **Base Year Rent Year Over Year Growth** rate). For example, the Year 2 value formula in cell d15 will be =c15*(1+d3), which equals (4,500,000) * (1 + .02). After you hit Enter, copy cell d15 and paste the formula to the right into cells e15, f15 and g15.

The interesting advantage of real estate cash flows is that the contractual nature of leases makes revenues easier to predict than for most businesses, as you can model when leases will be potentially renewed, expire, etc. Remember that many leases were signed in market conditions that were very different from the current environment, so in order to accurately forecast revenue, you must incorporate both lease-specific rental information and estimated future rents. As a result, you will not always see a smooth growth pattern for rental revenue. In fact, if tenants of high-priced rental space are vacating into an overbuilt market, rental revenue can significantly decline the following year. In our example, the fluctuations are due to assumed lease terminations and changing market rents.

Vacancy

In the Kathy Center example, three leases expire at the end of the 12th month of Year 1. You expect to re-sign two of the three tenants but think you will not renew the lease for the third space, resulting in a 3,000-leasable square foot vacancy (1%) starting in month 1 of Year 2. Therefore, you will not receive the projected gross potential rental revenue associated with the 3,000 square feet of physical vacancy in Year 2. You must subtract the expected gross potential rental revenue associated with the vacant space from the $4.59 million total expected gross potential revenue in Year 2 to calculate the **Net Base Rental Revenue** you expect to receive on occupied space. You perform the same calculation for each year based on your rent and vacancy expectations (Figure 5.3).

Not all vacancy is equal. Some vacancy exists even in a fully "stabilized" property. A **stabilized property** is fully occupied except for an expected "systemic" level of vacancy. The property's **net operating income (NOI)** is flat or growing relatively smoothly year-over-year and is indicative of the property's long-term future performance. An example of a stabilized 100-unit apartment building could be one with 2.5% yearly NOI growth, and 2-4% vacancy, as at any one time, some number of renters will be moving in and out as a part of normal **tenant turnover**. However, vacancy can also extend beyond normal turnover, particularly in weak markets and vulnerable properties. Such vacancy is often very lumpy, as when a corporation that leases half of your office building vacates the property. In addition, some space is effectively non-leasable.

A critical factor to remember about vacancy is its impact on other line items. For instance, as vacancies increase, operating expense reimbursements will decrease, as there are no tenants to pay the reimbursable expenses allocated to the vacant square footage. In addition, some cost items, such as electricity and phone service, will vary with vacancy. A similar relationship generally exists between vacancy and **ancillary income** (income from secondary sources), as with fewer people occupying the space, there will be lower demand for parking spaces, decreased washing machine usage, etc. Of course, ancillary income need not diminish with higher vacancy. For example, companies will still pay office landlords to utilize rooftops for antennae towers or signage. Therefore, you must carefully analyze each source of ancillary income to determine the appropriate relationship.

The interaction between vacancy and other line items is not limited to those detailed above, but these examples help you understand the interrelated nature of property performance. These interactions mean that **sensitivity analyses** that just change one assumption (e.g., What if rent is 10% lower?) without exploring the impact on other items can provide deceptive results. In a sense, properties are "living organisms," and you cannot make judgments on their investment risks and opportunities if you do not understand the realities of the real estate business. Real estate is not a spreadsheet, though a spreadsheet is a useful tool of the trade.

FIGURE 5.3

Kathy Center Cash Flow Statement					
OPERATING INCOME	Year 1	Year 2	Year 3	Year 4	Year 5
Rental Income:					
Gross Potential Rental Revenue	4,500,000	4,590,000	4,816,287	4,924,653	4,957,649
Vacancy	0	**(45,900)**	**(72,244)**	**(98,493)**	**(148,729)**
Net Base Rental Revenue	4,500,000	4,544,100	4,744,043	4,826,160	4,808,919

Online Companion Hands On: After having entered the Gross Potential Rental Revenue (GPR) in the Figure 5.2 tab, go to the Figure 5.3 tab, which builds on and links back to the Figure 5.2 tab (this same pattern is repeated for the subsequent Figures). You will note that Vacancy Rate % GPR assumptions are provided for you at the top of the tab. Fill in the Vacancy line, calculating it for each year as: −(that year's **Vacancy Rate % GPR**) * (that year's **Gross Potential Rental Revenue**). Then, calculate the **Net Base Rental Revenue** as: **GPR + Vacancy** (we add them because vacancy is represented as negative).

Percentage Rent/Overage

Total retail rent frequently is divided into **base rent** (and escalations thereon) and the additional rent component of **percentage rent** (a.k.a. **overage**). Overage lease clauses are specific to retail properties and stipulate that if gross sales for the tenant exceed a predetermined revenue threshold (the gross sales **breakpoint**), then a percentage of those incremental sales are paid to the landlord. The breakpoint is specified in the tenant's lease.

Based on negotiations with tenants, you expect the percentage rents from Kathy Center as summarized in Figure 5.4. The sum of the net base rental revenue and the percentage rent is the **Total Rental Income** you expect to receive from the property.

FIGURE 5.4

Kathy Center Cash Flow Statement					
OPERATING INCOME	Year 1	Year 2	Year 3	Year 4	Year 5
Rental Income:					
Gross Potential Rental Revenue	4,500,000	4,590,000	4,816,287	4,924,653	4,957,649
Vacancy	0	(45,900)	(72,244)	(98,493)	(148,729)
Net Base Rental Revenue	4,500,000	4,544,100	4,744,043	4,826,160	4,808,919
Percentage Rents	**93,305**	**66,209**	**66,925**	**64,003**	**65,425**
Total Rental Income	4,593,305	4,610,309	4,810,968	4,890,163	4,874,344

Online Companion Hands On: After completing Figure 5.3, go to the Figure 5.4 tab. Type in the Percentage Rents line dollar amounts as shown in Figure 5.4 above and calculate the **Total Rental Income** as: **Net Base Rental Revenue + Percentage Rents**.

Expense Reimbursements

Expense reimbursements go by multiple names: **tenant reimbursements**, **recovered expenses**, **cost recoveries**, and **pass-throughs.** Reimbursements are payments defined in the leases, made by tenants to the landlord for specified property expenses, such as insurance, property taxes, security, and utilities. These payments are for costs initially borne by the landlord and recovered from tenants as specified in their leases. These costs typically include not only suite-specific items, but also those for **common area maintenance (CAM)**. **CAM costs** are those costs associated with operating and maintaining a property's common space, such as the sidewalks and parking lots of Kathy Center. Each landlord defines CAM differently and allocates it as specified in the property's leases. Furthermore, while some CAM costs such as utilities, security, and trash removal at Kathy Center are common to all commercial property types, some properties incur property-type-specific CAM costs. For instance, a multi-story office building owner may incur costs associated with elevators, whereas a single-story warehouse owner does not.

The specifics of how CAM costs are repaid by tenants depends upon market conditions at the time the leases were signed, and on the negotiating strategies of the landlords and tenants. Your estimates for CAM cost reimbursements are displayed in Figure 5.5 in the **CAM Billings** line. In our example, the tenants in Kathy Center are expected to reimburse you for all common area maintenance. Looking at Figure 5.5, take note of how CAM Billings decrease as the vacancy level increases.

The local government levies property taxes based upon the **assessed tax value** of the center. They send you a tax bill, which you pay, and then pass on your tenants' respective shares as specified in their leases. This pass-through is often, but not necessarily, based on the tenant's proportionate share of leasable square footage. Your estimates of property tax reimbursements, which are assumed to be at 100% of cost, are displayed in Figure 5.5 in the **Property Tax Billings** line.

FIGURE 5.5

Kathy Center Cash Flow Statement					
	Year 1	Year 2	Year 3	Year 4	Year 5
OPERATING INCOME					
Rental Income:					
Gross Potential Rental Revenue	4,500,000	4,590,000	4,816,287	4,924,653	4,957,649
Vacancy	0	(45,900)	(72,244)	(98,493)	(148,729)
Net Base Rental Revenue	4,500,000	4,544,100	4,744,043	4,826,160	4,808,919
Percentage Rents	93,305	66,209	66,925	64,003	65,425
Total Rental Income	4,593,305	4,610,309	4,810,968	4,890,163	4,874,344
Expense Reimbursements:					
CAM Billings	**445,368**	**440,267**	**420,196**	**415,895**	**376,894**
Property Tax Billings	**390,428**	**370,123**	**351,126**	**346,681**	**330,128**

Online Companion Hands On: After completing Figure 5.4, go to the Figure 5.5 tab. Type in the amounts for the reimbursed **CAM Billings** and **Property Tax Billings** as shown. Corresponding expense lines for these two reimbursement lines will be entered further down the sheet.

Ancillary Income

Ancillary income is the income generated from all other activities conducted at the property other than rental of suite square footage. This may include revenue derived from billboards, parking facilities, laundry services, entertainment facilities, storage spaces, communication towers, pet fees, etc. You will often encounter truly unrealistic ancillary income forecasts and will need to modify them to be more reasonable. Be a skeptic and ask if the pro forma ancillary revenue forecast requires that the parking lot be fully occupied 24 hours a day, 365 days a year. An assumption of 100% occupancy is not likely to occur, as there will generally be vacant spaces in the parking lot over-night and during holidays. Or will every resident really use the paid laundry washer and dryer every day? Such lapses in business logic, or pure deception, are common. When evaluating these forecasts, always step back and do some simple math to verify that that the numbers make basic business sense. While ancillary income generally declines as vacancy increases, we show it as relatively constant in Figure 5.6.

FIGURE 5.6

Kathy Center Cash Flow Statement					
	Year 1	Year 2	Year 3	Year 4	Year 5
OPERATING INCOME					
Rental Income:					
Gross Potential Rental Revenue	4,500,000	4,590,000	4,816,287	4,924,653	4,957,649
Vacancy	0	(45,900)	(72,244)	(98,493)	(148,729)
Net Base Rental Revenue	4,500,000	4,544,100	4,744,043	4,826,160	4,808,919
Percentage Rents	93,305	66,209	66,925	64,003	65,425
Total Rental Income	4,593,305	4,610,309	4,810,968	4,890,163	4,874,344
Expense Reimbursements:					
CAM Billings	445,368	440,267	420,196	415,895	376,894
Property Tax Billings	390,428	370,123	351,126	346,681	330,128
Ancillary Income	**24,580**	**23,251**	**24,654**	**23,125**	**24,188**
Gross Income	5,453,681	5,443,950	5,606,944	5,675,864	5,605,554

 Online Companion Hands On: After completing Figure 5.5, go to the Figure 5.6 tab. Type in the amounts shown for **Ancillary Income**, then calculate the **Gross Income** as: **Total Rental Income** + **Expense Reimbursements for CAM Billings** + **Expense Reimbursements for Property Tax Billings** + **Ancillary Income**.

Credit Loss/Bad Debt

Credit loss, or "**bad debt**" must be deducted to reflect the anticipated non-payment of rent and other revenues. In quality properties, bad debt will usually be about 1-2% of the expected **Gross Income**. This percentage rises in a weak economic environment, or as your tenant quality profile deteriorates. While you do not know which tenants will fail to meet their rental obligations, or when, you must have an estimate of the expected default rate. Ask if a commercial tenant has lost a major contract, or taken on a lot of debt, or whether an apartment tenant has lost her job. It will generally be a different tenant every month that does not pay rent. In fact, if it is always the same tenant, it may be time to kick that tenant out of the building. To not allow for bad debt will lead to an overvaluation of the property's revenue capacity. Subtracting expected credit loss from Gross Income results in **Total Operating Income**, as shown in Figure 5.7.

FIGURE 5.7

Kathy Center Cash Flow Statement					
	Year 1	Year 2	Year 3	Year 4	Year 5
OPERATING INCOME					
Rental Income:					
Gross Potential Rental Revenue	4,500,000	4,590,000	4,816,287	4,924,653	4,957,649
Vacancy	0	(45,900)	(72,244)	(98,493)	(148,729)
Net Base Rental Revenue	4,500,000	4,544,100	4,744,043	4,826,160	4,808,919
Percentage Rents	93,305	66,209	66,925	64,003	65,425
Total Rental Income	4,593,305	4,610,309	4,810,968	4,890,163	4,874,344
Expense Reimbursements:					
CAM Billings	445,368	440,267	420,196	415,895	376,894
Property Tax Billings	390,428	370,123	351,126	346,681	330,128
Ancillary Income	24,580	23,251	24,654	23,125	24,188
Gross Income	5,453,681	5,443,950	5,606,944	5,675,864	5,605,554
Credit Loss	**(54,537)**	**(54,440)**	**(56,069)**	**(56,759)**	**(56,056)**
Total Operating Income	5,399,144	5,389,511	5,550,874	5,619,106	5,549,499

Online Companion Hands On: After completing Figure 5.6, go to the Figure 5.7 tab. You will see there are **Credit Loss % Gross Income** assumptions provided. Fill in the Credit Loss for each year, calculated as: −(that year's **Credit Loss % Gross Income**) * (that year's **Gross Income**). Then calculate the **Total Operating Income** as: **Gross Income** + **Credit Loss**.

OPERATING EXPENSES

Now that we have completed the income portion of the projection, we move on to expenses. Broadly defined, **operating expenses** are the costs required to effectively operate and maintain the property. It is important to understand how and why these costs change over time. The costs of items like security will generally correlate with inflation, while local property taxes historically increase more rapidly. Insurance costs can increase dramatically, while utility costs will vary over time depending on both inflation and property vacancy.

As stated above, **reimbursable expenses** are those initially borne by the landlord. For Kathy Center, while you expect full reimbursement for all CAM costs and property taxes for occupied space, you subtract these up-front landlord costs, as displayed in Figure 5.8 in the Reimbursable Expenses lines. But remember that you cannot recover costs from vacant space.

Common Area Maintenance

As discussed, **common area maintenance (CAM) costs** refer to upkeep expenses for areas and services that benefit all tenants. Examples include heating or cleaning building hallways, security, and parking lot maintenance. Malls provide a vivid example of CAM costs. Think of all the walking and lounging space that is not leased by Express, Nordstrom, Brooks Brothers, or other retail stores. Someone must clean, maintain, and provide security for such areas for the property to function. Tenants reimburse CAM costs as dictated by their leases.

Property Taxes

Property taxes are collected by the local government and must be paid regardless of whether the property generates any revenue. They are calculated based on a **millage rate** applied to the assessed tax value. A pro rata vacancy adjustment is made for vacancy non-recovery, as seen in the **Property Tax Billings** line in Figure 5.8. Landlords can appeal their tax assessment if they feel that it does not accurately reflect the level of property vacancy (i.e., if the property is being overvalued relative to its vacancy), but a reduction of the initial assessment is not guaranteed, and tax appeals are expensive and time consuming.

FIGURE 5.8

Kathy Center Cash Flow Statement					
	Year 1	Year 2	Year 3	Year 4	Year 5
OPERATING INCOME					
Rental Income:					
Gross Potential Rental Revenue	4,500,000	4,590,000	4,816,287	4,924,653	4,957,649
Vacancy	0	(45,900)	(72,244)	(98,493)	(148,729)
Net Base Rental Revenue	4,500,000	4,544,100	4,744,043	4,826,160	4,808,919
Percentage Rents	93,305	66,209	66,925	64,003	65,425
Total Rental Income	4,593,305	4,610,309	4,810,968	4,890,163	4,874,344
Expense Reimbursements:					
CAM Billings	445,368	440,267	420,196	415,895	376,894
Property Tax Billings	390,428	370,123	351,126	346,681	330,128
Ancillary Income	24,580	23,251	24,654	23,125	24,188
Gross Income	5,453,681	5,443,950	5,606,944	5,675,864	5,605,554
Credit Loss	(54,537)	(54,440)	(56,069)	(56,759)	(56,056)
Total Operating Income	5,399,144	5,389,511	5,550,874	5,619,106	5,549,499
OPERATING EXPENSES					
Reimbursable Expenses:					
Common Area Maintenance	**(445,368)**	**(463,183)**	**(481,710)**	**(500,978)**	**(521,018)**
Property Taxes	**(390,428)**	**(406,045)**	**(422,287)**	**(439,178)**	**(456,746)**

Online Companion Hands On: After completing Figure 5.7, go to the Figure 5.8 tab. Make the Year 1 amounts only for **Common Area Maintenance** and **Property Taxes** equal to the *negative* of their respective Reimbursement amounts. Then calculate the subsequent year values for each line item by applying the **Expense Year Over Year Growth** rate provided to the prior year's value. For example, Year 2's value is calculated as (Year 1 **Common Area Maintenance**) * (1 + Year 2 **Expense Year Over Year Growth** rate).

You may incur other operating costs associated with Kathy Center without the negotiated right to reimbursement from tenants. Your estimates for each of these **non-reimbursable expenses** are included in Figure 5.9. The sum of reimbursable and non-reimbursable expenses equals total operating expenses expected for Kathy Center. Note that depending on negotiations, different expenses may be reimbursable. For example, while insurance is not a reimbursable expense for Kathy Center, it may be for another property.

Insurance

You will generally obtain insurance to protect the property from natural disasters, tort liability, theft, fire, etc. You may also require each tenant to obtain individual policies for the interior of their space to cover potential liabilities including damage to inventory, customer accidents, employee mishaps, etc. These costs can be very volatile, so it is wise to require insurance to guard against them.

Utilities

Utility expenses include water, electric, gas, and oil usage. Since most modern buildings have separate utility metering for each tenant, you can easily calculate how much of the total property's utility bill each tenant owes related to their respective suite space. At Kathy Center, however, you are responsible for all utilities, excluding those covered by the CAM reimbursement. At another property, utilities may be fully recoverable expenses.

Property Management

The Management expense includes all costs associated with providing day-to-day managerial services. This line item represents either the costs associated with in-house management or the fee paid to a third-party management company.

FIGURE 5.9

Kathy Center Cash Flow Statement					
OPERATING INCOME	Year 1	Year 2	Year 3	Year 4	Year 5
Rental Income:					
Gross Potential Rental Revenue	4,500,000	4,590,000	4,816,287	4,924,653	4,957,649
Vacancy	0	(45,900)	(72,244)	(98,493)	(148,729)
Net Base Rental Revenue	4,500,000	4,544,100	4,744,043	4,826,160	4,808,919
Percentage Rents	93,305	66,209	66,925	64,003	65,425
Total Rental Income	4,593,305	4,610,309	4,810,968	4,890,163	4,874,344
Expense Reimbursements:					
CAM Billings	445,368	440,267	420,196	415,895	376,894
Property Tax Billings	390,428	370,123	351,126	346,681	330,128
Ancillary Income	24,580	23,251	24,654	23,125	24,188
Gross Income	5,453,681	5,443,950	5,606,944	5,675,864	5,605,554
Credit Loss	(54,537)	(54,440)	(56,069)	(56,759)	(56,056)
Total Operating Income	5,399,144	5,389,511	5,550,874	5,619,106	5,549,499
OPERATING EXPENSES					
Reimbursable Expenses:					
Common Area Maintenance	(445,368)	(463,183)	(481,710)	(500,978)	(521,018)
Property Taxes	(390,428)	(406,045)	(422,287)	(439,178)	(456,746)
Non-Reimbursable Expenses:					
Insurance	**(55,548)**	**(57,734)**	**(60,017)**	**(62,389)**	**(64,855)**
Utilities	**(105,114)**	**(109,355)**	**(113,755)**	**(118,334)**	**(123,097)**
Management	**(83,580)**	**(86,923)**	**(90,400)**	**(94,016)**	**(97,776)**
Total Operating Expenses	(1,080,038)	(1,123,240)	(1,168,169)	(1,214,896)	(1,263,491)

Online Companion Hands On: After completing Figure 5.8, go to the Figure 5.9 tab. Note the additional Management fee expense assumptions line at the top. Type in the negative values shown for the **Insurance** and **Utilities** lines. Next, calculate the **Management** expense line for each year as: (that year's **Management Fee % Reimbursables** assumption) * (that year's **Common Area Maintenance** reimbursable expenses + that year's **Property Taxes** reimbursable expenses). Then calculate the **Total Operating Expenses** line as the sum of all 5 of the Reimbursable and Non-Reimbursable Expense line items.

NET OPERATING INCOME (NOI)

Net operating income (NOI) is perhaps the most-discussed performance metric in commercial real estate, and is defined as Total Operating Income less Total Operating Expenses (Figure 5.10). NOI summarizes the property's ability to generate income, irrespective of the investment's debt and equity capital structure. Different owners may be able to achieve different NOIs from a property, depending upon their operating strategy and expertise. NOI is known as "the line," with operating income and expenses referred to as "above the line" items, and the capital and leasing costs items addressed in the next section referred to as "below the line" items.

FIGURE 5.10

Kathy Center Cash Flow Statement					
	Year 1	Year 2	Year 3	Year 4	Year 5
OPERATING INCOME					
Total Operating Income	5,399,144	5,389,511	5,550,874	5,619,106	5,549,499
OPERATING EXPENSES					
Total Operating Expenses	(1,080,038)	(1,123,240)	(1,168,169)	(1,214,896)	(1,263,491)
Net Operating Income (NOI)	**4,319,107**	**4,266,271**	**4,382,706**	**4,404,210**	**4,286,007**

Online Companion Hands On: After completing Figure 5.9, go to the Figure 5.10 tab. Calculate the **Net Operating Income (NOI)** line as: **Total Operating Income + Total Operating Expenses**. Then calculate the Year 1 cap rate (property income yield on price) as Year 1 **NOI** of $4,319,107 / Purchase Price of $48,500,000. You should get 8.91% as the result of that calculation.

CAPITAL AND LEASING COSTS

Property **capital and leasing costs**, also known as **capital items**, are the collection of property-related expenditures critical to attracting and retaining target tenants and to maintaining both a high property operating standard and the integrity of the physical plant. In other words, without sufficient readily-available budget for timely funding of required capital items, the competitiveness of the property in the marketplace would be compromised, and its physical deterioration would occur more rapidly than it should.

What makes this class of expenditures unique is that unlike utilities or management fees, capital and leasing costs are not relatively predictable or smooth amounts. They are erratic in terms of both timing and magnitude. For example, it is not a regular (e.g., every quarter or year) occurrence for a retail or office property's anchor tenant to let their lease expire, forcing the landlord to re-lease and build out tens (or hundreds) of thousands of square feet, incurring 6 or 7 figures in capital and leasing costs.

As unappealing as costs like this may sound to you as the landlord, the fact is that they are an eventuality, as leases operate on a calendar. Examples of physical plant-related capital items are replacement of key property system components like boiler units, HVAC cooling towers, and major repair or replacement of parking structures.

Even the best property managers and building engineers cannot see the future, so they do not know exactly when tenants will decide to vacate, or when systems or structures will no longer be usable. As a result, physical plant elements are maintained and inspected regularly (with these maintenance costs allocated to operating expenses), and property management separately funds a **capital reserves** account that is ready to deploy when needed. Capital reserves are sometimes referred to as **replacement reserves**, and their regular funding is required by lenders on mortgaged properties. From a property cash flow perspective, certain dollar amounts are funded into the reserves account each month. For example, for a newly-constructed multifamily property, a lender might require that $30 per unit per month be funded into the property's reserve account. The categories of costs for which reserves are funded are further defined below.

Tenant Improvements

Tenant improvements (TIs) are interior physical improvements that make tenant space habitable, useful, and pleasant. Newly-developed office and retail space is usually offered to the tenant as a "plain vanilla box" without furnishings, such as light fixtures, carpeting, etc. For completed buildings, the space is generally offered in "as is" condition (i.e., as left by the previous tenant). To entice a tenant to occupy a vacant space, the landlord will often agree to pay part of the tenant improvements. The negotiations over how much, if any, tenant improvements the landlord pays as a **TI allowance** to the tenant are dictated by market conditions. If the market is hot and the landlord has several potential tenants wanting the space, they will not have to offer much in the way of TIs. Since TIs are set when the lease is signed, if a cold market suddenly turns hot, the tenant will still receive the agreed-upon TIs.

Rarely will a new tenant desire the exact same interior fit-out as the previous tenant. Perhaps the most extreme example of these phenomena is a restaurant. Every restaurant operator has a philosophy on bar and kitchen design, as well as decor. The landlord may spend a lot of money on TIs for a tenant with a new restaurant concept, and 18 months later the landlord may have to pay to rip everything out after the tenant goes bankrupt. Then the landlord may have to offer big TIs (again) to attract a replacement tenant (which may or may not be a restaurant).

TI payment timing generally coincides with vacancy. Of course, while unexpected vacancy occurs, lease expiration dates are in black and white in the leases. Renewal leases generally require lower TIs than initial term leases. Depending upon the tenant and market conditions, people generally model the probability of tenant renewal between 25-75%. TIs are shown in Figure 5.11 increasing year over year for Years 1 through 3 as vacancy ramps up (and it is assumed space is re-tenanted) but tapering in Years 4 and 5 back to normal levels even though vacancy continues to grow. Remember, while vacancy requires TIs, it does not guarantee that their funding will occur, as that funding happens only if new leases are signed.

Leasing Commissions

Leasing commissions (LCs) are the fees you as the landlord pay to a broker or leasing company (sometimes a separate firm which you own) that leases your space. Leasing commissions will also generally correspond with your lease expiration schedule, as reflected in the lumpiness displayed in the Leasing Commissions line for Kathy Center in Figure 5.11. For example, the lease turnover in Year 3 is expected to result in relatively large leasing commissions, which are paid by the property to your management company. The landlord generally pays both landlord-side and tenant-side leasing broker commissions. Commissions are typically structured as a percentage of the total gross rent over the term of the lease, but the structure varies by market. Payment of LCs is generally half at lease signature and the balance at occupancy.

Capital Expenditures

Capital expenditures (cap ex) are dollars spent by the landlord for the repair or replacement of major property elements not located in tenant premises, such as the boiler in the basement, the air conditioning chiller on the roof, elevators, and the parking structure. There are many rules of thumb for capital expenditures. For instance, if you operate a property in the northern U.S., where there are significant weather changes during the year, you will need a higher reserve for cap ex than for a property located in a less variable climate. Weather changes increase the likelihood of parking lot damage, leakage, roof damage, etc. Or if you operate a property near the ocean, you will have higher cap ex needs due to the corrosive effects of the high salt content in the air. Older buildings will generally have higher capital expenditure needs than newer buildings, because it is harder to keep older buildings technologically competitive. Even the type of tenant impacts expected capital expenditures. For example, college students are much more "damage prone" apartment tenants than older adults. Of course, these are not all of the determinants of capital expenditures, but these examples give you an idea of the knowledge and experience you need to accurately forecast future cap ex needs.

The timing of some capital expenditures is predictable. For example, you may know when the elevators will need to be replaced. But more often, you will use your judgment and experience to estimate expected annual expenditures and size your reserve to the greater of the lender's minimum requirement and what you consider to be a "normalized" level.

UNLEVERED CASH FLOW

Unlevered cash flow is NOI after the deduction of capital and leasing costs. "Unlevered" refers to the lack of impact of any debt financing in the calculation of the cash flow, and as such, like NOI, unlevered cash flow also reports property performance irrespective of a transaction's debt and equity capital structure. In a forward-looking financial modeling context, unlevered cash flow is sometimes referred to as **NOI after normal reserves**, or **adjusted NOI** (where the adjustment referenced is the deduction of normal reserves).

It is important to know that while capital items are costs associated with owning and operating the property, in conformity with income tax rules, they are generally not included in the definition and calculation of "NOI" for office, retail and industrial properties. They are, however, typically included in the calculation of NOI for multifamily properties. Therefore, when discussing a property's cash flow, it is important to distinguish NOI before capital items from "NOI net of usual TIs, LCs, and cap ex," i.e., the unlevered cash flow. This variance is a common source of differences in reported cap rates, in that you may use NOI before these items are deducted, while someone else uses NOI after they are deducted to calculate the cap rate. Figure 5.11 extends the Kathy Center cash flow projection through unlevered cash flow.

FIGURE 5.11

Kathy Center Cash Flow Statement					
	Year 1	Year 2	Year 3	Year 4	Year 5
OPERATING INCOME					
Rental Income:					
Gross Potential Rental Revenue	4,500,000	4,590,000	4,816,287	4,924,653	4,957,649
Vacancy	0	(45,900)	(72,244)	(98,493)	(148,729)
Net Base Rental Revenue	4,500,000	4,544,100	4,744,043	4,826,160	4,808,919
Percentage Rents	93,305	66,209	66,925	64,003	65,425
Total Rental Income	4,593,305	4,610,309	4,810,968	4,890,163	4,874,344
Expense Reimbursements:					
CAM Billings	445,368	440,267	420,196	415,895	376,894
Property Tax Billings	390,428	370,123	351,126	346,681	330,128
Ancillary Income	24,580	23,251	24,654	23,125	24,188
Gross Income	5,453,681	5,443,950	5,606,944	5,675,864	5,605,554
Credit Loss	(54,537)	(54,440)	(56,069)	(56,759)	(56,056)
Total Operating Income	5,399,144	5,389,511	5,550,874	5,619,106	5,549,499
OPERATING EXPENSES					
Reimbursable Expenses:					
Common Area Maintenance	(445,368)	(463,183)	(481,710)	(500,978)	(521,018)
Property Taxes	(390,428)	(406,045)	(422,287)	(439,178)	(456,746)
Non-Reimbursable Expenses:					
Insurance	(55,548)	(57,734)	(60,017)	(62,389)	(64,855)
Utilities	(105,114)	(109,355)	(113,755)	(118,334)	(123,097)
Management	(83,580)	(86,923)	(90,400)	(94,016)	(97,776)
Total Operating Expenses	(1,080,038)	(1,123,240)	(1,168,169)	(1,214,896)	(1,263,491)
Net Operating Income (NOI)	4,319,107	4,266,271	4,382,706	4,404,210	4,286,007
CAPITAL & LEASING COSTS					
Tenant Improvements	**(36,200)**	**(57,629)**	**(152,145)**	**(46,696)**	**(18,629)**
Leasing Commissions	**(12,200)**	**(41,722)**	**(107,561)**	**(25,567)**	**(18,760)**
Capital Expenditures	**(103,400)**	**(323,565)**	**(190,919)**	**(24,947)**	**(10,975)**
Unlevered Cash Flow	**4,167,307**	**3,843,355**	**3,932,081**	**4,307,000**	**4,237,643**

Online Companion Hands On: After completing Figure 5.10, go to the Figure 5.11 tab. Type in the negative amounts as shown for **Tenant Improvements**, **Leasing Commissions** and **Capital Expenditures**. Then calculate the **Unlevered Cash Flow** line item as: **Net Operating Income (NOI)** + **Tenant Improvements** + **Leasing Commissions** + **Capital Expenditures**.

CAP EX VERSUS DEPRECIATION

It is important to distinguish between **cap ex** and **depreciation**. Cap ex reflects the property's actual wear and tear, for which you must spend money to keep the property in competitive condition. For example, when you replace worn out carpets, money comes out of your pocket to pay for the new carpeting. Depreciation, on the other hand, is a cost-allocation mechanism that provides the multi-year schedule on which you are allowed to deduct the total cost of the carpet for annual income tax calculation purposes. Depreciation is essentially a fiction, created by Congress to benefit taxpayers by serving as an **income tax shield** when calculating your **income tax liability** (what you will owe in income tax). Remember that age, design, location, tenancy, and luck determine actual capital expenditures in any given year, while tax rules alone determine depreciation. There are separate depreciation calculation rules for a property's purchase price, its TIs, and its cap ex.

If you underestimate required cap ex, you will find yourself with a building that is not competitive. To rectify this situation, you will need to unexpectedly increase cap ex, substantially reducing your cash flows relative to expectations. Accurately estimating required cap ex and having sufficient reserves will save you a lot of brain damage in future years. It is common to make simplifying assumptions, such as 3% of gross potential revenue will be required for cap ex. Will cap ex ever be exactly 3% of revenue in any year? Of course not, but it is an educated guess of what cap ex will be, on average, for a property like Kathy Center. Alternatively, you may use a certain dollar amount per square foot or per apartment unit as an estimate of annual cap ex.

Actual cap ex is irregular, with large expenditures in certain years, and smaller amounts in others. For instance, cap ex in a year when you replace an elevator, roof, or parking deck will be significantly higher than that for most years. Our model varies cap ex based on reasonable expectations. For example, cap ex in Year 1 is about 2.3% of gross potential revenue, rising to 7% in Year 2 as that year, major renovation is to take place with the electrical and water systems. Cap ex then drops to about 4% in Year 3 as renovations near completion. In the following two years, cap ex is less than 1% of gross potential revenues since no major maintenance is expected.

A common mistake made in the hotel sector is that whatever is assumed about cap ex, it consistently turned out to be too low, as hotels require ever greater expenditures for lobbies, bathrooms, furnishing, sound systems, technology, etc., to remain competitive. It might not seem like a lot of money on a per square foot basis, but an extra $0.20 per square foot on 300,000 feet is $60,000 per year. Would you like to notify your investors that you did not foresee this need and request a contribution from them to help cover the shortfall? Not likely.

Does forecasted depreciation tell you anything about actual cap ex? No. Future cap ex depends on the physical deterioration of sidewalks, elevators, carpeting, etc., while future depreciation allocations are determined by Congress and the IRS. Do you think that Congress conducted lengthy studies on the actual rate at which carpets need to be replaced? Of course not. The major discussion in Congress about depreciation was about how to collect the desired tax dollars in a way that gets them re-elected. Re-election is their pro forma! They may have testimony on the cap ex requirements from a variety of trade groups, but ultimately depreciation regulations reflect the political compromises necessary to get re-elected. If depreciation ever matches actual cap ex, it is by pure coincidence, much like "if you give a monkey a typewriter and enough time, it will eventually write *War and Peace*." Forecasted cap ex reflects expectations about future outlays; forecasted depreciation reflects the application of depreciation rules to past outlays.

The **taxable income** you report to the IRS is net of depreciation (i.e., after depreciation is deducted). Therefore, the higher your depreciation, the lower your taxable income and resultant tax bill. As a real estate owner, you want your allowable depreciation as high possible, as you prefer a lower tax bill for a given pre-tax cash flow. Therefore, every industry lobbies Congress for depreciation tax shields. In contrast, you want your cap ex to be as low as possible, while maintaining the property's competitive integrity. In fact, many of the operating expenses you incur are intended to keep future cap ex low. For example, when custodial workers vacuum the carpets, it reduces the damage dirt does to your carpets and extends their useful life.

In most countries, but not all, you are not allowed to depreciate land. Does land actually depreciate in value? It can. For example, what if you bought land thinking that a planned highway exit ramp would greatly improve access to your property, and the ramp is subsequently canceled? You bought the land believing you could develop a warehouse. However, without an exit ramp it is not a viable warehouse site, and the land is worth much less than you paid. That is a clear example of economic depreciation of land. Nevertheless, Congress says that you cannot depreciate land for income tax purposes, even in such instances.

How is future depreciation estimated? A (very) simple example illustrates the process. Remember that you bought Kathy Center for a purchase price of $48.5 million. Since you want your allowable depreciation to be as large as possible, you attempt to attribute as little of the $48.5-million purchase price to land as the IRS will allow. You could allocate none of the $48.5-million purchase price to land, and hence maximize your tax shield. But if you are audited, the IRS will retroactively make a "correct" land allocation and charge you interest and penalties on the taxes you saved due to your excessive depreciation. You will probably use an expert to select a "defensible" land allocation that is consistent with IRS norms.

PURCHASE DEPRECIATION

Assume that your tax expert says that 20% of the total purchase price must be allocated to land. This means that only 80% of the total purchase price is classified as **depreciable value** for tax purposes. Of that 80%, you need to distinguish the allocation of value between "structure" and "improvements," as well as specific allocations within the improvement category, as each has a different allowable depreciation rate. Structure generally refers to the building's frame, foundation slab, steel, brick, mortar, etc. Tax law requires you to depreciate the physical structure over its **depreciable life**, which is currently 27.5 years for residential properties and 39 years for all other property types. Note that a depreciable 39-year life means that $1/39^{th}$ (2.6%) of the value allocated to the structure is depreciable each year for 39 consecutive years. After year 39, you cannot depreciate the structure anymore. Improvements include elevators, furniture, carpeting, woodwork, lighting, etc. Tax law may allow you to depreciate such improvements over shorter periods. A 3-year depreciation allowance for improvements means that 33.33% of the allocated value is taken as depreciation each year for 3 consecutive years, and 0% thereafter.

You want to allocate as much of the $38.8 million depreciable value to improvements, but the IRS is vigilant about allocations. Your tax expert will establish the "correct" allocation based on IRS norms.

Figure 5.12 displays the allocation of the property purchase price for Kathy Center and associated purchase depreciation. Our example allocates 20% to land, 50% to structure (39-year depreciation), 20% to 7-year improvements, and 10% to 3-year improvements.

FIGURE 5.12

Kathy Center Purchase Depreciation Schedule					

Purchase Information

Purchase Price	**$48,500,000**	
Depreciation Allocation Totals:		
Land (20%)	$9,700,000	
Structure (50%)	$24,250,000	
7-year items (20%)	$9,700,000	
3-year items (10%)	$4,850,000	

	Year 1	Year 2	Year 3	Year 4	Year 5
Land	0	0	0	0	0
Structure	621,795	621,795	621,795	621,795	621,795
7-year items	1,385,714	1,385,714	1,385,714	1,385,714	1,385,714
3-year items	1,616,667	1,616,667	1,616,667	0	0
Depreciation from Purchase	$3,624,176	$3,624,176	$3,624,176	$2,007,509	$2,007,509

Online Companion Hands On: Find the blank formatted version of this Figure in the Online Companion, and note the Assumptions provided at the top of the tab. Type in 48,500,000 for the **Purchase Price** in cell c15, and then fill in the rest of the table. For the **Depreciation Allocation Totals** in cells c17-c20, multiply the **Allocation** % assumption by the Purchase Price for each category. For the annual line item amounts, enter 0 for Land for all years, and divide the total for each other line item by the associated **Schedule** length for that category. For example, for **Structure**, divide $24.25 million by 39 for each of the 5 years. However, for the **3-year items**, hard key in the value 0 for Years 4 and 5, as these items are depreciated fully by the end of Year 3. Last, total the line items to calculate the **Depreciation from Purchase** line.

The price you paid for the property reflects expected cash flows, including expected cap ex. Rarely do you approach the valuation of your property the way the IRS views it. Namely, how much is the land worth, how much is each improvement worth, and how much is the structure worth. It would be like asking, "How much of a cake's value is due to the sugar, flour, or milk?" It is the mix that creates the value of the cake, not the component parts. Your interest is the property's cash flow, while the IRS is interested in the discrete ingredients.

The depreciation exercise is merely to calculate your tax shield. It is essential to remember that depreciation and capital expenditures are two totally different things. It is as if you have one department filled with tax accountants who know nothing about the building's operation and are tasked with minimizing your taxes by carefully selecting the best depreciation allocations, while another department is filled with real estate engineers who focus solely on minimizing the costs of the physical deterioration of your building. And the two departments do not socialize! As the owner, you care about what both departments have to say, but for very different reasons.

DEPRECIATION OF TIs AND CAP EX, PART 1

In addition to the depreciation of the purchase price, the IRS requires the TI and cap ex costs to be "capitalized" (i.e., the amounts added to the property's balance sheet as capital assets) and for these new capital assets to be depreciated once they are put in service. Thus, for taxable income calculation purposes, instead of deducting the TI and cap ex outflow amounts dollar for dollar as they occur monthly (consider $36,200 spent over 3 months), you instead depreciate the total amounts over their appropriate depreciable lives per their respective **depreciation schedule** rules. In general, cap ex will fall under the "improvement" category, and each asset purchased or constructed using these funds will have a different depreciable life. As such, you will need to keep separate records for each asset acquired or constructed in each year. Obviously, this type of depreciation exercise quickly becomes tedious. There are tax professionals whose practices specialize in this **cost segregation analysis**. In our example, we assume that all cap ex is depreciable over 7 years.

For tax purposes, landlords "write off" (depreciate) TI costs as follows: 50% of the TI costs in the first year of the lease, with the remaining 50% depreciated evenly over years 2+. In our example, we will assume the total lease term to be 7 years. As a result, you expect to depreciate deductions for TIs and cap ex for ownership years 1 through 5 as summarized in Figure 5.13.

FIGURE 5.13

Kathy Center TIs and Cap Ex Depreciation Schedule					
	Year 1	Year 2	Year 3	Year 4	Year 5
Total TIs	18,100	31,831	83,892	43,846	33,704
Cap Ex	14,771	60,995	88,269	91,833	93,401
Depreciation from TIs and Cap Ex	$32,871	$92,826	$172,161	$135,679	$127,105

 Online Companion Hands On: After completing Figure 5.12, go to the Figure 5.13 tab. Populate the blue-shaded cells in rows 13-17 and 21-25 in the boxed *Depreciation Schedule Backup Detail* section. These table values should show as <u>negative</u> numbers. For the TIs, depreciate 50% of the amount spent in Year 1, and 50% evenly over the subsequent 6 years. For Cap Ex, the rule to reflect is: the Annual Spend / 7. After you fill out the table, link the totals into the **Total TIs** and **Cap Ex** lines in the Figure, changing the sign to positive by placing a subtraction operator in the formula, and sum the two lines to calculate the **Depreciation from TIs and Cap Ex** line.

Combining purchase depreciation with that for TIs and cap ex, the total depreciation deduction you can take over this 5-year period is displayed in Figure 5.14. All these depreciation items will show in Figures 5.16 - 5.18.

AMORTIZATION OF LEASING COMMISSIONS AND LOAN POINTS, PART 1

Similar to the treatment of TIs and cap ex, income tax law currently allows for the reduction of annual taxable income through the **amortization** of costs for leasing commissions and **loan points** (a fee paid to the lender for their underwriting). Leasing commissions (LCs) are expensed to reduce taxable income in a straight-line manner over the term of the lease (7 years in this example), and loan points are expensed in a straight-line manner over the term of the loan (also 7 years in this example). For instance, the LC amount of $12,200 in Year 1 is amortized annually in the amount of $1,743 per year (calculated as $12,200 / 7). Both of these amortization lines will show in Figure 5.17.

FIGURE 5.14

Kathy Center Total Depreciation					
Purchase Information					
Purchase Price	$48,500,000				
Percentage allocations					
Land (20%)	$9,700,000				
Structure (50%)	$24,250,000				
7-year items (20%)	$9,700,000				
3-year items (10%)	$4,850,000				
	Year 1	Year 2	Year 3	Year 4	Year 5
Land	0	0	0	0	0
Structure	621,795	621,795	621,795	621,795	621,795
7-year items	1,385,714	1,385,714	1,385,714	1,385,714	1,385,714
3-year items	1,616,667	1,616,667	1,616,667	0	0
Depreciation from Purchase	3,624,176	3,624,176	3,624,176	2,007,509	2,007,509
Total from TIs	18,100	31,831	83,892	43,846	33,704
Total from Cap Ex	14,771	60,995	88,269	91,833	93,401
Total Depreciation	**$3,657,047**	**$3,717,002**	**$3,796,337**	**$2,143,188**	**$2,134,614**

Online Companion Hands On: After completing Figure 5.13, go to the Figure 5.14 tab. Calculate the Total Depreciation line as: **Depreciation from Purchase + Total from TIs + Total from Cap Ex**.

LEVERED CASH FLOW

If Kathy Center is unencumbered by mortgage debt, and you were an income tax-exempt entity, there would be no need for additional analysis beyond the unlevered cash flow line (Figure 5.11). Also, if you were only interested in the property-level performance, as opposed to cash flows to equity, there would be no need to incorporate financing or tax considerations. However, since you are a taxable owner and you used debt financing to complete your purchase of Kathy Center, you will also want to know the **levered cash flows** (i.e., the expected **before-tax** and **after-tax cash flows** exclusively to equity). To calculate cash flows to equity, you need to incorporate debt and tax liabilities into your analysis, the latter of which will involve our depreciation and amortization calculations.

Debt Financing

Loan points, amortization, and interest payments resulting from use of debt financing have an impact on the calculation of after-tax equity cash flow. Assume you purchased Kathy Center for $48.5 million using an 80%

loan-to-value ("LTV") ratio. The resulting capital structure consists of a $38.8 million loan and your $9.7 million in cash equity. The loan is interest-only with a 5% interest rate and a 7-year term.

Loan Points

Loan points, or **origination costs** are the fees paid to the lender to compensate for the lender's underwriting costs. You were required to pay the lender a 50-basis point loan fee at the purchase and loan closing ("Time 0," the 1-day period that precedes Year 1). Thus, you paid the lender 0.5% of the face value of the loan, or $194,000 ($38.8 million * 0.5%), an immediate cash outflow at closing funded by equity. You will not recognize any additional cash outflows associated with loan points. Loan points do, however, have an impact on your future tax payments, as for tax purposes, you must amortize this fee over the 7-year term of the loan.

Debt Service Payments

As our example assumes an interest-only loan, we do not have to account for loan principal amortization. The loan carries a 5% fixed annual interest rate, resulting in a $1.94 million annual interest payment ($38.8 MM mortgage * 5% interest rate). You deduct this annual interest payment from your estimated unlevered cash flow, as you must make monthly payments to the lender to retain control of Kathy Center. Figure 5.15 displays the cash outflows associated with this debt service. Given this information, you can now calculate **before-tax levered cash flow**, which is the unlevered cash flow minus total debt service (interest payments and any principal amortization), as summarized in Figure 5.15. Note that because this example assumes an interest-only loan, there is no amortization of principal included in the Debt Service line.

FIGURE 5.15

Kathy Center Before-Tax Levered Cash Flow					
	Year 1	Year 2	Year 3	Year 4	Year 5
Unlevered Cash Flow	4,167,307	3,843,355	3,932,081	4,307,000	4,237,643
Debt Service	(1,940,000)	(1,940,000)	(1,940,000)	(1,940,000)	(1,940,000)
Before-Tax Levered Cash Flow	**$2,227,307**	**$1,903,355**	**$1,992,081**	**$2,367,000**	**$2,297,643**

 Online Companion Hands On: After completing Figure 5.14, go to the Figure 5.15 tab, and note the Assumptions at the top. Model in the **Debt Service** line as: **Debt * –Interest Rate**. Last, calculate **Before-Tax Levered Cash Flow** as: **Unlevered Cash Flow + Debt Service**.

TAXABLE INCOME

The final step in determining your after-tax levered (equity) cash flow for Kathy Center is the calculation of your expected annual **tax liability**. Assume that you purchased Kathy Center using a limited partnership structure. This is a **pass-through entity**, which means the tax liability is calculated for the property and is literally passed through to the individual partners in the limited partnership entity. If you were a non-taxable entity such as a pension fund or a university, there would be no need to calculate tax liability. You, however, are a taxable individual, and as such, are extremely interested in your expected tax bill to the IRS.

To determine your expected tax liability, you must calculate your taxable income, which is the income you receive from the property according to IRS rules. While you might expect taxable income to equal your before-tax cash flow (i.e., the actual money you receive from the property), the IRS sees it differently. Instead, several adjustments to before-tax cash flow are necessary to derive taxable income. Why? Because in some cases lobbyists were able to achieve beneficial rulings that help lower taxable income, while in other cases, the government passed laws to generate tax revenue which result in higher taxable income. As a taxpayer, you want taxable income as low as possible because your tax liability is calculated as your taxable income times your tax rate. Thus, the lower your taxable income, the lower your tax liability in that year.

DEPRECIATION OF CAP EX AND TIs, PART 2

As mentioned, tax law requires capitalizing cap ex and TIs once they are put in service and their subsequent depreciation. To avoid double counting the cap ex and TI expenses since they were previously deducted from NOI to get to unlevered cash flow, you must now add back the full costs of the cap ex and TIs in the periods in which they occur, as demonstrated in Figure 5.16. Similarly, you add back the full periodic leasing commission amounts, as these too were deducted upstream in calculating unlevered cash flow. Had you financed Kathy Center with an amortizing loan (instead of interest-only), you would add back the principal amortization payment amounts in the Plus: Principal Amortization line in this step as well. It is because the loan is interest-only that the figure below shows zeros for Plus: Principal Amortization.

FIGURE 5.16

Kathy Center Taxable Income Calculation Part 2a					
	Year 1	Year 2	Year 3	Year 4	Year 5
Before-Tax Levered Cash Flow	$2,227,307	$1,903,355	$1,992,081	$2,367,000	$2,297,643
Adjustments:					
Less: Depreciation (Purchase Price)	(3,624,176)	(3,624,176)	(3,624,176)	(2,007,509)	(2,007,509)
Less: Depreciation (TIs)	(18,100)	(31,831)	(83,892)	(43,846)	(33,704)
Less: Depreciation (Cap Ex)	(14,771)	(60,995)	(88,269)	(91,833)	(93,401)
Plus: TIs	36,200	57,629	152,145	46,696	18,629
Plus: Leasing Commissions	12,200	41,722	107,561	25,567	18,760
Plus: Cap Ex	103,400	323,565	190,919	24,947	10,975
Plus: Principal Amortization	0	0	0	0	0

Online Companion Hands On: After completing Figure 5.15, go to the Figure 5.16 tab. Fill out the lines for **Plus: TIs, Plus: Leasing Commissions** and **Plus: Cap Ex** by simply linking to corresponding name line items in rows 4, 5 and 6, respectively, but be sure to change the sign by including a negative operator in the formula so they show as positive. Enter all 0s for the **Plus: Principal Amortization** line.

AMORTIZATION OF LEASING COMMISSIONS AND LOAN POINTS, PART 2

The last adjustments necessary to calculate taxable income for Kathy Center are the amortization of LCs and loan points. As mentioned, LCs are amortized over their lease term (in our example, 7-year terms). Because LCs can occur in multiple operating periods (based on the subject property's occupancy dynamics), an LC cost amortization schedule is kept, tracking their cumulative amortization. At the point of sale (in our example, Year 5), any unamortized amount remaining will be expensed (deducted from taxable income) in a lump sum, such that the cost is fully amortized. Note the symmetry in the Total column in Figure 5.17 of the Plus: Leasing Commissions total of $205,810 and the Less: Leasing Commissions Amortization total, also a total $205,810 amount. As the spend and amortization amounts do not match contemporaneously, this equivalency is achieved by amortizing $146,574 in Year 5. Similarly, loan points are amortized (usually equally) over the life of the loan, and at sale a lump sum deduction will be taken for any unamortized loan points cost. In our example, the total loan fee of $194,000 is amortized over 7 years, so you see deductions of $27,714 annually from before-tax cash flow and a lump sum deduction in Year 5 to achieve full amortization.

FIGURE 5.17

Kathy Center Taxable Income Calculation Part 2b						
	Total	Year 1	Year 2	Year 3	Year 4	Year 5
Before-Tax Levered Cash Flow	$10,787,386	$2,227,307	$1,903,355	$1,992,081	$2,367,000	$2,297,643
Adjustments:						
Less: Depreciation (Purchase Price)	($14,887,546)	(3,624,176)	(3,624,176)	(3,624,176)	(2,007,509)	(2,007,509)
Less: Depreciation (TIs)	($211,372)	(18,100)	(31,831)	(83,892)	(43,846)	(33,704)
Less: Depreciation (Cap Ex)	($349,269)	(14,771)	(60,995)	(88,269)	(91,833)	(93,401)
Plus: TIs	$311,299	36,200	57,629	152,145	46,696	18,629
Plus: Leasing Commissions	$205,810	12,200	41,722	107,561	25,567	18,760
Plus: Cap Ex	$653,806	103,400	323,565	190,919	24,947	10,975
Plus: Principal Amortization	$0	0	0	0	0	0
Less: Leasing Commissions Amortization	($205,810)	(1,743)	(7,703)	(23,069)	(26,721)	(146,574)
Less: Loan Points Amortization	($194,000)	(27,714)	(27,714)	(27,714)	(27,714)	(83,143)

Online Companion Hands On: After completing Figure 5.16, go to the Figure 5.17 tab and note the Assumptions at the top. Link the **Less: Leasing Commissions Amortization** line to the **Total Leasing Cost Amortization** line in row 21; in Year 5, also deduct the **Still Unamortized at Year-end** value in row 24. Link the **Less: Loan Points Amortization** line to the Loan Points Amortization line in row 28; in Year 5, also deduct the **Still Unamortized at Year-end** value in row 30.

AFTER-TAX CASH FLOW TO EQUITY

After making all of these adjustments to before-tax cash flow, you can derive your taxable income from Kathy Center by summing the lines in Figure 5.17. You then apply the federal tax rate that corresponds to your income bracket to the expected taxable income from Kathy Center. For simplicity, assume your entire taxable income will be taxed at the tax rate of 21%. This simplification ignores the marginal tax system that is actually used in calculating the income tax liability. The resulting tax liability for Kathy Center is calculated in Figure 5.18. Subtracting the tax liability from pre-tax cash flow yields your after-tax cash flow to equity, shown in row 44.

What happens if the taxable income calculation results in a negative amount? That is a generated "loss," and the good news is that you do not pay income taxes if you generate a loss. In our example, the combination of the tax shields from depreciation, amortization and loan interest payments help generate a loss in the first 3 years of this investment. The even better news is that any unused loss amounts from one year can be carried forward and applied in the subsequent year. This is known as a **loss carry-forward**, and it is displayed in Figure 5.18 in the Less: Application of Suspended Losses line, where in this case it provides a 100% offset against the Taxable Income amount in Year 4. As losses can be carried forward, we track the Suspended Loss balance in a separate table (rows 8 through 12 in the Excel). In Year 5, there is an annual loss generated, and as it is the year of sale, we additionally apply all remaining unutilized Suspended Losses in that year. We note that in Figure 5.18, we now display all Less and Plus lines grouped with like-kind lines, as it is customary to do so.

FIGURE 5.18

Kathy Center After-Tax Cash Flow						
	Total	Year 1	Year 2	Year 3	Year 4	Year 5
Before-Tax Levered Cash Flow	**$10,787,386**	**$2,227,307**	**$1,903,355**	**$1,992,081**	**$2,367,000**	**$2,297,643**
Adjustments:						
Less: Depreciation (Purchase Price)	($14,887,546)	(3,624,176)	(3,624,176)	(3,624,176)	(2,007,509)	(2,007,509)
Less: Depreciation (TIs)	($211,372)	(18,100)	(31,831)	(83,892)	(43,846)	(33,704)
Less: Depreciation (Cap Ex)	($349,269)	(14,771)	(60,995)	(88,269)	(91,833)	(93,401)
Less: Leasing Commissions Amortization	($205,810)	(1,743)	(7,703)	(23,069)	(26,721)	(146,574)
Less: Loan Points Amortization	($194,000)	(27,714)	(27,714)	(27,714)	(27,714)	(83,143)
Plus: TIs	$311,299	36,200	57,629	152,145	46,696	18,629
Plus: Leasing Commissions	$205,810	12,200	41,722	107,561	25,567	18,760
Plus: Cap Ex	$653,806	103,400	323,565	190,919	24,947	10,975
Plus: Principal Amortization	$0	0	0	0	0	0
Taxable Income (Loss)	**($3,889,697)**	**(1,307,398)**	**(1,426,149)**	**(1,404,414)**	**266,587**	**(18,323)**
Less: Application of Suspended Losses	($4,137,961)	0	0	0	(266,587)	(3,871,374)
Net Taxable Income (Loss)	**($8,027,658)**	**(1,307,398)**	**(1,426,149)**	**(1,404,414)**	**0**	**(3,889,697)**
Less: Income Tax Liability *	$0	0	0	0	0	0
Plus: Depreciation (Purchase Price)	$14,887,546	3,624,176	3,624,176	3,624,176	2,007,509	2,007,509
Plus: Depreciation (TIs)	$211,372	18,100	31,831	83,892	43,846	33,704
Plus: Depreciation (Cap Ex)	$349,269	14,771	60,995	88,269	91,833	93,401
Plus: Leasing Commissions Amortization	$205,810	1,743	7,703	23,069	26,721	146,574
Plus: Loan Points Amortization	$194,000	27,714	27,714	27,714	27,714	83,143
Less: TIs	($311,299)	(36,200)	(57,629)	(152,145)	(46,696)	(18,629)
Less: Leasing Commissions	($205,810)	(12,200)	(41,722)	(107,561)	(25,567)	(18,760)
Less: Cap Ex	($653,806)	(103,400)	(323,565)	(190,919)	(24,947)	(10,975)
Less: Principal Amortization	$0	0	0	0	0	0
After-Tax Cash Flow	**$10,787,386**	**$2,227,307**	**$1,903,355**	**$1,992,081**	**$2,367,000**	**$2,297,643**

* Note: Profit-making real estate properties without a tax shelter must pay income taxes annually. In this example, losses are sustained in years 1 through 3, and income is fully sheltered in year 4 from suspended loss carry-forward. Year 5 is a loss-making year, and in addition, all unutilized deferred losses are applied as this writing off of all remaining losses is allowed in the year of sale. Consequently, income tax liability is $0 in all years shown, and before and after-tax cash flows in each year are equal to one another.

Online Companion Hands On: After completing Figure 5.17, go to the Figure 5.18 tab. Calculate the **Taxable Income (Loss)** line as: **Before-Tax Levered Cash Flow + all of the contiguous rows** in the block above the Taxable Income (Loss) line. Next, calculate the **Net Taxable Income (Loss)** line as the sum of Taxable Income (Loss) and Less: Application of Suspended Losses. Last, calculate the **After-Tax Cash Flow** line as: **Before-Tax Levered Cash Flow + Less: Income Tax Liability**. Note that while there is taxable income in Year 4, the prior year operating losses are applied to offset the amount one to one. When you are complete with the above, return to the Figure 5.2 tab and change the value of cell c15 to 6,500,000. Now return to the Figure 5.18 tab and observe how there is Income Tax Liability in all years since the property did not make a loss in any year, even with the additional lump sum deductions made for Leasing Commissions and Loan Points amortization in the sale year, Year 5.

THE CRAZY 1980s

It is useful to understand a bit of history. Our depreciation discussion provides some insight into the craziness of the 1980s U.S. real estate tax laws. Assume you purchased a property in the 1980s with Year 1 NOI yielding 9% on the purchase price. You allocated 20% of the purchase price to land, with the remainder allocated to structure and improvements as above, and the IRS Code allowed you to take roughly 8% of the purchase price as depreciation each year. With a 9% NOI return each year, you only had a 1% tax exposure (9% – 8%), excluding any tax shield from interest expenses. If you had any debt on the building you generated significant tax losses, even though the building was cash flow positive. Further, you could sell these tax losses to third parties from 1981 through 1986. This led property owners to intentionally create tax losses which were sold on a forward basis to people seeking to shelter taxable income (doctors, lawyers, etc.). The income derived from the sale of these tax losses lowered the effective acquisition cost for the property owner.

Real estate quickly became a business of manufacturing tax losses rather than satisfying tenant demand for space. It is hardly surprising that there was an incredible accumulation of excess supply during the 1980s, as it paid well to lose money!

Figure 5.19 demonstrates the 1980s scenario for a residential property, Leslie Heights. This property was bought for $100 million with 90% leverage. This high level of debt allowed the owner to acquire the property with little (if any) of their own money at risk. An $8 million annual depreciation allowance (8% of $100 million) was taken. The profit was derived purely from selling the tax credits. In particular, the owner could generate their equity requirement ($10 million) for the purchase essentially from the sale of the first two years of tax losses ($4.4 million annually). Note that the $600,000 pre-tax profit (also the after-tax profit) represents a 6% return on the $10 million equity. In addition, if the property appreciated at the rate of inflation (which was roughly 10%) for 3 years, and if the owner sold the property at the end of Year 3, the pre-tax annual equity internal rate of return (IRR) is seemingly 67% (see Figure 5.20). Note that all of this occurs even though annual interest payments exceed stabilized NOI by $1.8 million.

FIGURE 5.19

Leslie Heights Investment With Pre-1986 Tax Shelters	
Purchase Price	$100,000,000
Interest Payment Calculation	
Debt	90,000,000
Interest Rate	12.00%
Interest Payment	10,800,000
Taxable Income Calculation	
NOI	9,000,000
Depreciation	(8,000,000)
Interest	(10,800,000)
Taxable Income	(9,800,000)
Excess Tax Shelter Calculation	
Taxable Income	(9,800,000)
Tax Bracket Rate	50%
Value	4,900,000
Cash Flow from Operation	
NOI	9,000,000
Cap Ex	(2,000,000)
Interest	(10,800,000)
Tax Shelter Sales (90 cents on the $)	4,410,000
Net Cash Flow from Operation	**$610,000**

FIGURE 5.20

Leslie Heights Return on Equity Calculation				

Property Sale Net Cash Flow

Proceeds from Sale *(property grows at inflation: 100*1.1^3)*				133,000,000
Debt Payment				(90,000,000)
Net Cash Flow from Sale				43,000,000

Developer's Cash Outflows and Inflows

	Year 0	Year 1	Year 2	Year 3
Purchase Price	(10,000,000)			
Net Cash Flow from Operations		610,000	610,000	610,000
Net Cash Flow from Sale				43,000,000
Total Net Cash Flow	($10,000,000)	$610,000	$610,000	$43,610,000

Net Cash Flow: $34,830,000
Equity IRR: 67%

The industry collapsed once the tax law was amended in 1986 to eliminate these tax shelters, and banks became more disciplined in their lending. Figure 5.21 displays the same deal treated in the current tax framework. With the tax practices of old, you could achieve a 6% pre-tax return, while under today's structure you would realize a negative 38% return (i.e., a 38% loss of capital)! Not surprisingly, post-1986, development of new space quickly aligned with meeting property demand (rather than to an appetite for tax losses). Actually, the atmosphere of that time was even more ridiculous, in that the developer was paid for all future tax losses up front, rather than as they occurred. So, the developer cashed out very early in this sort of deal. Let's hope that those days never return.

FIGURE 5.21

Leslie Heights Investment With Pre-1986 Tax Shelters	
Purchase Price	$100,000,000
Interest Payment Calculation	
Debt	90,000,000
Interest Rate	12.00%
Interest Payment	10,800,000
Taxable Income Calculation	
NOI	9,000,000
Depreciation	(8,000,000)
Interest	(10,800,000)
Taxable Income	(9,800,000)
Excess Tax Shelter Calculation	
Taxable Income	(9,800,000)
Tax Bracket Rate	50%
Value	4,900,000
Cash Flow from Operation	
NOI	9,000,000
Cap Ex	(2,000,000)
Interest	(10,800,000)
Tax Shelter Sales (90 cents on the $)	4,410,000
Net Cash Flow from Operation	**$610,000**

Leslie Heights Investment Post-1986 Tax Law Change	
Purchase Price	$100,000,000
Interest Payment Calculation	
Debt	90,000,000
Interest Rate	12.00%
Interest Payment	10,800,000
Taxable Income Calculation	
NOI	9,000,000
Depreciation	(4,000,000)
Interest	(10,800,000)
Taxable Income	(5,800,000)
(Tax losses no longer apply)	
Cash Flow from Operation	
NOI	9,000,000
Cap Ex	(2,000,000)
Interest	(10,800,000)
Tax Shelter Sales - Not Applicable	0
Net Cash Flow from Operation	**($3,800,000)**

CLOSING THOUGHT

You must remember that your property-level pro forma must be a careful business analysis. It should be a preliminary assessment of the most likely results for net operating income. Have some humility and understand that even when carefully analyzed, the most likely outcomes are highly unlikely to occur. If things turn out better than expected, you can easily live with it; but if they are worse, it will be a problem. Addressing why and when it will be worse, and how you will deal with such situations, is much more important than just assembling "the numbers."

Numbers are easily manipulated to look good on paper. The difficult part is making them a reality, even for the most likely outcome. Football plays always work on paper. The playbook reads that Prushansky blocks Elliott, while Galloway throws a perfect spiral to Ferreira. But what really happens? Prushansky slips and misses the block. Under pressure, Galloway throws a wobbly pass, which Brasfield intercepts and runs for a touchdown! That is not in the playbook – but it happens. And it is all happening in inclement weather conditions. A playbook cannot tell you that Prushansky has a metal plate in his leg making it difficult for him to make that block. You have to know your players' weaknesses and strengths, understand what can go wrong, and plan for how you will adjust your strategy and personnel to deal with shortfalls. Likewise, to be a successful real estate investor you must intimately know your capabilities, market, property, and tenants. And just as in football, achieving the expected outcome requires tremendous planning, knowledge, diligence, energy, concentration, adaptability, and luck. Being average is hard work and a fulltime job.

 Online Companion Audio Interview: To hear a conversation about this chapter's content, go to the Online Companion and select the link for Chapter 5. Scroll down to the Audio Interview section and listen.

Chapter 6
Financial Modeling

"Believing a presented 26.24% IRR is silly; no one is 200 basis points accurate, much less 24 bps accurate." - Dr. Peter Linneman

WHAT IS FINANCIAL MODELING?

Financial modeling is the systematic projection and analysis of expected outcomes for an investment. The activity of financial modeling is used to assist in evaluating risks and opportunities. A detailed financial model provides a microscopic view of the financial elements of the property. Remember that the rows and columns in your financial model are only as useful as the quality of the information and judgment behind them. Just because they look authoritative on paper does not make them insightful, much less correct. Always be skeptical of your financial model, especially when you are inexperienced in the business. Be sure that you, not the rows and columns, make your investment decisions.

If a property's economics are very complex, even after comprehensive analysis, experts may not agree on its value. Smart investors, armed with similar information, frequently arrive at drastically different valuations because they perceive different degrees of risk and opportunity in the property. Like beauty, value is in the eye of the beholder, and price is negotiated. Most importantly, execution, not financial modeling, is ultimately the source of your returns.

Returns to equity are typically summarized across a few **key performance indicators (KPIs)**, measured after the hypothetical sale of the investment. KPIs are viewed in concert with one another. No single one of them is "the most important," as they each tell you something different about the performance of your invested capital. These equity KPIs are:

- Net Cash Flow (net profit/whole dollar profit);
- Internal Rate of Return (time-weighted average compounded annual return);
- Net Present Value (value created in discounted dollars);
- **Multiple on equity** (a.k.a. **equity multiple** and **multiple on invested capital**; how many times you get your investment back).

Preliminary analyses of potential investments are usually modeled on a before-tax basis for simplicity, as you want to focus your time and energy on the best prospective vehicles, without wasting time on in-depth analysis of mediocre opportunities. As you get more serious about a potential investment, you will extend the analysis to a monthly after-tax basis, given that taxes are inevitable.

THINGS CHANGE FOR A REASON

Students and young professionals generally put too much emphasis on the numbers and too little on the reasoning behind the numbers. As a result, meaningless "sensitivity tests" are often run, where the young analyst arbitrarily increases vacancy in increments of 10%, or decreases rental growth from 3% annually to 1%, or raises or lowers the exit cap in increments of 100 basis points, without ever pausing to think about what the world needs to look like for such changes to happen. Have you ever been shown false sympathy? Remember how easily you recognized it and how much it irritated you? A financial sensitivity analysis done without sincere thought is much the same.

Before you change the vacancy rate, ask yourself why the vacancy rate would increase. Is it because the economy is weak? Or has a big firm moved out of the area? Or is the property poorly located or of inferior design? Or are the rents too high? Like a good doctor, treat the disease, not the symptoms.

LESLIE COURT APARTMENTS

To illustrate the interaction between different line items in a good financial model, consider Leslie Court, a 100-unit residential rental apartment property. As of today (the "Time 0 | Model start" point in time in Figure 6.1), you are considering purchasing the building for $6.7 million at a 10.6% cap rate, using a $5.193 million mortgage with monthly payments. The building is in Colonial Heights, Virginia, a suburb of the state capital of Richmond. After a recent boom, Colonial Heights' market is rapidly weakening due to a recession and overbuilding. As a result, you believe the property's performance will weaken for the next two years before rebounding.

FIGURE 6.1

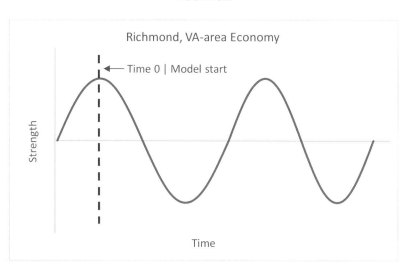

After careful analysis, you conclude that the local market will worsen over the next two years as new supply continues to exceed demand. You do not believe this pattern will reverse until the third year. Young analysts often only adjust the vacancy rate to reflect changing market fundamentals, but there are many other factors that change as overall market conditions change. The line items with the bold blue variables in Figure 6.2 highlight these elements. A well-constructed "dynamic" financial model allows you to change the input values of key **assumptions**, resulting in the model automatically recalculating corresponding projected cash flows, rates of return, or other performance metrics.

The most elegant models follow a logical path and can be easily interpreted, spot-checked, or updated by others. Overly complicated or multi-step formulas programmed into one cell of a worksheet run the risk of your model becoming a less-than-transparent "black box" to others. In such cases, it is best to break down each step and label the interim line items appropriately. Remember that line items can always be hidden in your worksheet before presenting the final report.

A general rule is to only input values in your blue bold assumption cells, as the rest of the model should flow from those assumptions exclusively. Resist the urge to "hard code" values into non-assumption cells, as chances are that you will have forgotten about your little tweak six months later when a dead deal is revived, and you need to re-run new assumptions.

While every transaction and corresponding analysis is different, the financial model and concepts presented in this chapter are meant to serve as a starting point for analyzing an investment in an income-producing real estate asset. The completed financial projection is shown in Figure 6.2, and the balance of this chapter walks through the related assumptions and calculations for each line item.

As seen in Figure 6.2, there is a Time 0 column, which is the point of closing on the acquisition. This is when the equity investment is made and can be thought of as "today." Additionally, a "forward" year column is included (Year 7), which allows you to value the sale of the property on the adjusted NOI for the new owner's first year of operation, which is Year 7 if you sell in Year 6. Sale valuation on a stabilized forward basis (as opposed to on "trailing" actual values) is customary for property types with lease terms of a year or longer. It is critical to understand that these Year 7 values, which terminate at adjusted NOI, impact before- and after-tax cash flow only to the extent that Year 6 sale proceeds are based on Year 7 adjusted NOI.

Adjusted NOI is used as the valuation basis of the next buyer's purchase price offer (as opposed to NOI before capital items), as capital items will be incurred by the next buyer to keep the building occupied and competitive. Additionally, a minimum reserves level will be required by the buyer's lender if they mortgage the property. In this example, there is a total assumed Year 7 capital items amount of $126,423 ($28,707 for TIs, $27,511 for Leasing Commissions, and $70,204 for Cap Ex), which blends to $1,264 per apartment unit. This adjusted NOI is our assumption today of what the next buyer's first year NOI will be in seven years. They key word is 'assumption,' so we may be materially mis-forecasting the Net Sales Price compared to what it will eventually be. As helpful as it would be, there is no "right price" for an asset written on a piece of paper secured in a hidden underground bank vault. As stated, value is in the eye of the beholder, and price is negotiated.

We note that the Figure 6.2 graphic on the next page does not show the same full set of line items between Net Taxable Income (Loss) and After-Tax Cash Flow as are shown in Chapter 5's Figure 5.18. This is for the sake of keeping the graphic legible on a single page. As shown in Chapter 5, After-Tax Cash Flow is Before-Tax Levered Cash Flow net of Tax Liability, and both of those lines indeed show in Figure 6.2 despite the exclusion of interim lines. However, we have included in the Online Companion Excel file an "expanded" version of Figure 6.2 for your reference as a comprehensive cash flow presentation template.

Further explanation is warranted relating to the Replacement Reserve ("RR") account that corresponds to the three line items with parenthetical note numbers in Figure 6.2. The nuance detailed below is best understood with the Figure 6.2 Excel file open to where the Replacement Reserve Account Detail Backup section starting in row 147 shows a $225,000 reserves contribution at closing. Above it, we note the following:

- o Parenthetical 1: Adjusted Net Operating Income (a.k.a. Unlevered Cash Flow) is defined as NOI (which is already net of the Replacement Reserve contribution) - TIs - Leasing Commissions - only the Cap Ex amount NOT covered by the Reserve Balance available (if any). As a result, if there are sufficient Replacement Reserves to fund the full annual Cap Ex, the Adjusted NOI will not be reduced by the Cap Ex amount in that year. For example, in Year 1, Adjusted NOI = $711,399 = NOI of $766,857 - TIs of $35,000 - LCs of $20,458 - Cap Ex of $75,264 + the use of $75,264 from the Replacement Reserve Account. The application of reserves to the cap ex outlay dollar for dollar make the net equation for Adjusted NOI in this example simply = $766,857 - $35,000 - $20,458.
- o Parenthetical 2: Plus: Cash Transfer to RR account – Based on how we specifically define Adjusted NOI, instead of carrying the "Plus: Cap Ex" line as shown in Chapter 5, we replace that line with the "Plus: Cash Transfer to RR account" line, which adds back only the Replacement Reserve contribution amount.
- o Parenthetical 3: Plus: Refund at sale of RR acct. bal. – This line is for the sweep to equity of any Replacement Reserve account balance remaining at sale. As a result, After-Tax Cash Flow is Before-Tax Levered Cash Flow net of Tax Liability, plus any remaining Replacement Reserve balance recouped at sale.

FIGURE 6.2

	Acquisition	Decline Stage		Recovery Stage		Stable and Sale		Forward
Leslie Court Apartments Cash Flow Projection	Time 0	Year 1	Year 2	Year 3	Year 4	Year 5	Year 6	Year 7
Base Rental Revenue Growth			-5.0%	1.0%	2.5%	3.5%	3.5%	3.5%
Base Rental Revenues		1,100,305	1,045,290	1,055,743	1,082,136	1,120,011	1,159,211	1,199,784
Expense Reimbursement Revenue		0	0	0	0	0	0	0
Gross Revenues		1,100,305	1,045,290	1,055,743	1,082,136	1,120,011	1,159,211	1,199,784
Vacancy % Gross Revenues		7.0%	14.0%	12.0%	10.0%	7.0%	5.0%	5.0%
Less: Vacancies		(77,021)	(146,341)	(126,689)	(108,214)	(78,401)	(57,961)	(59,989)
Net Base Rental Revenue		1,023,284	898,949	929,054	973,923	1,041,610	1,101,251	1,139,795
Ancillary Income Growth			-8.0%	-7.0%	-3.0%	5.0%	3.0%	3.0%
Plus: Ancillary Income		6,052	5,568	5,178	5,023	5,274	5,432	5,595
Effective Gross Income (EGI)		1,029,336	904,517	934,232	978,945	1,046,884	1,106,683	1,145,390
Operating Expense Growth			-2.0%	-1.0%	0.0%	4.0%	3.5%	3.0%
Less: Operating Expenses		(102,934)	(100,875)	(99,867)	(99,867)	(103,861)	(107,496)	(110,721)
Less: Real Estate Taxes	3.0%	(110,031)	(113,332)	(116,732)	(120,234)	(123,841)	(127,556)	(131,383)
Less: Replacement Reserve (RR)	4.5% of GR	(49,514)	(47,038)	(47,508)	(48,696)	(50,400)	(52,165)	(53,990)
Total Expenses		(262,479)	(261,245)	(264,107)	(268,797)	(278,103)	(287,217)	(296,094)
Net Operating Income (NOI)		766,857	643,272	670,125	710,149	768,782	819,466	849,295
Change in TI			8.6%	10.4%	-9.9%	-10.0%	-8.2%	-8.1%
Less: TI		(35,000)	(38,010)	(41,963)	(37,809)	(34,028)	(31,238)	(28,707)
Change in Leasing Commissions			27.0%	10.8%	18.0%	-1.7%	-14.8%	-3.3%
Less: Leasing Commissions		(20,458)	(25,982)	(28,788)	(33,969)	(33,392)	(28,450)	(27,511)
Change in Cap Ex			-8.9%	8.5%	3.6%	19.5%	-21.9%	-2.4%
Less: Cap Ex		(75,264)	(68,566)	(74,394)	(77,072)	(92,101)	(71,931)	(70,204)
Adjusted Net Operating Income (1)		711,399	579,280	599,374	638,371	701,362	759,778	793,077
Less: Loan Points	(51,938)	0	0	0	0	0	0	
Less: Debt Service Payment		(414,650)	(414,650)	(414,650)	(414,650)	(414,650)	(414,650)	
Before-Tax Levered Cash Flow		296,749	164,630	184,724	223,721	286,712	345,129	
Less: Depreciation (Purchase Price)		(201,818)	(201,818)	(201,818)	(201,818)	(201,818)	(201,818)	
Less: Depreciation (TIs)		(35,000)	(38,010)	(41,963)	(37,809)	(34,028)	(31,238)	
Less: Depreciation (Cap Ex)		(10,752)	(20,547)	(31,175)	(42,185)	(55,342)	(65,618)	
Less: Leasing Commissions Amortization		(20,458)	(25,982)	(28,788)	(33,969)	(33,392)	(28,450)	
Less: Loan Points Amortization		(7,420)	(7,420)	(7,420)	(7,420)	(7,420)	(14,839)	
Plus: Cash Transfer to RR account (2)		49,514	47,038	47,508	48,696	50,400	52,165	
Plus: TIs		35,000	38,010	41,963	37,809	34,028	31,238	
Plus: Leasing Commissions		20,458	25,982	28,788	33,969	33,392	28,450	
Plus: Principal Amortization		52,759	56,573	60,662	65,047	69,750	74,792	
Taxable Income (Loss)		179,032	38,456	52,482	86,042	142,282	189,810	
Less: Application of Suspended Losses		0	0	0	0	0	0	
Net Taxable Income (Loss)		179,032	38,456	52,482	86,042	142,282	189,810	
Less: Tax Liability	21.0%	(37,597)	(8,076)	(11,021)	(18,069)	(29,879)	(39,860)	
Plus: Refund at sale of RR acct. bal. (3)		0	0	0	0	0	60,995	
After-Tax Cash Flow		259,152	156,554	173,703	205,652	256,833	366,264	
Net Sales Price							9,143,710	
Less: Tax Liability							(678,594)	
Less: Outstanding Mortgage Balance							(4,814,167)	
Less: Initial Equity Investment	(1,783,188)							
After-Tax Levered Cash Flow	($1,783,188)	$259,152	$156,554	$173,703	$205,652	$256,833	$4,017,212	

Equity Investment Performance Indicators	Net Cash Flow	$3,285,919		Total Positive After-Tax Cash Flows	$5,069,107
	IRR	22.51%		Net Sales Proceeds % Total	72.02%
	NPV at 15%	$656,778			
	Multiple	2.84x			

BASE RENTAL REVENUE

One line item always hit by weak market conditions is rent. In soft markets, tenants will have to be enticed to rent space at your property through lower rents and other **landlord concessions**. These concessions may be free rent, lower security deposits, free AirPods, etc. Note that the change in base rental revenues is not smooth, with the biggest drops occurring as one moves from a hot to a cold market (Year 2 in our example). During market decline, base rental revenue falls rapidly until new supply shuts down, and demand begins to absorb the excess space. As shown in Figure 6.3, upon stabilization in Year 5, you expect rent to grow at 3.5% per year, slightly above the expected rate of long-term economy-wide inflation. Of course, there could be a big rent pop of say 6-9% if the economy recovers quickly or robustly. Your rent growth assumptions will vary based on property and market conditions.

FIGURE 6.3

Leslie Court Apartments Cash Flow Projection							
	Decline Stage		Recovery Stage		Stable and Sale		Forward
	Year 1	Year 2	Year 3	Year 4	Year 5	Year 6	Year 7
Base Rental Revenue Growth		-5.0%	1.0%	2.5%	3.5%	3.5%	3.5%
Base Rental Revenues	1,100,305	1,045,290	1,055,743	1,082,136	1,120,011	1,159,211	1,199,784
Expense Reimbursement Revenue	0	0	0	0	0	0	0
Gross Revenues	1,100,305	1,045,290	1,055,743	1,082,136	1,120,011	1,159,211	1,199,784

 Online Companion Hands On: Find the formatted, partially completed Excel version of Figures 6.2, 6.7, 6.8 (all on a single tab) in Chapter 6 of the Online Companion. Over the course of this chapter, you will complete the tab, as well as a separate tab for Figure 6.9, resulting in the calculation of four equity investment performance indicators: net cash flow, IRR, NPV, and multiple. These indicators are displayed on the bottom of the single tab for Figures 6.2, 6.7, 6.8.

Start with the lines shown above in Figure 6.3. First, make the **Base Rental Revenue Growth** rate assumptions inputs. Next, type in the <u>Year 1</u> **Base Rental Revenues** dollar amount as shown above, and then calculate the Year 2+ values by applying the growth rate to the prior year's value. For example, Year 2's value is calculated as (Year 1 **Base Rental Revenue**) * (1 + Year 2 **Base Rental Revenue Growth Rate**). We note that there is no **Expense Reimbursement Revenue** shown here (just enter 0s), which reflects the assumption that each apartment's utilities are individually metered and the tenants are billed directly by the utility companies. Last, fill in the **Gross Revenues** line, which is calculated as: **Base Rental Revenues** + **Expense Reimbursement Revenue**.

VACANCY

Vacancy generally moves inversely with the strength of the market. That is, the weaker the market, the higher the vacancy (Figure 6.4). In lesser-quality buildings, this is more pronounced, as tenants move up to higher quality buildings at rents that are at or below what the tenants are currently paying. While vacancy decreases **Net Base Rental Revenue**, its indirect effects also impact other line items.

FIGURE 6.4

Leslie Court Apartments Cash Flow Projection								
		Decline Stage		Recovery Stage		Stable and Sale		Forward
		Year 1	Year 2	Year 3	Year 4	Year 5	Year 6	Year 7
Base Rental Revenue Growth			-5.0%	1.0%	2.5%	3.5%	3.5%	3.5%
Base Rental Revenues		1,100,305	1,045,290	1,055,743	1,082,136	1,120,011	1,159,211	1,199,784
Expense Reimbursement Revenue		0	0	0	0	0	0	0
Gross Revenues		1,100,305	1,045,290	1,055,743	1,082,136	1,120,011	1,159,211	1,199,784
Vacancy % Gross Revenues		7.0%	14.0%	12.0%	10.0%	7.0%	5.0%	5.0%
Less: Vacancies		(77,021)	(146,341)	(126,689)	(108,214)	(78,401)	(57,961)	(59,989)
Net Base Rental Revenue		1,023,284	898,949	929,054	973,923	1,041,610	1,101,251	1,139,795

 Online Companion Hands On: Layer in the **Vacancy % Gross Revenues** assumption line, inputting the values as shown. Then calculate the **Less: Vacancies** line as: **Gross Revenues * −(Vacancy % Gross Revenues)**. Finally, calculate **Net Base Rental Revenue** as: **Gross Revenues + Less: Vacancies**.

ANCILLARY INCOME

Notice how in Figure 6.5 the 7% increase in the vacancy rate from Year 1 to Year 2 causes an 8% drop in **ancillary income**. This is not unexpected, for two main reasons. First, amenities such as your health club are predominantly used by your tenants. Hence, as vacancy increases, there are fewer tenants to join the club. Second, if the increased vacancy is due to a weak economy (rather than excess supply), tenants may not renew their memberships due to having less disposable income. During more prosperous times, such as the recovery period, the opposite is true. As a result, ancillary income often moves with greater volatility than rental income.

FIGURE 6.5

Leslie Court Apartments Cash Flow Projection							
	Decline Stage		Recovery Stage		Stable and Sale		Forward
	Year 1	Year 2	Year 3	Year 4	Year 5	Year 6	Year 7
Base Rental Revenue Growth		-5.0%	1.0%	2.5%	3.5%	3.5%	3.5%
Base Rental Revenues	1,100,305	1,045,290	1,055,743	1,082,136	1,120,011	1,159,211	1,199,784
Expense Reimbursement Revenue	0	0	0	0	0	0	0
Gross Revenues	1,100,305	1,045,290	1,055,743	1,082,136	1,120,011	1,159,211	1,199,784
Vacancy % Gross Revenues	**7.0%**	**14.0%**	**12.0%**	**10.0%**	**7.0%**	**5.0%**	**5.0%**
Less: Vacancies	(77,021)	(146,341)	(126,689)	(108,214)	(78,401)	(57,961)	(59,989)
Net Base Rental Revenue	1,023,284	898,949	929,054	973,923	1,041,610	1,101,251	1,139,795
Ancillary Income Growth		-8.0%	-7.0%	-3.0%	5.0%	3.0%	3.0%
Plus: Ancillary Income	6,052	5,568	5,178	5,023	5,274	5,432	5,595
Effective Gross Income (EGI)	**1,029,336**	**904,517**	**934,232**	**978,945**	**1,046,884**	**1,106,683**	**1,145,390**

Online Companion Hands On: Layer in the **Ancillary Income Growth** rate assumption line, inputting the values as shown. Next, enter the Year 1 value for **Plus: Ancillary Income**. Then calculate the **Plus: Ancillary Income** values for the subsequent years as (Prior year value) * (1 + current year's **Ancillary Income Growth** rate). Last, calculate **Effective Gross Income (EGI)** as: **Net Base Rental Revenue + Plus: Ancillary Income**.

OPERATING EXPENSES, REPLACEMENT RESERVES AND CAP EX

As discussed in Chapters 4 and 5, property operating expenses include costs such as insurance, real estate taxes, utilities, management fees, and marketing, among others. While operators always attempt to lower costs, this is particularly true during a recession. If the debt covenants for your loan require a minimum **debt service coverage ratio,** also known as **DSCR** (annual NOI divided by total annual **debt service expense**), there could be a violation in years when NOI is weak. As a result, operators will avoid flirting with breaking loan covenants by always seeking ways to squeeze out every dime of operating costs.

In weak markets, increased vacancy reduces **variable operating expenses**. The utilities expense, for example, will not be as high because there are not as many tenants using computers, hot water, lights, etc. In addition, you may reduce certain operating expenses by mowing the lawn yourself instead of using a gardener, or perhaps by mowing once every three weeks instead of every two weeks. **Fixed operating expenses**, such as insurance, do not change with the state of the market or the property's occupancy level. Cost-cutting measures should be assessed carefully. If the property deteriorates from a lack of maintenance, you may have greater repairs with which to contend in the future, attract lower quality tenants, or destroy the image of a brand that you spent years building.

As the market strengthens, operating expenses will increase. For example, you may need more staff to deal with greater tenant demand. It will take time to train new staff, and you may not hire the right people, so there may be employee turnover until you put the right team in place. These inefficiencies need to be reflected in your model. If the building requires a new roof or plumbing system, capital expenditures will be quite large. For this reason, **replacement reserves** are regularly funded into a dedicated account (with minimum amounts required by the lender). In weak markets, you may not have enough capital to pay for these essential, but expensive repairs. As a result, in weak markets, operators tend to postpone as much cap ex as possible. In the Leslie Court Apartments model, $10,000 of cap ex due to water damage is not made in Year 2. Therefore, it is expected that in Year 5, the typical $70,000 in cap ex is, instead, $92,000 to make up for this deferral. What if the damage is worse than expected and it is necessary to make repairs in Year 3? You may default on your loan! Also, if the water damage causes unhappiness with tenants, your vacancy may further increase. Figure 6.6 displays line items through cap ex.

In this example, we assume that $225,000 is contributed from equity at closing to pre-fund the Replacement Reserve ("RR") account, which resides at the mortgage lender's bank. This contribution is assumed to be a necessary condition of the funding of the acquisition loan. Seeding the RR account with funds at closing assures the lender that Year 1 cap ex will have a sufficient amount of dedicated funding from day 1 of property operation. The total annual contribution shown in the Less: Replacement Reserve (RR) line will be automatically swept monthly from revenues deposited into the property's main operating account (which also resides at the mortgage lender's bank) into the RR account. When cap ex needs arise, ownership will draw the required funds from the RR account. As such, in contrast to what we showed in Chapter 5, the annual cap ex spent does not reduce the property's Adjusted NOI (unlevered cash flow), assuming that the RR account balance is sufficiently funded at the time of the draw. If there are insufficient funds, then Adjusted NOI will indeed be impacted, as the property cash flow will be used to pay the cap ex bills. Any unutilized remaining RR account balance will be refunded to equity in the year of sale. A Replacement Reserve Account Detail Backup table is provided in the Online Companion.

FIGURE 6.6

Leslie Court Apartments Cash Flow Projection							
	Decline Stage		Recovery Stage		Stable and Sale		Forward
	Year 1	Year 2	Year 3	Year 4	Year 5	Year 6	Year 7
Base Rental Revenue Growth		-5.0%	1.0%	2.5%	3.5%	3.5%	3.5%
Base Rental Revenues	1,100,305	1,045,290	1,055,743	1,082,136	1,120,011	1,159,211	1,199,784
Expense Reimbursement Revenue	0	0	0	0	0	0	0
Gross Revenues	1,100,305	1,045,290	1,055,743	1,082,136	1,120,011	1,159,211	1,199,784
Vacancy % Gross Revenues	7.0%	14.0%	12.0%	10.0%	7.0%	5.0%	5.0%
Less: Vacancies	(77,021)	(146,341)	(126,689)	(108,214)	(78,401)	(57,961)	(59,989)
Net Base Rental Revenue	1,023,284	898,949	929,054	973,923	1,041,610	1,101,251	1,139,795
Ancillary Income Growth		-8.0%	-7.0%	-3.0%	5.0%	3.0%	3.0%
Plus: Ancillary Income	6,052	5,568	5,178	5,023	5,274	5,432	5,595
Effective Gross Income (EGI)	1,029,336	904,517	934,232	978,945	1,046,884	1,106,683	1,145,390
Operating Expense Growth		-2.0%	-1.0%	0.0%	4.0%	3.5%	3.0%
Less: Operating Expenses	(102,934)	(100,875)	(99,867)	(99,867)	(103,861)	(107,496)	(110,721)
Less: Real Estate Taxes	(110,031)	(113,332)	(116,732)	(120,234)	(123,841)	(127,556)	(131,383)
Less: Replacement Reserve (RR)	(49,514)	(47,038)	(47,508)	(48,696)	(50,400)	(52,165)	(53,990)
Total Expenses	(262,479)	(261,245)	(264,107)	(268,797)	(278,103)	(287,217)	(296,094)
Net Operating Income (NOI)	766,857	643,272	670,125	710,149	768,782	819,466	849,295
Change in TI		8.6%	10.4%	-9.9%	-10.0%	-8.2%	-8.1%
Less: TI	(35,000)	(38,010)	(41,963)	(37,809)	(34,028)	(31,238)	(28,707)
Change in Leasing Commissions		27.0%	10.8%	18.0%	-1.7%	-14.8%	-3.3%
Less: Leasing Commissions	(20,458)	(25,982)	(28,788)	(33,969)	(33,392)	(28,450)	(27,511)
Change in Cap Ex		-8.9%	8.5%	3.6%	19.5%	-21.9%	-2.4%
Less: Cap Ex	(75,264)	(68,566)	(74,394)	(77,072)	(92,101)	(71,931)	(70,204)

Online Companion Hands On: Layer in the **Operating Expense Growth** rate assumption line, inputting the values as shown. Next, enter the <u>Year 1</u> value for **Less: Operating Expenses**. Then calculate the values for the subsequent years as (Prior year value) * (1 + current year's **Operating Expense Growth** rate). Do the same for the **Less: Real Estate Taxes** line, but grow it at 3% annually, and the same for the **Less: Replacement Reserve (RR)** line, calculated as 4.5% of **Gross Revenues**. Calculate **Total Expenses** as the sum of the three expense lines. Lastly, calculate **Net Operating Income (NOI)** as the sum of **Effective Gross Income (EGI)** and **Total Expenses**. Note that how by Year 5, NOI has recovered and exceeds the Year 1 amount, and in Year 6, it has grown by almost 7% over the Year 1 level.

TIs AND LEASING COMMISSIONS

If you experience high vacancy, you will focus a great deal of energy on attracting tenants. One way to accomplish this is to increase marketing efforts. You may increase leasing commissions to motivate your sales force, hire additional leasing agents, or increase advertising. For this reason, leasing commissions generally increase as vacancy increases.

TIs for office and retail properties will also increase with greater vacancy, as when tenants leave, you will incur costs to attract tenants to re-lease the space. If leases are renewed, you will pay lower TIs than for new leases. For apartments, you may give away toasters or TVs or put in new appliances to attract customers, and as the market recovers, these costs will drop substantially. Again, these costs must be reflected in your analysis.

Figure 6.7 shows the **Less: TI** and **Less: Leasing Commissions** lines above Change In Cap Ex and then extends the analysis through **After-Tax Cash Flow** (the steps of which were discussed in detail in Chapter 5). As mentioned, it is important to note that the Year 7 values impact before- and after-tax cash flow only in that the Year 6 sale proceeds are valued off of the Year 7 adjusted NOI amount. Additionally, note that unlike the Kathy Center property in Chapter 5, Leslie Court has income tax liabilities it must pay.

Online Companion Hands On: Build in the lines for **Change in TI**, **Less: TI**, **Change in Leasing Commissions**, **Less: Leasing Commissions**, **Change in Cap Ex**, and **Less: Cap Ex**. For each of these sets of lines, enter the Year 1 amount shown in Figure 6.6, and calculate the values for the subsequent years as (Prior year value) * (1 + current year's **Change in** rate). The lines from **Adjusted Net Operating Income** down are already programmed for you. We note that the **Adjusted Net Operating Income** line references the Replacement Reserve Account Detail Backup table, which starts at row 147 on the tab.

To best appreciate Replacement Reserve account dynamics, replace the Time 0 Contribution input of $225,000 in cell d150 with a zero. As you do this, keep your eye on the Adjusted NOI line. You will notice it decreases in all years, as the contribution of around $50,000 in each year is insufficient to fully pay for the Cap Ex outlays of around $70,000 to $90,000 in each year. In the case of Year 1, if there is no contribution made at closing, the Adjusted NOI decreases from $711,399 to $685,649, a difference of $25,750, which is the shortfall amount between the $75,264 Cap Ex outlay and the $49,514 contributed to the RR account in Year 1. In other words, $25,750 of property income that would otherwise be cash flow must be used to invest in the property due to the insufficient reserves. Reinstate the $225,000 input so that your numbers tie to the printed Figures going forward.

FIGURE 6.7

	Acquisition	Decline Stage		Recovery Stage		Stable and Sale		Forward
Leslie Court Apartments Cash Flow Projection								
	Time 0	Year 1	Year 2	Year 3	Year 4	Year 5	Year 6	Year 7
Base Rental Revenue Growth			-5.0%	1.0%	2.5%	3.5%	3.5%	3.5%
Base Rental Revenues		1,100,305	1,045,290	1,055,743	1,082,136	1,120,011	1,159,211	1,199,784
Expense Reimbursement Revenue		0	0	0	0	0	0	0
Gross Revenues		1,100,305	1,045,290	1,055,743	1,082,136	1,120,011	1,159,211	1,199,784
Vacancy % Gross Revenues		7.0%	14.0%	12.0%	10.0%	7.0%	5.0%	5.0%
Less: Vacancies		(77,021)	(146,341)	(126,689)	(108,214)	(78,401)	(57,961)	(59,989)
Net Base Rental Revenue		1,023,284	898,949	929,054	973,923	1,041,610	1,101,251	1,139,795
Ancillary Income Growth			-8.0%	-7.0%	-3.0%	5.0%	3.0%	3.0%
Plus: Ancillary Income		6,052	5,568	5,178	5,023	5,274	5,432	5,595
Effective Gross Income (EGI)		1,029,336	904,517	934,232	978,945	1,046,884	1,106,683	1,145,390
Operating Expense Growth			-2.0%	-1.0%	0.0%	4.0%	3.5%	3.0%
Less: Operating Expenses		(102,934)	(100,875)	(99,867)	(99,867)	(103,861)	(107,496)	(110,721)
Less: Real Estate Taxes	3.0%	(110,031)	(113,332)	(116,732)	(120,234)	(123,841)	(127,556)	(131,383)
Less: Replacement Reserve (RR)	4.5% of GR	(49,514)	(47,038)	(47,508)	(48,696)	(50,400)	(52,165)	(53,990)
Total Expenses		(262,479)	(261,245)	(264,107)	(268,797)	(278,103)	(287,217)	(296,094)
Net Operating Income (NOI)		766,857	643,272	670,125	710,149	768,782	819,466	849,295
Change in TI			8.6%	10.4%	-9.9%	-10.0%	-8.2%	-8.1%
Less: TI		(35,000)	(38,010)	(41,963)	(37,809)	(34,028)	(31,238)	(28,707)
Change in Leasing Commissions			27.0%	10.8%	18.0%	-1.7%	-14.8%	-3.3%
Less: Leasing Commissions		(20,458)	(25,982)	(28,788)	(33,969)	(33,392)	(28,450)	(27,511)
Change in Cap Ex			-8.9%	8.5%	3.6%	19.5%	-21.9%	-2.4%
Less: Cap Ex		(75,264)	(68,566)	(74,394)	(77,072)	(92,101)	(71,931)	(70,204)
Adjusted Net Operating Income (1)		711,399	579,280	599,374	638,371	701,362	759,778	793,077
Less: Loan Points	(51,938)	0	0	0	0	0	0	
Less: Debt Service Payment		(414,650)	(414,650)	(414,650)	(414,650)	(414,650)	(414,650)	
Before-Tax Levered Cash Flow		296,749	164,630	184,724	223,721	286,712	345,129	
Less: Depreciation (Purchase Price)		(201,818)	(201,818)	(201,818)	(201,818)	(201,818)	(201,818)	
Less: Depreciation (TIs)		(35,000)	(38,010)	(41,963)	(37,809)	(34,028)	(31,238)	
Less: Depreciation (Cap Ex)		(10,752)	(20,547)	(31,175)	(42,185)	(55,342)	(65,618)	
Less: Leasing Commissions Amortization		(20,458)	(25,982)	(28,788)	(33,969)	(33,392)	(28,450)	
Less: Loan Points Amortization		(7,420)	(7,420)	(7,420)	(7,420)	(7,420)	(14,839)	
Plus: Cash Transfer to RR account (2)		49,514	47,038	47,508	48,696	50,400	52,165	
Plus: TIs		35,000	38,010	41,963	37,809	34,028	31,238	
Plus: Leasing Commissions		20,458	25,982	28,788	33,969	33,392	28,450	
Plus: Principal Amortization		52,759	56,573	60,662	65,047	69,750	74,792	
Taxable Income (Loss)		179,032	38,456	52,482	86,042	142,282	189,810	
Less: Application of Suspended Losses		0	0	0	0	0	0	
Net Taxable Income (Loss)		179,032	38,456	52,482	86,042	142,282	189,810	
Less: Tax Liability	21.0%	(37,597)	(8,076)	(11,021)	(18,069)	(29,879)	(39,860)	
Plus: Refund at sale of RR acct. bal. (3)		0	0	0	0	0	60,995	
After-Tax Cash Flow		259,152	156,554	173,703	205,652	256,833	366,264	

1. Adjusted Net Operating Income (a.k.a. Unlevered Cash Flow) is defined as NOI (which is already net of the Replacement Reserve contribution) - TI - Leasing Commissions - only the Cap Ex amount NOT covered by the Reserve Balance available (if any). As a result, if there are sufficient Replacement Reserves to fund the annual Cap Ex, the Adjusted NOI will not be reduced by the Cap Ex amount.

2. Based on the presence of a Replacement Reserve account and how we define Adjusted NOI, instead of carrying the "Plus: Cap Ex" line as shown in Chapter 5, we replace that line with the "Plus: Cash Transfer to RR account" line, which adds back only the Replacement Reserve contribution amount.

3. This line is for the sweep to equity of any Replacement Reserve account balance remaining at sale.

SALE VALUE

The calculation of the value upon sale, or the **residual value**, is critical, as a dominant portion of your cash flow derives from disposition. Figure 6.8 (which we display starting from NOI) shows in the very bottom right cell that over 72% of the property's cash flow is due to its residual value. To understand this residual value and how it is impacted by market conditions, it is necessary to determine how net sales proceeds are calculated.

FIGURE 6.8

Leslie Court Apartments Cash Flow Projection								
	Acquisition	Decline Stage		Recovery Stage		Stable and Sale		Forward
	Time 0	Year 1	Year 2	Year 3	Year 4	Year 5	Year 6	Year 7
Net Operating Income (NOI)		766,857	643,272	670,125	710,149	768,782	819,466	849,295
Change in TI			8.6%	10.4%	-9.9%	-10.0%	-8.2%	-8.1%
Less: TI		(35,000)	(38,010)	(41,963)	(37,809)	(34,028)	(31,238)	(28,707)
Change in Leasing Commissions			27.0%	10.8%	18.0%	-1.7%	-14.8%	-3.3%
Less: Leasing Commissions		(20,458)	(25,982)	(28,788)	(33,969)	(33,392)	(28,450)	(27,511)
Change in Cap Ex			-8.9%	8.5%	3.6%	19.5%	-21.9%	-2.4%
Less: Cap Ex		(75,264)	(68,566)	(74,394)	(77,072)	(92,101)	(71,931)	(70,204)
Adjusted Net Operating Income (1)		711,399	579,280	599,374	638,371	701,362	759,778	793,077
Less: Loan Points	(51,938)	0	0	0	0	0	0	
Less: Debt Service Payment		(414,650)	(414,650)	(414,650)	(414,650)	(414,650)	(414,650)	
Before-Tax Levered Cash Flow		296,749	164,630	184,724	223,721	286,712	345,129	
Less: Depreciation (Purchase Price)		(201,818)	(201,818)	(201,818)	(201,818)	(201,818)	(201,818)	
Less: Depreciation (TIs)		(35,000)	(38,010)	(41,963)	(37,809)	(34,028)	(31,238)	
Less: Depreciation (Cap Ex)		(10,752)	(20,547)	(31,175)	(42,185)	(55,342)	(65,618)	
Less: Leasing Commissions Amortization		(20,458)	(25,982)	(28,788)	(33,969)	(33,392)	(28,450)	
Less: Loan Points Amortization		(7,420)	(7,420)	(7,420)	(7,420)	(7,420)	(14,839)	
Plus: Cash Transfer to RR account (2)		49,514	47,038	47,508	48,696	50,400	52,165	
Plus: TIs		35,000	38,010	41,963	37,809	34,028	31,238	
Plus: Leasing Commissions		20,458	25,982	28,788	33,969	33,392	28,450	
Plus: Principal Amortization		52,759	56,573	60,662	65,047	69,750	74,792	
Taxable Income (Loss)		179,032	38,456	52,482	86,042	142,282	189,810	
Less: Application of Suspended Losses		0	0	0	0	0	0	
Net Taxable Income (Loss)		179,032	38,456	52,482	86,042	142,282	189,810	
Less: Tax Liability	21.0%	(37,597)	(8,076)	(11,021)	(18,069)	(29,879)	(39,860)	
Plus: Refund at sale of RR acct. bal. (3)		0	0	0	0	0	60,995	
After-Tax Cash Flow		259,152	156,554	173,703	205,652	256,833	366,264	
Net Sales Price							9,143,710	
Less: Tax Liability							(678,594)	
Less: Outstanding Mortgage Balance							(4,814,167)	
Less: Initial Equity Investment	(1,783,188)							
After-Tax Levered Cash Flow	($1,783,188)	$259,152	$156,554	$173,703	$205,652	$256,833	$4,017,212	

Equity Investment Performance Indicators			
Net Cash Flow	$3,285,919	Total Positive After-Tax Cash Flows	$5,069,107
IRR	22.51%	Net Sales Proceeds % Total	72.02%
NPV at 15%	$656,778		
Multiple	2.84x		

GROSS SALES PRICE, SALE INCOME TAX AND NET SALES PROCEEDS

As noted, the negotiated **gross sales price** (line A in Figure 6.9) is generally estimated by capping future stabilized adjusted NOI. Analysts often mistakenly use the same cap rate to estimate the **residual** ("reversion") **value** upon exit as what they used to determine their purchase price. The problem with this approach is that at sale, the building is older, and perhaps, not as competitive as when it was acquired years earlier. It also can justify wishful and nonsensical pricing. For example, using a 1% cap rate for both acquisition and disposition may seem like a good deal, but as the Japanese buyers of the 1980s painfully learned, there may be no one who is willing to pay the same crazy cap rate as you. So if you enter at a "1 cap," and exit at an "8 cap," you are dead.

For a stabilized property, the **exit cap rate** (**going-out cap rate** or **residual cap rate**) is generally somewhat higher than your **going-in cap rate**, reflective of it being an older and less sought-after building in the current competitive set. Interestingly for Leslie Court Apartments, while the going-in cap is 10.6% (adjusted NOI of $711,399 / purchase price of $6.7 MM), the exit cap is 8.5%. Isn't this contrary to what we just said? No. Specifically, you are purchasing while income is low and falling, and exiting after the building is stabilized. That is, your **purchase cap rate** is for a **non-stabilized property**, while your exit cap is for a stabilized property. Figure 6.9 shows the sale calculations for both **sale income tax liability** and net sales proceeds.

The first step to determine the income tax liability specific to the property sale is to arrive at the property's **net sales price** (line C), which is the gross sales price (line A) less **selling costs** (line B). Selling costs are primarily comprised of the sales **brokerage commission** but also include jurisdictional property transfer taxes. Commissions for investment sales brokers are negotiated amounts generally taken as a percentage of the gross sales price. A fee of less than 2% is assumed for this analysis, but if the transaction is a difficult sale, commissions can increase significantly. A weak market or property may not be the only reason for a challenging sale. If you have considerable deferred cap ex or have done a poor job of leasing the property, you may need to pay larger brokerage fees to sell the building.

The second step to determine sale income tax liability is to solve for the property's **adjusted cost basis** at the point of sale (line G). Adjusted cost basis is the original acquisition cost of the property (line D; the contract Purchase Price and transaction costs), plus capital expenditure amounts made (which include both tenant improvements and property-wide cap ex; line E), less **accumulated depreciation** (all depreciation taken to date) on the purchase price, TIs, and cap ex (line F).

Once we have the adjusted cost basis in line G, we can calculate the **gain-on-sale**, or **capital gain** (line H), as the net of the net sales price in line C and the adjusted cost basis in line G. There are two components to capital gain (and thus **capital gains tax**): depreciation "recapture" (line I) and property **appreciation** (the gain in property value; line J). Depreciation recapture is the total accumulated depreciation amount from which the property owner benefited by shielding taxable income. Depreciation recapture is currently taxed at 25%, producing the $413,644 capital gains tax amount in line L. The property appreciation capital gains tax basis in line J is the gain-on-sale (line H) less the depreciation recapture amount (line I). The property appreciation amount is currently taxed at 15%, producing the property appreciation capital gains tax amount of $264,951 in line M. The sum of the two resulting amounts in lines L and M is the **total sale income tax liability** (line N).

To solve for **net sales proceeds** (line T) the net sales price (line Q, which is the same as line C) is reduced by the **sale income tax liability** (line R, which is the same as line N) and any outstanding mortgage balance (line S). In our example, net sales proceeds are $3,650,948 (line T).

FIGURE 6.9

Leslie Court Sale Income Tax and Net Sales Proceeds Calculation			Line	Notes
Sale Income Tax Liability Accounting				
Gross Sales Price = (Year 7 Adjusted NOI / Cap Rate)		$9,330,317	A	
Less Selling Costs	2.00%	(186,606)	B	-% * A
Net Sales Price		9,143,710	C	A + B
Less Adjusted Cost Basis:				
Acquisition Cost		6,700,000	D	D4 from Fig 6.2, 6.7, 6.8 tab
Plus Tenant Improvements and Capital Improvements		677,373	E	Years 1-6 TIs and Cap Ex
Less Accumulated Depreciation		(1,654,575)	F	Years 1-6 Depreciation amounts
Adjusted Cost Basis		5,722,798	G	D + E + F
Gain-on-Sale (Capital Gain)		3,420,912	H	C - G
Components of Capital Gain:				
Depreciation Recapture		1,654,575	I	-F
Property Appreciation		1,766,337	J	H - I
		3,420,912	K	I + J
Capital Gains Tax on Sale:				
On Accumulated Depreciation	25.00%	413,644	L	Rate * I
On Property Appreciation	15.00%	264,951	M	Rate * J
Total Sale Income Tax Liability		**$678,594**	N	L + M
Net Sales Proceeds Calculation				
Gross Sales Price		9,330,317	O	A
Less Selling Costs		(186,606)	P	B
Net Sales Price		9,143,710	Q	O + P
Less Sale Income Tax Liability		(678,594)	R	-N
Less Outstanding Mortgage Balance		(4,814,167)	S	
Net Sales Proceeds		**$3,650,948**	T	Q + R + S

Online Companion Hands On: Complete the formatted, blank version of this Figure 6.9 found in Chapter 6 of the Online Companion Excel, using the description on the prior page and the Notes in the Figure as your guide. The **Less Outstanding Mortgage Balance** amount is the Year 6 Ending Balance, which you can reference in column R of the amortization schedule summary on the Figure 6.2, 6.7, 6.8 tab.

Now that you have completed Figure 6.9, return to the Figures 6.2, 6.7, 6.8 tab and look at the results in rows 132-135. If your values do not match those printed in Figures 6.7 and 6.8, you will need to retrace your steps to find your mistake(s), which can either be on your Figures 6.2, 6.7, 6.8 tab, or on the Figure 6.9 tab, or both. This "detective work" is a critical task in financial modeling, with the added challenge on the job of not having an answer key against which to check.

You will often search in vain for cap rates for **comparable transactions (comps)**, as they may not exist particularly in weak markets. Plus, not all comps will be at the same cap rate, and there is no guarantee you will realize the mean or median cap. Further, no website or professor can tell you exactly what to assume. Yet, you must assume something intelligent and defensible (which will be wrong), understand what can go wrong, and live with it. As Figure 6.10 shows, just a 50-bp increase in your exit cap to 9% can reduce your net cash flow to equity by more than $400,000 ($2,854,133 versus $3,285,919), your IRR by ~200 bps (~21% versus ~23%), your NPV by around $200,000 ($470,104 versus $656,778), and your multiple on equity by ~10% (2.60x versus 2.84x).

FIGURE 6.10

Leslie Court Apartments Cash Flow Projection - 9.00% Exit Cap							
	Time 0	Year 1	Year 2	Year 3	Year 4	Year 5	Year 6
After-Tax Levered Cash Flow	($1,783,188)	$259,152	$156,554	$173,703	$205,652	$256,833	$3,585,426

	Net Cash Flow	$2,854,133	
Equity Investment	**IRR**	20.62%	
Performance Indicators	**NPV at 15%**	$470,104	
	Multiple	2.60x	

Total Positive After-Tax Cash Flows	$4,637,320
Net Sales Proceeds % Total	69.42%

CLOSING THOUGHT

Never simply change a single line item or entry and think you are conducting a worthwhile sensitivity analysis. True insight requires a clear understanding of the ramifications and interdependencies between various line items. Focus on the "disease" that causes things to be worse and carefully work through each line item in view of the disease. You will focus more on bad outcomes because you can always live with things turning out better than expected. But even a meaningful analysis, complete with well-conceived scenarios, will never be right. You will always either be too low or too high, but your model allows you to systematically think about the property in a critical manner. As you gain business experience, you will become better at evaluating potential risks and how to best reflect those risks through financial models. Be patient. Your professional insight will improve over time.

 Online Companion Audio Interview: To hear a conversation about this chapter's content, go to the Online Companion and select the link for Chapter 6. Scroll down to the Audio Interview section and listen.

Chapter 7
Real Estate Due Diligence Analysis

"It's often a foregone conclusion left unchecked that comes back to bite you."
- Dr. Peter Linneman

WHAT IS DUE DILIGENCE?

Due diligence is the investigation made by a potential financial stakeholder prior to putting their capital at risk. Real estate courses often fail to cover due diligence, focusing instead on esoteric financing possibilities and option pricing models. But if you enter the real estate business, you will quickly find yourself engaged in due diligence efforts, as it is the foundation for making informed investment and lending decisions.

Due diligence involves both verifying and analyzing the facts about the property and the surrounding market and questioning the robustness of the assumptions made for your financial model. As such, due diligence serves as both a reality check and a challenge to your business plan. It also provides important insights concerning the property's risks.

There are many things to investigate before acquiring or developing a property. Where do you start? A due diligence checklist template helps, but creativity and awareness of the unique risks of each property are critical. Even for the most experienced players, no hypothetical should be out of bounds when stress-testing the premises on which an investment thesis is based. For instance, for a new highrise development opportunity, does a planned curved façade design potentially pose a sun-focusing risk that could be detrimental to neighboring properties, exposing you to lawsuits?

Assume you have developed a financial model for the next eleven years for your investment target. This pro forma summarizes expected revenues, expenses, capital improvements, leasing expenditures, debt service payments, etc. A critical aspect of due diligence is challenging your pro forma assumptions. Are the leases such that rents can truly grow by 5% in the third year? Can you sell the property when you want? How long will it take to sell the building? Will there be large capital expenditures? When and how can tenants get out of their leases? Are back-taxes owed by the seller? Have tenants provided signed **estoppel certificates** to confirm both their reimbursement obligations and that they are actually paying the contracted rents? Are there hidden legal liabilities? Is the property insurable? Due diligence is about identifying potential risks and addressing these types of questions before making an investment.

WRONG BUT USEFUL

Will the assumptions in your pro forma ever happen? Of course not! That is where careful analysis and risk management come into play. When real dollars are riding on your assumptions, you want to be extremely careful. In the end, the due diligence process provides information which helps you shore up your assumptions and determine whether the risks of acquiring or developing a property are more than offset by the opportunities it offers.

When you see a pro forma where a $2 million NOI in Year 4 doubles to $4 million by Year 7, you should be very curious about how this fortunate increase will be achieved. What specific factors make the increase possible; are they sustainable? Do the assumptions which yield this result make sense given the leases, the age of the property, and the market?

LITTLE MISTAKES + BIG NUMBERS = BIG PROBLEMS

Due diligence mistakes can be very costly. Often young professionals fall in love with the complexity and elegance of their financial models and neglect careful analysis of the property and its market. This invariably leads to expensive mistakes.

Sometimes your mistakes are apparent immediately, but more frequently, they will not show up until 12-36 months after you have closed the deal. Everything is running smoothly, when suddenly NOI begins to head south. Perhaps this is because the people in the area have moved elsewhere due to the local factory closing. Had you thoroughly performed market due diligence, you would have been aware of the weak state of the factory and either bid less or walked away from the deal. At a minimum, it should have been an outcome you considered when forming your bid. Of course, everyone makes mistakes. If you have not made any, it just means you have not done any deals. But if you make serious mistakes too often, you had better find another career.

What exactly goes into the due diligence process for real estate? A basic breakdown is:

- Title, Survey, Environmental, and Legal;
- Revenue;
- Operating Expenses;
- Capital Expenditures;
- Loan Documents;
- Neighborhood and Market.

TITLE, SURVEY, ENVIRONMENTAL, AND LEGAL

When you prepare to buy a property, it is important to know exactly what you are buying. Who owns it? What exactly do they own? Has it been owned prior to the current owner? Are there competing ownership claims? The way you obtain this information is by ordering a **property title search**. Title companies compile **title surveys** (reports) by searching public records. Knowing who owns the property is essential, because if you do not have each owner's title you may not own what you think you bought. The title search contains information on what each person owns, along with detailed legal property descriptions. A title document also contains additional information about the property, including its previous usage and ownership.

In the due diligence process it is your responsibility to understand what all this information means. This entails reading all of these documents, as well as all reference materials that describe any restrictions placed on the property. Deciphering all of this information is complex work that generally requires legal assistance. But reviewing and questioning your attorney's work is essential, as in the end, it is your money at risk.

You can purchase real estate either **encumbered** or **unencumbered**. Encumbered real estate has a **lien**, charge, or other financial liability attached to the property. For example, a mortgaged property is one in which a senior lender has a **security interest** on the property as long as the mortgage is outstanding. While encumbrances do not generally prevent the transfer of title, you had better know what encumbrances you are accepting before you acquire the property. There may also be physical encumbrances, such as telephone poles or utility towers on your property. All known encumbrances will be listed on the property's legal property description.

The title survey created from this information will display where improvements have been made, as well as what can potentially be added. **Easements** that have been granted will also be noted on this description. Easements are the right to do something on the property. It may be an **appurtenant easement**, such as the right for someone to cross through the property for transportation, ingress, or egress purposes. Another common easement is called easement "in gross," which is for the benefit of a person or company, rather than the benefit of another parcel of land. An example is an easement for public utilities. When performing due diligence, it is important to know who has what rights and what easements exist.

A hot topic in real estate is environmental contamination. If you are purchasing a residential property, chances are the owner has not been engaged in activities that cause severe environmental damage. So why do you have to be concerned about the potential environmental contamination of your property and the surrounding area? The property may have had a "dirty" use prior to becoming residential, or surrounding contamination may have entered the property below-ground. For example, was a previous owner a metals sculptor, or did a gas station formerly operate a block away from the site? It is possible that the sculptor illegally disposed of unused hazardous materials in the yard or that the gas station's underground storage tanks leaked and leached onto the property, contaminating both the site and the local aquifer. According to the current **Superfund Law**, as the new owner, you are liable for the damage regardless of whether you were the source or not. Why? Congress decided it is best to have things cleaned up first, and only then can you – as the new owner – sort out if you can collect from the original polluter later via a tort claim. These costs can be huge, and due diligence helps determine if these problems exist before you purchase the property.

There are several ways to conduct environmental studies: you search the public record; talk to people familiar with the property; hire consultants; and run your own investigations. If you walk the site and the grass is orange, it is not a good sign. When contracting a third-party service provider to conduct your investigations, you must be diligent of their cutting corners, especially when the market is hot and they are awash with clients. They may not interview enough people or not sample enough sites on the property. Your money is at risk, so it is your job to supervise them. Even if the seller says he has already checked everything and guarantees everything is fine, you must still perform your own due diligence, as the seller may not have sufficient assets to cover the damages they guarantee. Moreover, it is costly and difficult to prove that the seller engaged in fraudulent activity. Remember that the more severe the problem, the more likely the seller will try to convince you not to worry.

Just as you have to check for potential environmental defects, you also need to watch for structural defects. For example, some tall buildings have placed swimming pools on the top floors of their buildings. While beautiful and an attractive common amenity, pools can cause problems relating to enhanced mold spore growth. While not yet fully quantified, mold problems are now being compared to the asbestos contamination issue of a generation ago. Other questions to consider are: Is the roof in good condition? How about the HVAC system? The elevators?

A property should pass a structural integrity **Possible Maximum Loss (PML) test**, where the higher the building's score, the worse its structural integrity. If the score is above 19, it will be difficult to secure an accepting lender. Remember that lenders are risk-averse by nature. A warehouse is built like a big box, so if an earthquake occurs, the entire structure may fall like a stack of pancakes. Such a structural defect gives the building a PML in excess of 19, and bracing is required to provide sufficient support. If the PML is greater than 20, you may not want to purchase the structure because the cost of earthquake proofing the property may be prohibitively high. Sometimes, less sophisticated investors do not get the PML ratings in time and, therefore, lose substantial time and money bidding on a non-financeable asset.

You will also need to conduct legal diligence to determine if there are outstanding legal claims associated with the property. This includes worker injury claims, "slip and fall" claims, and lawsuits filed by tenants, vendors, or customers, etc.

REVENUES, OPERATING EXPENSES, AND CAPITAL EXPENDITURES

Revenues

After the physical aspects of the property have been thoroughly investigated, it is necessary to challenge your beliefs about how much cash flow the property can generate. Revenue can be broken into three components: creditworthiness of the tenants, current leases, and the long-term competitiveness of the property. For this last consideration, the location, design durability, and the flexibility of the property are critical, as these factors allow the value of the property to be maintained over time. The property may be currently leased to a great tenant at favorable terms, but the space may be difficult to re-lease because of poor design or location. For example, with an industrial warehouse, you want to make sure that the floors are truly flat, so that when tenants stack inventory 30 feet high, the pallets do not lean or collapse. Also, is it easy for trucks to enter and exit the facility? Does the property have sufficient clear height? Is it near a major highway interchange?

Is there a book or website that tells you what is a good location or design? No, but common sense and experience are good guides. You need to understand how the building will be used and the tenant's operating needs. For example, truck drivers generally cannot drive for more than an 8-hour shift. If your warehouse facility takes 30 minutes to enter and exit, the tenant will not be happy because that time could have been spent by their drivers in transit.

Your surroundings play a major role in property design, so there are no set rules of design. But experience dictates some lasting design elements. What is considered a "hot" design today may be passé in 10 years. As firms grow more sophisticated, and their operations change, so too will their design requirements. For this reason, it is important to be aware of the property's expansion and redevelopment options.

Contracts also play a large role in determining your revenues. If you own a strip retail center, your revenue will be largely dependent upon your tenant mix. If the property has a strong anchor, like Walmart, you will want to know if they have the right to terminate the lease or go dark. If so, under what circumstances? If a key tenant can go dark, then other tenants who have co-tenancy agreements may also leave the center. Since much of the center's profits derive from the smaller tenants, a dark anchor can destroy a center.

A different problem can occur in an office building. The property may have Citi as a major tenant, and at the end of their lease, they have the option to renew the lease for 15 years at 95% of "fair market value." What happens if the lease expires in a down market? Then you have no choice but to lock in the tenant at very low rents for another 15 years. This problem is exacerbated if the current lease states that the landlord provides tenant improvements at $50 per square foot upon renewal.

A careful review of the property's accounts receivable indicates who is in arrears (overdue on their rent) and for how long. If receivables are high, one or more of your tenants may be secretly facing bankruptcy. Will they void their leases in bankruptcy? Is their weakness an indicator of a larger economic decline in the area? Or perhaps a major tenant has a dispute with the current owner. A major problem with gathering receivables information is that the seller is usually slow to show you who is paying and who is not, as they want to collect as much of these receivables as they can before selling. Further, they are hesitant to expose the weaker aspects of their property. Oftentimes, accounts receivable reports are among the last data you will receive.

How do you learn about the demand side of the real estate business? Speak with tenants, local leasing agents, and brokers. In fact, working for a broker can be a great way to learn about tenants and their leasing needs. You will also gain some experience in what design features are relevant for tenants.

Operating Expenses

You should carefully explore the property financial statements and entity tax returns from the last 3-5 years. Carefully reading the leases is also critical because they articulate who pays for what. Will the tenant pay for utility bills or does the landlord? In a shopping center, tenants usually pay a share of all costs. For office buildings, each tenant tends to have a base year expense stop that reflects market conditions at the time the lease was signed. In that case, the landlord is responsible for that tenant's pro-rata percentage of shared expenses above the "base year stop."

Assume you want to construct Henderson Arms residential condominiums in downtown Philadelphia. Based on your work in the Philadelphia suburbs, you think that $125 per square foot is a reasonable estimate of construction costs. If you do not perform careful due diligence, you will be in for quite a shock when you realize it costs closer to $200 per square foot to build the structure! Why? Philadelphia is a union town. Union wages and work rules ramp up costs significantly. If you attempt to avoid union labor, you may find your project halted due to strikes or labor shortages. If you are building a medical facility and must install a multimillion dollar CAT scan machine, you will probably want the manufacturer of the machine to install it to avoid breaching the warranty. In this situation you may have to pay for a union member to stand and watch the installation process. Does the union worker add any value? No. Do you have to pay him? Yes. For this reason, you will have to adjust your pro forma expenditures accordingly.

After the September 11 attacks, insurance coverage and premiums changed for many properties. This means that coverage which was acceptable pre-9/11 is not adequate today. These changes will increase your insurance expenditures and decrease your NOI.

Another government policy that will alter expenditures is property taxes. When were they last raised? Are they up for revision? If the local government is looking for a quick way to increase revenues, they may consider increasing local property taxes. These increases will reduce your cash stream. You must assess the likelihood that your purchase triggers a new assessment and perhaps petition against it or agree to accept it and factor the higher real estate tax into your purchase offer.

In some cases, the property may be over-assessed. If your due diligence reveals this problem, then you will want to pursue a property tax reduction by requesting a **reassessment**.

Capital Expenditure Needs

Capital expenditure reserves are the cash amounts set aside for funding future capital projects such as major renovations or roof or elevator replacement. These contingencies reflect the fact that you know such outlays will occur, but not precisely when. These expenditures may result from severe damage due to a tornado or an unexpected collapse of the roof. The reserves also cover routine capital expenditures. How do you determine if your pro forma reserve is large enough? Go out and look at the structure and make a detailed analysis of what costs you think will be incurred. A reserve that is too small will make it difficult to get a loan or will squeeze you when you need money most.

LOAN DOCUMENTS

When buying a property, you may find that it is encumbered by debt. In certain cases, the debt is not transferable, which means the current owner cannot sell the property without paying off the debt. If the current owner needs cash right away to pay off the debt in full, then you probably will not be able to pay the owner piecemeal over time through an **installment sale** structure.

In some situations, the debt may be **assumable**, meaning that as the new owner you can take on the previous owner's debt. If you choose to do that, you must be wary. There may be covenants on the debt that prohibit certain operations you may wish to perform. If you are building a retail center and a covenant states that you cannot have parking lots, you will not be able to implement your plans. Sometimes the debt has an "equity kicker," where if the property generates a profit over some pre-determined amount, the lender receives a portion of the upside. If you do not want to share your profit, you may want to pay off the existing debt. But be wary because the loan may have a pre-payment penalty. If the debt is due in the distant future and is locked in at a high rate, this penalty can be quite large.

NEIGHBORHOOD AND MARKET

When you purchase a property, you are purchasing a part of the community. For this reason, you must be aware of what is happening in the community. If the area has experienced phenomenal growth due to the opening of a biotechnology firm, you must investigate whether that firm and industry are solid. Otherwise, you may put growth numbers in your pro forma that are impossible to achieve. Performing a neighborhood demographic analysis includes gathering data on income, traffic patterns, and population and employment trends. All of this aids you in doing a supply and demand analysis of the area. For example, a **trade area analysis** is conducted for contemplated retail developments to determine whether the area is "over-retailed" (overserved by other retail properties) or "under-retailed" (underserved by retail). A crude rule of thumb is that a market can support up to about 200 square feet of shopping space per person. If the subject city has a population of 400,000, is assumed to grow at 5% over the next 5 years, has no new construction in the pipeline, and currently has about 40 million square feet of retail, it has only about 100 square feet per person of shopping space. Thus, this town may be underserved in terms of retail space.

If the town has an upper middle-class demographic profile, and incomes are expected to grow, perhaps an upscale shopping venue is most appropriate. To determine the prime location of this center, traffic patterns are evaluated to assess where people regularly congregate or traverse. Gathering credit card receipt data from the town hall is another efficient means of determining where people shop. Always drive or walk around the neighborhood and observe the homes, cars, and stores in the area. Do this on different days and at different times, as the character and activity of the neighborhood may vary depending upon when you are there. For instance, is there a local farmer's market on certain days of the week that might hurt produce sales in the retail plaza you intend to develop? Perhaps this is why there is no produce market for several blocks. Also be cognizant of "virtual supply" in the market, such as AirBnB room inventory that does not show up on market reports but competes for traveler room nights.

CLOSING THOUGHT

All of the information required for responsible due diligence is not nicely organized on some website. You must get out, walk around, talk to brokers, read reports, drive or helicopter the area, and visit the property and town both at night and during the day. In short, you must be invested in the community in every sense of the word. You may engage local consultants to help you get up to speed if you are new to real estate or to update your understanding of the market. Doing your homework will require substantial creativity and dedication. In addition, you must be skeptical of what you read and hear. If you find a report saying that population is expected to double in three years, question that report, even if it is by a major firm. Their mistakes and typos can cost you a lot of money!

 Online Companion Audio Interview: To hear a conversation about this chapter's content, go to the Online Companion and select the link for Chapter 7. Scroll down to the Audio Interview section and listen.

Chapter 8
Analyzing Metropolitan Long-Term Growth Patterns

"Get a good pair of sunglasses and some sunblock if you want to build for the Boomers."
- Dr. Peter Linneman

Whether relying on recent headlines, conversations with friends, or gut feelings, real estate professionals must constantly formulate and refine their outlook about the market demand for their product, making operational and strategic adjustments as needed. Population and job growth drive residential, office, distribution, and retail demand. In short, growth fills space, supports real estate development, and is of high and perpetual interest to financial stakeholders in real estate.

A NATION OF CONSTANT POSITIVE POPULATION GROWTH

From 2010 through 2020, the U.S. population grew by about 20.2 million people and 10.9 million households. While the U.S. population growth rate has slowed from 0.89% in 2000-2010, to about 0.63% per year in 2010-2020, growth is a major distinguishing feature of the U.S. economy relative to other developed economies. In 2020, the total U.S. population was roughly 331.4 million. The U.S. Census Bureau projects U.S. populations of 353.8 million and 372.2 million by 2030 and 2040, respectively, for compounded annual growth rates of 0.66% and 0.51%. To put these figures in perspective, over the next 10 years, the U.S. will add the combined populations of Moscow and London or Beijing and Barcelona, or about 8.8 million households.

Growth requires significant real estate and infrastructure development. As shown in Figure 8.1, if this new population of 22.2 million people (through 2030) lives with the density of the Philadelphia Metropolitan Statistical Area (MSA), it will require over 1.2 million acres of new development. Alternatively, assuming population densities of the Miami or Los Angeles regions yields a new development requirement of 1.1 million and 1.9 million acres, respectively. If even lower densities are assumed, such as those of Atlanta and Phoenix, accommodating a population increase of 22.4 million will necessitate the development of 3.6 million and 5.1 million acres, respectively. We estimate that of this required land, more than 60% will be for residential use, with the remainder for office, retail, industrial, hotel, institutional and infrastructure, and open space.

FIGURE 8.1

Estimated U.S. Land Absorption Assuming MSA Densities (YE2020-2030)		
Estimated U.S. population growth		22,400,000
People per U.S. household		2.56
Estimated household growth		8,750,000
City	HH/Acre	Est. Required Acres
Philadelphia	7.0	1,248,817
Miami	7.7	1,136,302
Los Angeles	4.6	1,896,532
Atlanta	2.4	3,615,592
Phoenix	1.7	5,113,744

Source: Census, Linneman Associates

Not only will the population be larger, but it will also be richer. By 2030, the median consumer will likely have the income capacity of today's 70th percentile household. This means more gadgets, more travel, and certainly more cosmetic surgery. It also means that the housing stock designed 50-100 years ago will have an ever-harder time competing for these households. Similarly, if real wealth grows by approximately 40% to over $1.5 million per household by 2030, generational transfers will enable children and grandchildren to own their homes earlier, take more luxurious vacations, or retire far more comfortably than previous generations. Higher real incomes and real wealth will also increase the latent demand to live in the most desirable areas.

But there is no "national" U.S. real estate market, so real estate investors, lenders, and developers need to focus on what is happening in each specific area. In other words, looking at aggregate U.S. growth is interesting but does not allow demand to be evaluated on a sufficiently granular basis for making well-informed real estate investment decisions.

METROPOLITAN COUNTY POPULATION GROWTH

In 2006, Peter Linneman co-authored with Albert Saiz, a regression-based study in which they forecasted U.S. population by county and MSA through 2020. With the release of 2010 Census data in 2014, Linneman Associates updated the forecasts extending through 2030. MSA population as a percent of total U.S. population is the dependent variable, determined by local factors such as share of foreign-born residents, educational attainment, race and age share percentages, taxes per capita, voting trends, political party representation, weather characteristics, age of housing stock, proximity to an ocean or Great Lake, and geographic region (Figure 8.2).

FIGURE 8.2

Impact on Population Share Change 1990-2010 (Basis Point)		
Population change 1980-1990	+100bp	0.03
Population share change 1980-1990	+100bp	46.95***
Share foreign-born in 1990	+100bp	0.26
% with bachelor's degree or higher in 1990	+100bp	0.09
% with less than a high school diploma in 1990	+100bp	-0.13**
% white in 1990	+100bp	-0.05*
% over 65 years old in 1990	+100bp	-0.22**
% under 25 years old in 1990	+100bp	-0.32***
Income tax per capita / Income per capita in 1990	+100bp	-0.72
Sales tax per capita / Income per capita in 1990	+100bp	0.33
Presidential election vote over 55% Republican in 1992	If Yes	0.67
Presidential election vote below 45% Republican in 1992	If Yes	2.82***
All state senators Republican in 1990	If Yes	0.83
All state senators Democrat in 1990	If Yes	0.43
Average precipitation	+1%	-0.03**
January average temperature	+1%	0.02**
Average January sun days	+1%	-0.02***
Share housing older than 30 years in 1990	+100bp	-0.19***
Share housing newer than 11 years in 1990	+100bp	-0.04
County borders an ocean or a Great Lake	If Yes	-1.95**
Hills or mountains in county	If Yes	-0.28
Northeast	If Yes	0.96
South	If Yes	-1.07
West	If Yes	-5.96***
Observations		1,159
Adj R-squared		0.71

Source: Linneman Associates

*** significant at 1%, ** significant at 5%, * significant at 10%*

This statistical analysis provides an understanding of growth across U.S. metropolitan counties during the past 30 years. About 75% of all variation in county population growth is statistically identifiable. But growth surprises do occur and, in some cases, matter a lot. In the 1950s, who would have predicted that Benton County, Arkansas would emerge as the center of one of the biggest commercial empires in world history? Yet spurred by the phenomenal growth of Walmart, Benton County makes the Census list of top 70 counties by population growth. The point is that our statistical analysis will never predict who the next Sam Walton will be, or where he or she will be based.

The dependent variables in these studies capture attributes of an area that cause it to grow economically and attract employers and employees. Firm productivity varies across locales for several reasons: the skills and education of their population; accessibility to markets and transportation nodes; the impact of local public finances (taxes and expenditures); and **agglomeration economies**. The latter refers to firms becoming more productive if they locate closer to similar firms, enabling them to share information, infrastructures, and a pool of relevant workers, and to reduce the transportation costs of their common inputs and outputs.

2030 Forecast

Figure 8.3 reveals that the Atlanta, Washington, D.C., Dallas, New York City, Houston, Chicago, Richmond, and Minneapolis MSAs lead the pack in the 2030 population growth forecasts (versus 2016) on an absolute level, while Walla Walla, WA; Hinesville, GA; Carson City, NV; Valdosta, GA; Rapid City, SD; and Charlottesville, VA show the strongest percentage growth through 2030. No markets appear on both growth lists. Not surprisingly, the projected top percentage growth MSAs are relatively small, not meriting significant growth on an absolute basis. Combined, the top 10 percentage growth markets are expected to add only 1.5 million new people through 2030. On the other hand, the top 10 absolute growth markets will increase in population by 12.1 million on an aggregate basis through 2030. Of those, Richmond (65.1%), Virginia Beach (42.5%), Atlanta (41.1%), Washington, D.C. (32.4%), Minneapolis (22.8%), and Dallas-Fort Worth (20.3%) have the highest projected total percentage growth over the 17-year period. The aggregate sample population (274.8 million) in the statistical analysis represents about 85.0% of the total 2016 population of 323.1 million. The projection states that the major MSA urban population will experience a net increase of 58.1 million people, or about 21%, by 2030.

FIGURE 8.3

MSA Population Forecasts 2016-2030			
Highest Absolute Growth		Highest Percent Growth	
Metropolitan Statistical Area	Change in Population	Metropolitan Statistical Area	CAGR (%)
Atlanta-Sandy Springs-Roswell, GA	2,341,813	Walla Walla, WA	7.6
Washington-Arlington-Alexandria, DC-VA-MD-WV	1,969,272	Hinesville-Fort Stewart, GA	7.0
Dallas-Fort Worth-Arlington, TX	1,440,490	Carson City, NV	6.6
New York-Newark-Jersey City, NY-NJ-PA	1,372,866	Valdosta, GA	6.3
Houston-Sugar Land-Baytown, TX	940,934	Rapid City, SD	6.2
Chicago-Joliet-Naperville, IL-IN-WI	902,129	Charlottesville, VA	6.1
Richmond, VA	827,509	Lewiston, ID-WA	6.1
Minneapolis-St. Paul-Bloomington, MN-WI	803,535	Brunswick, GA	5.9
Riverside-San Bernardino-Ontario, CA	777,314	Albany, GA	5.8
Virginia Beach-Norfolk-Newport News, VA-NC	733,254	Wenatchee-East Wenatchee, WA	5.4
San Antonio-New Braunfels, TX	715,288	Athens-Clarke County, GA	5.2
Nashville-Davidson--Murfreesboro--Franklin, TN	713,207	Winchester, VA-WV	5.1
Charlotte-Concord-Gastonia, NC-SC	708,259	Macon, GA	4.9
Denver-Aurora-Broomfield, CO	650,672	Pine Bluff, AR	4.7
Phoenix-Mesa-Glendale, AZ	637,955	Idaho Falls, ID	4.6
Philadelphia-Camden-Wilmington, PA-NJ-DE-MD	590,790	Bismarck, ND	4.6
Indianapolis-Carmel-Anderson, IN	586,058	Grand Island, NE	4.5
St. Louis, MO-IL	586,034	Hattiesburg, MS	4.5
Kansas City, MO-KS	585,826	Amarillo, TX	4.3
Austin-Round Rock-San Marcos, TX	556,780	Kennewick-Pasco-Richland, WA	4.3
Cincinnati, OH-KY-IN	525,436	Warner Robins, GA	4.3
Louisville-Jefferson County, KY-IN	495,078	Jefferson City, MO	4.3
Orlando-Kissimmee-Sanford, FL	491,022	Victoria, TX	4.1
Columbus, OH	486,584	New Bern, NC	4.1
Las Vegas-Paradise, NV	481,067	Dalton, GA	4.0
Memphis, TN-MS-AR	467,133	Manhattan, KS	3.9
Baton Rouge, LA	436,686	Wichita Falls, TX	3.9
Sacramento--Arden-Arcade--Roseville, CA	432,851	Parkersburg-Vienna, WV	3.9
Portland-Vancouver-Hillsboro, OR-WA	388,177	Ithaca, NY	3.9
Albuquerque, NM	386,851	Hilton Head Island-Bluffton-Beaufort, SC	3.8
Boise City-Nampa, ID	367,061	St. George, UT	3.8
Baltimore-Towson, MD	366,566	Burlington-South Burlington, VT	3.8
Columbia, SC	358,830	El Centro, CA	3.8
Oklahoma City, OK	356,812	Yuma, AZ	3.8
Raleigh-Cary, NC	355,529	Mankato-North Mankato, MN	3.8
Knoxville, TN	352,706	Roanoke, VA	3.8
Jacksonville, FL	340,666	Farmington, NM	3.7
Birmingham-Hoover, AL	338,686	Morristown, TN	3.7
Tampa-St. Petersburg-Clearwater, FL	310,508	Columbus, GA-AL	3.7

Source: U.S. Census Bureau, Linneman Associates
CAGR = Compounded annual growth rate

Local Population Growth Insights

Between 2010 and 2019, the MSAs registering the greatest absolute population growth were Dallas-Ft. Worth, Houston, Atlanta, Phoenix, Washington, D.C., Miami-Ft. Lauderdale, Seattle, Austin, Orlando, and Denver. The MSAs with the greatest percentage growth during that period were The Villages (FL), Myrtle Beach, Austin, Midland (TX), and St. George (UT). Austin is notably on both lists. The analysis reveals that growth occurs where: people want to live and play; firms find it efficient to produce; necessary building approvals are relatively easy to obtain; potential growth can be accommodated; and other "wild card" factors.

Past Growth

The study found that the single most important factor in determining future population growth is past growth, a conclusion confirmed by prior studies. This persistence of population growth reflects the fact that growth begets growth. In fact, past growth accounts for 69% of the forces driving the 2030 forecasts. Specifically, agglomeration economies occur as firms cluster in a location and share a large pool of input resources, resulting in increased efficiency, greater innovation, and declining costs. For example, transportation costs associated with reaching customers and vendors are reduced, which in turn attracts related firms and customers. Large cities also tend to be attractive because of their concentrations of businesses, high and low culture, entertainment, transportation infrastructure, education, etc. Communities that allow growth are communities with both high levels of latent demand and a willingness to approve growth. The study found that big counties in major MSAs tend to dominate.

Economic Diversity

Local economies experience greater growth if they are economically diverse, as diversity increases the chance that an area is able to "ride the right horse." It is also true that the more diversified the economy, the less likely it is that an area becomes calcified by the social and political control of a single-industry constituency. This is exemplified by Houston, which has boomed as it transformed from a pure "oil city" to a diversified economy, while New Orleans remained tied to the oil industry and stagnated.

Immigrant Presence

Immigration is a primary driver of population growth. In the 1960s, most Americans claimed European or African ancestry, and the number of foreign-born households was relatively low. Between now and 2050, immigrants and their offspring will account for about half of the total growth in U.S. population, and Americans of European and African origin will become *primi inter pares* (i.e., first among equals) in a country of Mexican-Americans, Chinese-Americans, Korean-Americans, Indian-Americans, Filipino-Americans, and many others.

Ethnic networks lead people to move to areas where they have social contacts. Thus, metropolitan areas with large immigrant populations, for example, tend to attract yet more immigrants. In other words, immigrants tend to concentrate wherever previous immigrants have settled. Kinship ties, shared language, and the existence of common amenities and public goods make "immigrant enclaves" attractive to subsequent immigrants.

Biology and Age Distribution

The characteristics of the population of an area can predict population growth for simple biological reasons: younger populations tend to be more fertile, while the elderly experience higher mortality rates. The age distribution of the population is another predictor of future growth; that is, very young and very old populations tend to grow more slowly. Population growth is negatively related to both the share of people younger than 25 and the share of people older than 65, reflecting that households in their prime earning years are typically 25-65. Moreover, areas with a large proportion of older residents are less attractive to younger generations.

Weather

Some of the most powerful predictors of population growth are weather-related. Americans are steadily choosing sunnier and drier climates. Both the study's West regional indicator and "good weather" variables are strong predictors of population growth. All the weather variables (snowfall, precipitation, temperature, and sun days) are interrelated, with the number of sunny days in January being very important. In short, people are moving to "the bright and warm side."

Vintage of Existing Housing Stock

Areas with large amounts of new housing have three important attributes favoring growth: they are favorably inclined to development; they have a large recent demand relative to pre-existing housing; and their housing stock is more in-line with modern housing preferences. A very old housing stock that has survived was generally built for high-income families, and hence are of good quality. Since declining cities, such as New Orleans, Detroit, and Buffalo, have massive and valuable housing stocks, reduced housing demand translated into lower housing prices, making these cities a bit more attractive. However, areas with newer housing stocks generally experienced more growth.

Coastal Adjacency and Zoning

Counties adjacent to the coastlines of the Atlantic, Pacific, and Great Lakes tend to grow more slowly than inland counties. Coastal areas in the west and northeast often have restrictive zoning, which raises prices and discourages growth and change. Local opposition to growth is not a matter of having a majority of Democrats or Republicans, nor is it highly related to income. Counties that have grown over the past 20 years (controlling for the factors we have discussed above) tend to grow because of their openness to growth.

Educational Achievement

Cities with educated populations tend to grow faster, with counties having lower shares of high school dropouts growing more quickly. Education has an important long-run impact, but short-term changes in education levels are not powerful predictors of short-term changes in growth patterns. Metropolitan areas with highly-educated individuals are more productive, allowing them to pay higher wages, which attracts population inflows. On the other hand, highly-educated populations are often effective in curtailing residential development at the local level, stemming population growth. Many factors create an area's attractiveness, but even if underlying conditions change noticeably, reputation and growth will lag. For example, if a local government improves its educational system, its reputation will not immediately reflect this improvement.

Local Income and Sales Tax Rates

Tax rates are not uniform across municipalities. A high degree of taxation makes an area less attractive to both taxpayers and entrepreneurs. On the other hand, higher tax revenues may be associated with better public schools and other public services. Statistical analysis reveals that a higher local sales tax burden is associated with slower population growth.

Skilled Labor Force

Access to skilled individuals and production networks generates spillover economies. Thus, locating in areas where young workers want to live has become increasingly important in the 21st century. Similarly, agglomerations of people working on related problems help innovation and provide a deeper labor pool to accommodate growth. Areas with high levels of unemployment and high school dropout rates grow more slowly. Also, non-manufacturing employers tend to avoid areas with large manufacturing concentrations. This reflects both a mismatch of jobs skills and fear that the "old time" political influence of a large manufacturing sector will be used to hurt non-manufacturers.

Population Density

Population density matters in a complex way. Counties with very low densities tend to grow more slowly, but above a certain threshold, density is associated with slower growth. This population density threshold corresponds with a median county density of about 60 persons per square mile. Therefore, density increases growth up to about 60 people per square mile, after which amenity levels drop and population growth slows.

REGIONAL GROWTH VARIABILITY

Both national and local economies go through hot and cold periods. In 2007, Linneman Associates first published a study that attempted to answer the question: as the U.S. economy moves through cycles, which MSAs will over-react around trend growth on the up-cycle (but disproportionately suffer during down-cycles), and which will under-react, growing more steadily around their trends over the cycle? The analysis, which has been updated over the subsequent business cycles, provides a metric with which to manage risk expectations around generally smoothly growing pro forma analyses of local demographics.

Methodology

The analysis examines how various economic indicators behave in individual metropolitan areas based on national economic changes. For each MSA, Linneman Associates calculated a statistical equation, which summarizes how a 100-basis point change in the national variable affects the local indicator. The equation consists of a constant "alpha" for each market and a "beta," which is a multiplier applied to the national percent change in employment. The alpha indicates MSA growth that is independent of national growth. If there is no national job growth, then the alpha is the expected annual percentage change in MSA employment. The beta for the U.S. as a whole is defined as one. An MSA with a beta of one registers (on average) an increase of 100 bps in employment growth (plus its alpha) when national employment rises by 100 bps. A beta that is less than one indicates that the MSA does not boom (or bust) to as great an extent as the national economy, while a beta of greater than one indicates that such an MSA experiences swings of greater magnitude (compared to the local base) than the percentage changes at the national level.

These models are simple indicators of how coincident each MSA's economy is with movements of the national economy. They provide insight into the demand volatility around the local trend during unusual boom or bust periods (which occur but are never modeled in pro formas).

Insights

Figure 8.4 displays the average percentage job growth and standard deviation, employment growth R-squared, alpha, beta, and breakeven U.S. job growth rate for each MSA. Noteworthy in this analysis is the high degree of MSA employment growth predictability based on U.S. job growth, with a high R-squared indicating that simply knowing alpha, beta, and U.S. job growth disproportionally "explains" MSA job growth. The most predictable MSAs are Chicago, Charlotte, Atlanta, Cleveland, and Minneapolis, while the least predictable are Honolulu (by far), Knoxville, Albany, D.C., and Houston. In fact, Honolulu employment is almost uncorrelated with U.S. employment, reflecting that Hawaii is an economy largely independent of the U.S. mainland.

FIGURE 8.4

MSA	Growth	Standard Dev.	R^2	Alpha	Beta	Breakeven Point	Continent
Employment Growth Beta Analysis by MSA							
Albany-Schenectady-Troy, NY	0.6%	1.3%	0.48	(0.13)	0.53	0.24	Low α, very low β
Atlanta-Sandy Springs-Roswell, GA	2.0%	2.7%	0.89	0.32	1.52	(0.21)	Low α, high β
Austin-Round Rock, TX	3.7%	2.7%	0.68	2.26	1.32	(1.71)	High α, high β
Baltimore-Columbia-Towson, MD	0.8%	1.7%	0.68	(0.14)	0.82	0.18	Low α, low β
Baton Rouge, LA	1.9%	1.9%	0.22	N/A	N/A	N/A	N/A
Birmingham-Hoover, AL	0.8%	1.8%	0.84	(0.31)	0.98	0.32	Low α, low β
Boston-Cambridge-Newton, MA-NH	0.7%	2.0%	0.70	(0.35)	0.98	0.35	Low α, low β
Bridgeport-Stamford-Norwalk, CT	0.1%	1.9%	0.74	(0.91)	0.98	0.92	Very low α, low β
Buffalo-Cheektowaga-Niagara Falls, NY	0.3%	1.2%	0.53	(0.45)	0.50	0.90	Low α, very low β
Charlotte-Concord-Gastonia, NC-SC	2.0%	2.6%	0.90	0.41	1.45	(0.28)	Low α, high β
Charleston-North Charleston-Summerville, SC	2.1%	2.4%	0.60	0.81	1.10	(0.74)	High α, high β
Chicago-Naperville-Elgin, IL-IN-WI	0.7%	1.8%	0.94	(0.52)	1.02	0.51	Low α, low β
Cincinnati, OH-KY-IN	1.0%	1.6%	0.85	(0.09)	0.89	0.10	Low α, low β
Cleveland-Elyria, OH	0.2%	1.8%	0.89	(1.00)	1.04	0.96	Very low α, low β
Columbus, OH	1.5%	1.7%	0.87	0.35	0.96	(0.37)	Low α, low β
Dallas-Fort Worth-Arlington, TX	2.2%	2.3%	0.86	0.79	1.29	(0.61)	High α, high β
Denver-Aurora-Lakewood, CO	2.1%	2.4%	0.82	0.66	1.28	(0.52)	High α, high β
Detroit-Warren-Dearborn, MI	0.2%	2.7%	0.71	(1.32)	1.37	0.96	Very low α, high β
Grand Rapids-Wyoming, MI	1.5%	2.8%	0.71	(0.15)	1.41	0.10	Low α, high β
Greenville-Anderson-Mauldin, SC	1.3%	2.5%	0.83	(0.20)	1.36	0.15	Low α, high β
Hartford-West Hartford-East Hartford, CT	-0.1%	1.7%	0.53	(0.88)	0.74	1.19	Very low α, low β
Houston-The Woodlands-Sugar Land, TX	2.2%	1.9%	0.52	1.17	0.83	(1.41)	High α, low β
Indianapolis-Carmel-Anderson, IN	1.5%	1.7%	0.81	0.45	0.90	(0.50)	Low α, low β
Jacksonville, FL	1.9%	2.5%	0.87	0.35	1.41	(0.25)	Low α, high β
Kansas City, MO-KS	1.1%	1.5%	0.79	0.11	0.81	(0.14)	Low α, low β
Knoxville, TN	1.5%	1.6%	0.40	0.77	0.61	(1.26)	High α, low β
Las Vegas-Henderson-Paradise, NV	3.7%	4.4%	0.69	1.36	2.18	(0.62)	High α, high β
Los Angeles-Long Beach-Anaheim, CA	0.4%	2.3%	0.63	(0.74)	1.08	0.69	Very low α, low β
Louisville/Jefferson County, KY-IN	1.1%	1.9%	0.80	(0.05)	1.02	0.05	Low α, low β
Memphis, TN-MS-AR	1.0%	2.1%	0.81	(0.25)	1.14	0.22	Low α, high β
Miami-Fort Lauderdale-West Palm Beach, FL	1.6%	2.5%	0.85	0.17	1.37	(0.12)	Low α, high β
Milwaukee-Waukesha-West Allis, WI	0.5%	1.7%	0.86	(0.53)	0.92	0.57	Low α, low β
Minneapolis-St. Paul-Bloomington, MN-WI	1.3%	1.8%	0.88	0.17	1.00	(0.17)	Low α, low β
Nashville-Davidson--Murfreesboro--Franklin, TN	2.1%	2.2%	0.81	0.82	1.17	(0.70)	High α, high β
New Orleans-Metairie, LA	0.3%	5.4%	0.00	N/A	N/A	N/A	N/A
New York-Newark-Jersey City, NY-NJ-PA	0.6%	1.8%	0.66	(0.37)	0.90	0.41	Low α, low β
Oklahoma City, OK	1.5%	1.6%	0.69	0.63	0.79	(0.80)	High α, low β
Omaha-Council Bluffs, NE-IA	1.4%	1.3%	0.70	0.57	0.66	(0.86)	High α, low β
Orlando-Kissimmee-Sanford, FL	2.9%	3.1%	0.85	1.04	1.72	(0.61)	High α, high β
Philadelphia-Camden-Wilmington, PA-NJ-DE-MD	0.6%	1.5%	0.78	(0.30)	0.79	0.38	Low α, low β
Phoenix-Mesa-Scottsdale, AZ	2.6%	3.4%	0.83	0.63	1.88	(0.34)	High α, high β
Pittsburgh, PA	0.6%	1.0%	0.59	(0.08)	0.48	0.16	Low α, very low β
Portland-Vancouver-Hillsboro, OR-WA	1.8%	2.5%	0.82	0.29	1.33	(0.22)	Low α, high β
Providence-Warwick, RI-MA	0.4%	1.8%	0.70	(0.61)	0.90	0.67	Low α, low β
Raleigh, NC	2.8%	2.5%	0.82	1.33	1.35	(0.99)	High α, high β
Richmond, VA	1.3%	1.8%	0.82	0.21	0.99	(0.21)	Low α, low β
Riverside-San Bernardino-Ontario, CA	2.6%	3.0%	0.49	1.25	1.24	(1.01)	High α, high β
Rochester, NY	0.4%	1.2%	0.58	(0.33)	0.53	0.63	Low α, very low β
Sacramento--Roseville--Arden-Arcade, CA	1.7%	2.3%	0.56	0.49	1.03	(0.47)	Low α, low β
Salt Lake City, UT	2.6%	2.5%	0.75	1.09	1.31	(0.84)	High α, high β
San Antonio-New Braunfels, TX	2.4%	1.6%	0.74	1.51	0.81	(1.86)	High α, low β
San Diego-Carlsbad, CA	1.5%	2.1%	0.60	0.39	0.99	(0.40)	Low α, low β
San Francisco-Oakland-Hayward, CA	1.0%	2.6%	0.64	(0.41)	1.23	0.33	Low α, high β
San Jose-Sunnyvale-Santa Clara, CA	1.1%	4.0%	0.54	(0.79)	1.75	0.45	Very low α, high β
Seattle-Tacoma-Bellevue, WA	1.7%	2.4%	0.72	0.30	1.20	(0.25)	Low α, high β
St. Louis, MO-IL	0.7%	1.5%	0.87	(0.30)	0.82	0.37	Low α, low β
Tampa-St. Petersburg-Clearwater, FL	1.6%	2.8%	0.86	(0.09)	1.56	0.06	Low α, high β
Tulsa, OK	1.3%	2.2%	0.57	0.13	0.98	(0.13)	Low α, low β
Urban Honolulu, HI	0.7%	1.6%	0.15	0.18	0.37	(0.48)	Low α, very low β
Virginia Beach-Norfolk-Newport News, VA-NC	1.0%	1.4%	0.70	0.19	0.69	(0.28)	Low α, low β
Washington-Arlington-Alexandria, DC-VA-MD-WV	1.4%	1.5%	0.51	0.70	0.65	(1.07)	High α, low β
U.S.	1.1%	1.7%	1.00	-	1.00	-	

Figure 8.5 plots the alpha-beta combinations, coloring seven "alpha-beta continents." These continents group MSAs with similar alpha-beta combinations, with greater predictability reflected by larger MSA circles.

FIGURE 8.5

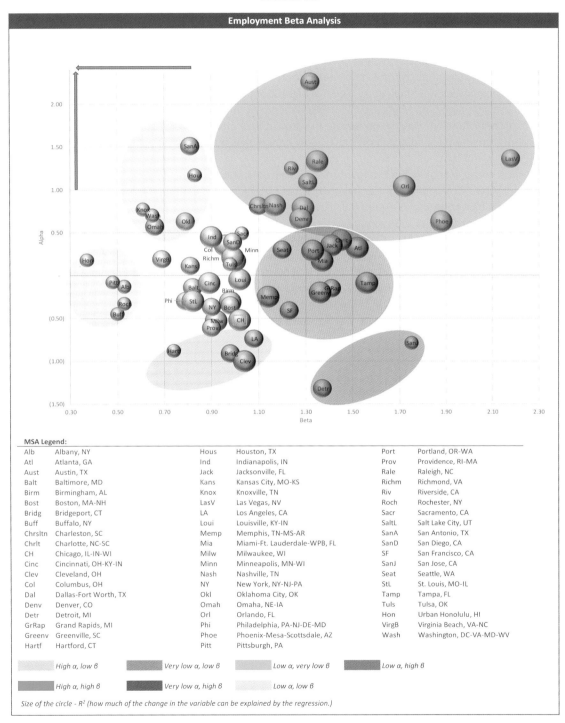

MSA Legend:

Alb	Albany, NY	Hous	Houston, TX	Port	Portland, OR-WA
Atl	Atlanta, GA	Ind	Indianapolis, IN	Prov	Providence, RI-MA
Aust	Austin, TX	Jack	Jacksonville, FL	Rale	Raleigh, NC
Balt	Baltimore, MD	Kans	Kansas City, MO-KS	Richm	Richmond, VA
Birm	Birmingham, AL	Knox	Knoxville, TN	Riv	Riverside, CA
Bost	Boston, MA-NH	LasV	Las Vegas, NV	Roch	Rochester, NY
Bridg	Bridgeport, CT	LA	Los Angeles, CA	Sacr	Sacramento, CA
Buff	Buffalo, NY	Loui	Louisville, KY-IN	SaltL	Salt Lake City, UT
Chrsltn	Charleston, SC	Memp	Memphis, TN-MS-AR	SanA	San Antonio, TX
Chrlt	Charlotte, NC-SC	Mia	Miami-Ft. Lauderdale-WPB, FL	SanD	San Diego, CA
CH	Chicago, IL-IN-WI	Milw	Milwaukee, WI	SF	San Francisco, CA
Cinc	Cincinnati, OH-KY-IN	Minn	Minneapolis, MN-WI	SanJ	San Jose, CA
Clev	Cleveland, OH	Nash	Nashville, TN	Seat	Seattle, WA
Col	Columbus, OH	NY	New York, NY-NJ-PA	StL	St. Louis, MO-IL
Dal	Dallas-Fort Worth, TX	Okl	Oklahoma City, OK	Tamp	Tampa, FL
Denv	Denver, CO	Omah	Omaha, NE-IA	Tuls	Tulsa, OK
Detr	Detroit, MI	Orl	Orlando, FL	Hon	Urban Honolulu, HI
GrRap	Grand Rapids, MI	Phi	Philadelphia, PA-NJ-DE-MD	VirgB	Virginia Beach, VA-NC
Greenv	Greenville, SC	Phoe	Phoenix-Mesa-Scottsdale, AZ	Wash	Washington, DC-VA-MD-WV
Hartf	Hartford, CT	Pitt	Pittsburgh, PA		

High α, low β	Very low α, low β	Low α, very low β	Low α, high β
High α, high β	Very low α, high β	Low α, low β	

Size of the circle - R² (how much of the change in the variable can be explained by the regression.)

High alpha markets tend to grow even if the U.S. is not growing. The highest alpha MSAs are: Austin, San Antonio, Las Vegas, Raleigh, Riverside-San Bernardino, Houston, Salt Lake City, and Orlando, all of which have alphas well in excess of 1.7% per annum. In contrast, low alpha markets require strong U.S. job growth rates in order to grow regionally and are led by: Detroit, Cleveland, Bridgeport-Stamford, Hartford, (perhaps surprisingly) San Jose, and Los Angeles. In fact, of the 59 markets that we analyzed, 26 have negative alphas, meaning that about 45% of MSAs only grow if U.S. employment is growing.

Of the 59 MSAs, 12 have betas near one (0.95-1.05), 22 have low betas (less than 0.95), and 24 have high betas (in excess of 1.05). It is noteworthy that all MSAs have positive betas, indicating that a rising U.S. employment tide does in fact lift all MSAs, though some much less than others. High beta markets tend to rapidly add jobs as the U.S. employment engine kicks into high gear. The five highest beta MSAs are Las Vegas, Phoenix, San Jose, Orlando, and Tampa. These very high beta MSAs are all heavily dependent on highly-cyclical sectors. For example, San Jose is dependent on tech funding, Detroit on autos, Houston on oil and gas, and Orlando and Las Vegas on high discretionary entertainment spending. In contrast, a low beta means more modest volatility, with lower magnitude employment booms and busts.

Not surprisingly, Honolulu has the lowest beta, again indicating that the geographically isolated Honolulu is its "own world." Aside from Honolulu, the five lowest beta MSAs are Pittsburgh, Buffalo, Albany, Rochester, and Knoxville in the light blue continent of Figure 8.5. Low beta MSAs generally have a strong government influence due to being a state or national capital. Government employment makes job growth less responsive to both economic upswings and downturns than MSAs with greater exposure to the more dynamic and volatile private sector.

In the latter stages of a U.S. job recovery, focusing on MSAs with the combination of relatively low betas, high alphas, and high R-squared statistics reduces cyclical demand risk (shown in the light green continent of Figure 8.5). In a downturn, low beta-high alpha MSAs experience lesser space demand declines, requiring higher rates of negative U.S. job growth in order to lose employment at the local level. In other words, these MSAs are more resilient to declines in national employment. Remember that negative net space absorption due to lost jobs must be made up in the recovery phase before net positive space demand occurs.

In contrast, during a recovery phase, high alpha-high beta MSAs are more desirable, as no new supply will generally occur anywhere for an extended period, and these MSAs experience the largest demand growth during recoveries.

The interaction between alpha and beta is summarized by the U.S. employment growth rate required to generate positive job growth in the MSA (Figure 8.6). Specifically, what minimum employment growth rate at the national level is associated with positive job growth for each MSA? The more negative this "breakeven" U.S. job growth rate, the stronger are the MSA's underlying growth fundamentals. The MSAs with the lowest breakeven U.S. job growth rates are San Antonio, Austin, Houston, Knoxville, and D.C. The MSAs with the highest required U.S. job growth rates to break even are Hartford, Detroit, Cleveland, Bridgeport, and Buffalo. Of the 59 MSAs, 33 (56%) have negative breakeven U.S. job growth rates. This bias towards negative breakeven job growth is reflected in an average annual U.S. job growth rate of 1.1%.

FIGURE 8.6

	Breakeven Point (% US Job Growth)
San Antonio-New Braunfels, TX	(1.86)
Austin-Round Rock, TX	(1.71)
Houston-The Woodlands-Sugar Land, TX	(1.41)
Knoxville, TN	(1.26)
Washington-Arlington-Alexandria, DC-VA-MD-WV	(1.07)
Riverside-San Bernardino-Ontario, CA	(1.01)
Raleigh, NC	(0.99)
Omaha-Council Bluffs, NE-IA	(0.86)
Salt Lake City, UT	(0.84)
Oklahoma City, OK	(0.80)
Charleston-North Charleston-Summerville, SC	(0.74)
Nashville-Davidson--Murfreesboro--Franklin, TN	(0.70)
Las Vegas-Henderson-Paradise, NV	(0.62)
Dallas-Fort Worth-Arlington, TX	(0.61)
Orlando-Kissimmee-Sanford, FL	(0.61)
Denver-Aurora-Lakewood, CO	(0.52)
Indianapolis-Carmel-Anderson, IN	(0.50)
Urban Honolulu, HI	(0.48)
Sacramento--Roseville--Arden-Arcade, CA	(0.47)
San Diego-Carlsbad, CA	(0.40)
Columbus, OH	(0.37)
Phoenix-Mesa-Scottsdale, AZ	(0.34)
Charlotte-Concord-Gastonia, NC-SC	(0.28)
Virginia Beach-Norfolk-Newport News, VA-NC	(0.28)
Seattle-Tacoma-Bellevue, WA	(0.25)
Jacksonville, FL	(0.25)
Portland-Vancouver-Hillsboro, OR-WA	(0.22)
Richmond, VA	(0.21)
Atlanta-Sandy Springs-Roswell, GA	(0.21)
Minneapolis-St. Paul-Bloomington, MN-WI	(0.17)
Kansas City, MO-KS	(0.14)
Tulsa, OK	(0.13)
Miami-Fort Lauderdale-West Palm Beach, FL	(0.12)
Louisville/Jefferson County, KY-IN	0.05
Tampa-St. Petersburg-Clearwater, FL	0.06
Grand Rapids-Wyoming, MI	0.10
Cincinnati, OH-KY-IN	0.10
Greenville-Anderson-Mauldin, SC	0.15
Pittsburgh, PA	0.16
Baltimore-Columbia-Towson, MD	0.18
Memphis, TN-MS-AR	0.22
Albany-Schenectady-Troy, NY	0.24
Birmingham-Hoover, AL	0.32
San Francisco-Oakland-Hayward, CA	0.33
Boston-Cambridge-Newton, MA-NH	0.35
St. Louis, MO-IL	0.37
Philadelphia-Camden-Wilmington, PA-NJ-DE-MD	0.38
New York-Newark-Jersey City, NY-NJ-PA	0.41
San Jose-Sunnyvale-Santa Clara, CA	0.45
Chicago-Naperville-Elgin, IL-IN-WI	0.51
Milwaukee-Waukesha-West Allis, WI	0.57
Rochester, NY	0.63
Providence-Warwick, RI-MA	0.67
Los Angeles-Long Beach-Anaheim, CA	0.69
Buffalo-Cheektowaga-Niagara Falls, NY	0.90
Bridgeport-Stamford-Norwalk, CT	0.92
Cleveland-Elyria, OH	0.96
Detroit-Warren-Dearborn, MI	0.96
Hartford-West Hartford-East Hartford, CT	1.19

(2.50)   (2.00)   (1.50)   (1.00)   (0.50)   -   0.50   1.00   1.50

Resiliency Analysis: Breakeven U.S. Employment Growth Rate

It is interesting to note that grouping employment into the aggregate of the 59 "major MSAs" and the less urban "rest of the U.S.," the major MSAs as a group have a beta of 1.07 versus 0.90 for the rest of the U.S., while they have essentially the same alpha. Thus, when the nation's employment grows, it disproportionately benefits the major MSAs, but downturns also hit them notably harder.

These analyses have important consequences for investors. Specifically, when the national economy is in a strong expansion phase, targeting office development in high employment beta MSAs provides the greatest space-demand upside. When national employment grows, Fort Lauderdale, West Palm Beach, Detroit, Austin, and Boston exhibit the highest employment growth betas and, thus, will experience the greatest regional percentage growth above that of the nation. During a national recession, on the other hand, low employment beta MSAs, such as New York, Philadelphia, Houston, St. Louis, and Washington, D.C., provide greater downside demand-risk protection.

A final factor to consider when thinking of space demand and cycles is that each MSA has a unique space absorption rate per job (Figure 8.7). That is, depending on the employment mix of the MSA, space absorption varies. In a downturn, other things being equal, MSAs with relatively low space absorption per job will have less space become vacant as job losses occur, while MSAs with high space absorption factors will see space demand expand most dramatically during periods of employment growth. For example, Austin is not only well-positioned for strong multifamily demand during the recovery phase because it is a high alpha-high beta MSA, but also because it has a high space absorption rate as measured by the expected number (or share) of apartment units rented per new job. In short, as the cycle gets "older," these space demand factors are useful in helping you think through your market risk exposure.

FIGURE 8.7

	Office SF/worker	Industrial SF/worker	Multifamily Units/worker	Retail SF/worker	Hotel Rooms/worker	Independent Living Units/worker	Assisted Living Units/worker
Space Absorption by Property Sector							
Atlanta	45	193	0.1418	49	0.0258	0.0027	0.0033
Austin	48	46	0.1906	58	0.0276		
Baltimore	52	144	0.1690			0.0073	0.0029
Boston	54		0.0804	26	0.0153	0.0036	0.0034
Charleston, SC	66						
Charlotte	88	159	0.0987	57			
Chicago	54	305	0.1261	47	0.0219	0.0061	0.0032
Cincinnati	26	257	0.1054	61		0.0050	0.0027
Cleveland	126	452	0.1063	76		0.0042	0.0041
Columbus	24	226	0.1290	42			
Dallas	66						
Dallas-Fort Worth		160	0.1797	50	0.0240	0.0063	0.0038
Denver	71	171	0.2544	59	0.0243	0.0056	0.0035
Detroit	48	245	0.1173	41	0.0146	0.0067	0.0024
Fairfield County	82						
Fort Lauderdale	31	105					
Fort Worth	23						
Fresno	67						
Houston	54	138	0.2186	56	0.0194	0.0034	0.0021
Indianapolis	25	240	0.1056	44			
Inland Empire	15	360	0.0980			0.0029	0.0040
Kansas City						0.0181	0.0058
Las Vegas		115			0.1324	0.0017	0.0017
Long Island	23	96					
Los Angeles	40	248	0.1846	42	0.0187	0.0029	0.0043
Memphis	25						
Miami	37	130	0.1060	48	0.0370	0.0112	0.0055
Minneapolis	31	51	0.0865	32	0.0149	0.0064	0.0057
Nashville	37	214	0.1372	36	0.0326		
New York City	85		0.2021	59	0.0235	0.0035	0.0047
North & Central NJ	52	196					
Orange County	51		0.1419		0.0296		
Orlando	29	91	0.1121	41	0.0804	0.0044	0.0033
Philadelphia	41	99	0.0575	44	0.0115	0.0090	0.0029
Phoenix	44	147	0.1398	63	0.0226	0.0074	0.0033
Pittsburgh						0.0048	0.0057
Portland	36	169	0.1035	44		0.0085	0.0077
Raleigh-Durham	51						
Sacramento						0.0038	0.0053
St. Louis	32	173	0.0861	48	0.0190	0.0068	0.0027
San Antonio						0.0049	0.0021
San Diego	46	112	0.2248	47	0.0345	0.0053	0.0039
San Francisco	134	57	0.1337	37	0.0413	0.0061	0.0076
San Jose	180		0.1125	34		0.0040	0.0018
Seattle	36	86	0.1621	34	0.0208	0.0079	0.0050
Tampa Bay	23	61	0.1253	52	0.0259	0.0071	0.0066
Washington, D.C.	95	37	0.1723	34	0.0310	0.0055	0.0024
Westchester County	34						
West Palm Beach	40						

Source: Linneman Associates

CLOSING THOUGHT

Real estate developers and operators are in the business of servicing population. The greater insight they can bring to their local demand outlook, the more confidently they can decide on their next steps.

 Online Companion Audio Interview: To hear a conversation about this chapter's content, go to the Online Companion and select the link for Chapter 8. Scroll down to the Audio Interview section and listen.

Chapter 9
The Use and Selection of Cap Rates

"'What is the bet?' is the critical question."
- Dr. Peter Linneman

BASIC CAP RATE VALUATION

For existing properties, you will usually begin your valuation analysis with simpler tools than a multi-year discounted cash flow (DCF) model. It is much like how you carefully sketch a building before you build it. This is partly for speed and simplicity, and partly because the distant future is difficult to forecast accurately (even though each year's numbers look equally authoritative on a spreadsheet). A simple standard valuation method is **income multiple analysis**, which estimates the value of a property by multiplying next year's "stabilized" NOI by the price-to-NOI multiple for which comparable properties are selling today. For instance, if a comparable property recently traded at 12.5 times its NOI (commonly written as 12.5x), you can multiply your property's NOI by 12.5 to approximate the price at which it might trade today. Thus, if your property had an NOI of $5 million, it would be valued on this basis at $62.5 million (calculated as $5 MM * 12.5).

However, **capitalization (cap) rates**, rather than income multiples, are generally quoted in real estate valuation analysis. The cap rate, which is expressed as a percentage yield, is the inverse (reciprocal) of the income multiple; that is, it is defined as stabilized NOI divided by property value (purchase price, either actual or anticipated). The cap rate equivalent of the 12.5x multiple in the example is 8% (calculated as 1 / 12.5) (Figure 9.1).

A low cap rate (e.g., 4%) reflects a relatively high price paid per dollar of property income (i.e., a relatively expensive cash flow stream to acquire), while a high cap rate (e.g., 10%) reflects a relatively low price paid per dollar of property income (i.e., a relatively inexpensive cash flow stream to acquire).

The real estate industry's usage of cap rates reflects its historic linkage to the bond market, as real estate derives its income from future promissory income streams in the form of leases. So just as the bond market commonly quotes yield, as opposed to multiple, when valuing bonds, the real estate industry generally quotes cap rates. If your $5 million NOI property traded at the $62.5 million valuation, it would be referred to as having traded at an "8 cap."

FIGURE 9.1

Capitalization Rate, Income Multiple and Valuation Equations
Cap Rate = Stabilized NOI / Value = 1 / Multiple
Multiple = Value / Stabilized NOI = 1 / Cap Rate
Value = Multiple * Stabilized NOI = Stabilized NOI / Cap Rate
Example: an "8 cap" = .08 = 8.00% = 12.5x Multiple

Property cap rates are not always whole numbers like 8%; a property could trade at a 4.17% cap rate, for example. Figure 9.2 shows a partial spectrum of capitalization rates, using 50-basis-point increments, and their equivalent income multiples.

FIGURE 9.2

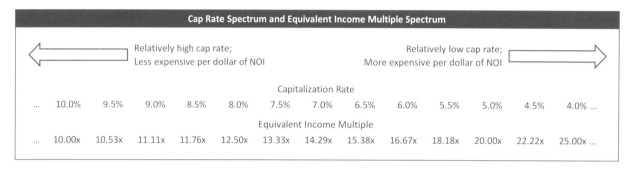

As introduced in Prerequisite I, to quickly calculate the value of a stabilized property, divide the property's **stabilized NOI** by the cap rate. And as defined in Chapter 5, "stabilized" means that the property's NOI reflects some systemic vacancy, is flat or growing relatively smoothly year-over-year, and that this NOI is indicative of the property's long-term future performance. Note that using the **cap rate valuation** method (income multiple analysis) is only appropriate when NOI is stabilized. If you "cap" (capitalize) an unstabilized NOI, this calculation generates nonsense values. For such properties, you must do a full DCF analysis to responsibly produce a meaningful valuation estimate.

For a stabilized property, you normally "apply" the cap rate (i.e., divide by it) to next year's NOI to estimate value, as this is the first full-year cash flow the property's new owner will receive. Therefore, the most commonly utilized equation for the cap rate is the property's projected NOI in ownership year 1 divided by the property's value.

Let's revisit our case study from Chapter 1, Felicitas Tower, with the 10-year lease to the U.S. government that is expected to generate $3 million annually in NOI, with no anticipated future NOI growth. Assume that the 10-year Treasury bond carries a yield of 1.6%, and that you feel you need a minimum NOI yield of 4.6% on the purchase price to invest in the property. The required 4.6% yield means that you need an additional 300 basis points of expected income return for the added risks presented by Felicitas Tower's future cash streams. Applying a 4.6% cap rate (a 21.7x multiple) to the property's stabilized NOI of roughly $3 million yields a property value of $65.2 million (calculated as $3 MM / 0.046) via the cap rate valuation methodology. Understand that your assessment of the property's opportunity and risk is reflected in this value calculation via the $3 million stabilized NOI that you capped at the 4.6% cap rate you selected. Figure 9.3 displays this valuation math.

FIGURE 9.3

Felicitas Tower Cap Rate and Multiple Valuation	
Assumptions	
Yield on 10-Year T Note	1.60%
Risk Premium	300 basis points (bp)
Cap Rate	1.60% + 300 bp = 4.60%
Multiple	1 / .046 = 21.7x
NOI	$3 MM
Valuation	
With Cap Rate	$3 MM / .046 = $65.2 MM
With Multiple	$3 MM * 21.7 = $65.2 MM

NOT EVERYONE AGREES

Property buyers desire high cap rates (i.e., low income multiples) for given property risk. This is because the higher the cap rate, the lower the purchase price for the stabilized income stream. On the other hand, sellers desire low cap rates (i.e., high income multiples), as they want the highest price possible for the stabilized income stream they are selling. It is common to have discrepancies between quoted cap rates from a property's buyer/seller pair. Why? Assume you bought the building in our example for $65.2 million. You might say you bought it for a 5.5 cap, but the seller of the building, who received the $65.2 million, might brag that they sold it for a 4.9 cap. How is this possible? Is someone lying? Maybe, but not necessarily.

There are several reasons purchase cap rate quotes can differ. For example, the seller and the buyer may have very different estimates of next year's NOI. Remember that each party derived their estimate of next year's NOI based on their independent analysis, and in most cases different parties will arrive at different NOI estimates. In addition, different investors may categorize certain costs as "operating expenses," while others may not. Specifically, are **normalized reserves** for cap ex, TIs, and leasing commissions deducted from NOI by one party (producing the **adjusted NOI**), but not the other? Or are they estimating differently what "normalized" levels are? Or perhaps the seller and the buyer may be using the NOI from different years in their calculations. Thus, although next year's NOI is the industry convention, the seller may quote the cap rate using this year's actual NOI, while the buyer may quote the cap rate for their purchase using next year's expected (higher) NOI. Further, the buyer and seller may use different definitions of "stabilized" NOI, as the term is a bit ambiguous. For example, the buyer might view next year's NOI as indicative of the stabilized performance of the property, while the seller may feel that NOI is not stabilized for 3 years. These examples demonstrate that you must be careful when comparing "market" cap rates.

When correctly applied to a stabilized property, the simple cap rate valuation approach produces roughly the same valuation estimate for a property as a more complex DCF analysis. However, if the property's expected NOI stream is complex, with irregular rental growth driving potentially high volatility, only DCF analysis can yield a credible and defensible value estimate.

REPLACEMENT COST

The denominator of the cap rate is the value (or sale price) of the building. In the case of our example, you used the cap rate to estimate a value of $65.2 million. In conducting your analysis, should you care what it cost to build Felicitas Tower? For example, if it cost $100 million to build the property three years ago, should this have any bearing on your assessment of the property's risk and opportunity? Probably not, as it is ancient history. In some ways, it is like your birth weight: interesting, but not terribly descriptive of who you are today. As a result, you will generally focus on conditions today rather than historic cost.

An important exception is a property's **replacement cost**, which is the hypothetical amount it would take to acquire the land and construct the exact same property today, including the cost of the LCs and TIs needed to attain the exact same tenant profile. What if Felicitas Tower cost $100 million to develop three years ago, and total development costs today are about the same? Your valuation of the property's stabilized cash flows indicates that the building is only worth $65.2 million. If your valuation is correct, it means that you are purchasing the property for a 35% discount to replacement cost. This means that rents must increase by roughly 53% before they will be high enough to justify new construction ($3 MM * 153% = $4.6 MM, capped at 0.046 = $100 MM). That is quite a cushion before new competition appears. But if Felicitas Tower was built in expectation of a less-than-competitive-return or if the development costs were significantly above market, you cannot use the $100 million cost as an estimate of replacement cost. For example, if the developer was inefficient, or substantially overpaid for land (such as an international player desperate to enter the U.S. market), rendering it a "white elephant" (costly and impossible to sell profitably) the original cost does not reflect the relevant replacement cost.

Of critical importance when calculating a property's replacement cost is the cost of land. If the original owner massively overpaid for the land, the relevant replacement cost must reflect today's realistic market land costs. Developers frequently overpay for land in the euphoria of a booming market. An extreme example occurred in Tokyo in the late 1980s, when developers paid $90 million for land while it cost just $10 million to build the structure. The land cost for a comparable site today is only $8 million, and despite construction costs having risen, land is still an outsized cost for a Tokyo building. Hence the relevant replacement cost with construction cost inflation is perhaps $30 million, not the original $100 million outlay. At a $30 million replacement cost basis, competition can profitably enter the market, while you are preparing to bid $65.2 million for a comparable building. If the government breaks its lease or fails to renew upon expiration, who will be willing to pay a rent that justifies your valuation when they can build a new property for about 55% less? In this case, you will be seriously concerned that competition will enter the market at a lower cost basis, allowing them to offer lower rents, while still generating an adequate return on their cost.

If, on the other hand, the structure is not a "white elephant," has an original development cost of $90 million, where the land component cost was originally $10 million, then even in the unlikely case that the land is completely worthless today, the property's replacement cost is $90 million. If you can acquire the building for $65.2 million, you acquire the property for a $24.8 million discount to replacement cost. Will the building ever be worth replacement cost again? Who knows? But there is some comfort in the fact that entrants cannot profitably build a competitive property for less than your purchase price.

The building's vintage is important to keep in mind when thinking about value relative to replacement cost. If the structure is 20 or more years old, it is likely no longer the most desirable product in its market, as it was not designed with today's technology, floorplans, desired natural light levels and modern amenities in mind. In other words, the replacement cost estimate you use should be based on today's costs. That is, how much would it cost to manufacture the product that will attract and retain the same tenant profile in today's market? The purchase price of an older building needs to be below replacement cost, perhaps by as much as 20-30%, because you will need to invest significant cap ex to bring it up to standard and reinstate its competitiveness.

GORDON MODEL: SIMPLE CAP RATE ESTIMATION

Let us return to the U.S. government-leased Felicitas Tower opportunity, but now assume that NOI grows modestly each year, instead of remaining flat. For example, the government lease contains provisions that dictate a roughly 1% increase in rent each year. In addition, assume that you believe the government will renew the lease at roughly similar terms forever. Will this really happen? Probably not but based on your analysis you may reasonably expect a 1% growth rate in NOI each year basically forever. We have effectively described a **perpetuity** cash flow stream.

As shown in Figure 9.4, the so-called **Gordon Model** or the **Gordon Growth Model**, named after Myron J. Gordon, converts perpetuity DCF analysis for a cash stream growing at a constant rate into a simple cap rate approximation by dividing stabilized NOI by the difference between the property's discount rate (r) and its NOI growth rate (g). The **discount rate** for a property is theoretically composed of four factors: the real (inflation-adjusted) long-term risk-free rate (approximated by the yield on a 10-year U.S. Treasury bond); expected economy-wide inflation; the risk premium associated with unexpected outcomes in the property's NOI; and the risk premium associated with the property's illiquidity relative to a 10-year Treasury bond.

FIGURE 9.4

Gordon Growth Model for Property Valuation *
Value = NOI / (property discount rate – NOI growth rate) = NOI / Cap Rate
Value = NOI / (r – g) = NOI / Cap Rate
Therefore: Cap Rate = (r – g)
*Assumes Stabilized NOI and constant NOI growth rate for perpetuity.

Assuming a property discount rate of 4.6%, we note that absent the assumption of property NOI growth, the discount rate here and the 4.6% cap rate from Figure 9.3 are equal to one another.

Figure 9.5 displays how to apply the Gordon Model to value the government-leased office building with an expected perpetual 1% annual rental growth.

FIGURE 9.5

Gordon Model Cap Rate and Multiple Calculation for Felicitas Tower	
Property Discount Rate (r)	4.60%
NOI Growth Rate (g)	1.00%
Cap Rate Calculation (r – g)	.046 – .01 = .036 = 3.60%
Multiple Calculation	1 / (.046 – .01) = 27.8x

Applying the resultant 3.6% cap rate to next year's NOI of $3.03 million (today's $3 million NOI grown by 1%) generates an estimated value for Felicitas Tower of $84.2 million (calculated as $3.03 MM / 0.036), which is $19 million (29.1%) more than the zero-NOI-growth case value of $65.2 million. It makes sense that a property assumed to have NOI growing by 1% every year should be worth more than the same property with no future NOI growth assumed. Alternatively, if you decide that the property's discount rate should be an additional 400 basis points higher than the risk-free rate (5.6% rather than 4.6%), but still assume the expected 1% perpetuity NOI growth, the Gordon Model yields a 4.6 cap (calculated as 5.6% – 1.0%), resulting in an estimated property value of $65.8 million (calculated as $3.03 MM / 0.046). Thus, the 400-basis point risk factor increase lowered the $84.2 million estimated value by 21.8%.

These examples demonstrate how opportunity (i.e., NOI and NOI growth; "g") increases value, while increased risk (a rising property discount rate; "r") decreases value. That is, even a little NOI growth adds a lot of value, and especially so for low-risk cash streams. This is illustrated in Figure 9.6, where we see that just 1% growth creates more than $12 million in property value.

FIGURE 9.6

Felicitas Tower Gordon Model Income Multiple Valuation With and Without Growth	
Discount Rate	5.60%
Growth Rate	1.00%
Multiple with growth	$1 / (r - g) = 1 / (.056 - .01) = 21.7x$
Multiple without growth	$1 / r = 1 / .056 = 17.9x$
Valuation	
NOI this year	$3.00 MM
NOI next year	$3.00 MM * 1.01 = $3.03 MM
Value with growth	$3.03 MM * 21.7 = $65.8 MM
Value without growth	$3.00 MM * 17.9 = $53.7 MM

The Gordon Model provides a "quick and dirty" calculation for estimating property value. Instead of using the Gordon Model, you could conduct a full DCF analysis of the steadily growing NOI, going out as many columns (years) as possible, and discounting them at your selected discount rate(s). The Gordon Model will generate almost the same answer as a full DCF analysis, as long as the property's NOI growth rate is fairly steady (stabilized) and small relative to the selected discount rate. If, however, the property does not meet these "stabilized" criteria, you must conduct a full DCF analysis to accurately assess its value.

Caveats: Looking at the Gordon Model formula, do you see any problems? For example, what if you think that the NOI growth rate (g) is greater than the property discount rate (r)? Using the Gordon Model of NOI / (r − g) yields a negative cap rate and hence, a negative value for the property, even though it has rapid income growth and low risk. This is clearly a nonsense result. Similarly, if the appropriate discount rate is equal to the NOI growth rate, the Gordon Model yields a 0% cap rate, suggesting the property value is infinite! Not likely. Also, using this model with a very high growth rate generates nonsense, as it is inconceivable that an asset's NOI can grow well in excess of the economy forever. If that were the case, eventually, the property's NOI would be larger than the economy!

LET YOUR COMMON SENSE PREVAIL

You must pay careful attention to NOI growth forecasts and the reasonableness of the assumptions utilized. I was once in a meeting where a non-real estate firm was pitching its very optimistic growth expectations. I asked how they intended to meet the sales objectives. The response was they would hire enough salespeople to meet their goals. As I listened, I estimated the sales volume an experienced salesperson could reasonably be expected to achieve, and how many such salespeople the firm would need over the next two years to achieve their forecasted sales. The number was 840 successful sales reps, without taking into account the long hiring process, training and ramp-up, unqualified hires, or that some would quit or die. And, oh yes, the firm currently had two salespeople. I quickly concluded that no matter how good their product was, it would be impossible to grow as projected, as they could never successfully hire, train, and retain eight qualified sales reps a week, every week, for the next two years. But such nonsense projections abound, frequently going unchallenged.

To effectively employ the Gordon Model in assessing value, the discount rate (r) must significantly exceed the NOI growth rate (g). If the property's NOI is expected to experience substantial growth in the next few years, as the market recovers or below-market leases roll over, it is not appropriate to use the Gordon Model because after these periods of higher-than-average growth, NOI will stabilize at a lower growth rate. Simple valuation metrics are powerful, but like a pair of shoes, one size does not fit all. If you have a size 10 foot, then do not wear size 3 shoes!

If NOI is not stabilized, do not use cap rate models to assess value. And always make sure your NOI growth and discount rates are sensible.

MARKET CHANGE

Thus far, we have been using a 1.6% yield for the 10-year U.S. Treasury bond. However, over the past decade, this rate has ranged as high as 3.58%. How does a higher risk-free rate impact real estate valuation analysis? Go back to the selection of the discount rates for Felicitas Tower. You began with the 10-year Treasury rate and adjusted for the additional risks associated with the property, including its illiquidity at the point of eventual sale. If the long-term Treasury rate increases by 100 basis points, your discount rate should also rise. If the long-term Treasury rate decreases by 4 basis points, your discount rates will remain unchanged for all practical purposes, as smart real estate investors only respond to significant changes in long-term Treasury yields rather than continually changing their discount rates for minor movements.

In addition, depending upon investors' level of fear and greed, the real estate **risk premium spread over Treasury yields** varies substantially. The risk premium margin over 10-year Treasury yields increases when investors seek safety in government bonds, driving their prices up and yields down. On the other hand, it decreases when investors perceive a decline in risk associated with real estate cash flows, causing them to move from government bonds into real estate positions. Looking at the cap rate spread over Treasuries reflects the relative pricing of real estate cash flow streams to those of government bonds.

A vivid example of spreads over Treasuries widening is displayed in Figure 9.7. The graph shows yield spreads proxied by the public company **REIT-implied cap rate**, which is a measure of yield calculated as the trailing 12 months' reported NOI adjusted for non-recurring items, divided by the market capitalization and outstanding debts, less the value of non-income producing assets. In February 2007, investor optimism ruled, and risk premiums were minimal (perhaps 50 basis points). A brief 18 months later, in September 2008, investor greed turned to total fear, and risk premiums skyrocketed (to perhaps 700 basis points).

FIGURE 9.7

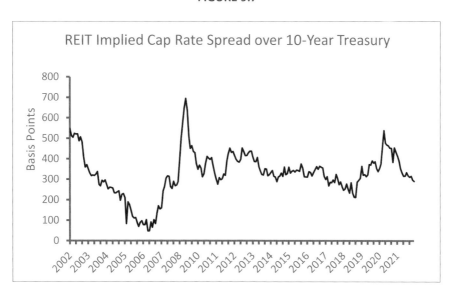

How do cap rates respond to changing long-term Treasury rates and risk premiums? Look again at the Gordon Model of NOI / (r – g). At lower discount rates (r) and relatively unchanged growth rates (g), you would expect cap rates (r – g) to fall (i.e., real estate values to rise). Intuitively, the return required to compensate for risk has decreased, while your long-term NOI stream has remained roughly the same. Figure 9.8 shows real estate cap rates (proxied by NCREIF-tracked, privately-owned properties) and 10-year Treasury yields since 1980.

As seen in the figure, as the long-term Treasury rates fell between 2002 and 2004, market cap rates for solid cash streams (proxied by NCREIF-tracked privately-owned properties) decreased by roughly 100 basis points for almost all property types. They fell even further as risk premiums subsided from 2004 through early 2007. Cap rates then exploded (i.e., rose, and property values dropped) in 2007 through 2009 despite falling Treasury rates due to an explosion in risk premiums across all assets. Interestingly, perhaps because of the appraisal lag, NCREIF cap rates declined during the pandemic.

FIGURE 9.8

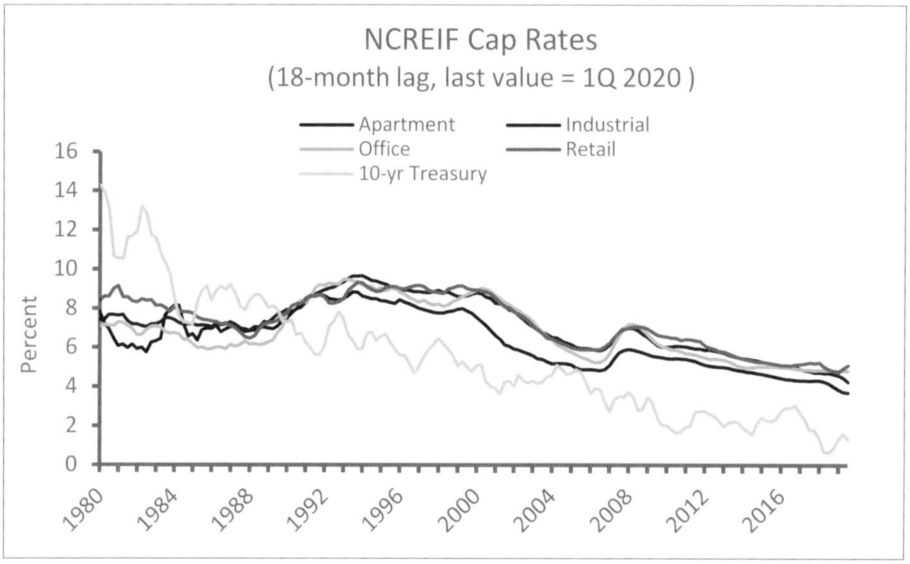

NCREIF Cap Rates
(18-month lag, last value = 1Q 2020)

Figure 9.9 provides the approximate cap rate ranges for stabilized properties as of early 2022. These rates change as the risk-free rate, property risk premiums, and expected NOI growth rates change.

FIGURE 9.9

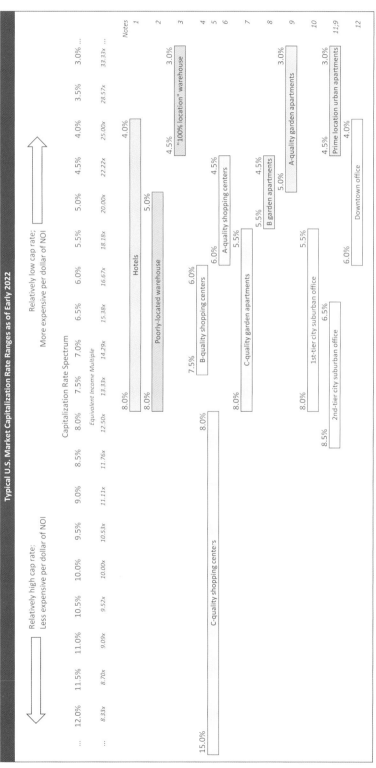

Notes on Figure 9.9

1 **Hotels:** Hotel properties are difficult to value due to their operating leverage. Hotels are in the 18-hour lease business, and they are essentially all fixed costs. Regardless of the occupancy from night to night, you are going to incur costs to continue to operate and maintain the hotel, the soap, the electricity, the marketing costs, etc. Therefore, a decrease in demand will cause a quick decline in prices. Hotels will be willing to lower prices to draw as many people as possible to cover as much of the fixed cost as possible. If you do not cut your prices, you will remain empty. This is a good example where cap rates and multiples are inappropriate valuation metrics because of unstabilized income. This is also an example of the numbers serving as a starting point. You could perform a DCF analysis on a hotel property right now. However, you are really going to have to start thinking about the risks and opportunities beyond the DCF. There is no way the model will be able to accurately capture the possible outcome for the property.

2 **Poorly-located warehouse:** Poor location with no easy access to the highway. Warehouses tend to have higher cap rates than other property types. This is because warehouses tend to have lower growth rates. Growth rates are lower because you can build a warehouse in roughly 8 months. A warehouse is generally a fairly simple structure to build. Therefore, demand can rarely exceed supply by a great margin for an extended period of time. If rents start to increase, developers can quickly build new product that will satisfy the demand. Furthermore, there is additional risk with a warehouse property. Specifically, warehouses only rent to a few large tenants, GE, Walmart, etc. Although those companies have excellent credit, your profitability is completely concentrated with a few tenants. If the tenant decides to leave, you are faced with an empty building and no cash flow. With no diversification, your tenant risk is incredibly high.

3 **"100% location warehouse":** near a major highway or exit ramp that leads to the property with ease.

4 **B-quality shopping centers:** pretty good retail strip centers.

5 **C-quality shopping centers:** empty Kmart, not well located.

6 **A-quality shopping centers:** good supermarket-anchored tenant with Walmart already in the competing market, so no fear of sudden entry and decline in customers.

7 **C-quality garden apartments:** usually has a good market. There is a significant increase in the cap rate for lower quality, B and C, properties. In a tough market, the A quality properties will be able to maintain occupancy. Although owners may have to lower rents to keep tenants, the B and C properties will have roughly the same occupancy. At lower rents, more people will be able to afford the A quality property and will move into the best buildings. As more and more people move to newer or higher quality buildings, the lower quality buildings will experience an increase in vacancy rates. With this higher risk, investors have historically required a higher return on these lower quality buildings, thus a higher cap rate. There is no exact definition for these quality rankings. This is just a phraseology the market uses to describe certain properties relative to other properties. It is just like saying someone is short. There is no pure definition of short.

8 **B-quality garden apartments:** usually has a good market.

9 **A-quality garden apartments / prime location urban apartments:** good location, recent design, does not rely on individual tenant credit, but tenants as a whole have good credit.

10 **1st-tier city suburban office:** suburban, good quality, smaller, fewer tenants, not as well located, not quite as liquid

11 **2nd-tier city suburban office:** small, two tenants, medium quality credit tenants, less liquid, lumpy lease expiration. There is a large spread on the second-tier office buildings. The city in which the property is located will have a significant impact on the property's cap rate.

12 **Downtown office:** prime towers, well-located, well-designed, top of the market, big building, lots of quality tenants, smooth lease expiration.

RESPONDING TO THE MARKET

Do you always have to adjust your discount and cap rates for significantly lower long-term Treasury rates or altered market risk premiums? Not if you believe the changes are unjustified and the market is wrong. You have every right to your view of the world. The only time you have to bid like everyone else is when you want to buy. Just as a baseball player does not have to swing at a pitch, even if it is a strike, you do not have to value things like other market participants. In fact, the truly great hitters know when to "take" a pitch, swinging only at pitches they believe they can successfully hit. In real estate, not bidding or purposefully offering a non-market bid is often the wise move.

A non-real estate example is the valuation of once high-flying WorldCom. Although WorldCom was not a real estate company, the same valuation issues apply. Historically, WorldCom perhaps had a discount rate of 35% and a growth rate of 17%, which implied an 18% cap rate, or a 5.6x earnings multiple. During the Tech bubble in the late 1990s, the market thought WorldCom had little risk and would conquer the world. As investors started to lower the discount rate to 20% and increase the long-term-growth rate to 20%, WorldCom's market value exploded. If you held a view of the world that WorldCom was already overvalued, you did not change your valuation of the firm, did not buy more shares, and hopefully sold or even shorted the stock. As the bubble burst, the market value of WorldCom collapsed because the discount rate soared, and growth estimates plummeted. The point is that you must always have a rational view of the world to avoid being influenced by market hysteria. At times, you may find yourself swimming alone against the current, but that may prove to be smarter in the end.

A LOOK AT THE PAST

The "**cash flow cap rate**" (as opposed to NOI-based cap rate) is a proxy for property income yields after normalized reserves are deducted for tenant improvements, leasing commissions, and capital expenditures. Remember, reported NOI does not always reflect these capital expenditure reserve contribution realities of property operation, so the distinction here is important. It is determined by discounting the property NOI-based cap rate by an approximated percentage of NOI set aside for reserves. In our analysis, we use the following discount factors: 0.68 for office; 0.83 for apartments; 0.69 for industrial; and 0.64 for retail. By analyzing the income stream net of these costs, we can regard the cash flow cap rate metric as the truest, most pure measure of a property's unlevered before-tax net income. In other words, it is (r − g) from the Gordon Model.

Figure 9.10 shows historic spreads of the cash flow cap rate over the 10-year U.S. Treasury yield. In the early 1980s, when you bought real estate, you not only acquired its income growth potential and risk but also accessed enormous tax benefits and the option to massively over-leverage the property. As a result, the value of a property reflected: the value of future operating income, plus the value of the tax benefits, plus the value of the option to over-leverage the property. During the early 1980s, cash flow cap rates for all property types were significantly negative (consistently 400-800 basis points lower than 10-year Treasuries), as their cash flow risk and potential were swamped by the value of the over-leveraging option and tax benefits. And this was despite high (and rising) vacancy which meant there was little hope for near-term cash flow growth. In this era, "forward" (next year's expected) cash flow cap rate spreads were not about real estate but, rather, about accessing tax benefits and purchasing the option to over-leverage.

When real estate's tax benefits were eliminated in 1986, forward cash flow cap rate spreads rose almost overnight by roughly 400 basis points for all property types. Nonetheless, forward cash flow cap rate spreads remained 200-400 basis points below Treasury yields, despite weak **property market fundamentals** (operating cash flows driven by rent and occupancy levels), due to the continued presence of the option to over-leverage. That is, purchasing a property provided operating income risk and opportunity as well as the option to receive grossly mispriced non-recourse debt. During this period, variations in spreads across product types grew, with retail and office cap rate spreads being roughly 200 basis points lower than those for apartments. This gap reflected the greater perceived credit quality of retail and office tenants relative to people who rent apartments.

In the early 1990s, real estate debt evaporated (Figure 9.11), and the sector no longer included an option to over-leverage. Therefore, the value attributed to that option disappeared. Instead, purchasing real estate included the requirement to under-leverage. Thus, even as construction ceased, and property fundamentals began modestly improving, forward cash flow cap rate spreads exploded, rising by nearly 400 basis points (Figure 9.10).

FIGURE 9.10

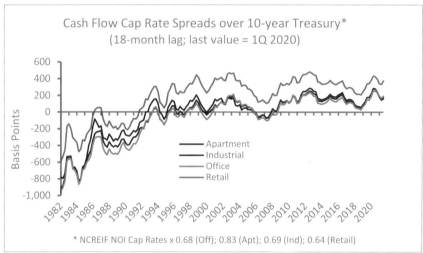

FIGURE 9.11

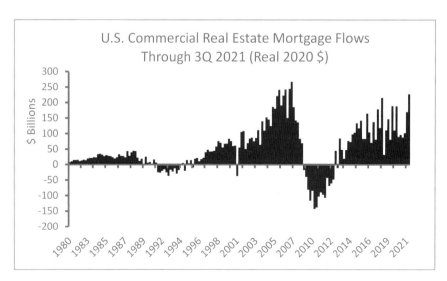

Retail and office forward cash flow spreads remained the lowest, while spreads for apartments remained the largest at nearly 200-basis points over Treasury.

By the mid-1990s, not only were real estate fundamentals improving, but real estate capital markets were also returning to equilibrium due to capital flows to CMBS, REITs, and opportunity funds. As a result, the period from late 1994 through the August 1998 Russian ruble crisis saw forward cash flow cap rate spreads for apartments moderate to 50-100 basis points. Retail spreads remained the narrowest, at -100 basis points, while office and industrial spreads were roughly zero.

While the late-1998 Russian ruble crisis had nothing to do with real estate, it caused cap rate spreads to rise by 100-200 basis points, as real estate capital markets were now connected with broader global capital flows. Hence, as global capital fled to safe government bonds, it abandoned relatively risky assets, including real estate. This pattern continued even as global capital markets stabilized, as the 1998-2000 tech bubble made the importance of positive cash flow seem passé.

As the tech bubble burst in 2001, cap rate spreads narrowed, falling by 50-75 basis points because cash flow became king. However, as property market fundamentals weakened following the 9/11 attacks, cash flow cap rate spreads rose temporarily. Cap rate spreads subsequently fell by 150-300 basis points across the board through early 2007 despite weakening property fundamentals. Subsequently, as risk premiums exploded during the Financial Crisis, cap rate spreads soared, seriously depressing property valuations. Spreads returned to more normal levels starting in 2010, though were higher than before the Crisis. It took mortgage flows until mid-2013 to reverse course from net negative to positive. As this occurred, cap rates fell notably and remained low through 2021. At the onset of the pandemic, cap rate spreads rose because 10-year U.S. Treasury yields dropped faster than the decline in cap rates. As vaccination rates rose, Treasury yields and cap rate spreads both reverted to pre-pandemic levels in 2021.

What is the historic relationship between cap rates and long-term Treasuries? If we focus on the "modern" real estate era, starting when real estate capital markets became connected to global capital markets and ignore the Russian ruble crisis, the tech bubble, and the credit crisis, the answer appears to be that stabilized cap rate spreads for institutional-quality ("Core") multifamily properties are expected to be in the 50-100-basis point range. The greater risk of these properties relative to long-term Treasury bonds is roughly offset by their cash flow growth potential. But substantial variations around this norm are generated by capital market abnormalities. Ironically, only brief periods over the past 25 years have been reflective of true real estate pricing, as opposed to periods driven by the option to over-leverage, the monetization of tax benefits, or other abnormal capital market conditions.

CONTRACTUAL INFORMATION

The analysis of real estate is more substantive and less challenging than for most industries, as real estate NOIs are often driven by existing leases. If you value a typical company, which let's assume sells bubble gum, you must make some very broad predictions about future income streams. For example, you may assume that sales will increase with inflation, a reasonable though imprecise assumption. With long-leased properties you can much more precisely predict future cash flows, as the leases are contractual obligations. They provide detailed information that, to a large degree, specify the operating costs, rental income, and many other critical aspects of future income. Once signed, these documents determine payment streams even if markets radically change. Hotels, self-storage and multifamily properties are notable exceptions, as the contract between the tenants and the landlord cover a much shorter period, making assessment of future cash flows much like that of a bubble gum company.

Numerous assumptions are necessary to reasonably forecast future real estate cash flows. For instance, you need to make assumptions regarding inflation, rents, vacancy, property taxes, utility costs, the time needed to re-lease, etc. Your research, experience, and judgment drive the selection of these unknowns. As you gain experience, usually by making mistakes, your analysis will become more than just a spreadsheet exercise; it will become the sophisticated analysis of a business.

The reward for this tedious analysis is that you will have a much clearer picture of the future income streams derived from a real estate asset than for most other companies. As a result, the spread on bids for real estate tends to be much tighter than those for most assets, as serious bidders generally have access to the same detailed lease information.

CLOSING THOUGHT

Even though real estate investors often have access to more substantive information about future income streams than what exists for most non-real estate companies, successful property investors must work desperately hard just to get actual outcomes remotely close to projections. Once you have estimated property value, determined a plan of action, and successfully purchased the property, you will work hard every day to execute that plan. Execution is where your skills and experience really come into play. Do you have expertise in running an office building? Do you have good tenant contacts? Are you familiar with the area? When the numbers fail to come to fruition, and tenants start to leave, or problems with the building arise, expertise with the property type and local market are critical in determining the success or failure of your investment.

The real estate investment process is like a football game. You may have a perfect game plan but translating that plan onto the field is a very different story. Saying you are going to block a superstar 300-pound defensive lineman is a lot easier than doing it! And completing a pass in the rain, on the run, as three defenders charge your quarterback is much more difficult than the pass appeared in the playbook. Remember that the great ones only make hard things look effortless; succeeding in the face of adversity is very difficult.

The numbers are just the start of true real estate finance and investment analysis. That is why the analyst calculating the numbers gets a relatively modest salary, while the CEOs get the big bucks!

 Online Companion Audio Interview: To hear a conversation about this chapter's content, go to the Online Companion and select the link for Chapter 9. Scroll down to the Audio Interview section and listen.

Chapter 9 Supplement A

A Disconnect in Real Estate Pricing?

Real estate pays a price for being connected to broader capital flows.
Dr. Peter Linneman – *Wharton Real Estate Review* – Spring 2004 Vol. VIII No. 1

Hardly a day goes by without talk of today's "disconnect" in the pricing of commercial real estate. The disconnect concerns the historic lows of cap rates, despite weak property fundamentals. As a result, while property cash flows decline, property prices remain high. The best example is the General Motors Building in New York City, which recently traded at a near 5% cap rate. However, this phenomenon is not limited to New York trophy office properties; it extends to strip shopping centers and suburban garden apartments.

WEAK FUNDAMENTALS

How weak are property market fundamentals? Focusing on publicly traded real estate companies, for which the best data is available, average funds from operations (FFO) are down over the past year by roughly 4% for office REITs and 5% for industrial REITs, while apartment REIT FFO are down by 7%. Only retail REITs have experienced FFO increases over the past year (6%). Over this period, "same store" NOIs are down by even more at apartment, office, and industrial REITs, with only retail REITs registering positive "same store" growth. These declines (for all but retail) are reflective of the rapid increases in property vacancy rates as the bubble economy exploded. [Figure 9A.1]

FIGURE 9A.1: U.S. VACANCY TRENDS BY SECTOR

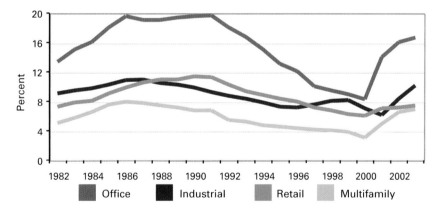

This weakness is also witnessed by the fact that the Linneman Real Estate Index stands at approximately 125, some 25% above a condition of market supply and demand balance. [Figure 9A.2]

FIGURE 9A.2: LINNEMAN REAL ESTATE INDEX

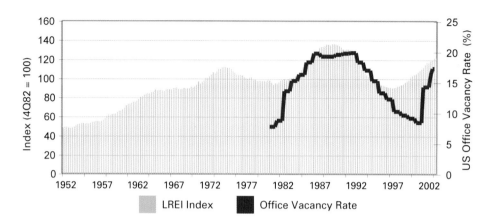

While this is lower than a decade ago, it is substantially higher than in 1999, and indicates substantial excess supply.

HOW STRONG IS PRICING?

Based on NCREIF data, cap rates are roughly 20% lower today than roughly 18 months ago. This represents a cap rate decline of 160 to 200 basis points for core properties over this period. While NCREIF data series are notoriously flawed due to lags induced by appraisal bias, it is clear that a substantial movement downward in cap rates has occurred over the past two years, precisely as property markets have been generally falling apart.

Turning to the valuations of public companies, implied cap rates for the major office industrial, retail, and apartment companies have also declined by roughly 20% over the past 18 months. This decline of roughly 160 to 200 basis points is consistent with the NCREIF data. In fact, it is surprising that the retail cap rates have fallen the least, despite their NOI fundamentals remaining strong. Instead, cap rates have fallen most dramatically for those property sectors where fundamentals have deteriorated the most, namely office and apartments. Over the past year, changes in the market pricing for private assets are generally in line with the pricing in public markets, with estimates of REIT market value relative to Net Asset Value (NAV) remaining in the range of 100, with the exception of modest public market premiums for retail.

These pricing patterns are clearly discernible among the day-to-day pricing of well-located, relatively well-leased properties owned by major REITs and institutional investors. However, the pricing for "questionable" properties in weak markets such as Silicon Valley, Austin, Texas, South of Market in San Francisco, Downtown Dallas, and severely challenged retail, indicates that "pure property" has not achieved the same type of strong pricing. In fact, it has been difficult to find bidders for such market-challenged properties, as low short-term interest rates have allowed their owners to keep their reservation prices high, in the hope that things will get better before their loans mature. Transactions for these weak properties have generally been on a "by the pound" basis, trading well below replacement cost of the property.

WHAT IS A CAP RATE?

A cap rate is the "stabilized" NOI generated by a property, divided by its value. This metric is relevant only for properties with stabilized NOI. If NOI is not stabilized, this concept lacks meaning as a valuation metric. For stabilized properties, the theoretical cap rate approximately equals a property's discount rate minus its long-term stabilized NOI growth rate. For example, if a property has a 10% discount rate and a 2% long-term stabilized NOI growth rate, its cap rate should theoretically be approximately 8%. This is the so-called **Gordon Rule**. Using this approximation of the theoretical cap rate for a stabilized property allows us to examine how the cap rate should have moved over the past two years, and to compare actual cap rate movements with the theoretically predicted movements. This, in turn, allows us to evaluate whether there is a "disconnect" in market pricing.

The discount rate for a property is theoretically composed of four factors: the real long-term risk-free rate (approximated by the yield on a 10-year U.S. Treasury bond); economy-wide inflation; the risk premium associated with unexpected outcomes in the property's NOI; and the risk premium associated with the property's illiquidity relative to a 10-year Treasury bond. These four elements add up to generate a property's theoretical discount rate.

Figure 9A.3 reveals that as recently as the beginning of August 2002 (90-day moving average), the yield on the 10-year Treasury bond was 5%.

FIGURE 9A.3: 10-YEAR TREASURY (3-MONTH MOVING AVERAGE)

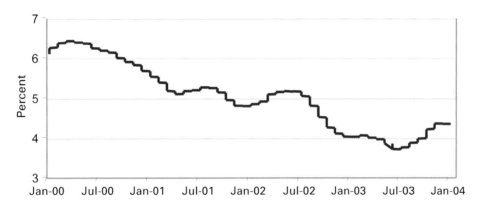

In contrast, from December 27, 2002 through October 9, 2003, the yield remained below 4%. The 10-year Treasury yield hit a low of 3.07% in early June 2003. In sum, over the past 14 months, the yield on the 10-year Treasury has been an average of roughly 110 basis points lower than during the previous two years, without any notable change in inflationary expectations. This decline in the yield on long-term Treasury bonds primarily reflects investor "flight to safety" in the face of the bursting stock market bubble and a string of financial scandals. In short, the combination of the global recession, 9/11 psychological trauma, corporate scandals, and the bursting of the stock market bubble worked to generate a cyclically high demand for relatively risk-free cash streams, of which the 10-year Treasury bond is the poster child. And while demand has surged for relatively risk-free investments, the supply of relatively risk-free assets experienced a cyclical reduction, as corporate cash flows and credit weakened throughout the recession. Thus, the declining yields on long-term, relatively risk-free assets reflect a relatively rare combination of an abnormally high demand for risk-free cash streams and a cyclically low supply of such cash streams.

The third element of the discount rate, the property-level NOI risk premium, has been differently impacted depending upon the nature of the property. To the extent that the property is fully leased on long-term leases to relatively strong-credit tenants, this risk premium has been largely unaffected by the current property market weakness. This is the case for properties like the General Motors Building, strip centers anchored by strong retailers, and office buildings leased to credit tenants with little lease rollover in the foreseeable future. In contrast, as property markets weakened, properties with significant lease rollovers, such as apartment buildings, have experienced notable increases in their NOI risk premium over the past two years. While it is impossible to know exactly how much higher the NOI risk premium should be, we suspect that it should be roughly 50 basis points higher. Finally, for properties facing major lease rollovers or with large amounts of vacant space, the NOI risk premiums have risen to such an extent that they are no longer stabilized properties. As such, cap rate valuation analysis is irrelevant for these properties.

With respect to the fourth component of the discount rate, namely the liquidity premium associated with the property, this continues to decline modestly for all but the most challenged real estate. This reflects the fact that as real estate becomes ever more connected to broader capital markets via CMBS debt funding, the public equity financing of REITs, and the continued investment of investors in real estate private equity funds, the real estate liquidity premium continuously declines. This connectivity means that for the first time in history, capital has remained available even as property fundamentals have weakened.

Combining these factors suggests that the theoretical discount rates for properties have declined by 135 basis points for safe properties and 85 basis points for more typical properties. [Figure 9A.4]

FIGURE 9A.4: THEORETICAL DISCOUNT RATE CHANGES (BASIS POINTS)

	Theoretical Discount Rate Changes (Basis Points)		
	Safe Property	Typical Property	Destabilized Property
Risk Free & Inflation	(110)	(110)	(110)
Property Specific Risk	0	50	150
Liquidity	(25)	(25)	0
Total Change	(135)	(85)	40

Thus, in spite of weakening fundamentals, the greater connectivity with global capital markets, combined with massively reduced long-term risk-free rates, has generated notable declines in real estate discount rates for all but the weakest properties.

The improved connectivity of real estate with global capital flows means that not only has real estate capital remained available, but also real estate has been a preferred asset class. Real estate's status as a preferred asset class over the past several years is vividly demonstrated by the fact that "mom and pop" private REIT syndicators have raised more than $10 billion over the past two years, in spite of approximately 15% front-end load factors. This is the Webster's Dictionary definition of a preferred asset class.

Real estate has been a preferred asset class despite its weakening property fundamentals because global capital flows to the sector that performs relatively—not absolutely—best. Thus, although real estate fundamentals have deteriorated over the past three years, compared to the collapse of the tech sector, the soaring default rates on corporate bonds, the shock of corporate malfeasance, and the poor performance of the broad stock market, real estate debt and equity has been a relatively attractive safe harbor. As a result, capital has flowed to real estate, as real estate's fundamentals were better than could generally be found elsewhere. This is a benefit real estate has earned by finally connecting with global capital markets. However, this connectivity can also work against real estate. There will soon come a time when, despite better real estate fundamentals, real estate will not be improving as rapidly as other sectors. The result will be a capital rotation into other sectors, even as real estate fundamentals improve.

The stabilized, long-term NOI growth rate, the third component of the theoretical cap rate, has remained largely unchanged over the cycle for properties with long-term leases to high-credit tenants. These "safe" properties have had the good fortune of not having leases rolling over into the current softness, or into the softness that will prevail in the next several years. For these "safe" properties, their lease structure protects them and, as a result, their stabilized NOI growth rate has been unaffected by the current market softness.

For more typical properties, with existing vacancies and notable lease rollovers during the next five years, long-term NOI growth rates are actually modestly higher today than several years ago. This is because by late 2001, it was apparent that substantial excess supply would occur in most property markets, and that NOI growth rates would weaken. But the worst years of this NOI deterioration have already occurred. Looking forward, the long-term expected NOI growth rate is modestly higher than two years ago. "The worst is behind us" effect means that over the past year, stabilized annual NOI growth rates for typical properties have risen by 50 to 100 basis points. While this may seem counterintuitive, it is obvious that expected long-term NOI growth rates are higher as one moves through the down phase of a cycle relative to the peak.

Returning to the Gordon model of the theoretical cap rate, namely the discount rate minus the long-term stabilized NOI growth rate, for "safe" properties the theoretical cap rate is roughly 185 basis points lower than prior to 14 months ago, while for more typical properties it is approximately 160 basis points lower. It is important to note that many properties that were considered "stabilized" two years ago are no longer remotely stabilized, and the cap rate valuation approach is irrelevant. The most notable examples are the once "hot" properties in Silicon Valley or the Boston tech corridor.

Our analysis suggests that, theoretically, cap rates should have fallen for most stabilized properties by roughly 20% over the past 14 months, in spite of weakening property fundamentals. Such movements do not reflect a "disconnect" in pricing, but rather a new connectivity with the theoretically expected outcome. [Figure 9A.5]

FIGURE 9A.5: THEORETICAL CAP RATE CHANGES (BASIS POINTS)

	Theoretical Cap Rate Changes (Basis Points)		
	Safe Property	Typical Property	Destabilized Property
Theoretical Discount Rate	(135)	(85)	40
Minus: Long Term NOI Growth	50	75	N/A
Equal: Theoretical Cap Rate Change	(185)	(160)	N/A

Importantly, the movements in actual cap rates over the past 14 months are basically in line with this expected movement.

Of course, this does not mean that every real estate transaction has been correctly priced. In fact, we suspect that some aggressive property buyers are incorrectly focusing their valuation analysis on short-term interest rates, which have declined by roughly 300 basis points. These purchasers are either knowingly or unknowingly using real estate to make a highly leveraged bet on short-term rates remaining at their historic lows. This may (or may not) prove to be a profitable bet. However, this is not real estate pricing, but rather the use of real estate as the vehicle through which to execute a highly leveraged yield curve arbitrage. This seems to explain the more "disconnected" transactions we have seen. But in general, we conclude that the broad pricing of both public and private real estate is "connected" today.

WHERE DO WE GO FROM HERE?

There are clouds on the horizon. The most notable cloud is that we expect long-term risk-free rates to rise 60 to 100 basis points over the next 12 months. In addition, as real estate begins its slow move through the upside of the cycle, the long-term stabilized NOI growth rate will modestly decline. Together, these factors suggest that cap rates will revert by 75 to 125 basis points over the next 12 to 24 months. This will be somewhat mitigated by the continued improved liquidity of real estate via public markets, securitized debt, and large liquid private equity funds. However, we believe that as other sectors of the economy improve, there will be a rotation out of relatively safe cash streams (including real estate) and into riskier assets. Stated differently, we expect a cyclical decline in the demand for relatively risk-free cash streams, at the same time that a cyclical increase in the supply of relatively risk-free cash streams occurs. This should result in a widespread cap rate reversion of roughly 100 basis points. This is the price that real estate pays for being connected to broader capital flows. We expect that this cap rate reversion will be widely heralded as a new "disconnect" in real estate pricing. People will ask, "How is it that as real estate fundamentals slowly improve, pricing is deteriorating?" The answer will be that in interconnected capital markets it is not enough to "do better;" rather, one must do better than the alternatives.

Chapter 9 Supplement B
The Equitization of Real Estate

What return does real estate deserve?
Dr. Peter Linneman – *Wharton Real Estate Review* – Fall 2006 Vol. X No. 2

At the beginning of 1990, federal bank regulators fanned out across the country in search of excessive real estate loans. Shocked by the poor underwriting and excessive loan-to-value ratios (LTV) that had been discovered in Texas, they had orders to impose sanity on the capitalization structure of real estate. Up to that point, real estate was basically a 100% debt business, with small amounts of equity required to get a project under way, and a history of abusive tax syndicates in the early 1980s. But equity underwriting of future cash streams was a rare commodity in the real estate industry as these regulators began to scrutinize banks and savings and loans across the country.

The regulators, armed with new federal lender regulations, were surprised at what they found at nearly every federally insured depository. Many lenders had provided real estate loans, particularly for development projects, at 100% of loan-to-cost, often with minimal underwriting and documentation. This meant that real estate owners had no equity invested yet had 100% of the upside. This capital structure made no sense and could be found in no other sector of the economy. Yet it was the common practice in commercial real estate, which represented one of the world's largest asset pools. Under intense regulatory pressure, banks announced that they were no longer making new loans, and many outstanding loans were in breach of covenants and must be repaid. Finding a 50% LTV loan was hard, even for properties with strong cash flow, and there was little hope of rolling over maturating debt. With the withdrawal of the industry's major capital source, property sales became almost nonexistent, and property values plummeted, although it was difficult to assess what "value" was, as so few properties were trading. This problem was exacerbated by the fact that the only properties on the market were being sold under duress by foreclosing lenders and government agencies, rather than by traditional property owners. As the 1990s dawned, the era of debt ended, and the era of real estate equitization began.

For a $2 trillion industry, this meant that as much as $500 billion of equity was necessary to replace debt and put the real estate industry's capital structure on par with other asset-rich, cash-flow businesses in terms of capital structure. The immediate reaction of most real estate owners was to view the problem as temporary and hope that lenders would soon revert to their old ways. But the more prescient realized that the world had changed, and that access to substantial equity would be required in this new era.

The obvious source of fresh equity should have been cash-rich pension funds. But those that had invested in real estate (remarkably, with little or no debt in an era when debt was massively underpriced) stood on the sidelines, as the value of their real estate portfolios plunged. Most had lost faith in their core real estate managers, who had repeatedly assured them that their properties could not fall in value. The open-end funds in which they invested were frozen as investors ran for the exits, and many managers were rocked by scandals involving properties being assigned artificially high valuations. Pension fund investors seeking to sell properties could do so only at substantial capital losses. In this environment, it was practically impossible for pension fund investors to commit additional funds for real estate. Quite simply, real estate lacked the transparency and track record to attract new money from these funds. Thus, at a time when these funds should have been aggressively purchasing real estate, most were looking to exit.

The equitization of real estate was seriously hampered by real estate having become a four-letter word—deservedly so, as it had almost brought down the U.S. financial system. This, combined with serious global equity investors having never followed real estate, meant that it was going to take time to develop a solid equity following. In addition, for most people real estate was synonymous with development. Hence, most global equity investors did not realize that real estate ownership involved relatively predictable operating cash streams for mature properties.

As the search for equity began in earnest, an obvious source was leveraged buy-out (LBO) funds. But these funds lacked real estate underwriting expertise and were hesitant to enter the industry at a time when a recession was under way. Further, LBO funds faced issues with their existing investments due to the recession. Another potential source for equity was high-net-wealth individuals. But most knew little about real estate and lacked the real estate underwriting expertise required to evaluate real estate opportunities in a meltdown environment. Their entry was further handicapped by the absence of an appropriate investment vehicle, and realistically there was not sufficient capital available through high-wealth individuals to replace the half trillion dollars of debt trying to exit real estate.

A logical source of equity for any capital-intensive industry is public markets. Over the years, public markets have invested in nearly every industry that provides a sufficient risk-return trade-off. But public market investors lacked an understanding of real estate, as they had never underwritten real estate in the era of 100% debt and tax gimmicks.

During the 1990s, real estate investment opportunities improved, since prices plummeted as distressed owners teetered on the brink of financial disaster. Not only were these owners going to lose their properties through foreclosures, but they would also lose the management fee streams associated with their properties and faced enormous tax liabilities. Many owners went bankrupt, while even more faced the prospect of bankruptcy.

EQUITIZATION

A modest equitization effort was under way through real estate private equity funds modeled after LBO funds. The first two funds were Zell-Merrill Fund I and Goldman Sachs' Whitehall Fund I. But these funds were small and difficult to raise and absorbed much of the available high wealth and institutional equity seeking to enter at that point. Several visionary real estate players, led by Kimco, understood that the stabilized cash streams associated with their stabilized properties were quite safe when delivered, and that safe cash streams could be relatively easily valued by the stock market. Thus arose the alternative of an initial public offering (IPO), which allowed sponsors to avoid bankruptcy. The execution of an IPO was daunting, time-consuming, and expensive, and the outcome uncertain. But if successful, the sponsor could use the offering proceeds (net of expenses) to reduce debt to 40% to 50% LTV (loan-to-value) and avoid personal recourse.

A successful IPO also salvaged the fee stream from properties that would otherwise have been lost to sale or foreclosure. These fee streams were converted into a value equivalent via shares in the newly public company. In addition, if properly structured as an UPREIT, the sponsor avoided punitive tax liabilities. Finally, with their low LTVs, the newly public company could obtain a corporate line of credit, which could be used to purchase properties from foreclosing financial institutions and distressed owners.

This new era of real estate equitization has four critical events: in 1989, the Zell-Merrill Fund I raised $409 million; in 1991, Goldman Sachs' Whitehall Fund I raised $166 million; Kimco's IPO in November 1991 raised $135 million; and Taubman's IPO in December 1992 raised $295 million. These four transactions set the tone for the modern real estate private equity fund and the modern REIT, respectively (Figure 9B.1).

At the beginning of the 1990s, REITs were an obscure, capital market backwater (Figure 9B.2). Out of roughly $2 trillion in industry value, equity REITs accounted for a mere $5.5 billion. In the early days of equitization, real estate pricing was tenuous at best. Burdened with a bad reputation, a poor track record, unproven sponsors, and complex investment vehicles, it is not surprising that public execution occurred at high cap rates relative to the risk. This pricing was consistent with the private pricing of real estate, which was dominated by distressed sales. For example, the typical REIT dividend yield at the end of 1993 was 6.2%. This implied an expected total return of roughly 10% for REITs, compared with a 5.8% 10-year Treasury rate, a 7.4% yield on BBB long-term bonds, and a roughly 9% total return expectation for diversified stock holdings. Thus, as 1993 ended, the expected total return for real estate investments was well in excess of those available for either stocks or bonds. This return premium was necessary to attract uninformed equity into real estate. As the initial REITs succeeded in avoiding bankruptcy while maintaining tax protection and management fee stream value, more IPOs occurred. At the same time, the success of the initial real estate private equity funds also attracted entrants, including the emergence of real estate mutual funds (Figure 9B.3).

FIGURE 9B.1: U.S. REIT EQUITY OFFERING PROCEEDS

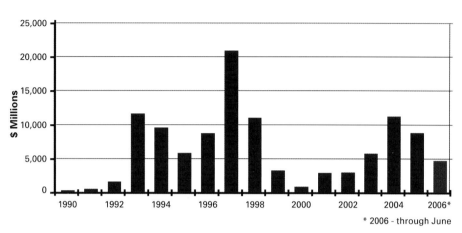

* 2006 - through June

FIGURE 9B.2: U.S. EQUITY REIT MARKET CAPITALIZATION

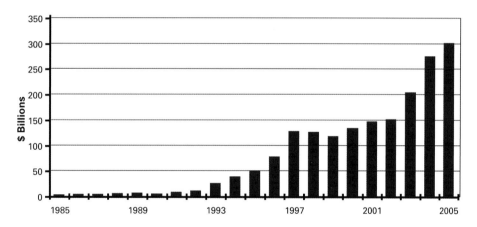

FIGURE 9B.3: NET INFLOWS TO REAL ESTATE MUTUAL FUNDS

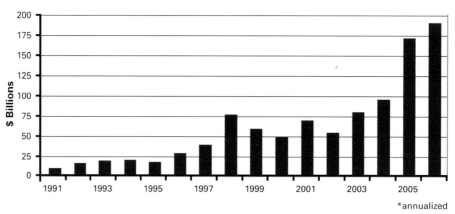

Source: AMG, Merrill Lynch. Note: 2006 data annualized

In a massive debt-for-equity swap, some $58.2 billion was raised by public companies from 1992 through 1997, with an additional $30 billion entering via real estate private equity funds. By the end of 1997, debt was returning to real estate markets, though in a very different form, and with lower LTVs. Specifically, commercial mortgage-backed securities (CMBS) were the primary debt vehicle, pooling individual mortgages that were cut into risk tranches and sold as securities into global debt markets (Figure 9B.4). These debt securities were also initially mispriced as global bond investors and rating agencies lacked an understanding of real estate underwriting. As a result, the spreads on CMBS debt were much higher than their corporate counterparts, despite the fact that relatively transparent hard assets backed these instruments. CMBS issues also had high subordination levels, causing real estate debt to remain expensive relative to the underlying risk. This was the price that was paid for the misconduct of real estate lenders in the previous decade. Typical CMBS LTVs were 50% to 70%, and equity was required in every project.

FIGURE 9B.4: HISTORICAL U.S. CMBS ISSUANCE

Source: Commercial Mortgage Alert

FIGURE 9B.5: CAPITAL FLOWS IN REAL ESTATE

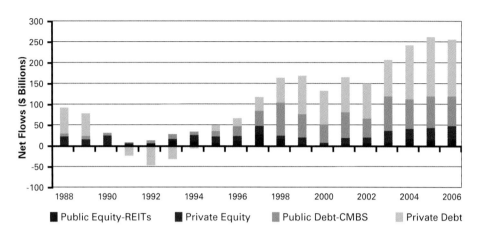

By the end of 1998, the first phase of the equitization of real estate was a success (Figure 9B.5). Equity had tentatively entered real estate via real estate private funds and REITs, while CMBS brought debt back to real estate with disciplined underwriting. And these vehicles had withstood the capital market dislocation of the Russian ruble crisis.

WHAT RETURN DOES REAL ESTATE DESERVE?

Real estate cash flow cap rates for both public and private real estate fluctuated between 8% and 10% from 1993 to the end of 2001. Since the end of 2001, they have steadily fallen, to approximately 4.7% today. In addition to this initial cash flow return, one anticipates receiving an appreciation return roughly equal to the expected rate of inflation. Over the past decade, this inflation has generally been 2% to 3%. Some observers have argued that real estate cap rates will revert to their historic norms of the past ten to fifteen years. But to answer whether cap rates will rise, one must address the risk-adjusted return for real estate.

Investors have three alternatives in terms of deploying their capital. First, they can invest in the equity claims on the corporations of the world. If we focus our analysis on the equity claims of U.S. corporations, the expected return for this claim is proxied by the expected returns for the broad U.S. stock market. Second, investors can invest in the debt claims of the same corporations, as well as various levels of government (state/local/federal). These debts claims are best proxied by the long-term BBB bond yield. Third, they can invest in the lease claims on the corporations and governments of the United States. These lease claims are primarily the lease claims held by the owners of real estate leased to government and corporate tenants. These lease claims, including the residual value, can be proxied by the ownership of a broad pool of cash flowing real estate such as the REIT index.

From a risk perspective, the debt and lease claims are far less risky than the equity claim, as corporations will pay their lease and debt claims prior to paying equity claims. As a result, the ownership of the debt and lease claims should command a substantially lower expected return than the ownership of the equity claim. Research by Jeremy Siegel of the Wharton School indicates that the expected return on the equity claim of U.S. corporations over the long-term is approximately 6% plus expected inflation. Thus, in a world of expected inflation of 2.5%, the total expected return for the ownership of the equity claim on U.S. corporations is today approximately 8.5%. Since no anticipated appreciation exists in the pricing of most debt claims, their total expected return is proxied by the BBB bond yield. In contrast, the ownership of the lease claim has both a cash flow component and an appreciation component reflective of expected appreciation.

Which is riskier, the debt claim or the real estate claim? Approximately 95% of the time, tenants will pay both their lease and debt claims in full. However, the remaining 5% of the time they will not fully honor these claims due to bankruptcy. Our analysis suggests that in bankruptcy the loss factor for real estate is slightly less than the loss suffered on the debt claim. To be conservative, we assume that bankruptcy losses are equal for the debt and the lease claim. This means that the total expected returns for the debt and the lease claims must be approximately equal. For example, if BBB bond yields are 7%, then the total return for real estate must also be 7%, comprised of 2.5% expected annual appreciation from inflation and 4.5% in current cash flow yield. Stated differently, the risk appropriate total expected return requires that the real estate cash flow return must be below the BBB yield by expected inflation.

Since BBB bond yields are 180 to 225 basis points over the 10-year Treasury yield, for today's 2.5% rate of expected inflation, the cash flow cap rate for real estate should be below the 10-year Treasury yield by appropriately price 25 to 70 basis points. That is, if real estate cash flow cap rates exceed the 10-year Treasury yield, real estate is underpriced!

Alternatively, one can analyze the appropriate pricing of real estate using the Capital Asset Pricing Model (CAPM). CAPM states that the total expected return for an asset is equal to the risk-free rate (10-year Treasury yield), plus beta times the market return net of the risk-free rate. Due to the longevity of real estate leases, and the differential supply and demand dynamics of real estate relative to other sectors of the economy, long-term real estate betas are 0.4 to 0.5. Since real estate reduces portfolio return volatility by not being perfectly correlated with market returns, the total expected real estate return should be less than for stocks, and above the 10-year Treasury, to the extent that beta exceeds zero. For example, for today's 10-year Treasury yield of 5%, and an expected stock market return of 8.5%, the total expected return for a real estate beta of 0.5 is 6.75%. Note that for a 2.5% expected rate of inflation, the cash flow cap rate for real estate must be approximately 4.25%; that is, the total expected return minus expected appreciation (in this example, 6.75% minus 2.5%). Note that this yields a cash flow cap rate that is 75 basis points below the 10-year Treasury rate.

These alternative approaches to analyzing the total expected return one deserves for real estate generate almost identical results. Namely, the total expected return on real estate should be roughly equal to the yield on BBB bonds, and the typical real estate cash flow cap rate should be 25 to 100 basis points below the 10-year Treasury yield. Higher expected returns mean that real estate is underpriced, while expected returns below this level indicate that real estate is overpriced.

Some argue that this analysis is correct for a diversified pool of real estate but does not hold for any single property. But this is also the case for every individual stock or bond. Since diversification can be achieved at the investor portfolio level, the total expected returns are reduced to the point where the analysis above applies for each asset class. This is particularly relevant for real estate, which prior to the equitization of real estate did not offer large, diversified investment opportunities. But investors today can diversify their ownership across a broad pool of REITs, real estate equity funds, and direct investments, and in doing so, push down expected real estate returns. This outcome is perhaps one of the greatest benefits of the equitization of real estate.

REAL ESTATE PRICING IN THE ERA OF EQUITIZATION

Throughout the era of equitization, the ownership of real estate has been substantially underpriced. In fact, from 1990 through 2002, the cash flow cap rate for real estate (that is, ignoring any expected appreciation) exceeded the total expected return for stocks. This was the case even though the equity claim is notably riskier than the lease claim. Underpricing continued through mid-2004, as the total expected return on real estate (cash flow cap rate plus inflationary appreciation) exceeded that of stocks. Only in the past two years, as cap rates have plunged, has this not been the case.

Figure 9B.6 displays the estimated cash flow cap rate spreads relative to the 10-year Treasury yield for differing types of real estate. Due to the appraisal lag in NCREIF data, these cap rates are lagged 18 months to provide a more accurate presentation of the timing (Figure 9B.7). Note that cash flow cap rate spreads were significantly negative in the early 1980s, when owning real estate was about purchasing not only cash flow but also access to mispriced debt and substantial tax write-offs. As the tax breaks were eliminated at the end of 1986, real estate cash flow cap rate spreads rose. However, the access to mispriced debt meant that real estate investors were willing to pay well in excess of the risk-adjusted price associated with the cash streams alone. As the 1990s dawned, cash flow cap rate spreads exploded, as not only were the cash streams more questionable in the recessionary economic environment, but also the ownership of real estate meant the lack of access to fairly priced debt.

Throughout the 1990s, real estate remained substantially underpriced as debt attempted to exit the market. During this period, anyone with access to equity and courage in their convictions realized a once-in-a-lifetime purchasing opportunity. As the equitization of real estate evolved into the mid-1990s, cash flow cap rates spreads narrowed but remained positive. However, by the end of the 1990s, real estate cash flow cap rate spreads moved upwards, as cash streams fell out of favor during the Tech Bubble. Only when the bubble burst five years ago did cash flow cap rate spreads begin to fall. Yet as recently as a year ago (the most recently available data given the appraisal lag), cash flow cap rates spreads were generally positive. This stands in stark contrast to theoretically justified negative spreads.

Figure 9B.8 displays estimates of average REIT total expected returns, calculated as the dividend yield plus expected appreciation (measured by the three-quarter moving average inflation rate.) Also displayed are the BBB bond yield, the 10-year Treasury yield, and the expected stock market return (measured by 6% plus expected inflation). Figure 9B.9 displays the spread between the average REIT dividend yield and the U.S. corporate BBB bond yield, while Figure 9B.10 shows the REIT AFFO yield over the 10-year Treasury. In the early days of the equitization of real estate, expected returns were 35% to 40% higher than deserved. By the time of the Russian ruble crisis, the mispricing had narrowed to about 20%, but as the bubble set in, underpricing soared to as much as 70%. In fact, between September 1997 and December 2000, expected real estate returns rose by 217 basis points, even as real estate operating fundamentals were improving. At the same time, Treasury yields fell by 48 basis points. This created a staggering period of mispricing. REIT implied total returns reached a high of 10.2% just before the bubble burst, at a time when 10-year Treasury yield stood at roughly 4.9%, BBB bond yields were at 7.5%, and expected stock returns were at 8.6%.

FIGURE 9B.6: CAP RATE SPREADS OVER 10-YEAR TREASURY

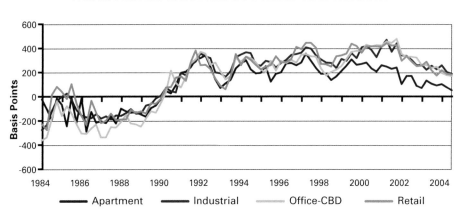

FIGURE 9B.7: NCREIF CAP RATES LAGGED 18 MONTHS

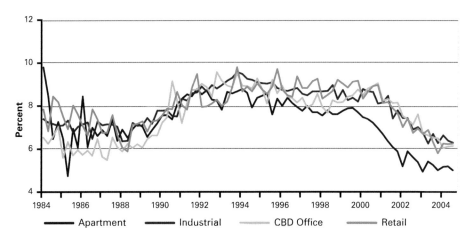

FIGURE 9B.8: YIELD COMPARISON

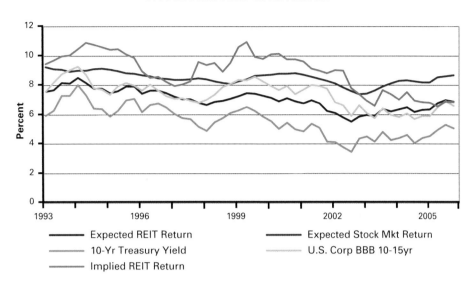

Expected REIT Return   Expected Stock Mkt Return
10-Yr Treasury Yield   U.S. Corp BBB 10-15yr
Implied REIT Return

FIGURE 9B.9: DIFFERENCE BETWEEN REIT DIVIDEND YIELD AND AVERAGE U.S. CORPORATE BBB

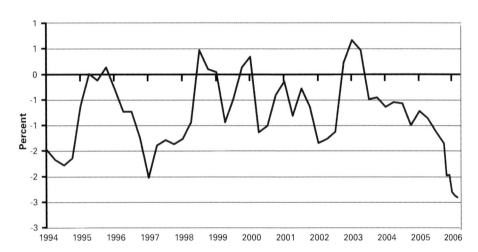

After the bubble burst, expected real estate returns steadily fell. But as expected real estate returns fell, BBB bond and 10-year Treasury yields also fell rapidly. As a result, between December 2000 and June 2003, real estate expected return rates fell by 232 basis points, while 10-year Treasury yields fell by 211 basis points, leaving real estate pricing still substantially out of alignment with the risk. Not until September 2003 did the expected real estate cash return equal the total expected return on stocks, and not until March 2006 did it approach the BBB bond yield. That is, until March 2006, real estate was underpriced despite four years of large and continuous declines in cap rates.

FIGURE 9B.10: DIFFERENCE BETWEEN REIT AFFO YIELD AND 10-YEAR TREASURY YIELD

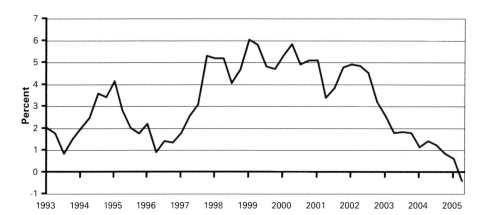

Over the past two years, real estate cash flow cap rates have continued to drift downward. At the same time, stock return expectations have risen modestly as inflation rose, while Treasury yields have risen by 90 basis points and BBB bond yields rose by 60 basis points. And only recently have cash flow cap rate spreads turned modestly negative. We believe that this modest negative cash flow cap rate spread will fall by another 25 to 50 basis points over the coming year. But for the first time in 16 years, real estate is not massively underpriced.

Figure 9B.11 displays the extent of real estate underpricing based upon CAPM, using a beta of 0.5 and an expected long-term dividend growth rate equal to the three-quarter moving average inflation rate. This more structured methodology yields the same story of considerable underpricing in the early-1990s, as equity began to flow into real estate. Underpricing lessened until the bubble. But CAPM reveals that during the bubble, there was enormous underpricing, disappearing only with the recent run-up in 10-year Treasury yields and the ongoing decline of cash flow cap rates. Figure 9B.12 illustrates an under-(over-)pricing matrix, assuming a beta range of 0.3 to 0.6 and long-term annual dividend growth of 2-3.5%.

FIGURE 9B.11: REIT UNDER- (OVER-) PRICING BASED ON CAPM

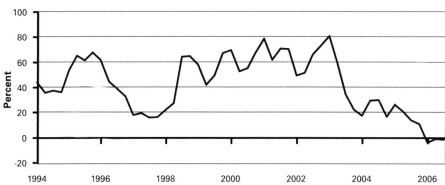

Assumptions: REIT beta = 0.5; Exp. REIT dividend appreciation = 3%; Exp. market rate of return = 6% + 3-quarter moving average Core CPI; Risk-free rate = 10-Yr Treasury

Theoretically, capital market adjustments occur instantaneously, as there is always enough "smart money" to arbitrage any mispricing caused by capital outflows. But the experience of the real estate industry reveals that the answer to the question, "How long will it take real estate equity to efficiently price real estate cash streams?" is

"About 15 years." This capital market adjustment took so long because knowledge was a rare commodity, and courage of investment convictions even more rarely met knowledge.

FIGURE 9B.12: REIT UNDER- (OVER-) PRICING THROUGH JULY 28, 2006

		Long-Term Annual Dividend Growth			
		2.0%	2.5%	3.0%	3.5%
Beta	0.3	1.7%	15.9%	34.6%	60.6%
	0.4	-6.3%	5.6%	20.9%	41.4%
	0.5	3.2%	-3.1%	9.7%	26.4%
	0.6	-19.1%	-10.4%	0.4%	14.2%

WHAT ABOUT MORTGAGE PRICING?

An interesting corollary is that if real estate expected total return should approximately equal BBB bond yields, then real estate debt (which holds the second loss position on real estate cash streams) should price substantially better than BBB bonds. Yet, until very recently, real estate debt was priced at a premium—not the expected discount—to BBB debt. Only recently has this reversed, as global debt markets have slowly come to better understand real estate. Not surprisingly, if real estate debt was substantially overpriced, real estate was underpriced.

Another way to see the mispricing of real estate debt over the last fifteen years is to note that the spreads on comparably rated CMBS tranches have generally been wider than comparable corporates. This reflects the lack of comfort with these instruments among both ratings agencies and investors, particularly in the early days when real estate was a four-letter word. But as real estate demonstrated that the high default rates of the late 1980s and early 1990s were not reflective of the risks of underlying cash streams, but rather excessive leverage, real estate debt pricing improved. This is also seen in declining subordination levels for CMBS.

A further demonstration of the mispricing of real estate debt is that REIT corporate debt has generally been rated around BBB. But this cannot be correct pricing if the underlying cash streams of real estate held by these companies is basically BBB in quality, and these REITs have only 40% to 50% LTVs. Instead, REIT debt was substantially overpriced due to systematic underrating by the rating agencies. This underrating is seen in the fact that there have been no defaults on REIT debt, while equivalently rated corporate debt has seen both defaults and transitions to lower ratings.

Given current leverage, it is likely that most REIT corporate debt should be rated A+ to AA. These ratings, and attendant pricing, will come in time. As it does, the advantages to being a public company will increase, as companies will be able to access fairly priced corporate debt.

WHY ARE REITS GOING PRIVATE?

Why are so many REITs going private (Figure 9B.13)? If today's REIT pricing is roughly correct, it is not that these private buyers are exploiting enormous underpricing. In fact, that opportunity was largely passed over by private equity players until recently, as their funds were too small to take on these opportunities. It is noteworthy that pricing today offers little in the way of positive leverage opportunities. In fact, negative leverage is often the case. In addition, the debt that private borrowers use costs approximately the same as public company debt. If anything, public companies can access debt more cheaply than private entities. In addition, the equity return required by most private buyers is generally the same or higher than that required by public equity. So, if there is no major return capital market arbitrage achievable by going private, why have so many companies gone private in the past eighteen months?

FIGURE 9B.13: RECENT REIT PRIVATIZATION

Acquired Entity	Buyer	Price ($Mil)
CarrAmerica (pending)	Blackstone Group	$5,600.0
Arden Realty (pending)	GE Real Estate	$4,800.0
Centerpoint Properties	Calpers, LaSalle	$3,400.0
Capital Automotive REIT	DRA Advisors	$2,960.8
Gables Residential	ING Clarion	$2,313.7
Storage USA	Extra Space, Prudential	$2,300.0
CRT Properties	DRA Advisors	$1,501.4
Town & Country Trust	Morgan Stanley, Onex	$1,500.0
Kramont Realty	Centro Properties	$1,103.9
Bedford Property (pending)	LBA Realty	$796.7
Prime Group Realty	Lightstone Group	$662.0

Source: Linneman Associates

The answer is threefold. First, many of these going-private REITs are sponsors who never wanted to go public and did so only to avoid bankruptcy. A decade later, these sponsors have aged, and most found that the public arena (particularly with Sarbanes-Oxley [SOX] headaches) is difficult. These entrepreneurial spirits were never comfortable operating a public company, with their requirements for reporting, strategy, and governance. Absent the bizarre world of the early 1990s, these sponsors would never have gone public. But the complete absence of debt and the need for large pools of equity drove them to survive by going public in the 1990s. Having survived, many had little appetite for the public world.

Interestingly, most of the going-private REITs are exits for these original sponsors. Most will pursue entrepreneurial deals funded either from their own capital or via equity provided by private equity firms. These entrepreneurs always felt hamstrung by the low debt levels imposed on REITs. Their exit is proof that real estate pricing has finally improved to the point where it is roughly in line with its risk, as otherwise these savvy real estate players would not have cashed out. Having achieved full value for their properties, they can gracefully exit the public playing field having served their—and their shareholders'—interests. To have sold when real estate was so obviously mispriced would have been a breach of their fiduciary and personal responsibility. Stated differently, these private transactions are evidence that real estate pricing is today in line with risk.

These going-private acquisitions also reflect that private real estate equity pools have finally grown to the point where they can make such purchases, as until recently private equity pools were insufficient to execute a meaningful going-private transaction. A further reason for going-private transactions is that as real estate pricing has come in line with the risk, private equity players have found it harder to achieve returns in excess of risk simply by acquiring real estate. As a result, some are now resorting to highly leveraged buyouts (LBOs), making a highly levered "bet" that cash flows will improve at 5% to 6% annually for the next three years, and cap rates will remain stable. These are classic LBOs of strong cash-flow streams. If they are right, and cap rates remain low while cash flows increase substantially, these going-private transactions will yield the 20% or greater equity IRRs they are seeking. If they are wrong, these transactions will underperform.

Going-private LBOs reflect the maturation of real estate capital markets, as LBOs have existed for years in other sectors. Just like traditional LBO funds, going-private REIT purchasers are willing to accept the risk of higher debt levels than the public market finds acceptable. If the behavior of LBO firms is an indicator, many of the acquired properties will enter public hands as the business plan is achieved.

Finally, some going-private transactions reflect that some of these REITs have missed opportunities to reposition their properties. This is because their entrepreneurial sponsors were so absorbed with the process of running a public company that they were sometimes unable to focus on the blocking and tackling of real estate. The private buyers hope to treat these assets with "loving care" or sell them to owners who will pay for the right to add value.

Nevertheless, there remains a major role for public real estate companies. In fact, new public REITs have entered the market even as others have gone private. The most creative public companies have demonstrated that, as we argued eight years ago, there is very little that a well-managed public company cannot do in terms of its capital structure that a private company can do; but there are things that a public company can do that a private company cannot. Thus, the best REITs are pursuing joint ventures with private capital, managing third-party assets, and operating value-added funds. These REITs have become efficient operating companies and the public market has provided them with unparalleled access to both public and private capital with a speed that is hard to match. Consider that a large REIT can raise a billion dollars in days, versus the months it takes even the best private equity funds to raise the same amount.

CHALLENGES REMAIN

Public real estate firms must resolve a number of issues. Foremost among these is to establish executive compensation structures that reward value creation and assure that top-quality management can be attracted and retained. This problem arises because the REIT IPOs in the 1990s squeezed compensation to achieve every penny in valuation. However, this created executive compensation schemes that were unsustainably low. While REIT compensation has improved, it has not kept pace with the opportunities available in the private market. Thus, much of the best talent remains private, or at public companies in other sectors (such as financial services).

Another problem is that only a few REITs have successfully incorporated meaningful value-add platforms. This includes not only development, but also leveraged subsidiaries, high-risk activities, and other value-creation activities. This reflects that most REIT management teams have been slow to demonstrate that they can create value. Similarly, they have been slow to move into alternative property types. As a result, unlike the best private equity players, most REITs are restricted to a single property strategy. While this is appropriate for some, others must convince public capital providers that they can successfully allocate capital and operate across property types. Further, while management fees may not be as stable as property cash flows, a successfully created management fee stream is extremely valuable. One need only look at the trading multiples associated with investment management companies. A major problem that arises in this context is the resolution of the inherent conflict of interest in fee management relationships. However, as REIT managers gain investor trust, this issue should be resolved.

Chapter 9 Supplement C

If Interest Rates Determine Cap Rates, Where Is the Evidence?
The Linneman Letter, Fall 2020 Vol. 20, Issue 3
Co-authored with Matt Larriva, CFA of FCP®, a privately-held national real estate investment company.

The positive relationship between location (location, location) and value is the best-known relationship in real estate, but the relationship between interest rates and cap rates is a close second. The supposedly positive connection is reiterated by brokers (CBRE), assumed by industry groups (NAREIT), posited by education sites (Investopedia), and examined by academic journals (Briefings in Real Estate Finance). At first blush, the presumption of a positive relationship seems reason- able. After all, real estate has a bond-like component in its perpetual income stream and the discount rate should be closely related to the interest rate. When the discount rate falls, value should rise, establishing a tight relationship between interest rates and real rates. Or, if that argument does not convince you, consider that the weighted average cost of capital presumably decreases proportionally with rates. If the WACC is used as a discount rate, then it will move roughly with rates (holding all else equal) and should also create a tight connection between cap rates and interest rates. And should those two relationships fail to satisfy you, then there is always the argument that decreased borrowing costs will force funds into the market and create a demand-pull inflation on pricing. With all these pricing mechanisms at work, the positive relationship should be a foregone con- clusion. But if real rates drive cap rates, then why is the empirical relationship so weak? And how could we have the same cap rates in grossly different real rate environments? For example, how did we have cap rates of 5.7% in January 2007, when the 10-year Treasury yield was at 4.7%, and cap rates 50 bps higher in July 2012 when the 10-year Treasury yield was 300 bps lower?

Background. Of course, all patterns have aberrations, and one contrary observation does not a proof make. But looking at the graph of the 10-year Treasury yield versus Green Street's major sector cap rates hardly shows a tight positive relationship (Figure 1). The same is true of real rates and all property cap rates (Figure 2).

FIGURE 1

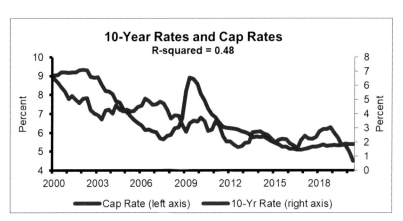

FIGURE 2

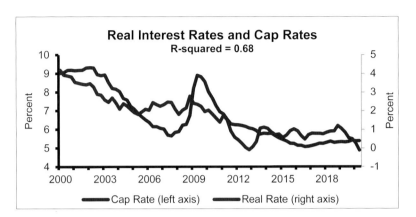

At first blush, an R-squared of 0.68 might suggest that the relationship is adequate. But then again, that same level of correlation exists in the relationship be- tween pool-drownings and Nicholas Cage films. And both relationships pale in comparison to the 0.95 R-square of cheese consumption and death-by-bed- sheet-entanglement (Figures 3 and 4).

FIGURE 3

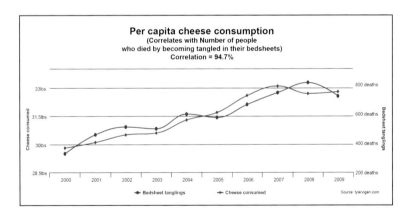

FIGURE 4

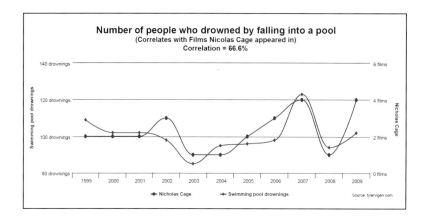

If Statistics 101 teaches us anything, it is that simple *correlation does not mean causation*. And if Advanced Statistics taught us anything, it was that grad school is very expensive when you are paying your own way. We also remember something about the perils of randomly correlated time series. On that note, the scatterplot of interest rates against cap rates warrants investigation (Figure 5).

FIGURE 5

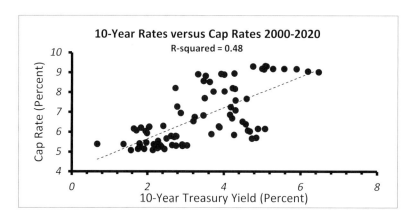

This plot appears to reflect the common wisdom that interest rates move with cap rates. But when we separate the interest rate and cap rate data by time period, a very different picture emerges. Specifically, as seen in Figure 6, three very separate patterns exist over time, each with negative (rather than the expected positive) relationships between 10-year yields and cap rates. The same phenomenon exists between cap rates and real interest rates (Figures 7 and 8).

FIGURE 6

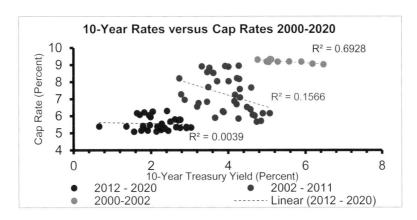

FIGURE 7

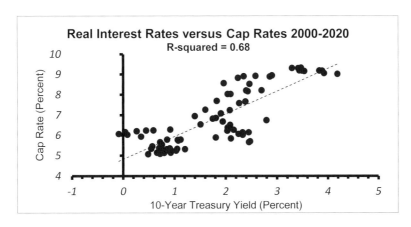

FIGURE 8

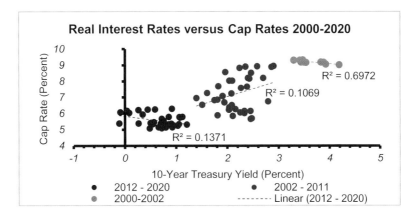

This is known in statistics as a lurking variable problem, or Simpson's paradox: a false pattern that appears when distinct relationships are comingled. Specifically, the time period of the observation tells us much more about cap rates than does than the interest rate. That is, one can estimate the cap rate with a much higher accuracy by simply knowing what time period one was trying to estimate. Knowing what the cap rate was in 2000, one could estimate with near-perfect accuracy what the cap rate would be in 2002 without knowledge of the 10-year Treasury yield. In fact, we find that both nominal and real rates, versus cap rates, show spurious patterns over time.

Statistically, one can often obviate the problems of spurious correlations by looking at the changes in the values, instead of the values. This exercise, with its 0.02 R-squared (Figure 9), reveals that cap rates are not driven by either real or nominal interest rates. Something else is determining cap rates.

FIGURE 9

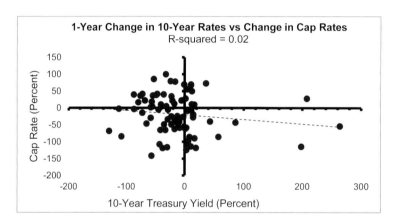

A stronger relationship. If not interest rates, what determines cap rates? To be sure, the inability of real rates to explain cap rates has been explored by a number of researchers over the past decade. Some authors find that the relationship between interest rates is weak but noteworthy; others cite interest rates as important only in certain circumstances. In this search for a more comprehensive understanding of the factors that drive cap rates, Linneman (2015), and Chervachidze & Wheaton (2013) independently arrive at a similar metric: the flow of funds into commercial real estate.

Linneman's thought experiment is helpful: if you knew for certain that three times as much capital was competing for the same real estate a year from now, what would happen to real estate values? His answer is that they would be roughly three times higher, irrespective of interest rates. Linneman then finds that the flow of commercial mortgage funds has by far the greatest empirical impact on cap rates. His statistical analysis uses the 10-year Treasury yield, outstanding multifamily and commercial mortgages as a percent of GDP, and the unemployment rate as potential explanatory variables. With these, he established a model that tightly forecasted cap rates for a variety of property types and allowed him to make the prescient statement in 2015:

> "...our bet is on the flood of liquidity, which could easily increase by more than 25%, keeping cap rates low even as other fundamentals exert upward pressure. So worrying about interest rates increasing appears not to be worth the effort. Instead, take advantage of the era of abnormally low rates by locking in debt financing for as long as possible, and watch the flow of mortgage funds as the key driver of changing cap rates."

In today's environment, where both real rates and nominal interest rates are uniquely low for as far as one can see, this result warrants revisiting. The aim here is to re-examine his fund flow model for robustness and ask if fund flows are simply another lurking variable. We utilize more cutting-edge statistical techniques than Linneman's original work, use better cap rate data (Green Street's transactional cap rate series for both apartments and offices) and examine how the model fares not just as a description of cap rates but also as a predictor of cap rates.

That last point is important. There is a distinction between a model which describes versus one that can predict. While we can describe the events of the past world conflicts—Antietam through D-Day—we struggle to forecast when and where such events will happen next. It makes the study of the events no less important, as we better understand market dynamics, but understanding World War II does not help one predict Operation Desert Storm. So too, it is possible that the fund flows explain cap rates but do not predict cap rates over the next year. We address both challenges.

Modeling Cap Rates as Functions of Different Variables. Linneman originally used the 10-year Treasury yield, the flow of mortgage funds relative to GDP, and unemployment rates to explain cap rates. We also use past values of the multifamily and office cap rates, fund flows (mortgage debt outstanding as a ratio of GDP), and U.S. unemployment rates.

This choice of variables is founded in economic theory, with cap rates determined by past cap rates, current supply and demand dynamics, and risk. We use one variable to capture each component. We regressed cap rates on earlier cap rates, the unemployment rate (to capture risk), and mortgage debt as a portion of GDP to capture the flow of funds. To model these variables, we use a more sophisti-cated statistical model, which allows for multivariate time series analysis and addresses an array of knotty statistical issues. For further reading on the specifics of our model, see our technical paper. The salient point is that statistics has a test of causality called Granger Causality which asks, "Am I better able to forecast cap rates if I know what funds flows are?" We find the answer is clearly yes, confirming Linneman's original experiment and empirical result.

Results: Does It Work? Does the model work descriptively? We examined the efficacy in forecasting one period ahead and conclude that the model tracks cap rates quite nicely and with very low errors. Note that this is the result of building a model on all the data available (2005-2020) and then using that model to forecast the series. While our study focused on the multifamily and office sectors, we believe (consistent with Linneman's original work) this analysis extends to other sectors.

The fit is excellent, though the model indicates a bigger jump in cap rates during the Financial Crisis than actually occurred. This is most likely because "extend and pretend" lender forbearance limited market discovery pricing. But also note that interest rates plunged during the Financial Crisis, while cap rates soared, contrary to the supposed positive correlation. To explore the predictive power of our model, that is its ability to forecast cap rates for periods beyond the data, we estimated a new model at each period using only the data prior to that period. In this way, we test the model's predictive ability *out-of-sample*. While the measures of fit decrease, they do so only marginally, and overall, the fit is good. This speaks to the efficacy of the model in capturing the dynamics of cap rates.

FIGURE 10

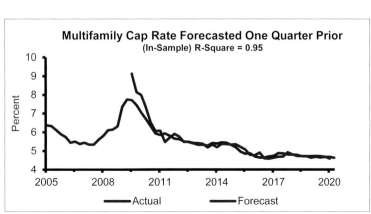

FIGURE 11

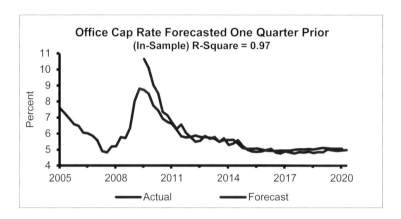

FIGURE 12

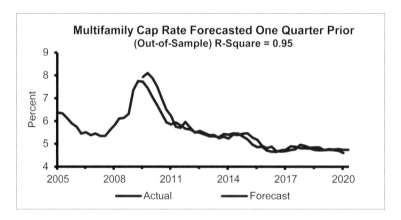

FIGURE 13

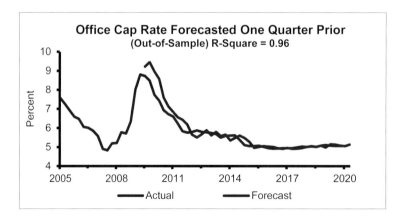

FIGURE 14

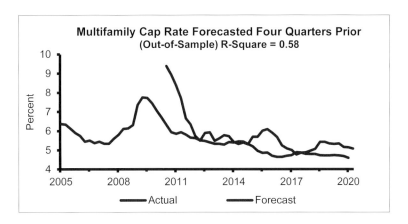

FIGURE 15

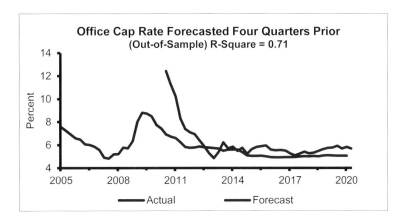

FIGURE 16

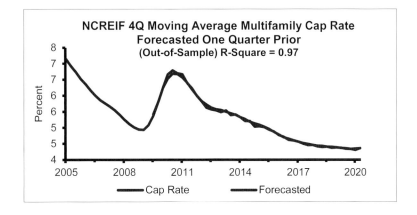

FIGURE 17

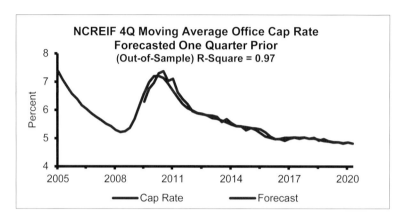

FIGURE 18

Cap Rate Response to a 100-bp increase in:	Mortgage Debt as a % of GDP	Unemployment
Multifamily Cap Rates	-22	1
Office Cap Rates	-65	3

FIGURE 19

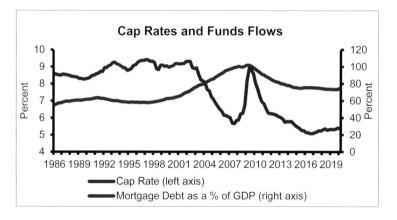

As to the more challenging test of evaluating the model's ability to forecast cap rates one year in the future, we evaluate the four-quarter ahead cap rate forecast and find that the forecasts are highly volatile during the Financial Crisis (again due to forbearance limiting price discovery) but are less noisy and more accurate outside in other periods. It is reasonable to ask, what is the efficacy of a model that has an R-squared of 0.6-0.7? Interestingly, this R-squared is similar to that of the original real rates versus cap rates graph, on which many practitioners have relied. The difference is, our fund flow model (above) is as relatively accurate predictively as the real rates model is descriptively. Furthermore, the fund flow model is strong statistically, validated out-of-sample, and is based on variables proven to statistically cause cap rates.

How helpful is it to have a four-quarter ahead cap rate forecast? One-year cap rate forecasts can aid fund managers with optionality as to when to exit, looking for additional return in a space where the difference between top and middle quartile performance is mere percentage points. This result also helps the individual buyers and sellers looking to purchase or sell. Such sellers have optionality as to time and would be served

We find that a change in the unemployment rate from 5% to 4% lowers cap rates by a negligible one to three basis points. Thus, even the 600-bp increase in the unemployment rated during the Financial Crisis only raised cap rates by 6-18 bps, and the inverse as unemployment fell. This is not really economically significant though it is statistically precise.

More importantly, we find that when mortgage debt grows 100 bps faster (slower) than GDP, cap rates fall (rise) by 22 and 65 basis points for multifamily and office properties respectively. If debt grows by 10%, relative to GDP, cap rates stand to compress by 220-650 bps. This is a dramatic impact.

So we clearly find that an increase in mortgage debt as a percent of GDP drives down cap rates, and an increase in unemployment slightly drives up cap rates. And this stands to reason, as these two variables provide insight to the risk side and the demand side of pricing, through unemployment and mortgage debt, respectively. In sum, we confirm Linneman's earlier finding that the connection between both multifamily and office cap rates and interest rates is weak, while the connection with flow of funds is the powerful driving force. Given that, we encourage investors to look to the flow of mortgages relative to GDP (specifically its change) as an indication of where cap rates should go in the near term and perhaps the longer term.

Our model finds that a spike in unemployment is very weakly negative for real estate valuation in the short term, but in the longer-term, the view on rates has not changed, as the flow of funds itself has been stable the past five years, with all real estate mortgage debt at 75% of GDP.

As monetary infusions spike, rates dive, and equity valuations move upwards, there is value to having a model which suggests a single variable of focus. As of 1Q 2020 there is an increase in the amount of mortgage debt as a percent of GDP. Granted, this is in large part due to the compression of GDP rather than the expan- sion of mortgage debt, but the model as stated accounts for this. And while unemployment is certainly wide of normal, the net impacts of these factors suggest stable-to-decreasing cap rates for the near-term.

Over the next year, we expect multifamily cap rates to drop 10 basis points while the office sector drops 20 basis points. There are, of course, ways that this dynamic can be muted. Two that come to mind are surprise inflation and cloudy price discovery via forbearance. The former may cause an exodus from real estate into higher-yielding asset types, while the latter may unhinge pricing from supply and demand dynamics. In all cases, we stand with George Box, who said, "All models are approximations. Assumptions, whether implied or clearly stated, are never exactly true. All models are wrong, but some models are useful. So the question you need to ask is not 'Is the model true?' (it never is) but 'Is the model good enough for this particular application?'" As interest rates approach zero, we submit the funds flow metric as a *useful* model in the current application.

Chapter 9 Supplement D
What Determines Cap Rates?

Dr. Peter Linneman – *The Linneman Letter* – Summer 2015 Vol. 15, Issue 2

In corporate finance, equity valuation is summarized by the price-earnings (P/E) ratio, which is the ratio of a firm's value (e.g., stock price per share) divided by its earnings. In real estate, valuation is generally described by the capitalization rate (familiarly, cap rates), rather than income multiples. The concept of the cap rate is simply the inverse of the traditional valuation multiple. That is, the cap rate is the income return of real estate, and is defined as stabilized net operating income (NOI) divided by the value of the property (purchase price, either anticipated or actual). The real estate industry's usage of cap rates reflects its historic linkage to the bond market, as real estate derives its income from future tenant promissory income streams. So just as the bond market commonly quotes yield, as opposed to multiples when describing bond values, the real estate industry generally refers to cap rates.

The cap rate (C) for a stabilized property can be shown to theoretically equal the discount rate (r) for the property's cash stream minus the perpetuity growth rate (g) of those cash streams.

$$C = r - g$$

The discount rate (r) is equal to the real long-term risk-free rate (Rf), plus expected economy-wide inflation (p), plus the operating risk of the asset (o), plus the liquidity premium associated with the asset's illiquidity versus the risk-free rate (l):

$$r = Rf + p + o + l$$

The expected long-term cash-flow growth rate (g) is expressed as the expected real cash-flow growth rate (c) plus economy-wide inflation (p):

$$g = c + p$$

Thus, basic algebra reveals that the cap rate is theoretically defined as:

$$C = Rf + o + l - c$$

Note that economy-wide inflation cancels out, as it is an equal component of both the risk-free rate and expected long-term cash-flow growth. Thus, inflation does not theoretically affect cap rates per se, as inflation increases both the discount rate and the cash-flow growth rate by the same amount. The cap rate is therefore equal to the real long-term risk-free rate, plus the property's operating risk and liquidity premiums, minus the real perpetuity expected cash-flow growth rate.

In analyzing these four components, the real perpetuity expected cash-flow growth rate (c) is the least volatile component of the cap rate. This is because "perpetuity" is, by definition, a very long time. The property-specific operating risk component (o) is tied closely to the macro or regional economy and is generally counter-cyclical. Specifically, cap rates tend to fall due to a decline in operating risk as the economy moves through the recovery phase of the business cycle. Turning to interest rates, historically, the real long-term risk-free rate (Rf) has been fairly constant at 200-250 bps, but has been abnormally low, and at times, even negative during the Financial Crisis. This reduction of 200-275 bps is historically unique, reflecting both the extraordinary flight to safety during the Financial Crisis, as well as unprecedented monetary policy activism. When the real return rose by about 100-150 bps in July 2013, it created upward pressure on cap rates, which was observed in both REIT and high-quality private asset pricing. However, our assessment is that the major movements of cap rates are attributable to changes in the liquidity premium (l). This component is highly counter-cyclical, plunging as the economy and capital markets boom and skyrocketing when they contract.

In 2015, we were among a minority that believes that cap rates, and equity multiples in general, would basically hold, even as interest rates rise. As support for this position we note that when value multiples were at similar levels in late 2006 and early 2007, the short-term rate was 5.3% and the 10-year yield was at 4.7%. That is, low cap rates (and high multiples) can co-exist with high interest rates. But for this to be the case, there must be an increased flow of funds, particularly of debt.

People correctly argue that, all other things being equal, a rise in interest rates should cause cap rates to rise by increasing the weighted cost of capital. But it is important to understand that "other things" do not remain equal as interest rates rise. In particular, as interest rates rise from artificially low levels, borrowers have a reduced incentive to borrow, while lenders have a notably increased incentive to lend. This incentive to lend manifests itself by changing "other things," including offering higher loan-to-value ratios, slower amortization, longer periods of interest-only payments, reduced covenants, narrower debt spreads, reduced underwriting standards, etc. These factors result in an increased flow of debt as rates rise from artificially low levels. This results in a reduced weighted cost of capital and more investor money chasing a limited supply of NOI and properties, resulting in higher prices. This was the case in 2006- 2007, when high interest rates stimulated a dramatic flow of debt.

When there is an extraordinary amount of liquidity pent-up in the largest money center banks, as interest rates rise these banks will notably increase lending incentives in order to increase the volume of loan originations. The resulting flood of debt, based on our research, more than offsets any negative impact of higher interest rates on cap rates.

The problem is that when the flow of debt eventually comes to an end, the process dramatically reverses. The contraction of debt is felt dramatically in the real estate sector, even when real estate is in supply-and-demand balance. This is because mortgage loans are roughly 60% of the real estate capital stack. As lenders pull back on originations, prospective buyers, as well as owners seeking to refinance are negatively and dramatically affected. If they are unable to refinance, existing owners face a capital shortfall, which is simply too large to be "instantaneously" filled. And to the extent it is filled, it is with expensive equity rather than cheap debt. This causes the cost of capital to temporarily skyrocket, forcing transactions to halt. As transactions cease, and loans default, the only transactions occurring are at temporarily depressed values to opportunistic equity buyers. These low value marks (i.e., high cap rates), in turn, further discourage lending, creating a feedback loop.

Given real estate's high overall leverage, even a 5-10% cyclical pullback in outstanding debt is simply too large to be absorbed without a severe impact on liquidity and pricing. This phenomenon underscores the fact that the flow of debt funds – more so than interest rates – is the dominant determinant of real estate pricing, as even very low rates cannot offset the absence of debt in terms of the weighted average cost of capital.

The Fed's artificially low interest rate policy resulted in a lot of frustrated "would be" investors. These are people and firms who would like to borrow at these low rates, but find that they are not credit worthy, and hence are unable to get loans. Most have become so frustrated that they have stopped trying. As the Fed allows rates to rise, we will see an upward movement along the debt supply curve, and lenders will have greater incentive to lend. Thus, higher interest rates result in more funds flowing to borrowers. The result will be fewer frustrated "would be" borrowers, more outstanding debt, and a great flow of debt that will offset any impact of rising interest rates on cap rates (and equity multiples). Hence, it is not hard to understand why even as rates rise from artificially low levels, more debt will be issued.

Chapter 10
Development Pro Forma Analysis

"Be prepared to adjust if you want to succeed."
- Dr. Peter Linneman

DEVELOPMENT

We next turn our attention to the creation of properties (i.e., development). While all of the concepts discussed so far apply directly to development (since the development process produces operating assets), there is also risk and opportunity unique to the development business.

Figure 10.1 summarizes the development pro forma for Celina Gardens, a 250-unit suburban garden apartment complex being built for sale as condominiums. The development is **speculative** ("spec") in nature, meaning there are no units under contract prior to the start of construction. Spec development of an operating asset is when no space is committed to be leased in advance of construction. The projection presents the story of the transaction from start to finish using 6-month time intervals. Planning and construction are projected to take 24 months, and sellout of the condominiums is expected to span the 12 months after the completion of construction. The financial model assumes a total development cost of $28.58 million and total net sales revenue of $37.19 million, rendering a pre-tax profit of roughly $8.61 million. While the pro forma in Figure 10.1 lists the major cost categories, a full development project pro forma would include more detailed line items.

FIGURE 10.1

Projected Opening Date: Start of Month 25

Celina Gardens Condominiums Development Projection

6-Month Period Starting with:	Year 1		Year 2		Year 3		Total
	Month 1	Month 7	Month 13	Month 19	Month 25	Month 31	
Land and Hard Construction Costs							
Land Acquisition	(3,050,000)						
Engineering	(20,000)	(375,000)					
Construction	(145,000)	(11,354,895)	(9,004,531)	(1,689,566)			
Soft Construction Costs							
Architect	(50,000)	(1,150,000)					
Rezoning	(120,000)	(10,000)					
Fees	(200,000)	(135,000)					
Furniture		(6,000)	(8,500)				
Development Overhead	(102,000)	(55,000)	(65,000)	(205,000)			
Legal	(351,000)	(251,000)	(20,000)	(55,000)			
Loan Interest	(851)	(46,840)	(54,000)	(55,000)			
Total Development Costs	($4,038,851)	($13,383,735)	($9,152,031)	($2,004,566)	$0	$0	($28,579,183)
Total Net Revenues	$0	$0	$0	$0	$18,596,678	$18,596,677	$37,193,355
Net Cash Flow	($4,038,851)	($13,383,735)	($9,152,031)	($2,004,566)	$18,596,678	$18,596,677	$8,614,172
PV of Costs at 3.00%							($27,618,122)
PV of Revenues at 7.00%							$30,883,186
Project NPV							$3,265,063

Online Companion Hands On: Go to the Online Companion page for Chapter 10 and scroll down to the Excel Figures section and download the Excel file. In the tab for Figure 10.1, holding all other inputs constant, manually iterate on the Land Acquisition input in cell f15 to solve for the maximum amount that can be paid if the Project NPV in cell d34 must be $4.5 million. What about if costs were discounted at 2% and revenues at 6%? An alternative to changing the input manually is to use Excel's Goal Seek tool, setting cell d34 to 4,500,000 by changing cell f15.

THE TWO BUSINESS PHASES OF DEVELOPMENT

During its initial stages, a real estate development generates negative cash flows, as a great deal of money is paid for the acquisition of the land and the creation of the building, while little or no revenue is generated. The little revenue that might be present is known as **interim income**, as it is expected to terminate, usually at the start of construction. An example of interim income is running a parking lot on your site while you are waiting for your building permits. A benefit of interim income is that it can be used as a development source of funds. Nonetheless, interim income is very minor relative to the costs incurred. By itself, all (or almost all) cash outflow is a bad business! It is development's "second" business (i.e., operating or selling a completed property), which is expected to yield substantial positive cash flows that make development financially attractive despite its various risks.

Phase I: The Negative Cash Flow Business

The first 24 months of the Celina Gardens project are comprised of securing the land, and the planning and construction of the building. During this time, the development company pays lawyers to draft a land purchase and sale agreement, and to apply for zoning approvals and entitlements. The developer also pays architects and engineers to draw up plans and submit them for building permits, and eventually, they pay construction contractors to build the building.

Development schedules vary based on the length of the approvals process, the securing of financing, the property and construction type, and the construction process itself. Figure 10.2 summarizes typical time frames for the planning and construction of different building types.

FIGURE 10.2

Typical Planning and Construction Schedule Lengths	
Property Type	Schedule
Warehouse	9-18 months
Garden Apartments	1-2 years
Suburban Office	18-36 months
CBD Office and Highrise Residential	2-4 years
Strip Center	18-30 months
Regional Mall	3-6 years

The main cost categories incurred during property development are **land acquisition costs**, **hard costs**, and **soft costs**. Land acquisition costs include the purchase price of the site and associated transfer costs. Hard costs are best thought of as costs relating to construction, such as materials and labor. The largest hard cost is the cost of construction. This cost covers expenditures for hiring construction workers (labor), as well as purchasing the concrete, steel, and other materials required to build the property. These costs tend to occur over the months of construction in the shape of a bell curve (Figure 10.3 left graph) and accumulate over the life of a project like in an S curve (Figure 10.3 right graph – note the different y-axis). When the land is being cleared, construction costs are relatively low. As more labor- and capital-intensive work takes place, costs begin to soar. As the finishing touches are added, costs top out.

FIGURE 10.3

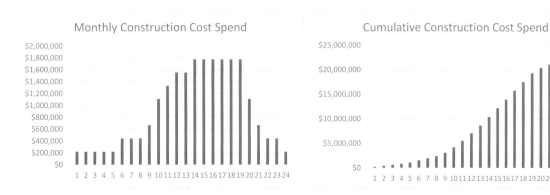

Soft costs are broadly defined as indirect costs. The largest soft costs generally include architects, engineers, and construction loan interest costs. The bulk of design and engineering fees generally occur at the onset of the process. These functions are important for planning and approvals, but unless major problems or changes occur, they become less significant over time.

The property will not generate any significant revenue until construction is completed and a large share of the development costs are paid with borrowed funds. With this debt comes interest incurred on the outstanding loan balance. As more money is borrowed to pay for construction costs, interest costs rise. But how can this interest be paid if there is no revenue? The answer is that the interest on the construction loan **accrues**, or accumulates, each month over the life of the loan. Effectively, the lender loans the developer money to pay the interest which is due. This additional borrowing for interest is "capitalized," or added to the principal balance owed, with interest in each subsequent month charged on the new total principal balance. As a result, the loan principal increases until the property generates enough cash flow to service or repay the debt, or to re-finance the property with a permanent loan that pays off the construction loan all at once. This type of loan in which the principal owed rises in each successive month is referred to as a **negative amortization loan** (see Prerequisite III for interest calculation details).

Development overhead encompasses expenses such as project management salaries, back-office work, accounting, etc. The development process also requires lawyers who perform due diligence analysis, such as checking titles and deeds prior to land closing. If complex environmental issues arise, legal fees rise substantially. A more detailed pro forma would describe these fees with much greater specificity. Legal fees will also be incurred for obtaining the construction loan and for review of marketing and leasing documents.

Rezoning costs are associated with changing zoning ordinances or if any variances are sought for non-conforming use of land. Land is often **optioned** to reduce the developer's risk while zoning approvals are sought. Specifically, the developer options, rather than purchases, the land during the approval phase to reduce the risks and defer the large land closing payment (in many cases the developer does not have the funds yet to go to closing). The option contract gives the developer the exclusive right to acquire the land at a specified price and date and prevents the landowner from marketing the site during the option term. A non-refundable option amount of 3-10% of the total land price is typically paid up front, with the remainder due at the developer's option at some future land purchase closing date. Often, the option requires that all approvals be in place before the developer exercises the purchase right.

Phase II: The Positive Cash Flow Business

Upon completion of construction and the receipt of a **certificate of occupancy** allowing tenants to move in, the second phase of development begins. Specifically, the property changes to the business of operating a building or selling for-sale product. As much has been already said about income-producing property operation, we will not repeat it here. With respect to the unit-sales business model of single-family homes and residential condominiums, the unlocking of positive cash flow is achieved through marketing and selling the individual units, typically through an on-site marketing center. In the case of Celina Gardens, we are projecting to sell out the condominium units after construction is complete, in months 25 through 36.

CERTAINTY OF CASH FLOWS

Which part of development's cash flow is more certain: the planning and construction phase cash outflows, or the cash inflows of the operation or unit sales of the completed product? Unfortunately, the outlays associated with the planning and construction phase are much more certain than the NOI or sales proceeds which occur upon completion. Since planning and construction costs are relatively certain to occur, the appropriate discount rate for this negative cash flow phase is quite low, as the discount rate always represents the riskiness associated with the corresponding cash flows.

As a result, buying the land and soft and hard costs should be discounted at the 2-year Treasury rate, as this is the risk-free rate for the 24-month planning and construction phase. In the case of Celina Gardens, we use the 2-year Treasury rate plus a 270-basis point risk premium as the discount rate for these costs. If the 2-year Treasury rate is currently 0.3%, it yields a 3% discount rate for the development costs.

Another way to understand why a very low rate is the appropriate discount rate for the development phase is to consider a developer who asks, "How much money do I need to invest today to be absolutely certain I will be able to cover all development costs with the invested capital plus the interest it earns?" To be certain that no payment shortfall occurs during the development phase, the money must be invested in very low-risk instruments, like short-term Treasuries. In this example, to safely have enough to cover the $2,004,566 of total development costs incurred during months 19-24, the developer needs to set aside $1,992,593 in Month 1 to make up the $11,973 difference with the interest earned on the 2-year Treasury over 24 months. As a result, a low discount rate must be applied to the relatively certain planning and construction costs.

In contrast to the planning and construction expenses, the positive cash flows derived from operating or selling out the property upon completion are much less certain. The business of forecasting the building's sales proceeds two years into the future is difficult, even for the best analyst. The same goes for the NOI and eventual sale of an office property. Who is going to occupy the space? What will market rent and TIs be in two years? What will operating expenses be? What will be the credit of the tenants? When will rental payments begin? What new competitive product will come online in the meantime? And if you think this is difficult to project two years into the future, what about five or more years?

This is not to say that the project will not be very successful, but there may be cost overruns, construction delays, weakened market conditions, or leasing or sales problems which hurt future cash flows. This future cash flow uncertainty requires that you apply a notably higher discount rate to the positive cash flow phase than is used to discount the negative cash flows incurred during the planning and construction phase. Of course, if the development process took two days, you could apply the same discount rate to the positive cash flow business as to the negative cash flow business with little harm. However, longer development projects necessitate varying discount rates to accurately estimate the present value of the development. It also means that development IRRs are meaningless, as the IRR calculation inappropriately assumes a single discount rate applies to all years. Yet, developers and lenders use it because of its mathematical elegance (or perhaps because ignorance is bliss).

In some cases, the discounting of a development's future operating cash flows can be tempered. Recall that revenue generated from an operating asset derives primarily from the rent and cost recoveries paid by tenants. If you lease the building to Apple or the U.S. government you are leasing to high credit tenants, and hence reduce the risk of not being paid. In contrast, if you lease the building to start-up company Wish & A Prayer, Inc., you should utilize a high discount rate. Perhaps you will lease to Apple, but not for three years until their current lease runs out, and in the interim, you will lease to Wish & A Prayer. In this case, the discount rates you use will differ as the tenancy of the property changes over time. Figure 10.4 shows a 12% discount rate used for Wish & A Prayer, Inc., and a lower 8% discount rate used for Apple, even though the Apple cash flows start four years into the future operation of the property.

FIGURE 10.4

Different Quality Tenants and Discount Rate Risk						
	Year 1	Year 2	Year 3	Year 4	Year 5	Year 6
Tenant	Wish & A Prayer, Inc.			Apple		
Rent	$1,000	$1,000	$1,000	$1,000	$1,000	$1,000
Appropriate Discount Rate	12.00%	12.00%	12.00%	8.00%	8.00%	8.00%

Figure 10.5 shows two different NPV calculation methods for Celina Gardens. Total development costs in today's dollars are $28.58 million (the left-most value). These costs are discounted at 3% in the middle column, yielding a present value of $27.62 million, and at 7% in the right-hand column, yielding a present value of $26.43 million. This roughly $1.18 million difference persists in the resulting NPVs given the revenues are discounted at 7% in both cases, making the project appear more lucrative in the all-7% discount rate case (a $4.45 million NPV versus $3.27 million NPV). In other words, if the development costs are incorrectly discounted at the same 7% rate as the cash flows from condo sales, costs are being understated in today's dollars. If you do not analyze your costs and revenues properly, you can end up entering a thin-margin deal or even lose money. While Celina Gardens is financially feasible under both methods, it is misleadingly profitable when costs are discounted too aggressively.

FIGURE 10.5

Celina Gardens Pro Forma Net Present Value Calculations			
	Today	At 3% Discount Rate	At 7% Discount Rate
Total Development Costs	($28,579,183)	($27,618,122)	($26,432,321)
PV of Revenues @ 7%		$30,883,186	$30,883,186
NPV		$3,265,063	$4,450,865
		(Correct)	(Incorrect)

REVENUE RISK MITIGATION

Like all investors, real estate developers are in the business of risk. To the extent they can do so profitably, developers seek to mitigate revenue risk in their projects. A primary method they employ is **pre-leasing** and **pre-sales** of their product when it is still just an architectural rendering on a brochure, or any time past that point but before the construction is complete. Such contracts are much riskier than leases or sales for existing properties, as only if numerous conditions are met is the tenant legally obligated to sign the actual lease or the pre-sales buyer obligated to go to closing.

Pre-Leasing

A **pre-lease** obliges the tenant to sign a pre-agreed lease if the building receives a certificate of occupancy by a specified date, is built in accordance with the agreed-upon design specifications, and has an agreed-upon tenant profile. The advantage of pre-leasing to the developer is that some of the uncertainty of future cash flows and tenant credit risk is mitigated. Offsetting this advantage is that rents are locked in years in advance, meaning that if market rents rise over time (which is probably the developer's expectation), the developer cannot take advantage of the higher rents.

Your ability to pre-lease critically depends upon market conditions. For example, if there are an abundance of leases expiring in existing buildings over the next two years, successful pre-leasing is easier. To attract pre-lease tenants in a weak market, you will need to offer substantial concessions. For example, in addition to cutting rents, you may have to offer the tenant better space in the building or alter designs to meet the tenant's desires. On the other hand, if the market is tight and space is not readily available, you may receive a premium, as in such a market, you help solve the tenant's business problem – the lack of sufficient operating space.

In addition, a pre-leased commercial tenant must still be in business (and not in bankruptcy) when it is time to start paying rent. For example, during the late 1990s dotcom boom, many start-ups had Candy Land dreams and signed pre-lease agreements for large blocks of office space. But as the bubble burst, most dissolved, and their pre-leased space went vacant. The surviving few found themselves committed to space at rents well above market. In the face of their dire circumstance, these firms scrutinized their pre-lease agreements to find ways of getting out of their obligations, claiming they did not have to comply with the pre-lease agreement because: the building was completed late, or the design was not exactly as anticipated, or perhaps the developer did not get enough "quality" firms to lease at the building. If in bankruptcy, the tenant can void the lease, leaving you with vacant space and a negative cash flow project. In fact, absent the pre-lease, you may not have developed the building. Hence, while pre-leasing can reduce your development risk, it can also lull you into a false sense of security.

Pre-leasing strategies are less relevant for multifamily properties. Retail space, in contrast, is generally pre-leased (e.g., regional malls require approximately 80% pre-leasing before starting construction). Everything else falls somewhere in between.

Pre-Sales

With for-sale residential developments such as condominiums, developers can pre-sell a minority share of unit inventory based off the strength of their marketing program. Pre-sold units are typically priced at a discount to pro forma pricing for completed units, so while it is nice to have some future absorption lined up, developers are presumably leaving some money on the table. Signed pre-sale contracts not only prove out demand for the product, but in some states such as Florida, buyer cash deposits are allowed (with certain conditions) to be used to fund construction, reducing the developer's equity requirement. In some markets and points of the real estate cycle, construction lenders will not release any funding until a threshold percentage of the project is pre-sold at pricing that confirms loan repayment feasibility. In this situation, the revenue risk mitigation is lender-enforced.

DELAY RISK

Assume you are able to find a commercial tenant who is willing to pre-lease. If the property is ready for occupancy on time and meets all the pre-lease specifications, the tenant executes the lease upon building completion, provided that the tenant is not bankrupt. But if the completion is delayed, even by a few months, the tenant may no longer be obligated to execute the pre-agreed lease. Two years may seem like sufficient time to get the development done. However, many things can happen during development, and most of them are bad. Developers must carefully plan for the foreseeable and perhaps more importantly, unforeseeable delays.

A developer generally works with more than fifteen regulatory bodies to obtain all the necessary planning and construction approvals. This process is expensive and time consuming, as regulatory bodies on the state, municipal, and Federal levels often have more pressing priorities than your development. In addition, these regulatory bodies often have conflicting missions, opinions, and agendas. A month, week, or even a day delay beyond the time you allotted for a particular regulatory process can snowball into additional delays and costs, perhaps resulting in the loss of a pre-leased tenant. Remember that the time pressures created by pre-leases are your problems, not the regulators', as you were the one who agreed to the pre-lease arrangements.

In addition to numerous regulatory approvals, a developer must also worry about the timing involved with financing the property. To help cover construction costs, you will almost certainly obtain a construction loan. How long will it take to close this loan? If you have trouble finding suitable construction financing, you risk pre-lease negotiations breaking down or delaying completion and, hence, losing a pre-leased tenant.

Assuming that you find a lender that will lend 65% of the development costs, the loan documents will stipulate that your equity dollars must go in first and in full prior to the first dollar of the loan funding. This is because if anything goes wrong during the development, your equity is completely at risk. By requiring the equity to go in first, the lender attempts to align the developer's incentives with their interests. Keep in mind that the equity investors receive all of the upside if the project succeeds.

When thinking about what can go wrong with financing a development, consider all of the possibilities. What if the loan officer in charge of your loan goes on vacation during the week you need to close your loan? What if the loan officer has a family or medical emergency that renders them unavailable for a month? You were expecting the loan to close in the next 5 days, but these factors may delay the loan closing. Construction will generally not commence until you have a construction loan in place to assure that checks can be written for the concrete, steel, bricks, contractors, construction workers, and other construction costs. Your time constraints are your problem, not the lender's. A good developer understands and plans for the human aspects of the development process that can destroy their timeline.

Another human aspect of development is the interaction you will have with numerous vendors, including contractors and construction trades. For example, if business is hot for contractors, they may accept more projects than they can service, creating costly delays for your project. On the other hand, in a slow construction environment, contractors and construction workers may purposely delay the construction process to prolong their employment. A classic example is discovering that concrete was "accidentally" poured into the plumbing after it has been installed. To rectify this "mistake" the construction company will have to replace the fixtures and pipes. This will not only increase your costs, but the delayed completion may also cause you to miss pre-lease deadlines.

Another risk that results in delay is that your contractors may go bankrupt. For example, you made a down payment on the electrical work, and your electrician files for bankruptcy two weeks into their work. You simply become another unsecured creditor of the electrical contractor hoping (in vain) to recoup payment. In addition, you must spend time and money finding another reliable, financially solvent electrical contractor on short notice.

Completion delays are damaging even if you do not have pre-leases, as you cannot collect rent or close on units until the building is completed. Hence, the longer it takes you to finish, the longer it takes to realize positive cash flows from the project; plus, you will incur additional interest costs and suffer "image" problems ("behind schedule," "in trouble," etc.). Development is an incredibly "public" endeavor – your success or failure is on display to everyone who passes your site, for better or for worse.

OPPORTUNITY

Why take on these and many other development risks? Because development, if done in a timely and efficient fashion, can compensate you handsomely for the risk. Development attempts to make the final product (a building) more valuable than the ingredients (land, steel, concrete, labor, and other materials). As such, successful development is true value creation.

If the developer can, for example, "**build to** a 10" and "**sell to** an 8," they create a lot of value. What does this mean? Build to an *X* means that projected NOI for the property upon stabilization divided by the expected total development cost equals *X*%. So to build to a 10 means that your stabilized annual NOI return is 10% of the total development cost. Remember that expected stabilized NOI is in the eye of the beholder. Some buildings are considered stabilized only when they reach 97% occupancy, others when they achieve 92% occupancy, and still others when they are at 88% occupancy. Stabilized NOI is contingent upon the market, location, and type of building, as well as who is using the term. Most simply think of a stabilized building as one that has not only completed the construction phase but has also had sufficient time to achieve economic maturity.

Let's go through the simple mathematics of calculating the developer's expected "build to" **return on cost**, often referred to as the **yield on cost** or **going-in cap rate**. Figure 10.6 shows that if you have a total projected development cost of $10 million and expect stabilized NOI to be $1 million, the going-in cap rate is 10%.

FIGURE 10.6

Going-In Cap Rate* Calculation
Going-in cap rate = Projected Stabilized NOI / Projected Total Costs
Build to a 10% = $1,000,000 / $10,000,000

* Alternately referred to as the Yield on Cost, Return on Cost, or the Build to Return

It is highly unlikely that the total development cost for the building will end up equaling the projected $10 million. Similarly, it is unlikely that actual stabilized NOI will be the projected $1 million. Yet, these are your informed expectations. In the end, the concrete will be more expensive than you thought, the steel cheaper than expected, and rents will be above (or below) your expectations. Even for the most experienced and diligent developer, these numbers are merely estimates, not guarantees, of what will happen.

To "sell to an *X*" means that stabilized NOI divided by your projected sales price upon stabilization is *X*%. Note that the stabilized NOI used is the same as that used in calculating your expected return on cost. The concept of "sell to an 8" is the same as having a **going-out cap rate** of 8%. An example of selling to an 8 is shown in Figure 10.7.

FIGURE 10.7

Going-Out Cap Rate Calculation		
Sell to an X	=	$\dfrac{\text{Projected Stabilized NOI}}{\text{Projected Sale Price}}$
Sell to an 8	=	$\dfrac{\$1,000,000}{\$12,500,000}$

In Figure 10.7, if the projected stabilized NOI is $1 million and the "sell to" cap rate is 8%, the expected sale price upon stabilization is $12.5 million. This means you expect a $2.5 million value creation from the development, calculated as the difference between the $10 million in projected development costs and the $12.5 million expected sales price. Value creation in development is no different than baking a cake. You combine the ingredients (sugar, eggs, and flour) and hope that you create a cake that is sufficiently more valuable to customers than the ingredients to make it worth your effort. Similarly, development is taking a collection of inputs (steel, wood, land, and labor) and creating a building which you hope tenants will find sufficiently useful to generate enough value creation to compensate you for the risks. Developers typically seek 150-200-bp spreads on the "build to" and "sell to" cap rates.

The "build to" and "sell to" calculations are critical calculations for a developer. While you will utilize detailed spreadsheets to summarize projected revenues and costs, these "build to" and "sell to" calculations effectively summarize the developer's assessment of value creation potential. These ballpark calculations will almost always yield very similar results as complex net present value spreadsheet calculations. In fact, if they do not, you should carefully examine your spreadsheets.

The $2.5 million expected value creation on the $10 million in projected costs in our example means that you expect a **gross development profit margin** of 25% for the project. The calculations of gross development profit margin using both cap rates and dollar values are shown in Figure 10.8.

FIGURE 10.8

Gross Development Profit Margin Calculation	
Gross development profit margin = (Expected going-in cap rate / Expected going-out cap rate) − 1	
(Expected going-in cap rate / Expected going-out cap rate) − 1 = (Expected value at sale / Expected cost) − 1	
= (10 / 8) − 1 = 25%	= ($12,500,000 / $10,000,000) − 1 = 25%

The opportunity to achieve a meaningful profit margin is why developers accept the risks of development. Expected gross profit margins for development projects are typically 15-25%. This is significantly higher than the returns on Treasury notes, but so are the risks. Your assessments of risk and opportunity are critical in deciding whether to develop. Who you are, the development experience and expertise you possess, your investment criteria, your comfort with specific types of risks, sources of capital, and how well you can cope with the many problems that will occur during the development process determine whether you will undertake a development project. In fact, these considerations are far more important than the expected returns, as if you lack the ability to resolve the many headaches that arise during the development process, your pro forma profit will quickly disappear.

Thus far, we have purposefully not discussed financing structure because it is essential to understand the "business" of real estate before you can contemplate how best to finance it. While leverage can dramatically increase returns on equity, it also substantially increases equity risk. Remember, if a development project is a bad business idea, financing is almost never going to save it. A bad piece of real estate is almost always a bad development deal.

OPTIONS AND DEVELOPMENT

Development is in many ways like an option contract. When you own or control a parcel of land, its value increases as the likelihood of profitable development increases. For example, a tenant may come to you and ask you to develop a building for them. Or a change in zoning may make your site more valuable as a development. Or the construction of a highway exit ramp near your property may put the development value of your land "in the money." A substantial, and elegant, theoretical literature of option models for real estate development has evolved. The spirit of this literature is that while there is no (or little) cash stream from raw land, future growth and the volatility of future growth creates development value for land. To value this option, this literature uses variations of the Black-Scholes option pricing model. When valuing development opportunities with such models, the value is higher: the greater the growth in the local economy; the longer the hold period; and the greater the volatility of local growth.

Unfortunately, these parameters are basically impossible to measure for development parcels. Take growth volatility as an example. You may know that Philadelphia is a market with relatively little growth volatility, while Houston has a great deal of growth and volatility. So, other things equal, land in Philadelphia tends to be worth less than land in Houston because there is a chance that a sharp economic upswing will occur in Houston. But how much of a discount for your particular Philadelphia site is justified relative to a comparable site in Houston? You cannot answer this question, because there is no reliable data with which to estimate the volatility facing your property, both because properties are very idiosyncratic, and because return data does not exist for your site. As a result, while development option pricing is a nice intuition to bear in mind, concentrate on understanding the risks and opportunities offered by your property. Your brain is a powerful portable computer, and as you gain experience and information from watching others, reading, thinking, and succeeding or failing on your projects, you will formulate a sophisticated approach to development valuation.

THE DEVELOP VERSUS BUY ANALYSIS FRAMEWORK

Development is riddled with potentially stomach-turning risk, and it is not for every real estate investor. If the goal of investing in income-producing real estate is to gain ownership of a recurring, growing cash flow stream, why doesn't everyone prefer to acquire existing cash-flowing properties instead of going through the multi-year development process of manufacturing the cash flow stream? Common sense tells us there must be a greater financial reward in the latter, at least over a certain timeframe in certain circumstances.

To investigate this, we can approach the question with the following simulation: assume that you are comparing the acquisition of an existing property generating a 5% annual yield, which continues in perpetuity. As an alternative, assume you could develop a new property of the same type to a 6.5% yield (a 5% cap rate plus the developer's targeted 150-basis point spread), which also remains constant forever. You could do a simple comparison of cumulative annual operating cash flow to equity over 15 years on an unlevered basis. If you did so, you would find that it is not until year 14 that the development's cumulative cash flow overtakes that of the acquisition. Introducing 2% annual cash flow growth in both cases reveals that it takes the full 15 years for the development project's cumulative operating cash flow to overtake the amount generated by the acquisition. While this might seem counterintuitive, this imbalance toward acquisition occurs and essentially remains the case even with 70% debt assumed in both scenarios, as well as with 70% debt and 2% annual cash flow growth. Further, in all four scenarios, the 15-year NPV of the development is lower than that of the acquisition, due in part to the lack of any positive cash flow during the planning and construction period.

So is a financial preference for development justified? The answer lies in the implementation of a particular investment strategy as it relates to the value creation objective. If you, as the developer, want to recoup your capital as quickly as possible, you can refinance the property upon stabilization, simultaneously paying off the construction loan and taking cash out of the property while retaining ownership of future cash flows (a "**cash out refinancing**"). You could possibly even take out a loan large enough to not only return all your invested equity, but also to provide a return (profit) on that equity at the point of refinancing. Alternatively, you can sell the property upon stabilization, a so called "**merchant builder**" strategy, recouping your equity through the sale and making a sizable profit. In both cases, you can use the recouped equity and any profits to invest in your next development.

It is important to remember that academic thought experiments like this are based on multiple assumptions that may never come to pass in reality. The financial attraction of development is ultimately the opportunity to create a value premium over acquiring and holding properties by embracing additional risk. Empirically proving this value premium out is impossible because no two properties or investments are the same, and you cannot make two different investments with the same capital at the same time.

CLOSING THOUGHT

If after weighing the risks and opportunities of development, you still want to be a developer, the next questions are: "Where should I start?" and "How should I start?" If you really want to be a developer, perhaps you should not go to Midtown Manhattan to start your career, even though Manhattan is a fun and exciting place. After all, it is already built! A developer is in the business of servicing population, economic, and political growth. Therefore, the best opportunities are where there is sustained growth. This means places like Chester, Virginia, or Victorville, California, or Albuquerque, New Mexico. These types of places may not be the sexiest, but they are where the greatest development opportunities are located. Just as if you want to be a dairy farmer, it is unlikely that you will find great opportunities in Manhattan, so too with development.

Assuming you pick an appropriate location to launch your development career, how do you start? To succeed in developing new products, it is essential that you understand the market's product offerings. If you wanted to create a new beer, you would taste a lot of beer. You would also study brewing and fermentation processes and how they have changed over time. You would study the labeling, advertising, and marketing strategies of beers. That is, you would learn the beer business from the ground up. In the same way, if you want to develop real estate, get close to the tenants and the operation of properties to understand what works, why, and what product niches are underserved. Understand that even an idiot can develop a "unique" product. For example, develop a structure without doors or windows! A successful developer knows what works and generally makes minor improvements on successful products. Rarely do they create a highly "unique" product. To be a successful developer, copy what works and strive to do it cheaper, faster, and better.

Perhaps the most common question I hear is some variation of, "Even though I want to be a developer, can't I start my career in investment banking, so I can enjoy Manhattan and make those big Wall Street bucks?" The short answer is that working at a prestigious investment banking firm is a great place to learn finance, but probably not the best place to lay a career foundation for becoming a real estate developer. Imagine that you want to someday be the head coach of the Philadelphia Eagles. Would you start your career in the entertainment group at Morgan Stanley? Very doubtful. You would probably start as an assistant coach for a high school or college team and work your way up. Similarly, if you someday want to be a great developer, work with a firm that specializes in the ownership, operation, or creation of property. Many great financiers, but very few great developers, began their careers at investment banks. If you want to become a developer, go to a good local, regional, or national real estate firm and start learning the business from the ground up (literally) one day at a time.

 Online Companion Audio Interview: To hear a conversation about this chapter's content, go to the Online Companion and select the link for Chapter 10. Scroll down to the Audio Interview section and listen.

Chapter 11
Development Feasibility Analysis

"In the battle between fear and greed, greed wins about 80% of the time."
- Dr. Peter Linneman

DEVELOPMENT FEASIBILITY ASSESSMENT

With a better understanding of many of the potential risks and opportunities associated with commercial real estate development, you can now analyze specific development projects. As with analysis of existing properties, a spreadsheet is merely a helpful tool to organize information. Remember that your assumptions are just informed guesses. As such, your spreadsheet serves as a template to challenge your beliefs and against which you can assess the risks and opportunities. Before you begin the arduous task of modeling the detailed cash flows for a development project, you should always perform a simple **development feasibility analysis**. If the development does not "pencil" (show a sufficient level of return relative to risk) based upon this simple "back of the envelope" analysis, I promise you that it will not work any better after hours, days, or weeks of arduously modeling it in the rows and columns of a more detailed multi-period analysis. If the simple analysis suggests it could work, then create a detailed spreadsheet and begin your in-depth market and financial analysis.

SIMPLE CALCULATIONS

Assume that as a developer of office buildings in downtown Phoenix, you have decided that you need to build to a 10 (i.e., a 10% expected stabilized NOI rate of return on expected total costs) to undertake the Muk Office Plaza development project summarized in Figure 11.1A. This reflects your belief that comparable existing stabilized properties are selling at 8-8.5% cap rates, and you feel a 15-20% development profit margin is required to offset the risks of development. Take a moment to study Muk Office Plaza, paying special attention to the amount of square footage that is not leasable (Figure 11.1B).

As you know, you can only receive rent on leasable space, which depends upon the building's design. Space used for elevators, the lobby, mechanicals, and stairwells does not generate income. The building's **loss factor** (i.e., how much gross square footage of the building is unleasable) also depends upon your leasing strategy. For instance, if you decide to split a floor in the office building between six tenants rather than rent the entire floor to a single tenant, the loss factor rises as you must provide hallway access for the tenants. With one tenant, common area hallway space is reduced, and you can collect rent on more of the space. However, multiple tenants provide greater diversification which offsets the risk of having an entire floor vacant for any period of time. You assume for preliminary purposes that Muk Office Plaza will have a 30% loss factor. Put another way, the building will be 70% economically "efficient."

FIGURE 11.1A

Expected Development Cost and Operating Assumptions for Muk Office Plaza	
Land Cost	$30 per GSF (building gross square foot)
Hard Costs	$90 per GSF
<u>Soft Costs</u>	<u>$30 per GSF</u>
Total Development Cost	$150 per GSF
Building Size	100,000 GSF
Loss Factor	30% of GSF
Leasable Square Feet	70,000 SF
Stabilized Vacancy	5% of Leasable Square Footage
Occupancy *(1 – Vacancy)*	95% of Leasable Square Footage
Leased Square Feet	95% * 70,000 = 66,500 SF
Annual Rent	$30 per Leasable Square Foot
Annual Operating Cost	$10 per GSF

FIGURE 11.1B

Muk Office Plaza square footages

Based upon your knowledge of the market, you anticipate that total development costs will be about $150 per building gross square foot (GSF). Included in this figure are land, hard costs, and soft costs. Thus, in order to generate at least the necessary 10% return on total development costs (i.e., "build to a 10 cap"), the property must at least generate an expected stabilized NOI of $15 per gross square foot. This "build to" calculation, which was introduced in Chapter 10, is shown in Figure 11.2.

FIGURE 11.2

Build to x% Return* Calculation
Build to x% Return = Projected Stabilized NOI / Projected Total Costs
Build to a 10% = $15.00 per GSF / $150.00 per GSF

Alternately referred to as the Yield on Cost, Return on Cost, or the Going in Cap Rate

What NOI can you expect from the property? The key top line component of NOI is expected rental income, which is primarily determined by market conditions. Unless this is an enormous project, you will probably not significantly impact market rent. But remember that your building adds to market supply and will itself place some downward pressure on market rents. Assume that based on your knowledge of the local market, you determine the expected rent (i.e., "market rent") is $30 per leasable square foot (LSF) per year (office, retail and industrial rents are typically quoted on this annual basis, except in California where monthly rents are quoted). However, you must adjust the rent per leasable square foot to reflect vacant space to get to an **effective rent per leasable square foot**. As shown in Figure 11.3, assuming a 5% vacancy rate (95% occupancy rate) upon stabilization, you estimate effective rental income of $28.50 per leasable square foot by multiplying $30 per leasable square foot by 95%. Ancillary income (not shown in this calculation) derived from rooftop billboards, cellular signal antennas, parking, and vending machines must also be included if it is expected to be a major source of revenue. Remember, the higher your stabilized vacancy, the fewer people in the building to contribute to ancillary income.

FIGURE 11.3

Effective Rent per Leasable Square Foot Calculation
Effective Rent per Leasable SF =   Market Rent per Leasable SF * (1 – Stabilized Vacancy %)
= $30.00 * (1 – .05)   = $28.50

Based upon your knowledge of local operating costs (utilities, repairs and maintenance, real estate taxes, insurance), you estimate annual operating costs net of tenant recoveries of approximately $10 per gross square foot. That is, you will have to pay roughly $10 per building square foot even if the space is vacant as you must pay real estate taxes, insurance, snow removal, and other costs regardless of whether or not the property is fully occupied. For consistency in calculating NOI per square foot, you must convert rent per leased square foot to rent per gross square foot. If only 70% of the property is leasable (due to the 30% loss factor), a $28.50 rent per leased square foot is equivalent to $19.95 in **effective rent per gross square foot**, as shown in Figure 11.4.

FIGURE 11.4

Converting Effective Rent per Leasable Square Foot to Effective Rent per Gross Square Foot
Effective Rent per Gross SF = Effective Rent per Leasable SF * (1 – Loss Factor %) = \$28.50 * (1 – 0.30) = \$19.95 per GSF

As shown in Figure 11.5, with expected effective rent per gross square foot income of \$19.95 and expected operating costs net of recoveries of \$10 per gross square foot, you expect stabilized NOI per gross square foot of \$9.95. This implies an expected **yield on total development cost** ("yield on cost"; the build to return) of 6.63% (i.e., \$9.95 / \$150).

FIGURE 11.5

Stabilized NOI per Gross Square Foot Calculation
Stabilized NOI per GSF = Rental Revenues per GSF – Operating Costs per GSF = \$19.95 PSF – \$10.00 PSF = \$9.95 PSF

Does this project pass an initial examination? Not if you require a 10% stabilized NOI return on cost to compensate for taking on development risks. Based on this simple yield on cost analysis (Figure 11.6), the project does not offer enough potential return to make it worth the risk (i.e., It does not pencil).

FIGURE 11.6

Expected Yield on Total Development Cost Calculation
Expected Yield on Cost = Expected Stabilized NOI / Expected Total Costs = \$9.95 / \$150.00 = 6.63%, which is less than the required 10.00%

If you undertake the project, you expect an unacceptable compensation for the development risks. Stated bluntly, why would you take on all of the risks of development, when based on your market analysis you know you can buy comparable existing stabilized buildings for an 8-8.5 cap? By the way, note that this analysis took you less time than you need to warm up your PC for a full spreadsheet analysis.

SOLVE BACKWARDS FOR REPLACEMENT RENT

How high does the market rent have to be for the Muk Office Plaza to be potentially viable? You can solve backwards for this **replacement rent** per gross square foot, as well as its equivalent per leased square foot.

Since stabilized NOI must equal $15 per gross square foot for you to receive a 10% return on total costs of $150 per gross square foot, market rents per gross foot must rise to $25 if expected operating costs are $10 per gross square foot. This back solving is shown in Figure 11.7.

FIGURE 11.7

Replacement Rent per Gross Square Foot Calculation
Replacement Rent per GSF = (Build to Return * Expected Total Cost) + Expected Operating Costs = (10% * $150.00) + $10.00 = $15.00 + $10.00 = $25.00 per GSF

How does replacement rent per gross square foot translate into replacement rent per leased square foot? Think about it as having to still generate the same NOI for your required yield on cost, but the NOI derives from fewer square feet. Algebraically, the numerator (NOI) is the same, but the denominator is leased square feet, which is a subset of gross square feet and leasable square feet. Dividing the same NOI by a smaller square footage value naturally yields a larger rent per leased square foot than rent per gross square foot.

As Muk Office Plaza is 100,000 gross square feet, we know that total required projected rent is $2.5 million ($25 per GSF * 100,000 GSF). Since 30% (or 30,000 gross square feet) of the building is unleasable and another 5% of the leasable space (3,500 square feet) is assumed to be vacant, then total leased space is 66,500 square feet (100,000 − 30,000 − 3,500). Therefore, rent per leased square foot must be $37.59 ($2.5 MM / 66,500) for the expected return on costs to be 10%. A more elegant way of calculating this conversion is shown in Figure 11.8.

FIGURE 11.8

Replacement Rent per Leasable Square Foot Calculation
Replacement Rent per Leasable Square Foot = Replacement Rent per GSF * (1 / (1 − Loss Factor)) * (1 / (1 − Vacancy)) = $25.00 * (1 / (1 − 0.3)) * (1 / (1 − 0.05)) = $37.59 per Leasable Square Foot

Since the replacement rent per leasable square foot must be at least $37.59 for the project to generate your required returns, current market rents of $30.00 PSF must rise by roughly 25% before replacement rent is achieved. If rents rise 3% per annum, this will take 7.6 years to achieve. Of course, since operating costs, rent, construction costs, and other factors change daily, while $37.59 per leasable square foot may be sufficient to justify development today, it may not be adequate tomorrow. As a result, developers regularly re-evaluate projects to determine their feasibility.

This simple feasibility analysis is fast and accurate and with a little practice, can be done in your head. If your spreadsheets produce significantly different results from this analysis, carefully check the rows and columns, as there is something wrong in them. This analysis saves you the time and trouble of performing the detailed analysis, which if done correctly in this example, will only confirm that you cannot remotely achieve your desired profitability given current market conditions.

A COMMON MISTAKE

Avoid simply **trending** recent rental data points (i.e., extrapolating them at the same slope) when conducting feasibility analysis. Developers frequently lose sight of the fact that rent is driven by supply and demand fundamentals rather than trend lines. Look at Figure 11.9 and assume that you passed on our example development in Year 2 because you felt that the $30 market rent was too low. You continue to monitor rents over the next several years, and the pattern shown evolves.

FIGURE 11.9

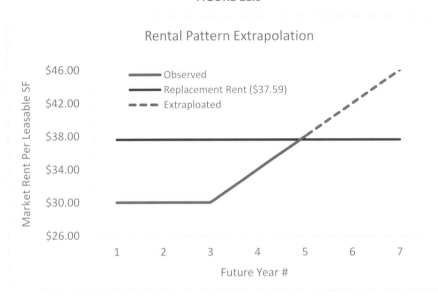

Specifically, after flat rents of $30 per leasable foot in Years 1 through 3, as the economy picked up, rents rose to $34 in Year 4 and to $38 in Year 5. While rents in Year 4 remained too low to justify development, Year 5 rents had risen above replacement rent.

Looking at this rental trend (in early Year 5), you might infer that since market rent increased by $8 per square foot over the past two years, or by 26.7%, while contemporaneous inflation was only about 2-3% per year, this must be a strong market with great rental growth potential. You project continued rental growth through Year 7, as indicated by the dashed line. Forecasting market rent of $42 per square foot in Year 6 and $46 per square foot in Year 7, you conclude that if you start development now (early Year 5), you will receive rent of roughly $46 per leasable square foot upon completion in Year 7. This forecasted market rent is well in excess of the $37.59 per leasable square foot required to justify new construction. Deciding it is time to build, you note that if necessary, you can pay more than the $30 per gross building square foot for the land you originally assumed and still generate your 10% target return.

Does this analysis make sense? Of course not. Once rents rise above replacement rent, developers will do what they do best: Develop! Just as you see development opportunity, so too will other developers. If it makes sense for you to build, it will make sense for others as well. Thus, as demand growth pushes rents above replacement rent, supply will increase with a lag. As this new space comes online, rents will tend to revert to replacement rent, rather than continue the upward trend. To believe that rents will continue to rise well beyond replacement rent ignores the basics of supply and demand. In fact, if enough developers use this faulty analysis to justify development, excessive development will occur, and rents will fall below replacement rent.

Figures 11.10 and 11.11 depict realistic potential rental rate growth outcomes. Note that rental rate growth should taper off as rents approach replacement rent. Figure 11.10 shows an overshoot of rents as supply lags demand, with reversion to replacement rent, while Figure 11.11 shows an overshoot of rents followed by a decline to below replacement rent due to excessive development, with ultimate reversion to replacement rent.

FIGURE 11.10

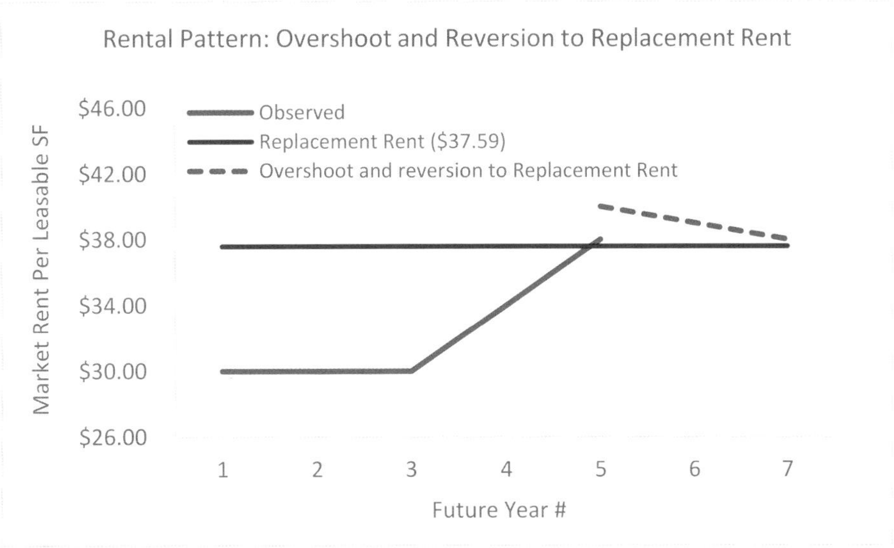

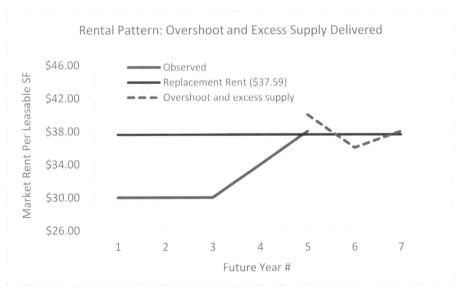

FIGURE 11.11

Although simply extrapolating at the same slope may seem to be an obvious error in a classroom, this type of rental trend analysis is common practice. Would a rational person accept this trend analysis? No. But neither would a rational person drink to excess and sleep with their head on the toilet. Yet some of you do it! In the morning you say that you will never do it again, but next weekend some of you do it yet again. In the same way, no matter how obvious it may appear, if you are overly anxious to develop, you will frequently neglect market dynamics. It happens time and time again.

LAND COST

Where analytic sloppiness costs you, as a developer, is in the price you pay to purchase the development site. Based on the faulty trend analysis, you believe you will receive $46 per leasable square foot for your office space when it is completed in Year 7. In your haste to take advantage of this "great opportunity," you may overpay for land. Recall that your original analysis indicated that you would pay about $30 per building gross square foot for the land. To assure that you are not outbid for the "can't miss" development site, you submit a higher bid for the land, raising your development costs. When market rents turn out to be $38, rather than $46 per leasable foot, your realized return falls below your 10% return on cost threshold.

You must always carefully calculate what you can afford to pay for a development site as a function of the market environment and your required expected return. Just as with replacement rent, you can determine the maximum amount you are able to pay for the development site by making land cost the unknown variable and solving for the maximum you can pay and still receive your targeted 10% return on total development costs. This specific application of back solving is known as **residual land valuation**, and it answers the question "What can I afford to pay for the land given my required yield?"

Continuing the Muk Office Plaza example, as shown in the NOI Calculation section of Figure 11.12, if market rent is $38 per leasable square foot, the expected rent per gross square foot is $25.27, calculated as ($38 * 0.7) * (0.95). At $10 per gross square foot of operating costs, expected NOI per gross square foot is $15.27 ($25.27 – $10). Thus, to achieve the 10% yield, total development cost can be $152.70 per gross square foot.

As shown in the bottom section of Figure 11.12, you can pay up to $32.70 per buildable gross square foot for the development site (given the assumed $120 per gross square foot of hard and soft costs). Note that to the extent you borrow to pay the extra $2.70 per gross foot for the land, your interest costs (hence, your soft costs) will be very modestly higher. Specifically, if you borrow 65% of the total costs at a 6% interest rate for one year, your soft costs will be $0.11 per gross square foot (calculated as $2.70 * 0.65 * 0.06) higher than your original $30 per gross foot soft cost estimate.

FIGURE 11.12

Residual Land Valuation of Muk Office Plaza Development Site

Assumptions
Required Return: 10%
Leasable space (Efficiency %): 70%
Vacancy: 5%
Market Rent: $38.00 per Leasable SF
Effective Rent per Leasable SF: $38.00 * (1 − .05) = $36.10
Operating costs per GSF = $10.00
Soft Costs: $30.00 per GSF
Hard Costs: $90.00 per GSF

NOI Calculation
Rent per GSF = Effective Rent per Leasable SF * (1 − Loss Factor %)
         = $36.10 * (1 − .30) = $25.27

NOI per GSF = Rental Revenues per GSF − Operating Costs per GSF
         = $25.27 − $10.00 = $15.27

Maximum Land Cost Back Solve Calculation
Required Return = NOI / (Soft Costs + Hard Costs + Maximum Land Cost)
Maximum Land Cost = $x

10% = $15.27 / ($30.00 + $90.00 + $x)
10% * ($120 + $x) = $15.27
$12.00 + ($x / 10) = $15.27
($x / 10) = $3.27
Maximum Land Cost per GSF = $x = $32.70

Online Companion Hands On: Complete the formatted, blank version of this Figure 11.12 found in Chapter 6 of the Online Companion for the Assumptions set given at the top of the tab.

As shown in Figure 11.13, if the development site's allowable **Floor Area Ratio (FAR)** is 1, the maximum land price of $32.70 per gross square foot means you can pay $1,424,412 per acre (1 acre = 43,560 square feet; $32.70 * 43,560). If the FAR is 2, you can pay up to $2,848,824 as you can build twice as much square footage, and if the FAR is 0.5 you can only afford to pay up to $712,206.

FIGURE 11.13

Land Price for a 1-Acre Development Site at Differing Floor Area Ratios			
Maximum Land Cost per building GSF	$32.70	$32.70	$32.70
Floor Area Ratio (FAR)	0.5	1	2
Building size	21,780 GSF	43,560 GSF	87,120 GSF
Maximum Price able to pay (Max. Land Cost * GSF)	$712,206	$1,424,412	$2,848,824

Regardless of the landowner's asking price or competing bids, $32.70 per building gross square foot is the most you should be willing to pay for the site in this example. When multiplied by the maximum 100,000 GSF building size the site allows, this equals $3,270,000. This simple backwards arithmetic helps avoid the mistake of overpaying for land.

Do the calculations above mean that land should, or will, be sold for $32.70 per building gross square foot? That is not your decision, as it is up to the landowner. But if you must offer more than $32.70 per building gross square foot, do not do the deal! If you pay more, you are setting yourself up for future self-inflicted punishment. And never forget that the other bidders for the land may be idiots.

AN EXAMPLE: ANOOP COURT

Next let's consider the development budget for a 258-unit multifamily development project, Anoop Court. As shown in Figure 11.14, the budgeted total cost of the project is $30,000,000 or $116,279 per unit. If comparable apartment communities in the market are selling for $95,000 per unit, does it make sense to build? Of course not, as building would destroy value. If you built in this scenario, the cake would be worth less than the cost of the ingredients. You would only build if after careful study you felt that the units were worth at least 15-20% above your cost. Note in Figure 11.14 the % Total column indicates the project percent share of each major cost category: land at roughly 8%, hard costs at roughly 65%, soft costs at roughly 24%, and construction loan interest at roughly 4%. These proportions are illustrative of the general cost category ratios to total project cost that you should expect when underwriting a real estate development transaction. But every deal is unique, presenting its own exceptions. For instance, construction interest is partly a function of how long construction takes. For a 5-year project, construction interest might consume 10% of the total budget. Similarly, if the land is especially "irreplaceable," it could consume up to 35% of the budget.

FIGURE 11.14

Anoop Court Development Sources and Uses of Funds			
SOURCES OF FUNDS	Total	% Total	Per Unit
Equity	7,500,000	25.00%	29,070
Construction Mortgage	22,500,000	75.00%	87,209
Total Sources of Funds	**$30,000,000**	**100.00%**	**$116,279**
USES OF FUNDS	Total	% Total	Per Unit
Land Acquisition	**$2,326,923**	**7.76%**	**$9,019**
Hard Costs			
Rezoning Costs	250,000	0.83%	969
Construction	18,000,000	60.00%	69,767
Contingency	912,500	3.04%	3,537
Total Hard Costs	**$19,162,500**	**63.88%**	**$74,273**
Soft Costs			
Architecture & Engineering	2,250,000	7.50%	8,721
Permits	437,000	1.46%	1,694
Utility Fees	255,000	0.85%	988
Owner Allowances	150,000	0.50%	581
Construction Loan Fee	225,000	0.75%	872
Lending Inspection	50,000	0.17%	194
Transfer/Recordation	259,457	0.86%	1,006
Real Estate Taxes	200,000	0.67%	775
Consultants	575,000	1.92%	2,229
Insurance	23,420	0.08%	91
Marketing	500,000	1.67%	1,938
Furnishings, Fixtures & Equipment	350,000	1.17%	1,357
Borrower Legal	50,000	0.17%	194
Lender Legal	250,000	0.83%	969
Development Overhead	1,000,000	3.33%	3,876
Contingency	657,488	2.19%	2,548
Total Soft Costs	**$7,232,365**	**24.11%**	**$28,032**
Construction Interest	**$1,278,212**	**4.26%**	**$4,954**
Total Uses of Funds	**$30,000,000**	**100.00%**	**$116,279**

HARD COSTS

FIGURE 11.15

Anoop Court Development Hard Costs Budget Summary			
	Budget	% Total	Per Unit
Hard Costs			
Rezoning Costs	250,000	0.83%	969
Construction	18,000,000	60.00%	69,767
Contingency	912,500	3.04%	3,537
Total Hard Costs	**$19,162,500**	**63.88%**	**$74,273**

As discussed in Chapter 10, hard costs are comprised primarily of material, labor, equipment, and contractor fees related to the site and building. They can also include items such as rezoning costs incurred if you want the property to be used in a manner that does not conform to current zoning. Such rezoning not only raises the cost of development, but also raises the risk. This is because it extends the approval process, and there is always a chance that your rezoning request will be denied. Note that you may sometimes see rezoning costs listed as soft costs and architecture and engineering ("A&E") costs listed as hard costs, demonstrating that the exact classification of costs is less critical than being certain to account for all costs.

While hard costs are impacted by the market prices of drywall, steel, and labor, your costs are also a function of **value engineering** and project oversight. Value engineering is the process of reducing construction costs where possible without destroying the value of the final product. Too often, developers incorporate costly features for which tenants are unwilling to pay. Such developments regularly win design awards as their developers go bankrupt.

How do you estimate hard costs? In part by going out and seeing what has been built, what succeeded, what mistakes were made, and by identifying the high-quality but low-cost contractors and vendors, etc. If you are developing a 20,000-square foot building, find out how much similar buildings have cost to construct and study how you can build it cheaper yet better. Generally, you will engage a specialist to estimate these costs, but the better you understand the property type and local market, the potentially more accurate and lower your development hard costs estimate will be.

FORECASTING HARD COSTS

Hard costs are market-specific, as labor costs vary by geography, reflecting each market's supply and demand for specialist contractors and laborers. Hard costs are also determined by the market's union- or non-union status for construction trades and the competitiveness of contractors in bidding for work. Contractor pricing is impacted by the current state of the real estate cycle and how busy the contractor is at the time of the request for bids. Hard costs are also project-specific, as development costs vary across property types and building design.

While every development is one of a kind, and every hard costs budget is unique, it is instructive to see how costs have trended historically on a more generic basis when contemplating how they might change going forward. The Linneman Construction Cost Index (LCCI) reflects a hypothetical building consisting of lumber (5%), concrete (5%), gypsum (10%), iron and steel (10%), labor (50%), and land (20%). Linneman Associates tracks the costs of these components (except land) using producer price indices from the U.S. Bureau of Labor Statistics. For land, Linneman Associates sets the 1995 base value to 100 and assumes that it has increased by CPI (all goods) over time. We then add up the nominal values of the component indices to arrive at the nominal LCCI, which is converted to a real basis using CPI. The LCCI can be plotted on the same graph with the Turner Building Cost Index (TBCI), published by Turner Construction, which tracks the overall cost of construction on a national basis, taking into account major cost categories such as "material prices, labor rates, productivity, and the competitive condition of the marketplace." To compare these on an apples-to-apples basis, as with the LCCI, the TBCI is converted to a real basis using CPI. Figure 11.16 fits a linear trend line to each series. As of the end of 3Q 2021, the Linneman Index is well above trend, while the Turner Index is modestly above trend.

FIGURE 11.16

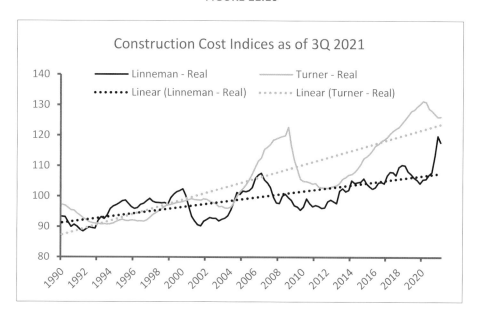

As both of the fitted lines have positive slopes, it is generally correct to assume that as time passes, construction hard costs will continue to increase. But the plotted data series show many steep reversals, so it is not irrational to project that hard costs at the point of signing a construction contract will be notably higher or lower than they are at the point of running a feasibility analysis. As hard costs are typically greater than half of the development budget, it is prudent when assessing development feasibility to assume that at the very least, hard costs will grow at CPI on a compounded basis until the point when the construction contract is signed and executed.

SOFT COSTS

As discussed in Chapter 10, soft costs are indirect development costs. There are many categories of indirect costs, including development fees to fund developer overhead, consultants, and a **contingency reserve**. The contingency reserve is set up because, "I don't know what unexpected event is going to happen, or when, but I had better set something aside, because experience says that I should expect the unexpected." You never know what will go wrong with your development, but something surely will. More complicated developments will generally require larger contingency reserves. Similarly, redevelopments of older properties generally require larger contingency reserves than new developments, as you never know what lurks behind those walls. You will note back in Figure 11.15 that there is also a hard costs contingency line item.

When estimating costs, you need to carefully assess each cost category. This is a tedious yet essential task for even small developments, much less a $30,000,000 development. Figure 11.17 shows top-level soft costs budget categories for Anoop Court.

FIGURE 11.17

Anoop Court Development Soft Costs Budget Summary			
	Budget	% Total	Per Unit
Soft Costs			
Architecture & Engineering	2,250,000	7.50%	8,721
Permits	437,000	1.46%	1,694
Utility Fees	255,000	0.85%	988
Owner Allowances	150,000	0.50%	581
Construction Loan Fee	225,000	0.75%	872
Lending Inspection	50,000	0.17%	194
Transfer/Recordation	259,457	0.86%	1,006
Real Estate Taxes	200,000	0.67%	775
Consultants	575,000	1.92%	2,229
Insurance	23,420	0.08%	91
Marketing	500,000	1.67%	1,938
Furnishings, Fixtures & Equipment	350,000	1.17%	1,357
Borrower Legal	50,000	0.17%	194
Lender Legal	250,000	0.83%	969
Development Overhead	1,000,000	3.33%	3,876
Contingency	657,488	2.19%	2,548
Total Soft Costs	**$7,232,365**	**24.11%**	**$28,032**

TIMING

Your lenders will require you to inject your equity before allowing you to draw upon your loan. Your loan officer will ask the following questions:

- "What is the money for?"
- "How much equity is ahead of my loan?"
- "How large of a loan do you want?"
- "When exactly do you need the money?"
- "When and how do I get paid back?"

"When do you need the money?" and "When am I going to get repaid?" are particularly key questions. Capital sources need to know precisely when you expect to incur the development costs to track the timing of your loan. You do not draw on the loan before you need the money because as soon as you take the money, the interest clock starts ticking on the outstanding principal balance. On the flipside, you do not wait too long because if you have a cash shortage during development, things can get very messy. Construction will grind to a halt if you cannot pay your bills or if you default on your loan, and the entire project will be at risk, if not dead.

The costs during a development project are not the same every week. Typically the **run rate**, that is, how much is being spent daily (or weekly, or monthly) is low in the beginning, rising as construction gets into full swing, and then stabilizing upon completion at your interest-carry cost. Figure 11.18 is a graphical portrayal of the expected timing and relative magnitude of development costs over the life of development.

FIGURE 11.18

DESIGN

Property design is an important aspect that affects both your costs and revenues. How do you decide what floorplans to use? Should you offer one-bedroom or two-bedroom units, or a mix of both? If a mix, in what ratio? Should you put in big kitchens or big bathrooms? A large lobby or a small one? How many elevators are needed? Where are they located? What types and sizes of windows? Should the property include a pool? What type of HVAC system? Plus a million more such questions. The answers are not found in a book or on a magical website. And while architects can design what you need, they will rarely know what you need. So how do you discover the right design? Get in your car (or walk) and visit competitive properties in the area. See and understand what works and why. Constantly visit apartment complexes and tell the leasing agent, "I am interested in a one-bedroom unit. May I see them? What is the rent? What are their best-selling features?" Speak with potential tenants and see what they want and what they value. This will give you an idea of what is selling and what is not. Looking at a floor plan or photos of a kitchen is different from seeing it in person. In short, immerse yourself in the product.

Design affects your loss factor. How efficiently you create space substantially impacts your costs and income. Sometimes design will affect how many rooms you build. Suppose you have 600 square feet of "extra space" after creating the perfect design plan. Perhaps you can turn that space into a studio unit or design one superior two-bedroom unit. Be creative and explore alternative solutions in your head and on paper before committing to construction. It is cheap to throw away paper but very expensive to rectify design flaws once they are built.

CLOSING THOUGHT

What is the most important aspect of a development to analyze? Development cost? Interest rates? The return on cost? Market rent? Your detailed pro forma? The dynamics of the local economy? NPV? IRR? The answer is everything and a lot more. When real money is at stake, you need to research and analyze the factors influencing the risks and opportunities. Asking which "one" to focus on is like asking which characteristic to use in drafting a basketball player. Is it a person's height, arm span, speed, jumping ability, strength, endurance, shooting ability, motivation? To only focus on any one such characteristic would be ludicrous. It is the entire package of skills (and luck) that ultimately determines success on the court. Real estate development is no different. If the project appears to yield negative or minimal returns, walk away. But once a deal "pencils" and you decide to pursue it, everything matters.

Each property type, geographic region, and street location offers specific challenges. What makes a great developer is avoiding properties for which you have no viable design solution and more efficiently delivering better-designed space than your competitors. That is, just like any other business, if you give the customer a product they want faster, cheaper, and better than the competition, you will generally succeed.

 Online Companion Audio Interview: To hear a conversation about this chapter's content, go to the Online Companion and select the link for Chapter 11. Scroll down to the Audio Interview section and listen.

Chapter 12
Real Estate Company Analysis

"People are the ultimate assets."
- Dr. Peter Linneman

Assume you manage FJCL Real Estate Company, which owns 70 operating office properties, and you are asked by your shareholders to value the company and produce a consolidated financial report. To that end, you roll up the 70 property-level pro formas, with each line item reflecting the sum of the revenues, the expenses, and debt across the properties. How will this aggregate pro forma differ from what you saw at the property level?

DIFFERENCES BETWEEN PROPERTY- AND COMPANY-LEVEL CASH FLOWS

The first significant difference is company-level overhead. At the property level there is no line item reflecting the costs of running your company, although the property-level analyses reflect the administrative expenses related to operating each building. However, you must pay your corporate staff, rent corporate office space, and engage outside accountants and lawyers for corporate matters. This overhead is referred to as **corporate general and administrative (G&A)** expense.

Some line items may occur both on the property- and company-level pro formas but will capture different definitions of cash flows. For example, cap ex on a company level reflects both the sum of property cap ex as well as company-level cap ex for desks, chairs, computers, and other things at your corporate offices. Likewise, depreciation on the company pro forma reflects both property-level depreciation as well as depreciation on carpets, lamps, furniture, etc. at your administrative offices.

If you have corporate debt in addition to individual property debt, these corporate-level obligations will not appear on any property pro formas but must appear in the business entity analysis. In contrast to a mortgage, which is secured by a building as collateral, the firm may also have corporate debt that is not secured by real estate. The risk of such unsecured debt reflects the risk of the company's net cash flows, as well as its operating and financial reputation.

There may also be income generated at the company level that is not related to property revenue. For example, the company may derive income from stocks, bonds, or other owned non-real estate assets. Or perhaps you have been able to license your company's name for merchandising. For example, if you license your name to a golf ball or bottled water manufacturer, this income stream will appear at the company level. You may also receive management fees, development fees, and leasing commissions from your properties or third-party properties you service. These examples reveal that you must first roll up the individual property pro forma financial statements and then incorporate corporate-level line items in order to properly analyze your consolidated real estate company.

Figure 12.1 presents the pro forma model for FJCL, whose 70 properties comprise about 12 million square feet of U.S. office space. When FJCL produces an internal consolidated financial analysis, it rolls up the detailed information the firm possesses for each property. In contrast, a "Wall Street" analyst model does not possess the detailed information for each of FJCL's properties necessary to perform a roll-up. Why doesn't the Wall Street analyst just ask FJCL for the detailed data required for each property-level pro forma and then roll them up? Quite simply, FJCL will not provide such detailed private information, as one of its most coveted assets is this detailed information. Armed with this information, competitors could replicate FJCL's marketing and tenant retention strategy. For example, if competitors knew when FJCL's tenants' leases expire and at what rents, they would know exactly when and how to capitalize on that information. Wall Street analysts must rely on publicly-available information to model future performance, but this is not the same quality information that is available for internal purposes. As a result, Wall Street analyses provide relatively imprecise financial descriptions of companies.

FIGURE 12.1

FJCL Company Projection Model ($ in 000s)					
	Year 1	Year 2	Year 3	Year 4	Line
Forecasting Variables					
Existing properties revenue growth	0.0%	5.3%	4.4%	3.3%	A
Acquisitions during period	$0	$11,200	$20,000	$30,000	B
Developments during period	$0	$22,500	$37,800	$50,000	C
Rate of return on new acquisitions	0%	8.5%	8.5%	8.5%	D
Rate of return on new development	0%	8.0%	8.0%	8.0%	E
Dispositions during period	$0	($30,000)	$0	$0	F
Cap rate on dispositions	NA	9.2%	9.0%	9.0%	G
Rents – Existing properties	$287,450	$302,612	$316,097	$331,527	H
Rents – New acquisitions	0	952	1,700	2,550	I
Rents – New developments	0	1,800	3,024	4,000	J
Rents – Dispositions	0	(2,760)	0	0	K
Subtotal	287,450	302,604	320,821	338,077	L
Parking	12,712	11,501	11,501	11,789	M
Other	6,301	6,305	6,308	6,965	N
Property operating expenses	(100,605)	(97,009)	(103,418)	(112,604)	O
Property NOI	**205,858**	**223,401**	**235,213**	**244,227**	P
Fees from noncombined affiliates	1,508	1,609	1,618	1,656	Q
Interest income	4,012	2,502	2,000	2,000	R
General and administrative	(11,564)	(13,113)	(12,912)	(13,645)	S
EBITDA	**199,814**	**214,399**	**225,919**	**234,238**	T
Debt service expense	(72,876)	(82,519)	(82,253)	(84,802)	U
Amortization of financing costs	(500)	0	0	0	V
Depreciation	(57,500)	(68,200)	(69,712)	(73,218)	W
Impairment on securities and assets held for sale	(12,685)	0	0	0	X
Net income before minority interest	56,253	63,680	73,954	76,218	Y
Minority interest in operating partnerships	(7,612)	(10,136)	(10,085)	(10,800)	Z
Minority interest in partially-owned assets	(812)	(500)	(500)	(500)	AA
Income from investment in limited partnerships	6,908	10,712	6,600	6,800	AB
Gain (loss) on sale of real estate	0	8,125	0	0	AC
Net income before pref div and extra items	54,737	71,881	69,969	71,718	AD
Preferred dividends	(5,700)	(5,600)	(4,500)	(4,500)	AE
Net income before extraordinary items	**$49,037**	**$66,281**	**$65,469**	**$67,218**	AF
Performance Indicators					
Rental expense as % of revenues	35.00%	32.06%	32.72%	33.97%	
NOI Growth		8.52%	5.29%	3.83%	
Growth in EBITDA		7.30%	5.37%	3.68%	

COMPANY-LEVEL NET INCOME PROJECTION

The company pro forma in Figure 12.1 displays the forecasted results obtained from applying assumptions from the top block of Forecasting Variables to base year information. Let's examine a few of the key forecasting variables that are used to arrive at company-level net income.

Existing Properties Revenue Growth

Forecasted rent growth on existing owned properties is driven by the assumptions in the "Existing properties revenue growth" line at the top of the projection (Line A). Commingled rents from existing operating assets are shown in the "Rents – Existing properties" line item (H). Absent detailed lease information, Wall Street analysts can only make educated guesses of future rental growth that in the long run are roughly equal to expected inflation. There is absolutely no chance that FJCL will actually achieve such smooth rental growth. This vividly demonstrates how detailed lease information enhances careful real estate analysis. Without such information, Wall Street simply performs "bubble gum company" analysis. Such analysis, when well done, works best for apartments and hotels, as they have short-term leases. However, this type of analysis is less suited for office, warehouse, and retail properties, where long-term leases determine the timing of revenue changes.

Acquisitions and Developments and Rates of Return

Growth beyond what can be achieved at existing properties can be generated via acquisitions and development. As FJCL acquires properties, it adds both revenues and expenses. FJCL also develops new properties that generate additional income and expenses. For example, $11.2 million is FJCL's estimate of their acquisitions during Year 2. Will $11.2 million be the actual amount? Of course not. It is merely an educated guess. If they acquire more than expected, the line item "Rents – New acquisitions" (I) will be higher than the pro forma, and vice versa. Similarly, if FJCL develops more properties than their $22.5 million estimate for Year 2, the line item "Rents – New developments" (J) will be higher than currently projected.

In addition to the amount of acquisition and development activity expected, you need to project the return and future income generated by these activities. Applying the "Rate of return on new acquisitions" (D) and "Rate of return on new development" (E) assumptions to the forecasted level of acquisitions and developments, and using assumptions about FJCL's cost structure, you forecast the expected rental income and operating costs associated with expansion activities. These amounts show up in the two "Rents – New" lines (I and J), and net (of disposition-related) amounts show up in the "Parking," "Other," and "Property operating expenses" lines M, N and O.

Dispositions During the Period

The "Dispositions during period" assumptions line item (F) represents the expected property sales activity of FJCL, which will impact expected future cash flows. Disposition activity is illustrated in Year 2 of the pro forma with the sale of property valued at $30 million. When a disposition occurs, FJCL receives cash proceeds from the sale as an immediate cash inflow. This is captured in the "Gain (loss) on sale of real estate" line (AC). But after the property is sold, it generates no future NOI, lowering expected future rental income, which is reflected in the negative value in the "Rents – Dispositions" line (K). Dispositions also lower operating costs, interest payments on secured debt, and depreciation associated with the properties sold, and this is reflected in the associated line items on a net basis.

Below the "Property operating expenses" line (O), we arrive at the aggregate "Property NOI" line (P). Property NOI is the rental revenue from existing and net new properties, plus any ancillary property income, minus property operating costs. Below the Property NOI line item, the calculated subtotals and net amounts will reflect the impact of corporate-level items.

Fees from Noncombined Affiliates

The first corporate item is "Fees from noncombined affiliates" (Q). FJCL corporate receives fees from certain partners and co-investors for managing properties, as FJCL owns 25% of several properties they manage, with unrelated investors owning the remaining shares of each. The fees they derive for such management services are reflected here.

EBITDA

A company's **EBITDA** is its earnings before interest, tax, depreciation and amortization. EBITDA (row T) is calculated as Property NOI plus noncombined affiliate fee income, plus interest income from non-real estate assets such as bonds, minus company-level G&A expenses. The "Interest income" and "General and administrative" lines sit directly above EBITDA in rows R and S, respectively. It is important to remember that EBITDA is not the same as Property NOI.

Debt Service Expense

After calculating EBITDA, you need to deduct the cash flows related to financing. The company's total debt payments are the sum of the interest and principal payments made for each existing property mortgage, as well as payments on any unsecured corporate debt and lines of credit, plus the debt service payments associated with additional debt the company expects to undertake for new developments and net (of dispositions) acquisitions. In addition, some of the existing debt will mature. Therefore, you need to estimate how much new debt and refinancing the company will undertake and at what terms. You must remember to incorporate interest payments for existing and future corporate-level debt. This is all summed in row U, "Debt service expense."

Amortization and Depreciation and Impairments

"Amortization of financing costs" (i.e., loan origination fees) in row V and "Depreciation" (W) on existing assets, newly acquired and developed properties, and corporate assets like chairs, desks, computers, etc. are both deducted from EBITDA. Note that you must include depreciation on anticipated future cap ex and TIs, net of the discontinued depreciation of any assets sold.

Cap ex occurs not only at existing properties but also at newly developed and acquired properties and corporate assets. This amount must be adjusted for disposed assets. It is common to assume that a certain percent of gross revenues will be required for cap ex, with the percentage varying by property type, geography, age, and other factors. This method will not fully capture the realities of cap ex but is generally the best that one can do.

Deducted below depreciation is the "Impairment on securities and assets held for sale" (X), which is the impaired value of any stocks and bonds and other assets (including properties) whose fair value is less than the net carrying value shown on the company's balance sheet. This is the final negative adjustment to EBITDA before getting to the "Net income before minority interest" line (Y).

Minority Interest

Generally Accepted Accounting Principles (GAAP) state that for operating partnerships and assets in which the company owns a controlling share, the company must report those items on the balance sheet as if they hold 100% ownership in those assets. Given the company really owns less than 100%, management must make an adjustment to reflect the portion of operating partnership and asset income they receive. Similarly, unconsolidated minority position income also needs to be added. These adjustments are shown in the two "Minority interest" lines Z and AA.

After deducting minority interest items, adding income from "Income in investment in limited partnerships" (AB) and including gains (losses) on sale of properties (AC), the last adjustment in determining company earnings is the deduction of company "Preferred dividend" payments (AE). When this is done, we arrive at the company's pre-tax income, "Net income before extraordinary items" (AF).

VALUE OF A COMPANY

The value of a real estate company can be greater or less than the value of its properties. This is because when you own a company, you own both its properties and its management. If management adds value beyond the value of the properties, the value of the company is greater than the properties. The converse is also true.

While all management believes they add value, this is simply not the case. As an example, consider properties in England which generally have a very low-risk lease structure. Specifically, the leases run for 25 years, are triple net, the tenant is responsible for all cap ex, and tenants must return the property in its original condition or better. The tenant can escape the lease only by liquidation bankruptcy, and rental rates are adjusted every five years to market rents. However, rents can only be adjusted upward upon these reviews. This means if market rents have fallen since the last rent review, rents remain at their current level for the next five years; if rents have risen, they are adjusted upward to market rates.

A company which owns a large portfolio of properties leased in this manner to high-credit tenants provides a very safe income stream. Yet British property companies generally trade at substantial discounts to their property values. Why? It is because the management of many of these public companies often destroys value by reinvesting these relatively safe cash streams in high-risk developments. By investing in high-risk developments, management believes that they are creating value. But in fact, they may be destroying value, as investors who desire low-risk cash streams avoid these property companies for fear that their safe cash streams will be lost in high-risk developments. In the extreme, imagine the discount at which a government bond fund would trade if the cash flows from these bonds were invested in start-up biotech firms.

In the case of real estate, particularly when it is well-leased, of high quality, and well-located, management's value-added potential is relatively limited. After all, how much can you improve the value of a fully-leased building which has the U.S. government as its tenant for the next 20 years? Sure, you can control your costs a little better and exploit favorable refinancing opportunities, but compared to typical operating businesses, there is less potential upside for value added by management.

The primary ways in which management can add value beyond the properties are: executing strategies involving substantial and efficient lease-up; property repositioning; development; opportunistic acquisitions or dispositions; operational cost controls; and the ability to take advantage of favorable financing windows. A high value-added real estate strategy successfully executed, such as development or redevelopment, can add about 15-20% in value. A well-executed cost control and refinancing strategy for a fully-leased building can probably add 5-15% to value. While these margins are small compared with businesses such as high-tech companies, when executed with leverage and on a large asset base, the value enhancements are substantial. For example, if the value added by efficient management of publicly-traded real estate companies is 10% of their $400 billion asset value, this amounts to $40 billion in value enhancement. Similarly, on a $1 billion private equity fund, a 20% value-added margin represents $200 million.

FUNDS FROM OPERATIONS

As depreciation and gains or losses on the sale of real estate make a huge impact on reporting of Net income before extraordinary items, the business has adopted two non-audited measurements to better reflect the real-time "free cash flow" of real estate companies from their ongoing core operations. **Funds from Operations (FFO)** is the first of these two metrics, and it reflects funds from operations available to equity owners on a pre-income tax basis.

FFO is equal to Net income before extraordinary items, but before minority interest income, gain or loss on sale of real estate, depreciation, amortization and any impairments on assets held for sale. To compute FFO from Net income, we add these values back to Net Income, except for gains on sale of real estate, which we deduct. We note that FFO is not perfect, as it fails to reflect cap ex requirements, tenant improvements, and leasing commissions that are a normalized part of operations. Consequently, two companies with the same FFO may have very different free cash flows, as their cap ex, TIs, and leasing commissions may differ significantly. The company FFO calculation for FJCL is shown in Figure 12.2.

FIGURE 12.2

FJCL Company FFO Calculation ($ in 000s)				
	Year 1	Year 2	Year 3	Year 4
Net income before extraordinary items	49,037	66,281	65,469	67,218
Minority interest in operating parterships (OPs)	7,612	10,136	10,085	10,800
(Gain) loss on sale of real estate/other adjustments	0	(8,125)	0	0
Depreciation (incl. OP depreciation) and amortization	58,000	68,200	69,712	73,218
Impairment on assets held for sale	12,685	0	0	0
Funds from Operations (FFO)	$127,334	$136,492	$145,266	$151,236

ADJUSTED FUNDS FROM OPERATIONS

Adjusted Funds from Operations (Adjusted FFO; AFFO), also known as **Funds Available for Distribution (FAD)** or **Cash Available for Distribution (CAD)**, is the second of these two non-audited metrics. AFFO is used to measure a real estate company's cash available for distribution to shareholders without a deterioration of its asset base. It is regarded as a closer measure of cash flow or economic profitability than FFO and is calculated as FFO less expected recurring cap ex, TIs, and leasing commissions, with adjustment for "straight-line rent" and Financial Accounting Standards 141/142/143.

GAAP reporting requires that rent from leases is straight-lined (i.e., the total rent over the lease term is divided by the term, and the resulting average rent is used as the reported rent for each year). As a result, reported rents from leases that that have contractual escalations are over-stated in the early years, and under-stated in the later years. The straight-line adjustment removes this artificial distortion to better reveal cash flow.

Lastly, there are adjustments made for Financial Accounting Standards 141/142/143. These adjustments require the company to account for: above or below market leases of newly acquired assets, goodwill and other intangible assets from acquisitions, and the retirement (and associated costs of retirement) of tangible long-lived assets. Figure 12.3 shows the AFFO calculation for FJCL.

FIGURE 12.3

FJCL Company AFFO/FAD Calculation ($ in 000s)				
	Year 1	Year 2	Year 3	Year 4
Funds from Operations (FFO)	**127,334**	**136,492**	**145,266**	**151,236**
Cap Ex, TIs and Leasing Commissions	(15,619)	(21,025)	(23,014)	(20,736)
Straight-line rent adjustment and FAS adjustments	(6,616)	(7,900)	(7,900)	(7,900)
Adjusted Funds from Operations (AFFO/FAD)	**$105,099**	**$107,567**	**$114,352**	**$122,600**

DCF VALUATION

When evaluating the value of a real estate company, you value the company's ability to generate recurring cash streams. This is no different from valuing any other company. Thus, you forecast future cash streams for the company, including growth in net cash flow derived from net acquisitions, refinancings, and development, and discount these future cash streams at the appropriate discount rate. The discount rate will generally be modestly lower than that for individual properties, particularly for a large company, as the law of large numbers makes the expected returns statistically more likely for the company's portfolio than for any individual property. The value of this company reflects the cash flow-generating ability of existing assets, as well as management's ability to add value. To obtain the value of the equity of the company, deduct the value of liabilities. Figure 12.4 displays the estimated FJCL equity value via DCF of $1.34 billion.

FIGURE 12.4

FJCL Company Valued by Simple DCF ($ in 000s)				
	Year 1	Year 2	Year 3	Year 4
EBITDA	199,814	214,399	225,919	234,238
Cap Ex, TIs & Leasing Commissions	(15,619)	(21,025)	(23,014)	(20,736)
Operating Cash Flows	184,195	193,374	202,905	213,502
Sale Cash Flow *(Year 4 Op. CF / .08)*				2,668,772
Total Cash Flow	184,195	193,374	202,905	2,882,274
PV of Cash Flows at 11.00%	2,369,894			
Average Debt Outstanding (in Year 4)	(1,027,810)			
Equity Value	$1,342,084			

In Figure 12.4, the equity value is calculated by first determining the expected cash flows of FJCL. If FJCL does not generate enough cash to cover all expenses, it will not be able to pay its operating obligations. To approximate the cash flows, we take EBITDA and adjust for expected cap ex, TIs, and leasing commissions. The expected cash flows are discounted by an 11% rate, while the terminal value is calculated using an 8% cash flow cap rate (derived from the Gordon Model using an 11% discount rate and a 3% growth rate). This residual value is then converted into present value at an 11% discount rate. Note that EBITDA accounts for the value of management by incorporating the income generated from new acquisitions, dispositions, and capital improvements.

If you value FJCL without accounting for future acquisitions, developments, refinancings, and dispositions, you will be ignoring the potential value added by management. If management chooses lucrative acquisitions, prudent dispositions, and profitable development projects which contribute to the growth of profits, they add value to the firm. This is reflected via the "Rents – New acquisitions," "Rents – New developments," and "Rents – Dispositions" lines (I, J and K in Figure 12.1). With the inclusion of these line items, the firm's value will be greater than the value of the existing portfolio of assets. If you do not take these factors into account, the equity value will be less than the $1.34 billion amount indicated.

CAP RATE VALUATION

Capping Year 4 stabilized NOI, adjusted for cap ex, at an 8 cap yields an equity value of $1.43 billion, as shown in Figure 12.5. In solving for the equity value, the debt in Year 4 is subtracted from Year 4 "Capped Stabilized NOI." Realize that the cap rate (or multiple) approach and the DCF analysis are both reliant on the risk and growth assumptions for the company. You examine recent market comparables when selecting the cap rate to use in your calculations. The cap rate approach is a good approximation for the equity value of the firm. Currently, the cap rate/multiple approach values FJCL at a 6.62% premium over the DCF valuation, providing a reasonable level of confidence given that both valuations are in the same ballpark.

FIGURE 12.5

FJCL Company Valued by Cap Rate ($ in 000s)		
Stabilized EBITDA		234,238
Less: Cap Ex, TIs and LCs		(20,736)
Stabilized NOI in Year 4		213,502
Cap Rate (r – g)	(11% – 3%)	8.0%
Capped Stabilized NOI		2,668,772
Debt in Year 4		(1,237,790)
Equity Value		$1,430,982
Equity Value with DCF		*$1,342,084*
% Difference between Equity Values		*6.62%*

NET ASSET VALUE

Net Asset Value (NAV) is a commonly-used approach to valuing a real estate company. This approach assumes that management neither adds nor subtracts value. Figure 12.6 presents a calculation of NAV for FJCL.

As displayed in Figure 12.6, there are a number of value sources in the company. First are its existing properties. Their aggregate value is estimated by capping (stabilized) NOI, which simply assumes that, on average, the NOI for all properties is stabilized. In the case of FJCL, a 9% cap rate is used.

The company may also derive net income from property management or development services that are being offered to third parties. The value of these income streams is achieved by applying a market multiple to the stabilized net income generated from each business activity. These activities will merit different multiples from those used to value the real estate. For example, property management services may have a 2-5x valuation multiple, while property ownership merits a 9-11x multiple. The management service multiple is lower because management contracts are usually cancelable on 30-day notice. If you had a development-for-fee or a management-for-fee business, you would similarly value each net income stream separately.

In the case of FJCL, there are 3 other income streams to which multiples are applied: Parking (4.7x); Management fees from noncombined affiliates (4.8x); and Other (5.6x).

Total company value is the sum of: the capitalized value of the properties and all other income; the capitalized value of the development business; the value of land; and your cash position. The latter 3 are shown in the "Add other assets" section of Figure 12.6. To calculate NAV, you deduct the value of the company's debt and other liabilities. FJCL's NAV is $1.43 billion, 6.93% higher than the DCF valuation estimate of $1.34 billion.

FIGURE 12.6

FJCL Company NAV Components and Calculation ($ in 000s)	
	Baseline
Property Ownership Cap Rate	**9.00%**
NOI Stabilized in Year 4	244,227
Value of property portfolio	**$2,713,631**
Add value of other income:	
Parking	11,789
Parking Multiple	**4.70x**
Fees from Noncombined Affiliates	1,656
Fees from Noncombined Affiliates Multiple	**4.80x**
Other	6,965
Other Multiple	**5.60x**
Value of other income	**$102,361**
Add other assets:	
Development project underway	50,000
Land held for future development or sale	6,762
Other investments in unconsol. subsid. (Year 4)	6,800
Cash and equivalents	8,452
Other miscellaneous assets	10,142
Value of other assets	**$82,156**
Gross value of assets	**$2,898,148**
Deduct:	
Total liabilities	(1,447,031)
Preferred stock	(16,000)
Net Asset Value	**$1,435,117**
Equity Value with DCF	*$1,342,084*
% Difference between NAV and DCF	*6.93%*

 Online Companion Hands On: Complete the formatted, blank version of this Figure 12.6 found in Chapter 12 of the Online Companion. Given the Assumptions provided, what is the company NAV?

Unfortunately, NAV is not as precise as it seems, as it is very sensitive to the cap rates and multiples chosen to convert the incomes into value. As Figure 12.7 reveals, a 50-bp shift in the cap rate alters FJCL's value considerably. Lowering the property cap rate by 50 bps, the NAV becomes roughly $1.6 billion, and raising the property cap rate by the same increment decreases the NAV to roughly $1.3 billion. Shifts in the multiples used to value other income streams impact value similarly. Since no one knows the exact cap rate and multiples to use for these different value sources, two intelligent and meticulous analysts could disagree by a small amount and the NAVs would differ substantially. Further, the NAV approach ignores the value of management (by design).

FIGURE 12.7

FJCL Company NAV at Three Property Cap Rates ($ in 000s)			
	Baseline	Higher Value	Lower Value
Property Ownership Cap Rate	9.00%	**8.50%**	**9.50%**
NOI Stabilized in Year 4	244,227	244,227	244,227
Value of property portfolio	**$2,713,631**	**$2,873,256**	**$2,570,808**
Add value of other income:	*(Same in all cases)*		
Parking	*11,789*		
Parking Multiple	*4.70x*		
Fees from Noncombined Affiliates	*1,656*		
Fees from Noncombined Affiliates Multiple	*4.80x*		
Other	*6,965*		
Other Multiple	*5.60x*		
Value of other income	***$102,361***		
Add other assets:	*(Same in all cases)*		
Development project underway	*50,000*		
Land held for future development or sale	*6,762*		
Other investments in unconsol. subsid. (Year 4)	*6,800*		
Cash and equivalents	*8,452*		
Other miscellaneous assets	*10,142*		
Value of other assets	***$82,156***		
Gross value of assets	**$2,898,148**	**$3,057,773**	**$2,755,325**
Deduct:	*(Same in all cases)*		
Total liabilities	*1,447,031*		
Preferred stock	*16,000*		
Net Asset Value	**$1,435,117**	**$1,594,743**	**$1,292,295**
DCF Equity Value	*$1,342,084*	*$1,342,084*	*$1,342,084*
% Difference between NAV and DCF	*6.93%*	*18.83%*	*(3.71%)*
% Difference from baseline NAV		*11.12%*	*(9.95%)*

The only way you will ever know what the "correct" cap rates or multiples are for the firm is to liquidate it, as it is only worth as much as somebody is willing to pay for it. Liquidating a firm could take 6 months to 2 years, depending on the size of the company. When selling the firm, you would also be selling management (for better or worse).

NAV also fails to reflect hidden tax, debt, and environmental liabilities. For example, pre-payment penalties associated with debt are not deducted. Nor are substantial capital gains taxes that must often be paid by the company upon sale. Also, there may be environmental liabilities or employee severance contracts associated with liquidation. As a result, if calculated NAV is different from the market value of the assets by more than 10-15%, there is a possibility that the assets are substantially over- or underpriced. But if the estimated NAV is within 10-15% of the market value, the market value is probably a better indicator of value.

CLOSING THOUGHT

What makes a property company potentially more valuable than the value of their properties? In short, it is the ability to squeeze even more income out of these properties than competitors (who establish market values) and the ability to find and successfully execute value enhancing transactions. That is, people! When you own a pool of properties, you only have the claim on those assets, while when you own the company, you also own the claim on the creativity and execution skills of the people at the company. These people may either create or destroy value. So, when approaching the valuation of a property company, you must look to the value of all its assets, including the people.

 Online Companion Audio Interview: To hear a conversation about this chapter's content, go to the Online Companion and select the link for Chapter 12. Scroll down to the Audio Interview section and listen.

Chapter 13
Distressed Real Estate Loan and Bankruptcy Basics

"Have both a professional and private life to balance the ups and downs of each."
- Dr. Peter Linneman

What happens if a borrower is unable to make the scheduled debt service payments or repay the loan at maturity? Lenders and borrowers have several options available to them in these distressed situations. This is a highly technical and ever-changing area of law, and this chapter is simply an introduction to the basic concepts.

DISTRESSED LOAN RESOLUTION OPTIONS

A mortgage becomes **delinquent** when the agreed upon debt service payments have ceased being made when they are due. Delinquency is an outcome that lenders generally expect to occur on 3% or fewer of their loans when the economy is healthy. Over the last 30 years, delinquency rates have spiked for commercial real estate mortgages to as high as almost 12% in bad economic periods. If after a certain period, the borrower fails to **cure** the delinquency by making all missed payments to bring the loan payments **current**, they are in **default** on the loan, and the loan is referred to as a **non-performing loan (NPL)**.

Loan default certifies distress with the source of the debt service payments. This is likely due to weakness in the tenant rental stream. We will discuss the options available in the U.S. for resolving loan default situations, one of which involves staying the course, while others involve dissolution of the lender-borrower relationship. In all cases, the lender seeks to be made whole for what the borrower owes. It is said that Rule number 1 of lending is "Do not lose the money," and Rule number 2 is "Do not forget Rule number 1."

Loan restructuring

The loan was underwritten with a happy ending, not a tragic one. If lender underwriting standards were strict, it is presumed all the applications with even a moderate probability of ending badly were rejected. As such, there is a case to be made for staying the course with the borrower and holding the loan to maturity. What are the circumstances that led to the default? Can the loan be **restructured** so that it can once again be current and ultimately repaid? If the borrower is a quality operator and the economy is recovering, it is likely they will be able to service a restructured loan. It can be tricky to restore the debt service stream, as finding new tenants to quickly soak up tens or hundreds of thousands of vacant square feet for any property type takes time, even in a strong economy. In addition, borrower and lender relationships become strained during default.

If the lender is committed to holding the loan, they can restructure the interest rate and/or the amortization term to reduce the monthly debt service payment to make it affordable to the borrower. This **loan modification** can be done temporarily and undone once the ability to pay in full (per the original terms) has been restored. Both lowering the interest rate and extending the amortization term would naturally provide the most relief to the borrower.

Dissolution options

If the lender cannot or does not desire to restructure, they may allow the borrower to pay off the loan at a discount (and the lender writes off the loss and moves on). Alternatively, the borrower may give the property back to the lender to liquidate (writing off any loss), or the borrower may sell the property to pay off the lender. A sale that does not generate sufficient proceeds to pay back the full owed amount is known as a **short sale**. Short sales require lender approval.

Lenders are not in the business of owning and operating real estate – they are in the business of loaning capital and making a spread on the interest they charge. When they foreclose on and take back a property for which they have a loan, the loan disappears from the asset side of their balance sheet, and the property appears on the liability side as **real estate owned (REO)** . The REO department of banks is essentially a loan graveyard, staffed by REO specialists charged with liquidating the properties rapidly, after which the bank writes off any losses on the associated loans. As an alternative to foreclosure and liquidation, lenders may entertain a cash offer from a **distressed loan investor** whose business model is buying loans from banks at discounts to the unpaid principal balances. Selling a loan to an investor keeps the debt in place on the property, makes the investor the new note holder, and legally removes the lender from the equation. The lender will still write off any loss on the loan.

BANKRUPTCY

A final option available to resolve a bad loan situation is for the borrower to file for **bankruptcy**. Bankruptcy provides legal protection for borrowers from their creditors. Bankruptcy law provides a structured mechanism by which debtors unable to meet the terms of their credit agreements can attempt to resolve their debts and other liabilities. It can make sense for mortgage borrowers to file for bankruptcy if there is no near-term way for them to restore the debt service stream, or if, as happens during capital crunches, they are unable to refinance their debt upon maturity or to pay off the loan via cash funds or sale of the asset.

A first lien real estate lender has contractual rights to the cash flow and the property as collateral throughout the life of the loan. For example, a senior lender generally has the right to **foreclose** on the property if the borrower violates the terms of the loan agreement. In foreclosure, a lender with a first security position can theoretically take control of the property and auction it off. The first payments from the sale go to the government to settle any outstanding tax or environmental claims against the asset, as the government always has a "super position." A distressing element of bankruptcy is that a bankruptcy sale is treated as the sale of the asset, hence triggering capital gains taxes for the borrower, even though the debtor generally receives no income from this liquidation. Imagine having to come up with millions of dollars in tax payments but having no source of income with which to pay these taxes! This is the so-called "phantom income" problem.

Remaining sale proceeds are used to pay the lawyers and brokers hired in the foreclosure and sale process. Finally, the lender theoretically receives all principal and interest owed to them plus related expenses. After these obligations are satisfied, any money left goes to repay the owners of the next priority position. This process continues until all **junior creditors** (those with positions subordinate to the senior debt) are paid what they are owed, assuming there are sufficient net proceeds received from the sale. The last party to receive proceeds from the sale, assuming there is any excess beyond the repayments made, are the common equity holders (i.e., the residual interest holders).

Bankruptcy law varies significantly across countries as well as across states in the U.S. For instance, Canada and the U.K. are extremely unforgiving to a defaulting borrower. At one time, borrowers in the U.K. who were unable to meet loan agreements were considered criminals, as not fulfilling a loan agreement was viewed as a form of fraud. In the U.K. today, borrowers do not go to jail for violating the terms of a loan agreement, but the bankrupt borrower will be quickly replaced by a trustee who operates the entity with the sole objective of maximizing recovery for the debt holders. This creates a strong bankruptcy framework for lenders.

In contrast, the "defaulting criminals" that fled the U.K. came to America and established a more borrower-friendly system. Their view was that their bankruptcy was not due to their malfeasance but, rather, due to unexpected temporary setbacks. Thus, historically the United States has had a relatively forgiving bankruptcy framework for borrowers. There are two basic types of U.S. bankruptcies, Chapter 7 and Chapter 11, named after the respective sections of the IRS Code. In a **Chapter 7 bankruptcy**, the debtor ceases all operations, goes completely out of business, and a trustee is appointed to sell the property and other assets to pay off obligations with sale proceeds. **Chapter 11 bankruptcy** law was created in 1978 to formalize the business reorganization framework. Chapter 11 law codified the view that reorganization of the business is generally preferred to liquidation. As such, the U.S. Chapter 11 bankruptcy process attempts to conserve going-concern value, generally requiring a consensual plan of reorganization. This reflects the nation's social policy to protect equity holders from temporary setbacks. These laws are the underpinning of all contracts, including mortgages, leases, and labor contracts. As such, it is incumbent for management to use the full force of bankruptcy law to protect equity owners from setbacks.

Perhaps not surprisingly in view of this history, one of the key provisions of the U.S. bankruptcy code is that once a borrower enters into Chapter 11 bankruptcy, secured lenders cannot immediately seize their collateral. This is why people refer to "seeking bankruptcy protection." Why, if the loan document says the lender can seize their collateral, are they unable to do so? Simply stated, bankruptcy law trumps the loan contract. Once U.S. bankruptcy is declared, bankruptcy law effectively dictates the terms of the loan agreement.

U.S. bankruptcy law allows the defaulting borrower to remain in control of business decisions (subject to bankruptcy court oversight) until the point is reached when the bankruptcy court rules that either a successful reorganization has occurred or that a successful reorganization is impossible. Instead of assigning a trustee to work on behalf of the lenders, U.S. bankruptcy law works with the borrower in an attempt to regenerate value beyond liabilities. To this end, U.S. bankruptcy law provides a 180-day exclusivity period, during which time only the debtor is allowed to submit a reorganization plan. This exclusivity period will be extended beyond 180 days as long as the bankruptcy court determines that a reorganization by the borrower is not futile. As a result, the defaulting borrower is entrusted with creating a plan to save the company for at least 180 days and perhaps several years. This framework is much less lender-friendly than U.K. bankruptcy law.

BORROWERS' RIGHTS

U.S. bankruptcy law also allows for **debtor in possession (DIP) financing**. This allows the defaulting borrower to subordinate existing debt claims to new debt which is taken on to operate the business while it attempts a successful reorganization. For instance, there could be a case where a property owner is unable to meet debt payments in the middle of a value-add lease up because they lose a major tenant who stops paying rent. If the property owner seeks bankruptcy protection, the senior lender cannot unilaterally seize and auction off the project. The property owner may be able to obtain additional debt senior to existing debt to help fund needed tenant improvements and leasing commissions. DIP financing is possible (with the blessing of the bankruptcy court) even if existing senior loan documents expressly prohibit any debt being senior. Again, bankruptcy law trumps contract law. The theory is that the former first mortgagee is protected, in spite of subordination of their debt, as completing the lease up adds sufficient value to enhance the owner's ability to service the debt and pay back the original loan. But while this is the intent, it is not always the outcome.

Under Chapter 11 bankruptcy protection, the borrower does not have to pay interest on their loans, as bankruptcy law again takes precedence over loan contracts. As a result, an overleveraged company facing significant interest payments can achieve substantial cash flows while in bankruptcy. Under the oversight of the bankruptcy court, the company can channel this money towards salaries, TIs, leasing commissions, capital expenditures, vendors, and other non-lenders to keep the business operating. Under Chapter 11 protection, the borrower also has the right to reinstate their mortgage at the original interest rate. This is particularly advantageous to the borrower in an environment where interest rates have risen since the loan was originally made.

Bankruptcy law also takes precedence over key lease terms. For example, a retailer called Modest may have signed a lease for $5 per square foot that runs an additional 15 years, with two renewal options prohibiting subleasing. Under Chapter 11 bankruptcy protection, Modest can vacate the space and sublease to Kindergym Playzone for $8 per square foot, yielding a $3 per square foot profit for Modest on the lease. Under Chapter 11 bankruptcy protection, Modest has the right to sublease as long as the sublease agreement is deemed reasonable by the bankruptcy court. This is despite the fact that the landlord may have a lease provision stating that Modest's lease is terminated if the company goes into bankruptcy. Again, bankruptcy law trumps all. Lease terms prohibiting subleasing and causing lease termination upon tenant bankruptcy are unenforceable without the bankruptcy court's agreement, as the lease is viewed as a tenant asset, and it is the bankruptcy court's job to supervise the attempt to maximize the value of all assets.

An office tenant, Alexis LTD, may have a lease with rent due on the 16th of the month. If Alexis goes into Chapter 11 bankruptcy on the 15th, they can decide to not pay rent while under bankruptcy protection, and the landlord has no immediate eviction right. Further, in an attempt to achieve solvency, Alexis can walk away from its obligations, irrespective of the lease document. Also, bankruptcy law limits landlord back rent collections to a maximum of roughly 18 months.

Rockefeller Center in the 1990s offers a glimpse into the cold realities of the U.S. bankruptcy process. The lender had a first position against the property for $1.3 billion, secured by the entire property and all its leases. There was roughly $20 million in trade debt and some "slip and fall" insurance claims. The simplicity of the borrower's capital structure in the Rockefeller Center situation meant a "fast" foreclosure was possible. Yet, even in this case it took roughly 14 months to consummate the foreclosure. With more complex capital and lease structures, this process would have taken considerably longer, with $50,000-$100,000 in legal and advisory bills piling up monthly. In contrast, if Rockefeller Center was in the U.K., the foreclosure would have been completed in a few weeks (as was the case with Canary Wharf).

BANK OF AMERICA VERSUS LA SALLE STREET PARTNERS

This is an important case for real estate bankruptcy, illustrating several key aspects of bankruptcy law. In this 1999 U.S. Supreme Court case, La Salle Street Partners defaulted on the mortgage secured by a property which was located between two other properties they owned. For operating reasons, La Salle wanted to retain the defaulting property. While in bankruptcy, La Salle proposed a plan of reorganization under which they recognized the **absolute priority rule**, which states that no junior creditor will receive consideration until all senior creditors are paid in full, and no equity holder will receive consideration until all creditors have been paid in full (including interest). La Salle proposed contributing fresh capital in exchange for the 100% ownership of the property as it exited bankruptcy. This is called the **new value exception** to the absolute priority rule.

In this case, there was a significant **deficiency claim**. That is, the value of the property was not sufficient to repay the entirety of the creditors' outstanding debt. If the debtor classified the deficiency claim as **unsecured debt** (debt not backed by an underlying asset), the debtor could never receive either the 51% creditor approval or the two-thirds creditor class approval which are necessary to obtain court approval for a reorganization plan. This is because there are usually very few unsecured creditors for real estate. Furthermore, if the debtor classified the deficiency claim as unsecured debt, it would allow the deficiency claimants to overpower the other unsecured creditor class members, making it very difficult to achieve the necessary reorganization approvals. To circumvent this problem, the debtor placed the deficiency claim in a separate class from the unsecured creditors, while offering the unsecured creditors 93 cents for every dollar owed, which virtually assured acceptance by a sufficient number of creditor classes. The debtor offered only 3 cents on the dollar for the deficiency claim.

Not surprisingly, the secured lender objected to this plan. The debtor tried to use the **cram down rule** against the sole dissenting party, as the bankruptcy code allows the bankruptcy court to force a dissenting party to accept a plan.

One of the questions in the case was whether the debtor could classify the deficiency claim as a separate class rather than as unsecured debt. The second issue was the new value exception. The bankruptcy court, the U.S. District Court, and the U.S. 7th Circuit Court all confirmed the reorganization plan. However, the U.S. Supreme Court overturned their rulings. The Supreme Court ruled that the original equity owners had no right to contribute this new value simply because they were the original equity holders. This ruling reduced the availability of the new value exception to current owners. The court held that the new value exception requires a "market test." That is, if you want to use the new value exception, you have to offer the new equity position to the market and not simply offer it as the original owner. This market test clearly detracts from the exclusive right of the original equity holder to use the new value exception. Unfortunately, the courts have yet to establish a clear definition of "testing the market."

SECTION 11.11B

Section 11.11B of the bankruptcy code is particularly important for real estate. Most mortgages that enter bankruptcy are **non-recourse mortgages**, which means that the creditor can only look to the property to recoup owed principal and interest. The lender cannot go after the debtor's personal assets to satisfy claims and, thus, cannot file a deficiency claim for insufficient value from the property. However, under Chapter 11 bankruptcy statutes, both recourse and non-recourse lenders are permitted to file for a deficiency claim. Under section 11.11B, the lender can waive its deficiency claim. For example, assume you are a lender with a $10 million mortgage against a building that is only worth $5 million today. Therefore, you have a secured claim of $5 million and an **unsecured deficiency claim** worth $5 million, entitling you to receive settlements as both a secured creditor and an unsecured creditor. As the lender, you can waive your $5 million unsecured deficiency claim, which results in a single $10 million secured claim. However, the return on that claim will only have a present value of $5 million. In other words, the stream of payments promised under the debtor's reorganization will only have a present value of $5 million. So why would you waive the deficiency claim? The primary reason is you believe that the debtor will fail again, in which case you retain your $10 million secured claim. If you accepted the deficiency claim and the property subsequently defaults, you only have a $5 million secured claim. This option is available only under Chapter 11 protection.

CLOSING THOUGHT

Not all real estate transactions go according to plan and have happy endings where all the stakeholders profit. While Chapter 11 bankruptcy provides strategic opportunities unavailable via Chapter 7 liquidation, it is not an easy ride. The bankrupt entity must provide a viable plan for keeping the company alive and deal with the bankruptcy court. Keep in mind your equity holders may lose faith in you and seek your ouster as manager. There is a good chance they will get little if any of their money back. Imagine trying to raise money for future deals after that! Moreover, a bankruptcy situation may generate ill-will with investors, who may feel that you cheated them, even if you didn't. Hence, the effect on your reputation can be substantial. Bankruptcy is a very complicated and highly nuanced legal field and varies wildly across states and countries, with some states providing absolute foreclosure rights and others having no foreclosure law. While the general principles of lending are clear enough, bankruptcy law can change everything. As a borrower, you can use bankruptcy both offensively and defensively, so be sure to understand your rights and restrictions under bankruptcy laws before taking out a loan.

 Online Companion Audio Interview: To hear a conversation about this chapter's content, go to the Online Companion and select the link for Chapter 13. Scroll down to the Audio Interview section and listen.

Chapter 14
Should You Borrow?

"Embrace the 11th Commandment: thou shalt not take yourself so seriously."
- Dr. Peter Linneman

Debt, equity, and property values are inextricably linked, and it is critical to understand the sources of debt and the rationale for and against encumbering a property with a mortgage.

SOURCES OF DEBT CAPITAL

Of the roughly $3.1 trillion in commercial real estate mortgages outstanding, roughly 61% are held by banks, 14% by insurance companies, 13% by asset-backed securities issuers and finance companies, 9% by mortgage REITs, and 3% by government entities. In 1970, before the rise of the **commercial mortgage-backed securities (CMBS)** market, banks provided 49%, while insurance companies provided 30% of the debt capital. In terms of relative risk profile and asset quality, life companies are typically regarded as originating the lowest-risk loans on the highest-quality properties in the market, followed by banks (higher risk, lower quality), and then by CMBS issuers (highest risk, lowest quality).

A real estate entrepreneur seeking debt for a transaction will usually speak with a bank or work with a mortgage broker to assess their alternatives. Debt capital flows to real estate are cyclical, with rising interest rates increasing lender incentives to deploy funds. While senior debt is typically 60%-70% of the capitalization of a real estate transaction, when property values are rising and transaction volume increases, capital flows to real estate swell and lender credit committees raise their first mortgage loan-to-value ratios. In so doing, they have greater financial exposure as a percentage of the current real estate value. In other words, the extent to which one can **leverage** a real estate transaction with debt is generally tied to the current and anticipated future trajectory of real estate pricing. With greater debt flows, property values tend to rise. This tendency creates a self-reinforcing LTV and value mechanism, which pushes values upwards in times of easy money, but downwards when LTVs decline.

THE FOUR REASONS TO USE DEBT IN A TRANSACTION

Now that you are beginning to understand some of the dynamics that exist between a lender and a borrower, ask yourself why someone would borrow to purchase a property. Why would anyone go through all of the negotiations, headaches, and operating restrictions that come with dealing with lenders? There are four primary reasons to borrow:
- You simply do not have enough money to buy the asset.
- Even if you have enough money to purchase the asset, you want to diversify your investments.
- You desire the tax shield that comes with interest payments.
- You seek to enhance the return on your equity.

Let's examine each of these interrelated rationales for borrowing.

Do Not Have Enough Money

The simplest reason to borrow is that you do not have enough money to purchase the asset. You have found the perfect investment opportunity but lack sufficient capital to buy the property. Remember that buying a building with predictable cash flows costs a great deal of money. Not everyone can afford to pay for the property solely through their equity, and borrowing bridges the gap.

Alternatively, you may want to develop a property in the hope that it will generate significant cash flows upon completion. A developer incurs substantial negative cash flows before the project is completed, leased, and generating revenues, and may not have enough money to cover the upfront costs.

In short, real estate is a capital-intensive business, and debt enables you to buy or build real estate that you otherwise could not afford solely with your own money.

Diversification

You may be fortunate enough to have sufficient capital to buy or build the property on which you are focused. Suppose you have $10 million in savings and identify a wonderful opportunity to purchase a $10 million building. While you like the asset, you may not want to commit 100% of your wealth to real estate. Even if you want to put all of your wealth in real estate, you may not want it all in a single property. By using 75% non-recourse debt you can spread your $10 million across four $10 million properties. This diversification lowers your geographic, tenant, lease expiration, and asset risk exposure, improving your overall portfolio risk profile.

Investing in multiple properties may also create economies of scale in terms of property operations. For instance, you can spread your back-office expenses over multiple properties. Similarly, by engaging a painter or other contractor for four buildings, rather than one, you may be able to negotiate a lower price per unit.

Investing in multiple properties may also enhance your revenues. For example, with more tenant relationships you can offer alternative space when a tenant's lease expires. By moving a tenant to a larger (or smaller) space in one of your other buildings to satisfy their expansion needs, you will retain more tenants and enhance your revenues.

Interest Tax Shield

Another reason people borrow is to shield taxable income. Of course, this reason is not unique to real estate, as the IRS allows you to deduct all interest payments from your taxable income, not just those from mortgages. The greater your debt, the higher your interest deductions and the lower your tax bill. But remember, you are only allowed to deduct interest, not principal payments.

Enhanced Equity Returns

If things "go right," you can enhance your equity returns via debt financing. To illustrate, assume you are considering three alternative **capital structures** (a.k.a. "capital stacks") for the $10 million purchase of Sterling Towers: capital structure 1 is 100% equity; capital structure 2 is 50% equity and 50% debt; while capital structure 3 is 10% equity and 90% debt, as summarized in Figure 14.1.

FIGURE 14.1

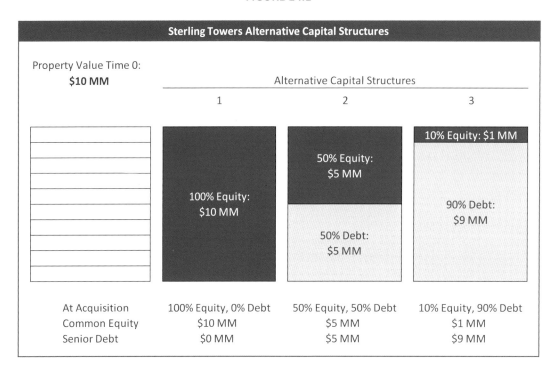

The two components of **total returns to equity** are capital appreciation and annual cash flow. **Capital appreciation** is the return you earn as the building's value increases (or decreases), while the **cash flow return** is driven by the cash flows generated by the property, net of any debt service.

CAPITAL APPRECIATION

Assume that you believe the property will increase 10% in value over a two-year period, at which point you will sell the property. This capital appreciation assumption is independent of which capital structure is employed, as the valuation relates to the property and not the capital sources. After all, the building does not know how much debt is on it! With 10% appreciation, the building is expected to be worth $11 million in two years, as seen in Figure 14.2. This value gained is shown as "earned equity" in the Figure and the original equity investment is now labeled as "bought equity."

FIGURE 14.2

Sterling Towers Alternative Capital Structures With 10% Capital Appreciation

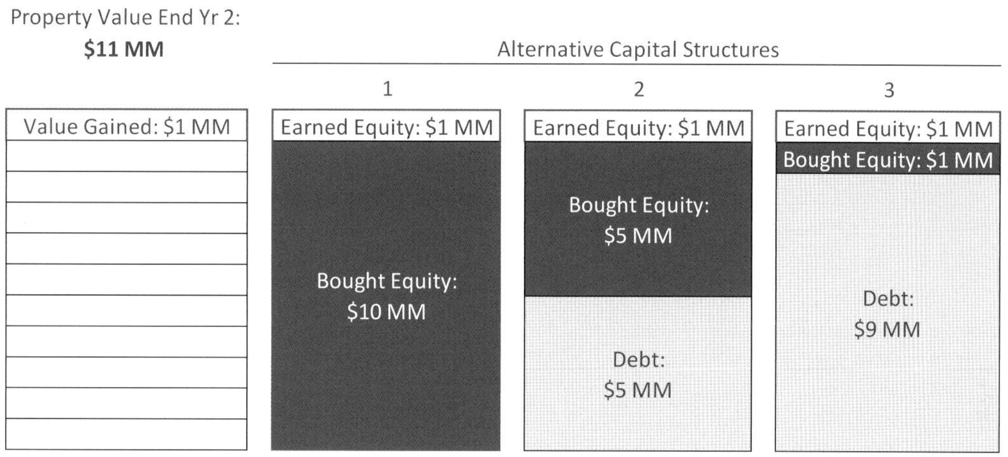

Property Value End Yr 2:
$11 MM

Alternative Capital Structures

	1	2	3
Value Gained: $1 MM	Earned Equity: $1 MM	Earned Equity: $1 MM	Earned Equity: $1 MM
			Bought Equity: $1 MM
	Bought Equity: $10 MM	Bought Equity: $5 MM	Debt: $9 MM
		Debt: $5 MM	

	1	2	3
At Acquisition	100% Equity, 0% Debt	50% Equity, 50% Debt	10% Equity, 90% Debt
Common Equity	$10 MM	$5 MM	$1 MM
Senior Debt	$0 MM	$5 MM	$9 MM
Debt Repayment	$0 MM	($5 MM)	($9 MM)
Equity Value	$11 MM	$6 MM	$2 MM
Equity Returns			
Multiple	1.10x	1.20x	2.00x
Total	10.00%	20.00%	100.00%
Annualized	4.88%	9.54%	41.42%

For capital structures 2 and 3, you must repay any debt you owe from the proceeds of the anticipated $11 million sale in two years. For capital structure 1, there is no debt to repay because you did not take out a mortgage to purchase the building. For structures 2 and 3 you must repay $5 million and $9 million, respectively (the Debt Repayment line). Thus, your residual equity value net proceeds after any debt repayments for structures 1, 2, and 3 are: $11 million, $6 million, and $2 million, respectively (the Equity Value line).

At first glance, the $11 million Equity Value provided to you by capital structure 1 seems more lucrative than the other two capital structures. But you cannot directly compare this with the equity values of the other two capital structures because you initially contributed different amounts of equity capital: the entire $10 million for capital structure 1; $5 million for capital structure 2; and only $1 million for capital structure 3. To make an apples-to-apples comparison, you need to calculate the expected equity return from the capital appreciation. This is equal to the money you expect to receive from the sale, minus the debt you borrowed, minus the money you put into the deal, divided by the money you put into the deal, as illustrated in Figures 14.3 and 14.4. In other words, it is the percent change between your original equity investment and the net residual value (after debt is paid) at sale.

FIGURE 14.3

Residual Equity Value and Equity Return from Capital Appreciation
Residual Equity Value = Property Sale Value – Debt Repayment
Equity Return from Capital Appreciation = (Residual Equity Value / Original Equity Investment) – 1

FIGURE 14.4

Equity Return Calculations ($ in MM)
Capital Structure 1: = ($11 – $0) / $10 – 1 = 10%
Capital Structure 2: = ($11 – $5) / $5 – 1 = 20%
Capital Structure 3: = ($11 – $9) / $1 – 1 = 100%

Figure 14.4 shows that capital structure 3 is the most beneficial to equity, with a 100% total return, versus 10% and 20% returns for capital structures 1 and 2, respectively. All else held constant, the greater the debt, the greater the potential magnification of equity return. Remember that the anticipated return from expected capital appreciation was for a two-year period. You can calculate the annual equity capital appreciation using the **compounded annual growth rate (CAGR)** calculations, as summarized in Figure 14.5.

FIGURE 14.5

Annualized % Return (CAGR) Calculations for 3 Capital Structures		
Compounded Annual Growth Rate (CAGR) formula: = (1 + Total Return) ^ (1 / # of years) – 1		
Capital Structure	Total 2-year Return	Annualized Return
1	10%	4.88%
2	20%	9.54%
3	100%	41.42%

Online Companion Hands On: Go to the Online Companion and select the link for Chapter 14. Scroll down to the Excel Figures section and download the Excel file and open it to the Figure 14.5. Using the CAGR formula, calculate the annualized returns for each of the Total Return values assuming a 2-year hold.

Note that the greater the proportion of debt, the higher is the expected equity appreciation return. This is because the expected total gain on the property ($1 million) is the same for each of the three simulated capital structures, while the equity you have in the project is lower with greater debt. Thus, debt provides you the opportunity to leverage the property's expected appreciation into a greater equity return, as illustrated in Figure 14.6. The graph shows how a certain level of property value appreciation (x-axis) translates into equity value appreciation (y-axis) at four different levels of debt: 0% LTV, 30% LTV, 60% LTV and 80% LTV. For instance, with no debt (the blue line), a 5% property value appreciation renders an equal 5% equity value appreciation, whereas with 80% debt (the red line), the same 5% property value appreciation renders a 25% appreciation in equity value, a 5x magnification.

FIGURE 14.6

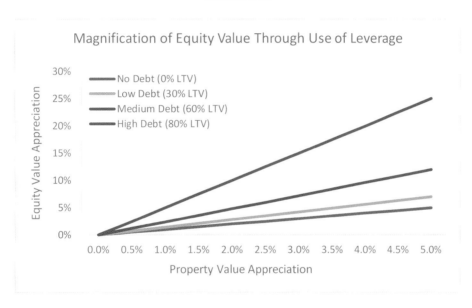

One of the great mistakes that plagues real estate borrowers is that when debt is plentiful, many borrowers forget that debt has both a price (the interest rate) and risk. That is, these greater expected leveraged equity returns are not risk-free! To see this, ask what happens if instead of the anticipated 10% increase in value, the property value depreciates by 10% over 2 years due to an unexpected downturn in the economy and a tenant bankruptcy (Figure 14.7).

If this occurs, after two years of hard work, you will only be able to sell the property for $9 million, even though you originally paid $10 million. This means the property realizes a loss of $1 million in value, irrespective of the capital structure. The residual equity value will then be $9 million, $4 million, and $0 for capital structures 1, 2 and 3, respectively. So a 2-year total decline in property value of 10% generates total negative equity appreciation returns of −10%, −20%, and −100% for structures 1, 2 and 3, respectively. These 2-year losses amount to negative compounded annual growth rates of −5.13%, −10.56%, and −100% for structures 1, 2 and 3, respectively.

FIGURE 14.7

Sterling Towers Alternative Capital Structures With 10% Capital Loss			

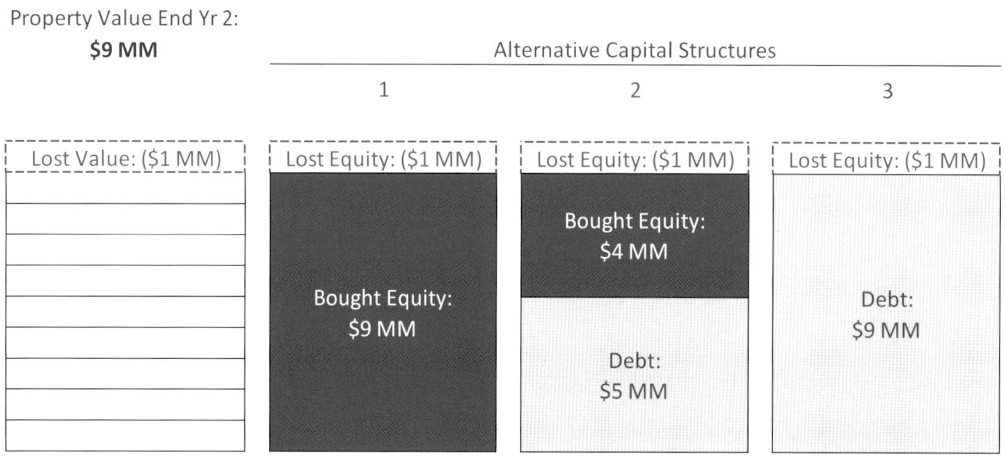

Property Value End Yr 2: **$9 MM**

Alternative Capital Structures

	1	2	3
Lost Value: ($1 MM)	Lost Equity: ($1 MM)	Lost Equity: ($1 MM)	Lost Equity: ($1 MM)
	Bought Equity: $9 MM	Bought Equity: $4 MM	Debt: $9 MM
		Debt: $5 MM	

	1	2	3
At Acquisition	100% Equity, 0% Debt	50% Equity, 50% Debt	10% Equity, 90% Debt
Common Equity	$10 MM	$5 MM	$1 MM
Senior Debt	$0 MM	$5 MM	$9 MM
Debt Repayment	$0 MM	($5 MM)	($9 MM)
Equity Value	$9 MM	$4 MM	$0 MM
Equity Returns			
Multiple	0.90x	0.80x	0.00x
Total	(10.00%)	(20.00%)	(100.00%)
Annualized	(5.13%)	(10.56%)	(100.00%)

The lesson is that if the property value declines, the more debt you had on the property, the worse your equity appreciation returns will be, as illustrated in Figure 14.8. The four series plotted below 0% represent the equity value decreases associated with property value declines of the stated percentages. In fact, relatively small and temporary value declines can wipe out an investor's entire equity position when high leverage is employed. And if the debt comes due or a covenant is violated during such temporary value declines, the borrower will be unable to successfully refinance the property. The result is that either fresh equity must be infused in a down market (when capital is generally expensive) or the owner will lose a good long-term property through foreclosure by the lender.

FIGURE 14.8

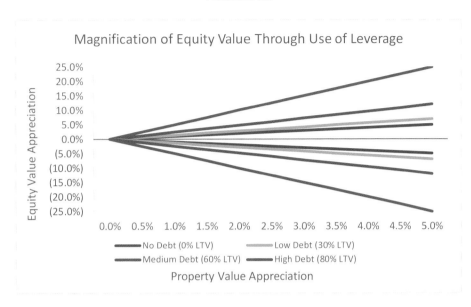

Magnification of Equity Value Through Use of Leverage

Y-axis: Equity Value Appreciation: 25.0%, 20.0%, 15.0%, 10.0%, 5.0%, 0.0%, (5.0%), (10.0%), (15.0%), (20.0%), (25.0%)

X-axis: Property Value Appreciation: 0.0%, 0.5%, 1.0%, 1.5%, 2.0%, 2.5%, 3.0%, 3.5%, 4.0%, 4.5%, 5.0%

Legend: No Debt (0% LTV), Low Debt (30% LTV), Medium Debt (60% LTV), High Debt (80% LTV)

The key insight about leverage and equity appreciation returns is that in good times, debt is cheap and can significantly "juice" your pro forma equity returns; but during downturns your losses are magnified with increased debt. Stated differently, while debt is your friend on the way up, it is your enemy on the way down. This reality was underscored in the 2008-2009 U.S. Financial Crisis. Since debt substantially increases the investment risk for the equity holder, equity must demand a substantially higher return as leverage increases. The reason debt increases equity risk is because the lender gets paid first, leaving the equity holder's cash flows in a riskier second payment position. In fact, until the lender gets paid in full, the equity holder receives nothing. It is critical for you to remember that financing decisions and project investment decisions are not the same. Instead, they are separate, critically important, issues. Always calculate both unlevered and levered expected returns so that you can understand the extent to which expected equity return derives from property performance versus leverage.

CASH FLOW RETURN

Now let's look at the second component of equity returns: the equity cash flow return. The real estate industry frequently uses the terms **positive leverage** and **negative leverage** to describe the effects of debt on cash returns.

Positive Leverage

Positive leverage simply means that the annual property cash flow yield percent (NOI after normal reserves / Purchase Price) is greater than the annual interest rate paid to the lender. For example, if you borrow at a 5% annual interest rate for a property whose annual cash flow yield is 10%, you realize a 5% (10% – 5%) positive spread on every dollar borrowed.

To illustrate the effects of positive leverage, we return to the $10 million Sterling Towers purchase. Assume that based on your analysis and negotiations with the lender, you decide to use capital structure 2 (50% loan-to-value; debt of $5 MM) to purchase the property, and the lender charges you 5% on an interest-only basis. As a result, you must pay $250,000 in interest each year ($5 MM * 5%). If you purchase the property at an 8 cap (after reserves), it generates $800,000 in annual NOI ($10 MM * 8%). In this case, you have positive leverage, as the 8% property return exceeds the 5% interest rate. Effectively, you are borrowing a dollar at 5% and investing it at an 8% cash return, generating a 3% cash spread on every dollar borrowed.

How does positive leverage affect your current equity return? In our example, subtracting the $250,000 interest payment from the projected NOI of $800,000 leaves a before-tax cash flow to equity (cash flow net of debt service payments) of $550,000. In this case, the equity investment is $5 million ($10 MM purchase price – $5 MM in debt), so the **cash-on-cash yield** is 11% ($550,000 of cash flow to equity / $5 MM equity investment), which is substantially higher than the property's 8% yield, as seen in Figure 14.9.

FIGURE 14.9

Cash-on-Cash Yield Calculation	
NOI	$800,000
Interest	($250,000)
Cash Flow to Equity	$550,000
Equity Investment	$5,000,000

Cash-on-Cash Yield =
Cash Flow to Equity / Equity Investment

= 550,000 / 5,000,000 = 11.0%

Positive leverage increases your cash-on-cash yield if the investment meets your pro forma expectations, with your $5 million equity investment earning an 11% return even though the property only generates an 8% return. Combining this expected annual cash-on-cash yield (11%) with the expected annualized capital appreciation gives you a quick estimate of your anticipated **total annual return**. For example, if you assume you are taking the 50% LTV loan, you can quickly estimate your equity's expected total annual return as 11% from cash flow plus the 9.54% CAGR from expected appreciation (seen in Figure 14.5), for an anticipated total annual return of 20.54%.

If this quick calculation yields an annual equity return that is sufficient in view of the risks of the property and capital structure, you then construct a detailed financial model to more closely analyze the risks and opportunities of the investment. Since NOI is generally expected to grow over time, the expected IRR will be higher, but this quick calculation serves as a sanity check, and saves valuable time and energy.

Negative Leverage

Negative leverage refers to situations where the property generates a lower cash flow percentage yield than the interest rate on borrowed dollars. Assume that the property is a hotel purchased for an 8 cap on February 1, 2020, with $5 million in equity and $5 million of debt carrying a 5% interest-only interest rate ($250,000 in annual interest payments). However, instead of the 8% property-level return you anticipated, the property is struggling to generate a 1% NOI return, as after Covid-19 exploded, vacancy skyrocketed, room rates fell by 25%, and the food and beverage business deteriorated, while most of your operating expenses such as maids, doormen, electricity, security, and other expenses continued.

Because of these declining revenues and fixed costs, the building is only generating $100,000 in NOI ($10 MM * 1%). Thus, your before-tax cash flow to equity is –$150,000 ($100,000 – $250,000). Hence, your cash-on-cash yield is –3% (–$150,000 / $5,000,000). As a result of the negative leverage, you have a –3% return on your cash, versus the property's positive 1% NOI return. This means that you must come "out of pocket" an additional $150,000 annually to cover the difference between the property's NOI and your interest payments. In this case, the negative leverage forces you to inject additional equity to keep your ownership position alive, while you hope that NOI improves. Each $150,000 check you write is additional equity and as such, increases your equity investment above the original $5 million. As a result, the denominator for all subsequent equity return calculations is higher than the original $5,000,000.

If you do not have the $150,000 required to fund the shortfall in this example, you can seek an equity partner. But your negotiating position will be weak, as few want to invest in a deal where they are losing money out of the gate. Particularly if this shortfall occurs unexpectedly, and you need money in a hurry to survive, you will not have much negotiating power. This is a major risk associated with debt, particularly with negative leverage.

Having negative leverage is not necessarily a bad thing. For instance, development is almost always a negative leverage business, as during the initial lease-up, your NOI is negative (i.e., no or low income and lots of operating costs), and you continue to incur interest payments during lease-up. Nonetheless, you borrow because you believe the property will ultimately yield sufficient cash flows and capital appreciation to offset the risk of debt and temporary negative leverage.

JAPAN AND POSITIVE LEVERAGE

The Japanese real estate market from 1997-2007 offers a vivid example of positive leverage at work. This example also helps you understand that declining cash streams are tricky to evaluate but can still have substantial value. In fact, even a property with little or no residual equity value after debt repayment can still be extremely valuable because of the cash flows it provides during the hold period.

The Japanese economy experienced almost no growth from 1990-2007. As a result, real estate demand was basically stagnant during this period. However, the real estate supply in Japan grew by about 2% per year during this time. What happens to rents if supply grows, while demand remains essentially flat and there is no economy-wide inflation? Rental rates decrease. Of course, it was not guaranteed that net rents would continue to decline, as many believed that the Japanese economy was about to turn around. But let's assume that the expectation was that net rents would fall by about 2% annually as the economy continued to stagnate.

Assume that in late 2002, you purchased $100 million of Japanese real estate at a 7 cap, so your expected NOI for the next year was $7 million. If the economy performed as you expected, net rents would decline by about 2% annually. Figure 14.10 displays the expected NOI for each of the next 4 years after your acquisition.

FIGURE 14.10

NOI Projection for $100 MM Japanese Property Portfolio			
Year	2003	2004	2005	2006
NOI	$7.00 MM	$6.86 MM	$6.72 MM	$6.59 MM

If you financed 85% of the total purchase price interest only at a 4% interest rate (which was very possible), you invested $15 million ($100 MM – $85 MM) in equity, and your annual interest payment was $3.4 million.

Let's first evaluate the expected cash-on-cash yield for 2003 (the first year of ownership). With $7 million in year 1 NOI, you expected to earn $3.6 million after making your $3.4 million interest payment. On the $15 million equity, this is a 24% annual cash-on-cash yield! This is positive leverage at work, as you borrowed at 4% and invested in a building that was generating a 7% cash flow. With 85% leverage you are able to leverage the 7% property return into a 24% cash-on-cash yield.

Calculating the expected cash-on-cash yield for each additional year, you can see in Figure 14.11 that the cash-on-cash return was expected to decline as the NOI declined due to the decreasing net rents. In fact, the cash-on-cash yield was expected to decrease to 21.3% by 2006, but that's still a nice equity yield. After all, the Japanese long-term Treasury bond barely yielded 1%, so if you expected to earn a 21.3% cash-on-cash yield on your property purchase in 2006, it seemed like an attractive bet, despite declining returns.

FIGURE 14.11

Forward Cash-on-Cash Yield Projection on Japanese Properties				
Year	2003	2004	2005	2006
NOI	$7.00 MM	$6.86 MM	$6.72 MM	$6.59 MM
Interest	($3.40 MM)	($3.40 MM)	($3.40 MM)	($3.40 MM)
Cash Flow to Equity	$3.60 MM	$3.46 MM	$3.32 MM	$3.19 MM
Cash-on-Cash Yield	24.0%	23.1%	22.1%	21.3%

But you have a problem, as the property is probably declining in value as NOI falls. Assume that you believed you could sell the building for a 7 cap at the end of 2006. To forecast the sales value, you capped pro forma 2007 NOI, which equals 2006 NOI "grown" one year at –2%. This implied an expected sale price of $92.3 million (($6.59 MM * (1 + –2%) / 7%). After you repaid the $85 million debt, you expected to only have $7.24 million of your original $15 million equity investment left.

That is, from the sale you expected to lose more than half ($7.76 million) of your initial equity investment, so your expected equity return from capital appreciation over the four-year hold period was –51.6%, or an annual expected equity capital gain of –16.6%. Negative capital appreciation is called **capital depreciation**. In this case, leverage severely hurt you in terms of capital depreciation, while positive leverage greatly enhanced your cash-on-cash yield. Figure 14.12 shows the expected total equity return for each year (all of which are net positive because operating cash flow returns are included), assuming the property is sold in that year at a 7 cap.

FIGURE 14.12

	Japanese Portfolio Equity Returns at Various Sale Years			
Sale Year	Before Tax Cash Flow	NOI	Before Tax Net Sales Proceeds	Before Tax Equity IRR
2003	$3.60 MM	$7.00 MM	$13.00 MM	10.67%
2004	$3.46 MM	$6.86 MM	$11.04 MM	11.05%
2005	$3.32 MM	$6.72 MM	$9.12 MM	11.46%
2006	$3.19 MM	$6.59 MM	$7.24 MM	11.90%

This example provides a glimpse of the dilemma that the Japanese market presented to property investors: eroding property values but attractive cash-on-cash returns derived from highly positive leverage. If the economy was to rebound or cap rates fell, it would be a home run. On the other hand, if the market deteriorated more than expected, or cap rates rose, it would be a failed investment, barring another capital infusion.

HOW MUCH SHOULD YOU BORROW?

How much debt should you use to fund your real estate investments? There is no single answer. Instead, the decision to borrow depends on both who you are and the nature of the property. For instance, if you are a developer, the tax shields from debt are not useful to you during development as they are for properties with strong NOIs, as the development phase generates little in the way of taxable income to shelter. On the other hand, as a developer, you may need debt because you do not have enough money to fund the development and additionally desire to diversify your risk exposure. A developer may also borrow to enhance the return from expected capital appreciation when they sell the building.

Alternatively, since pension funds are non-taxable entities, they have no use for the interest tax shield provided by debt. Further, cash-rich pension funds often do not need debt to fund their investments. Since pension funds do not actively operate properties, potential economies of scale are not particularly important. However, pension funds often borrow non-recourse debt to diversify as well as to enhance their expected returns.

In contrast, a real estate private equity fund may borrow to finance deals they could otherwise not afford and utilize leverage to enhance expected equity returns. Furthermore, since these funds are usually structured as tax pass-through partnerships, their taxable investors benefit from the debt tax shelter. Thus, such funds historically tend to use leverage in the 65-75% range.

The reasons for borrowing are not mutually exclusive. If you understand why you want to use debt, you will be able to determine how much and what type of debt you should use. But if you fail to understand what you are trying to achieve with debt, you are ultimately headed for disaster, as you are taking leveraged risks without a clear purpose. By understanding why you want or are willing to incur debt, you can customize your financing to meet your needs.

MEZZANINE FINANCE

Mezzanine finance is a highly customized area of financing. But what is mezzanine finance? It helps to understand mezzanine finance if you know the origins of the term mezzanine. In the department stores built between 1900 and 1929, such as John Wanamaker, Marshall Fields, and Macy's, the first floor was extremely spacious, with high ceilings and elaborate décor intended to impress customers. High-end women's clothing was displayed on the first floor, while high-end men's clothing could be found on the second floor and marked-down goods were relegated to the basement. The second floor was a long climb because of the high ceilings on the first floor, and because there were originally no elevators or escalators, people actually had to walk up the stairs! People would get tired of walking up three flights of stairs to get to the men's department, so many stores incorporated a mezzanine balcony around the interior wall of the first floor. People could stop and catch their breath while shopping on the mezzanine, before continuing up to the second floor. Because of insufficient space, the store displayed some high-end men's clothing, as well as less popular women's clothing on the mezzanine level. Thus, the mezzanine was used for a bit of everything in between.

That is the spirit of mezzanine financing. In our analogy, the "first floor" is first priority senior debt (which is exclusively secured by the real estate itself), while the "second floor" is straight common equity (secured by nothing but the potential success of the legal entity owning the property). The mezzanine includes every other imaginable type of "middle" financing that is not secured by the real estate. Mezzanine is any type of **junior debt**, whether holding the second, seventh, or other unsecured position. Mezzanine is also **preferred equity** where you have specified rights above common equity, but below senior debt. Mezzanine is also **convertible debt** where you hold debt, but you have the right to convert into common equity at specific terms. Mezzanine is also **participating debt**, where you receive an interest payment each year and also participate in any property income above a specified level. Of course, if the borrower gives the mezzanine lender a share of income or a portion of the capital appreciation, the lender has to give something in return, such as a lower interest rate, higher LTV, or more favorable borrowing covenants.

The only things that limit the type of mezzanine products are your creativity and the market. After all, the market can reject a creative financing product, just as customers can reject department stores selling Christmas lights on the mezzanine on March 1st. For such an offering, you are probably not going to find too many buyers. So too with most mezzanine financing products for most properties. Remember, the bulk of real estate financing is generally either straight senior secured debt or common equity. But sometimes your needs merit a customized mezzanine financing.

Mezzanine financing is used mainly by borrowers seeking higher LTVs and who can creatively negotiate "mezz" terms. However, the benefits of mezzanine financing come with both greater risk and higher cost. For example, assume you are purchasing a $10 million office property, but you only have $1 million in equity and need to borrow the rest. The senior secured lender offers you a 75% LTV mortgage ($7.5 million) at a 6% interest rate. Thus, you need a $1.5 million mezz piece to purchase the property. The mezzanine lender is willing to provide you with the remaining 15% LTV, but at an 11% interest rate, as the mezzanine lender is taking additional risk due to their subordination to the senior secured lender. Based on this capital structure, your weighted average cost of debt capital is 6.83% (as calculated by .83 * 6 + .17 * 11), as summarized in Figure 14.13.

FIGURE 14.13

Debt Capital Structure			
	% of Total Debt	Value	Interest Rate
Mezzanine Loan	16.67%	1,500,000	11.00%
Senior Secured Loan	83.33%	7,500,000	6.00%
Total | Weighted Average	100.00%	$9,000,000	6.83%

 Online Companion Hands On: Select the tab for Figure 14.3 in the Online Companion Chapter 14 Excel file. In the blank cell for the weighted average Interest Rate, calculate it as: (Mezzanine Loan % Total Debt * 11%) + (Senior Secured Loan % Total Debt * 6%).

Thus, mezzanine financing is helpful in satisfying your borrowing needs but raises your weighted average borrowing costs from 6%, had you only used straight senior secured, to a blended 6.83%. In addition, at the higher leverage inclusive of mezzanine financing, you are more exposed to equity erosion should property values decline.

To calculate your **weighted average cost of capital (WACC)** for this capital structure, assume you require a 14% annual return on your equity capital. This results in a weighted average cost of capital for the project of 7.55%, as summarized in Figure 14.14.

FIGURE 14.14

Weighted Average Cost of Capital			
	% of Total Capital	Value	Interest Rate
Equity	10.00%	1,000,000	14.00%
Debt	90.00%	9,000,000	6.83%
Total | Weighted Average	100.00%	$10,000,000	7.55%

Online Companion Hands On: After you have completed the exercise for Figure 14.13, go to the Figure 14.14 tab. Use the SUMPRODUCT function as a shorthand solution to solve for the weighted average cost of capital. The first array you reference will be the range of **%s of Total Capital**, and the second array will be the corresponding **Interest Rate** values. Note that this function could have been used for the exercise in Figure 14.3, and vice versa for the Figure 14.3 longhand method.

CLOSING THOUGHT

Debt can be your friend in good times but an unforgiving enemy in bad times. Real estate's relatively stable cash streams lend themselves to equity's prudent use of leverage to enhance returns and diversify a portfolio. However, never forget that real estate is a long-term asset and, as such, your capital structure should have a sizable slice of the longest form of liability – equity. This equity cushion is essential to see you through the tough times that will inevitably and unexpectedly occur. At least 3 times in the last 35 years, real estate has failed to meet the stress test of maintaining equity value when financed in excess of 55-65% LTV. Yet, the industry continually strives to achieve higher leverage levels and is surprised each time extreme economic and capital market distress wipes out large numbers of equity holders and their lenders. It is true that those who ignore real estate history are condemned to relive it.

Online Companion Audio Interview: To hear a conversation about this chapter's content, go to the Online Companion and select the link for Chapter 14. Scroll down to the Audio Interview section and listen.

Chapter 15
The Use of Debt and Mortgages

"Stick to what you know but keep learning to expand what you know."
- Dr. Peter Linneman

You need to understand the fundamentals of the real estate business before you can select the appropriate financing structure. If you do not understand the risks and opportunities of a property, you will never be able to efficiently select your financial structure.

Ask yourself, "What is the best financial outcome a secured first mortgage lender can expect from their loan?" The very best they can expect is to get their money back and the timely payment of interest. Their upside is limited to the complete receipt of the principal plus their lending spread (generally 110-250 basis points over comparable maturity Treasury bonds) in interest payments. Too often, lenders forget that if the building vastly outperforms expectations, the lender receives nothing more than what is contractually defined in the mortgage documents. But if the property fares worse, they may not do this well and could lose much of their money. This yields the asymmetric lender risk/reward distribution displayed in Figure 15.1 for a loan made at Treasury plus 180 basis points. Whether the probability of outcomes is more like the area under the blue curve or that under the gray dotted line, the maximum possible return is the same.

FIGURE 15.1

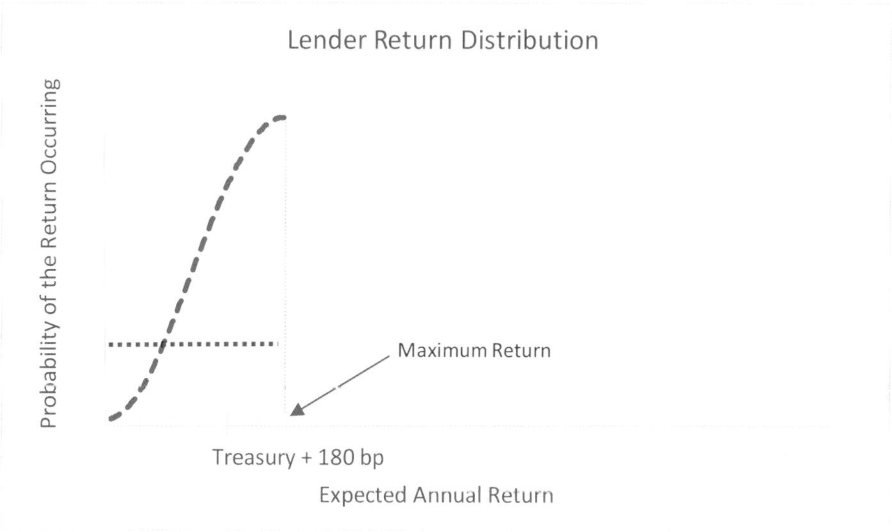

Lender Return Distribution

Probability of the Return Occurring

Maximum Return

Treasury + 180 bp

Expected Annual Return

INTEREST TYPES AND SHORT-TERM VERSUS LONG-TERM DEBT

Loan interest rates for both short- and long-term loans can be **fixed** or **floating** (a.k.a. "variable"). Fixed is exactly what it sounds like – a nominal rate locked in for the duration of the loan period. Floating rates, on the other hand, adjust with the debt markets, and the rate the borrower pays is reset at a negotiated time interval. Base variable interest rates used for U.S. floating-rate debt have typically been LIBOR or a rate associated with shorter-term U.S. Treasuries. (As of this writing, from the year 2022 forward, it is expected that the Secured Overnight Financing Rate (SOFR) will replace LIBOR as the benchmark floating debt rate.)

The **term** of a mortgage is the amount of time over which borrowed principal can remain outstanding. The loan term is specified in years. Short-term mortgage debt is generally 3-5 years in length, and long-term debt is generally 10 to 30 years. Short- and long-term debt are each suited to a different borrower case profile, and each carry their own potential risks and opportunities. Borrowers with very long-term investment horizons for acquiring a stabilized core asset tend to select long-term debt with a fixed interest rate. They are most comfortable with a constant debt service obligation, even if the interest rate is marginally higher than if they were to use shorter-term debt (which it typically is, all else equal). Life companies are major providers of long-term, fixed-rate debt, as its duration matches the length of their insurance policy payout liabilities. Short-term debt with a floating interest rate appeals to borrowers on the other end of the investment horizon and risk spectrum, as their mandates allow for making near-term bets on interest rate levels remaining as is or falling and for repaying the loan once significant property value has been created. Banks prefer to issue floating-rate debt to match their floating-rate liabilities.

From the borrower's perspective, risks of locking in a long-term, fixed-rate mortgage include overpaying for the loan if interest rates fall during the term and being subject to expensive penalties if you repay the loan before the scheduled maturity date. Another short-term debt risk, whether fixed or floating, is that the loan can come due for repayment in a down market, when getting a replacement loan or selling your asset are not possible. If the debt is floating, there is also the risk that rates rise during the term, resulting in more expensive capital and lower cash-on-cash returns. Borrowers can try to negotiate an **interest rate cap** to set a ceiling on their interest rate. Conversely, lenders can establish an **interest rate floor** to mitigate the risk of rates falling.

INTEREST CALCULATION BASES

There are three commonly used methods for calculating interest. Historically, the most prevalent has been **30/360**, which takes the nominal interest rate and divides it by 360 days to get the daily equivalent rate, then multiplies this daily rate by 30 to get the monthly rate. This is the least expensive calculation basis for the borrower. The second method is **Actual/365** (a.k.a. 365/365), wherein the monthly rate is calculated by taking the annual interest rate, dividing it by 365 days, and then multiplying that daily rate by the number of days in the current month. As leap years occur every four years, the actual annual rate ends up slightly higher than the 30/360 method, thus this is slightly more expensive to the borrower. The third and most expensive to the borrower is **Actual/360** (a.k.a. 365/360), in which the annual rate is divided by 360 days (not 365) and then multiplied by either 365 or 366.

KEY LOAN SIZING RATIOS

Given their limited upside, lenders must focus on limiting their downside. As a result, a secured lender will **underwrite** (assess) a prospective loan's size based on many key ratios and offer the borrower the smallest loan amount resulting from the various loan size tests. The five most commonly-used ratios for sizing loans are: loan-to-value or loan-to-cost, debt yield, interest coverage, debt service coverage, and fixed charges.

Loan-to-Value and Loan-to-Cost

Loan-to-Value (LTV) is the principal amount of the loan divided by the estimated property value. The loan-to-value ratio reflects how much equity cushion the lender believes they have before the loan is "underwater" (i.e., the property value has fallen below the outstanding loan amount). For instance, if the lender believes the value of the property is $100 million and they wish to maintain a maximum LTV of 65%, they will lend the borrower up to $65 million. Typically, the LTV for secured first mortgages ranges from 50-70%, depending on the property, the state of the market, and the strength of the investment sponsor's track record.

A key step for the lender is to determine the property's value. If the loan is being made to support a purchase, the lender will generally utilize the purchase price as the value. Of course, if the buyer is overpaying (a common problem in hot markets), this value cushion can quickly disappear. Even more problematic is the assessment of value for refinancing (refi), as there is no "arm's length" purchase transaction to establish value of that particular property. In this case, an **appraisal** is usually done to provide a valuation based on comparable sales or income capitalization. However, appraisals are lagged and always wrong, as they are nothing more than (hopefully) informed and unbiased professional estimates. In other words, they do not set price, as only an arm's length property sale can establish actual market value. The result is that appraisal-based valuations tend to be notably overstated in hot capital markets, as lenders are eager to put out money to both aggressive buyers and refinancers. Hence, when capital markets cool, much of the apparent equity cushion can quickly evaporate, leading to larger than expected lender losses.

For construction loans, instead of using LTV, lenders use the **loan-to-cost (LTC)** ratio as the parameter for the largest allowable loan size. As with LTV, the LTC is expressed as a percentage (e.g., a 60% LTC). Loan-to-cost differs from loan-to-value in that construction lenders are providing funds towards an approved budget of the costs of land acquisition and development, not the appraised value or sale price of the property upon construction completion. Construction loans are typically between 55% and 70% LTC, also depending on the project, the state of the market, and strength of the sponsor.

For both LTV and LTC, the concept of an **eligible loan cost** applies. Eligible loan costs are those costs for property elements that have collateral value to the lender and, thus, liquidation value in the event of a foreclosure. For instance, undeveloped land has liquidation value, as does a completed building. Origination fees paid to a third-party mezzanine lender, or an acquisition fee charged by the deal sponsor for their services, do not. As a result, these transaction costs are typically excluded from the value or cost amounts by which the LTV or LTC percentages are multiplied to size the loan.

Debt Yield

Debt Yield is another metric used by lenders to size their loans. Debt yield is also expressed as a percentage (e.g., 10%). It is calculated as the first year's NOI divided by the loan amount. You can think of the debt yield as the "lender's cap rate," as it is the property NOI yield on the lender's "purchase price" (i.e., the loan size). Targeted debt yields run from 8% to 13%.

Interest Coverage Ratio

Interest Coverage Ratio is the property NOI divided by the annual interest payment. This ratio indicates how many times NOI can cover the interest obligation and gives the lender an idea of how much of an income cushion the borrower has in terms of their ability to pay the interest on the loan. The higher the ratio, the greater the cushion and the safer the lender feels. For instance, a property with a $10 million NOI and $6.25 million in annual interest payments has an interest coverage ratio of 1.6x ($10 MM / $6.25 MM). Lenders will often underwrite based on a minimum interest coverage ratio mandated by their internal credit committee. A minimum interest coverage ratio of 1.2x for a property generating NOI of $10 million yields a maximum interest payment of $8.33 million ($10 MM NOI / 1.2x interest coverage ratio). Typical interest coverage ratios are 1.2x to 2.0x for secured first mortgages.

An interest coverage ratio of 1.25x means that the property's NOI could fall by 25% and would still generate sufficient income to cover interest payments. However, if an income decline occurs as the loan is coming due, any refinanced replacement loan would be underwritten with a reduced property value to achieve the same interest coverage from its reduced income.

Debt Service Coverage Ratio

Debt Service Coverage Ratio (DSCR) is the annual NOI of the property divided by the annual debt service payment inclusive of both principal and interest. If the hypothetical $65 million loan had an interest rate of 7% and a 20-year amortization period, it would have an annual debt service payment of approximately $6.14 million, assuming payments are made annually. With $10 million in NOI, the property would have a DSCR of 1.63x. Debt service coverage ratios generally must exceed 1.2x for placement of secured first mortgages.

 Online Companion Hands On: Using the PMT function in Excel, solve for the annual debt service payment on the $65 million loan assuming the annual interest rate of 7% and 20 years of amortization. Since mortgages are paid monthly, divide the interest rate by 12 to determine the monthly interest rate ("**rate**" in the Excel function) and multiply the amortization term in years by 12 for the total number of months ("**nper**" in the Excel function) over which the loan is paid. Then multiply the result of the function by 12 to get the annual payment amount, calculated on a monthly basis, of $6.05 million.

Fixed Charges Ratio

Fixed Charges Ratio is the property NOI divided by all fixed charges incurred annually. Thus, the fixed charges ratio will include all debt service payments as well as other fixed charges the borrower incurs, including ground lease and operating lease payments and payments on unsecured debt. Assume that in addition to the $6.14 million debt service in the previous example, the borrower pays $1 million in annual ground lease payments and another $1 million interest on a second mortgage on the property. With $10 million in NOI, the property has a 1.23x fixed charges ratio ($10 MM in NOI / ($6.14 MM debt service + $1 MM ground rent + $1 MM second mortgage interest)).

What are the "right" LTV, interest coverage, DSCR, and fixed charges ratios? That depends on the lender, the borrower, and the property. For instance, some lenders are willing to exceed the industry norms, while others lend very conservatively. For each ratio, the lender will analyze the fundamentals of the property and the competitive market and lend according to their risk profile and return expectations. The borrower must always remember that while higher LTVs and lower coverage ratios generate larger loan proceeds, they also increase the risk that financial distress and foreclosure will occur. There is no free lunch.

OTHER KEY LOAN TERMS

While these loan sizing ratios are important, **loan covenants** are often far more important and contentious. To limit the downside of the risk profile illustrated previously, lenders demand as many loan covenants as possible. Covenants are the terms or clauses of the loan agreement. There are **positive covenants** ("things you must do") and **negative covenants** ("things you cannot do") in a loan agreement. Lenders hope these covenants never become an issue, as if they do, it means there is a problem. It is much like parenting. You do not want to impose a lot of restrictions on your children as you would prefer they voluntarily behave like angels. Yet good parents must impose certain restrictions to help avoid instances when children might act unsafely or inappropriately. Despite your teenage protests, if your parents had not imposed a 12 a.m. curfew, too often you would have come home at 4 a.m. The lender is in the same position. In general, loan documents specify that if any covenant is violated, the lender has the right to **accelerate** the loan (i.e., demand full repayment prior to maturity).

Lenders must consider situations that help them avoid potential losses from a borrower's careless behavior. While the headline numbers (the interest rate, amortization, fees, and loan amount) are important, as the borrower, you are going to spend much of your time negotiating covenants with the lender. In fact, it is relatively easy to identify an excessively "hot" debt market, as standard loan covenants disappear in the rush by lenders to get money out the door. While this might seem advantageous to borrowers, such overheated markets (e.g., the early 1970s, late 1980s, and 2005-2007) are usually followed by ice-cold loan markets, with little debt available to refinance maturing loans or support property prices. As a result, the seemingly great loan on offer in a red-hot loan market may simply lure the borrower to overpay for a property, only to default into the teeth of the subsequent ice-cold debt market.

COMMON NEGATIVE COVENANTS

Prepayment Penalty

If the borrower pays off a fixed interest rate loan prior to maturity, they must generally pay a pre-determined cash **prepayment penalty.** This covenant protects lenders from massive prepayments if interest rates drop. Specifically, if such prepayments occur, the lender effectively loses the difference between the original interest rate and the lower interest rate at which they must re-deploy the funds prematurely returned. The penalty generally ensures that the lender receives the originally agreed upon interest rate (or better). In some instances, the loan may contain a **lock-out clause**, which is the complete prohibition of early repayment for a specified period of time. Prepayment penalties are common with long-term loans (and less so with short-term or floating rate debt) because long-term lenders such as life insurance companies generally try to match the asset-liability durations on their balance sheet. Getting repaid for a loan prematurely introduces a mismatch. Prepayment penalties are discussed in more detail later in the chapter.

Distributions

The lender may restrict the distributions paid to equity holders. For example, assume a building is generating $8 million in NOI annually, and interest is absorbing $3.5 million of that income. The lender may require you to set aside an additional $3.5 million in reserves or in an escrow account to further ensure your ability to meet future interest payments or capital expenditure needs. These reserves provide the owner, and thus the lender, a cushion for hard times.

Operating Restrictions

The lender will frequently specify certain operating levels below which the property cannot fall without the loan being accelerated. For example, occupancy cannot drop below 80%, or rents cannot fall below specified levels. The reason is that lenders worry that a desperate borrower might sign below-market leases, hence deteriorating the value of their collateral. Why would a borrower ever sign a below-market lease? While both parties want the property to operate successfully, when it does not, lender-borrower interests and priorities can become increasingly misaligned. For example, the borrower may derive leasing commissions and management fees from the lease which may exceed their loss in equity value. This is particularly a concern when the property is in trouble and there is little remaining equity value. In anticipation of such possibilities, the lender imposes loan covenants that protect their collateral by making it difficult for the borrower to act inappropriately.

Operating restrictions may also restrict tenant quality. For example, assume a landlord wants to lease to start-up Wish And Prayer Inc. because of high rents and an upfront leasing commission. The problem is that Wish And Prayer is a very low-credit company. Remember that debt holders do not benefit from the property's upside but are exposed to the property's downside risk. To mitigate their collateral risk, lenders may require that the building be leased to specific tenants or tenants of a specified minimum credit quality.

Additional Debt

The lender may not let you obtain additional financing without their permission. Even if the lender has a secured first position, they worry about any additional debt (which is subordinate to their mortgage) that you may incur, as a greater debt burden may prohibit you from making future first-position loan payments. In addition, the second loan could have payments due a day before when the first lender's payments are due. As a result, although the lender has a secured first position, critical cash flow could go to the second lender due to timing.

COMMON POSITIVE COVENANTS

Deposits

The lender could require you to keep the property operating account or corporate checking account at their bank. The lender could further require you to maintain minimum balances in those accounts.

EBIT, Cash Flow, or NOI

These restrictions require that the property maintain minimum levels of EBIT (earnings before interest and taxes), cash flow, or NOI. Such minimum thresholds provide the lender with a cushion and a check on the status of the collateral.

Leases

The lender may require that the borrower provides copies of all new pending leases prior to execution. This restriction allows the lender to ensure that the borrower's leasing execution is consistent with the business plan presented when the loan was originated.

LOAN TERMS

Secured

A **secured loan** is secured by recourse to the assets of the property. If the borrower fails to repay the loan, the secured lender is entitled to foreclose on the secured assets to satisfy their claim. Which assets? The lender will secure against the building, the capital improvements, the land, and the leases – in other words, everything owned by the lender's special purpose business entity that took title to the property during the foreclosure process. Upon taking control of the property, the lender will claim the leases because they are the direct sources of the property's cash flows. Remember that the cash flows, to a large extent, are derived from the leases rather than from the bricks and mortar.

Recourse

If the loan is solely secured by the property's assets, it is referred to as a **non-recourse** loan. This means the lender only has recourse to the property's assets and cannot seize any of the borrower's personal assets to recoup losses. Absent additional collateral, the outstanding loan balance effectively becomes a **put option** for the borrower. That is, if the property value falls below the loan balance, the borrower can, de facto, sell the property to the lender for forgiveness of the loan balance. As a result, lenders need to bear in mind that they are effectively making a standing offer to purchase the asset at a price equal to the loan balance.

Alternatively, the lender might also secure the loan against the personal assets of the borrower. In this case, if the borrower does not repay the loan, the lender can seek to possess and liquidate the borrower's personal assets to cover any losses on their loan, with the specifics of the process covered by state and federal bankruptcy codes. This is called **recourse** lending. Even if you as the owner structure your special purpose company as a limited liability entity, you can agree (unhappily) to additionally place your personal or other assets at risk with a recourse loan. Recourse can be full or partial in nature, with the former making all personal assets eligible for seizing, and the latter pledging as additional collateral only the assets specified in the loan agreement. Most first mortgages are non-recourse, except for specifically carved out "bad boy" acts by the borrower (e.g., fraud, theft of rents/security deposits/insurance proceeds, environmental pollution) and completion guarantees for development.

Guarantees

Lenders sometimes require that the borrower **guarantees** certain events such as construction completion or leasing to a specific level of occupancy. For example, lenders often require that the developer guarantees the receipt of a certificate of occupancy for their property. Once this certificate is received, tenants can legally move into the newly constructed building, and the borrower is released from recourse action against their personal assets. However, failure to complete the project allows the lender to pursue the borrower's personal assets.

Receivables

In addition to the leases, the lender may have rights to outstanding lease payments, meaning that any monies owed by tenants to the landlord accrue to the lender to satisfy their loan losses.

Draws

For construction loans, as the borrower, you must generally present the lender with supporting documentation on the use of loan proceeds. Any money you ask for in a **draw request** must have a legitimate and fully documented purpose for the requested loan funding to be considered or approved. Examples are copies of permits or a **pay requisition** packet from the general contractor. For acquisition loans that also allow for delayed draws for capital costs relating to the occupancy of new tenants (so-called "good news money"), the borrower will need to provide as proof the signed lease, which includes the interior space fit-out specifications **work letter** and the signed broker leasing commission agreement.

Amortization

Instead of borrowers paying only interest in their periodic debt service, most loans have a specific **amortization schedule** that details the repayment of the borrowed principal over a fixed term. With an amortizing loan, the borrower makes a payment each month (or quarter) that is composed of both principal and interest. It is common, though not always the case that the total amount is the same for each payment. For example, you may have a $50 million loan with a 6% annual interest rate, a 10-year maturity, and a 30-year amortization schedule. The amortization schedule specifies the number of years over which the principal is repaid. In the case of a 30-year amortization schedule, your cumulative payments will completely pay off the loan at the end of 30 years. But how does this work if the loan matures in 10 years? You calculate the constant monthly payment factor, called the **loan constant**, as if the loan will be completely paid off over 30 years, but the final month's payment at the end of the tenth year is equal to the usual payment plus a **balloon payment** equal to all remaining principal owed.

Calculating loan constants used to absorb a great deal of time utilizing a complicated equation. However, the advent of cheap computing power, spreadsheets, and the Internet make such schedules easily available. Just go to Google and enter "mortgage constant calculator" and click on one of the free and easy-to-use calculators. All you need to do is enter the loan amount, interest rate, loan term, and desired years to amortize, and the monthly (or annual) payment throughout the life of the loan is calculated by multiplying the constant by the loan amount.

Lenders may offer an amortizing loan that is structured as an interest-only ("I/O") loan in the early years of the loan period. These up-front I/O "teaser periods" reduce the debt service burden to the owner in the early years of operation. This can be particularly useful for a transitional property that has significant vacancy upon acquisition, as the borrower does not yet have a full NOI stream with which to service the debt. The length of I/O periods are another basis on which lenders compete with one another for placing their funds with borrowers.

Insurance

This is a critical issue, particularly since the September 11, 2001 terrorist attacks. A common loan covenant requires that the borrower must maintain all insurance on the property that is "customary and typical," in an amount sufficient to cover the loan balance. Such insurance means that in the event of an insurable disaster, the borrower will receive insurance payments that are sufficient to repay the loan in full. The lender generally does not care if you insure beyond this amount. They just want their money paid back in full (i.e., to be "made whole").

Before September 11th, few paid much attention to terrorism insurance, which was largely provided as part of the property's umbrella insurance coverage. After September 11th, many building owners were unable to obtain terrorism insurance or could only obtain it at a premium payment of perhaps 2% of the value of the property. This implies a probability of roughly one out of every fifty buildings being blown up each year! If the borrower cannot get terrorism insurance or is unwilling to pay the premium, are they in breach of the loan covenant requiring "customary and typical" insurance? Yes, in the eyes of the lender, and if the borrower has breached the contract, the lender may have the right to accelerate the loan. At first, some borrowers thought they wanted lenders to accelerate the loan so they could refinance the building at a lower interest rate without a prepayment penalty. However, borrowers quickly realized they would also need terrorism insurance before a new lender would make a loan. Similar problems frequently occur with respect to hurricane and earthquake insurance following major disasters.

Sweep

Any money that comes into the property must generally be paid to the lender until contractual loan obligations are satisfied. Imagine that the rent is paid on the 15th of the month, and the loan payment is due on the 16th of the month. If the owner knows they are about to default, they will deposit the rent check elsewhere on the 15th and then default on the loan on the 16th. The lender can protect against such behavior by requiring the property operating account be housed at their bank and by instituting a **sweep** provision, which allows the lender to take all cash inflows until the borrower's loan obligations are satisfied.

LOAN POINTS

The lender will generally charge a fee, commonly called **loan points** or **origination fees**, for processing the loan. This is designed to cover the lender's costs associated with conducting due diligence, credit checks, and environmental analysis, as well as the time and energy of its employees. The lender will charge the borrower a fee that is quoted in basis points to cover these costs. The typical loan fee is 30-100 basis points of the total amount of the loan. Do not confuse this fee with the interest rate paid on the loan. The loan points are paid at closing for originating the loan. The interest rate is charged for the use of the lender's money for the term of the loan. From a cash flow perspective, loan points are an upfront outflow. From an accounting perspective you generally amortize the loan points over the life of the loan.

THE REFI DECISION

Refinancing is the replacement of one debt facility with another. Deciding whether to prematurely refinance your mortgage can be a very difficult decision. By refinancing, you may be able to take a loan larger than the outstanding balance of the in-place loan. You do this to withdraw cash from the equity in the property. The IRS allows the owner to take distribution of these **excess loan proceeds** and re-deploy them as they wish, without paying any capital gains taxes until the sale of the property. This is what is known as taking a "cash out" loan.

Consider the case where you have a $70 million mortgage on a property which was worth $100 million seven years ago, when you took out a 10-year mortgage. Today the property is worth $170 million and after 8 years of amortization, the outstanding loan balance is $60 million. Thus, your current LTV ratio is a mere 35%. By refinancing the property at a 70% loan-to-value, you could receive a $119 million mortgage. Thus, after retiring your existing $60 million loan balance, the refinancing generates $59 million in net proceeds. If the loan is non-recourse, this money goes into your pocket absent any contemporaneous taxes, irrespective of how the property performs in the future.

In addition, by refinancing, you can lock in today's interest rate on a new long-term mortgage. However, you also give up the option that rates may be even lower when your current mortgage matures. Further, early refinancing entails fees and may trigger substantial prepayment penalties. Also, to the extent that you borrow more money than the remaining principal at the time of the refinancing, you will have a higher mortgage payment than on your existing loan. In other words, if you take excess loan proceeds and then go buy yourself a boat or a piece of land for your next development, this does not mean that you no longer owe that amount on the loan related to the collateral property. On the other hand, the new loan (excess proceeds taken or not) generally provides an effective tax shield, as it will have a repayment schedule with greater interest expense, and you will once again be in the early (high tax shielding) years of the amortization schedule. In short, the early refinance decision requires you to carefully consider what objectives are most important to you as well as to determine the desired risk-return profile for your property ownership.

There are two common reasons to undertake an early refinancing. The first is that, as in our previous example, your property has risen substantially in value, allowing you to notably increase the amount of debt on your property. Note that absent a refinancing, the existing $60 million mortgage, which has two years to maturity, locks in your first collateral position at a massively underleveraged 35% LTV level. While you could use mezzanine financing to tap into this underleveraged value, the fact that you cannot access your first lien position means that the pricing on mezzanine financing will not be as attractive as if you could pay off your loan and refinance using the first lien right on the full $170 million value.

The second common reason for premature refinancing is that mortgage interest rates have fallen significantly relative to what you are paying on your existing mortgage. For example, if you have a 10-year mortgage with two years to maturity at an 8% interest rate, while the current interest rate on a 10-year mortgage is 5.7%, every dollar borrowed at the old rate costs you 2.3% in additional interest (pre-tax). If you refinance at the current lower rate and lock this rate in for 10 years, you substantially lower the cost of your debt. If the amount of the loan and all other terms were the same and refinancing were costless, you would always refinance when interest rates fall. Thus, there are two key questions. How expensive is it to refinance relative to the savings you achieve from refinancing at the current rate? Are other loan terms (including the amount borrowed) of the existing mortgage equal to or better than those offered on the new loan?

The most common problems associated with prematurely refinancing are: the time and energy involved, fees, more stringent loan terms, and prepayment penalties. However, time, energy and fees, while substantial, are really a matter of time shifting. That is, you are going to have to refinance when your loan matures, so an early refinancing simply means you are doing it sooner. As a result, it is only the time value of these items which are of relevance. Hence, these factors tend to be relatively unimportant in the decision to prematurely refinance.

In general, there is no reason to believe that terms and covenants for the new loan will be systematically more onerous than the existing loan. Some will be better; others worse. But since debt markets are sometimes either overheated or super cold, terms must be carefully evaluated on a case by case basis to ascertain whether the new loan is more attractive in this regard.

Prepayment penalties are usually the major problem facing premature refinancing. Fixed rate mortgages with maturities greater than three years generally have substantial prepayment penalties. These penalties come in many forms, but all variants effectively require that the lender receives (at least) the present value of the future interest payments over the remaining term of the loan. The discount rate used in these present value calculations is the short-term U.S. Treasury rate, resulting in a penalty payment substantially in excess of the true present value of future mortgage payments (because the Treasury rate is lower than the rate on a newly-minted comparable loan's interest rate). These prepayment penalties reflect the lender's desire to receive the payment stream specified in their loan.

Although there is generally little opportunity for debt service payment savings via premature refinance (due to the penalty's artificially low discount rate), carrying out the refi may still make sense. There are four general cases where this is true. The first is when you can convince the lender that issuing you a new long-term fixed-rate loan, which generates origination fees and places money for the lender today, is better for them than if you refinance your loan with a competitor when it matures. But you will only refinance with them now if the lender waives the prepayment penalty. This sometimes occurs in a highly competitive lending market, particularly when your current mortgage has only a short term remaining, as the loan officer may be pressed to place new funds to meet personal compensation production targets.

A second scenario arises when you believe (perhaps correctly, perhaps incorrectly; only time will tell) that interest rates are at unsustainably low levels. As a result, despite the origination costs and prepayment penalties associated with replacing the current loan, you decide to lock in today's long-term rates before they disappear. This tends to be relevant only when the remaining term on your mortgage is short. For example, you may be willing to suffer the prepayment penalty for the remaining year on your current loan to lock today's very attractive interest rate for the subsequent nine years. Essentially, you are only moderately worse off for the next year. You believe you will be much better off for the ensuing nine years and that if you wait until maturity to refinance, interest rates will be much higher. The shorter the remaining term of the existing loan and the more unsustainably low you believe today's rates are, the more likely you are to execute an early refinancing.

A third case, despite fees and penalties, occurs when you desire to pull out capital on a non-taxed, non-recourse basis, to access substantially underleveraged appreciation in your property. In this case, you are deciding to take your money off the table tax-free, and the loan points and prepayment penalties associated with the premature refinancing are simply the cost of doing so.

A fourth case supporting premature refinancing is driven by your improved credit quality as a borrower. As the new owner of the property, you can borrow at notably lower rates due to a superior credit rating or access to cheap capital. For example, if Apple purchases a property, they may achieve a lower interest rate due to their superior credit. Alternatively, perhaps you were a young start-up when you took out the mortgage, while today, you are a preferred customer of the lender. It is important to keep in mind that these four possibilities are not mutually exclusive. For example, it is possible you want to refinance because you believe rates are too low and your credibility with banks has improved, and you desire to take cash out of the property to fund other investment activities.

 Online Companion Hands On: Using Excel, solve for the maximum refinancing loan proceeds for a property that has an NOI of $5 million and a cap rate of 6% for valuation purposes. Assume 30-year amortization and a 5% interest rate. Run these three loan sizing tests assuming monthly payments and the following constraints: maximum 70% LTV; minimum 1.20x DSCR; minimum 10% Debt Yield. Choose the lesser of the three resulting loan sizes. See Chapter 15 in the Online Companion for the solution.

PREPAYMENT PENALTIES

Early refinancing decisions are challenging and necessitate full understanding of what you are trying to achieve, along with the requisite number crunching to determine if the present value of the benefits outweigh the present value of the costs. The primary cost is the prepayment penalty on the original loan. Penalties can take the form of a percentage of the outstanding balance (typically a declining percentage as the maturity date approaches), defeasance, and yield maintenance. **Defeasance** involves a substitution of collateral: Treasury bonds for the real estate. "Defeasing" the loan requires that the borrower uses proceeds from the refinance to purchase a portfolio of U.S. Treasuries sufficient to make all of the remaining loan payments. The Treasuries are pledged to the original lender, who then releases the real estate from the lien of the mortgage. The loan's promissory note, which remains outstanding after the defeasance, and the portfolio of securities are assigned by the original borrower entity to a successor borrower entity that makes the remaining debt service payments through the bond interest stream and eventual portfolio liquidation.

Yield maintenance is a way to prepay the loan and make the lender whole on the unpaid interest that they would have received if the borrower had not prepaid. The borrower pays the lender the unpaid principal amount, and also pays the lender the present value of the scheduled amortizing debt service payment amounts over the remaining term versus a replacement interest rate. The discount rate typically used in prepayment penalty formulas is the yield on a very short-term Treasury note, as is the reinvestment rate. Using such a short-term rate as the discount rate, rather than a longer-term maturity rate, builds in a substantial prepayment penalty by under-discounting future interest payment streams. Further, the use of a short-term U.S. Treasury rate as the reinvestment rate rather than the higher rate for a comparable mortgage imposes a notable penalty.

REFINANCING IN A DOWN MARKET

Refinancing in a down property market, which usually coincides with a cold debt market, is a serious challenge. Not only may the property be worth less than the loan balance (i.e., be "underwater"), but higher underwriting standards will often make it impossible to refinance the loan balance. In such cases, tedious and often hostile negotiations will transpire between the borrower and lender. The tenor of these discussions is usually the lender saying, "Just pay me," and the borrower saying, "I can't, and it's not my fault; just give me time." This is a highly nuanced area and is never pleasant. But oftentimes, re-striking a deal with an honest and competent borrower is a better solution than foreclosing and conducting a distressed property sale in a down property market. About once a decade, this type of systemic problem arises and is solved by a combination of extended maturities and equity infusions. In the 2008-2010 cycle, many lenders "extended and pretended," extending loan maturities as long as borrowers made debt payments. Why? The properties were cash flowing enough to cover monthly payments, and both parties believed that capital markets temporarily understated the value of the properties, making an accurate valuation impossible. As a result, many insolvent borrowers remained in business and survived the frozen capital markets.

CLOSING THOUGHT

Will the lender get all of the terms they desire? Probably not. But given the secured lender's asymmetric return profile, you should expect them to get most of what they request. Frequently, the terms discussed above are offered on a "take it or leave it" basis. However, when lenders get aggressive, they frequently compromise the restrictiveness of their covenants. Similarly, when borrowers feel that they cannot lose on their projects, more restrictive covenants are accepted and recourse guarantees are frequently provided.

 Online Companion Audio Interview: To hear a conversation about this chapter's content, go to the Online Companion and select the link for Chapter 15. Scroll down to the Audio Interview section and listen.

Chapter 16
Sources of Long- and Short-Term Debt

"The machine is rarely the problem; the people operating the machine are usually the problem."
- Dr. Peter Linneman

Thus far, we have discussed debt financing only in the contexts of a senior mortgage secured by, or a mezzanine loan placed on, a single asset. However, the process of loan origination does not always stop with individual property-level underwriting. In fact, a substantial secondary market exists for loans that have been put in place on properties. The creation, rise, collapse, and rebirth of the **commercial mortgage-backed security (CMBS)** market reflects significant changes in real estate capital sources over the last 30+ years.

CAPITAL EVOLUTION

In 1970, if you were looking for money to purchase real estate, you would primarily look to commercial banks and life insurance companies. Commercial banks held federally insured deposits, and in return, the federal government imposed numerous regulations on the commercial banking industry. One of the most important regulations barred commercial banks from making equity investments, as regulators viewed equity as too risky. Despite modern portfolio theory's views of diversification, government regulators viewed a 100%-debt portfolio as safer for banks than having any equity. Therefore, commercial banks could only receive federal insurance on their deposits if their investments were debt, generally secured loans to local borrowers.

Banks issued debt secured by accounts receivable, cars, single-family homes, and commercial real estate. Commercial banks have short-term liabilities, as depositors can withdraw their deposits at any time. Therefore, in 1970, banks were primarily responsible for originating construction loans, as the short-term and finite nature of the construction period matched their short-term deposit liabilities.

At that time, banks were generally not permitted to have more than one office location. Even in the most progressive states, banks could only have a few branch locations within their home county. With a single office location, most banks primarily originated local loans, as they had staff only in that area to evaluate loan applications. So, if you owned a bank in Grand Island, Nebraska, it was unlikely you made any loans outside of your county, let alone in New York, Los Angeles, Philadelphia, or D.C. The large banks located in major U.S. cities had the same constraints but had larger deposit bases and served a larger local market. Senior bank managers knew the local borrowers and personally conducted business with them. Even if better opportunities existed in other markets, regulatory restrictions made it difficult to lend outside of the bank's immediate geographic area, so most local banks simply attempted to develop lending relationships with the "best" local borrowers.

The other major sources of money at that time were the large life insurance companies. Life insurance companies take in policy premiums, invest to earn a return spread, and return the money when a policyholder dies. Actuarially, a person's lifetime is a long-term liability. Therefore, life insurance companies are logical long-term lenders (3 to 20 years), as they seek to match their long-term liabilities with long-lived assets. Life insurance companies have historically been heavily regulated by the states as a result of the fear that an insurer will collect premiums from policyholders and bet on very risky assets. If the bets pay off, the insurer wins; if they lose, the insurer will be unable to pay on its policies. As a result, most state regulators require insurers to limit equity investments to roughly 25% of total investments, with the remainder of their portfolios primarily composed of long-term debt.

Given the heavily regulated nature of these two major sources of capital, an abundance of money flowed into real estate lending. While there were other capital sources, such as university endowments, charitable foundations, high net worth individuals, and a few pension and mutual funds, commercial banks and life insurance companies were the dominant sources of capital. In fact, U.S. pension funds had few assets in 1970.

Today, the structure and regulation of capital sources has changed dramatically. For instance, banks operate nationally and freely invest in equities. While, in real terms, banks and life insurance companies control more assets than ever, they are no longer the primary sources of capital. Instead, today, if you are looking for capital for your projects, you will also look to pension funds, mutual funds, endowments, and sovereign wealth funds. Pension funds and mutual funds control roughly 65% of all assets in the U.S., while banks and life insurers have gone from roughly 70% of all assets in 1970, to less than 35% today.

Pension funds and mutual funds are also regulated, but these regulations are primarily "prudent man" and disclosure regulations. Specifically, mutual funds are allowed to invest in anything as long as fund managers fully disclose and abide by their stated investment criteria. For example, if a mutual fund manager discloses that they will only invest in AAA bonds, the mutual fund basically is prohibited from investing in lower-rated bonds. Mutual funds have proliferated, investing in a variety of debt and equity investments, including real estate debt and equity.

Since pension funds are tax-exempt entities, the IRS is concerned with pension funds taking over businesses and wiping out corporate tax revenues. Therefore, pension funds are generally prohibited from actively owning businesses. As a result, most pension funds primarily invest via securities and private equity funds.

FOLLOW THE MONEY

Real estate needs to follow the money because it is a very capital-intensive business. It is not surprising that the nature of real estate financing has changed dramatically as the sources of capital have changed. With 65% of the money in the U.S. held by pension funds and mutual funds, the real estate industry had to figure out a way to access these deep pools of capital with a preference for securitized investments. CMBS is the vehicle used to achieve this goal with respect to real estate debt. The CMBS market did not exist in 1970 and still does not exist in most countries, as if banks are the only source of debt capital, CMBS serve little purpose.

HOW IS A CMBS ISSUANCE CREATED?

Suppose you are a commercial mortgage lender. You have contacts and relationships with numerous borrowers, as well as the capacity to underwrite loans. However, having originated 50 $10 million mortgages, you exhaust your $500 million capital base. If you could package your 50 mortgages and sell them to the countless fixed income mutual funds and pension funds and use the sale proceeds to originate more loans, you could capitalize on your underwriting expertise. Pension and mutual funds generally lack loan origination and underwriting capacity but are major investors in fixed income securities. Thus, if you can match your mortgage origination skills with their deep pockets, you can underwrite a lot more mortgages, and potentially generate a lot more profit.

Each mortgage you issue is secured by a warehouse, apartment, mall, or other real property. Assume that the average loan-to-value ratio is 65% with an interest coverage ratio of 1.4x. Of course, these ratios vary across the individual loans, but none of the loans has an LTV above 70% or a debt service coverage ratio below 1.3x. Further assume that the weighted-average interest rate across the 50 mortgages is 7%, and that, for simplicity, all the loans have prepayment prohibitions, no amortization, 10-year terms, and the same origination and maturity date. Each of these simplifying assumptions illustrates the incredible nuances that one ultimately encounters with actual CMBS packaging, as to the extent that these assumptions do not hold, the bookkeeping and math becomes much more complex. In reality, all mortgages will not have the same maturity, interest rate, amortization schedule, LTV, or covenants.

Since each mortgage is secured by the property's leases and loan documents, this is a tremendous amount of paper! This is why you see increasing standardization in the loan documents for loans that are part of a CMBS securitization. For example, no loan in a CMBS issuance can have a DSCR below 1.3x or exceed 70% LTV, and no one borrower can have more than a few properties in the pool. These standardized terms make it easier for the pension funds and mutual funds looking to invest in your CMBS issue to understand the pool of mortgages.

Given the assumed loan pool, you expect to receive $35 million in interest payments each year for the next 10 years ($500 million * 7% interest rate), and at the end of the 10th year, the $500 million principal will be repaid. Remember that your core competence is as a loan originator. If you have the human resources to underwrite and originate $500 million in loans each quarter, but only have $500 million available to lend, you cannot lend beyond your current portfolio. Therefore, rather than tie up your $500 million for the next 10 years, while your origination expertise sits idle, you decide to package and sell your existing loans. By capitalizing on your underwriting skills, you can originate more loans with the sale proceeds.

HOW DO YOU SELL?

To facilitate the sale of your mortgage pool, you create a new company called a **special-purpose bankruptcy-remote entity (SPE)** that will ultimately own the pool of mortgages. You first transfer your 50 mortgages to the new SPE in exchange for 100% of its ownership. The SPE's bankruptcy-remote structure means that, other than fraud, if something goes wrong with the assets, investors generally cannot go after either your personal assets or your loan origination company. You then put your ownership of the SPE, which owns the 50 mortgages, up for sale to the highest bidder. Specifically, you will try to convince pension funds and fixed income mutual funds to acquire the SPE. By focusing on these large institutional fixed income capital sources that desire long-term assets, you will generally obtain a better price for the SPE than if you only marketed to dedicated real estate money sources.

Your $500 million-mortgage pool generates $35 million annually, or a 7% yield. If you can sell the ownership claims on the SPE to investors for a pro forma 6.5% IRR on their investment, you can reap substantial profits. After all, the buyers of the SPE do not care what interest rate you received on the mortgages, as to them, it is just a company with $35 million in cash flow (with underwritten expected shortfalls) in each of the next 10 years, with an additional $500 million in cash flow at the end of the 10th year). The buyers will compare this investment with others of similar risk and expected cash flows. As the seller, you will try to get the buyer to offer as high a price (accept as low a return) as possible.

You will generally engage a CMBS sales and marketing specialist, such as an investment bank, to market to potential buyers and to determine pricing for an ownership claim in the SPE. If the company is sold for a 6.5% IRR over the 10-year hold, you will receive $518 million in gross proceeds, as shown in Figure 16.1.

FIGURE 16.1

CMBS Pool Price Determination ($ in MM)								
Loan Principal Amount ($500)	Issuance	Year 1	Year 2	Year 3	Year 4	Year 5	...	Year 10
Pool Purchase Price	($518)							
Interest Payment Stream 7.00%		35	35	35	35	35		35
Return of Principal								500
Total Purchaser Cash Flow	(518)	35	35	35	35	35		535
Purchaser IRR	6.50%							
Net Cash Flow To Purchaser	$332							

Online Companion Hands On: Find the formatted, blank version of this Figure in Chapter 16 of the Online Companion and complete it. The **Interest Payment Stream** values are calculated as: **Loan Principal Amount * –Interest Rate.** Key in the **Return of Principal** amount of 500 in Year 10. Sum the **Pool Purchase Price, Interest Payment Stream** and **Return of Principal** lines to calculate the **Total Purchaser Cash Flow.** Run the **IRR function** and then manipulate the **Pool Purchase Price** value and observe how the IRR changes (pools are priced by buyers using this back-solving approach where a targeted IRR is achieved by raising or lowering the purchase price). Last, sum all **Total Purchase Cash Flow** amounts to calculate the **Net Cash Flow to Purchaser.**

PROFIT FROM THE CMBS PACKAGING

What was the cost of this process? First, you had to originate the $500 million in loans, pay lawyers and accountants to create and certify the SPE, and pay fees to the sales agent for marketing the securities. If the costs of creating and selling the securities are $8 million, you net $10 million in profit, as seen in Figure 16.2.

FIGURE 16.2

Lender Economics for a Sample CMBS Issuance ($ in MM)	
Starting loan underwriting capacity	$500
Individual loans originated	(500)
CMBS packaging/issuance costs	(8)
CMBS pool sale proceeds	518
Net profit	$10
Ending loan underwriting capacity	$500

As a result of the sale, you can pull out $10 million in profit and still have $500 million for new originations. If you originate, package, and sell $500 million in mortgages each quarter, you can generate $40 million in profits from sales, plus the profit from loan origination fees on the $2 billion lent over the course of the year. At a 20-basis point loan origination fee profit, this amounts to an additional $4 million in your pocket (4 * $500 MM *.002) annually. Thus, your total annual net profit from this business is $44 million ($40 million from the four sales and $4 million from origination fees). Note that you only required $500 million in capital to fund your $2 billion in annual mortgage originations. In our example, securitization allows you to generate $44 million in profit, while if you originated the $500 million in loans and held them, you would only generate $36 million in profit in the first year and $35 million for the remaining 9 years. Hence, the more frequently you can originate and sell, the greater are your profits. The example in Figure 16.3 shows lender profit over 10 years of $432 million (an 8.56% IRR) when issuing 4 $500 million CMBS pools per year, versus profit of $351 million (a 7.03% IRR) when holding a single $500 million origination amount to maturity. Issuing CMBS at that pace yields the lender a 23% improvement on their return on assets. Note that the IRR on the hold-to-maturity scenario exceeds the interest rate due to the origination fee profits.

FIGURE 16.3

Lender Profit Comparison: Holding Loans to Maturity vs. Multiple CMBS Pool Issuance ($ in MM)									

Hold Loans to Maturity

		Origination	Year 1	Year 2	Year 3	Year 4	Year 5	...	Year 10
Loans Originated		($500)							
Origination Profit		0.20%	1						
Interest Payment Stream	7.00%		35	35	35	35	35		35
Return of Principal									500
Total Lender Cash Flow		(500)	36	35	35	35	35		535
Lender IRR		7.03%							
Lender Profit		$351							

Issue CMBS Pools

		Issuance	Year 1	Year 2	Year 3	Year 4	Year 5	...	Year 10
Loans Originated		($500)	(2,000)	(2,000)	(2,000)	(2,000)	(2,000)		(2,000)
Origination Profit		0.20%	4	4	4	4	4		4
CMBS Pools per year		4							
Pool packaging/issuance costs		($8)	(32)	(32)	(32)	(32)	(32)		(32)
Pool Sale Proceeds	$518		2,072	2,072	2,072	2,072	2,072		2,072
Interest Payment Stream	0.00%		0	0	0	0	0		0
Return of Principal									500
Total Lender Cash Flow		(508)	44	44	44	44	44		544
Lender IRR		8.56%							
Lender Profit		$432							

Online Companion Hands On: Find the formatted, blank version of this Figure in Chapter 16 of the Online Companion and complete it. First fill out the **Hold Loans to Maturity** section. Calculate the Origination Profit as **–Loans Originated * Fee Rate**. Calculate the **Interest Payment Stream** values as: **–Loans Originated * Interest Rate**. Key in the **Return of Principal** as a positive value in Year 10. Total the cash flows for the Origination column and subsequent years, run the IRR on them, and sum the cash flows to find the **Lender Profit**.

Next fill out the **Issue CMBS Pools** section. Calculate the **Loans Originated** as: initial **Issuance Amount * CMBS Pools per year**. Calculate the **Origination Profit** as annual **–Loans Originated * Fee Rate**. Calculate the **Pool packaging/issuance costs** as: initial **Pool packaging/issuance cost * CMBS Pools per year**. Calculate the **Pool Sale Proceeds** as: initial **Proceeds Amount * CMBS Pools per year**. Calculate the **Interest Payment Stream** values as: **–Loans Originated * Interest Rate**. Key in the **Return of Principal** in Year 10 as a positive value. Total the cash flows for the Issuance column and the subsequent years, run the IRR on them, and sum the cash flows to find the **Lender Profit**.

Manipulate the **CMBS Pools per year** variable to observe how the Lender IRR and Lender Profit change with a higher and lower frequency of pool issuances.

IT'S ABOUT SPECIALIZATION

Securitization allows for a return to specialization, with you, for example, specializing in origination, someone else in packaging, someone else in marketing the deal, and yet others in holding and servicing the loans. Prior to the emergence of CMBS, lenders made the loan, held it, and did all the bookkeeping until maturity. CMBS allows different people to serve different functions: you can originate the loan without holding it; you can hold it without originating it; or you can manage it without either originating or holding it.

The management of the entity is typically outsourced for a fee to two different specialists. One company, the **servicer**, is responsible for assuring that the borrowers are in compliance with their loan documents and for taking appropriate actions if the borrower is in default. The servicer also makes sure that investors and the IRS receive all pertinent information in a timely manner. The other management specialist is the **special servicer**, who takes control of the administration of any non-performing loans. The special servicer receives a small fee for being prepared to take over non-performing loans as well as an incentive-related fee for dealing with any defaults that arise.

The CMBS process is the creation and sale of new special purpose companies that own pools of mortgages. The more companies you can profitably sell in a year, the more money you can make. The business model attempts to take advantage of your specialization skills, whether you are the servicer, the special servicer, the originator, the packager, or the ultimate investor. A profit can be made if there are enough buyers willing to invest in these companies. This ultimately requires quality mortgages, efficient packaging and marketing, and effective servicing. In this sense, CMBS is no different from soda bottling. You could make your own bottles, but there are companies that specialize in bottling, and you, therefore, buy from them because they can do it more efficiently. And if the soda inside the bottles is of poor or inconsistent quality, ultimately people will stop buying the product, no matter how sleek the bottles or effective the marketing.

Originally, government agencies and banks with disastrous balance sheets primarily utilized the CMBS process to securitize existing mortgages. The next step was to originate mortgages with the intent to quickly securitize the loans. Wall Street stepped in, using their sales and marketing skills to create an active CMBS market. From 1997-2007, many investment banks purchased mortgages from banks, life companies, and mortgage brokers, and directly issued loans as well. This allowed them to pool large volumes of mortgages and quickly sell and recycle their available capital. From a marketing perspective, investment banks were ideal issuers, as they specialize in selling securities with well-networked sales teams and sophisticated research support to push those securities to the market. Of course, some CMBS purchasers employed independent research analysts to help sort through the many available CMBS offerings.

Perhaps the key marketing tool for debt securities is a bond rating from a major rating agency, such as Moody's or S&P, which theoretically, independently assesses the likelihood of the debt holder receiving interest and principal as promised. It is not a rating of whether the securities are a good investment. The CMBS packager pays the rating agencies a fee to rate the securities. These rating agencies are incredibly important, as many buyers can only invest in AA or better rated securities.

CREATING TRANCHES

The rating agencies are critically important when the CMBS issuance is targeted towards multiple buyers of different risk profiles. In our original example, you created a company which sold a single class of ownership claims to pension funds and fixed income mutual funds. However, if the loan pool is large enough, it is possible to slice it up into multiple ownership classes in an attempt to appeal to a much broader set of investors. This is referred to as **tranching** the CMBS pool. Tranching, which is the CMBS industry norm, involves the creation of 8-15 separate ownership claims of differing priority on the commingled stream of cash flows from the underlying pool of mortgages. For example, you can create a highly preferred ownership claim ("super senior"), a second ownership claim subordinate to the first claim, another ownership claim subordinate to the second ownership claim, and so on.

In this case, the first ownership claim is entitled to its contracted cash flow before the subordinate investors receive any money from the pool. That is, if there is insufficient cash flow resulting from defaults or non-payments on the underlying mortgages, tranched CMBS investors will not share the loss equally. Rather, the most senior claims will receive their money first, while the most subordinated ownership claim only receives their contractual payments if the proceeds are sufficient to pay all senior tranches in full first. If the most subordinated ownership claim is insufficient to absorb the entire shortfall, then the next lowest ownership claim incurs subsequent shortfall losses. This continues up the ownership classes, like fire consuming a building from the basement up.

Clearly, the most senior ownership claim has the most protection from not receiving their contractual payments because of the subordinated owners. The actual structuring of the different tranches is highly technical, as some ownership claims may be entitled to only interest payments, while others receive only principal payments, some contractual payments may float with LIBOR/SOFR, etc. Nevertheless, the basic concept of tranching is very simple. You create and sell ownership rights of varying seniority rather than a single ownership right to the whole company.

The rating agencies apply simplistic models to determine the likelihood of losing money for the various ownership claims. For example, the 60% most senior claims on CMBS cash flows typically receive "investment grade" AAA ratings (the lowest risk, "highest" rating), with another 10% rated AA, 10% rated A, 10% rated BBB, and roughly 8% in the BB range. The latter is considered "non-investment-grade," as is the last 2% ownership claim, effectively the common equity of the company. Namely, they receive all the money not promised to the more senior ownership classes and are in the first loss position. This is the riskiest ownership position.

The lower the subordination, the lower the rating. The higher the rating, the lower the contractual payment rate promised to the investor (i.e., the tighter the yield spread over comparable duration U.S. Treasury yields). That is, the higher the ownership claim, the more the investor is willing to pay for its relatively more certain contractual cash flow stream. Cutting up the underlying cash flows (the $35 million annual payment) does not create or destroy risk, as the cash flow stream itself is unchanged. However, while the LTV on the overall pool is unchanged by tranching, you have created a de facto lower LTV and higher effective interest coverage for the most senior ownership claim, as they receive their money first at the expense of the subordinate ownership claims.

Tranching will generally generate a better price than the $518 million (in our example) that you realized by selling a single ownership claim, as you will find investors who are willing to pay a premium for the customized assets, particularly for the highest-rated ownership claim. Returning to our original example, assuming the 10-year Treasury yield is 5% and the super senior 60% of the $500 million was sold at an IRR pricing of 5.8%. This 60% is rated AAA and offers the lowest risk to investors, justifying a lower required rate of return. The remaining $200 million consists of a $50 million AA-rated tranche selling at a 6.2% IRR, a $50 million A-rated tranche selling at a 6.4% IRR, a $50 million BBB-rated tranche selling at a 6.8% IRR, a $30 million BB-rated tranche selling at a 7% IRR, while the last $20 million is an unrated tranche that sells for a 9% IRR, as summarized in Figure 16.4.

FIGURE 16.4

Tranched CMBS Pool Example			
Tranche	% of Total Pool	Value	Buyer IRR
AAA	60%	$300 MM	5.8%
AA	10%	$50 MM	6.2%
A	10%	$50 MM	6.4%
BBB	10%	$50 MM	6.8%
BB	6%	$30 MM	7.0%
Unrated	4%	$20 MM	9.0%
Total/Average	100%	$500 MM	6.2%

Based on this information, as shown in Figure 16.5, we back solve to see that the tranched CMBS pool sells for $529.1 million.

FIGURE 16.5

Tranched CMBS Pool Price Determination ($ in MM)									
Loan Principal Amount ($500)		Issuance	Year 1	Year 2	Year 3	Year 4	Year 5	...	Year 10
Pool Purchase Price		($529.1)							
Interest Payment Stream	7.00%		35	35	35	35	35		35
Return of Principal									500
Total Purchaser Cash Flow		(529.1)	35.0	35.0	35.0	35.0	35.0		535.0
Weighted Purchaser IRR		6.20%							
Net Cash Flow To Purchaser		$320.9							

 Online Companion Hands On: Find the formatted, blank version of this Figure in Chapter 16 of the Online Companion and complete it. Manipulate the **Pool Purchase Price** input to back solve until you achieve the targeted Weighted Purchaser IRR of your choosing.

The weighted-average expected IRR for this tranched issuance is 6.2%. The yield (7%) is higher than the IRR, as the investors pay above par for the cash flow stream ($529.1 million) and expect to receive only $500 million in principal back in the 10th year.

If you can successfully tranche and sell this CMBS issuance at a 6.2% weighted IRR, you generate $29.1 million in proceeds in excess of the $500 million face value of the loans. Compared to our initial example, where you sold the single CMBS ownership claim at a 6.5% IRR for $518 million, you can generate an additional $11.1 million from tranching the ownership claims.

You may have an additional $3 million in fees due to the increased marketing costs, additional documents, a more involved rating process, and extra servicing costs due to the added complexity of the deal. As a result, the tranching results in a net increase of $8.1 million in additional profits. In total, this process generates $19.1 million in profits ($529.1 MM in sales minus the $511 MM cost of creating and selling, plus $1 MM in origination fees). As shown in the bottom section of Figure 16.6, if you generate 4 turns on your $500 million during the year, you earn a total of $76.4 million in annual net profit ($19.1 MM * 4 times a year) (Total Lender Cash Flow line). This is a 15.3% annual return on your $500 million in assets ($76.4 MM / $500 MM). At 5 turns a year, you could generate $95.5 million in total profits, for a 19.1% annual return on assets. At 6 turns, you could generate $114.6 million total net profit, for a 22.9% annual return on assets. Thus, the more frequently you can create and sell a CMBS pool, the more profit you earn.

FIGURE 16.6

Lender Profit Comparison: Untranched vs. Tranched Multiple CMBS Pool Issuances ($ in MM)									
Issue Untranched CMBS Pools									
		Issuance	Year 1	Year 2	Year 3	Year 4	Year 5	...	Year 10
Loans Originated		($500)	(2,000)	(2,000)	(2,000)	(2,000)	(2,000)		(2,000)
Origination Profit		0.20%	4	4	4	4	4		4
CMBS Pools per year		4							
Pool packaging/issuance costs		($8)	(32)	(32)	(32)	(32)	(32)		(32)
Pool Sale Proceeds	$518		2,072	2,072	2,072	2,072	2,072		2,072
Interest Payment Stream	0.00%		0	0	0	0	0		0
Return of Principal									500
Total Lender Cash Flow		(508)	44	44	44	44	44		544
Lender IRR		8.56%							
Lender Profit		$432							
Issue Tranched CMBS Pools									
		Issuance	Year 1	Year 2	Year 3	Year 4	Year 5	...	Year 10
Loans Originated		($500)	(2,000)	(2,000)	(2,000)	(2,000)	(2,000)		(2,000)
Origination Profit		0.20%	4	4	4	4	4		4
CMBS Pools per year		4							
Pool packaging/issuance costs		($11)	(44)	(44)	(44)	(44)	(44)		(44)
Pool Sale Proceeds	$529.1		2,116.4	2,116.4	2,116.4	2,116.4	2,116.4		2,116.4
Interest Payment Stream	0.00%		0	0	0	0	0		0
Return of Principal									500
Total Lender Cash Flow		(511.0)	76.4	76.4	76.4	76.4	76.4		576.4
Lender IRR		14.84%							
Lender Profit		$753							

DEFAULT DYNAMICS

Thus far, we have assumed no defaults on the underlying mortgage pool. Assume instead that 2% of the total pool defaults at the end of the 10th year, when the $500 million principal payments are due. That is, $10 million of the $500 million in mortgages do not pay according to the loan agreement. In this case, the non-payments have no impact on the AAA, AA, A, BBB, BB, but will wipe out half of the $20 million non-rated tranche due at the end of the 10th year. While the non-rated tranche would have received all of their annual interest payments in this example, they lose half of their investment in the final year. This example illustrates the benefits of subordination for the higher rated tranches. If each class had the same ownership rights, each tranche would have suffered a 2% loss of their initial investment, while with subordination, only the lowest-rated tranche incurs a loss. Figure 16.7 shows how lower tranches bear losses to their maximum capacity, prior to the next lowest tranche suffering losses, by simulating pool default rates of 2%, 5%, and 11%.

FIGURE 16.7

Losses Borne by CMBS Tranches at Differing Default Rates ($ in MM)								
			Pool Default Rate					
			2.00%		5.00%		11.00%	
Tranche	% Total	Value	$10 Loss		$25 Loss		$55 Loss	
	Pool		Losses Borne by Tranche					
AAA	60%	$300	$0	Loss %	$0	Loss %	$0	Loss %
AA	10%	50	0		0		0	
A	10%	50	0		0		0	
BBB	10%	50	0		0		5	10%
BB	6%	30	0		5	17%	30	100%
Unrated	4%	20	10	50%	20	100%	20	100%
Total	100%	$500	$10		$25		$55	

Online Companion Hands On: Find this Figure in Chapter 16 of the Online Companion and manipulate the **Pool Default Rate** in any column to get a feel for the relative safety of the more senior tranches.

Tranching conceptually works because there is a deep pool of money seeking AAA rated paper. For instance, many corporations invest their cash exclusively in such securities. Similarly, many mutual funds and money market funds are restricted to very highly rated debt securities. Even funds that are not limited to very highly rated bonds invest their cash positions in the AAA and AA securities as a hedge against lower-rated assets. This high demand tends to generate attractive pricing (from the issuer's perspective) for the highly rated tranches. This is similar to a liquor store just outside a college campus. The liquor store can charge higher prices (within reason) as students are willing to spend their parents' hard-earned money for their preferred "asset."

On the other hand, there are very few buyers of the lower-rated tranches, especially those rated below BBB (the investment grade threshold). You are basically selling these highly subordinated tranches to specialized real estate investors, as the lowest tranche is the first loss position after the equity in the property. Thus, investors in the most subordinated tranche need to understand the security as a real estate investment.

THE EVOLUTION OF THE U.S. CMBS MARKET

The U.S. CMBS market crashed spectacularly in late 2008, after an equally spectacular run from 2003 through mid-2007. The cause of this crash and subsequent CMBS market freeze was remarkably simple: poorly underwritten, low-quality mortgage pools were oversold by investment banks and overrated by the rating agencies. In this regard, the failure of CMBS was no different from the demise of any company which oversells a product of ever deteriorating quality. By mid-2007, super senior ratings were being awarded to the most senior 80-90% of the ownership claims. This occurred even as interest coverage ratios eroded to below 1.15x due to LTV increases to 85% on the underlying mortgages. To make matters worse, the majority of mortgages had no amortization, resulting in large balloon payments at maturity. Yet, even as product quality deteriorated, pricing increased as investors took undue comfort in the AAA ratings assigned by the conflicted and overwhelmed rating agencies.

The lesson is not that the CMBS concept is flawed but rather, the key for long-term success is to under-promise and over-deliver. The failure to do so erodes confidence in the product and destroys demand until the problem is clearly resolved.

CLOSING THOUGHT

For a CMBS issue to succeed, it must be large enough to appeal to fixed income buyers, who are generally interested only in relatively large issues. Most bond desks will not buy unless the CMBS offering is at least $200 million. Size also helps in that it provides a more diverse pool of properties, markets, and maturities.

On the other hand, overzealous mortgage lenders who turn a blind eye to market signals can kill the CMBS market. If the broad set of fixed income investors demand a 6.5% IRR for the associated risk, you work backwards and determine that you need borrowers to accept a 7% interest rate on their loans if you are to profitably originate and package CMBS. But if lenders are willing to lend to borrowers at 4%, the CMBS issue will never take place because no one will borrow from you at 7%, and you cannot profitably sell the CMBS issue for a 6.5% IRR if you are only receiving 4% in interest income. For example, the evolution of CMBS in Germany was hindered by their old state-owned Landesbanks. You can imagine that government-owned banks were not terribly efficient and that considerable political lending took place. In this lending environment, CMBS did not generally work because the Landesbanks offered significantly lower mortgage rates than were available through CMBS issuances. In addition, there were few pension or mutual funds in Germany willing to purchase CMBS pools. So for years, there was little in the way of a CMBS market in Germany.

A final word is in order on the diversification advantage of a CMBS pool. Never forget that while a CMBS pool may offer diversification, if the underlying mortgages are worthless, then the pool is worthless as well. Further, if a mortgage default arises due to circumstances which are unique to the individual property, the CMBS mortgage pool provides diversification benefits for investors. However, the bulk of mortgage defaults are historically due to cyclical, rather than property-specific, problems. As a result, the diversification advantages of a large mortgage pool are largely illusory, as when an economic recession occurs, all properties tend to be battered by the economic storm.

 Online Companion Audio Interview: To hear a conversation about this chapter's content, go to the Online Companion and select the link for Chapter 16. Scroll down to the Audio Interview section and listen.

Chapter 17
Ground Leases as a Source of Finance

"Judgment is far more important than intellect."
- Dr. Peter Linneman

Ground leases are a relatively rare, but interesting, dimension of real estate finance. Generally, real estate transactions involve the acquisition of a **fee simple ownership interest**, which is the purchase of both the building and the land on which it sits. However, when there is a **ground lease** in place, the land title does not transfer, and the land is leased by the building owner from the third-party landowner. For example, in Hawaii, China, New York, and London, many buildings are owned "subject to" ground leases. The separation of the ownership of land and structure can create problems and leads to some nuances in the financial analysis.

To illustrate the dynamics of a ground lease, assume you are interested in purchasing the apartment building, Seaview Apartments, summarized in Figure 17.1. If the land were owned fee simple, there would be a single ownership claim on the property's NOI.

FIGURE 17.1

Seaview Apartments Acquisition Subject to Ground Lease	
Property NOI	$8.00 MM
Property Value including Land	$100.00 MM
Acquisition Cap Rate	8.00%
Senior Mortgage LTV	65.00%
Senior Mortgage Amount	$65.00 MM
Interest Rate	5.40%
Annual Interest Payment	$3.51 MM
Ground Lease Details:	
Annual Lease Payment	$3.00 MM
Term	70 years
Lease Payment Growth	3% every 10 years

Based on your analysis, you determine that the $8 million stabilized NOI for the property (including the land) is worth $100 million (an 8 cap or 12.5x multiple). To finance your purchase of the building, you obtain a 10-year, $65 million interest-only first mortgage on the property. With the 10-year Treasury rate at 3.6% (yes, risk-free rates can rise to this level), you negotiate a 5.4% interest rate (180 basis points above Treasury), which means you will pay $3.51 million in interest per year. In this example, you have a loan-to-value ratio of 65% ($65 MM mortgage / $100 MM estimated property value) and a 2.28x interest coverage ratio ($8 MM NOI / $3.51 MM interest payment).

Assume that instead of a fee simple ownership for the property, the apartment complex is subject to a $3 million annual ground lease payment to the landowner. If you fail to make the $3 million payment, the landowner has foreclosure rights on your building, as stipulated in the ground lease. Generally, the terms of the ground lease allow the landowner to take ownership of the building to satisfy their claim if you fail to meet the terms of the ground lease. Post-foreclosure, only if the value of the building exceeds the present value of the landowner's lease claim will the building owner receive the excess value. In some ways, a ground lease is similar to a mortgage, as both have fixed payment streams that have priority over equity claimants, and failure to pay causes a contractual default that triggers specific remedies.

Because ground leases generally specify that the landowner receives any structures remaining on the land at the end of the lease, they tend to have very long terms (e.g., 99 years). They are not infinite because of legal technicalities. Ground leases tend to be renegotiated every 10-20 years at the request of the lessee, because as the expiration date approaches, the landowner may have little incentive to extend the lease. If you encounter a situation where the landowner takes control of the building due to lease expiration, you can be certain that one of the parties misplayed their hand many, many years earlier. Either someone was very sloppy or procrastinated too long.

Most ground leases have relatively simple rental payment structures. However, even if a ground lease does not provide a mechanism for increasing the ground rent over the term of the lease, the rent usually rises upon renegotiation. If you are the lessee and are only obligated to pay $3 million per year for 90 years, why would you ever agree to an increase? Remember that the landowner has the right to take your building at the end of the lease. Therefore, you will renegotiate the ground lease from time to time to extend the maturity and protect the value of your building. You do not play Russian roulette with the ground lease for a valuable building, as a modest ground rent increase is preferable to losing the entire building. Thus, even if the property has a 70-year ground lease with a 3% increase in the ground rent every ten years, you will more than likely renegotiate new terms for the ground lease sometime in the next 20 years.

What NOI is realized by the building owner given the terms of this ground lease? After the $3 million ground lease payment, the relevant NOI is $5 million ($8 MM – $3 MM), rather than the full $8 million NOI associated with fee simple ownership. In essence, the ground lease is an operating expense, as to operate the property, you must pay your ground lease obligation. An advantage of the ground lease structure in the U.S. is that the ground rent payment is tax-deductible, while owning the land provides no tax shelter since land is not a depreciable asset.

VALUATION OF AN OPERATING ASSET SUBJECT TO A GROUND LEASE

How do you value an operating asset subject to a ground lease? Note that while the land is valuable, you have no claim to that value. There are several alternative methods to estimate the value of your building, two of which back solve to the building value on a residual basis.

Method #1: Ground Lease Payment DCF

The first method of valuing the building is to calculate the value of the land from the landowner's perspective through a DCF analysis of the ground lease payments over the 70-year term (incorporating expected renegotiations), and subtract this value from the value as if it were an owned property fee simple. This approach is illustrated in Figure 17.2.

The discount rate the landowner applies to the ground lease payments is notably lower than the discount rate on the NOI stream for the fee simple ownership structure, as the landowner owns a priority slice of the property's cash stream. Therefore, the landowner's expected rental stream has much less risk than the property under a fee simple structure. Remember that as the building owner you have to pay your ground lease or lose your building! Although the ground lease payments are not riskless, the landowner should receive payment as long as the NOI remains above $3 million.

In our example, a 7.3% discount rate is assumed to be sufficient to compensate for the risk of the leasehold interest. Applying the Gordon Model, for a 3% increase in ground lease payments every ten years (a 0.329% compounded annual growth rate), the terminal value in year 30 is equal to $46.83 million ($3.28 / (0.073 - 0.00329)). Discounting the ground lease payments and the terminal value to the present and summing them, results in a land value of $42.48 million. This implies a building value of $57.52 million ($100 MM − $42.48 MM).

FIGURE 17.2

Seaview Apartments				
Ground Lease Payment Discounted Cash Flow-based Residual Building Valuation				
		Year 1 ...	Year 10 ...	Year 20 ...	Year 30
Ground Lease Payment		$3.00 MM	$3.09 MM	$3.18 MM	$3.28 MM
Terminal Value		0	0	0	$46.83 MM
Total Cash Flow		$3.00 MM	$3.09 MM	$3.18 MM	$50.11 MM
Land Value at 7.30%	$42.48 MM				
Property Value	**$100.00 MM**				
Less Land Value	($42.48 MM)				
Building Value	$57.52 MM				

Online Companion Hands On: Find the blank, formatted version of this Figure in Chapter 17 of the Online Companion, and note the Assumptions provided at the top of the tab. Model the 30 years' worth of **Ground Lease Payments** with 3% growth every 10 years, and insert the Year 30 **Terminal Value**, calculating it as: Year 30 **Ground Lease Payment / Terminal Cap Rate**.

Next, in cell c15, apply the **NPV function** to the **Total Cash Flow** line, capturing all values for years 1-30, to get the **Land Value**.

Deduct the **Land Value** in cell c18 from the **Property Value** in cell c17 to get the residual **Building Value** in cell c19. The **Building Value** is its Present Value.

Method #2: Ground Lease Payment Capitalization

The second method of valuing the building is simply to cap the stabilized ground lease rental payment and subtract this value from the property value under a fee simple ownership structure. Applying the Gordon Model with a 7 cap (lower than the property 8 cap due to lesser risk to the landowner) on the $3 million payment indicates the ground lease is worth $42.86 million ($3 MM / 0.07), as shown in Figure 17.3. Note that this is quite close to the $42.48 million in land value achieved by the previous DCF-based analysis.

FIGURE 17.3

Seaview Apartments Ground Lease Payment Capitalization-based Residual Building Valuation	
Annual Ground Lease Payment	$3.00 MM
Cap Rate	7.00%
Land Value ($3.00 MM / 0.07)	$42.86 MM
Property Value	$100.00 MM
Less Land Value	($42.86 MM)
Building Value	$57.14 MM

Subtracting this estimated land value from the value of the property fee simple implies that the building subject to the ground lease is worth approximately $57.14 million (versus $57.52 MM from the first method).

Method #3: Building Net Operating Income DCF

As shown in Figure 17.4, a third approach is a DCF analysis of the building NOI (NOI after ground lease payments), using a relatively high discount rate. For this analysis, you assume the building NOI grows roughly with inflation at 1.5% annually. Therefore, you project 30 years of NOI for the property and subtract the ground lease payments. Given the 7.3% discount rate used to value the ground rent payments, a 10.75% discount rate for the NOI after ground lease payments is sufficient to compensate for the added risk of the building owner's interest.

For the building owner's terminal value in year 30, you use a 9.25% exit cap rate. This 125-bp premium over the 8% fee simple cap rate captures the physical deterioration of the building after 30 years and the additional risk of the building owner's position. Discounting both the 30 years of expected NOI after ground rent and the terminal value at the 10.75% discount rate results in a building value of $57.75 million. This is close to the results of the two previously discussed methods.

FIGURE 17.4

Seaview Apartments Building NOI Discounted Cash Flow-based Building Valuation				
	Year 1 ...	Year 10 ...	Year 20 ...	Year 30
Property NOI	$8.00 MM	$9.15 MM	$10.62 MM	$12.32 MM
Ground Lease Payment	($3.00 MM)	($3.09 MM)	($3.18 MM)	($3.28 MM)
Terminal Value	0	0	0	$97.75 MM
Total Cash Flow	$5.00 MM	$6.06 MM	$7.43 MM	$106.79 MM
Building Value at 10.75% $57.75 MM				

Online Companion Hands On: Find the blank, formatted version of this Figure in Chapter 17 of the Online Companion, and note the Assumptions provided at the top of the tab. Model the 30 years' worth of **Property NOI** with 1.5% growth per year, **Ground Lease Payments** with 3% growth every 10 years, and insert the Year 30 **Terminal Value**, calculating it as: Year 30 (**Property NOI** + **Ground Lease Payment**) / **Terminal Cap Rate**. Then sum the three lines in the **Total Cash Flow** line. Next, in cell c19, apply the **NPV function** to the **Total Cash Flow** line, capturing all values for years 1-30, to solve for the **Building Value**.

Method #4: Building NOI Capitalization

A final method to solve for the building value is to cap the $5 million of stabilized "building NOI" ($8 MM net of the $3 MM ground lease payment). The cap rate to apply to the $5 million building NOI must be higher than the 8% cap rate for the property fee simple, as the certainty of the landowner's lease payments being stripped away is greater than the certainty of the building-only NOI. In this case, we use an 8.75% cap rate and arrive at the same $57.14 million building value derived in the second method (Figure 17.5).

FIGURE 17.5

Seaview Apartments Building NOI Cap Rate-based Building Valuation	
Property NOI	$8.00 MM
Ground Lease Payment	($3.00 MM)
Building NOI	$5.00 MM
Building Cap Rate	8.75%
Building Value ($5.00 MM / 0.0875)	$57.14 MM

You can analyze the situation using any of these methods, but the cap rates and discount rates selected for the alternative analyses must be internally consistent relative to the risk associated with each cash stream. Which answer is "right"? None of them; after all they are all just models. Only time will tell the true value.

A word to the wise: do not subtract the ground lease liability twice! That is, if you subtract the ground lease expense from revenues as an operating cost, do not subtract land value from the building valuation. Remember the land and property are worth $100 MM together.

Figure 17.6 summarizes the four valuations. Of course, as the ground lease payment changes so too will the building's value.

FIGURE 17.6

Seaview Apartments		
Comparison of Subject to Ground Lease Building Valuations		
Property Value: $100 MM including Land Value		
Building Valuation Method	Rate	Building Value
Ground Lease Payment DCF	7.30% Discount Rate	$57.52 MM
Ground Lease Payment Cap	7.00% Cap Rate	$57.14 MM
Building NOI DCF	9.25% Cap Rate, 10.75% Discount Rate	$57.75 MM
Building NOI Cap	8.75% Cap Rate	$57.14 MM

FINANCING OF PROPERTY SUBJECT TO A GROUND LEASE

Now consider financing the property's acquisition. The terms upon which you agreed with the lender for a fee simple purchase are completely out of whack for the purchase of the property subject to the ground lease. If you attempt to borrow $65 million to purchase the building subject to the $3 million annual ground lease it is a 113.8% LTV ($65 MM / $57.1 MM), as the $42.9 million-land value is not yours to give as collateral. In addition, the interest coverage ratio for such a loan is only 1.42x ($5 MM / $3.51 MM), as $3 million of the $8 million NOI goes towards ground lease payments. Of course, the lender will know about the ground lease obligation and will use $5 million, not $8 million, as the relevant NOI when calculating interest coverage for your purchase subject to the ground lease. As a result, lenders will not lend as much to purchase a property subject to a ground lease as for fee simple ownership.

The good news is that since you are purchasing the property subject to a ground lease, instead of purchasing fee simple, you only need about $57 million to purchase the building, rather than the $100 million required for the purchase of the building and the land. If you purchase the building for $57 million subject to the ground lease using a 65% LTV mortgage, you will receive a $37 million ($57 MM * 65%) loan. But the lender will charge a higher interest rate or impose tougher covenants on this loan since the ground lease payments increase the building's NOI risk. Assume the lender charges a 30-basis point higher interest rate (hence a 5.7% interest rate, 210 basis points above Treasury), resulting in a $2.11 million annual interest payment each year. With $5 million pro forma NOI net of $3 million in ground lease payments, the pro forma interest coverage ratio is 2.37x.

The lender may demand that the landowner agrees to subordinate their ground lease claim to the mortgage. This subordination means that the landowner accepts a lower position in terms of rights to both the collateral and the cash flows throughout the life of the loan. Subordinating their land means that if you default on your mortgage, the lender not only has recourse to your building but also to the landowner's land to satisfy their mortgage claim. This highlights the fact that the details of a loan contract are everything. Even though the interest coverage ratio mathematically remains at 2.37x, such contractual terms with the lender make the coverage ratio effectively much higher.

Such a mortgage proposal might be acceptable to both the borrower and the lender, but what about the poor landowner? You want the landowner to agree to receive his ground lease payment after the lender, and in the event that you default on your mortgage, they could lose their land to the lender. What do you think the landowner is going to say to this proposal? A good bet is, "No Way!"

You begin to see the problems involved with separate owners of the land and the building. You can only give one absolute first lien, but both the lender and the landowner want that position. When you split ownership of the land and the building, it is hard to make everyone happy. That is why the ground lease structure is relatively rare and usually inefficient.

CLOSING THOUGHT

Although ground leases are not used in most U.S. real estate transactions, understanding their associated complexities makes you a more informed analyst. Be sure to carefully evaluate the details of the ground lease before recommending or choosing to invest in a situation where they are involved.

 Online Companion Audio Interview: To hear a conversation about this chapter's content, go to the Online Companion and select the link for Chapter 17. Scroll down to the Audio Interview section and listen.

Chapter 18
Real Estate Owner Exit Strategies

"Get rich slowly; it lasts longer."
- Dr. Peter Linneman

Smart real estate investors spend considerable time thinking about their exit strategy prior to acquiring or developing a property to avoid the "roach motel" phenomenon: you can get in, but you can't get out. Exiting an investment allows you to free up your equity and move on to (hopefully) better things!

WHY EXIT?

Why might you decide to exit? After all, you spent a lot of time assessing whether you wanted to invest, and even more time operating the property after the purchase. But if you are a developer, for example, you are in the business of creating buildings and may need equity for new developments. So developers need an exit strategy which allows them the opportunity to free up their capital for future developments. Thus, once the property is stabilized and generating a solid return, a developer may need to exit to build again. Besides, another entity, such as a REIT or local operator, may have a comparative advantage in managing stabilized properties, while developers will do best when they focus on their own core competency.

Another reason to exit is to alter your risk-reward profile. For example, a developer specializes in taking development risks. However, once the building is stabilized, this type of risk is gone. Similarly, an older building in need of repositioning has more risk than a new building. If you are unwilling or unable to deal with the complexities, costs, and challenges posed by an older building, you will want to exit. If you are purchasing a new strip center as part of your strategy to only own the best property in the market, as demographics, the local economy, consumer preferences, competitive centers, and tenants change, you may need to exit based on this new information, as the building will no longer match your investment criteria.

Another example is that opportunistic investors generally desire to exit once value has been added (e.g., through renovations or operational efficiencies), to generate higher IRRs. All private equity funds must have an exit strategy, as most have finite lives of 7-12 years.

There are also "old-fashioned" reasons to exit. For example, people exit inherited estate properties, as the beneficiaries rarely want the headaches of managing real estate. In addition, change-of-life situations such as a divorce or partnership dissolution frequently force people to exit their investments, so you will be well-advised to have a strategy in place.

HOW TO EXIT

What is the best exit strategy? To illustrate the pros and cons of several alternative exit strategies, assume that 3 years ago, you bought a poorly-managed property, Jessica Crest, for $100 million with the expectation of substantially enhancing property value through active management and re-leasing. You purchased the building with $40 million of equity and a $60 million interest-only mortgage. For tax purposes, your accountant allocated $75 million of the purchase price to the structure (depreciable), and $25 million to land (non-depreciable). The capital structure and depreciation allocations are summarized in Figure 18.1.

FIGURE 18.1

Jessica Crest $100 MM Investment Property			
Capital Structure		Depreciation Allocations	
Equity	$40 MM	Land	$25 MM
Debt	$60 MM	Structure	$75 MM

After three years of hard work, you have successfully repositioned the property, and its value has indeed risen to the expected $140 million, increasing your equity from $40 million to $80 million ($140 MM – $60 MM of debt), as illustrated in Figure 18.2.

FIGURE 18.2

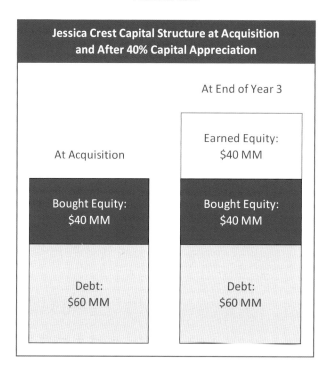

Having successfully executed your business plan, you now have a problem: it is highly unlikely you can double your equity again via this property over the next 3 years. Meanwhile, you have identified another mismanaged property and want to repeat the repositioning strategy. Purchasing the identified property requires that you come up with $40 million in equity, which you do not have, as all of your money is tied up in Jessica Crest. How do you access this built-up equity in Jessica Crest?

DISPOSITION

One option is the outright **disposition** (sale) of the fee simple ownership interest in Jessica Crest. If you decide to sell Jessica Crest, you have to go through the process of finding a buyer. Depending on the building and market, a "typical" sales process requires three to twelve months. To prepare the property for sale you must gather your documents and contracts, prepare financial statements, have an accounting firm audit those statements, perhaps create a sales book, hire lawyers to negotiate and structure the sale agreement, possibly hire a broker to help sell the property, spend time negotiating with buyers, etc.

In addition to the time and energy involved, the sales process has significant costs, as lawyers, accountants, and brokers do not work for free. Many of the costs of these services are relatively fixed. As a result, fees as a percentage of the total sales price tend to be larger for smaller properties and smaller for larger properties. In general, 2%-5% is a good estimate for the transaction costs associated with selling a property, but keep in mind the actual percentage fluctuates with property value. If you have a large trophy asset, like Rockefeller Center, the fees as a percentage of value will be substantially less because the amount of work and value added by the brokers are not large relative to the value of the property. If, however, you have a $5 million property, then the fees can easily exceed 5%. Assume that you estimate that selling Jessica Crest will cost you $3 million in fees.

Assume that after 6 months of searching for a buyer, you successfully sell Jessica Crest for $140 million. You will use the $140 million in **gross sales proceeds** to repay the $60 million mortgage. If the buyer uses debt financing to purchase the building, there are technical complications in the final closing, as the buyer will be unable to pay you until they receive their mortgage. However, the buyer's lender will not provide a mortgage until they have a first lien on the property, which cannot be given until you sell the property and repay your loan. To solve this problem, you will simultaneously close the sale, repay your existing loan, and transfer the first lien to the purchaser's lender.

Assuming that you are not a non-taxable entity such as a pension fund, another major payment you have to make upon sale is your long-term **capital gains tax**. Under U.S. tax code, there are two components of the capital gains tax. The first component is the actual gain you achieve on the building. In this case you paid $100 million for the property and you sold it for $140 million. This $40 million gain is (currently) taxed at 15%, or $6 million in taxes. But remember that the capital gains tax rate changes over time as tax law evolves.

The second capital gains tax component (under current law) is that you have to pay taxes on the property's **accumulated depreciation**. You have been depreciating the building over the past three years to shield income from ordinary income taxes. The government (currently) requires that you pay a 25% tax rate on accumulated depreciation. Depreciating the $75 million you attributed to structure over a 39-year schedule ($1.923 million per year), means that you have taken $5.769 million in total accumulated depreciation over the past 3 years. In reality, the accumulated depreciation will be larger than $5.769 million, as not all non-land value will be attributable to the long-lived structure. Other non-land value is allocated to shorter-lived improvements such as furniture, fixtures, and equipment (FF&E). The shorter the depreciation schedule, the higher the allowable percentage of item cost written off in each year. For simplicity, we assume that the total accumulated depreciation at the point of sale is $5.769 million. The government will tax this amount at a 25% tax rate, or $1.442 million in taxes. Combining these capital gains tax components, you will pay a total of $7.442 million in capital gains taxes upon the $140 million sale (Figure 18.3).

FIGURE 18.3

Jessica Crest Disposition Capital Gains Taxes Calculation	
Capital Gains Tax Rate	15.00%
Accumulated Depreciation Tax Rate	25.00%
Depreciation Allocation to Structure	$75.00 MM
Depreciation Schedule	39 years
Tax on Gain	
Property Appreciation ($140 MM – $100 MM)	$40.00 MM
Capital Gains Tax at 15.00%	$6.00 MM
Tax on Depreciation	
Annual Depreciation	$1.923 MM
Accumulated Depreciation over 3 years	$5.769 MM
Depreciation Tax at 25.00%	$1.442 MM
Total Capital Gains Taxes	$7.442 MM

Thus, as shown in Figure 18.4, after repaying the loan, paying all fees and paying the IRS, you are left with $69.56 million of the $140 million in gross sales proceeds. This post-sale cash amount can be thought of as your net equity or **wealth position**.

FIGURE 18.4

Jessica Crest Disposition Net Equity Calculation	
Sales Revenue	$140.00 MM
Debt	($60.00 MM)
Fees	($3.00 MM)
Capital Gains Tax	($6.00 MM)
Depreciation Tax	($1.44 MM)
Net Equity/ Wealth Position	$69.56 MM

Online Companion Hands On: Go to the Online Companion and select the link for Chapter 18. Scroll down the page to the Excel Figures section and download the Excel file. Complete the formatted, blank Figure to solve for the Net Equity of the property owner given the Assumptions provided at the top of the tab. The Net Equity after Sale is $37.054 million.

In addition, you may face a prepayment penalty for repaying your loan prematurely. This analysis assumes that you have no prepayment penalty because given your repositioning strategy, you probably would have selected a floating rate loan that allowed you to sell the building with little-to-no prepayment penalty after roughly 3-4 years. This exemplifies how the type of debt selected depends on your investment and exit strategy.

Upon completion of the sale, you have sufficient funds to execute the other repositioning deal, as you have $69.56 million and only needed $40 million in equity for the new project. However, freeing up your money came at a cost. Specifically, even though you doubled your equity from $40 million to $80 million on the investment, you only have $69.56 million in your pocket due to the substantial leakage from fees and taxes. Are there exit alternatives available which reduce these leakages from sale? And what will the costs be?

REFINANCING

An alternative exit strategy for the Jessica Crest property is **refinancing** (i.e., replacing the in-place loan with a new loan). If the original lender was willing to lend $60 million on the $100 million Jessica Crest property (a 60% LTV) prior to repositioning, a lender should be willing to lend you substantially more once Jessica Crest is stabilized and worth $140 million. Instead of selling the property, assume you obtain a new 65% LTV ($91 million) first mortgage. In this case, after repaying the original lender, you are left with $31 million in "excess" refinancing proceeds ($91 MM in new debt minus $60 MM of original debt repaid).

While the refinancing process is much cheaper than the sales process, as you do not have to pay the transfer taxes and brokerage fees, you probably will have a loan fee of 50 basis points on the new mortgage, as well as legal and accounting fees. But even if you pay $1 million in refinancing costs, it is a notable reduction from the costs associated with the sale option. Plus, if you refinance, you postpone paying capital gains taxes, as they are only triggered upon sale. This is the major advantage of the refinance option relative to a sale.

Given the time value of money, you generally prefer to defer the inevitable tax liability. In fact, the longer you think you will hold the building, the more attractive is the refinance option. For example, if you plan to sell the building tomorrow, the refinancing option makes no sense because you simply pay $1 million in refinancing fees, as well as the sale-related fees and taxes. But if you plan to hold the property for 60 years, the present value of the deferred capital gains tax liability from refinancing now is effectively zero.

As shown in Figure 18.5, upon refinancing Jessica Crest, you realize net refinancing proceeds of $30 million ($31 MM in excess proceeds minus $1 MM in fees), which is at your disposal for new investments. However, although you avoid the incremental $2 million in fees and the $7.442 million in capital gains taxes incurred if you had sold, the $30 million in net proceeds from refinancing the property are $39.56 million lower than the $69.56 million in net proceeds derived from an outright sale. Where did the remaining money go? The answer is that you still own a $49 million equity position in Jessica Crest after refinancing, as the building is worth $140 million against a $91 million loan (Figures 18.5 and 18.6).

FIGURE 18.5

Jessica Crest Refinancing Net Equity Calculation	
New Property Value	$140.00 MM
New Debt at 65% LTV	$91.00 MM
Repayment of Old Debt	($60.00 MM)
Equity to Holder	$31.00 MM
Fees	($1.00 MM)
Capital Gains Tax	$0
Depreciation Tax	$0
Net Refinancing Proceeds *	$30.00 MM
Equity in Jessica Crest	$49.00 MM
Net Equity	$79.00 MM
* Available for new projects	

FIGURE 18.6

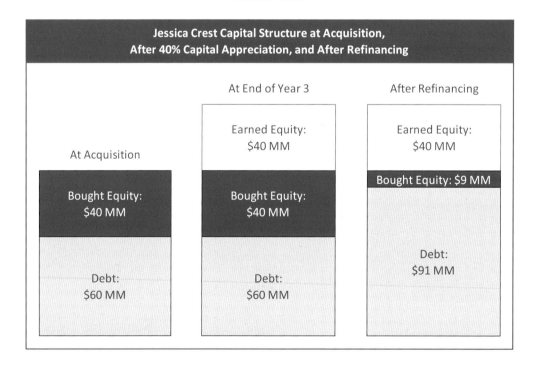

Jessica Crest Capital Structure at Acquisition, After 40% Capital Appreciation, and After Refinancing

Therefore, your total wealth position after refinancing is $79 million ($30 MM in cash from the refinancing plus $49 MM in equity in the property), which is higher than the $69.56 million from selling the building.

Yet, after refinancing you still have a problem, as you need $40 million in cash for the new repositioning deal. Therefore, refinancing does not always meet your objective. Of course, if the increase in value were greater, or the refinancing LTV were higher, the refinancing option may achieve this goal. Or if you only need $30 million for your next investment, refinancing is very effective. But in our example, too much value remains tied up in Jessica Crest for refinancing to achieve your objective.

What can you do to solve this equity gap? You could take on a smaller repositioning project or sell a slice of either Jessica Crest or the new project to an equity partner. A problem with finding an equity partner is there are relatively few buyers of **minority interests** in privately owned properties, as relatively few investors want an illiquid ownership stake, particularly where their vote will never impact decisions.

Of course, investing $40 million in another property is not every investor's objective, and thus the refinancing option is very attractive for investors who are happy to retain an interest in the stabilized property. For those happy to take $30 million out of Jessica Crest and keep the $49 million equity position, the refinancing option is perfect because of the lesser value leakage. Remember that there is no single objective for all investors. Numbers are important, but who you are and what you are trying to accomplish will ultimately dictate your exit strategy.

LIKE-KIND EXCHANGE (1031 EXCHANGE)

There is a third exit possibility that is U.S.-specific. Under current U.S. tax code, IRS Section 1031, you can pursue a so-called **like-kind exchange**, which essentially allows you to sell your property free of state and federal income taxes if you purchase a "similar" property within a prescribed period of time, hence forestalling capital gains taxes until you ultimately break the ownership chain. Also, the "1031 exchange" allows you to restart your depreciation schedule. This is particularly helpful if you have a building that is nearing the end of its depreciable life. Under the like-kind exchange principle, you can exchange your property partnership interest for an IRS-qualified partnership interest in a different partnership. If correctly executed, this legally-technical exchange process defers your capital gains tax until you sell your new interest.

Using the Jessica Crest example, you would sell the $140 million Jessica Crest building exactly as before. You will pay the sale-related fees and retire the debt, but you do not pay the capital gains taxes immediately if you successfully find a building for purchase which qualifies under the tax code for a 1031 exchange. Volumes of tax law dictate the circumstances under which you can effectuate a like-kind exchange and defer taxes, and the nuances constantly change.

There are some general guidelines you can use to understand the application of like-kind exchange as an exit strategy, but you must make certain that the new property is being held for investment or productive use. The property cannot be acquired with the intent of being resold after a short time period. One of the criteria is the items exchanged must generally be the same business. For example, you cannot sell Jessica Crest and buy an oil and gas company, stocks, or bonds and treat it as a like-kind exchange. Broadly speaking, whether a property is considered like-kind is up to the "nature and character of the property, not its grade or quality" (IRS Code Sections 1031(a)-1(b)). You may do exchanges on both unimproved and improved property. The IRS does not consider real estate outside the United States as like-kind property.

There are two noteworthy margins that people try to capitalize on via like-kind real estate exchanges. The first is to sell a stabilized building, while purchasing a building where there is opportunity to add value. In our example, you would look to sell your stabilized Jessica Crest property for the poorly-managed, partially-leased building you wanted to reposition. As long as you can get the IRS' blessing of the repositioning purchase as a qualified like-kind exchange, you have satisfied your strategic objective of purchasing the new value-added project while deferring your capital gains taxes on the sale of Jessica Crest.

The second opportunity is to sell your property and buy a stabilized building that offers a better refinancing opportunity and a reduced management burden. The poster child transaction in this case is to exchange a multi-tenant corporate office complex for a new building that is leased on a long-term basis exclusively to the U.S. government. The upside of this building is that lenders are willing to lend against it as collateral at a higher LTV ratio than on Jessica Crest, due to the higher tenant credit and long-term lease of the government. Figure 18.7 illustrates such an exit strategy.

FIGURE 18.7

Jessica Crest Like-Kind Exchange Net Equity Calculation	
Part 1: Sell Jessica Crest Asset	
Sale Price	$140.00 MM
Debt (60% LTV)	($60.00 MM)
Fees	($3.00 MM)
Capital Gains Tax	$0
Depreciation Tax	$0
Equity Freed	$77.00 MM
Part 2: Buy U.S. Government-Leased Asset	
Purchase Price	$140.00 MM
Debt (75% LTV)	($105.00 MM)
Equity in Asset	$35.00 MM
Equity Freed	$77.00 MM
Equity in Asset	($35.00 MM)
Fees on Purchase	($1.00 MM)
Equity for new projects	$41.00 MM
Net Equity	$76.00 MM

As before, you sell Jessica Crest for $140 million, repay the $60 million loan, and pay $3 million in fees. But you will not pay capital gains tax in this example, as long as the "replacement" purchase of the government-leased building qualifies as a like kind exchange. As a result, as shown in Part 1 of Figure 18.7, you net greater proceeds from the sale of Jessica Crest within a like-kind exchange exit than from the sale in the straight disposition strategy ($77 MM versus $69.56 MM shown in Figure 18.4).

As shown in Part 2 of Figure 18.7, you buy the government-leased building for $140 million with a combination of $35 million of equity from the Jessica Crest sale and $105 million in senior mortgage debt (a 75% LTV). You will incur $1 million in fees to borrow the $105 million, allowing you to take $41 million out of the new property while retaining your $35 million equity position for a total wealth position of $76 million. Although the $76 million derived from the like-kind exchange is less than the $79 million net value from a refinancing (due to the higher fees associated with selling Jessica Crest), you are able to achieve your objective, as the $41 million pulled out of the property provides you the $40 million necessary to purchase and reposition another property (and put $1 million in your pocket). You also are able to focus your energy on the repositioning exercise because the government-leased property you own is a relatively low-headache management task. In contrast, with a straight refinancing you still have to actively manage the Jessica Crest property.

A major drawback is that other bidders looking to protect their tax position will also be attracted to the exchange property. As a result, the price of a poster child transaction replacement property is generally bid up to the point where some of your tax savings are often passed on to the seller in the form of a higher price. It should also be noted that it is nearly impossible to find a property worth the same as yours. For this reason, any excess gain is taxed, with this excess known as the "Boot."

To execute a 1031 exchange, you appoint an independent specialist known as a "QI," or **qualified intermediary**, to help sell the property. The qualified intermediary's purpose is to set up an agreement, so that an escrow or closing agent transfers the property to a buyer and that the sales proceeds go directly to the qualified intermediary. If this were not so, the 1031 exchanger would be taxed on the proceeds. The exchanger has to acquire a new property within a limited number of days. The new property must be designated as a "replacement" by the exchanger, and this designation must be sent to the person from whom the exchanger will acquire the property. This is known as the "identification" process. The exchanger must identify a property that is not owned by a subsidiary or employee of the exchanger. The IRS Code has a detailed description of the people from whom the property cannot be purchased, known as "disqualified persons." While there are many types of like-kind exchanges, conceptually they are merely technical variants.

EXCHANGE FOR PUBLIC COMPANY SHARES

Another possible exit strategy is to exchange your ownership interest in Jessica Crest for a monetarily equivalent ownership interest in a publicly-traded company. For instance, you could exchange the $140 million Jessica Crest property for common shares in publicly-traded Boston Properties. If this transaction is structured properly, you will again be able to defer taxes and will not recognize capital gains on the transaction until you sell your Boston Properties position. Your tax basis from Jessica Crest will carry over to your interest in Boston Properties and your capital gains will be determined based on the proceeds from its sale versus the old basis. However, to achieve such deferral of capital gains can require rather complex structuring. You will generally receive dividend rights and voting rights equal to your pro rata share of the acquiring public company. This transaction provides you with a small slice of ownership in a larger, more diversified pool of assets. However, you will not have control of the property and will generally lose the property management fees you previously earned from the property. Figure 18.8 summarizes the four exit strategies discussed so far.

FIGURE 18.8

Jessica Crest Comparison of Common Exit Strategies				
Jessica Crest property value at end of Year 3: $140.00 MM				
	Taxes at Exit		After Exit	
Exit Type	Capital Gains	Depreciation	Wealth Position	# of Controlled Properties
Fee simple disposition	Yes	Yes	$69.56 MM	0
Refinancing	No	No	$79.00 MM	2
Like-kind exchange	No	No	$76.00 MM	1
Exchange for public company shares	No	No	$77.00 MM	0

GO PUBLIC

The alternative to the four types of exits discussed so far is to take your company and properties public. As discussed in more detail in Chapter 21, to do so, you will need a much larger pool of assets than just Jessica Crest. Your company must consist of a large pool of diversified properties in a particular property type, or the investor community will probably be unwilling to purchase your stock at the initial public offering (IPO). Furthermore, the pool of assets will need to be structured in a manner dictated by the public market: low debt, predictable cash flows, independent governance, and high reporting transparency. If your portfolio lacks these qualities, it is unlikely you will be able to receive fair value from the public market investor community.

In addition, an IPO takes 12-18 months. If your IPO succeeds, you will incur total fees equal to about 10% of the total money raised. In fact, you will incur $500,000-$1 million in expenses whether you successfully complete an IPO process or not. If you pursue an IPO, you are subject to the vagaries of the market during the process, which will impact pricing and timing. If the market weakens, you may be unwilling to issue equity at substantially reduced prices. On the other hand, if the IPO is successful, you will be able to access public capital markets and use the proceeds to purchase additional properties or pay down debt.

GOVERNMENT TAX INCENTIVE PROGRAMS

Over the course of a career, real estate investors will likely encounter various government tax incentive programs, some of which might influence their evaluation of the attractiveness of the four common exit strategies discussed in detail. One such program that is currently in place in the U.S. is the Opportunity Zone Program, created by the 2017 Jobs Act, which is designed to benefit communities where incomes are below state medians. In a simplified manner, this program generally allowed investors to re-invest realized capital gains (such as those related to the disposition of a property) into a new property in a particular geography and defer those original capital gains tax liabilities until 2026, and also receive a reduced tax rate. Additionally, if the investors hold the new property investment for 10 years, any capital gains for the new investment would not be taxable. While each of the programs one will encounter will be highly specialized, they are likely to all be variations on the theme of "pay certain taxes later or not at all."

CLOSING THOUGHT

Selecting an exit strategy is critical. The optimal strategy depends on your objectives. While the numbers and calculations are important, exit is ultimately a personal decision. Two people looking at the same numbers on the sale option and the refinance option may make completely different decisions based on their objectives. Like most things in real estate investing, selecting an exit strategy is definitely not a one size fits all exercise!

 Online Companion Audio Interview: To hear a conversation about this chapter's content, go to the Online Companion and select the link for Chapter 18. Scroll down to the Audio Interview section and listen.

Chapter 19
Real Estate Private Equity Funds

"Find out who you are and stay true to your values."
- Dr. Peter Linneman

The **real estate private equity fund** ("R.E. P.E. fund") is a major source of capital for the real estate industry. These investment vehicles, which are also known as **opportunity funds**, are among the largest owners of real estate in the country, holding an estimated $500 billion of real estate equity and well over $1 trillion in U.S. assets as well as substantial portfolios abroad.

EVOLUTION

Historically, individual real estate properties were purchased and developed with lots of debt and minimal cash equity investment from very small single-transaction investment groups known as **syndicates**. For example, if you needed equity to fund a development project, you would go to your brother, your cousin, and your neighbor to raise the necessary sliver of equity. This structure worked well when lots of debt was available for real estate projects. If you had access to almost 100% debt financing, which was not uncommon from 1960-1990, you could probably find the necessary equity, especially if you had an established track record. For example, with 99% leverage, if you wanted to do a $50 million project, you only had to come up with $500,000 in equity. While that is a lot of money, an established player should be able to raise $500,000 in equity or they should not be in the business.

In addition to the availability of debt financing, from 1981-1986, IRS depreciation laws allowed property owners to depreciate the structure over a 15-year period. Combined with even shorter depreciation schedules for the in-structure improvements, you could probably write off the entire building (excluding the land allocation) in 7-10 years for tax purposes. That is, assuming 80% of the value of the property was non-land, and if you are able to write the building off for tax purposes over ten years, that is about 8% of the value of the property written off each year. Thus, the owner of an 8-cap property could completely shelter all income solely via depreciation! Combined with debt financing of 90-100% loan-to-value, the tax shields from interest payments and depreciation generated enormous tax losses and modest cash flows each year. Until 1987, you could sell these tax losses for cash on a forward basis to people like doctors and dentists, who valued the losses to shelter their ordinary income from taxes. You could probably get 30-90 cents for every dollar of tax loss you sold. Therefore, you were often able to raise the necessary equity through small equity syndicate sales of the tax losses, while still retaining most of the property's upside for yourself.

In 1986, Congress extended depreciation schedules and generally prohibited the sale of tax losses except for low-income housing and historic preservation. The swish of the President's signature on this tax bill eliminated the primary source of real estate equity. In the early 1990s, when lenders finally realized they had been vastly mispricing their real estate loans and began offering only 50-70% LTV mortgages, it meant large chunks of equity were suddenly required to own or develop real estate.

Since the early 1990s, you have generally needed a large amount of equity to own or develop real estate. For example, a 35% equity slice on a $50 million project requires $17.5 million. This is a lot more than the old $500,000 requirement, and you cannot raise a dime of it from the sale of tax losses. Raising $17.5 million in equity is a much more difficult and sophisticated exercise than raising $500,000. You also run the risk that while you are raising the required equity for the deal, you may lose the property to a better-capitalized competitor. For example, a high net worth individual or institutional investor may write a check to fund the project while you are still tweaking your Powerpoint investor presentation. After all, one of the advantages of a multi-billion-dollar balance sheet is that you generally have sufficient equity for your real estate purchases.

In this new capital environment, investors that have equity with certainty often have an advantage. This is because although the investor putting together an equity syndicate might be willing to bid more for a property, the seller may accept a lower bid from a well-capitalized bidder to ensure a quick closing. If you can achieve even a 1-3% lower purchase price on a building with an expected 11% annual return, you realize almost one-third of a year's return up-front simply by being able to quickly write a check. This capital advantage led to the creation of real estate private equity funds, which raise large pools of equity prior to investing to ensure ready access to equity.

A BIT OF HISTORY

The real estate private equity fund business started with the first Zell-Merrill fund in 1988. Today there are perhaps 2,000 professionals working in the business (excluding accountants), versus maybe 50 in 1992. From 1992 to 2021, these funds grew from almost no assets to more than $500 billion in equity. However, the business reached a degree of maturity, with funds raising up to $125 billion annually in aggregate equity commitments, to be invested over roughly the first three years of a fund's lifetime.

These funds raise money from pension funds, foundations, university endowments, and high net worth individuals. They receive specific **investment commitments** from these investors, drawing down the promised commitment on an "as needed" basis through **capital calls**. The minimum investment commitment is usually $1 million, meaning relatively few individuals directly invest in these funds, though millions have a stake via their pension funds.

Investors invest in a limited partnership vehicle managed by the fund **sponsor**, who serves as the **general partner (GP)** responsible for all operations. If a **limited partner (LP)** investor fails to satisfy a call on their funding commitment, the investor forfeits many of its rights and economics.

The fund does not take all of the committed money upfront because it would have to invest the excess funds in low-yielding cash until it was needed for the higher-return real estate investments, dragging down fund return performance. Although pension funds and other institutional investors would rather the real estate opportunity fund put the committed capital to work in a predictable manner, institutional investors are generally better suited to handle the excess cash position than are the private equity funds. In addition, pension funds and other institutions have lower total expected portfolio returns than real estate private equity funds.

Historically, real estate private equity funds have marketed that they will generate a 20% IRR and a 2.0x equity multiple over the life of the investment. Lately, these return targets are creeping downwards. These high target returns were originally necessary to lure investors back into a business that no one trusted in the early 1990s. However, the truth is that realized returns have been far less, often only single digit. In fact, the liberal usage of debt to generate returns means that many funds have lost money in weak property markets.

The typical fund promises to liquidate all property holdings within 7-10 years, as investors like knowing when they will get their money back. The problem with this liquidation structure is that while the properties may be great investments, the market could be weak as the fund's termination date nears. To resolve this problem, sponsors and investors generally can agree to an extension period of up to three years pending a vote of the majority of the limited partners. Although weak market conditions may persist beyond three years, most investors prefer to take reduced returns and close out the fund.

The sponsor markets the fund, requesting funding commitments. The sponsor retains the right to raise less, or more, than their investment commitment target. For example, their target may be a fund size of $1 billion, but they can raise more or less depending on circumstances. Assuming they raise exactly $1 billion in commitments, the fund strategy is to invest the $1 billion in equity commitments over the subsequent 2-4 years. The fund will leverage this equity when making its real estate investments. At a 2:1 leverage target (i.e., 67% LTV), the fund will have roughly $3 billion in investment power over the 2-4-year investment period.

Once the fund has invested most of its capital, the sponsor will attempt to raise a new fund. The investors in the second fund invest in a separate limited partnership and have no claims on the assets held in the sponsor's first fund. It takes roughly 12-18 months and, perhaps, $1 million in out of pocket costs from the time you begin to seriously plan a fund to the time you close funding commitments. And there is no guarantee that the fund will be successfully raised.

There are covenants in the fund's partnership documents that permit the sponsor to raise a new fund only after roughly 85% of the fund's capital is invested. This is designed to assure that the attention of the sponsor remains on the current fund. Of course, the sponsor wants to ensure a seamless transition to its next fund, as they do not want to be "out of the market" for 12-24 months while they raise the new fund.

The sponsor generally invests in the fund alongside the investors. The amount that institutional investors require the sponsor to commit depends on many factors, including the capital base of the fund sponsor. For example, investors expect a large and well-capitalized sponsor to put much more into its $2 billion fund than a young real estate entrepreneur who is raising a $30 million fund. This difference reflects the investor's desire to make sure the sponsor's loss is significant to the sponsor if the fund fails to perform. The upper-end investment among sponsors is 25-50% of total equity commitments, while the low end is 1-3%.

WHO ARE THEY?

There are three broad groups of fund sponsors today: those associated with investment banks; those associated with investment houses; and dedicated real estate players.

Investment Banks

The number of players in this group of funds has declined due to regulations but still includes Morgan Stanley (MSREI) and Goldman Sachs. Investment bank sponsors attempt to exploit their access to investors (especially their network of high net worth individuals), deal flow, and capital market expertise. How did they get those connections? Investment banks have sales and asset management groups that have long focused on providing investments to high net worth individuals. With these established networks, it is relatively easy for investment banks to approach existing clients who seek portfolio diversification. Given that investment banks' competitive advantage is raising money, they frequently partner with real estate professionals to run their funds.

Another advantage of investment banks is access to deal flow. For example, investment banks are frequently intermediaries for companies or governments looking to sell properties. Therefore, investment bank-sponsored funds see a lot of large property sale offerings. The so-called "Chinese Wall" between investment principals and transaction agents within the investment bank is riddled with holes, as the private placement memorandum of every investment bank-sponsored fund describes proprietary deal flow derived from the firm's high net worth client relationships. Finally, these shops are experts in corporate finance and have the expertise to add value by creatively financing and selling complex deals. The investment banks once held a more prominent role in the real estate private equity world than they do today. Their decreased presence is largely due to the Volcker Rule component of the Dodd-Frank Wall Street Reform and Consumer Protection Act, which came into effect in 2015. Specifically, the Volcker Rule restricts U.S. banks from making certain kinds of speculative investments that do not benefit their customers.

Investment Houses

The name-brand investment houses have come to have a major presence in the real estate private equity world over the last 20 years. Players in this group of funds include sponsors such as: Blackstone, Carlyle, Cerberus, Apollo, Angelo Gordon, TPG, and Oaktree. Funds at these investment houses are generally stand-alone vehicles which are part of a larger family of funds, including corporate LBO funds, venture capital funds, hedge funds, and distressed debt funds. The advantage of having multiple funds under the umbrella of a single investment company is that you are raising money for all the funds under one brand from the same investor base. To the extent they have performed well on other funds, their track records enhance credibility with capital sources for their real estate fund, as they can go to a pension fund and say, "Remember how well you did in my LBO fund? Why don't you invest some of the money you made there in my real estate fund?" Credibility and reputation are critical in the fundraising business, and brand recognition facilitates the process, as pension funds and endowments, the two largest sources of investment capital, are not in the business of taking risks. Remember that the individuals running investments for these institutional capital sources are generally not incentivized to take risks. If a pension fund invests in an unknown real estate fund and loses money, the employee who made the decision might get fired. But a poor return, or even a loss, via a name brand fund is more easily forgiven.

Dedicated Real Estate Players

Well-known players in this group of opportunity funds include: Starwood, Lonestar, Westbrook, AEW, Lubert-Adler, Walton Street, Colony, O'Connor, and Crow Holdings. Historically, the people who head these funds have worked in real estate most of their lives and are also skilled at raising money. They tend to be relatively focused real estate investors whose comparative advantage is identifying opportunistic investments and property-level expertise.

RETURN WATERFALL

In their capital raising marketing material, a fund sponsor lays out their fund's **investment cash flow waterfall** distribution structure. This cash waterfall provides a mechanism for how fund proceeds will be split between the investors and the sponsor for the purposes of returning invested capital and paying out profits. The waterfall structure provides an important financial incentive to the fund sponsor to strive to guide the fund to its fullest investment returns potential over its 7-10-year life. Take as an example the hypothetical $100 million Urban Fund, whose investors are ArrowCo Pension and the fund sponsor Urban Renaissance ("UR"). Collectively these two investing groups are known as "the money," as they both invest capital into Urban Fund. The sponsor of the Urban Fund commits to its investors (including itself) that they will receive all distributable cash flows until all capital is returned, plus a **preferred return (a "pref")** on all commitments drawn. This preferred return is typically an IRR-based **hurdle rate** and is usually 7-11% annually. Below we assume that the annual preferred return is 9%.

If the investments do not generate sufficient cash flow to pay the full 9% hurdle return on the invested equity (i.e., if the preferred return hurdle dollar amount is not achieved), all sub-9%-level proceeds generated by operating cash flow, refinancing, and sale still go to "the money" (which includes the sponsor's investment) **pari passu** (i.e., pro rata/proportionate to the amount they invested, simultaneously). If the investments generate more than the preferred rate of return (i.e., the cash flows "clear the hurdle"), "the money" and the sponsor split the residual profits in a prescribed manner. The fund sponsor's share of this excess profit beyond that for their cash investment position is referred to as a **promote** or **carried interest**. The promote is the mechanism that provides the sponsor a financial incentive, as it is a share of profits awarded to the sponsor for their "sweat." This promote structure can result in the sponsor receiving a materially disproportionate share of the fund's profits relative to their cash investment.

Figure 19.1 identifies key elements of the Urban Fund, which has $100 million in equity commitments, $90 million from ArrowCo Pension and $10 million from the sponsor (Urban Renaissance).

FIGURE 19.1

Urban Fund Description	
Fund Name:	Urban Fund
Fund Sponsor:	Urban Renaissance
Fund Investment Size:	$100.00 MM
Investors ("the money"):	ArrowCo Pension $90.00 MM
	Urban Renaissance $10.00 MM
Annual Preferred Return:	9.00% IRR
Sponsor Promote:	20.00%

Assume for simplicity that the fund invests all its capital at Time 0 and liquidates all properties simultaneously exactly one year later. In so doing, the fund generates $25 million in total profits after all costs and repayment of debt. This $25 million profit equals a 25% annual return and IRR, which exceeds the 9% IRR preferred return hurdle. Since the 9% preferred return is exceeded, profits above the pref level are split 80/20, with "the money" receiving 80% and the sponsor receiving their "promoted interest" of 20% of these profits.

The sponsor's promote is typically structured in one of two ways. In the most common waterfall structure (preferred by sponsors), "the money" and the sponsor split all profits, <u>including</u> those of the preferred return, 80% to "the money" and 20% to the fund sponsor, as long as "the money" receives all of their invested capital back and the preferred return. If the fund does not exceed the preferred return hurdle rate, no sponsor promote is earned, and profit distributions are paid 100% to "the money," split pari passu (90% to ArrowCo and 10% to UR in our example).

There is an alternative waterfall structure with the payout of 80% to "the money" and 20% to the sponsor just on the **residual split**, that is, only the profits in excess of the preferred return distribution.

As shown in Scenarios 1 and 2 in Figure 19.2, the alternative promote mechanics are irrelevant if the fund does not generate profits in excess of the preferred return. Line E for these two scenarios shows that assumed actual fund profits are only $9 million. As a result, the entire $9 million profit is required for the preferred return tier, leaving nothing for the residual split (Line K). Consequently, Line U in the Profit Summary section shows that UR receives no promote in either of these two scenarios.

FIGURE 19.2

Urban Fund Profit Splitting Under Different Waterfall Structure Scenarios ($ in MM)					Line
		Applies globally across all structures and scenarios:			
Total Investment ("the money")	Share	$100.00			A
ArrowCo Pension contribution	90.00%	$90.00			B
Urban Renaissance (UR) contribution	10.00%	$10.00			C
Targeted Preferred Return IRR to "the money"	9.00%	$9.00			D
Scenario		1		2	
80/20 Waterfall Structure		Common Structure		Alternative Structure	
Actual Fund Profits		$9.00		$9.00	E
Preferred Return Exceeded?		No		No	F
		PREFERRED RETURN			
		Share	Amount	Share	Amount	
To "the money"		100.00% *	$9.00	100.00%	$9.00	G
Pro Rata share to ArrowCo Pension		90.00%	$8.10	90.00%	$8.10	H
Pro Rata share to UR		10.00%	$0.90	10.00%	$0.90	I
Promote to UR as Sponsor		0.00%	$0.00	NA	NA	J
		RESIDUAL SPLIT			
		Share	Amount	Share	Amount	
Available to split			$0.00		$0.00	K
Distributed to "the money"		80.00%	$0.00	80.00%	$0.00	L
Pro Rata share to ArrowCo Pension		90.00%	$0.00	90.00%	$0.00	M
Pro Rata share to UR		10.00%	$0.00	10.00%	$0.00	N
Promote to UR as Sponsor		20.00%	$0.00	20.00%	$0.00	O
		PROFIT SUMMARY			
"The money"					
Preferred return		$9.00		$9.00	P
Residual split		$0.00		$0.00	Q
Total		$9.00		$9.00	R
Return on Investment		9.00%		9.00%	S
Share of total fund profits		100.00%		100.00%	T
UR Sponsor					
Promote		$0.00		$0.00	U
Share of total fund profits		0.00%		0.00%	V
ArrowCo Pension					
Preferred return		$8.10		$8.10	W
Residual split		$0.00		$0.00	X
Total		$8.10		$8.10	Y
Return on Investment		9.00%		9.00%	Z
Share of total fund profits		90.00%		90.00%	AA
UR as "money" and Sponsor					
Preferred return		$0.90		$0.90	AB
Residual split		$0.00		$0.00	AC
Promote		$0.00		$0.00	AD
Total		$0.90		$0.90	AE
Return on investment		9.00%		9.00%	AF
Share of total fund profits		10.00%		10.00%	AG

* Is 80% if "the money" has all capital returned and achieves the Pref. Return; otherwise is 100%, not allowing any promote.

Online Companion Hands On: Find the completed version of this Figure in Chapter 19 of the Online Companion, and study the Calculation notes provided to the right of the "Line" column of the table. Change the blue inputs to see how the profit splits behave.

The pie charts in Figure 19.3 show that the proportions of "dollars in" and "dollars out" of the fund are the same, as the promote is not triggered due to the insufficient returns. As a result, as shown in the bar graph, ArrowCo, UR, and Urban Fund all earn 9% returns.

FIGURE 19.3

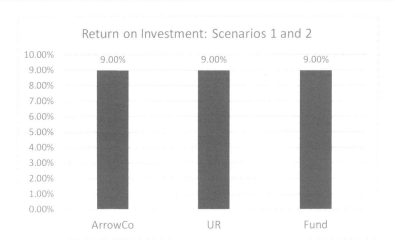

Reviewing Scenario 3 (Figure 19.4), we display the outcome for the structure when fund profits are assumed to be $25 million (i.e., exceeding the preferred return hurdle). In this case, all profits are split 80% to "the money" (Line G) and 20% to the sponsor (Line J). The 80% is shared pari passu based on equity investment shares (90% to ArrowCo and 10% to UR; Lines H and I). For this waterfall structure in this scenario, it appears that ArrowCo does not receive its 9% preferred return of $8.1 million ($90 million * 0.09). However, final distributions are determined and adjusted on a **look-back** basis (i.e., trued up as needed after the fund has fully liquidated). As noted in the footnote of Figure 19.4, if total profits over the life of the fund are not sufficient to return all capital and generate the preferred return, then the initial split to "the money" (Line G in Scenario 3) would be 100% rather than 80% (i.e., Scenario 1 in Figure 19.2).

Remaining with Scenario 3, Line K shows $16 million available for the residual split and reflects total profit, net of the $9 million preferred return that is first distributed. The remaining $16 million of profits is split between the 80% ($12.8 million) share that goes to "the money" (Line L) and the 20% ($3.2 million) promote that goes to the sponsor (Line O). In this scenario, due to the sponsor's promoted 20% participation in the preferred return (Line J), UR receives a total $5 million promote (Lines J and O, shown in AD), which when added to their share of the preferred return (Line AB) and residual split (Line AC), yields $7 million in total profits (Line AE). This is a 70% return on the UR cash investment ($7 MM / $10 MM) (Line AF) and a 20% return on the ArrowCo investment ($18 MM / $90 MM) (Line Z).

FIGURE 19.4

Urban Fund Profit Splitting Under Different Waterfall Structure Scenarios ($ in MM)					Line
		Applies globally across all structures and scenarios:			
Total Investment ("the money")	Share	$100.00			A
ArrowCo Pension contribution	90.00%	$90.00			B
Urban Renaissance (UR) contribution	10.00%	$10.00			C
Targeted Preferred Return IRR to "the money"	9.00%	$9.00			D
Scenario		3		4	
80/20 Waterfall Structure		Common Structure		Alternative Structure	
Actual Fund Profits		$25.00		$25.00	E
Preferred Return Exceeded?		Yes		Yes	F

	PREFERRED RETURN				
	Share	Amount	Share	Amount	
To "the money"	80.00% *	$7.20	100.00%	$9.00	G
Pro Rata share to ArrowCo Pension	90.00%	$6.48	90.00%	$8.10	H
Pro Rata share to UR	10.00%	$0.72	10.00%	$0.90	I
Promote to UR as Sponsor	20.00%	$1.80	NA	NA	J

	RESIDUAL SPLIT				
	Share	Amount	Share	Amount	
Available to split		$16.00		$16.00	K
Distributed to "the money"	80.00%	$12.80	80.00%	$12.80	L
Pro Rata share to ArrowCo Pension	90.00%	$11.52	90.00%	$11.52	M
Pro Rata share to UR	10.00%	$1.28	10.00%	$1.28	N
Promote to UR as Sponsor	20.00%	$3.20	20.00%	$3.20	O

	PROFIT SUMMARY			
"The money"				
Preferred return	$7.20		$9.00	P
Residual split	$12.80		$12.80	Q
Total	$20.00		$21.80	R
Return on Investment	20.00%		21.80%	S
Share of total fund profits	80.00%		87.20%	T
UR Sponsor				
Promote	$5.00		$3.20	U
Share of total fund profits	20.00%		12.80%	V
ArrowCo Pension				
Preferred return	$6.48		$8.10	W
Residual split	$11.52		$11.52	X
Total	$18.00		$19.62	Y
Return on Investment	20.00%		21.80%	Z
Share of total fund profits	72.00%		78.48%	AA
UR as "money" and Sponsor				
Preferred return	$0.72		$0.90	AB
Residual split	$1.28		$1.28	AC
Promote	$5.00		$3.20	AD
Total	$7.00		$5.38	AE
Return on investment	70.00%		53.80%	AF
Share of total fund profits	28.00%		21.52%	AG

* Is 80% if "the money" has all capital returned and achieves the Pref. Return; otherwise is 100%, not allowing any promote.

Online Companion Hands On: Find the completed version of this Figure in Chapter 19 of the Online Companion, and study the Calculation notes provided to the right of the "Line" column of the table. Change the blue inputs to see how the profit splits behave.

The pie charts and bar graph in Figure 19.5 illustrate the attractiveness of the outcome for the sponsor in Scenario 3. This scenario is best for UR, with 28% of fund profits and a 70% return on their cash investment, part a return on cash invested and part due to their sweat.

FIGURE 19.5

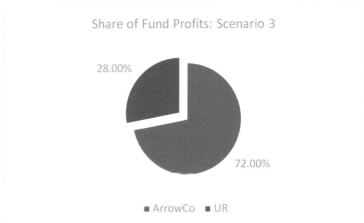

Note in the bar graph that not only does UR outperform the fund, but ArrowCo Pension (necessarily) underperforms the fund. This is by design, as the preferred return hurdle was cleared and ArrowCo "forfeited" a portion of what would otherwise be their pari passu profits to UR for its promote. This is a de facto management incentive program.

Scenario 4 in Figure 19.4 shows the alternative promote structure when fund profits are assumed to be $25 million (Line E). In this scenario, Line K shows $16 million available for the residual split, reflecting total profit net of the $9 million preferred return that is first distributed exclusively to "the money" (Line G). The remaining $16 million of profits is split between the 80% ($12.8 million) share that goes to "the money" (Line L) and the 20% ($3.2 million) promote that goes to the sponsor (Line O). In total, in Scenario 4, ArrowCo Pension receives $19.62 million of the profits (Line Y), which is a 21.8% return ($19.62 MM / $90 MM) (Line Z), while UR receives $5.38 million of the profits (Line AE), a 53.8% return ($5.38 MM / $10 MM) (Line AF). Figure 19.6 shows the profit splits and return on investment for the entities in this scenario.

FIGURE 19.6

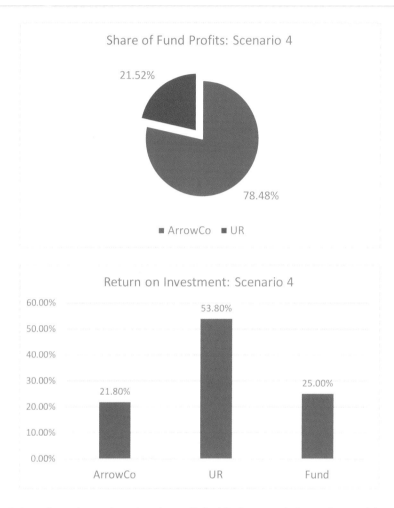

Which structure is best for primary investor ArrowCo? All else equal, ArrowCo would prefer to have the alternative structure modeled in Scenarios 2 and 4 (but with the profit level of Scenario 4). Scenario 4 provides the same fund-level $25 million profit as in Scenario 3, but ArrowCo does marginally better in return on investment (21.8% versus 20.0%).

INVESTOR PROTECTIONS

How much profit is too much for limited partners to forfeit to a sponsor? In Scenario 3 of the Urban Fund example, the sponsor walked away with a profit share that was almost 3 times the share of capital they invested (28% of fund profit versus 10% of fund investment). That is a very rich payout to the sponsor, who put little capital at risk relative to the primary investor.

To prevent the "casual forfeiture" of millions to tens of millions of dollars if the fund performs wildly above the preferred return level, limited partners typically require that the fund limit the total share of fund profits that can be distributed to the sponsor for their promote. Generally, the sponsor's promote distributable share is capped at a maximum of 20% of total fund profits. Part and parcel with distribution of profits above the preferred return is the proportion at which those excess cash flows are paid. In our example we have simulated that all properties are sold simultaneously, thus our discussion of an 80% split to "the money" and 20% promote to the sponsor after the preferred return is devoid of this nuance.

In reality, the sale of the fund's properties will be staggered over the latter few years of the fund's life. And in reality, there are alternative rates at which the sponsor's promote distributions can reach the 20% threshold of total fund profits. For example, if the sixth property sale in the portfolio propels the fund performance above the preferred return level, should the sponsor get 100% of those next distributable dollars until the maximum promote 20% share of total fund profits is reached? If not 100%, what about 80% or 50% (or anything greater than 20%, as a reward for a job well done exceeding the pref)? This issue is addressed by the **catch-up** provision, which stipulates what the split will be. The lower the share that goes to the sponsor, the lower the risk to the investor that they might end up (as seen in retrospect at the end of the fund life) over-allocating profits to the sponsor. Such a scenario often triggers a **claw-back**, which returns the excess share of total profits to "the money" to comply with the promote percentage cap on distributions received by the sponsor.

CLOSING THOUGHT

Like every aspect of the real estate business, the real estate private equity fund business is highly technical and nuanced. The key to their success is their ability to formulate and execute strategies that yield returns substantially in excess of those available via public real estate companies. As is the case for all real estate investments, the private equity structure is only as good as the players' ability to execute.

 Online Companion Audio Interview: To hear a conversation about this chapter's content, go to the Online Companion and select the link for Chapter 19. Scroll down to the Audio Interview section and listen.

Chapter 20
Investment Return Profiles

"You don't need to be 100% right when you buy if you are invested for the long haul."
- Dr. Peter Linneman

A commonly asked job interview question for business school students is, "If you had $100 million, how and where would you invest?" While there is not a "right" answer to the question, there is a well-reasoned response that reveals, at the very least, the student's knowledge of investment alternatives and their risks and opportunities. Limiting the "how" to major commercial real estate vehicles and the "where" to the U.S., how would you answer?

STUDY #1: INVESTMENT VEHICLE AND LIMITED PARTNER PERFORMANCE

In "Understanding the Return Profiles of Real Estate Investment Vehicles" (*Wharton Real Estate Review* Fall 2003), along with Deborah Moy, I presented simulated investment returns for: Unlevered Core (NCREIF), Core Plus, REITs (NAREIT), and Value-add funds. Assume that $100 million is invested in each of these vehicles for a 7-year investment horizon. Estimating cash flows based on assumptions about leverage, growth rates, cap rates, management fees, and cash flow payout ratios, we note that because Value-add funds take greater up-front risks, with the expectation of greater profits late in the investment horizon, their returns are generally negative in the early years.

The result is that Value-add funds will under-perform relative to NCREIF and NAREIT in their early years, even if they ultimately exceed their business plan. The need to reserve judgment on performance of these funds until later in their investment horizon can frustrate employees of limited partner investors, as many receive bonuses based upon annual investment performance. This delayed "day of reckoning" may allow weak Value-add managers to raise additional funds, as it is difficult to determine if the current weak performance is temporary or permanent. Nonetheless, we determined that under four distinct market conditions, the Value-add vehicle tends to outperform the other vehicles, and that the true risk of the Value-add investments is not the prospect of "disastrous" market conditions, but the inability of the manager to truly "add value."

QUALITATIVE DIFFERENCES

It is important to note the qualitative pros and cons of each investment alternative (Figure 20.1). For example, REITs are the most liquid, though the illiquidity of the other investment vehicles is often mitigated, particularly by Value-add funds, through re-financing, which is a much simpler and tax-advantaged transaction than a sale.

FIGURE 20.1

Pros and Cons of Alternative Investment Vehicles				
	Core	Core Plus	REIT	Value-add
Return Potential	Low	Medium	Medium	High
Liquidity	Low	Low	High	Low
Leverage	Low	Medium	Medium	High
$ Cost-Averaging	No	No	Yes	No
Investment Transparency	Medium	Medium	High	Low
Reporting Control	Sponsor	Sponsor	SEC	Sponsor
Operating Control	Medium	Medium	Low	Low
Diversification	Low	Medium	High	Medium
Alignment of Interests	Low	High	Medium	High

Investment transparency includes knowing how much capital investors will put to work, versus their investment commitment. For example, if an investor wants to invest $100 million in REITs, $100 million of securities (less fees) can be quickly purchased. However, with Core, Core Plus, and Value-add funds, an investor can agree to commit $100 million, but the amount put to work depends on the availability of desirable investments (and the ability to win control of those investments). As a result, we categorize the Core and Core Plus funds as both having medium investment transparency, while Value-add funds have low transparency.

With regard to reporting, REITs must adhere to rigorous SEC guidelines. That is not to say that the other vehicles have no reporting but, rather, that reporting is dictated by each investor and sponsor. For example, separate account fund reporting can be as demanding as SEC reporting criteria. Multiple investors in commingled funds can also dictate reporting requirements, although collaborative and consistent investor reporting is relatively difficult. A major limitation of Value-add fund reporting is the lack of a meaningful return benchmark.

The greatest investor operating control is associated with Core funds. Core assets are the most stable and easiest to "understand" from a cash flow perspective. REITs offer no operating control but allow easy exit. Direct Core Plus investments allow operating control and less cash flow volatility. At the other end of the spectrum, the Value-add funds offer no operating control, high cash flow volatility, and difficult exit. Core funds have less diversification because of their focus on stabilized, core assets. Diversification of the other vehicles varies, because while those vehicles have greater flexibility in which property types to invest, diversification may or may not be a primary goal. Lastly, the interests of the investor and the manager are most closely aligned for REITs, Core Plus, and the Value-add funds, due to de facto sponsor promote structures.

THE SET-UP

The base case market scenario assumptions for each investment vehicle simulation are summarized in Figure 20.2. The investor commits $100 million of equity in each of the four real estate vehicles, which have different investment strategies, capital structures, cash flow payout ratios, management fees, and promote structures. The simulated NAREIT and Core Plus investment vehicle own the same quality properties as the unlevered Core scenario, but are levered 50% and 65%, respectively. In addition, the REIT portfolio grows over time, as the REITs retain 30% of their cash flow to purchase additional stabilized, core properties (i.e., a 70% cash flow payout ratio) that are also 50% levered. Once stabilized, the Core Plus properties are refinanced with 70% debt, and net proceeds are distributed to investors.

FIGURE 20.2

Base Case Investment Vehicle Simulation Assumptions and Results				
	Core	Core Plus	REIT	Value-add
Purchase Price - Year 0	$28,748,910	$82,139,743	$57,497,820	$95,829,700
Purchase Price - Year 1	$34,512,500	$98,607,143	$69,025,000	$115,041,666
Purchase Price - Year 2	$36,738,590	$104,967,399	$73,477,179	$122,461,966
Reserve for Negative CF	$0	$0	$0	$16,234,039
LTV	0.0%	65.0%	50.0%	70.0%
Equity Committed	$100,000,000	$100,000,000	$100,000,000	$102,480,769
Equity Invested	$100,000,000	$100,000,000	$100,000,000	$100,000,000
Interest Rate	n/a	6.0%	6.0%	6.3%
Going-in Cap Rate (Stabilized)	8.0%	8.0%	8.0%	n/a
Residual Cap Rate	8.0%	8.0%	8.0%	8.0%
Yr 0 Inv Residual in Yr 5	$31,741,120	$90,688,914	$69,005,082	$129,135,749
Yr 1 Inv Residual in Yr 6	$38,866,680	$111,047,658	$84,653,780	$129,135,749
Yr 2 Inv Residual in Yr 7	$42,201,091	$120,574,547	$94,686,642	$129,135,749
Cash Flow Payout Rate	100%	100%	70%	100%
Management Fee*	0.5%	1.5%	0.5%	1.5%
Carried Interest (Promote)	n/a	10%	n/a	20%
NOI Growth Rate	2.0%	2.0%	2.0%	2.0%
Pre-Promote IRR	10.5%	16.3%	13.0%	20.0%
Equity Multiple (over 7 years)	1.6x	1.94x	1.79x	2.17x
Years to Double Equity	8.7	7.2	7.8	6.5

Management fee on committed capital for Core Plus and Value-add; on invested capital for Core and REITs.

The hypothetical investments are made over 3 years, rather than assuming all committed capital is immediately invested. Specifically, each vehicle is assumed to have three staggered investment phases of five years each. Acquisitions occur in years 0, 1, and 2 and are sold in years 5, 6, and 7, respectively. Note that the Value-add fund experiences negative operating cash flow during the first 2 years of each stage of investment (during redevelopment), before stabilizing in the third year. That is, the properties purchased up-front experience negative operating cash flow in years 1 and 2 and stabilize in year 3. The properties purchased in the beginning of year 2 experience negative cash flow in years 2 and 3, stabilizing in year 4, and the third-stage investments experience negative cash flow in years 3 and 4, stabilizing in year 5. Specifically, we set the first-, second-, and third-year NOIs of each investment phase of the Value-add fund to $0, $2 million, and $9.7 million respectively.

In the base case for the Value-add fund, NOI is set so that combining all three investment phases generates a 20% gross IRR over the 7-year investment horizon (before the general partner promote). Given our assumed operating cash flow, debt, and interest rate in the base case, the 3-year staggered investments of the Value-add fund generate an aggregate cash flow of –$16.2 million, which is set aside from the equity commitment as a reserve. As a result, only $86.2 million of the equity commitment is used for acquisitions. This amount is invested evenly over three years, or about $28.7 million per year.

The Value-add vehicle is used as the starting point for the amount invested in each of the other funds each year. Because Value-add investments are unstabilized in the early years, the investor must tap into the committed capital to cover operating cash shortfalls. These shortfalls ($5.8 million in year 1 and about $8 million in year 2), plus the actual capital placed by the Value-add fund ($28.7 million in each of the first three years), determine the capital placed by the other vehicles.

Management fee calculations for the Core fund and REITs are based on "placed" capital, while Core Plus and Value-add fund fees are based on "committed" capital. Although the actual cash investments are staggered for the Core Plus and the Value-add vehicles, the management fees for both are based upon the commitment of $100 million, not merely the amount that has been placed. As a result, in the early years, the effective management fee for these vehicles is significantly higher than 1.5% per year. In fact, because about $28.7 million (including the operating cash shortfall of the Value-add fund) is placed in the first year, the effective management fees of the Core Plus and Value-add funds start out at about 5.25% of invested capital. Then as capital is returned to the investor through re-financing (for the Value-add fund) or liquidation, the management fee is adjusted accordingly, often bringing the effective management fee lower than 1.5% toward the end of the investment horizon. We examine investor returns net of sponsor promote incentives and fees.

MARKET SCENARIO COMPARISONS

As shown in the Pre-Promote IRR line at the bottom of Figure 20.2, at the base case assumptions, the equity IRRs of the Core, Core Plus, and REIT vehicles over the 7-year investment horizon are 10.5%, 16.3%, and 13%, respectively. As indicated earlier, the Value-add vehicle is set up to generate a 20% IRR. Comparing the Core, Core Plus, and Value-add vehicles on an unleveraged basis, we observe that Core (10.5% equity IRR) outperforms Core Plus (8.7% equity IRR), simply because of the slightly higher management fee of the Core Plus vehicle. With an 8.9% unlevered IRR, the REIT fund performs slightly better than the unlevered Core Plus portfolio, but also worse than the unlevered Core vehicle. In contrast, without leverage, due to fees, the Value-add fund IRR drops to 7.8%.

We examine hypothetical Base, Strong, Weak, and Disaster real estate market scenarios. These scenarios reflect different annual NOI growth rates and residual cap rates, as summarized in Figure 20.3. In the Strong market scenario, NOI is assumed to grow by 3% (versus 2% in the Base case) annually, and the investor enjoys significant appreciation through a 7% (versus 8%) residual cap rate. In contrast, the Weak market scenario assumes that the annual NOI growth rate falls 100 basis points short of the base case, while the residual cap is 100 basis points higher. In the Disaster scenario, real estate market conditions soften dramatically, resulting in annual NOI growth of negative 2%, combined with a 9% residual cap rate. Each of these four real estate scenarios occur over a 7-year investment period.

FIGURE 20.3

Market Scenario Assumptions		
	NOI Growth Rate	Residual Cap Rate
Strong	3%	7%
Base	2%	8%
Weak	1%	9%
Disaster	(2%)	9%

Although we have "standardized" the initial capital outlays across investment vehicles, it is still difficult to compare the four sets of cash flows year to year, without ignoring the additional complexity of the Value-add fund of purchasing, refinancing, and selling different properties at overlapping times of the hold period. For example, in year 5 of the Value-add vehicle, properties purchased at the beginning of year 1 are sold, but properties purchased at the beginning of year 3 are refinanced. Thus, benchmarking the Value-add portfolio against the Core or the REIT portfolio at that time is not a fair comparison. However, we are able to consistently examine three metrics: the IRR, the equity multiple over the hold period, and the time path of the cash flows (including how long it takes to get investor capital back).

The 7-year pre-promote equity IRRs under each of the four market scenarios are summarized in Figure 20.4. In all cases, the Value-add fund yields the highest IRR, while the Core strategy (NCREIF) yields the lowest in all but the Disaster scenario. That is, if the investor seeks safety from substantial value declines, the unlevered Core strategy is best. If we change the residual cap to 10% (worse than the Disaster scenario), combined with a −2% annual NOI growth rate, the value of the Core unlevered portfolio declines by 30% and generates the highest IRR (1.9%) of the four vehicles, roughly equal to the Value-add fund (1.7% IRR).

FIGURE 20.4

Scenario Comparion: Pre-Promote Equity IRR (7-Year Horizon)				
Case	Core	Core Plus	REIT	Value-add
Strong	14.1%	24.3%	17.7%	29.0%
Base	10.5%	16.3%	13.0%	20.0%
Weak	7.2%	7 7%	8.5%	12.2%
Disaster	3.5%	-5.4%	0.5%	7.1%
Range in bps	1063	2974	1723	2189

Indicates best return in each case.
Indicates worst return in each case.

In the Disaster scenario (a 9% residual cap rate and −2% annual NOI growth), the Core Plus vehicle falls victim to its higher debt service and higher management fees, resulting in the lowest IRR of the four alternatives. In contrast, even though the Value-add fund uses more leverage than the Core Plus alternative, its performance is buffered by its value-add execution (assuming they successfully stabilize the portfolio). Thus, the "real" disaster situation for the Value-add fund is failure to achieve stabilization. That is, if a Value-add fund fails to add value, the returns are very disappointing except perhaps in the Strong market case, where a buoyant market saves the day.

Comparing equity multiples across all scenarios, the Value-add fund performs the best, requiring the shortest amount of time to double one's equity. On the other end of the spectrum, the Core vehicle is the weakest performer except in the Disaster case. And when Disaster strikes, the Core Plus vehicle is the weakest (Figure 20.5).

FIGURE 20.5

Scenario Comparison: Pre-Promote Equity Multiple (7-Year Horizon) & Years to Double				
Case	Core	Core Plus	REIT	Value-add
Strong	1.88x / 7.5	2.67x / 5.2	2.2x / 6.4	2.81x / 5.0
Base	1.6x / 8.7	1.94x / 7.2	1.79x / 7.8	2.17x / 6.5
Weak	1.39x / 10.1	1.37x / 10.2	1.47x / 9.5	1.67x / 8.4
Disaster	1.17x / 11.9	.8x / 17.4	1.02x / 13.7	1.36x / 10.3

Indicates best return in each case.
Indicates worst return in each case.

Under the Base, Weak, and Disastrous market conditions, the Core investor does not receive their full investment back until year 7 when the portfolio is liquidated. However, under Strong market conditions, the Core portfolio generates sufficient cash flow to fully return equity capital at the end of year 6. With the Core Plus vehicle, investors get their money back in six years, assuming Base or Strong market conditions, and 7 years under Weak market conditions. However, Core Plus investors suffer a notable loss under Disastrous conditions. REIT investors will be in the black after six years of Base case or Strong conditions, but not until a liquidity event in year 7 with Weak or Disastrous conditions. The Value-add investor's capital is fully returned in year 5 under Base and Strong market conditions and year 6 under the Weak and Disaster scenarios. This is despite negative cash flows in the first three years of the investment period.

THE IMPACT OF SPONSOR PROMOTES

Core Plus and Value-add fund structures provide the general partner sponsor a **promote** (a "sweat equity" profit share) in exchange for portfolio management, asset selection, the oversight of major capital improvements, lease-up decisions, and the orchestration of turn-around strategies and refinancing decisions. How do these promotes alter the returns realized by limited partner investors? To evaluate this question, we analyzed a typical promote structure for a Value-add fund, using the following fund cash flow distribution waterfall:

1) A 10% cumulative preferred return to investors
2) The return of investor capital
3) 50% of remaining cash flows go to the general partner's "catch-up," until the general partner has received 20% of all profit distributions (not including the return on their invested capital)
4) Thereafter, profits are split, with 80% going to investors and 20% going to the fund's general partner.

For the Core Plus vehicle, the promote structure reflects the following cash flow distribution waterfall:

1) A 9% cumulative preferred return to investors
2) The return of investor capital
3) 50% of remaining cash flows go to the general partner's "catch-up," until the general partner has received 10% of all profit distributions (not including the return on their invested capital)
4) Thereafter, profits are split, with 90% going to investors and 10% going to the fund's general partner.

The final two profit distributions in each structure are the general partner's promote, an incentive-based compensation to the sponsor for exceeding the (cumulative) preferred return. The promote structure allows a 50% **catch-up** of cash flows to the general partner until they have received their full profit share. Beyond this "catch-up," additional cash flows are split between the limited and general partners either 80/20 (Value-add) or 90/10 (Core Plus). While neither the investment's equity cash flows nor IRR are affected by the promote structure, the split of profits between investors and the general partner varies depending upon investment performance.

FIGURE 20.6

			Limited Partner IRR Pre- & Post- Promote			
Case	Core	REIT	Core Plus		Value-add	
			Pre-	Post-	Pre-	Post-
Strong	14.1%	17.7%	24.3%	21.5%	29.0%	21.8%
Base	10.5%	13.0%	16.3%	14.3%	20.0%	15.2%
Weak	7.2%	8.5%	7.7%	7.6%	12.2%	9.5%
Disaster	3.5%	0.5%	-5.4%	-5.4%	7.1%	6.1%

As shown in Figure 20.6, in the Base market scenario, the Value-add limited partner's post-promote equity IRR is 15.2%. Even after paying the promote to the general partner, the Value-add fund generates the highest IRR in the Base case. In addition, because of the refinancing upon stabilization, Value-add investors benefit from an earlier extraction of cash flows. For the Core Plus investment in the Base scenario, the equity IRR for limited partners is 14.3%, net of the general partner promote, which is still higher than the 13% return for the REITs. The most conservative investment approach, unlevered Core, is by far the weakest performer for the Base case, with an IRR of 10.5%.

In the Strong real estate market scenario, where the residual cap rate is 100 basis points lower, and the annual NOI growth rate is 100 basis points higher each year, the Value-add fund generates a total IRR of 29.0%. Net of the general partner promote, the investor's IRR drops to 21.8%. For the Core Plus vehicle, the equity IRR is 24.3% and 21.5%, pre- and post-promote to the limited partner investor, respectively. That is, the Core Plus post-promote sponsor return in the Strong scenario is 150 basis points higher than the Value-add fund pre-promote Base market scenario return of 20%. In addition, the Core Plus investor still fares better after the promote than the REIT investor (who receives a 17.7% IRR), as well as the unlevered Core investor (who only achieves a 14.1% IRR) in a Strong market. In fact, with the Core (NCREIF) investment vehicle, we observe that a Strong market scenario provides unlevered investor returns less than that achieved by Core Plus investors in the Base scenario, vividly demonstrating the upside limitation of the unlevered Core strategy.

Turning to the Weak real estate market scenario, returns for Core Plus are insufficient for the general partner to earn their promote until year 7. That is, performance does not exceed the preferred return hurdle until liquidation, leaving the limited partner investor with an IRR of 7.6% (versus 7.7% before the promote). In this scenario, the Value-add fund modestly exceeds the preferred return hurdle in year 6, a year earlier than the Core Plus investor. As a result, the general partner earns a larger share of the profits than the Core Plus general partner under the same conditions, causing the limited partner's IRR to drop to 9.5% (versus a pre-promote investment equity IRR of 12.2%). Under the Weak market scenario, REITs generate an investor IRR of 8.5%, while the unlevered Core once again performs the worst at 7.2%. That is, even if markets are weak (100-bp higher residual cap rate, and 100-bp lower NOI growth each year), the Value-add fund performs notably better than the alternatives, while the unlevered Core strategy substantially underperforms.

If a real estate market Disaster strikes (9% residual cap rate, −2% annual NOI growth rate), implying a portfolio value decrease of about 10% from the Value-add fund purchase price, the promote structure does not kick in for the Value-add fund until year 7. The Value-add pre- and post-promote IRRs are 7.1% and 6.1%, respectively. For the Core Plus fund, returns are insufficient to yield profit participation for the general partner in the Disaster scenario. As a result, post-promote returns for investors are identical to pre-promote returns of −5.4%). In short, the Core Plus vehicle is penalized for its relatively high leverage. Note that the original $100 million Core portfolio drops in value to about $78 million after 7 years in the Disaster scenario. Because of its conservative capital structure, the unlevered Core strategy generates the second highest IRR of 3.5%, with the Value-add fund providing a 6.1% post-promote IRR, as even though the Value-add fund utilizes the highest leverage ratio, its low acquisition price buffers the IRR. The strength of moderately leveraged real estate is demonstrated by the fact that the REIT strategy still ekes out a 0.5% IRR under this Disaster scenario.

The four simulated market scenarios (Base, Strong, Weak, and Disaster) cover a broad range of market conditions. If the Value-add fund is able to execute its stabilization strategy, it provides the best risk/return trade-off, while the unlevered Core provides superior capital preservation. REITs provide the most liquid investment of the four investment vehicles, while Core Plus generally performs slightly better than REITs on the upside but provides less liquidity. Even post-promote, the limited partner investor in a Value-add fund fares substantially better than other vehicles (assuming stabilization is successfully achieved) in the Base scenario or better real estate markets, while the unlevered Core strategy performs the worst in all but the Disaster scenario.

SENSITIVITY ANALYSES

When structuring the partnership agreement, how critical is the preferred return hurdle for limited partners? As seen in Figure 20.7A, a preferred return range of 7% to 10.5% for the Core Plus fund generates an equity IRR for the limited partner, ranging from 14.2% to 14.6%. In comparison, 8% to 11.5% preferred returns for the Value-add fund result in a 15.2% to 15.3% IRR with the Value-add fund. In the Strong case (Figure 20.7B), the same preferred return range corresponds to no change in the Core Plus vehicle and a swing of only 10 basis points in the IRR for the Value-add fund limited partners. In the Weak case (Figure 20.7C), the IRR swing resulting from a change in the preferred return hurdle varies by 60 and 30 basis points between the lowest and highest assumed preferred hurdle for the Core Plus and Value-add funds, respectively. In the Disaster case (Figure 20.7D), since the preferred return hurdle is never achieved for the Core Plus vehicle, it is irrelevant over the range of outcomes we examine. That is, market conditions do not allow for a strong enough performance to even reach a 7% return hurdle. In the Value-add vehicle, the Disaster case IRR varies by 100 basis points for the given range of preferred return hurdles.

FIGURE 20.7A

Base Case Preferred Return Sensitivity			
Core Plus Base Case		Value-add Base Case	
Pref. Ret.	IRR	Pref. Ret.	IRR
7.0%	14.2%	**8.0%**	15.2%
7.5%	14.2%	8.5%	15.2%
8.0%	14.2%	9.0%	15.2%
8.5%	14.3%	9.5%	15.2%
9.0%	14.3%	10.0%	15.2%
9.5%	14.4%	10.5%	15.3%
10.0%	14.5%	11.0%	15.3%
10.5%	14.6%	11.5%	15.3%

FIGURE 20.7B

Strong Case Preferred Return Sensitivity			
Core Plus Strong Case		Value-add Strong Case	
Pref. Ret.	IRR	Pref. Ret.	IRR
7.0%	21.5%	**8.0%**	21.8%
7.5%	21.5%	8.5%	21.8%
8.0%	21.5%	9.0%	21.8%
8.5%	21.5%	9.5%	21.8%
9.0%	21.5%	10.0%	21.8%
9.5%	21.5%	10.5%	21.8%
10.0%	21.5%	11.0%	21.8%
10.5%	21.5%	11.5%	21.9%

FIGURE 20.7C

Weak Case Preferred Return Sensitivity			
Core Plus Weak Case		Value-add Weak Case	
Pref. Ret.	IRR	Pref. Ret.	IRR
7.0%	7.1%	**8.0%**	9.5%
7.5%	7.2%	8.5%	9.6%
8.0%	7.3%	9.0%	9.6%
8.5%	7.5%	9.5%	9.7%
9.0%	7.6%	10.0%	9.7%
9.5%	7.7%	10.5%	9.8%
10.0%	7.7%	11.0%	9.8%
10.5%	7.7%	11.5%	9.8%

FIGURE 20.7D

Disaster Case Preferred Return Sensitivity			
Core Plus Disaster Case		Value-add Disaster Case	
Pref. Ret.	IRR	Pref. Ret.	IRR
7.0%	(5.2%)	**8.0%**	6.1%
7.5%	(5.2%)	8.5%	6.3%
8.0%	(5.3%)	9.0%	6.5%
8.5%	(5.3%)	9.5%	6.6%
9.0%	(5.3%)	10.0%	6.8%
9.5%	(5.3%)	10.5%	7.0%
10.0%	(5.3%)	11.0%	7.1%
10.5%	(5.3%)	11.5%	7.1%

These simulations demonstrate that the limited partner's equity IRR is driven far more by real estate market conditions than the preferred return hurdle. In short, a 100-basis point higher or lower preferred return is not nearly as critical as investors often believe, as its differential impact on the IRR comes into play only within a very narrow performance range. But if a Value-add sponsor insists on a low hurdle, it may be a sign of low confidence in their performance prospects.

How does the general partner "catch-up" impact the limited partner's return? Recall that we assume in step three of the cash flow distribution waterfall that "50% of remaining cash flows (after preferred returns and return of capital) go toward the general partner's 'catch-up' until the general partner has received 20% (10% for Core Plus) of all profit distributions." What if these allocations are changed to 25% or 75% rather than 50%? How are the equity IRRs of the limited partner investing in each vehicle impacted under varying real estate market conditions?

Figure 20.8 illustrates a range of catch-up allocations and the resulting limited partner IRRs for the Core Plus and Value-add vehicles under the Base case market conditions. On the one extreme, when 0% of the excess profits (after preferred return and return of capital) are allocated toward the catch-up, the limited partner maximizes his IRR. As the catch-up allocation increases, the LP's IRR decreases. However, from the perspective of the limited partner, if enough cash flow is generated to allow the general partner to reach his maximum promote, then the limited partner's "downside" IRR is capped. In the Base case, the general partner of the Core Plus vehicle achieves the maximum 20% promote when 75% of the excess profits are allocated toward the catch-up. Even at a higher allocation percentage to the general partner, the limited partner is no worse off under the same market conditions, because the general partner allocations will have already "caught up" to the designated promote share. Similarly for the Base case Value-add fund, the general partner achieves his maximum promoted share at a 50% allocation. Thus, given the portfolio's performance in the Base case market conditions, the limited partner's IRR will be no less than 14.2% and 15.2% under the Core Plus and Value-add fund vehicles, respectively.

FIGURE 20.8

Base Case: LP 7-Year Equity IRR		
Catch-Up Alloc.	Core Plus	Value-add
0.0%	16.3%	20.0%
5.0%	15.3%	17.7%
10.0%	14.9%	17.3%
15.0%	14.6%	16.9%
20.0%	14.5%	16.5%
25.0%	14.5%	16.1%
50.0%	14.3%	15.2%
75.0%	14.2%	15.2%
100.0%	14.2%	15.2%

The allocation percentage that goes toward a general partner's catch-up is a way to smooth limited partner cash flows. At the extreme, if 100% of all excess cash flows are allocated to the general partner catch-up, then the limited partner receives no profit share for an extended period. This discontinuity is unattractive to most limited partner investors. However, the difference between a 25% and a 50% catch-up allocation is not as critical as avoiding the 100% allocation.

The Base, Strong, Weak, and Disaster scenarios are driven by real estate market conditions, specifically in annual NOI growth rates and residual cap rates. These variables significantly impact investor returns. Figure 20.9A and Figure 20.9B illustrate Core Plus sensitivity tables for even more extreme market conditions. Specifically, the residual cap rate varies between 6.5% and 10%, while the NOI growth rate varies between negative 3% and positive 4% (for all 7 years). The resulting limited partner equity IRRs are color coded for each of the Base, Strong, Weak, and Disaster scenarios, but incremental IRRs are also shown in the matrix for combinations within those ranges.

FIGURE 20.9A

Core Plus Equity IRR Pre-Promote								
Residual Cap Rates								
	6.50%	7.00%	7.50%	8.00%	8.50%	9.00%	9.50%	10.00%
-3.0%	9.1%	5.4%	1.5%	-2.4%	-6.7%	-11.4%		
-2.5%	10.9%	7.3%	3.7%	-0.1%	-4.0%	-8.1%	-12.8%	
-2.0%	12.6%	9.1%	5.7%	2.1%	-1.5%	-5.3%	-9.4%	-14.1%
-1.5%	14.3%	10.9%	7.6%	4.2%	0.8%	-2.7%	-6.4%	-10.5%
-1.0%	15.9%	12.6%	9.4%	6.2%	3.0%	-0.3%	-3.8%	-7.4%
-0.5%	17.4%	14.2%	11.1%	8.0%	5.0%	1.9%	-1.3%	-4.7%
0.0%	18.9%	15.8%	12.8%	9.8%	6.9%	3.9%	0.9%	-2.2%
0.5%	20.3%	17.3%	14.4%	11.5%	8.7%	5.9%	3.0%	0.2%
1.0%	21.7%	18.8%	16.0%	13.2%	10.4%	7.7%	5.0%	2.3%
1.5%	23.1%	20.2%	17.5%	14.8%	12.1%	9.5%	6.9%	4.3%
2.0%	24.5%	21.6%	18.9%	16.3%	13.7%	11.2%	8.7%	6.2%
2.5%	25.8%	23.0%	20.3%	17.8%	15.3%	12.8%	10.4%	8.1%
3.0%	27.1%	24.3%	21.7%	19.2%	16.8%	14.4%	12.1%	9.8%
3.5%	28.4%	25.7%	23.1%	20.6%	18.2%	15.9%	13.7%	11.5%
4.0%	29.6%	27.0%	24.4%	22.0%	19.7%	17.4%	15.2%	13.1%

(Row labels on left: Annual NOI Growth Rate)

Legend: Strong · Base · Disaster · Weak

FIGURE 20.9B: WITH 50% CATCH-UP ALLOCATION

Core Plus Limited Partner Equity IRR Net of Promote								
Residual Cap Rates								
	6.50%	7.00%	7.50%	8.00%	8.50%	9.00%	9.50%	10.00%
-3.0%	8.3%	5.4%	1.5%	-2.4%	-6.7%	-11.4%		
-2.5%	9.8%	7.2%	3.7%	-0.1%	-4.0%	-8.1%	-12.8%	
-2.0%	11.3%	8.3%	5.7%	2.1%	-1.5%	-5.3%	-9.4%	-14.1%
-1.5%	12.8%	9.8%	7.4%	4.2%	0.8%	-2.7%	-6.4%	-10.5%
-1.0%	13.9%	11.3%	8.5%	6.2%	3.0%	-0.3%	-3.8%	-7.4%
-0.5%	15.1%	12.7%	10.0%	7.6%	5.0%	1.9%	-1.3%	-4.7%
0.0%	16.5%	13.9%	11.5%	8.9%	6.9%	3.9%	0.9%	-2.2%
0.5%	17.8%	15.1%	12.9%	10.4%	8.0%	5.9%	3.0%	0.2%
1.0%	19.1%	16.4%	14.1%	11.8%	9.4%	7.6%	5.0%	2.3%
1.5%	20.4%	17.7%	15.2%	13.2%	10.9%	8.7%	6.9%	4.3%
2.0%	21.6%	19.0%	16.5%	14.3%	12.3%	10.1%	8.1%	6.2%
2.5%	22.8%	20.3%	17.8%	15.5%	13.7%	11.5%	9.5%	7.8%
3.0%	24.1%	21.5%	19.1%	16.8%	14.7%	12.9%	10.9%	8.9%
3.5%	25.2%	22.7%	20.4%	18.1%	15.9%	14.2%	12.3%	10.3%
4.0%	26.4%	23.9%	21.6%	19.3%	17.2%	15.2%	13.6%	11.7%

(Row labels on left: Annual NOI Growth Rate)

Legend: Strong · Base · Disaster · Weak

Gray shaded section indicates no post-promote impact on the IRR

Comparing Figures 20.9A and 20.9B, it is apparent that equity IRRs for the Disaster cases of the Core Plus vehicle are identical for pre- and post-promote. This is because performance under such onerous market conditions does not merit any profit participation to the general partner. However, the limited partner's Strong case equity IRR of the Core Plus strategy declines by 280 basis points between the pre- and post-promote payment. Similarly, the Core Plus Weak and Base case limited partner IRRs drop by 10 and 200 basis points, respectively.

Figures 20.10A and 20.10B illustrate the same analysis for the Value-add fund, with equity IRR sensitivity tables driven by changes to the residual cap rate and the annual NOI growth rate assumptions, before and after the promote payment, respectively. Once again, we examine market condition combinations, where residual cap rates range from 6.5% to 10%, and annual NOI growth rates range from negative 3% to positive 4%. Even in the Disaster case, cash flows are sufficient to achieve a general partner promote distribution, decreasing the limited partner distribution by 100 basis points. The more the performance of the Value-add fund improves, the greater the spread between pre- and post-promote IRRs. Specifically, the Weak case pre-promote IRR to the limited partner is 12.2% but declines by 270 basis points to 9.5% upon payment of the general partner's promote. The Base Case for the Value-add fund exhibits a 480-basis point decline, with a 20% initial IRR and a 15.2% IRR net of promote. Following the same pattern, the Strong case equity IRR decreases by 720 basis points between the pre- and post-promote cash flow to the limited partner.

FIGURE 20.10A

		6.50%	7.00%	7.50%	8.00%	8.50%	9.00%	9.50%	10.00%
	Value-add Fund Equity IRR Pre-Promote								
	Residual Cap Rates								
	-3.0%	23.9%	19.5%	15.4%	11.8%	8.4%	5.3%	2.5%	-0.1%
	-2.5%	24.7%	20.3%	16.3%	12.7%	9.3%	6.2%	3.4%	0.8%
	-2.0%	25.6%	21.2%	17.2%	13.5%	10.2%	7.1%	4.3%	1.7%
	-1.5%	26.4%	22.0%	18.0%	14.4%	11.0%	8.0%	5.2%	2.6%
Annual NOI Growth Rate	-1.0%	27.2%	22.8%	18.8%	15.2%	11.9%	8.8%	6.0%	3.4%
	-0.5%	28.0%	23.6%	19.7%	16.0%	12.7%	9.7%	6.9%	4.3%
	0.0%	28.8%	24.4%	20.5%	16.9%	13.6%	10.5%	7.7%	5.1%
	0.5%	29.6%	25.2%	21.3%	17.7%	14.4%	11.3%	8.5%	6.0%
	1.0%	30.3%	26.0%	22.1%	18.5%	15.2%	12.2%	9.4%	6.8%
	1.5%	31.1%	26.8%	22.8%	19.3%	16.0%	12.9%	10.2%	7.6%
	2.0%	31.8%	27.5%	23.6%	20.0%	16.7%	13.7%	11.0%	8.4%
	2.5%	32.6%	28.3%	24.4%	20.8%	17.5%	14.5%	11.7%	9.2%
	3.0%	33.3%	29.0%	25.1%	21.5%	18.3%	15.3%	12.5%	9.9%
	3.5%	34.0%	29.7%	25.8%	22.3%	19.0%	16.0%	13.3%	10.7%
	4.0%	34.7%	30.5%	26.6%	23.0%	19.8%	16.8%	14.0%	11.4%

◻ Strong   ◻ Base   ◼ Disaster   ◻ Weak

* Annual growth rate applies after stabilization

FIGURE 20.10B: WITH 50% CATCH-UP ALLOCATION

		6.50%	7.00%	7.50%	8.00%	8.50%	9.00%	9.50%	10.00%
	-3.0%	17.6%	14.8%	11.8%	9.5%	7.1%	5.3%	2.5%	-0.1%
	-2.5%	18.3%	15.3%	12.3%	10.2%	7.5%	5.7%	3.4%	0.8%
	-2.0%	18.9%	15.9%	12.9%	10.7%	8.2%	6.1%	4.3%	1.7%
	-1.5%	19.6%	16.4%	13.6%	11.2%	8.8%	6.5%	4.9%	2.6%
	-1.0%	20.3%	17.0%	14.2%	11.7%	9.5%	7.1%	5.3%	3.4%
	-0.5%	21.0%	17.5%	14.9%	12.2%	10.0%	7.7%	5.7%	4.3%
Annual NOI Growth Rate	**0.0%**	21.6%	18.0%	15.6%	12.7%	10.5%	8.3%	6.1%	4.8%
	0.5%	22.3%	18.7%	16.2%	13.3%	11.0%	8.9%	6.7%	5.1%
	1.0%	22.9%	19.3%	16.8%	13.9%	11.4%	9.5%	7.3%	5.5%
	1.5%	23.6%	20.0%	17.3%	14.6%	11.9%	9.9%	7.9%	6.0%
	2.0%	24.2%	20.6%	17.8%	15.2%	12.5%	10.4%	8.5%	6.5%
	2.5%	24.9%	21.2%	18.3%	15.8%	13.1%	10.9%	9.1%	7.1%
	3.0%	25.5%	21.8%	18.8%	16.4%	13.7%	11.3%	9.5%	7.7%
	3.5%	26.1%	22.5%	19.2%	17.1%	14.3%	11.9%	10.0%	8.2%
	4.0%	26.7%	23.1%	19.8%	17.7%	14.9%	12.5%	10.4%	8.8%

Value-add Fund Limited Partner Equity IRR Net of Promote
Residual Cap Rates

Strong   Base   Disaster   Weak

* Annual growth rate applies after stabilization
Gray shaded section indicates no post-promote impact on the IRR

STUDY #1 CONCLUSION

The unlevered Core vehicle merits investment if you fear market disasters imperiling one's capital. This downside protection comes at the price of limited upside. Comparing Core Plus and REITs, Core Plus performs slightly stronger on the upside but is less liquid, and worse on the downside than REITs. The Value-add fund generally presents the best risk-reward balance, *if* successful stabilization is achieved and if the investor is willing to risk capital loss in exchange for greater upside.

This brings us back to square one: how should we compare return performance of these alternative vehicles? We have shown that interim performance is useful for only the most conservative strategies, while more opportunistic strategies are unfortunately much more difficult to evaluate until their investments are fully liquidated. Therefore, a strong tolerance for short-term weak performance, combined with patience, is the key to pursuing more aggressive investment strategies. Assessing the ability to execute among Value-add funds is the first hurdle in pursuing the riskiest of the four strategies.

STUDY #2: PROPERTY RISK AND OPPORTUNITY

How "at risk" are different property investments to an economic downturn? To address this question, Linneman Associates examined a variety of simplified investment profiles. Specifically, we simulated the returns for an 8-year hold period for 3 hypothetical multifamily investments: a class A property with a low yield and high NOI growth in a Gateway market ("Gateway A"); a class A property with a mid-range yield and medium NOI growth in a secondary market ("Secondary A"); and a class B property with a high yield, but low NOI growth, in a tertiary market ("Tertiary B"). We chose to model multifamily because of the simplicity of mark-to-market rents, though our insights can be generally applied to other property types. Each investment is analyzed for a Base Case with constant (but different for each property) NOI growth. For all investments, we assume a purchase price of $100 million, cash flow margins of 83% of NOI (reflecting on-going capex), and exit transaction fees of 3%.

The Gateway market A investment has a going-in cap rate of 4%, NOI growth of 4% per annum for 8 years, and an exit cap rate of 4.5%. The Secondary market A investment has a going-in cap rate of 6%, NOI growth of 2.5% per annum, and an exit cap rate of 6.5%. The Tertiary market B investment has a going-in cap rate of 7.5%, NOI growth of just 1.5% per annum, and an exit cap rate of 8%. For each property, we overlay 3 leverage scenarios: no leverage, 50% LTV, and 75% LTV. This yields a total of 9 "Base Case" scenarios. In both the 50% and 75% LTV scenarios, we assume 10-year debt with a 3.5% interest rate and 30-year amortization.

We simulated how returns and (interest and debt) coverage ratios are affected by reduced NOI growth due to a cyclical downturn. We refer to these 9 scenarios as the "Realistic" scenarios, as NOI never grows smoothly upward forever. These scenarios assume –6% NOI growth in years 3 and 4 (i.e., an aggregate 11.6% NOI decline spread over those years) of the investment horizon. Thereafter, the originally modeled growth rates resume through year 8 (Figure 20.11).

FIGURE 20.11

Economic Downturn "At Risk" Simulation NOI Growth Rate Assumptions							
Base Case Economy	Year 2	Year 3	Year 4	Year 5	Year 6	Year 7	Year 8
Gateway A	4.0%	4.0%	4.0%	4.0%	4.0%	4.0%	4.0%
Secondary A	2.5%	2.5%	2.5%	2.5%	2.5%	2.5%	2.5%
Tertiary B	1.5%	1.5%	1.5%	1.5%	1.5%	1.5%	1.5%
Realistic Case Economy	Year 2	Year 3	Year 4	Year 5	Year 6	Year 7	Year 8
Gateway A	4.0%	-6.0%	-6.0%	4.0%	4.0%	4.0%	4.0%
Secondary A	2.5%	-6.0%	-6.0%	2.5%	2.5%	2.5%	2.5%
Tertiary B	1.5%	-6.0%	-6.0%	1.5%	1.5%	1.5%	1.5%

In total, we simulated 18 investment scenarios and their corresponding return profiles: 3 different investments, with 3 leverage ratios and 2 economic environments. The scenario assumptions and results are summarized in Figure 20.12.

FIGURE 20.12

Hypothetical Investment Analysis: Multifamily Performance Metrics										
Assumptions					Results					
Market	LTV	Economy*	Going-in Cap Rate	Residual Cap Rate	Equity IRR	Equity Multiple	% of Return from Cash Flow	Average Interest Coverage	Average Debt Coverage
Gateway A	0%	Base	4.0%	4.5%	5.2%	1.44	21.2%	n/a	n/a
Gateway A	50%	Base	4.0%	4.5%	6.3%	1.60	11.1%	2.9x	1.7x
Gateway A	75%	Base	4.0%	4.5%	8.5%	1.98	(4.1%)	1.9x	1.1x
Secondary A	0%	Base	6.0%	6.5%	6.0%	1.50	29.0%	n/a	n/a
Secondary A	50%	Base	6.0%	6.5%	8.0%	1.71	25.4%	4.1x	2.4x
Secondary A	75%	Base	6.0%	6.5%	11.6%	2.22	19.6%	2.7x	1.6x
Tertiary B	0%	Base	7.5%	8.0%	6.6%	1.53	34.2%	n/a	n/a
Tertiary B	50%	Base	7.5%	8.0%	9.1%	1.78	34.5%	4.9x	2.9x
Tertiary B	75%	Base	7.5%	8.0%	13.9%	2.36	33.7%	3.3x	1.9x
Gateway A	0%	Realistic	4.0%	4.5%	2.5%	1.19	22.3%	n/a	n/a
Gateway A	50%	Realistic	4.0%	4.5%	1.2%	1.10	8.7%	2.5x	1.5x
Gateway A	75%	Realistic	4.0%	4.5%	(0.1%)	0.99	(24.6%)	1.6x	1.0x
Secondary A	0%	Realistic	6.0%	6.5%	3.7%	1.28	30.1%	n/a	n/a
Secondary A	50%	Realistic	6.0%	6.5%	3.6%	1.28	26.4%	3.6x	2.1x
Secondary A	75%	Realistic	6.0%	6.5%	4.1%	1.35	17.7%	2.4x	1.4x
Tertiary B	0%	Realistic	7.5%	8.0%	4.5%	1.34	35.3%	n/a	n/a
Tertiary B	50%	Realistic	7.5%	8.0%	5.2%	1.39	36.6%	4.4x	2.6x
Tertiary B	75%	Realistic	7.5%	8.0%	7.3%	1.57	37.2%	2.9x	1.7x

Source: Linneman Associates
Base case economy assumes constant positive NOI growth rates in each scenario.
Realistic case economy assumes -6% NOI growth in years 2 and 3. All other years match the Base case.
Coverage ratios are based on NOI.

While highly simplified, this analysis provides realistic insights on the impacts of leverage, property type, and the economy. As to leverage, as long as original pro-forma growth occurs, increased leverage increases both the equity IRR and the equity multiple. For example, as seen in the top block of rows in Figure 20.12, the Gateway A property generates an equity IRR of 5.2% with no leverage, 6.3% with 50% leverage, and 8.5% with 75% leverage, while the equity multiple increases from 1.4x to 1.6x to 2.0x, respectively, over the 8-year hold.

One noteworthy impact of leverage is that higher leverage notably reduces the proportion of IRR derived from annual cash flows. This is particularly true for the Gateway A investment, where high leverage converts this low-yield investment into a pure residual bet (−4.1% share from cash flow). The Secondary A property sees its proportion of return due to a cash flow drop by one-third with high leverage, to 19.6%. However, because of high positive leverage, the Tertiary B property experiences essentially an unchanged Base Case return share from cash flow of roughly 34%. This greater cash flow return greatly reduces risk, as it is money in your pocket rather than money at risk until exit. Even though debt coverage ratios (before cap ex) are above "1.0x" in all scenarios, in the

Base Case, the ratio only averages 1.1x at a 75% LTV. As such, assuming capital expenditures of 17% of NOI for multifamily, the cash flow-to-debt service coverage ratio averages just 0.9x over the 8-year period for the Realistic case. That is, the highly levered low-yield investment cannot always cover debt from cash flow even when debt is very cheap.

These simulations indicate that in the Realistic Case, higher leverage does not always translate into higher IRRs and higher equity multiples. Specifically, in the Realistic Case, the Gateway A property generates an equity IRR of 2.5% with no leverage, declining to a 1.2% IRR with 50% leverage, and a −0.1% IRR with 75% leverage. This occurs because the Gateway A property has a lower going-in yield, and absent growth, its cash flows are unable to support the debt service associated with 75% leverage in the recession years. The equity multiples also decline for the Gateway A property in Realistic conditions as leverage rises. In fact, in this scenario, the return is totally dependent on value appreciation. In the Realistic scenario, the Secondary A property exhibits modestly increased IRRs and notably decreased cash flow return shares as leverage increases from 0% to 75%. Interestingly, the Realistic scenario with 50% leverage for the Secondary A property generates almost identical returns to the no-leverage scenario. That is, the equity IRRs and the equity multiples are roughly equal with both no leverage and 50% leverage.

The Tertiary B property exhibits strong increases in both the equity IRR and equity multiple as the LTV increases due to its high positive leverage. Specifically, higher going-in yields provide a cushion against the 2-year decline in NOI. For this property, the proportion of return derived from operating cash flow is relatively constant at about 35-37% regardless of leverage or state of the economy.

Evaluating returns across property types, the Tertiary B property outperforms Gateway A and Secondary A properties over the longer hold. That is, in both economies, the highest equity IRRs are generated by the Tertiary B property, regardless of leverage or economy. Similarly, the Tertiary B property also generates the highest percentage share of return from operating cash flows, reducing its risk by making it less dependent on value appreciation. This is due to the higher going-in yield generating high cash-on-cash returns, particularly at higher leverage. In contrast, when comparing properties under similar economic conditions, the least attractive scenario generating the lowest comparable returns is the highly leveraged Gateway A investment, particularly in a Realistic case, where you bet on high growth which fails to occur.

It is important to bear in mind that this analysis fails to capture the fact that the Tertiary B property has the lowest liquidity. Hence, exit (or refinancing) at the modeled cap rates may not be possible, particularly during the cyclical downturn. Nonetheless, this analysis reflects the power of high yields in a low-interest rate environment — even with slow growth.

As displayed in Figure 20.13, we also calculated how far NOI growth must decline in years 3 and 4 in order to yield a 0% IRR for each scenario. Not surprisingly, as leverage rises, a less severe downturn is required to result in a 0% IRR. In other words, leverage increases investment risk because higher debt service drains cash flow. In order for the Gateway A investment to achieve a 0% IRR, NOI would have to decline for 2 consecutive years by 14.7% with no leverage, 8.2% with a 50% LTV, and just 6.0% with a 75% LTV. For the Secondary A investment, NOI would have to drop by 18.2%, 11.9%, and 9.6%, respectively, while the Tertiary B investment would require comparable NOI declines of 20.2%, 14.2%, and 11.9%. Thus, high yield-slow-growth investments can survive notably steeper NOI declines.

FIGURE 20.13

2-Yr NOI Decline Needed for 0% IRR in Realistic Case			
	Unlevered	50% LTV	75% LTV
Gateway A	(14.7%)	(8.2%)	(6.0%)
Secondary A	(18.2%)	(11.9%)	(9.6%)
Tertiary B	(20.2%)	(14.2%)	(11.9%)

We conducted a similar analysis to determine how far NOI must decline in the Realistic Case before interest and debt coverage fall below 1.0x (Figure 20.14). That is, how bad can the economy get before an investor is forced into default, even before any capital expenditures are made? As previously discussed, the Tertiary B property cash flows are more insulated than the Secondary A cash flows, which in turn, are more insulated than the Gateway A cash flows. Therefore, the Tertiary B investment can withstand the largest NOI declines before defaulting. The good news is that for all except one scenario, significant declines in NOI would have to occur before coverage problems arise.

With 50% leverage, debt coverage would be insufficient only if NOI declined by 35% for the Gateway A property, 56% for Secondary A property, and 65% for the Tertiary B property. The only scenario that is truly at risk of not covering debt service is the Gateway A property with 75% leverage, where only a 3% NOI decline is needed before default.

FIGURE 20.14

Year 3 NOI Decline Resulting in Insufficient Interest Coverage or Debt Coverage in Realistic Case *				
	50% LTV		75% LTV	
	Interest Coverage	Debt Coverage	Interest Coverage	Debt Coverage
Gateway A	(60.0%)	(35.3%)	(40.0%)	(3.0%)
Secondary A	(72.9%)	(56.2%)	(59.4%)	(34.4%)
Tertiary B	(78.1%)	(64.6%)	(67.2%)	(47.0%)

"Insufficient" is defined as coverage ratios less than 1.0x.

Our final analysis examined what exit cap rate is necessary to produce the same equity IRRs for the different investments and LTVs (Figure 20.15). We used Gateway A with 0% leverage as our benchmark in each economy. Specifically, we targeted an IRR of 5.2% in the Base Case and 2.5% in the Realistic Case.

To produce the same IRR in the Base Case economy (constant NOI growth) as the Gateway A property with no leverage, both the Secondary A and Tertiary B investments require a much higher exit cap rate than in the original exercise. Additionally, as leverage rises in the Base economy, exit cap rates required to achieve the baseline unlevered IRR target also rise. This indicates that as leverage increases, more weight is given to the residual value in order to maintain a constant IRR. However, in the Realistic case, the opposite is true: to maintain a constant IRR, required exit cap rates decrease as leverage increases, re-emphasizing the fact that the residual value becomes increasingly important when NOI declines.

FIGURE 20.15

	Orig. Residual Cap Rate	Base Economy			Realistic Economy		
Residual Cap Rate Needed for Uniform IRR (Benchmark: Gateway A, 0% LTV)							
		0% LTV	50% LTV	75% LTV	0% LTV	50% LTV	75% LTV
Gateway A	4.5%	4.5%	4.8%	5.0%	4.5%	4.2%	4.2%
Secondary A	6.5%	7.0%	7.5%	8.0%	7.3%	6.8%	6.8%
Tertiary B	8.0%	9.2%	10.0%	10.7%	9.9%	9.2%	9.1%
Equity IRR Benchmark		5.2%	5.2%	5.2%	2.5%	2.5%	2.5%

CLOSING THOUGHT

There is no "right" way to invest in real estate. Each strategy and its associated vehicle and each market environment pose unique risks and opportunities. Success comes from having a clear strategy and putting a skilled team in place to implement the required tactics. Of equal importance to execution is to not lose focus or resolve when things look bleak, and to stay humble and aware when things are so good that they "can't get any better than they are."

 Online Companion Audio Interview: To hear a conversation about this chapter's content, go to the Online Companion and select the link for Chapter 20. Scroll down to the Audio Interview section and listen.

Chapter 21
REITs and Liquid Real Estate

"It is easy to raise money if you're not the one doing it."
- Dr. Peter Linneman

Although the U.S. real estate business has been around since colonial times, the REIT (Real Estate Investment Trust) tax status was created by Congress in 1960, and large and well-traded public real estate companies have only emerged since the early 1990s. In 2021, according to the National Association of Real Estate Investment Trusts, "REITs…collectively own more than $3.5 trillion in gross real estate assets across the U.S., with stock-exchange listed REITs owning approximately $2.5 trillion in assets."

There are three REIT categories: equity REITs, mortgage REITs; and hybrid REITs. Equity REITs, the dominant format, own and operate income-producing real estate and tend to be low-leverage investors. Mortgage REITs lend money directly to real estate owners or extend credit indirectly through the acquisition of loans or mortgage-backed securities. The revenue from mortgage REITs primarily derives from interest on the mortgages they own, while equity REITs derive their profits from rental streams. Hybrid REITs pursue a bit of both strategies. Key differences between publicly traded real estate companies and real estate private equity vehicles are: investments in private equity funds are much less liquid; private equity funds seek higher equity returns; since there are no investment minimums for public real estate companies, they provide an opportunity for all types of investors to invest in real estate; and investors in public real estate typically own both the real estate assets and the management team.

HISTORY OF REITs

The REIT tax classification was created to make investments in large-scale, income-producing real estate accessible to all investors. REITs, however, were not a major force until the early 1990s, as banks, insurance companies, tax syndicates, and pension funds provided the bulk of capital for real estate up until then.

Until wildly undisciplined bank lending led to the collapse of real estate markets in 1990, REITs were a niche financial vehicle with a mixed history of booms and busts. For example, from 1970-1974, bank-sponsored REITs made speculative development loans that ended with the mortgage REIT bust of 1974. After that, there was little REIT activity until the early 1990s. Prior to the 1990s, abundantly available debt meant that the major owners of real estate did not need to access large pools of equity to own or develop real estate. In addition, since real estate owners had tax losses due to high debt and large depreciation allowances, the REIT structure's **single taxation** feature offered no advantage. Only when lending rationalized and depreciation tax breaks disappeared, did many of the leading owners of real estate turn to public equity markets.

When lenders began requiring that transactions be composed of 25-50% equity, many leading property owners went public to efficiently access the equity necessary to de-lever their over-levered portfolios. This resulted in greater real estate market liquidity and transparency. The total equity market capitalization of REITs exploded from $12 billion at the end of 1990, to roughly $1.49 trillion at the end of 2021, as properties shifted from private to public ownership. As of August 2016, publicly traded REITs were recognized as part of a discrete business sector, and were moved into a newly-created "Real Estate" classification in the Standard & Poor's Dow Jones Indices. The Real Estate sector represents nearly 4% of the equity market capitalization of the S&P 1500 and is included in all major market indexes.

Until the early 1990s, real estate was largely debt financed. If you could buy $1 billion worth of real estate for $1 of equity and finance the rest via non-recourse debt, wouldn't you take that deal, almost irrespective of the real estate? Of course! If the value of the portfolio rises by just 1%, you make a $10 million profit on a $1 investment.

And if the value falls, you only stand to lose a dollar (and perhaps a bit of reputation). When 90-110% LTV loans were the industry norm, owners did not have to be particularly good at operating real estate. Instead, the critical skill was the ability to convince lenders to lend you money.

As excessive debt financing disappeared, large pools of equity and the ability to efficiently operate properties became critical ingredients for success. As a result, many real estate entrepreneurs began to specialize in a particular property type or geographic region. After all, if you have to put a significant amount of your own money into a deal, you want to invest where you believe you have a core competency. In addition, equity sources have increasingly funneled their capital to the best operators who share an alignment of interests.

REIT IPO BASICS

As the 1990s began, there were few notable public REITs. Today, REITs are well-established and a big part of the "Who's Who" of the real estate business. The reason for this change is that until the early 1990s, the real estate business sustained itself on tax gimmicks and excessive debt and was not seen as a legitimate asset class by the global capital markets. Foolish tax legislation and undisciplined lending by the banks, savings and loan institutions (S&Ls), and life insurance companies led to massive overbuilding in the 1980s. As the economy softened in the early 1990s, financial regulators literally shut down real estate lending. This caused a virtual collapse in a real estate industry that was comprised primarily of highly leveraged developers reliant on continued debt refinancing to repay their maturing debt. But as mortgages matured in the early 1990s, no new loans were available to repay these maturing obligations.

For many leading real estate operators, there were only two viable financial options: filing a Chapter 11 bankruptcy or filing an S-11 Initial Public Offering (IPO) prospectus with the SEC. The strategy for going public was to sell the majority equity claim to their assets and use the IPO's net cash proceeds to repay the maturing debt. For those nimble enough to successfully complete an IPO, an S-11 was far more attractive than Chapter 11. The volume of real estate public offerings was very rapid, with $19.5 billion raised in 117 IPOs from 1992-1996. Once de-levered, these newly public real estate companies were able to purchase additional real estate, both by using their shares as currency to purchase properties from distressed owners unable to navigate their own IPO, and via the cash raised in secondary stock offerings.

To see how the IPO process works, consider Chan Realty, which owns a portfolio worth $100 million when valued at a 9 cap. However, this $100 million valuation was only theoretical. The actual value of these properties is highly uncertain, as the absence of debt means that there are very few viable purchasers for the properties. Hence, a large margin of error exists in assessing the value of the portfolio. This margin is easily plus or (more dangerously) minus 10% in volatile market conditions. Even at the questionable $100 million valuation, the once proud multi-millionaire Ms. Chan faces a severe financing squeeze, as she has $98 million in mortgages against these properties. To make matters (much) worse, she has $56 million in debt maturing in the next 24 months, of which $30 million is personally guaranteed. And this $98 million debt burden is the same whether the properties were worth $100 million or only $90 million. What can Ms. Chan do to repay this maturing debt and free herself from the personal guarantees that could leave her penniless?

If she declares Chapter 11 bankruptcy, the process will buy her perhaps 12-24 months, during which time market conditions might improve. However, absent a major market turnaround, she will eventually lose the properties securing the maturing mortgages, the management fee streams associated with these lost properties, and her other assets due to her personal recourse. This is not to mention being subject to capital gains taxes triggered by the foreclosures. Alternatively, she can attempt to sell some of her prized properties to generate enough cash to pay off the maturing obligations. But the success of this strategy is highly questionable in a market populated with few strong buyers and many distressed sellers. Further, upon sale, she would lose the management fees on these assets, have to pay capital gains taxes, and remain personally liable for any debt repayment shortfalls.

She considered selling limited partnership interests in her properties to pension funds, insurance companies, or high net-worth individuals, and she was told "No thanks, we have our own real estate woes" and "If I didn't invest in your real estate partnerships when things were supposed to be good, why would I invest now?" These potential capital sources were also troubled by the failure of real estate operators to return capital via sale, as too often these operators keep the properties to generate management fees, arguing that it is never the right time to sell. In addition, no lender will provide more than a 50% LTV loan, and at such an LTV, Chan Realty clearly lacks sufficient capital to repay the near-term maturing debt. Since Ms. Chan's wealth is primarily her properties, she lacks the resources to repay the loan gap with a personal equity infusion. She faces some decisions.

An answer is perhaps an IPO sale of publicly traded common equity in her properties. This solution gives individual investors control in the capital decision via the sale of their individual shares. If the IPO generates sufficient proceeds, Ms. Chan will be able to pay off her $56 million in maturing debt, eliminate personal recourse obligations, de-lever her portfolio, maintain control of the management fee stream, and avoid capital gains taxes. The key is that absent extreme leverage, these assets provide the relatively predictable cash flow stream that investors seek. Also, if public markets have rebounded, Wall Street will probably value the assets higher than private buyers, as private markets historically lag public real estate pricing. With a dash of transparency, a pinch of good corporate governance, a slick roadshow, and some luck, investors just might buy Ms. Chan's IPO offering in pursuit of low-leveraged, relatively predictable cash streams.

Ms. Chan rolls her property partnerships into a new entity, Chan REIT. She then (successfully) sells $60 million in publicly traded common equity claims in this new entity via an IPO, with the proceeds designated to pay off the $56 million of maturing debt and roughly $4 million in IPO fees.

How does this solve Ms. Chan's problem of salvaging her slim (and questionable) equity stake? After all, the IPO's $4 million in fees were greater than her theoretical $2 million equity sliver. The answer is that she did not lose control of her properties to either third-party buyers or foreclosing lenders, and she still owns the fee stream associated with managing these assets. This management fee stream, which would become valueless as assets are sold or foreclosed, is also rolled into Chan REIT, valued at an appropriate multiple, separate from the valuation of the properties. Since her management fees are roughly $650,000 (5% of property revenue) a year, at a 7.0x multiple, Ms. Chan's fee stream is worth roughly $4.55 million, as shown in Figure 21.1. Thus, in exchange for her contribution of this fee stream to Chan REIT, Ms. Chan receives a 2% (for example) equity ownership of Chan REIT. Chan REIT is now an internally managed public company, with Ms. Chan as the Chairperson and CEO, for which she is compensated with a package of salary, bonus, and stock options. As part of the IPO, she agrees not to compete with Chan REIT and that she will not sell her equity ownership for a period of 12 months.

Figures 21.1 through 21.4 summarize the IPO cash flows, resulting corporate capital structure, and equity ownership shares.

FIGURE 21.1

Value of Chan's Management Fee Stream	
Portfolio Revenue	$13.00 MM
Management Fee (5%)	$0.65 MM
Valuation Multiple	7.0x
Management Fee Stream Value	$4.55 MM

FIGURE 21.2

Chan REIT IPO Summary	
Property Value (+/- 10%)	$100.00 MM
Management Fee Stream Value	$4.55 MM
Debt	($98.00 MM)
Net Pre-IPO Equity	$6.55 MM
IPO Equity Raised	$60.00 MM
IPO Fees	($4.00 MM)
Debt Repaid with IPO Proceeds	$56.00 MM
Chan REIT Debt post-IPO	$42.00 MM

FIGURE 21.3

Chan REIT Post-IPO Summary		
Pre-IPO Value	$104.55 MM	
IPO Fees	($4.00 MM)	
Value of Chan REIT	$100.55 MM	
Debt	$42.00 MM	41.8%
Equity	$58.55 MM	58.2%

FIGURE 21.4

Chan REIT Post-IPO Ownership	
IPO Investors	98.00%
Chan	2.00%

Thus, although the IPO drained $4 million in value due to IPO fees, it liquefies the value of Chan's management fee stream, allows all maturing debt to be repaid in a timely manner, and frees Ms. Chan of her personal guarantees. In addition, she has a well-paid job with a company that is sufficiently deleveraged (only 41.8% debt) to take advantage of other distressed owners, and no capital gains taxes are triggered in the process.

You may be looking at Chan REIT's ownership structure and wondering why she would settle for 2% (in this example) REIT ownership, when she formerly owned 100% of her properties and 100% of the management company which owned the property management fee stream. The answer is that 2% of something is a lot more than 100% of nothing! Plus, as a key employee she receives annual grants of restricted shares and stock options, and as a common shareholder, 2% of the dividends paid by the deleveraged company. Also, if ownership is correctly structured, Ms. Chan defers paying the capital gains taxes that would have been due had she declared bankruptcy or sold the properties, as these taxes are deferred until Ms. Chan sells her ownership in Chan REIT.

Post-IPO, the Chan REIT can obtain a $16 million corporate line of credit from the lenders to whom Ms. Chan endeared herself by repaying her debt while many others were defaulting. With this line of credit, Chan REIT could purchase an additional $16 million in real estate and still maintain a 50% corporate leverage level. When Chan REIT reaches roughly 50% debt, it plans to issue a **secondary equity offering** (sale of shares after the IPO) to pay down the line of credit, restoring borrowing capacity on the line of credit for further acquisitions.

To be sure, the process of Ms. Chan's IPO was hardly a walk in the park. Ms. Chan spends roughly a year preparing it and is at risk of its failure to raise sufficient funds to repay the maturing debt. But, if successful, she is in an enviable position relative to other debt-laden property owners. Post-IPO, she can approach distressed owners and offer to purchase their properties in exchange for tax-deferred equity ownership interests in Chan REIT. This would allow them to gracefully exit without triggering capital gains taxes and simultaneously avoid the costs, uncertainties, and headaches of either bankruptcy or their own public offering. If Chan REIT acquires these properties for ownership interests in Chan REIT, it also generally assumes the debt on the properties. To retire this debt, the Chan REIT can either use its line of credit or "float" (issue and sell) additional equity shares. Both routes are relatively fast, cheap, and easy because Chan REIT is now a modestly leveraged public company with a transparent balance sheet. Also, since secondary equity offerings are much faster and cheaper than IPOs, Chan REIT has a cost advantage over distressed owners contemplating survival via their own IPO. The main challenge facing Chan REIT is execution, as managing a public real estate company in a rapidly changing market means that if you fail operationally, you become very visible prey for bigger and savvier fish.

REIT INCOME TAX ADVANTAGES AND OPERATING RESTRICTIONS

All companies attempt to minimize their income tax liability. From a tax perspective, non-real estate companies are basically C-corporations or partnerships. As a C-corp, corporate net income is taxed at the corporate level. Whatever money a C-corp has after paying corporate taxes can be retained or distributed as desired. If a C-corp decides to pay a portion of these funds in dividends, the shareholders (if they are taxable entities) pay income taxes on their dividend income. This is referred to as **double taxation**, as the government taxes profits at both the corporate and the shareholder level. If no dividend is paid, only a single corporate tax is assessed.

Alternatively, partnerships do not pay taxes at the corporate level, but instead pass through all tax liabilities directly to the owners. If the property earns taxable income, the owners will be taxed pro rata on these profits, regardless of whether this income is distributed to the owners. Since there is no corporate tax payment, these structures are single taxation structures. The problem is that if the firm retains the earnings, the owners have a tax liability with no distribution to pay the taxes. As a result, these structures avoid double taxation, but owners can owe taxes without receiving any income.

The REIT tax structure offers the possibility of avoiding corporate taxes without generating tax liabilities for owners, absent income distributions. This sounds perfect, right? So, why isn't every company in America a REIT? The answer is that to qualify as a REIT under the tax code, a company must satisfy a long litany of operating restrictions. Two of the most important operating restrictions are: the firm must primarily be in the business of owning and operating real estate; and the firm must pay out at least 90% of its taxable income in dividends (some of which may be paid in stock).

Who is impacted by the first restriction? Think about homebuilders (or builders in general). For a homebuilder to qualify as a REIT, they cannot sell the homes they build, as to qualify as a REIT they must own and operate their properties (i.e., single-family homes). However, most homebuilders are in the business of building and selling, not owning and operating. Similarly, commercial property developers rarely choose to be REITs, as most developers are in the business of building and selling their properties upon stabilization (the **"merchant builder"** business model). In addition, the combination of relatively high debt levels and minimal (if any) cash flow during the development period generates little taxable income requiring shelter from corporate taxes. Therefore, from the standpoint of a developer, there is generally little advantage and many operating drawbacks of being a REIT.

Since a REIT's primary business must be owning and operating real estate, this tax structure is not available to most companies. For example, Microsoft owns a lot of real estate, but that is not their primary business. If Microsoft put their real estate in a separate and independent subsidiary that owns and operates those facilities, the subsidiary could qualify as a REIT, but not the parent company.

To qualify as a REIT, the firm cannot be in the business of "trading" real estate. The definition of the word "trading" is a bit ambiguous, as a REIT is allowed to sell some of its assets from time to time. This restriction can be problematic. For example, a REIT may want to purchase 12 of the 45 properties in a portfolio being sold, but the remaining 33 properties do not fit their strategy. However, to purchase the 12 desirable properties it must purchase the entire portfolio because that is what is being sold. If they acquire the entire portfolio and sell the 33 undesirable properties as quickly as possible, they may endanger their REIT status, as the IRS may view these sales as a trading business.

If a company loses their qualified status, the IRS will demand back taxes, interest on those taxes, and perhaps penalties. The company can also be barred from becoming a REIT again for at least five years. This restriction is designed to prohibit firms from constantly switching status to minimize taxes.

Another major operating restriction is that a REIT must distribute 90% of its taxable income as dividends. Hence, while it does not pass through its tax liability, a REIT must distribute a large portion of available cash flow to shareholders. Shareholders are then taxed (if they are taxable entities) on this dividend income. Remember that a REIT's taxable income will generally be notably lower than cash available for distribution due to, among other reasons, depreciation. As a result, a REIT may generally distribute as little as 50-70% of their available funds and still comply with the 90% of taxable income dividend restriction.

As a real estate operator, why might you dislike the REIT dividend restriction? The obvious downside is that if you are required to distribute large dividends, then you are not able to retain that capital to grow your business. For example, you pay accountants to calculate how much you must pay out in dividends to remain a REIT, and then you have to pay investment bankers to raise money to grow your business. That's expensive! Even worse is if you select REIT tax status and unknowingly violate one of the many operating restrictions. During the IPO process, not only did you pay out money that you could have used to fund growth, but the government still collects corporate taxes, interest on those taxes, and penalties. As a result, firms generally maintain a cushion with respect to the REIT operating restrictions. In short, REITs achieve single taxation, but at a price.

Figure 21.5 summarizes pros and cons of the different business entity tax statuses.

FIGURE 21.5

Pros and Cons of Different Business Entity Tax Statuses		
	Pros	Cons
C-Corp	- Can retain more cash flow for growth - Simpler corporate structure - No limitations on the types of businesses performed	- Pay corporate tax
REIT	- No corporate tax	- Large Dividend payments - More dependent upon equity specialists to raise growth capital - Numerous operating restrictions
Partnerships	- No corporate tax	- Tax liability without distribution - Cumbersome governance structure

REIT VERSUS PUBLICLY TRADED REAL ESTATE COMPANY

Becoming a REIT is simply a tax status election. Publicly traded REITs are governed by the same SEC and listing rules as all other publicly traded companies and are "normal" companies in every way except taxation.

REITs do not have to be public companies. In fact, there are many private REITs. Choosing REIT status is a separate decision from the decision to list on a public exchange. The REIT decision revolves around the gains from single taxation (estimated at 3-5% of the value of the assets) versus the costs of the operating restrictions. If you believe more value is created by avoiding double taxation than is destroyed by the operating restrictions, you will select REIT status. One reason why most private companies are not REITs is that to qualify as a REIT, you must have at least 100 shareholders, and no 5 shareholders taken together can control 50% or more of the equity. In contrast, most private real estate companies have heavily concentrated ownership, very often within a single family. If the controlling family wants to become a private REIT, they must substantially dilute their equity stake. As a result, most owners opt for a partnership structure. To ensure compliance with these ownership restrictions, most REITs have bylaws which limit ownership concentration. This ownership structure restriction is also a key reason why companies like Microsoft do not create REITs to operate their real estate, as they would dilute their control over these operating assets.

In a similar manner, public real estate companies do not have to be REITs. For example, publicly traded developers are generally not REITs, as the tradeoff between tax benefits and operating restrictions does not favor REIT status. Never forget that REIT status is about taxes, while the decision to be public is about access to capital.

PUBLIC VERSUS PRIVATE AND LARGE VERSUS SMALL

The decision to go public depends on the desire to access large pools of anonymous capital to fuel growth, versus the willingness to adhere to the rules imposed on public companies. What are these rules? They are many, including: reporting executive salaries; providing detailed audited financials; disclosing material information such as planned financings, developments, and major tenant lease expirations; describing material mistakes made in the course of business; and paying lawyers and accountants to create documents for the SEC. Not only is this expensive, time consuming, and potentially embarrassing, but it also provides information that your competitors can use against you. In addition, you must disclose everything of material importance (good and bad) that the company does, and everyone does stupid things sooner or later! As a private company you do not have to do any of these things. As a private company, you may write a report for your investors, but the exercise is much cheaper, shorter, less painful, and private.

IPOs are expensive. The investment banks you hire will take 6-7% of the gross proceeds of the IPO. In addition, you pay lawyers, accountants, and other related fees. In total, an IPO can easily cost 10% of the gross proceeds raised. Thus, if you could sell 50% of your company's equity, 5% of the value of the firm's equity disappears during the IPO process. This value loss means that you had better have very productive uses for the money you raise. In addition, it costs perhaps $1 million annually in documentation and filing costs to be public. If your firm has a 10x value multiple, that $1 million annual outlay represents a further $10 million in equity value eaten up by lawyers and accountants.

If your business strategy requires substantial amounts of equity, access to the vast pool of equity capital available via public markets can outweigh the many costs of being public. For example, if your business needs $8 billion in equity to execute its business plan, being public is a viable answer, as it is very difficult to find a small group of private investors that can provide $8 billion. The beauty of the public equity market is that it efficiently pools the resources of millions of relatively small investors to achieve your otherwise unattainable $8 billion equity goal. The irony is that a group of ten very rich investors may not be able to provide the $8 billion you need for your business plan, but 100,000 not so rich investors can. In contrast, if you only need $800,000 in equity to execute your strategy, you would never incur the costs associated with being public.

Some companies incur the costs of being public without realizing the benefits of being public. This is because investors in public markets tend to avoid small companies with illiquid shares. Thus, if you are public but not large enough to effectively access large pools of public money, you bear the costs, yet receive few of the benefits of being public.

From time to time, a very dumb debate rages about whether a large real estate company is better than a small one. I supposedly began this debate in 1997 when I wrote an article entitled *Forces Changing the Real Estate Industry Forever*, which is discussed in Chapter 22. This article argued that there were economies of scale in real estate, particularly in terms of capital costs, to be exploited. My point was that economies of scale would drive consolidation until sufficient scale was achieved. I argued that visionary managers would procure financing for their projects based upon the ability to generate economic value via operating efficiency, and that the "weeding out" of small and inefficient companies would occur as they are taken over by more efficient firms. It is important to recall that this was written when the typical public real estate company had an equity market capitalization of just a few hundred million dollars. Over the next decade, I was proven correct that a company with a market capitalization of a few hundred million dollars was not big enough to justify being public.

Modest cost savings in real estate, as with every industry, can provide significant competitive cost advantages over the long term. It is cheaper for one firm to raise $2 billion than for twenty small competitors to raise $100 million due to redundant fees, time, and expenses. These cost advantages provide larger public firms that own "commodity" real estate properties with a competitive advantage that is particularly valuable in weak property markets because they may not have otherwise been able to attract sufficient capital to execute their business plans.

An essential feature of being an efficient real estate company is flexibility. As leverage increases, so do loan covenants which decrease operational flexibility. Thus, to achieve the benefits of being a public real estate company over the long term, it pays to keep debt levels low. This is particularly true for REITs, as they realize no tax shield from interest deductions. The real estate collapse of 2008-2010 demonstrated this simple truth, as low-leveraged REITs survived, while the absence of new debt killed many highly leveraged private firms.

As firms get larger, they are increasingly able to purchase services and supplies more cheaply. Purchasing supplies such as paint, fixtures, janitorial services, landscaping, security, and power in mass quantities reduces operating costs on a unit basis. Overhead may also be more efficiently amortized, increasing the value of the firm. In addition, as firms become larger, they may be better able to relocate tenants to another property in their portfolio, reducing the risk of losing a prized tenant to a competitor. Further, by having a large portfolio of real estate assets, firms attain greater tenant and geographic diversity, generating more predictable cash streams. Against these advantages is the phenomenon that larger firms are generally less entrepreneurial and far more bureaucratic. Smaller competitors often exhibit greater flexibility, which offsets the potentially superior purchasing power, systems, and capital market access of larger firms.

For a large public company, the cost advantages of greater liquidity and better access to capital do not have to be huge to be meaningful. A 1% cost reduction at a 10x multiple on a $100 million in revenue translates to $10 million in value added. But remember that size provides an opportunity for, not a guarantee of, success. Do the economies of scale for real estate companies dissipate at some threshold? Probably, but surely not until a firm's market capitalization reaches several billion dollars. Is a $100 million REIT large enough to achieve economies of scale? Surely no. How about a $10 billion REIT? Surely yes.

The argument over whether to be a large or small public company is much like asking whether a big body is better than a small body. It depends on what you want to do. If you want to be a ballerina, you are better served by a smaller, supple body; if your goal in life is to be a sumo wrestler, you will require a much larger body. Similarly, if your business strategy is to be the best owner of three garden apartments in the western Cincinnati suburbs, becoming a big public company will probably detract substantial value. On the other hand, if your business plan is to efficiently operate 70 regional malls scattered across the U.S., then being a large public firm is beneficial. It all comes down to your business strategy and your ability to execute that strategy.

The existence of publicly traded real estate helps curtail oversupply. Why? Since publicly traded companies make numerous disclosures, market transparency is improved. These disclosures provide better information, which helps keep supply in check. But there will always be periods of excess supply, as public disclosures do not stop stupidity; they just document it. In the long run, public disclosures and the associated research will lessen excess supply risk because foolish development projects will tend to be punished upon announcement rather than upon completion. As one sees competitors being punished for announcing foolish projects, other management teams are less likely to make similar mistakes.

TAXABLE REIT SUBSIDIARY

Suppose a REIT is in the business of owning and operating top quality apartment buildings, and management desires to provide a service to tenants where pets will be walked, groomed, and fed. The REIT intends to charge tenants a fee for this service, but a qualified REIT can only offer "the customary and typical services" of a real estate company. If competitors do not offer this service, the IRS may rule that it is not "customary and typical." If strict interpretation of the "customary and typical services" rule is applied, a REIT can never be a service leader.

To remedy this disadvantage, REITs can offer ancillary services as long as they do not become the company's primary business, and as long as the REIT carves out the income from such services into a taxable subsidiary. Simply stated, "non-real estate" income cannot be sheltered from taxes by REIT status.

The IRS requires that relationships between the REIT and the subsidiary reflect "market" terms. Is there room for manipulation? Of course. For example, a REIT can offer dry cleaning drop-off and pick-up services to tenants via its taxable REIT subsidiary. The REIT can charge this subsidiary rent that (just coincidentally) equals the profit of the subsidiary for usage of a very tiny amount of storage space. Therefore, the REIT will attempt to push the subsidiary's rent as high as possible until the IRS says, "no way."

UPREIT STRUCTURE

There is a widely used REIT structure known as an **UPREIT**. For most practical purposes there is no meaningful operational difference between a REIT and an UPREIT. An UPREIT is simply designed to allow a REIT to acquire buildings from partnerships without triggering capital gains taxes for the sellers. Recall that if a partnership property is acquired by exchanging buyer shares for the seller's partnership units, the transaction is a taxable event, as it is not viewed by the IRS as a "like-kind" exchange. To avoid creating a capital gains tax liability on such a transaction, the UPREIT structure essentially creates a tax-sheltered master "umbrella" partnership between the selling partnership and the purchasing REIT. The REIT owns the master partnership, which in turn owns all of the seller's property interests or partnerships, which are exchanged with the seller for ownership units in the master partnership. While the legal nuances are many, when the acquisition is structured in this way, it is viewed by the IRS as a like-kind exchange.

The only reason REITs use the UPREIT structure is to avoid capital gains tax for sellers of partnership properties that desire REIT equity ownership instead of cash proceeds. In the early 1990s, the question existed as to whether the IRS would view this structure as acceptable. However, once the IRS blessed this structure it quickly became the industry norm. Typically, an ownership unit in the REIT's master partnership is convertible into a REIT share. Thus, if your ownership of the master partnership units represents 1% of the fully diluted shares of the REIT, you receive 1% of the REIT's dividends, votes, and upon conversion, 1% of the REIT's shares. As such, the master partnership is generally a pass-through vehicle. While variations of this structure exist, they are mostly legal in nature and have little impact on either the strategy, operation, or basic governance of the REIT. Figure 21.6 is a diagram of the UPREIT structure.

FIGURE 21.6

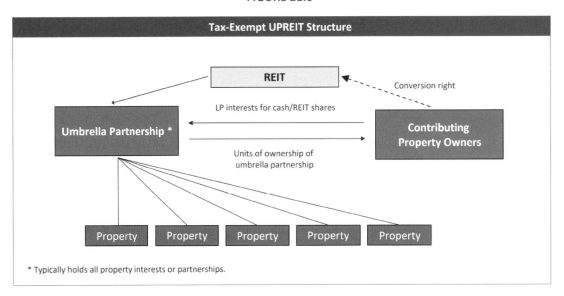

RETURN ON CAPITAL VERSUS RETURN OF CAPITAL

There are two commonly used investment concepts that merit attention: "return of capital," and "return on capital." Return of capital focuses on when, and with what certainty, investors receive their invested capital back. Return on capital focuses on the return investors earn while their invested capital remains at risk. Of course, since money is fungible, the money received by an investor is not economically earmarked as one or the other (except for tax and accounting purposes) – each dollar is just money received. But investors typically think about how long it takes to "get their money back," how they "get their money back," and "how much they earn on their money."

Public real estate companies primarily focus on the "return on capital." This is because the individual investor substantially controls the timing of their return of capital through the decision to sell their shares. In contrast, private operators, developers, and private equity funds generally place more focus on the return of investor capital, as investors in such non-traded investments generally do not control the exit decision. All real estate operators attempt to maximize risk-adjusted returns, but public companies place a relatively greater focus on generating ongoing cash streams, while private operators must also consider when and how to exit ownership of the property.

CLOSING THOUGHT

Investor returns for REIT shareholders primarily come from dividend payments, with moderate long-term share price appreciation. REITs are designed to deliver tax-efficient, relatively reliable dividends. The typical dividend yield is about 5-9%. While the explosive growth of the 1990s is unlikely to be replicated, public REITs will continue to evolve and grow in importance. Today, real estate is now not only liquid but also de facto traded every time an S&P contract is traded. But being a REIT or publicly traded real estate firm is not a magic elixir. If you are a poorly performing private real estate partnership, you will almost certainly be a poorly performing public REIT. Changing your tax status or ownership structure is never a cure for weak operational skills.

 Online Companion Audio Interview: To hear a conversation about this chapter's content, go to the Online Companion and select the link for Chapter 21. Scroll down to the Audio Interview section and listen.

Chapter 22
The Forces Changing the Real Estate Industry Forever

"Those who know how and when to adapt have the best chance of thriving."
- Dr. Peter Linneman

In 1997, I published a widely cited article in the *Wharton Real Estate Review* that stated that the commercial real estate industry was then undergoing a critical industrial transformation that would last another 20-25 years. This turned out to be the case.

Prior to 1986, the U.S. commercial real estate business was fueled by financial gimmicks such as unsustainable tax write-offs, mispriced debt, overleveraged properties, and inside deals with friendly local bankers. These features created highly fragmented ownership. As recently as 1990, 95-110% LTVs were the norm. This excessive debt financing was even available for speculative development projects, allowing real estate entrepreneurs to achieve wealth through acquisition and development, regardless of whether they created economic value.

Economic catalysts for the structural change in the U.S. real estate business started around 1990, primary of which were the withdrawal, en masse, of lenders (and the industry's subsequent collapse); regulatory changes in the banking and insurance industries; and the emergence of mutual funds as a preferred investment vehicle.

REAL ESTATE IS A CAPITAL-INTENSIVE BUSINESS

Commercial real estate development and acquisitions typically involve tens of millions of dollars, meaning that real estate is a highly capital-intensive business. Every capital-intensive industry has experienced a critical transition period typically lasting 20-30 years, triggered by factors such as the emergence of a visionary leader (e.g., petroleum and the automobile), wars (e.g., aerospace), capital requirements to meet rapid growth (e.g., steel and railroads), regulatory changes (e.g., utilities, banks, and rail), and excess capacity (e.g., tires). These transitions were rarely as quick or smooth as suggested in high school history books. The transition of these capital-intensive industries was driven by the search for cheaper capital and resulted in stronger and more rational industries. Operators who understood these forces created great wealth for their investors. The natural results in each industry's evolution were greater transparency, consolidation, and much lower leverage. The same has been the case for real estate over the last 25 years.

THE "FORCES" WHICH CHANGED REAL ESTATE

There have been three main forces changing the structure of the real estate industry over the last 25 years.

Force #1: Shifting of Control of Capital

The first among the "forces" is the control of capital dramatically shifting from debt provided by local commercial banks and life insurance companies, to equity provided by pension funds and mutual funds. In 1970, the combined asset base of commercial banks and life insurance companies accounted for 53% of all U.S. assets, while the combined asset base controlled by pension funds and mutual funds was a mere 14%. By 1997, assets held by commercial banks and insurance companies had fallen to 35% but jumped to a staggering 44% at pension funds and mutual funds. And this trend continues. This dramatic shift in the control of the nation's assets and capital had a significant impact on the real estate industry, given its ongoing need to access large amounts of capital. Of particular significance is the fact that pension funds and mutual funds invest primarily in highly liquid, mark-to-market assets, while commercial banks and life insurance companies historically use non-mark-to-market debt instruments. The shift of capital control from institutions that utilized non-mark-to-market debt vehicles to those that invest via publicly traded equities, corporate debt, and alternative private equity funds was a powerful "force" that required real estate companies to evolve in order to access the necessary capital. The primary instruments in this regard are publicly traded real estate companies, commercial mortgage-backed securities (CMBS), unsecured commercial real estate company debt, and real estate private equity funds.

Force #2: Consolidation of Capital

A second "force" changing the real estate business is the consolidation that has occurred in the U.S. financial sector. The number of FDIC-insured commercial banks in the U.S. dropped to less than 4,400 in 2020, compared to the 9,600 in 1996 and over 13,500 in 1970. In addition, the largest 100 banks controlled 49.7% of all U.S. commercial real estate assets in 1970; this figure jumped to 61.7% in 1996, and by year-end 2014, the largest 5 banks alone controlled approximately 44% of all U.S. commercial real estate assets, just shy of the amount held by the top 100 banks less than 40 years earlier.

As seen in Figure 22.1, the consolidated banks now hold 61% of existing commercial mortgages, versus 57% in 1997 and 49% in 1970. In contrast, insurance companies held 30% of outstanding commercial mortgage debt in 1970, declining to 19% in 1997 and a mere 14% in 2021. Asset-backed securities (ABS), finance companies, and mortgage REITS now account for 20% of commercial mortgages, versus just 3% in 1970.

FIGURE 22.1

Holders of Commercial Mortgage Assets - Percent Share				
($ Billions - Nominal)	1970	1997	2016	3Q 2021
Total Commercial Mortgages	$86,503	$826,355	$2,570,917	$3,194,500
Banks	49.4%	57.4%	59.6%	61.2%
Insurance Companies	30.4%	19.5%	13.9%	14.4%
Pension & Retirement Funds	2.4%	1.3%	0.8%	0.6%
ABS Issues and Finance Cos.	0.6%	11.8%	13.7%	13.0%
Mortgage REITs	2.3%	0.8%	6.7%	6.7%
Other	14.9%	9.2%	5.3%	4.1%
	100%	100%	100%	100%

Source: Federal Reserve Board, Linneman Associates

The impact of the financial sector's consolidation and the rise of equity mutual funds on the real estate industry cannot be overstated. It meant far fewer "friendly local bankers" with the mission of supporting local owners and developers. Local real estate operators no longer had an inside track to the capital they needed simply by virtue of belonging to the right local country club, church, or charity board. Increasingly, national, and even international financial bases are essential as capital markets have consolidated and globalized. This force encouraged larger, more transparent companies with strong balance sheets.

Force #3: Prevailing of Basic Economics

The final "force" that radically changed the real estate industry was that "business basics" ultimately prevailed. Specifically, acquisitions and speculative developments no longer command 95-110% non-recourse debt levels priced at single-A bond spreads. This means that real estate ownership requires substantial equity, particularly for development, causing firms to focus on core competencies. Operators with vision, access to rationally priced capital, the lowest operating costs, and good risk management ultimately prospered, eliminating many of the weakest competitors.

This was a harsh message to an industry raised on excessive debt and speculative development. To survive and prosper required substantial equity, a comparative expertise, and greater operational efficiency. Gone was the era when 100% LTVs allowed developers to develop and own an array of property types with little if any equity. In a world that required at least 25% equity, real estate participants would have to decide where to allocate their scarce equity and concentrate on accessing large capital pools.

In 1997, my message was that not all industry participants were going to survive, much less prosper, and that many players needed to figure out how and when to exit. And there are only two ways to exit: when you want to or when you have to, with the former option being clearly more profitable. My message was that the winners would embrace these changes, while the losers would yearn for a world that would never return.

THE KEYS TO SUCCESSFUL LONG-TERM REAL ESTATE OWNERSHIP

The mantra of the real estate industry has long been that the key to successful real estate ownership is "location, location, location." However, past collapses of real estate values vividly demonstrate that location does not guarantee successful ownership. As seen in the 1995 Rockefeller Center bankruptcy, a great location does not guarantee an owner's success (though a bad location generally ensures failure).

If not location, then what? The simple answer is that the same elements which determine success in other capital-intensive industries (such as petroleum, automobiles, steel, tires, rail, and aerospace) determine success in real estate. Broadly speaking, successful ownership in capital-intensive industries is driven by:

- Visionary leadership and the ability to sell that vision;
- Low long-term capital costs relative to competitors;
- Low overhead relative to competitors;
- Enhanced revenue opportunities relative to competitors;
- Successful risk management;
- Operating efficiency.

The most successful operating companies in capital-intensive industries are those that can bring to bear these six elements on behalf of their investors. Firms that do not do so dissipate their investors' wealth over the long term and exit the industry (either voluntarily or involuntarily).

Managerial Vision and Ability to Sell It

As is the case with other capital-intensive industries, the real estate industry has a limited number of visionary leaders, who also possess the ability to sell their vision to their employees and the capital markets. The industry's assets become concentrated in the hands of this select group as it evolves. As was the case in other capital-intensive industries in the early years of their transformations, in the early 1990s, the real estate industry had far too many mediocre operators controlling too many assets.

The consolidation of capital-intensive industries has historically been particularly rapid during periods of industry distress because that is when only the strongest can effectively access the capital needed to survive and grow. In normal times, the consolidation process continues, though at a slower rate, as some weak operators see the handwriting on the wall and sell their assets while they still have value. As a result, they receive prices greater than their assets are worth to them but less than they are worth under the control of the strongest industry operators. As the industry recovers, the "forced" consolidation process slows — until the next period of industry distress. One of the reasons why industry evolutions take so long is that several periods of distress are required to fully shake out the weakest operators.

In capital-intensive industries, the importance of "great ideas" relative to the "capital required to execute these ideas" is low. Thus, to generate the greatest value from the limited capital allocated to the industry, it is essential to generate the biggest bang per "great idea." When capital was irrationally allocated to the real estate industry, it was possible for many mediocre operators to survive and prosper. However, real estate has joined the ranks of other industries where capital is more or less efficiently rationed. Once capital demands a return, only those most skilled at predictably generating returns ultimately survive! Portfolios of assets lacking leadership and the ability to obtain visionary-driven growth tend to trade at discounts. The most obvious examples of this phenomenon are closed-end mutual funds, which generally trade at 20-30% discounts to their liquidation values. This is because value derives from the visionary enhancement of assets, rather than the mere holding of assets. Those operators with the ability to add the greatest value to their assets — as Warren Buffett has done at Berkshire Hathaway — ultimately outbid mere asset collectors for managerial talent, tenants, and additional properties.

The value of managerial vision (and the ability to sell this vision) in the real estate industry increases as consolidation occurs; cash flow payout ratios to owners decrease; more equity is used; and binding debt, operating, and financing covenants decline. Why? If a property company borrows heavily and pays out its entire cash flow, it has little borrowing capacity, and therefore is restricted in its operations by debt covenants. This means that when management identifies value-enhancing opportunities (which generally require the deployment of significant amounts of capital), they cannot be executed without time-consuming and expensive capital market activities. Since capital market "windows of opportunity" do not generally coincide with operating and investment "windows of opportunity," many value-enhancing opportunities slip away for the lack of capital. As a result, firms constrained in their ability to exploit opportunities without going back to the capital markets will struggle, while those with ready access to capital will prosper.

As retained earnings grow and cash flow payout ratios decline, corporate balance sheets are strengthened. In turn, borrowing capacity rises and restrictive operating covenants decline through the use of unsecured debt with easily satisfied covenants. The value attached to the operator's ability to identify operating and investment opportunities also greatly increases. Similarly, real estate private equity funds that are able to assemble large pools of capital can act quickly to take advantage of investment opportunities. As a result, these operators have a reduced cost of capital (from both time and rate savings), increasing the competitive pressures on mediocre operators.

The size of the company is also important. Today a large real estate company has more than $3 billion in assets, an unused line of credit of $50 million, and an 80% cash flow payout ratio. Such a firm, if public, has annual retained earnings of roughly $32 million a year and nearly $100 million readily available to pursue investment opportunities, eliminating the need to access the capital markets. This represents only about: 500 multifamily units, a couple modest sized office properties, or several decent strip centers. This underscores the advantage of large public real estate firms and private equity funds. The lack of an effective opportunistic margin for value-added management is stark among: smaller firms; operators with higher cash flow payout ratios; and operators with less borrowing capacity.

Envision a real estate operator with $20 billion in assets (comprised of 70% equity), a cash flow payout ratio of only 65% on its 9% equity return, a $350 million unused line of credit, and $700-$800 million for opportunistic deployment each year. With this capital margin, management's ability to find opportunities and the capital required to execute are more in balance. An effectively managed company with this profile will have value notably in excess of the value of its assets.

Low Capital Costs Relative to Competitors

As owning real estate is extremely capital-intensive and given the low ratio of significance of "ideas" to "capital," a better mantra for success in the industry might be "cheap capital, cheap capital, cheap capital." As proof of this proposition, consider that during the 1980s, when unlimited debt capital was essentially given free to real estate operators, the most successful operators were those who accessed the greatest amount of this mispriced capital. Of course, the problem was that many of them did not exit before the debt became rationally priced! That is, once capital was not free, they were not able to successfully operate — even if they had great locations.

There are three components of the cost of capital:

- the cost of debt;
- the cost of equity;
- the cost associated with raising capital.

The cost of debt is the most easily understood of these costs. Companies with the best histories of financial performance and the healthiest balance sheets are rewarded with lower debt costs. Firms that are able to achieve investment grade ratings for their debt, without sacrificing the risk profile of their assets, are able to realize capital cost savings associated with the greater depth and liquidity of the investment grade debt market.

An additional, often forgotten, cost of debt is the loss of operating cash flows associated with the reduced operational flexibility of restrictive debt covenants and security pledges. This hidden cost can be large, particularly in opportunistic periods. Conservatively underwritten investment grade unsecured debt imposes the least binding operating covenants, and hence the lowest hidden capital cost from debt restrictions. This is a powerful force which drives firms to use unsecured debt and provides a substantial capital cost advantage, which is not always appreciated.

A firm qualifying for a BBB+ rating for its unsecured debt has a lower interest rate and fewer operating restrictions worth perhaps 100 basis points (bps) over its strongest unrated competitors. For a company with $3 billion in assets, of which 30% is debt, a 100-bp debt cost advantage represents $9 million a year. At a 20x equity valuation multiple, the ability to use such debt increases equity value by $180 million (6% of $3 billion). Even greater value increases are obtained as the debt rating rises above BBB+.

There are two components of the cost of equity: the annual dividend and the expected annual appreciation. The pricing of equity capital reflects the pricing of risk. Factors that lower risk lower the cost of equity capital. When all firms are privately owned and provide little in the way of standardized or detailed disclosures, no firm is at a competitive capital cost disadvantage due to the lack of transparency. However, once major competitors become transparent, providing detailed (often public), standardized, and regular disclosures, equity pricing becomes more efficient. This is why no industry has ever reverted to private ownership once a major portion of the industry has gone public. In fact, the presence of major publicly owned competitors has always sped up the evolution of more firms in the sector going public, so that they can maintain a competitive cost of equity.

The advantage of being a transparent firm grows over time, as the history of verifiable sustained financial and operational performance grows. The longer firms are transparent, the greater the operator's understanding of the need to consistently disclose information and effectively communicate with providers of equity capital about the risks associated with their equity.

An advantage of public real estate firms, in terms of the cost of equity capital, is enhanced liquidity. Increasing liquidity is one way in which equity owners reduce their risks. The value of liquidity is greatest for the largest and most heavily traded companies. The industry's consolidation partially reflects operators striving for larger equity bases through increased liquidity, in order to lower their capital costs.

Returning to the example of a $3 billion-asset firm comprised of 70% equity, if the equity capital cost advantages associated with disclosure and liquidity for a public firm versus a private competitor are only 100 bps, this amounts to a $21 million equity cost savings (1% of $2.1 billion). Again, at a 20x equity value multiple, this represents an equity value gain of $420 million (14%) equity value enhancement.

The third component of capital costs is the cost associated with raising capital. Given the fixed cost dimension of many of these costs, clear economics of scale exist in raising capital. Ten $1 billion companies, each requiring $100 million in growth capital (debt and equity combined) per year will have a blended cost of raising funds on the order of $50 million. If instead, two $5 billion firms each raise $500 million, they will have a blended cost of perhaps $40 million. If a $10 billion firm raised $1 billion it will have a blended cost of only $25 million.

At a 20x equity multiple, $25 million in capital costs savings create $500 million in equity value for a $10 billion operator, relative to the aggregate value of its ten $1 billion competitors. This amounts to a 5% equity value enhancement. These economies of scale of raising capital are a powerful driver of consolidation in capital-intensive industries. In most capital-intensive industries, dividends as a percent of cash flow are on the order of 35%. Since REITs must legally pay out 90% of their taxable income, as a practical matter, they must pay out a minimum of about 55% of their cash flow (90% * 65%). Thus, in the absence of significant operating diseconomies of scale, real estate operators using the tax-advantaged REIT structure need to grow much larger than firms in other capital-intensive industries in order to increase their access to retained earnings. Maintaining high cash flow payout ratios and remaining a fragmented industry needlessly enriches capital-raising intermediaries at the expense of capital owners. This is particularly true given the fact that the best operators need to grow in order to maintain their depreciation base.

Most observers of the real estate industry fail to appreciate that capital costs (for both debt and equity) account for roughly 85% of the total costs of a real estate company. Consider the long-term competitive outcome between two Class A garden apartment competitors. Assume that for the reasons previously described, the first has lower debt and equity costs, by 100 bps each. If the second firm's weighted-average capital costs are 11%, this 100-bp lower cost is a 9% cost advantage on 85% of all costs. Given the commodity nature of Class A garden apartments, this 7.7% total cost advantage of the lower capital cost firm represents a formidable long-term competitive advantage.

The advantage of having the lowest capital costs in a capital-intensive industry tends to be self-reinforcing. This is because low capital cost firms can use this cost advantage to reduce rents in order to obtain and retain tenants, make more capital expenditures on a timely basis to maintain the competitive position of their properties, purchase properties at higher prices, outbid their competitors for the best managerial talent, and engage in more advertising. Because of their lower capital costs, they can do all these things and still financially outperform their higher cost competitors! The operating advantages derived from lower capital costs are particularly valuable in times of industry distress, underscoring why industry consolidation is greatest during down cycles. Notable recent examples of this phenomenon were seen in the tire industry in the 1980s, the banking industry in the early 1990s, and of course, the real estate industry in the early 1990s and again since the Financial Crisis.

As the real estate industry continues to evolve, firms with the lowest capital costs competitively dominate, leaving high cost of capital operators the same three choices faced by high capital cost firms in other capital-intensive industries:

- to live with needlessly low valuations for their assets and face eventual competitive ruin;
- to sell their properties to lower cost operators before their properties erode competitively;
- to move into sectors where their higher capital costs do not impair their competitiveness because the major players do not operate in these assets.

The strategy of shifting to specialty niches is perhaps best exemplified by the evolution of the (also very capital-intensive) steel industry, which turned to public capital markets and experienced rapid consolidation relatively early in its history. As it consolidated, the production of commodity steel products became completely dominated by the largest, lowest cost of capital firms. Any high capital cost firm which attempted to compete in commodity product lines was eliminated. However, many smaller firms with relatively high capital costs survived and prospered by moving out of commodity steel products and into specialty steel products and fabrication. A similar challenge faces many of today's operators of the best apartments, offices, hotels, warehouses, and retail centers. They can survive by selling their commodity assets to lower capital cost operators and redeploying their operating skills where they are not in direct competition with the low capital cost operators.

Many real estate owners wait too long before selling their assets to operators with lower capital costs. They will convince themselves that they are doing "just fine" while markets are strong, only to be forced to sell at "fire sale" prices when their operating margins are squeezed and capital is unavailable during down markets. These high cost operators are better served to sell sooner in order to realize the highest value from their assets, and refocus on properties not targeted by the low capital cost firms.

Firms with intermediate capital costs face a difficult strategic problem. Initially these firms prosper competitively by beating out competitors with higher capital costs. The fact that their competitors with lower capital costs are doing even better seems of little consequence, as they are doing "just fine." However, as the industry's competitive process evolves, ever more high capital cost competitors are eliminated. As this occurs, intermediate capital cost firms slowly become the highest capital cost operators left in the business, and eventually it is their turn to be eliminated by competitive pressures! Industrial history is full of examples of firms which hung on too long while they were moderately successful, only to be forced out during the first downturn, when they became the highest capital cost firms left in the business. These firms would have served their owners much better had they merged with (or sold) their operations to the lowest capital cost firms during a strong market and before they became the high capital cost firms.

It should be noted that combining real estate operations with real estate development can potentially impose a capital cost disadvantage. This is because development is a 150-300-bp riskier business than the operation of developed properties. Capital markets tend to price all marginal flows of capital into businesses that develop at higher rates due to the fungibility of money (i.e., a dollar is a dollar). That is, even though the firm may say the money will not be used for development, the fungibility of funds means the firm can effectively use the capital for development. This capital cost "penalty" associated with combining development and ongoing operations means that these activities should only be combined where the business competency advantage is sufficiently large to offset this capital cost disadvantage. This will not generally be the case in markets for commodity products.

In sum, the cost of capital is lower for larger, more liquid firms with established disclosure and financial performance records (i.e., capital market "brands"). Given the high proportion of total costs accounted for by capital costs, the need to reduce capital costs has been a major driver of the consolidation of the real estate industry over the past 25 years.

Lower Operating Costs Relative to Competitors

Given the fact that capital costs represent, by far, the largest component of costs, competitive advantages associated with operating costs tend to be of secondary importance. However, in a commodity business, every operating cost savings is competitively valuable. Consolidation may allow for purchasing advantages in terms of supplies (paint, carpet, etc.), legal services, accounting services, insurance, systems, personnel training, employee benefits, and advertising. Obtaining a 10% reduction in these operating costs through effective consolidation provides a competitive advantage of approximately 1.5% of total costs. For a company with an operating cost of $30 million and a 20x equity valuation multiple, a 10% operating cost savings creates $60 million in equity value ($3 MM * 20), or an almost 6% equity value enhancement for a $1 billion asset operator.

Lower Overhead Costs Than Competitors

Overhead reductions are a driver behind the consolidation in every industry. Overhead savings from consolidation are direct and substantial. One CEO, one CFO, one head of marketing, one head of acquisitions, one director of investor relations, one human resource department, one audited statement, one investor report, etc. All told, these cost savings easily total $5-$20 million annually. At a 20x multiple, this represents the creation of equity value of $100-$400 million through overhead reduction. Value gains of this magnitude are the equivalent to 1-2 years'-worth of solid cash flow growth. The gains from overhead reduction should not be dismissed lightly, particularly by high and intermediate capital cost firms, and those firms lacking visionary leaders. These firms are well-advised to stabilize and then sell to more efficient operators during strong market periods in order to capture a portion of the value created via the combined entity's overhead cost savings.

Enhanced Revenues Relative to Competitors

Another force driving the consolidation is potential revenue enhancement associated with consolidation. Revenue enhancements have long existed in the regional mall business and are increasingly being realized in the strip and community center sectors, as larger real estate operators provide a national relationship base. As global tenants become more prevalent, larger real estate owners with national relationships and reputations will be able to increasingly exploit revenue enhancement opportunities in the office and industrial sectors. The multifamily industry has not been able to successfully develop brand loyalty similar to that found in the auto, tire, or hotel industries.

An important revenue-related competitive advantage of larger firms is slowly evolving in the office market. As corporate tenants move to ever shorter leases in the search for greater operating flexibility, larger portfolios of office space are required to efficiently diversify the risk of higher tenant turnover. Single-property operators will find it difficult to hedge such leasing risks, and thus will need to charge relatively high premiums for short leases. In addition, as tenants move to shorter leases, lenders will correctly tend to reduce their loan levels on secured properties. This will require single-property office operators to use more equity to finance such properties.

In contrast, the operator of a large portfolio of office properties can approach the risk of shorter leases on a "statistical" basis, charging relatively low premiums for short-term leases — hence making his properties more attractive to corporate tenants. Also, larger operators can float unsecured debt, thereby partially offsetting the need for increased equity.

Successful Risk Management

Another source of competitive advantage is relatively efficient risk management. In the real estate industry, this means that as regional and national (and ultimately international) portfolios are assembled in areas of core competency, the cost of capital will decline. Note that the advantage of asset diversification is limited by the extent of operational competency. However, the ownership of larger portfolios in areas of core competency reduces risk by spreading tenant risk, improving informational flows, and perhaps by bestowing some degree of pricing discipline. Further, asset diversification across markets of operating competence also buffers the firm's cost of capital against movements caused by short-term imbalances in local markets.

It is important to note that consolidation into larger public firms will not make the industry immune from periods of excess, as periods of excess capacity still exist periodically in the auto, tire, aerospace, and steel industries. However, the consolidation of these industries has lessened the degree of excess capacity creation by reducing the number of independent decision makers. With fewer, larger decision makers, each firm is more acutely aware of its impact on market capacity. Also, the superior information flows associated with greater transparency make it more readily apparent to capital sources that excesses are occurring, allowing capital markets to reprice risk. This raises the cost of capital for firms in the sector, making further capacity expansion less financially attractive. Again, this disciplinary process tends to occur more rapidly in industries dominated by larger firms than in industries with fragmented private ownership.

Operating Efficiency

Real estate operators, like comparable firms in other capital-intensive industries, are operating (rather than trading) businesses. As such, they need to reduce the "market timing" mentality which characterizes many real estate operators. A more realistic goal is to be a very good operator in both good times and bad. If investors desire to trade during different parts of the operator's or industry's cycle, this is best achieved by creating liquidity for the ownership claims which accommodate trading without disrupting the operating effectiveness of the entity. It is impossible to build a great long-term operating company with a trader's mindset. This was a major flaw of the real estate pension fund advisory business in the 1980s.

PROOF OF THE "FORCES" AT WORK

Growth in Company Size, Liquidity, and Prominence

As consolidation has occurred, the size of real estate companies has increased drastically. At the end of 1996, the largest publicly traded real estate company was Simon Property Group, with a total equity market capitalization of $3.1 billion and a firm value of $5.4 billion. As of year-end 2021, the largest publicly traded real estate company was American Tower Corporation, which had a total market capitalization of $118 billion, while the value of Blackstone's global real estate portfolio was nearly $450 billion.

The total equity market capitalization for public REITs now stands at around $1.49 trillion at year-end 2021, with enterprise value approaching $2.5 trillion today, versus $150 billion two decades earlier.

Real estate private equity funds and publicly traded real estate companies have equitized the industry. In 1996, only 21 publicly traded real estate companies had a market capitalization over $1 billion. By year-end 2017, the largest 25 REITs all possessed market capitalizations in excess of $10 billion. Similarly, in 2001, only 3 real estate companies were part of the S&P 500. By year-end 2021, this number stood at 31, in addition to large private equity managers Blackstone, Starwood, Lone Star, Colony Capital, and other mega-private equity shops. In 1997, private equity funds controlled perhaps $10 billion of real estate versus more than $2 trillion today. Real estate private equity funds are easily the largest owners of privately held real estate in the U.S.

The increasing prominence of public company-owned real estate, which we foresaw, is demonstrated by the monthly trading volume of the NAREIT composite index. In 2001, the index was approximately $15 billion; by year-end 2021, it had risen to nearly $200 billion. It is interesting to note that this increase in value is primarily attributable to the extraordinary increase in the number of assets owned by U.S. publicly traded companies. Since 1996 the percentage of warehouse space owned by publicly traded companies has risen from approximately 3% to almost 10%. Public ownership of office space has risen from 1.8% to approximately 7.6%, public ownership of apartments from 4.6% to 8%, and public ownership of strip retail from approximately 8.3% to 13.5%. The percentage of publicly owned hotels has grown from approximately 8.3% to almost 20%, and public ownership of malls has grown from approximately 22% to nearly 35%. Most of these public holdings are of higher quality properties in the major U.S. markets, and two giant mutual fund companies (Vanguard and BlackRock), alone, account for 10-20% of the equity of all public real estate companies.

Further evidence of the role of public company-owned real estate is that the average trading volume of the NAREIT Composite index exceeds $15 billion each month. This compares to the $25-40 billion of private real estate transactions that occur annually. Also, while a handful of public real estate companies have gone private, these have been — as I hypothesized — exceptions to the rule. Taken together, these figures demonstrate a dramatic change in a remarkably short period of time.

No Reversion to Excessive Leverage

A fundamental premise of the thesis behind the 1997 article was that substantial levels of equity would be required for the ownership and development of real estate. This has proven true over the last 25 years and has driven the creation of large public and real estate private equity firms.

Today's most highly leveraged real estate owners would have been laughably under-leveraged 25 years ago. For example, the relatively highly leveraged ownership positions of real estate private equity funds utilize approximately 55-70% debt, while debt levels for publicly traded real estate companies hover between 15-40%. In contrast, a "conservatively" leveraged property in 1990 was 80% and, more typically, 90% to 110% leveraged. Debt coverage ratios have improved even more dramatically, including for the most aggressive borrowers.

This equity cushion proved its worth during the Financial Crisis. Even though vacancy rates fell to levels not seen since 1993, the fallout in the real estate industry was relatively limited. Delinquency rates on office mortgages were 0.4% in 2010 versus 8.5% in 1993.

It is important that long-lived real estate assets be matched with substantial amounts of the longest liability — equity — because when downturns occur, there is no way that owners can adjust their cost structures to maintain profitability. Harvesting the long-term value of properties requires substantial equity cushions to see one through the inevitable hard times.

Growth in Transparency

The maturation of the CMBS market and the use of unsecured corporate bonds linked the pricing of real estate risks to that of the broader debt markets. The amount of outstanding non-agency CMBS debt has risen from approximately $87.6 billion in 1997 to approximately $616.9 billion as of Q3 2021, with an additional $750 billion of government agency-issued CMBS. As predicted, this growth has meant that balance sheets similar in size to those in other capital-intensive industries now characterize the real estate industry.

Publicly traded real estate debt and equity have created an analyst community that scrutinizes the supply and demand fundamentals for the major property markets. This information flow has put a damper on the optimism of developers and development lenders. The continuous public market pricing of debt and equity has also raised awareness among capital providers of the cost of capital for new developments. In this regard, real estate is becoming more like other capital-intensive industries. It has served, albeit imperfectly, to keep excess supply conditions in check in most real estate markets better than during past cycles.

IS BIGGER BETTER?

Are larger firms necessarily more efficient? Of course not. However, many once-local real estate businesses have successfully been acquired by and woven into national platforms, and companies operate at scales previously thought impossible. The "forces" article stimulated academic research that has explored real estate scale economies. Though limited, this research reveals evidence of scale economies achievable at least up to firm sizes of several billion dollars.

Remember that for a firm with a 20x multiple, a 1% improvement represents $20 million in value per $100 million in revenue. In addition, those firms with unsecured debt instruments saw their spreads narrow where each 100 bps is worth $10 million per $100 million in debt. In short, at least at a number of major property companies, the scale economies I predicted appear to be at work.

After decades of debt-financed development, development now requires 25-50% equity. Combining development with stable real estate cash streams is a challenging financial structure. For example, a primary reason that many U.K. public property companies trade at large discounts to liquidation value is that while the English lease is an extremely low-risk asset, sought after by low-risk investors, most U.K. public property companies use these very low-risk cash flows to fund high-risk developments. Because of this mismatch, investors are unable to access their low-risk cash streams. Imagine the extreme case of a development company that utilized the proceeds from a government bond fund to fund speculative developments. Certainly, such a fund would trade at a substantial discount to its liquidation value, as its logical clientele — low-risk investors — would avoid it due to the development risk.

Another major challenge for public real estate companies with substantial development activities is the need to shut down the overhead burden of development when excess supply market conditions exist. All too often, these groups become self-perpetuating overhead burdens. Firms that fail to perform this shutdown will be severely punished by capital markets.

A major unanswered question is whether a development company can successfully exist as a stand-alone public company. While real estate development offers a higher risk profile than stabilized real estate, it does not provide a massive risk premium, because many people enjoy being developers. As a result, the margins earned on developments may not be large enough to attract large-scale capital into development. In addition, development tends to be very cyclical, resulting in limited revenue in down economies. For many years, this was the case in homebuilding. However, as debt has become less available, homebuilding has been increasingly dominated by the largest companies. Between 1993 and 2021, the market share of the top ten homebuilders grew by 3.26x from 9.2% to 30.0%.

CLOSING THOUGHT

Industry structure responds to economic fundamentals. Primary in this regard is the need for large amounts of equity. This has caused the real estate industry to become more public, more transparent, and more consolidated. In short, the industry morphed into a structure consistent with a concentrated lending community and equity providers that prefer public companies and private equity funds, rather than privately held firms. As this occurred, the professionalism of the industry massively increased. Hence, the proliferation of real estate courses and the need for young professionals to master a core set of business skills.

 Online Companion Audio Interview: To hear a conversation about this chapter's content, go to the Online Companion and select the link for Chapter 22. Scroll down to the Audio Interview section and listen.

Chapter 23
Corporate Real Estate Decision Making

"Why ever do less than the best you can?"
-Dr. Peter Linneman

By now you may have decided to pursue a career in retail, medicine, or law; anything but real estate. However, you will find that in each of these careers you will still have to deal with real estate issues. For example, if you are a lawyer and the lease on your office is expiring in a month, what do you do? Where should you locate your practice? How much space do you need? Should you buy, build, or lease this space? Thus, every business faces corporate real estate decisions, not just big corporations with specialized staffs.

WHAT TYPE OF SPACE DO I NEED?

One of the key issues that arises is determining what type of space you need. If you plan to service mostly family clients, such as a primary care physician, you will probably look for office space in a suburban location near a major medical center. But you might also consider space in a strip center near your home and convenient to your client base. If you work for a food distributor, you will probably look for a warehouse facility that also can be used as office space. This decision process is similar to what you went through when narrowing your list of potential colleges. You start with a list of locations and properties based on your general knowledge, gather data, and analyze the specifics to find the right fit for you. A broker with knowledge of the space available in the market may be helpful in this process.

Determining retail space needs is particularly tricky, as many retailers are re-evaluating the decision of whether to locate in a mall, a strip center, or an open-air town center. This decision has become increasingly difficult as competition and consumer preferences evolve.

WHERE SHOULD I LOCATE?

Another key decision is where to locate. The location decision depends upon the type of property you need. Assume you are in charge of real estate for Walmart, and you have to select a new warehouse. The first factor you must analyze is the customer base that the warehouse will service. Specifically, the warehouse will service current and future Walmart stores in the southeastern Pennsylvania market. You need to make judgments on the extent and timing of store expansions (and shrinkage) in this region. Your goal is to minimize the cost of transporting and storing the merchandise being sent from the warehouse to your stores. These costs include drive times, fuel consumption, labor costs, and rent.

To reduce costs, you might combine your warehouse and retail spaces. Is this prudent? There will be two dimensions of your analysis of this alternative. The first is the relative costs of renting more space at the retail location to house the products versus the reduced shipping costs of transporting goods. The second is the cost associated with directly transporting goods from the vendor locations to the warehouse facility versus directly to your retail locations. For example, smaller lot shipments may not qualify for significant quantity discounts that are available if the vendor ships to a centralized warehouse. Your job is to minimize the combined costs and headaches of transportation and storage space, while maintaining a quality retail environment and sufficient inventory.

You will generally select warehouse facilities close to major highway interchanges to facilitate transportation, both into and out of the warehouse. You will need to consider whether to utilize one large warehouse versus multiple smaller locations throughout the area. A single facility reduces the cost and effort dedicated to receiving and shipping goods but increases the distance to store locations. With a little consideration, you begin to see the detailed analysis demanded by business location decisions.

Suppose you are responsible for selecting a location for a new Costco store. You will carefully analyze the accessibility of alternative sites, focusing on finding a convenient location for the consumers that fit your customer profile. You need to factor both current and future customers (i.e., growth) into your analysis. Therefore, you may decide to locate in an area that currently has a relatively small, but rapidly growing, population. Frequently you will have to decide between a site that best satisfies existing demand versus a site with greater, but uncertain, future demand. One reason why so many "Mom and Pop" retailers go bankrupt is because they poorly assess the best location for their store. Often they have a solid retail idea but select a location that dooms the business.

Of course, you cannot simply locate near your customers and expect success. If you decide to locate in a heavily saturated market and sell commodity goods, it is unlikely you will survive. Why will customers select you over existing competitors? As a result, you often select a site with less competition, even if it is accessible to a smaller customer base. The point is that both demand and supply are important in location analysis. It is no surprise that large grocery chains and retailers perform sophisticated analyses of current and future demographic trends, and that they study competitive locations to determine which will best address those trends.

In addition to supply and demand, you must also consider the availability of your required inputs, namely labor and finished goods. You will attempt to locate where you can find enough employees to properly staff your business, as well as a location that is accessible to deliveries from your warehouses. If it is difficult for trucks to reach your store and/or unload products, you will find it difficult and costly to run your business. Hindrances to truck traffic, including weight restrictions, narrow streets, school zones, and poorly designed loading docks must all be factored into your analysis. If trucks are forced to unload in front of your store it can significantly detract from your retail curb appeal and hurt sales. Hence, the attractiveness of retail facilities with rear-loading facilities.

What if you are in the market for office space? Once again, you must worry about employees, clients, and customers visiting your office, as well as efficiently delivering your services and products to customers. If you are evaluating the best location for your law firm, you must make sure that your staff will be able to conveniently get to work. Otherwise, you will inconvenience your employees, which over the long term will make it difficult for you to attract and retain the best talent. This becomes a significant problem in a strong labor market when employees are more selective about where to work. Remember that a strong economy is the worst time to lose staff, as most service firms make their best profits in a strong environment, and replacing personnel is most difficult in such times.

The same is true for those customers who may travel to your office for meetings. If you are a service company, you are in the business of catering to clients, a mission that becomes infinitely more difficult if clients believe that visiting your office is an unpleasant hassle due to poor location, security, traffic, HVAC, or other design concerns.

Another major consideration is access to your client base. For example, a plumber that is close to the residential center has a substantial advantage over competitors who are not. Not only can he reach clients faster, but people will also notice his shop driving home. Proximity to an airport, train station (especially in Europe and Japan), and/or a highway is critical if you need to travel long distances to your customers.

A key factor that often dictates office location, particularly for headquarter decisions, is CEO ego. It may be more profitable to locate in a B-quality building in the suburbs, but the CEO wants a grand building with a granite lobby in the premier office district to boost his or her ego. While this does not always happen, it is reflective of the real world. In contrast, with the exception of shared office/warehouse facilities, ego rarely plays a role in the warehouse location selection decision. Executives frequently justify their office "ego-decisions" by saying a quality structure shows corporate quality and attracts clients. While it is true that quality space helps attract clients, many ego-driven executives go overboard.

You will also find countless studies of the optimal location for a corporate headquarters done by many firms that ultimately conclude that the ideal business location is about a mile from the CEO's residence. What a coincidence! Executives frequently act in their best interests and often dictate location decisions that make their life convenient at the expense of the firm. Retail properties do not suffer from this problem as seriously, as they are generally driven by fundamental supply and demand analysis, with the exception of Mom and Pop stores which often select nearby locations simply because they do not know better.

HOW MUCH SPACE DO I NEED?

Simple calculations based on "typical" square footage used per employee is a starting point in determining the amount of space you require. Space design and utilization are also significant factors in this process. For instance, the size of seats in sports stadiums continues to decrease (even as customer bottoms increase), while the number of seats increases. As demand for tickets increases, owners want to fit as many people in the stadium as possible. The total usable square footage of a sports venue depends on the ability of architects and designers to maximize the number of seats within the space and still satisfy building and safety codes. So too with all space, from apartment units to office suites.

Design is particularly important with respect to the **loss factor**. The existence of load-bearing columns, ducts, and wiring, as well as the number and location of stairwells and elevators dictate how much usable space you will have for a given amount of gross space. The greater the loss factor, the more gross space you will need. Extravagant headquarters generally have large loss factors. Inefficient loss factors reflect features such as large atrium lobbies, quirky angles, and round façades, as it is very difficult to effectively utilize round or triangular structures.

Cost is also a factor in the space decision. In New York, there is an abundance of young workers in cubicles, effectively working in the hallway. This is because space is so expensive that employers attempt to cram as many people as possible in a given space. But in places where space is cheap, like suburban Kansas, most workers have offices, rather than cubicles. Design regulations will also impact space usage. For example, German law requires that all workers have access to direct sunlight (even though the sun rarely shines). This makes the use of interior cubicle space basically impossible.

The market will partially dictate how much space you require. For instance, when there are numerous vacancies, and market rents and lease terms are soft, landlords seek to mitigate tenant losses. As a tenant, you can exploit such conditions by stocking up on "discounted" space, assuming you have the financial ability to carry the space until you grow into it. By leasing more space to house future expansion, you can both capitalize on the cheap rents and provide better quality space for your employees. As the market improves and firms actively lease before a full market recovery takes hold, demand for space generally outpaces the economic recovery.

Tenants also use weak markets to upgrade the quality of their space while market rents are low. Such quality shifts are common in office markets where tenants move from a building with slow elevators, poor HVAC, and other problems, to a newer building with higher quality amenities. Warehouse upgrades consist primarily of moving closer to a major highway interchange or to buildings with better clear heights.

Dramatic quality shifts for hotels can occur in a weak market environment. For example, Friday and Saturday nights are generally the weakest nights for urban hotels due to the lack of business customers. As they cut room rates in the face of a weak economic and tourism market, some urban hotels see stronger demand from high school and college students who can now afford to take their "dates" to these newly affordable, classier digs. This type of quality shift can drastically damage your profitability over the long run, as hotel customers are sensitive to the clientele, and if regular patrons notice an abundance of college and high school students, you can expect a rapid decline in property reputation and reduced high-end demand. Similar shifts can occur with respect to families with children shifting up into quality hotels.

The same quality shift dynamics take place at residential properties. Landlords generally prefer mature, reliable, upscale tenants. However, as rents decline in a soft market, a younger, noisier, and far more destructive tenant base can afford the property. Landlords often rent to these tenants to mitigate the reduction in demand from preferred customers, but an image erosion for the property can occur as the tenant mix changes. This can seriously impair the long-term value of the property.

SHOULD I OWN OR RENT?

Having determined what type of space you want, how much space you want, and where you want to locate, you need to determine whether to own your space (assuming you have the capital necessary) or rent it. Most users of real estate that have the means to own their real estate do a miserable job evaluating the own versus rent decision, performing a fundamentally faulty analysis.

Faulty Own Versus Rent Model

Assume the company Linneman Associates is interested in finding a suitable headquarters in Philadelphia. If the firm's executive management decide to purchase the $100 million building, they are interested in occupying, it will require $40 million in equity, with the remainder financed with a non-amortizing $60 million non-recourse mortgage, which carries a 6% interest rate. This means that the company will pay $3.6 million per year in interest payments in addition to the costs of operating the building. If the company purchases the property, it may engage a real estate firm to manage the property. Alternatively, the company may use in-house staff to manage the property. In either case, assume that the operation of the property costs $2 million a year.

Assuming the company is a taxable entity, they can use the mortgage interest payments as a tax shield. Assuming a 21% corporate tax rate, this means they will avoid $756,000 in taxes each year ($3.6 MM * 21%). The company can also use the property's depreciation as a tax shield. Assuming 80% of the $100 million is allocated as non-land value for tax purposes, and that the combination of structure and improvements gives an average depreciable life of 20 years for the non-land allocation, the company takes $4 million in depreciation a year (($100 MM * 80%) / 20) for 20 years, resulting in $840,000 in annual expected tax savings ($4 MM * 21%).

Summing the expected cash inflows and outflows as displayed in Figure 23.1, the company finds that in year 1, it expects a net payment of $44 million ($40 MM equity investment + $3.6 MM in interest + $2 MM in operating expense – $756,000 in tax savings from the interest shield – $840,000 in tax savings from the depreciation shield). Performing this calculation for the second year results in a net payment of $4 million ($3.6 MM in interest + $2 MM in operating expenses – $756,000 in tax savings from interest – $840,000 in tax savings from depreciation). If the company holds the property for 10 years, and ignoring inflation in operating costs, management estimates the same net outlay as that for year 2 in each of the remaining 8 years.

FIGURE 23.1

Owning Linneman Associates Headquarters, Excluding Sale ($ in MM)						
		Year 1	Year 2	Year 3	...	Year 10
Equity Investment		(40.00)				
Interest		(3.60)	(3.60)	(3.60)	...	(3.60)
Operating Expense		(2.00)	(2.00)	(2.00)	...	(2.00)
Interest Tax Shield		0.756	0.756	0.756	...	0.756
Depreciation Tax Shield	Total	0.84	0.84	0.84	...	0.84
Total Cash Flow	($80.04)	($44.00)	($4.00)	($4.00)	...	($4.00)

Linneman Associates also assumes that it can profitably sell the building at the end of the 10th year. Users almost always assume that the building will be sold for a profit, as no one ever loses money on a pro forma sale! Assuming a sale for $130 million (2.7% compounded rate of annual appreciation), minus $3 million in selling fees and $60 million in debt repayment, the net sales proceeds are $67 million. Since the company is a taxable entity, management calculates an expected accumulated depreciation and capital gains tax payment of $14.5 million ($4 MM in depreciation * 10 years * 25% accumulated depreciation tax rate, plus $30 MM in actual capital gains * 15% capital gain tax rate), which results in net cash proceeds of $52.5 million, as summarized in Figure 23.2.

FIGURE 23.2

Sale of Linneman Associates Headquarters	
	Year 10 Sale
Sale Revenue	$130,000,000
Fees	(3,000,000)
Debt Repayment	(60,000,000)
Accumulated Depreciation Tax	(10,000,000)
Capital Gains Tax	(4,500,000)
Net Proceeds	$52,500,000

Combining the operating and sale cash flows, and applying a 10% discount rate, the company then calculates the NPV of owning the building as −$40.73 million (Figure 23.3).

FIGURE 23.3

Owning and Selling Linneman Associates Headquarters ($ in MM)						
		Year 1	Year 2	Year 3	...	Year 10
Cash Flow		(44.00)	(4.00)	(4.00)	...	(4.00)
Cash Flow from Sale	Total	0.00	0.00	0.00	...	52.50
Total Cash Flow	($27.54)	(44.00)	(4.00)	(4.00)	...	$48.50
NPV at 10.00%	($40.73)					

Alternatively, the company calculates the NPV for the rental option, assuming that rent provides a landlord with an 8% yield on the $100 million building and an 80% operating profit margin. Therefore, the annual rent is $10 million per year, with $2 million in operating costs (the same as for the user) to generate an $8 million net operating income ($10 MM − $2 MM) on the $100 million building. Ignoring inflation in operating costs, the company's rent is set at $10 million per year for the 10 years it plans to stay in the space. The estimated NPV for this rental stream over the 10 years of occupancy, using a 10% discount rate, indicates a −$61.45 million NPV (Figure 23.4).

FIGURE 23.4

Faulty Analysis: Renting Linneman Associates Headquarters ($ in MM)						
		Year 1	Year 2	Year 3	...	Year 10
	Total					
Rent Payment	($100.00)	(10.00)	(10.00)	(10.00)	...	(10.00)
NPV at 10.00%	($61.45)					

At this point, all too many users say, "This is a no brainer! Why rent at the cost of a negative $61.45 million NPV, when buying yields only a negative $40.73 million NPV?" This faulty analysis is the basis for many corporations owning instead of renting.

What Is the Problem?

What is wrong with this analysis? Quite simply, enough things to almost fill a chapter in a textbook. Most importantly, in the own analysis, the user did not take into consideration their opportunity cost of tying up $40 million of equity and $60 million in borrowing capacity during the 10 years of ownership. The company could have used this $40 million and borrowed an additional $60 million to invest in its core business rather than real estate. In the analysis above, equity is treated as free (i.e., a zero cost of capital)! Is it surprising that the buy option results in a massively better NPV if ownership is given a $40 million equity subsidy in the form of zero capital costs? But you cannot legitimately compare an investment with free capital and costs (the own option), with one that is only made up of costs (the rent option). You must either remove the investment aspect of the own option or credit the rent option for the return realized on the $40 million in available equity, presumably utilized in core operations instead of toward the building purchase.

Another serious analytical error is that the ownership analysis assumes property value appreciates by 30% over 10 years, while the rental analysis implicitly assumes little or no value increase if the building is owned by a landlord (same rental income in Year 10 as in Year 1). Specifically, for the property value to increase by 30%, one would expect rental rates would also substantially increase by the 10th year. Also, the analysis assumed the user and the landlord have the same property operating costs, even though the landlord is a real estate specialist. Taken together, these errors render the analysis hopelessly flawed, though widely employed.

Corrected Own Versus Rent Model

Intuitively, you should generally expect that the NPV for renting is better (i.e., less negative) than the NPV associated with owning. After all, the expected property appreciation is roughly the same irrespective of who owns the asset. Also, the user is not in the real estate business and will tend to have higher operating costs than a professional landlord. Furthermore, the opportunity cost of owning is very high for the user, given that a firm should be able to generate higher expected returns from core business operations than real estate. If not, maybe they should switch to the real estate business! A correct analysis will incorporate this higher expected return on equity in the core business. What about the depreciation and interest deduction advantages of ownership? The professional landlord takes advantage of the same deductions, and if markets are highly competitive, they will be forced to pass these savings along to tenants in the form of lower rents.

Returning to our example, assume that the annual opportunity cost of capital is 12% in the firm's core business. Therefore, $12 million per year in positive inflows is added to the rental option (the $100 MM in retained capital investment capacity * 12%) minus the 21% corporate tax paid on these expected profits. In addition, one must credit the $756,000 annual tax shield they receive on the interest payments on the $60 million borrowed for the core investment. In addition, they receive a depreciation tax shield from the $100 million invested in their core business. If these core investments have a 10-year depreciable life, it generates $2.1 million annually in depreciation tax shield. The company will also realize a gain in the value of the investment in the core operations after 10 years. In this case, they expect to sell the business in Year 10 at $53.75 million (3% expected compounded annual appreciation). These changes to the original rental option analysis are itemized in the partially corrected analysis shown in Figure 23.5.

FIGURE 23.5

Partially Corrected Analysis: Renting Linneman Associates Headquarters ($ in MM)						
		Year 1	Year 2	Year 3	...	Year 10
Investment in Operations		(40.00)				
Rent Payment		(10.00)	(10.00)	(10.00)	...	(10.00)
Interest Payment		(3.60)	(3.60)	(3.60)	...	(3.60)
Interest Tax Shield		0.756	0.756	0.756	...	0.756
Depreciation Tax Shield		2.10	2.10	2.10	...	2.10
CF from Normal Operations		12.00	12.00	12.00	...	12.00
Tax on CF from Normal Operations		(2.52)	(2.52)	(2.52)	...	(2.52)
Investment in Operations Remaining	Total	0.00	0.00	0.00	...	53.75
Total Cash Flow	$1.11	($41.26)	($1.26)	($1.26)	...	$52.49
NPV at 10.00%	($23.41)					

Since you would expect a real estate specialist to operate the property more efficiently than the user, assume the landlord's operating costs are 10% lower than if the company owns the property. This implies $1.8 million in annual operating expenses (ignoring inflation) ($2 MM in operating expenses from rental option * (1 – 10%)). In the original faulty rental analysis, the landlord leases the building at a rent that yields an 8 cap. Using this same assumption in this partially corrected rental analysis, the landlord can charge a lower initial rent and still achieve an 8 cap given the 10% lower operating costs. After all, the property value ($100 million) has not changed. To reach $8 million in NOI in year one, the landlord need only charge $9.8 million in rent ($9.8 MM rent – $1.8 MM operating expense = $8 MM NOI).

Holding the cap rate constant, to generate the assumed 30% expected property appreciation over 10 years, NOI must increase. Given an 8 cap, the NOI in year 10 must reach $10.4 million for the property value to appreciate by 30% ($10.4 MM / 8% = $130 MM). This implies a rent of $12.2 million in year 10 ($12.2 MM rent − $1.8 MM in operating expenses = $10.4 MM NOI). Assuming the rent increases at a constant rate over the 10 years, the company models a 2.46% annual rent increase each year, as shown in the fully corrected analysis in Figure 23.6.

With this corrected rental analysis, the company uses a 10% discount rate to calculate the expected net cash flows to determine the expected NPV of the rental option.

FIGURE 23.6

Corrected Analysis: Renting Linneman Associates Headquarters ($ in MM)						
		Year 1	Year 2	Year 3	...	Year 10
Investment in Operations		(40.00)				
Rent Payment		(9.80)	(10.04)	(10.29)	...	(12.20)
Interest Payment		(3.60)	(3.60)	(3.60)	...	(3.60)
Interest Tax Shield		0.756	0.756	0.756	...	0.756
Depreciation Tax Shield		2.10	2.10	2.10	...	2.10
CF from Normal Operations		12.00	12.00	12.00	...	12.00
Tax on CF from Normal Operations		(2.52)	(2.52)	(2.52)	...	(2.52)
Investment in Operations Remaining	Total	0.00	0.00	0.00	...	53.75
Total	($8.51)	($41.06)	($1.31)	($1.55)	...	$50.28
NPV at 10.00%	($28.05)					

Online Companion Hands On: Go to the Chapter 23 page of the Online Companion, and complete the analysis with the Assumptions given, calculating the NPV of both the own and rent options. Should the company own or rent their space?

As intuitively expected, the rental option yields a better (i.e., less negative) NPV than the ownership option (−$40.73 million for the ownership option versus −$28.05 million for the corrected rental option). Based on both common sense and financial analysis, you would expect most, if not all, corporate users would rent rather than own. Simply put, given limited capital, it is generally better for a company to invest in its core business than in real estate.

ONE SIZE DOES NOT FIT ALL

While we have a sound framework with which to assess the NPVs of owning versus renting, no two corporate real estate decisions are identical. Each corporate real estate decision depends on the returns of the firm's core business, the nature of the specific real estate market, the type of real estate, and the firm's income tax profile. Firms with low cash flow multiples and core-business rates of return, needing a highly specialized property in a non-competitive market (e.g., a factory in a suburb of a third-tier city), are better off owning their real estate than renting it. The other assumptions that underpin the "better to own" conclusion include: high expected real estate appreciation; lower property operating costs for the company than for a landlord; and a higher landlord rate of return (if the company were to own) than the company's core business rate of return. If these are true, it is better to own corporate space than invest in their lower-return core business.

These conclusions are based on the decision model I published in the Spring 2008 Wharton Real Estate Review, which put forth the following relationship that expresses the differential after-tax present value profitability ($\Delta\pi$) of leasing (πL) versus self-ownership (πO):

$$\Delta\pi = \pi L - \pi O = (1\text{-}t)\, V\, [(r + \alpha e)M - gN] - t(D+A).$$

The terms shown are as follows:

- t = the corporate tax rate;
- V = the property value;
- r = the rate of return on core corporate operations;
- αe = the corporate owner's proportional operating costs relative to landlords;
- M = the company's core operation valuation multiple;
- g = the landlord's expected rate of return;
- N = the real estate's cash flow multiple;
- D = the present value of the tax savings associated with the depreciation allowance provided to owners of corporate real estate;
- A = the present value of the expected after-tax appreciation on the corporate real estate.

Three simulations demonstrate the own versus rent decision yielded by this model (Figure 23.7). First, consider the case of a "typical" firm. Assume it has a 21% corporate tax rate, a 12% core return, and a 13x cash flow multiple. The property return is 9% and has a 13x cash flow multiple. Landlords have 10% lower operating costs than corporate owners due to the commodity nature of the real estate and depth of the property market, while self-provision operating costs are 3% of value. The property is expected to appreciate 3% annually, and there is a 20% effective capital gains tax, 2.5% of non-land is depreciable annually, and land accounts for 30% of the real estate value. For this company/property/market combination (Case 1), leasing generates a present value greater profit equal to 24% of the value of the real estate. That is, every $100 million deployed in corporate real estate destroys $24 million in corporate value.

Case 2 assumes a company with a mere 8% core return, and a 7x core cash flow multiple. In addition, the company is evaluating a highly idiosyncratic piece of real estate for which their operating costs run 4% annually of the real estate value and are 10% lower than what a landlord's would be to operate the property. The property is expected to appreciate at 5% annually. Due to a non-competitive real estate market, the landlord's return is 12%. All other parameters are the same as in the first case. In this case, the ownership of corporate real estate generates a higher present value profit equal to 93% of the value of the real estate. That is, owning $100 million of real estate generates higher present value profits of $93 million. Note that it is difficult to envision a more attractive case for ownership, as there is substantial arbitrage, lower owner operating costs, and substantial property appreciation associated with owning.

FIGURE 23.7

Differential After-tax Present Value Profitability of Renting vs. Owning				
Case		1 Typical situation	2 Loaded towards owning	3 Loaded towards renting
Example		Consulting firm	Specialized assets	Tech company
Δπ – Differential Renting to Owning (positive value = better to rent)		**24%**	**(93%)**	**41%**
Common assumptions across all cases:				
t – the corporate tax rate	0.210			
V – the property value	1.000			
B – annual non-land depreciation allowance rate	0.025			
s – capital gain tax rate	0.200			
T – years owned property is held	40.000			
l – land (non-depreciable) share of value	0.300			
d – discount rate for tax shield (reflects risk of tax law change)	0.080			
Unique assumptions:				
r – the rate of return on core corporate operations		0.120	0.080	0.140
M –the company core operation valuation multiple		13.000	7.000	18.000
a – owned property annual capital appreciation rate		0.030	0.050	0.030
N – the after-tax real estate cash flow multiple		13.000	15.000	10.000
e – landlord specialization efficiencies relative to owned property pre-tax costs		0.100	(0.100)	0.200
α – owned property real estate costs as a proportion of value		0.030	0.040	0.030
n – discount rate for real estate appreciation		0.100	0.080	0.120
g – the landlord's expected rate of return		0.090	0.120	0.050

Case 3 considers a firm leasing space in a highly competitive property market (g = 5%), where landlord efficiencies are high (e = 20%), real estate multiples are low relative to core business multiples, and core returns are high (r = 14%). In this instance, the arbitrage associated with shifting capital from real estate to core operations, combined with reduced rents attributable to landlord efficiencies, create a 41% present value profit gain associated with renting real estate. That is, $100 million of corporate real estate ownership destroys $41 million in corporate value. These results are summarized in the bar chart in Figure 23.8.

FIGURE 23.8

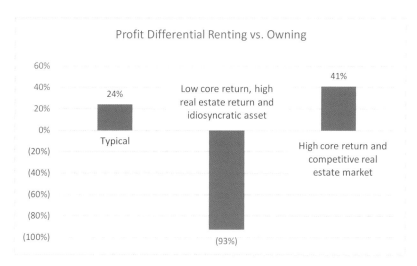

PROPENSITY FOR CORPORATE OWNERSHIP OF REAL ESTATE

Why do so many companies, particularly outside of the U.S., own their space if it is generally economically beneficial to rent? As amazing as it may sound, one reason is that most companies have never done the correct analysis. Bad analysis leads to bad decisions.

On the other hand, some firms truly have free capital for real estate. Universities, for example, often receive capital from alumni who are willing to donate substantially more capital for the naming rights to buildings than for scholarships and academic programs. For example, if alumni are willing to donate $4 million for academic programs and scholarships, but $40 million for a named building, $36 million of the capital for the building is effectively free. Therefore, major universities are extensive owners of their real estate, as there is a large element of free capital. In addition, as tax-exempt entities, universities rarely pay local property taxes, which are a major component of real estate operating costs. As a result, they may have lower operating costs than a taxable landlord despite their lack of real estate expertise.

Another reason universities tend to own their real estate is that few landlords are comfortable owning an asset with such a specific purpose as laboratories and classrooms. If you lease a building to a university for classrooms, and the university walks away from the lease, considerable reworking of the space will be required. In contrast, it is much easier to re-lease a plain vanilla warehouse, office building, or apartment complex. Therefore, to the extent that the space you require is relatively unique, and your rental market is not highly competitive (meaning that rents will be relatively high), the ownership option makes better sense.

In a similar manner, users of complicated space, such as factories or casinos, often own their properties, as they believe that any realistic lease will be too inflexible to effectively deal with the constant tweaking which is essential to keep those spaces at maximum productivity. For example, in the case of a casino, gaming, restaurant, entertainment, and hotel configurations are regularly modified to accommodate changing strategies. There is substantial value associated with the operational flexibility of ownership. In the view of most resort and casino operators, the operating flexibility and control benefits of ownership outweigh the apparent savings of the lease option.

A unique benefit that comes with ownership is the secrecy of operations. For instance, Michelin was once the only producer of radial tires in the U.S., and they would not let any outsiders into their production plants. Their concern was understandable, but no landlord would sign a lease that states that under no circumstances can the landlord gain access to their property.

SYNTHETIC LEASES

There is a third option for meeting your corporate real estate needs, namely a **synthetic lease**. A synthetic lease allows a company with an economic and tax ownership position to hide the ownership (and the accompanying debt) from shareholders. A synthetic lease is a type of contract that attempts to convince the IRS that you own the real estate, while at the same time satisfying the Securities Exchange Commission (SEC) (hence securities holders) that you rent it. You want to convince the IRS that you own the building so that you can take depreciation write-offs and use interest payments to shield your taxable income. But why would you want to convince the SEC that you do not own the building? In the eyes of the SEC, real estate ownership means you are putting the sizeable low yielding asset (the property) and the corresponding liability (property-level debt) on your balance sheet. Having this liability on your balance sheet may violate your corporate debt loan covenants. Also, without the asset on your books, your return on book equity and assets are higher. Sound fishy? It is — but it is not illegal — yet. Hiding assets and liabilities from your shareholders and bondholders simply leads to inaccurate valuations and wasteful capital misallocations.

Synthetic leases evolved out of very detailed nuances of SEC and IRS regulations. Tax and accounting specialists have spent countless hours designing ways to satisfy both the SEC and the IRS criteria. One of the simplest techniques amounts to setting up a new special purpose entity (SPE), which is essentially a protective entity between the corporation and the property. The SPE only exists for this purpose, and the property is the only asset owned by the SPE. The SPE is financed with a minimum nominal equity contribution of say 3%, which primarily comes from the parent firm, with the remaining 97% coming from debt that is secured by the property and is also guaranteed by the corporate parent. The SPE uses these funds to purchase the building, with the parent corporation leasing the building from the SPE at a rent equal to the debt service payments and a nominal return on equity.

If structured correctly, the corporation is renting the building from an independent company (the SPE). If all goes as planned, the SPE will repatriate dividends to the parent company and make the scheduled interest payments. As long as you conform to the rules, the IRS allows the parent company to take the depreciation from the building and use the interest payments to shield their taxable income. At the same time the SEC will not require you to record either the SPE's debt or property on the parent's balance sheet as long as the lease is structured in conformity with the rules of an operating lease: the lease cannot transfer ownership; the lease cannot contain an option to purchase the building at a bargain price; the lease term is less than 75% of the estimated economic life of the building; and the present value of lease payments is less than 90% of the fair market value of the building. This will allow the company to effectively hide significant amounts of debt (and loan guarantees) and assets from both shareholders and bondholders, as individually, most properties are not large enough to be material for disclosure. In an extreme example, a company with zero debt on its balance sheet could be heavily levered, with thousands of "immaterial" SPEs financed with off-balance sheet debt and corporate guarantees.

FOR HOW LONG SHOULD I LEASE?

Assuming you have decided to lease, for how long should you lease the space or the entire building? In general, the longer the lease, the better rental deal you will be able to achieve. This is similar to the lower unit pricing of bulk items at Costco. Larger quantity items generally cost less per ounce than the same product in a smaller package, as the manufacturer gets an assured sale, saves on packaging, distribution, warehousing, and competition, and shares those savings with the consumer. It is no different with real estate. In general, if you sign a 10-year lease, you will get a better deal than if you sign 5 two-year leases, because the landlord gets assured occupancy, will save on legal and accounting costs, and will be forced by competition to share those benefits with the tenant. A longer lease also provides the tenant some negotiating leverage. However, by signing a long lease, the tenant gives up the operational flexibility of exiting when they no longer need the space. If you know for certain that you will need the space for a long period of time, then you should sign a long-term lease. But in a world of frequent mergers and acquisitions, bankruptcies, rapidly changing products, and increased global competition, few tenants know how long they will need their space. An exception is the U.S. government. As a result, the U.S. government generally signs long-term leases.

Signing shorter leases provides substantial option value to the tenant, though this is difficult to accurately value. You must value the expected economic savings from the longer leases versus the expected benefit of increased operating flexibility.

THE CORPORATION OF YOU

Even if you do not become a business owner who needs to make corporate real estate decisions, you need to realize that you are also the "CEO of you," and you will likely consider owning a home at some point. While renting has attractions such as landlord-provided maintenance and repairs, and common amenities like a pool (that you do not have to clean or open and close), life has a funny way of "happening to us" and changing our real estate needs. In the blink of an eye, we find ourselves with a serious significant other, possibly with plans for having a child. Suddenly a pool crowded with young folks drinking beer is less important, and a good school district is more important. With new priorities, the question of moving arises and, thus, whether to rent or own. You can always rent a house or another apartment in a good school district but are then faced with the adult concern of "throwing your money away" on rent year after year and helping the landlord to build equity and wealth, while you build none.

Owning a residence, whether a condominium, townhome, or detached house comes with its own benefits and trade-offs. Benefits include the income tax shelter from mortgage interest payments and the ability to build equity in the property. However, since there is no guarantee that the home value will increase during the term of your intended ownership, you are making a bet the same way you would as an investor with an investment property. The fundamental difference is that even if the value does not always go up, the house always provides the significant utility of shelter, safety, and a place to call home.

Regarding homeownership as a purely financial decision requires NPV analysis to compare renting and owning. Several academic models have addressed this issue, but all naturally fall short because the modeling constraints are unrealistic, and there is no variable for "emotion." As much as we want to think of our homes as investments, we do not always buy them rationally. Often we buy homes with our hearts, based on our life circumstances, and not our heads. Generally, it is the kitchen or Jacuzzi (which will never get used) that will sell the home (or not), and in the case of families not doing homeschooling or private school, it is the combination of the kitchen and the public school district ranking. The best way to think about your home is first as a safe place for you and your family, second as an income tax shelter, and third as an investment. Thus, even if the third factor does not pan out, the first is the most important, and the second is a nice predictable bonus.

CLOSING THOUGHT

The use of real estate is ubiquitous. The more successful you become in your chosen field of endeavors, the more time you will spend dealing with your real estate needs. Never forget that it is a highly specialized area, and that your expertise is running your business, which may not be developing, owning, and operating real estate. If it is not, unless you have no viable choice, keep your scarce capital employed in your core business and leave real estate operations to professionals.

 Online Companion Audio Interview: To hear a conversation about this chapter's content, go to the Online Companion and select the link for Chapter 23. Scroll down to the Audio Interview section and listen.

Chapter 24
Some Observations on Real Estate Entrepreneurship

"When asked if real estate entrepreneurs are born or made, my answer is always Yes."
- Dr. Peter Linneman

I have been a small-scale entrepreneur for 40 years and taught real estate entrepreneurship for nearly 20 years. In addition, over the past 42 years I have befriended and observed innumerable entrepreneurs, including many legendary figures. I have read numerous books by and about entrepreneurs, as well as scholarly papers on the topic. I offer here some observations on entrepreneurship.

"Can entrepreneurship be taught?" is a common question. It is generally asked with a knowing smirk by someone who misunderstands the purpose of education. The answer is "Of course it can." Education, at its core, is about efficiently passing along "what is known" on a topic. This involves a set of focused lessons that advance the student's learning process. Assuming that focused lessons are twice as efficient as trial and error, 60 hours of student time in a class (20 in class and 40 outside of class) can generate the equivalent of 120 hours of insight. This amounts to a mere two weeks of full-time work. However, if a course can achieve in a week what would otherwise require two weeks to learn through experience, it is a huge success. Yet in the context of a career, two weeks is a drop in the bucket.

Another important educational goal is to assist students in discovering their strengths, weaknesses, and passions, and to help them to determine if they have "what it takes." If the 60 hours committed to a course can save years of pursuing false dreams, or light a fire under someone, the course has been successful. In this context, I am reminded of the Monty Python skit in which a mousey chartered accountant tells a career counselor that he wants to become a lion tamer. After the career counselor disabuses him of the idea that lions are cute animals that sit on your lap and play with string by showing him a man-eating lion, the accountant realizes that chartered accountancy is perfect for him. Better to learn such lessons in the comfort of a classroom than to be eaten alive on the job.

Entrepreneurship can be effectively taught, but while you can teach someone to play football and to better understand and love the game, you cannot teach them to be Tom Brady. Teaching can expose, inform, and excite, but it cannot create virtuosos. Being a professional, much less a superstar, in any walk of life requires a combination of education, innate skill, and a lifetime of honing one's game. Just as few young football players ever achieve superstar status, few entrepreneurs ever achieve the level of success of Albert Ratner, Steve Ross, Steve Roth, Alfred Taubman, or Sam Zell.

By inspiring and helping budding entrepreneurs understand the challenges they will face, how to approach these challenges in a disciplined manner, and how to avoid making the "well-known" mistakes, it is possible to help them along the path to becoming an entrepreneur. As an educator, the goal is to guide them, so they make mistakes that others have yet to make. Students need to understand that making errors is what entrepreneurs do, and that success comes from solving, not avoiding, problems.

ARE THERE ENTREPRENEURIAL TRAITS?

All too often, people seek a cookbook approach to entrepreneurship: "Just do these things and you will become a billionaire!" But this is as foolish as saying someone will be a star quarterback if he is the right height, weight, speed, IQ, and so on. While these factors tend to be correlated with success, they are far from perfect predictors. There is no formula for great quarterbacks, as they come in many sizes and shapes. But there are no great 5-foot, 120-pound pro football quarterbacks. The same is true for entrepreneurs: they come in many different packages, with certain personality traits correlated with success and others associated with failure.

Entrepreneurs are usually intellectual arbitrageurs rather than inventors. That is, they are more likely to tweak existing ideas than to create new concepts out of whole cloth. Thus, Steve Wynn's brilliant resort/casinos appropriate and combine the best elements of large-scale resorts, boutique retail, and quality entertainment venues in a way that enhances their complementarities. Alfred Taubman's shopping malls likewise combined elements found in ancient arcades with modern merchandising concepts found in the world's best downtown shopping areas. Neither created entirely new concepts but, rather, put together existing components in a new way.

Successful entrepreneurs generally look at things differently from other people. While most people see how things are, entrepreneurs see how they could be better. As a result, entrepreneurs must be able to sell their personal vision to their audience (employees, vendors, customers, capital sources, and advisors), who does not necessarily share it. Absent the ability to sell effectively, entrepreneurs will fail to muster the resources necessary to implement their idea. Entrepreneurial sales ability involves being able to describe the vision in a simple, yet sophisticated, manner. A great entrepreneur is able to package his or her ideas into a presentation that is so simple that it can be grasped by an intelligent child. What could be simpler, for example, than Sam Walton's vision of everyday low prices built around economies of scale?

The ability to sell does not require PowerPoint or a thick consultant report. It does require many hours of thought about how to express a complicated idea in a simple manner. When I fail to understand an entrepreneur's pitch, it usually means that they are not ready for success. I encourage students who are preparing a pitch to think about the selling of televisions. Televisions are highly complex pieces of equipment that work due to an amazing combination of high-level electronics and physics. Yet how is one sold? The customer is told, "Push this button to turn it on and this button to change channels." No one would buy a television if the sales pitch consisted of electrical flow charts and discussions of wave theory.

The ability to present complex ideas with simplicity is a critical trait of entrepreneurial success. But just as important is the ability to persevere after repeatedly being told "no." As social animals, we all love to be told "yes." In fact, most people do everything possible to avoid being told "no"; the easiest way to do this is to conform. Thus, entrepreneurs proposing unusual and untested ideas are constantly being told "no" by customers, vendors, potential employees, government officials, and capital sources. Yet, entrepreneurs are not deterred by rejection or temporary setbacks, a quality which requires somewhat odd "social wiring."

Entrepreneurs believe that they cannot fail, because they will (somehow) figure out a way to make things work. Entrepreneurs view each "no" as a missed opportunity for the naysayer, not a personal failure. And yet most entrepreneurs are terrified of failure. This fear also forces them to be more flexible and pragmatic than most people, constantly altering their approach as they move forward. Anything to avoid the ultimate "NO!"

Successful entrepreneurs are willing to make decisions, knowing that they will need to change course many times on the fly. They are like a great quarterback scrambling for his life, yet still able to see things evolving around him so he can make a play. This adaptability is apparent in another quality of entrepreneurship. Entrepreneurs tend to believe that "the answer" is less important than the ability to quickly adapt if an initial answer leads them awry. It is perhaps the reason why most lawyers and academics are poor entrepreneurs, as their training teaches them to search for the answer rather than selecting an answer, with a mind to changing it if need be.

The entrepreneur perceives risks differently from other people. Just as a great quarterback knows he will take some big hits if he is going to throw touchdowns, the successful entrepreneur knows there will be a lot of bumps on the road to success. And like a great quarterback, his fear is not about getting hit (which is what a normal person fears) but, rather, that he will not complete the pass. Stated differently, entrepreneurs are more afraid of failure than they are of getting hurt.

Entrepreneurs have a rare capacity to absorb their social and business environment. This is essential, as it allows them to see opportunities that others fail to see. Entrepreneurs tend to be avaricious readers of newspapers, trade periodicals, magazines, and analytical reports. Their reading even includes seemingly unrelated fields such as novels and history. Entrepreneurs do not read to learn the "story" but to understand how things "fit together." This reading forms a mosaic of the world in which they live, helping them identify the missing pieces of the mosaic that provide business opportunities.

Entrepreneurs also tend to seek the advice and counsel of various experts. This includes not only lawyers, accountants, bankers, architects, and economists, but also those in seemingly unrelated fields: doctors, scientists, historians, artists, and writers. Again, these advisors provide the entrepreneur with additional pieces for their mosaic. The ability to create a mosaic of life is one of the most consistent elements I have found in observing entrepreneurs. Interestingly, entrepreneurs are less interested in mastering the analysis provided by these inputs than in abstracting bits and pieces to form their ever-changing mosaic.

Contrary to popular belief, entrepreneurs are not dreamers. They are extreme pragmatists. They do not imagine a perfect world where everything goes right and everybody wants their product. Instead, most are brutally realistic in their appraisal of the challenges they face. When someone tells me that everyone needs their product, I know I am listening to an unsuccessful pitch; no one has a product that everyone needs. Entrepreneurs realize this and possess the flexibility and vision to take on the challenges that would discourage others.

Entrepreneurs are an unusual blend of studied pragmatic opportunism and blind determination. Once they have identified an opportunity and determined that it is realistic, they act with a sense of urgency. In fact, what distinguishes a good entrepreneur from a good corporate executive is the sense of urgency in pursuing a course of action. A good corporate executive in a well-established firm will meticulously scrutinize a business opportunity, consulting numerous committees before embarking on a course of action. In contrast, the entrepreneur acts quickly, as it is only a matter of time before others see the same opportunity and will perhaps attack it with greater resources than the entrepreneur possesses. We have all observed an entrepreneur execute a project with great success, and wonder, "Why didn't I do that?" The opportunity was obvious, the market demand was obvious, and yet most people did not pursue it. The challenge for entrepreneurs is to act before established corporations get around to addressing the opportunity.

Entrepreneurs must be smart enough to process information and identify opportunities. But being an entrepreneur is not about being a genius. One needs an IQ of 120, but not 150. Entrepreneurs come from many different social backgrounds, ranging from scions of wealthy families to new immigrants, and from places as diverse as Manhattan and Fayetteville, Arkansas. Today, most entrepreneurs are college graduates, though in previous generations this was not the case. Even so, entrepreneurs do not always hold advanced degrees. I know successful entrepreneurs who have studied business administration at Wharton, music at Julliard, fine arts at the University of Southern California, and English literature at Amherst. It is neither education, super-intelligence, nor heredity that typifies entrepreneurs. What is common to every entrepreneur I have ever met is a total passion for what they are doing. It is both their work and their entertainment. It is how they make friends as well as how they make their living. It is what they live to do rather than what they do to live.

WHAT MAKES SAMMY RUN?

Students often believe that entrepreneurship is about getting fabulously rich overnight. But almost every entrepreneur's story is one of an "overnight" success that took 10 to 15 years. It only seems like overnight, because their stories did not appear in Forbes or Fortune until they were already established. This creates the impression that success — as opposed to notoriety — is instantaneous. This false impression is compounded by the fact that the typical person's exposure to entrepreneurs is primarily through magazines and news profiles. But the successful entrepreneurs highlighted in the media are newsworthy, precisely because they are atypical. Bill Gates and Steve Jobs are not typical entrepreneurs, nor are Trammell Crow, Mel Simon, Don Bren, or Gerald Hines. It is precisely their uniqueness that makes them interesting. Their success is beyond the dreams of even very successful entrepreneurs. The truth is that most successful entrepreneurs are in their fifties and sixties and have net worth in the range of $1-20 million after many years of hard work and struggle. While this is notable financial success by any normal standard, it is far from what students have in mind when they think of entrepreneurial success.

Entrepreneurs' passion is to be successful, rather than to get rich, in whatever they are pursuing. Money, though comforting, is a by-product of achieving entrepreneurial success. In fact, there are entrepreneurs who pursue non-profit or purely humanitarian endeavors. Sister Theresa was a great entrepreneur. She had passion, intelligence, and a vision of what could be done. She was terrified that she might fail in fulfilling her mission. Both she and Bill Gates are legendary entrepreneurs; one died poor, while the other ended up the richest man in the world. But both were extraordinary entrepreneurs.

I used to tell my students that, with a few exceptions, the mere fact that they were at the University of Pennsylvania means they would be able to earn enough to live a comfortable life. But it was not clear if they would have fun. I note that if they want to be an entrepreneur to get rich quick, they are making a big mistake, as they can make far more — at least in the short term — by working for McKinsey, Goldman Sachs, Apple, or Google. They would work the same hours, with less risk and higher compensation. The question is whether they would be as happy. A real entrepreneur would not be.

I used to begin my entrepreneurship course by asking students why they want to be entrepreneurs. The most typical answer is, "I want to be my own boss." This may be a necessary condition for being an entrepreneur, but it is hardly sufficient motivation. Many people want to be their own bosses, but most lack the courage, vision, and passion to be entrepreneurs. It is this passion that explains why so many entrepreneurs remain active, often almost to the end of their lives. Their jobs are what they are, who they are, and what they do for fun. As they get older and enjoy the benefits of a lifetime of entrepreneurial success, they may put in fewer and more flexible hours, but with no less passion. In fact, many entrepreneurs stay on well after the market has passed them by, and their personal mosaic is a tattered ruin. One needs to look no further than Henry Ford, a great entrepreneur, whose belief in the black Model T lasted a decade or more past its useful life, and who nearly destroyed the Ford Motor Company. Ford's story is a reminder that being your own boss often means having a bad boss, since most entrepreneurs are poor managers. They are so passionate about doing what they are doing that they fail to focus on the need to manage, frequently including themselves.

BETTER, FASTER, CHEAPER

Entrepreneurs do not possess identical skill sets. Some, like Gerald Hines, Steve Wynn, and Alfred Taubman are brilliant with products. They master how real estate functions and how to improve the physical product from a cost and usage perspective. They understand how properties will be used and possess the rare skill of putting themselves in the place of the consumer. Consumer empathy is important, not only for high-end hotels, Class A office buildings, and luxury resorts, but also for mobile home communities, strip centers, and affordable housing. Most people lack the ability to understand, respect, and empathize with consumers' behavior and are, thus, unable to fulfill and enhance the consumer's experience. Those who provide a unique and superior value experience reap great rewards. Izzy Sharpe's Four Seasons Hotel chain is a perfect example of this phenomenon.

Another defining attribute of entrepreneurs is the ability to control production processes, time schedules, and costs. Such entrepreneurs make generic products, but they do it faster, more reliably, and more cheaply than their competitors. They possess the ability to control cost overruns before they occur and to adapt to the unknowable events that will challenge timely product delivery. An example is Ron Caplan of Philadelphia Management, who consistently delivers residential re-developments at a significant cost advantage over his competitors.

Another skill that defines some entrepreneurs is an ability to sell, even if their property is inferior to, or more expensive than, that of their competitors. Great marketers not only describe their product in an appealing manner but are also able to get customers to execute agreements. They are closers. They stand in marked contrast to most people, who are often good at describing the product of choice but have difficulty closing the sale.

Another type of entrepreneur, although rarely found in the real estate field, excels at managing people. Such entrepreneurs have the ability communicate their insights, skills, and passions to large numbers of employees. Sam Walton is perhaps the greatest example. Not only did he have a great business model, but he was also able to take it to extraordinary scale by creating a managerial environment that could replicate his vision. If one can make 10,000 people only 10% more productive, and each worker produces $50,000 annually, the value creation is $50 million annually, representing a present value of $500 million or more.

Some entrepreneurs are great risk analysts. This sounds simple, but great risk analysts are able to evaluate and manage both the upside and the downside of their vision in light of their limited capital (both financial and human). Jay Pritzker and Sam Zell come to mind in this regard. Such entrepreneurs focus on how to limit their downside, how to get out in a way that does not cripple them if they are unsuccessful, and how to identify the investments most worth making. These investment decisions are not simply based upon internal rates of return and net present values, but also on understanding what can go wrong and how to survive. For students, this is the most alluring type of entrepreneurship, because they believe that their courses in risk analysis have prepared them for this task. However, being able to calculate an IRR or NPV is very different from having a feel for the opportunities of the market and being able to constantly adapt to changing conditions.

A final defining skill of some entrepreneurs is being a master deal maker. Deal-making is exemplified by legendary real estate entrepreneurs such as Mel Simon or Edward DeBartolo. There is seemingly no obstacle that a great deal maker cannot overcome. This takes enormous resourcefulness and social connectivity. It requires understanding what others are seeking and how to help them achieve their goals without compromising one's own objectives. It requires a belief that deal making is a positive-sum game. It is also the reason that great deal makers are rare in the socialist countries of Western Europe as well as Japan, where a zero-sum mentality prevails.

Each of the above skills is rare, even among highly intelligent and educated individuals, but entrepreneurs must possess at least one of these skills to succeed. A small group of entrepreneurs possess two of these entrepreneurship skills, and legends are made of those who possess more than two. It is unrealistic for teenagers playing high school football to believe that they will become the next Peyton Manning. A far more realistic goal is to first play on a college team, and if very successful, receive a scholarship to a Division I university, and then if extremely successful, make it to the NFL as a substitute for a season or two. It is the same for entrepreneurs. The young entrepreneur's goal should not be to be the next Bob Toll or Barbara Corcoran, but rather to be successful in developing one's own skill in a pursuit about which he or she is passionate.

The greatest difficulty in teaching entrepreneurship is to avoid creating the impression that success as an entrepreneur is the result of having a Big Idea. Was Ray Kroc's idea to franchise restaurants that made hamburgers of consistent quality throughout the country a Big Idea? Or Sam Walton's plan to sell quality merchandise at the lowest prices in town? Or Warren Buffett's strategy to make long-term value investments? Hardly. What distinguished these entrepreneurs and made them legends was not their idea but, rather, their execution of the idea: "It's the singer not the song." Tens of thousands of young men are big enough and strong enough to play professional football, but most cannot make it for the lack of execution — reliability, perseverance, consistency. Unlike Big Ideas, execution is neither glamorous nor easy to teach. Execution requires attention to detail, commitment, and a fanatical exploitation of one's skills. Don Bren's source of success is his commitment and attention to details. In football, great athletes who are well trained and able to repeatedly execute mediocre plays are more valuable than mediocre players who lack skills but, on occasion, execute a great play. The same holds true for real estate entrepreneurship.

Entrepreneurial success is rarely about doing "something new." Most real estate entrepreneurs succeed by doing something better, cheaper, or faster. If an entrepreneur can do any one of these three, he or she will be successful.

In terms of execution, getting the right people to do the right jobs is the key to success. This entails selecting not necessarily the best talent but, rather, the best talent for the assignment at hand – people who share the vision and fit the budget. Too often, managers are dazzled by résumés and ignore the compatibility of a résumé with the task at hand. In addition, one's social networks and business relationships are critical in terms of successful execution, since entrepreneurs are not institutions and must rely on a broad network rather than their own firms.

Great entrepreneurs are instinctive network builders. Most entrepreneurs treat people well irrespective of their job or status in life, and they help people simply because they can. They do not engage in a "tit for tat," in marked contrast to many corporate managers who do favors only if they believe the favors will be repaid. I urge students to treat the assistants of the executives with whom they want to interact as well as, or better than, how they treat the executives themselves. This advice eludes most students (and most corporate employees). They do not understand that if executive assistants dislike them, the "big boss" will dislike them too, as bosses respect their assistants' opinions. This is not to suggest that entrepreneurs are saints, or that all of them are easy to work with. After all, they are human. But entrepreneurs generally treat people with greater sincerity and respect than most corporate managers, creating a support network to offset their lack of institutional infrastructure.

The fact that entrepreneurial success depends upon execution rather than Big Ideas, leads most academics to under-estimate entrepreneurs. But in fact, in every endeavor in life, virtuosity is defined by execution rather than an idea. Milton Friedman was smart and had many ideas — some of them big — but his stature as an economist derived from his skill in executing his research agenda. Even in the "idea business," execution trumps ideas.

Great athletes adapt to different game conditions, weather conditions, and opponents, finding a way to prevail. The same is true of great entrepreneurs. They make decisions, fully aware that their decisions are flawed. But unlike Hamlet, entrepreneurs realize that the question is not "To be or not to be?" but rather "What's next?" It is entrepreneurs' high tolerance for change that allows them to succeed where others fail. But this tolerance for change can also become their enemy, as they can underestimate the market's resistance to change. This is because the only thing most people hate more than change itself is the person responsible for the change. Thus, to be able to continually adapt and change requires entrepreneurs to have relationships and employees that are compatible with the entrepreneur's pattern of behavior. They must constantly sell and motivate people about the necessity to change, despite natural resistance to change.

The entrepreneur rarely says, "It's okay, because we've always done it this way," but frequently asks, "Why don't we try this?" This characteristic can be risky and has led to the downfall of many entrepreneurs, as they can find it difficult to know when not to change. This becomes more difficult the more one succeeds, as we all tend to believe our headlines. Entrepreneurs are constantly at risk of hubris, believing they can achieve anything to which they set their minds. For this reason, it is essential for entrepreneurs to have advisors who are perceptive, loyal, and brutally honest (though perhaps leavening their advice with honey). The need for such advisors grows the more successful the entrepreneur becomes. The successful entrepreneur must rein in the human tendency to avoid dissent.

WHAT ARE THE RISKS?

Everyone takes a shower in the morning. Most get into a car, drive to work or play, ride in elevators, and sit in their kitchen or dining room to eat. Each of these activities presents the risk of serious bodily injury, and perhaps even death. Yet, most of us go through the day without thinking we took a risk. This underscores the difference between risk, perception of risk, and the management of risk. Many things that are quite risky are not generally perceived as risks, partially because we take steps to mitigate and manage risks (seatbelts, elevator safety features) and partially because the activities are routine. Entrepreneurs see the risks they face in a similar manner.

Entrepreneurs manage risk by specializing in a particular market or product type. Today's world is too complex for anyone to master all geographies and product types. Successful real estate entrepreneurs who cut across geographies and product lines invariably started as a specialist in a single geography or in a single product, slowly growing beyond that niche. Even the prolific developer Trammell Crow spent his early years building everyday warehouses in his hometown of Dallas, branching out only after establishing a competency and track record in this niche.

One of the most difficult things to convey to students is that in order to be successful entrepreneurs, they will have to specialize to develop a knowledge and skill base that allows them to effectively manage risk. This frustrates students, who are worried about being pigeonholed, but in this case, being pigeonholed is simply being knowledgeable. Great real estate entrepreneurs must know every deal in their market. They must know every tenant who is looking for space. They must know the capital sources seeking to do business in their product niche and market. They must know each building in their market, why it works, and its limitations. Although amassing this knowledge base is time-consuming, it is critical, since no one can master multiple markets, particularly early in their career. It is a common and usually fatal mistake of young entrepreneurs to fail to specialize.

Another way entrepreneurs manage risk is to use other people's money, exchanging their sweat equity for a slice of the profit they create for others who do not possess their knowledge and skill base. This underscores the need for an identifiable expertise, as without specialized knowledge, why would anyone entrust the entrepreneur with their money? But entrepreneurs also put their money at risk side-by-side with their investors because they believe in their own vision. One of the quickest ways to distinguish a true entrepreneur from a fake is to determine if they have their money side-by-side with their investors. An entrepreneur's investment may not be as large as that of other people, but real entrepreneurs believe in their vision and want to put their money to work in their deals rather than let it sit in a well-diversified portfolio of stocks and bonds.

While entrepreneurs face many risks, perhaps none is greater than the risk to one's reputation. This is because a reputation is difficult to establish but very easy to lose. It takes a long time to build trust, but trust can be lost in an instant. And reputation is the most valuable asset an entrepreneur possesses, as it yields increasing returns over one's career. I was once asked by a student how to build a great business network and reputation. I responded that if you always do the very best you can to fulfill what you said you would do, help others (simply because you can rather than because you believe it will directly benefit you), and do this for the next thirty years, you will have a great reputation and network. In short, a great reputation takes 25 to 30 years to create.

Young entrepreneurs receive little cash compensation relative to what they could be earning working for a major company. They may even have to be spending out of pocket for payroll and operating expenses. I am constantly asked by recent graduates with high-paying jobs in management consulting or investment banking how they can receive cash compensation equivalent to their current pay but get the upside reward of an entrepreneur. My answer is that they can't. As Ron Terwilliger tells his partners, entrepreneurship is a "get rich slow" exercise. In the beginning, this means a relatively meager lifestyle compared to one's corporate peers. Entrepreneurship is about building a business, not making a quick killing. There simply is not enough money to be made in early entrepreneurial opportunities. Instead, early entrepreneurial opportunities generally help outside investors get rich while establishing the foundation for a long entrepreneurial career. Early entrepreneurial opportunities are best viewed as investments in human capital, building the track record, reputation, and expertise that will generate more profitable opportunities in the future.

Entrepreneurs face significant political, product, and market risk. By knowing everything that is happening in their market and by building relationships with local tenants and information sources, entrepreneurs mitigate their operating risk. Similarly, by becoming an integral part of their community, entrepreneurs develop a network that helps them to understand how important issues and market dynamics affect them and their goals, as well as how to legitimately influence political outcomes. This is particularly important for developers. Entrepreneurs involve themselves in community service, as it provides them with introductions to key players in their community. This is not to suggest that they are not interested in their community but, rather, that in addition to doing good, these networks also help them do well. Again, it is a positive sum relationship.

Great entrepreneurs study competitive products and competitors, both to analyze what these competitors do well and to determine what opportunities they leave in their wake. They must understand the difference between fads and market realities, for while money can be made from fads, long-term success cannot (unless you are Ron Popeil, the legendary inventor of gadgets sold on TV). Great entrepreneurs avoid the pitfalls of fads by concentrating on market fundamentals. Think of Warren Buffett, who during the early 2000s Tech Bubble stayed true to value, investing in non-tech companies even when it was temporarily out of favor.

Entrepreneurs seek the advice of experts, not to generate voluminous reports that can be put in a file in case a lawsuit occurs (as many large corporations do) but, rather, to gain insights. This input filters into their mosaic of life. Developer-entrepreneurs also understand that paper is cheap, but bricks and mortar are expensive. That is, they spend endless hours analyzing the details of the transaction on paper before committing to construction.

Perhaps the ultimate risk-mitigant is the entrepreneur's passion. After all, if they are not excited about what they are doing, why should others be excited? If they are unclear as to why they are doing things, how can they expect others to share their vision? In the end, entrepreneurs manage risk by doing it "for themselves" rather than doing it "for money." While most entrepreneurs desire to make money (and lots of it), money is the derivative of their success. Most entrepreneurs' passion allows them to see that there is plenty of money to go around if they can successfully execute their vision. They seek a win-win exercise for all parties involved. For only by making it a win-win exercise will they have repeated success as an entrepreneur. This is particularly true, as win-lose situations do not enhance reputation as effectively as win-win situations. In an unspoken way, great entrepreneurs understand that they will ultimately spend a great deal of time trying to figure out how to effectively give away their money, so a fixation on making more at the expense of their reputation is not worth the possible short-term gain.

RAISING CAPITAL

Real estate is highly capital-intensive. Development and buying buildings and land require capital well in excess of the entrepreneur's wealth. Hence, successful real estate entrepreneurs must raise outside capital. Raising money is rarely fun, but if the entrepreneur is passionate about the objective, has realistic goals and can explain the vision in a clear manner, money will come. Failure to raise capital generally reflects failure in at least one, if not all, of these categories.

To raise money also requires a reputation commensurate with the task at hand. If an entrepreneur's reputation is "small," so too must be the project. As reputation grows with success, so too will the capital that can be raised. The entrepreneur also must be able to tell his or her story clearly and concisely in two or three simple sentences. What is the opportunity and why have others not pursued it? Why will the entrepreneur be successful in the pursuit of this opportunity? How does the plan compare with what others are already doing?

In my experience, a complicated pitch reflects a lack of understanding of the business opportunity. One of the easiest ways for an entrepreneur to convincingly convey his or her story is to risk a significant amount of his own net wealth in the project, side-by-side with the money of investors. The failure to do so is often —and should be — a death knell for capital raising.

Raising money takes time. While a project may be of utmost importance to the entrepreneur, it is just another capital commitment consideration for the people from whom they are seeking capital. Capital sources will rarely have the same sense of urgency about a project. Therefore, a successful entrepreneur must be respectful of the timeline of capital sources and, yet, be insistent on moving the process along. Sometimes this means that fundraising will have to be concluded at a lower level than initially intended. But "declaring victory" is important when raising capital, as it allows the entrepreneur to establish that he has done something other than spend years trying to raise money.

In many ways, capital raising is less about raising money for the current opportunity than raising it for an opportunity two or three projects down the line, when the entrepreneur's reputation is more established. This is particularly true with respect to institutional capital sources, which are hesitant to invest with young entrepreneurs. Hence, when meeting a potential capital source, even though the entrepreneur is telling the lender about the opportunity at hand, he must realize that the lender's logical answer for this opportunity may be "no." It may take one or more proven successes before the entrepreneur can establish a successful relationship with a lender.

Entrepreneurs must master leverage, which can be either a great friend or a cruel enemy. Generally, entrepreneurs think in terms of financial leverage, with greater debt enhancing their expected returns. But great entrepreneurs understand that nothing ever goes according to plan. As a result, debt that is wonderful on the upside is very unforgiving on the downside. And the entrepreneur's key asset — reputation — is even more dependent on his or her behavior in bad times than in good times. Winning gracefully is easy; losing gracefully takes class.

Great entrepreneurs understand that despite their best efforts, they will experience difficult times, and that the key to success is to survive the inevitable downturns. They must have the relationships and capital or cash flow necessary to make it through the hard times. Hence, the importance of "getting rich slowly," as taking on less debt means the entrepreneur will survive the downturns.

Another type of leverage is managerial leverage: identifying the right people, putting them in positions where they can grow and succeed, motivating them effectively, and facilitating their success. Managerial leverage can be enormously profitable but requires keen judgment and generosity. Great entrepreneurs have staffs who want them to succeed – not because if the entrepreneur succeeds, they will receive better compensation – but because they are on the entrepreneur's side. Great entrepreneurs understand that they need excellent people around them, especially during the hard times. If an entrepreneur is successful in terms of both financial and managerial leverage over a prolonged period, he or she will become a legend.

CLOSING THOUGHT

Being an entrepreneur is not about a bank account, nor is it about prestige or headlines. It is about a life journey of enjoying what one is doing. It is about the opportunity to help people, whether they are customers, employees, partners, or capital providers. It is about developing long-term relationships. It is about retiring not when one can, but when one wants. This is what it means to be an entrepreneur.

So where does all this leave us? Entrepreneurship can be taught, with future entrepreneurs aided by such courses. But entrepreneurs will never be created by books, case studies, and lectures. Yet, entrepreneurship courses serve a vital purpose: to underscore the importance of entrepreneurs to the growth and dynamism of our economy. They are agents of change who challenge existing conventions. Their successes lead to new conventions, producing greater wealth and prosperity for society. Even their failures invigorate the economy by marking the path forward. Courses in entrepreneurship demonstrate that entrepreneurs succeed not by luck (as we all have luck) but, rather, by their focus and determination to capitalize on their luck. Entrepreneurs are not the kings of the system but, rather, they constantly challenge the kings, keeping the established business class ever vigilant. In short, they are the underappreciated drivers of progress, and this should be taught to all members of the business community.

 Online Companion Audio Interview: To hear a conversation about this chapter's content, go to the Online Companion and select the link for Chapter 24. Scroll down to the Audio Interview section and listen.

Chapter 25
Real Estate Cycles

"Don't lose your cool about things you cannot possibly control."
- Dr. Peter Linneman

Real estate cycles are widely misunderstood despite their recurring impacts on real estate markets. The better you understand cycles, the more humble you will become about the accuracy of your beautiful financial models, as these models rarely (if ever) incorporate cycles. Actually, they regularly reflect up cycles but never down cycles.

You have heard discussions of real estate cycles in the media, but like most of the authors of these stories, you probably did not really understand what was being reported. For example, when someone says, "We are at the bottom of the real estate cycle," does it mean real estate is overvalued? Undervalued? While press pieces frequently make such assertions, it is very difficult to know if a property is undervalued. The truth is that when you purchase a property with substantial vacancy in a recessionary market and when capital is scarce, within a few years, you will either be labeled a fool who paid too much by trying to "catch a falling knife," or a visionary who accurately foresaw a booming recovery and the return of cheap capital. You may believe that the property is cheap, but never forget that the Winner's Curse is that no one, including a lot of smart investors, is outbidding you. All that is known with certainty is that buildings take time to build; leases eventually expire; and if things get better fast enough, property values will rise quickly. However, there are considerable lags in the supply and demand responses for space and capital, and being a contrarian investor is both risky and lonely.

WHAT ARE CYCLES?

Real estate cycles are prolonged periods of property supply and demand imbalance. Every product, from pumpkins to office towers, experiences times of supply and demand imbalance, with a long-term tendency to gravitate towards market balance. For some products, this adjustment occurs in a matter of weeks; for others, it requires many years. Real estate imbalances fall into this latter category. In fact, real estate markets are rarely near equilibrium.

It is a week before Halloween, a time when demand for pumpkins is greatest. But for some reason, jack-o-lanterns are a bit out of fashion this year. Consequently, there are too many pumpkins relative to demand. What happens? Faced with an oversupply of soon-to-rot pumpkins, grocers slash their prices, inducing some additional consumers to buy pumpkins. Also, as prices plummet, some pumpkin farmers find alternate uses for their pumpkins, such as selling to pumpkin meal canners. In fact, prices may fall so much that some marginal farmers may not even harvest their pumpkins, leaving them to rot on the vine. If an excess pumpkin supply still exists after Halloween despite major price cuts, any unsold pumpkins will soon rot. As a result, the supply and demand for pumpkins is back in rough equilibrium within a few weeks.

CONTRACTUAL AGREEMENTS AND MARKET FRICTIONS

Contrast the market dynamics for pumpkins with those for real estate. Real estate, unlike pumpkins, takes years to plan, build, and lease. Further, properties do not "rot" in a few weeks if they are unused. Imagine developing a new office building in Emchar Hills, New Jersey, where demand had grown rapidly for 6 years, and supply and demand were roughly in balance when you commenced construction a year ago. But sadly, the economy in Emchar Hills badly weakened shortly after construction began. Thus, instead of surging demand exceeding supply (as you expected), you must lease your property into a market with notable excess supply. As a result, you are experiencing almost no leasing interest (in stark contrast to your financial model's rosy predictions).

What happens? The long-term nature of real estate leases means that faced with weak demand, landlords are hesitant to lease in today's depressed market for (say) a 10-year lease term. In addition, even if you drastically lowered your rents, very few tenants will move to your property in the short run, as most are locked into long-term leases at their current premises. So, you lower rent a little, or offer concessions like tickets to a football game, a dinner at the best restaurant in town, or a couple of months of "free rent." After all, who knows exactly what the next decade will bring? Do you really want to lease all of your space at today's low rents and lose the possibility of better rents for the next decade? Under these market conditions, rents fall slowly, supply begun in good times continues to come onto the market with substantial vacancy, no old buildings "rot," and investors nervously await an uncertain market rebound.

Another important phenomenon is also at work. There is an older, sub-quality building in town that happens to be fully leased for the next 6 years at solid rental rates, because it had the good fortune of being fully re-leased when the market was red hot and quality space was scarce. Interestingly, the rent paid in this lower quality building may be much higher than what you can get today for space in your fabulous new building. Will the owner of this lesser quality property have to lower rents to "market levels" to keep their tenants from moving to your higher quality property? Of course not, as their building is fully leased with 6-year leases. So the worst building remains substantially fully leased at relatively high rents, while the best and newest building languishes with substantial vacancy and poor rents. Strange indeed.

Will this situation last forever? Probably not. Just as the least attractive pumpkins will rot, given enough time, the least efficient property will be eliminated. But this market adjustment can take a very long time, because when leases at the weakest property expire in 6 years, demand may again exceed supply. As a result, the existing tenants will decide to stay where they are for several more years, giving the property a further extension on its economic life. Thus, by sheer luck of timing, inefficient buildings and owners can survive and even thrive beyond expectations, while the newest properties can struggle for frustratingly long periods. As long as the weakest survive, supply remains unchanged, even in the face of weak demand. This means that things move very slowly, and relatively predictably, as only demand growth (which is also inherently slow) will tend to close the supply-demand gap.

DEMAND ADJUSTMENTS

Let's explore demand adjustments on a "national" level in the U.S. "National" is in quotes, because there is no "national" real estate market in the U.S. or elsewhere. Nonetheless, focusing on the national dynamics allows us to easily examine the market adjustment process.

The U.S. population is roughly 330 million and had historically grown by about 1% a year, but over the last decade, had averaged just 0.6% per year. Roughly one-third of U.S. population growth is driven by immigration, while two-thirds is from births in excess of deaths. Not everyone in the U.S. has a job, as some people are retired, others are in prison, and many are too young to work. Consequently, there are about 148 million jobs in the U.S.

A 0.6% growth rate on a population of 330 million means about 2.0 million new people each year. In turn, due to the age structure of the population, this population growth translates to roughly 1.8 million new jobs each year, as these "new" people work to feed, house, and clothe themselves and their families.

Will the U.S. add 1.7 million new jobs every year? Of course not. Some years it may add only 800,000. In another year, it will add 2.4 million. Occasionally it will even lose jobs, as when it lost 8.7 million jobs from September 2008 through December 2009. But roughly 1.8 million is the sustainable job growth rate given an annual population growth of roughly 2.0 million people. Thus, if 6 million jobs are added over a two-year period, while the economy added 5 million people, it is great fun, but not sustainable.

In 2000, U.S. office space supply roughly equaled demand for the first time in almost two decades (Figure 25.1). In addition, the demand for office space was growing rapidly due to economic growth fed by the last gasps of the tech bubble. Of course, supply equaling demand did not mean there was zero vacancy, as at zero vacancy, supply is too low relative to demand. In 2000, the U.S. office vacancy rate was about 6%, and roughly 6 million jobs had been added during the preceding two years. It was the "dotcom era," when nonsense was accepted as sensible. Developers justified developments with elaborate financial models that were driven by overly optimistic assumptions of soaring job growth. They believed such demand would quickly fill their new buildings, and some even accepted what would end up being worthless stock options in place of cash for rent.

FIGURE 25.1

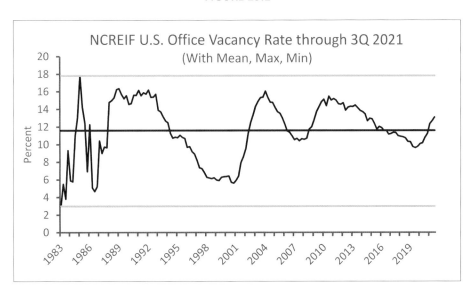

Suppose that in 2000, you were the developer of a 200,000-leasable square foot building. How many jobs do you need to fill a typical 200,000 square foot building? Think back to your last office cubicle. It may have been small, perhaps 9 feet by 9 feet (81 square feet). But there was also common space for boardrooms, bathrooms, hallways, copy rooms, servers, elevators, stairs, etc. In addition, your bosses had much larger offices. Taking all this space into account, a typical U.S. office employee requires approximately 200-250 square feet. This space usage is contingent upon the nation, culture, building design, and region, with offices in New York City being smaller than offices in Ashland, Ohio. Despite all the variables, a good rule-of-thumb is that a building with 200,000 leasable square feet requires roughly 1,000 workers to fill it (200 leasable square feet per worker).

With the economy adding 3 million jobs per year, you felt comfortable that you could easily find the 1,000 jobs you need to fill your new building. These may be either new workers, or employees transferring from other buildings as leases expired. But can 3 million jobs per year be added to the U.S. economy forever? Of course not. If you look at the total amount of office square footage completed in 2001-2003, it would have taken about 3.5 million new jobs in each of those three years to fill that space under development. But remember that the U.S. only averages about 1.8 million new jobs a year. This was a clear case of excessive development in the absence of a recession (but the absence of a recession does not mean job growth will be double the average).

You may have even correctly concluded that this pace of job growth was unsustainable, but thought, "Hey, I only need 1,000 jobs. That's a drop in the bucket, even in bad times." The problem occurs when you have 4,000 similar developers scattered across the country thinking the same thing, in which case, new supply quickly results in overbuilding.

So what happened in 2001-2003? Instead of 10-11 million new jobs being created, in line with development expectations, the U.S. lost about 2 million jobs after the dotcom bubble burst. This was roughly a 13 million-job shortfall versus expectations, or about 10% of total U.S. employment. As a result, the office market quickly went from about an 8% vacancy rate, to roughly 18% (revisit Figure 25.1). That was roughly the original vacancy rate plus the new supply excess as a proportion of total jobs. Note that the expected new jobs that were not created were far more numerous than the jobs that were lost during the recession.

Unfortunately, this excess supply does not disappear like pumpkins after Halloween. Thus, to get back to balance, the U.S. needed to add roughly 13 million jobs and halt new construction. This meant that even if construction completely halted (which it never does), it would take roughly 7 years of normal job growth to restore supply-demand balance. Of course, this excess supply was not evenly spread across markets, with tech havens such as Silicon Valley hit the hardest. Nonetheless, high office vacancy was prevalent in varying degrees throughout the nation until 2007.

By mid-2007, vacancy rates had fallen after 5 years of strong demand growth and little new supply. So what happened? First, supply pipelines grew by about 3% of the existing stock. At the same time, the U.S.'s economic Great Recession wiped out more than 6% of all U.S. jobs. This collapse in demand plus the supply expansion quickly added about 1,000 basis points (10 percentage points) to the U.S. office vacancy rate. Once again, new supply ceased, but it took several years of economic growth to restore balance. Meanwhile, property owners and lenders struggled, and in retrospect, the original financial models are laughable.

What happened to all of that vacant office space? Eventually, it was absorbed, destroyed, or re-used as residential or institutional space. In the meantime, the "cycle" of rental decline and recovery corresponds to job growth trends, often with a lag. Real estate cycles do not have to happen, but once underway, they play out slowly due to the gradual nature of demand growth, long-term leases, and the fixity (permanence) of supply.

To better understand cycles, it is necessary to constantly gather information, and monitor trends. Publications such as *The Linneman Letter* provide such information for a variety of local markets and property types. Vacancy rates indicate whether markets are improving (falling vacancy) or weakening (rising vacancy). Useful statistics are **gross absorption** (the total amount of square footage tenants newly occupy over a given period of time) and **net absorption**, which measures the difference between the total newly-occupied square footage and the total square footage vacated over the same period (i.e., how much vacant supply was leased). *The Linneman Letter* and similar research publications forecast market supply and demand by assessing local economic growth and the new supply pipeline. This information helps you better understand your market and raises your awareness of the challenges "behind the numbers" in your pro forma. It is also important to remember that there will always be good investment opportunities, even in bad markets, while bad deals abound in great markets.

STRUCTURAL OFFICE DEMAND HEADWINDS?

Over the years, some have purported that there are clear drivers for a systemic and sustained reduction in the future need for office space. These drivers relate to the consistent advent of technology as a contributor to worker productivity, the increasing use of **open plan** floor layouts, and more recently, pandemic-driven working from home. Technology has indeed infiltrated the workplace relentlessly over the last three decades, as well as enabled home office connectivity, but the prediction that technology's benefits towards worker productivity in and out of the office would slash office space demand has been proven wrong. While there has been a downward trend in the occupied office space per office worker in the U.S. over the last 30 years, other factors have countered that trend. Specifically, the ongoing shift in the U.S. workforce from manufacturing to the service sector, coupled with overall job growth, has overwhelmed the impact of per-worker space allocation reductions on a net basis.

It is important to note that there is a natural "floor" to per-worker square footage allocation, as firms are competing for the best talent, and one of the ways to entice talent and keep employees happy is with an attractive working environment that also has visual privacy and sound separation from others. Additionally, the economics clearly support providing more space to attract and retain top high-producing office workers. For instance, if additional office space costs a firm $50 a year per square foot after taxes, and the incremental amount of space under consideration for attracting another star profit center worker is 200 square feet, as long as that worker generates more than $10,000 in incremental after-tax profit a year, the increased space consumption makes economic sense. A star employee is likely to generate 5 to 15 times the breakeven amount.

The Covid-19 pandemic that began in 2020 reduced global office space utilization dramatically, as many companies and institutions implemented work-from-home policies. As the global service economy adapted rapidly (and mostly successfully) to interacting primarily over Zoom and Microsoft Teams, the press at large and some real estate business insiders started to debate whether traditional office space had much of a future post-pandemic. As Covid-19 cases dropped, numerous back-to-office pronouncements were made by Google, Morgan Stanley, and other major companies, only to walked back when new variants emerged. At year-end 2021, nearly two years into the pandemic, the share of people in the office varies by city, but most are averaging 25-35% of pre-pandemic levels, according to the Robin Return to Office Report.

While productivity in many cases can be maintained or even improved by working from home, there are several downsides to not physically being in the office. The first is that communication can be more laborious and challenging when physically remote, and that online collaboration software does not work flawlessly, as many of you have likely experienced personally. High-level problem-solving sessions, in particular, are generally most productive when collaborators meet face to face. While there was no competitive disadvantage to working remotely when most others were doing the same, there will be a huge competitive disadvantage associated with hiring, integrating, doing deals, pitching (and retaining) customers, etc. for those who continue to be remote. Furthermore, office politics will resume, and people will want to be there to protect and advance their interests. Perhaps most compelling is the fact that workers' families want them anywhere except home!

There are many reasons why people will go back to the office, the most fundamental of which is that we are social beings. In addition, as an increasing number of workers return to the office, others will feel competitive pressure to follow. Just as education in classrooms is superior to virtual education, productivity is much higher at the office than at home for the vast majority of employees. Those who are highly disciplined and self-motivated can efficiently work from home, but most are unable to do so due to poor home office conditions (e.g., slow internet, barking pets, clinging kids, etc.) or a lack of discipline. These workers lose 20-30% of their productivity when they work from home. Two-income households found the partners booking "conference room" time in their own homes to avoid overlapping Zooms. And while all of us would like to think we are highly self-disciplined, the fact is that not everyone can maintain the same level of focus and industriousness at home as they can at the office. Additionally, while initially the work from home phenomenon gave many a newfound appreciation for their household members, this in person "honeymoon" ran its course for most, with many concluding that when they made their marital vows "for better or for worse," they did not agree to "for better or for worse, and all day every day."

PERMITS AND REGULATIONS

While smart developers attempt to match new supply to forecasted space demand, their efforts encounter substantial friction. A major source of friction is the time it takes to develop a building, as construction, planning, and obtaining financing are not instantaneous. As a result, new properties continue to come on-line even after markets plummet, as they were started a year or two earlier when the market looked great. If supply could easily match demand in the real estate market, they would move together and vacancy would be constant, as seen in the two contemporaneous graphs in Figure 25.2.

FIGURE 25.2

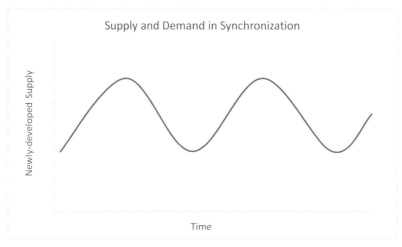

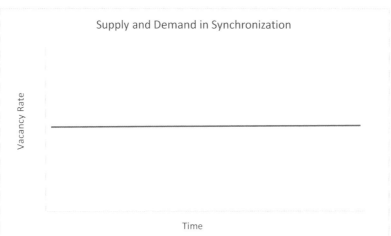

However, due to production and information lags, mismatches in the timing of supply and demand occur, with supply soaring even as demand plummets. Such supply and demand imbalances are reflected in the vacancy rate, as displayed in the two contemporaneous graphs in Figure 25.3.

FIGURE 25.3

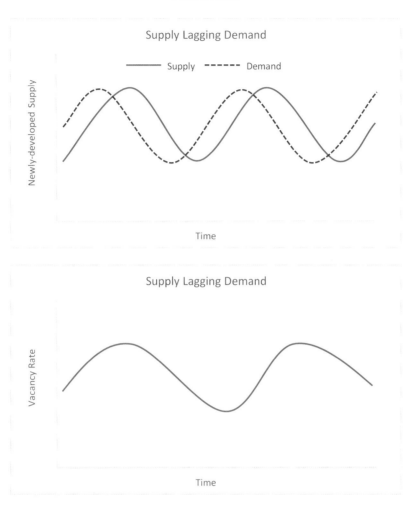

Another major source of market friction is the development regulatory process. Developers must receive many permits, certificates, and approvals before construction can commence. Even a highly skilled developer becomes entangled in a web of conflicting and changing regulations. How does this affect cycles? Imagine you have spent 6 months getting your financing in place, after a year was spent obtaining the necessary permits and approvals, and you are now ready to start construction. Your equity has already been invested, primarily in the land acquisition and approval process. Two years earlier, when you embarked on the project, the supply and demand picture looked great, and your development pro forma appeared conservative. At that time, you believed several major local tenants were going to expand and seek space in your building. Just before you commence construction, you discovered that several other developers share your vision and are starting 5 similar properties. Some of these competitors started their planning process at nearly the same time as you, while others started later (or earlier), but took less (or more) time to clear regulatory hurdles. You know that if the local economy cools, it cannot support all of the planned developments. Should you stop? Will any of the other developers stop? Often the answer is no, as some of this space is already pre-leased. In other cases, the leases are "almost signed." In most instances, the remaining money for construction comes completely from lenders who have already legally committed their money. If this is the case, developers will generally build despite the looming excess supply, as their only hope to recover their equity is to spend the lender's money to complete the property and hope for the best. The resulting market dynamics are as shown in the two contemporaneous graphs in Figure 25.4.

FIGURE 25.4

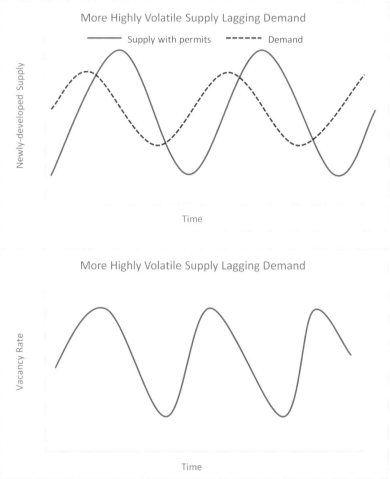

Regulations make the development process longer, more cumbersome, and riskier, meaning that the volatility of supply will generally exceed that of demand. Hence, it will take a long time to absorb the supply mistakes, leading to longer periods of market imbalance.

Another source of friction is complex building designs. For example, it is quicker to build the typical single-family home than a complicated mixed-use property. Regional malls, for which the average planning and building time is several years, compensate for this complexity by rarely developing speculatively, requiring roughly 80% pre-leasing before beginning construction. However, even pre-leasing can backfire, as many of these tenants may go bankrupt prior to the project's completion.

CAPITAL CYCLE

A fundamental truth is that if a developer gets money, they will build; a corollary is that if debt is cheap and plentiful, real estate owners will overpay and overleverage. These two truths underscore the inextricable linkage between the states of the economy, capital markets, and the boom and bust of property prices.

Developers often cry that "there is no money." That is generally untrue, although there is often a shortage of funds willing to back a **speculative** (non-pre-leased or non-pre-sold) development in a weak or recovering market. Most smart money has gone to the same schools (both academic and "of hard knocks") as you and understands the business. They see what is occurring in the market and have their own views on whether the market will recover in 3 or 5 years. Generally, smart players agree on the "big picture" that the market will recover. The devil is generally in the detail of determining when recovery will actually occur – plus or minus a year or two.

Having substantial equity is a tremendous advantage, especially during down cycles, as equity allows you both to survive the bad times and the luxury of your upside convictions being wrong by a year or so. Having capital when lenders and institutional equity are conservative allows you to fund your developments and acquisitions, even during down cycles. Of course, if you are correct (or lucky), and an earlier than expected demand recovery occurs, your space will benefit from a rapidly tightening market. If you are wrong, you will realize sub-standard returns (at least temporarily).

If there is too much money chasing too few opportunities, investors will ultimately be disappointed. Borrowers are always lured by cheap and plentiful debt, but generally the beneficiaries of such debt markets are land and property sellers who exit into the teeth of a bidding frenzy fueled by cheap debt. Conversely, too little money may be a sign of short-term illiquidity and an opportunity to purchase at bargain prices. For this reason, it is important to track the supply of real estate capital.

The Linneman Real Estate Index (LREI, published quarterly in *The Linneman Letter*) measures capital market balance by calibrating commercial real estate debt relative to the ultimate driver of space demand, economic activity (proxied by GDP). The index rises when outstanding mortgage debt rises more rapidly than the economy grows ("easy money") and declines when money is tight relative to economic growth. It proxies the availability of capital to a capital-intensive asset class. The LREI is near 100 when supply and demand conditions for real estate capital are in rough balance (e.g., 1982 and 1999). As the index rises notably above 100, it indicates an excess supply of real estate capital. For example, an index value of 110 means that there is roughly 10% too much capital relative to underlying real estate demand.

In Figure 25.5, we overlay the office vacancy series from Figure 25.1 with the LREI and see that the LREI rapidly rose from 1982 through 1988, with the expansion of real estate capital outstripping demand growth by more than 40%. Not surprisingly, given this flood of capital, vacancy rates soared, as this excess capital was largely transformed into bricks and mortar. However, the index began to decline in 1989, as lending ceased, and the economy gradually grew into the capital stock. By 1994, the index indicated a moderately undersupplied real estate capital market, which lasted through 1999. Not surprisingly, this was one of the best periods ever for purchasing real estate, as capital availability was about 10% less than what was justified by demand. Even though vacancy rates fell through early 2001, capital availability had outpaced demand by about 10% by early 2001, with most of this excess capital being used to fund new developments for tech bubble tenants. By year-end 2001, there was a nearly 20% oversupply of real estate capital relative to underlying demand, and this rose to about 45% as debt securitization created a massive excess from 2005-2007. The LREI peaked at 170 in 2009 and bottomed at 134 in 2014 (a 21% decline) as the Financial Crisis drove substantial deleveraging of commercial real estate. Because banks resumed lending, the index subsequently rose to 155 through the first quarter of 2020. Then due to the extreme contraction in GDP during the pandemic shutdown, the LREI shot up to 174 in the second quarter of 2020. It dropped to 156 in the third quarter of 2021 as restrictions were loosened and GDP grew.

The Fed pumped trillions into the banking system through **quantitative easing** ("QE injections") in response to both the Financial Crisis and the pandemic and allowed banks to reduce Tier 1 capital levels. Unlimited bank reserves meant that banks absorbed problem loans as regulators encouraged unprecedented bank forbearance. This has prevented cascading foreclosed loans from depressing asset values. But while banks, life insurance companies, Freddie Mac, and Fannie Mae have largely given forbearance, securitized debt experienced greater distress.

FIGURE 25.5

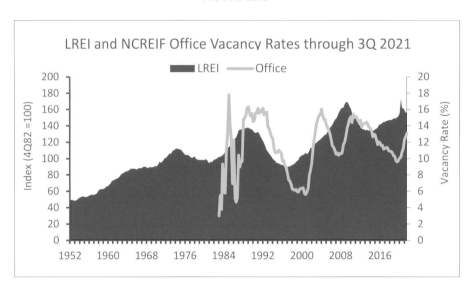

WHAT LED TO THE 2008-2009 FINANCIAL CRISIS?

As I wrote in the Spring 2008 issue of *The Linneman Letter*, the origins of what we retrospectively call the 2008-2009 Financial Crisis are tied to three main phenomena that arise at least once a decade. The first is the triumphing of fear over greed. Both fear and greed are fundamental to human nature, and they are constantly warring inside the world's capital markets. In the 20 years prior to 2007, fear defeated greed four times: the 1987 stock market crash, the S&L collapse in 1990, the Russian ruble crisis of 1998, and the terrorist attacks of 9/11. The three most recent triumphs of fear are reflected in the labeled peaks shown in Figure 25.6, when there was a flight to safety (government bonds) driving Treasury yields down and credit spreads up. Figure 25.6 shows the junk bond spread over the 10-year Treasury and the REIT Dividend.

FIGURE 25.6

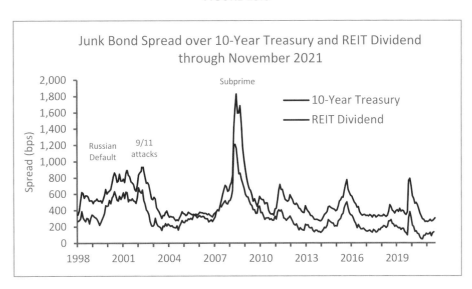

By 2007, investors came to the realization that if lenders were willing to lend at high LTVs and with razor-thin interest rate spreads and limited credit checks, greed had gone too far. If these low-credit borrowers could get mortgages (many on speculative homes), it meant that all good lending options had been exhausted. Fear soared as people realized how low underwriting standards had fallen and how the credit ratings agencies fell prey to their own greed by giving high ratings to massive pools of risky residential mortgages. The corresponding spike in the junk bond spreads in Figure 25.6 are breathtaking.

The Financial Crisis was triggered by defaults on these **subprime** residential mortgages, whose mortgage market share nearly quadrupled from 2001-2006 (Figure 25.7).

FIGURE 25.7: SUBPRIME MORTGAGE VOLUME

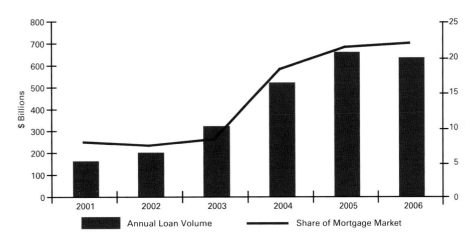

Source: Bloomberg, Mortgage Bankers Association

Subprime home loans traditionally allowed borrowers such as a small lawn care business sole proprietor or a service worker (e.g., a waitress, golf caddy, or charter boat captain) to qualify for a home loan even though their underreported cash income put them "out of formula" for traditional income-to-debt mortgage ratios. Such borrowers do not qualify for conventional loans for a property commensurate to their income, as they often have large amounts of unreported cash income and generally lower credit scores. In addition, subprime loan applications are relatively light on income, asset, and liability documentation requirements versus those for conventional loans (subprime loans are often marketed as "stated income" loans). To compensate for the extra risk, lenders charge a higher rate on subprime loans (100 to 250 basis points).

But subprime mortgages, per se, were not the issue. It was the massive growth in subprime borrowing from 2002-2006 by **speculative homebuyers** that set the table for the collapse. Figure 25.8 shows the share of subprime borrowing by credit score band. Note the decreasing slope of the dark blue series (scores of 540 and below, the lowest-score category tracked) from 2002-2006 in particular which was the result of more subprime loans going instead to higher credit borrowers.

FIGURE 25.8: SUBPRIME BORROWER CREDIT SCORES

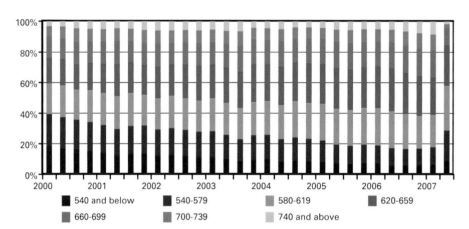

During these years of rapid property value growth and abundant mortgage capital, perhaps a million homes were bought by speculators with the hope of flipping the properties to the other buyers within a few months, making a fat profit by riding the wave of rising home prices. Mortgage lenders competed aggressively to deploy capital to this growing borrower base, offering 95% LTVs with low- and no-documentation requirements. Some 30% of these loans had low "teaser" rates that would reset after a designated period. To accommodate the demand, loan officers often misstated in their underwriting that the loans would be for the borrowers' primary residences instead of investment properties. This enabled loan officers to underwrite the mortgages with higher LTVs than what is allowable for investment properties.

Both fraudulent borrowers and lenders sought enormous profits. Big bonuses were paid to loan officers, and they replicated their successes through multiple rounds by having the investment banks repackage the subprime loans into **residential mortgage-backed securities (RMBS)**. These securities were highly rated on the justification that the pools were geographically diversified across the U.S., and thus uncorrelated. They were then marketed as high-grade packages sold to institutional investors around the world. The sale of the mortgage securities provided lenders a fresh batch of capital with which they could repeat the execution of their formula.

The large global investor appetite for these RMBS issuances was a symptom of the second phenomenon tied to the origins of the Financial Crisis – namely, there was more money than brains at work. The world economy had never grown as rapidly as it did in 2002-2007 (Figure 25.9), but the investment infrastructure lagged the expansion of investable wealth. When this happens, investors typically rely on ratings agencies and on "who else is investing" rather than conducting their own due diligence to determine investment risk. Institutional investors needed higher-yielding vehicles than the artificially low U.S. government bond rates, and Wall Street was more than happy to assist.

FIGURE 25.9

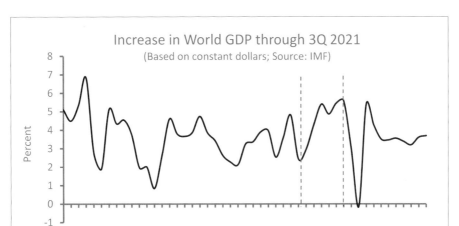

When housing price growth reached the point where the market saw properties were overvalued, and as the big block of adjustable-rate mortgages began to reset, the party was over. Unsurprisingly, speculators stopped making payments on their fraudulent "primary residence" investment properties. As defaults rose, the extent of poor underwriting became clear, and investors became fearful about what else had potentially been oversold and overrated. As fear quickly replaced greed, institutional investors effectively went on strike and stopped buying "risk assets" and parked their money in government securities instead, driving credit spreads up (Figure 25.10).

FIGURE 25.10: MONTHLY SPREADS OVER TREASURY IN THE CMBS MARKET

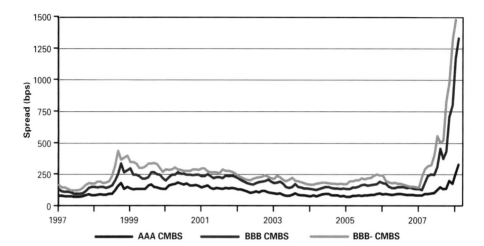

As credit spreads rose, institutional investors were subject to **margin calls**. A margin call is the immediate requirement for a securities holder to produce a significant amount of cash to offset the loss of value in accounts in which they purchased securities using borrowed funds. These margin calls further shook the markets.

Margin calls are related to the third phenomenon tied to the origins of the Financial Crisis, which is that most assets, such as cash streams on buildings, the returns to homeownership, and corporate profits, are long-term in nature, but most liabilities, such as bank deposits, are of much shorter duration. This fundamental asset-liability mismatch in the financial system means that mismatched investors run the risk of not only having their debt be subject to margin calls, but also that they will be unable to refinance existing debt positions upon their maturity. As long as greed is winning, this mismatch is not a systemic problem since values generally increase when greed prevails, allowing comfortable refinancing and few margin calls. However, when fear defeats greed, asset values drop and investors with mark-to-market debt must sell assets to pay it down. As investors sell, they further force asset prices down, causing a ripple effect, as happened through 2009 in the U.S. and internationally. The U.S. capital markets suffered an erosion of credibility, and the dollar fell in value as securitization, ratings, underwriters, hedge funds, collateral, and liquidity were shown to be incomplete, incompetent, conflicted, and occasionally corrupt.

Greed is part of the human condition. As expected, the markets recovered over time as smart, highly liquid investors started to say "at these prices these assets are a steal," and off we went again to a new cycle of fear shifting to greed.

CLOSING THOUGHT

Market conditions are easier to analyze on a national basis, because at a local market level, you have the vagaries of what specific areas are hot. For example, if Lex Wexner had started The Limited in Akron (rather than Columbus, Ohio), and if Bill Gates and Jeff Bezos had founded Microsoft and Amazon in Cleveland (rather than Seattle), the real estate markets of Akron, Cleveland, Columbus, and Seattle would all be very different, but the U.S. economy would be roughly the same. Similarly, the chemical industry may be in the dumps, but if your market is primarily driven by telecom demand, you may not be greatly affected. Thus, it is easier to predict demand nationally than locally, as you know that a Comcast headquarters is going to be somewhere, but it is much more difficult to accurately predict if it will locate in Philadelphia, for example; and if so, it is even more difficult to accurately forecast which submarket and building they will select.

The best market analysts are humble in the face of cycles. Remember that people rarely model a down cycle in their 10-year pro-formas, but they will almost certainly experience a cycle over this time period. Surviving these down cycles will result in a long and prosperous career in real estate. Remember that equity cushions are the ultimate key to this survival.

 Online Companion Audio Interview: To hear a conversation about this chapter's content, go to the Online Companion and select the link for Chapter 25. Scroll down to the Audio Interview section and listen.

Chapter 26
There Are a Lot of Right Ways to Do It

"Do the right thing simply because it is the right thing to do."
- Dr. Peter Linneman

ETHICS IN REAL ESTATE?

Yes, there are ethics in real estate. In fact, you are well advised to behave ethically if you want to have a long and successful career. At the end of the day, "the deal" is always secondary to people and relationships. More money has been lost on "great deals" done with the wrong people, than doing the wrong deal with great people. This is particularly true in real estate, where you have relatively predictable cash streams and a smaller opportunity to create value. Therefore, if you cheat investors, constantly tie them up in knots, or make it difficult to operate, you will have a troubled track record.

Your reputation is all you have in business. As a young person, your problem is that you have no reputation. You may believe that you do because of the way you have lived your life, but people in the industry have not been with you and rarely can call anyone they know and respect to verify your reputation. For example, they will not call your buddies, parents, or high school teacher because they do not know them. Potential business partners may call one of your professors, but since they generally do not know your professors very well, they will take their recommendation with a grain of salt. And in most cases, your professor does not know you very well. The true challenge you face early in your career is not how to do deals and make a lot of money but, rather, how to build a reputation as someone with whom people want to do business.

A lot of young people ask me: "How do I get a contact base like yours?" or "Why do people ask you for help?" or "Why do people respect your opinions?" Trust me, I did not begin my career with great (or any) contacts, nor did people ask me for help, or request to hear my opinions. A successful network is created very slowly. You do it by doing the right things for people, even if there is nothing in it for you. This includes helping their son or daughter, or giving free advice gladly, or introducing them to someone with a common business or social interest, all performed without any expectation of reward. It is about under-promising and over-delivering. These are the foundations of a reputation.

A reputation is not a con; you cannot fake it over the long run. You must want to be the person whose reputation you create, and not just perform "good acts" when it is convenient.

As you begin your career, your goal should be that in 15-20 years, people will trust you and put their faith (which you will discover is more important than money) in you. The problem with reputation is that it is very slow and difficult to build but can be lost unbelievably fast. This is particularly true in the modern world of viral social media, which is based on emotion rather than research and facts. You could do the right thing for 20-30 years, building trust and loyalty, and then do one thing that people view as wrong, and in a matter of hours, uninformed tweets can seriously tarnish your reputation. Guard your reputation more carefully than you guard your money, because if you retain your reputation, you can always regain your money.

In my experience, investors and partners are much more forgiving if you lose their money than if you treat them badly. This is because people understand that even the smartest investors sometimes lose money. While they do not like it, they accept it. But if they feel you mistreated them, lied to them, misinformed them, or took advantage of them, they are unforgiving, even if you make money for them. Ethics in real estate is not just about doing what is legal; that goes without being said. It is about doing what is right.

RIGHT AND WRONG

Everyone must develop their own sense of right and wrong with respect to business. Obviously, there is the golden rule of "Do unto others as you would have them do unto you," but each of you has a different perspective as to what you want done to you. You must find your way, make your decisions, and attempt to behave consistently. No one expects you to be nominated for sainthood at the end of your career. But at the end of your career, you hope people do not say, "This person cheated me" or "This person mistreated me." You would like to believe that the worst somebody will say at the end of your career is "very tough, but always fair."

If you never have an ethical dilemma during your career, you are probably being unnecessarily conservative. You are in the business to make money, and making money legitimately and fairly means you are going to encounter conflicts. The point is not to avoid all conflicts, as that is not fair to your investors, lenders, or employees. Alternatively, if you have an ethical dilemma every hour, sooner or later you are going to cross the line. So if you are always having ethical problems, back off a little; and if you are never having them, push harder. Research shows that some of you have a hard time identifying ethical challenges. Therefore, you will be well-served to have a couple of people in your life that you respect and with whom you regularly consult to see things you may miss.

Hopefully, you are not thinking, "Someday, I plan to cheat people." If, as a student, you are planning to con the world, you will have a very difficult career, and nothing you read here is likely to change your mind. It is the same as if when walking down the aisle to get married, you are planning a midnight rendezvous with a member of the wedding party.

Whatever guidelines or anecdotes one provides, most of you believe such situations will never happen to you. But unfortunately ethical issues sneak up on you. What is the best way to deal with these problems? Be alert as to how and why they arise and watch how people you respect resolve them. Preparation is your best defense.

BRIBES

What about corruption? Is there corruption in U.S. real estate? Ever been to New Orleans? Bribes may get things done, but jail time and the loss of reputation are heavy prices to pay. Even if you are doing business abroad, you are prohibited by U.S. law from engaging in bribery and the willful ignorance of your partner performing corrupt acts.

Most corruption occurs when you need a permit or approval, as the regulator has the power to halt or delay profitable business activities. Thus, development is much more susceptible to a corrupt environment than is operating a building, as many approvals are required to complete a development. Under U.S. law, you can pay **accommodation fees** but are not allowed to pay bribes. The question is, where is the line? If you take a local politician to a basketball game, it is generally viewed as an accommodation, but if you give him a brown paper bag filled with $10 million in cash in an alley, it is a bribe! There is a lot of ground in between, and this is where tough calls arise.

In some ways, investing abroad is similar to what many of you faced as college freshmen. As high school seniors you knew how to survive the system, with its many explicit and implicit rules. But as a freshman in college, you had a hard time adjusting because you did not know what acceptable behavior was. This "freshman feeling" is a taste of what you will feel entering an international market. You do not know exactly who to befriend; who to avoid; what is legal; or what is acceptable. To lessen the cost of transition, many businesses form partnerships with locals, but be very careful about whom you choose as your partner.

BUT EVERYBODY IS DOING IT!

The following is a true story, although I have changed the names, numbers, and places to protect the innocent. I was assisting a prominent U.S. investment group, who owned the best building in the developing country of Feli. The good news was that they owned the best building in Feli; the bad news was they owned the best building in Feli, as Feli is a very rough place. Rents in Feli were about $50 net per square foot, and the newly completed building was about 15% leased when the economy of Feli absolutely collapsed. If you had space for rent in Feli, you were in trouble, because no one was renting.

Their local partner said they could rent a large block of space for about $40 a foot to a high credit tenant. The problem was that Feli had a value-added tax which applied to rent. This tax amounted to about $14 per square foot, resulting in a net rent of $26 per square foot. While this was lower than the pro forma net rent of $50, it was better than nothing. As we debated whether to wait and see if rents picked up or to take the $26 per square foot for 5 years, the local partner suggested that instead of calling the $40 per square foot payment "rent," we should structure it as $1 per square foot rental payment and a $39 per square foot payment for "consulting services," as consulting was exempt from the value-added tax. Structured in this manner, the net rent was just under $40 per square foot. Needless to say, our local partner swore that this was common practice.

Would you accept this structuring proposal? While this may (or may not) be tax fraud for which you risk becoming a long-term "guest of the state," the other risks associated with this transaction far outweighed the benefits. The biggest risk? Damage to our reputation!

How long did it take us to decide? Two minutes. This was not a holier than thou decision. If we used this structure, a number of people would "have us." At the very least, the tenant and our partner would know about this transaction, as would the lawyers and local brokers. Any one of these people could hold this over our heads. The reward simply did not justify the risk, as we had all worked too long building reputations to lose it like this.

PERVERSE INCENTIVES

A classic example of an ethical dilemma in the real estate industry is when you are selling a fully leased property, while having extensive conversations with two major tenants about developing a new property for them. While you do not have pre-leases, you are pretty sure that these tenants will move to your planned building when their leases expire in two years. Should you reveal this information to the buyer? If you do, the deal may fall through, or you may receive a substantially lower price. Obviously, if the prospective buyer asks you, "Are you in discussions about tenants moving to a new property?" and you lie, that is fraud. The question is whether you should volunteer this information. Should you say, "Here is a building for sale, but I am pretty sure that two of the key tenants will soon re-locate to a new building I am developing," when you do not really know for sure what they will decide? What damage are you doing to your reputation if the tenants leave for your new project after sale? The buyer will be upset, and people in business discuss relationships, especially when they are angry. These discussions are not necessarily "bad-mouthing" but, rather, a way for people who do not know a potential partner to find out the type of person with whom they will be working. If people discuss you in a negative context too often, you get the reputation as a person with whom no one wants to do business and will find your opportunity set shrinking.

There are people, who if things do not go according to plan, will sue as a part of their business strategy. They figure that they do this all the time and are used to it, while you may be intimidated by a lawsuit. They view it as just another business tool. They are like guys, who in pick-up basketball games, call a foul every time they miss a shot regardless of a foul being committed. Is this the way you want to conduct your business? You have to decide if what you extract from constant lawsuits against your partners, lenders, employees, and investors is worth the damage to your reputation. Will it destroy your reputation? Probably not. Will it affect your reputation? Absolutely.

FAVORITISM

Should you favor the people with whom you do business? Do you turn a smiling eye to an executive that gives you a consulting contract? Do you give favorable treatment to somebody who is paying you? Do you help somebody who is paying you, such as a tenant or investor, get their child into college? You can look at things like this in a lot of ways. You can say, "I will not be a part of that," but then people will view you as unhelpful. On the other hand, you can say that the university has to accept someone, and this applicant is as good as anyone else, and if you can be a tie-breaker and help someone you know, so be it. You will have to frequently sort through these types of issues during your career.

DO NOT EXPECT THANKS

There was an instance when I was doing work for one the world's largest corporations. I had done a pretty good job and billed them for my services. Shortly after sending the bill, I received a check for the exact amount of my invoice. I was paid, they were happy with my work, and everything was wonderful. The next day I received a second check for the exact amount as I had received the previous day. For a minute, I thought, "Gee, maybe I had actually done some other work and it was owed to me," and maybe "They were so happy with my work they decided to double my pay as a bonus!" However, the second check was clearly an error. Given the size of the corporation, they probably would never realize that they had made a mistake. It was a trivial amount for them but a significant amount for me.

What should I do? Taking the check was not only wrong but might be theft, though I could simply record it as a credit against any future billings. So, I sent them a letter stating that they overpaid me and returned the second check. After sending this check I felt I was the world's most noble person, and that they would be so grateful they would send me a bonus. However, I never heard a word about the check, as no one wanted to admit it was their fault. How do you think it looks for them to tell their boss, "We double-paid Peter Linneman, but he is such a swell and honest guy that he gave it back"? The boss would question their competence and double-check all their work in search of similar mistakes. While I believe I would have done the same thing had there been three more zeros at the end of the check, I fortunately did not have to face that situation.

CONFLICT OF INTEREST

You are working on a deal and suddenly find yourself on both sides of the deal. This can happen whether you are an advisor, lender, or bidder. For example, you may be on the board of a lender, but at the same time, are working with a firm that is going to that bank for a loan. If you are an active businessperson, you will frequently encounter conflict of interest situations. No one is upset when you have a conflict of interest. The question is how you deal with it. A word to the wise is to avoid situations where continual conflicts could regularly arise. For example, you should know before you agree to advise two major New York City office property owners, that there is a high chance that these companies will someday bid on the same asset.

When a conflict situation arises, declare it early, often, and clearly. Ask yourself, "What are the conflicts? How did they arise? What business do you do with the parties?" Make certain that both parties understand the situation fully and are clearly supportive of your continued involvement. If not, either pick a side or bow out altogether. Your reputation in dealing with such situations will affect how people deal with you when the tables are turned.

CLOSING THOUGHT

The goal is not to be a saint but, rather, a legitimate, respected professional. People will slowly come to understand what it means to deal with you, and they hopefully will enjoy the experience. Reputation is a rare asset that can generate great profits over the course of your career. Stay focused on your guiding principles, and carefully choose the people with whom you deal. When in doubt, it does not hurt to ask if your mother would be proud of your behavior.

 Online Companion Audio Interview: To hear a conversation about this chapter's content, go to the Online Companion and select the link for Chapter 26. Scroll down to the Audio Interview section and listen.

Prerequisite I
The Basics of Discounted Cash Flow & Net Present Value Analyses

Discounted cash flow analysis (DCF) postulates that the value of a property is equal to its expected future cash flows discounted to present dollars. DCF is premised upon two basic concepts: the only source of value for a property is its ability to generate future cash flows; and a dollar received today is more valuable than a dollar received tomorrow. However, simply making these assumptions does not necessarily make them true. While it is often true that future cash flows are the sole determinants of a property's value, some investors value a property for more than its income potential. For example, an investor can attribute a psychic value (as with a piece of art) to a property. In other instances, pride of ownership will influence value (thus the expression "trophy property"). If these reasons are reflected in future cash streams (i.e., the best building always sells for more), it fits the DCF methodology. However, as is sometimes the case with trophy properties, if an investor values the "bragging rights" of ownership, they will pay more than the value indicated by DCF analysis. Does this make them bad investors? Not if they value the "bragging rights."

> **works with** alexa
>
> To hear spoken definitions of the book's **bolded key terms**, launch Amazon Alexa and say **"Alexa, open Commercial Real Estate Glossary."**

TIME VALUE OF MONEY

The second concept underpinning DCF is formally known as the **time value of money**, which states that a dollar amount received today (referred to as **Time 0**) is worth more than that same nominal dollar amount received tomorrow or at any other point in the future. Why? Because if you have, for example, $100 at Time 0 (the **present value**), you can invest those $100 and expect to have more than $100 in the future, as the investment is expected to yield a positive return. Thus, other things equal, you would prefer a property to produce income earlier rather than later, and you "discount" dollars received in the future to reflect this preference.

How much less valuable is $100 received tomorrow than $100 received today? That is, by how much should you discount future dollars? A bit of background is helpful.

The **future value** is how much $100 today is expected to be worth some time in the future. For instance, if you invest $100 today in a low-risk project generating a 4.0% expected annual return, you expect to have $104 at the end of one year (the original $100 plus $4 earned over the year). Rationally you would be indifferent between receiving $100 today and $104 dollars one year from now if you felt that the 4.0% return was a fair return for the risk associated with investing in this manner for one year. You can express the future value (FV_1) of the original $100 ($CF_0$) one year from now as:

$$[\text{Eq. PI.1}]$$

$$FV_1 = CF_1 = CF_0 * (1 + r_1)$$

where r_1 is the return you need to receive in Year 1 to just make it worth the risk of investing in this project. Equation PI.1 tells you that given an appropriate **risk-adjusted** 1-year rate of return (r_1), you can calculate how much a particular cash flow today will be worth in one year. Figure PI.1 illustrates graphically the concept of future value where the arrow indicates how the current cash flow grows into the future at the Year 1 rate (r_1).

FIGURE PI.1

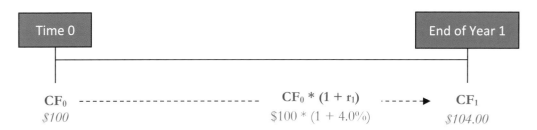

Extending this example to a 2-year timeline, suppose that the expected annual return you required is 4.5%. You start with $100 in the investment and earn a **compound return** of 4.5% for two years, yielding a value of $109.20 at the end of Year 2. That is, the future value at the end of Year 2 of $100 invested in this particular risk profile over two years is $109.20. The 2-year future value is higher than just adding $4.50 twice to $100 (yielding exactly $109.00) due to the compounding of the return. Compounding means you are generating a return on the 4.5% return earned in the first year. Specifically, the $4.50 of interest from the first year generates 20 cents of interest in the Year 2 ($4.50 * 4.5%). We also note that in this example you felt a modestly higher annual return than 4% was required for you to undertake a 2-year investment horizon.

Online Companion Hands On: Go to Textbook.GetREFM.com/toc/ and select the link for the Online Companion to Prerequisite I. Scroll down to the Excel Figures section and download the Excel file and open it. Complete the exercise given on the Fig PI.1 tab, and do the same for Figure PI.2 on the Fig PI. 2 tab when you are ready.

Expanding Equation PI.1 to incorporate Year 2, you can express the Year 2 future value (FV_2) of $100 ($CF_0$) today as:

[Eq. PI.2]

$$FV_2 = CF_2 = CF_0 * (1 + r_2) * (1 + r_2)$$
$$FV_2 = CF_2 = 100 * (1 + 4.5\%) * (1 + 4.5\%)$$
$$FV_2 = CF_2 = \$109.20$$

where r_2 is the expected annual return you need to receive to make it worth the risk of you investing for the 2 years. In Equation PI.2, the $100 initial investment earns 4.5% interest in Year 1 to generate the future value one year from today of $104.50, and this becomes the $109.20 at the end of Year 2. Figure PI.2 illustrates graphically the concept of compounding and future value for a 2-year investment.

FIGURE PI.2

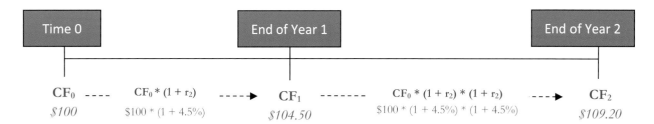

Expanding this example to a 3-year timeline, assume that the required annual expected rate of return necessary to invest the $100 in an opportunity for 3 years is 3.9%. In this case, if you leave the $100 invested for 3 years, it grows to $112.16 at the end of the Year 3. Thus, the future value of $100 today given this 3-year risk profile is $112.16 in 3 years. Expanding Equation PI.2 to incorporate the Year 3, you can express the Year 3 future value (FV_3) of $100 ($CF_0$) today as:

[Eq. PI.3]

$$FV_3 = CF_3 = CF_0 * (1 + r_3) * (1 + r_3) * (1 + r_3)$$
$$FV_3 = CF_3 = 100 * (1 + 3.9\%) * (1 + 3.9\%) * (1 + 3.9\%)$$
$$FV_3 = CF_3 = \$112.16$$

where r_3 is the expected annual return you need to receive to make it worth the risk of investing for the three years. Figure PI.3 graphically represents this Year 3 of investing.

FIGURE PI.3

Time 0	End of Year 1	End of Year 2	End of Year 3

CF_0 - - - - - - - - → CF_1 - - - - - - - - - - - - → CF_2 - - - - - - - - - - - - - - - - - → CF_3

$100   *$103.90*   *$107.95*   *$112.16*

$CF_0 * (1 + r_3)$ $CF_0 * (1 + r_3) * (1 + r_3)$ $CF_0 * (1 + r_3) * (1 + r_3) * (1 + r_3)$

*$100 * (1 + 3.9%)*   *$100 * (1 + 3.9%) * (1 + 3.9%)*   *$100 * (1 + 3.9%) * (1 + 3.9%) * (1 + 3.9%)*

Online Companion Hands On: Select the Fig PI.3 tab in the Excel file and complete the exercise.

You can extend Equation PI.3 to calculate the future value for any year, where each subsequent year you are reinvesting at the expected annual return that sufficiently compensates you for rolling over your investment. Expressed generically, the future value in year T is equal to the previous year's cash flow times the required expected annual rate of return in year T.

[Eq. PI.4]

$$FV_T = CF_T = CF_0 * (1 + r_T) * (1 + r_T) * (1 + r_T) * ...... * (1 + r_T)$$, where there are T number of $(1 + r_T)$ factors

or

[Eq. PI.5]

$$\text{Future Value (in year T)} = CF_T = CF_0 * (1 + r_T)^T$$

Figure PI.4 illustrates the generic formula for future value for a constant rate r_T :

FIGURE PI.4: GENERIC FORMULA FOR FUTURE VALUE

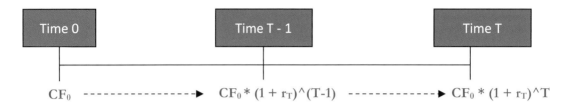

where the exponent for period 1 (the first period after Time 0) is always 1 and the exponent for the second-to-last period (Period T-1) is always (T-1). In the graphic above period 1 and the second-to-last period are one and the same, but naturally not all timelines have only 2 periods.

Although we have used years thus far, you can use quarters, months, weeks, or days as your time unit as long as you are consistent in your application of the equation. For example, if you use months to represent time, you must apply a monthly required rate of return to monthly cash flows.

PRESENT VALUE

With this background, you can calculate the future value of a dollar today for the required expected annual returns reflective of the risks of a particular investment. But how much is the **present value** of a future dollar (i.e., the value today of a future dollar)? In our investment example, if you could either receive $104 in one year or $100 today, which would you pick? Since we said that 4% is the return required to make you indifferent between receiving $100 today and $104 one year from today, the options are equivalent. That is, at 4% assumed annual growth (and assuming you do not need the $100 in capital between today and one year from now), receiving $104 one year into the future is equal to $100 today. Rearranging Equation PI.1, the present value of future cash flow received one year from today is expressed as:

[Eq. PI.6]

$$\text{Present Value} = FV_1 / (1 + r_1) = CF_1 * (1 + r_1)^{-1} = CF_1 / (1 + r_1)^1$$

where the **discount rate** (i.e., the required expected annual return) is r_1 and the **discount factor** is $(1 + r_1)^{-1}$.

Applying Equation PI.6 to our example, $104 in one year is equal to $100 today, that is, it has a present value of $100:

$$\text{Present Value} = FV_1 / (1 + r_1) = CF_1 * (1 + r_1)^{-1}$$
$$\text{Present Value} = \$104 * (1 + 4\%)^{-1} = \$104 * 0.9615 = \$100.$$

So in this example, $100 is the present value, the discount rate is 4.0%, and the discount factor is 0.9615, calculated as: $1 / (1 + 0.04)$. Figure PI.5 illustrates graphically the concept of present value, where the arrow indicates that the future cash flows are discounted back to the present using the required rate of return (r_1).

FIGURE PI.5

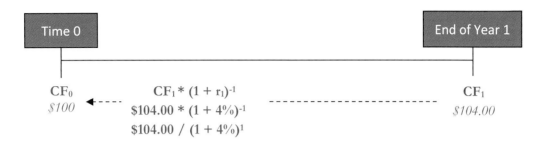

Online Companion Hands On: Select the Fig PI.5 tab in the Excel file and complete the exercise.

In our 2-year example, what is the present value of the future $109.20 held for 2 years? Again, you said that you are indifferent between receiving $100 today and $109.20 two years from today if you deem the required annual return is 4.5%. Therefore, the present value of $109.20 two years from now for this risk profile is $100. Rearranging Equation PI.2 and solving for the present value of cash flow received two years from today yields:

[Eq. PI.2]: $FV_2 = CF_2 = CF_0 * (1 + r_2) * (1 + r_2)$
$FV_2 = CF_2 =$ Present Value $* (1 + r_2) * (1 + r_2)$

[Eq. PI.7]

Present Value $= FV_2 * ((1 + r_2) * (1 + r_2))^{-1} = CF_2 / ((1 + r_2) * (1 + r_2))$.

In this case, the discount factor is $((1 + r_2) * (1 + r_2))^{-1}$.

Present Value $= FV_2 * ((1 + r_2) * (1 + r_2))^{-1} = CF_2 * ((1 + r_2) * (1 + r_2))^{-1}$
Present Value $= \$109.20 * ((1 + 4.5\%) * (1 + 4.5\%))^{-1} = \$100$.

So the discount factor is 0.916 and the present value is $100 at the 4.5% discount rate.

Figure PI.6 illustrates the concept of discounting cash flow in Year 2 back to the present using the required rate of return for each year.

FIGURE PI.6

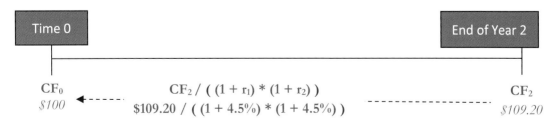

Online Companion Hands On: Select the Fig PI.6 tab in the Excel file and complete the exercise.

Expanding our example to Year 3, if you receive $112.16 at the end of year three at the previously discussed risk profile, you would be indifferent between $100 today and $112.16 in three years. Applying our formula to this example yields $112.16 in three years equals $100 today, where the discount factor is $((1 + r_3) * (1 + r_3) * (1 + r_3))^{-1}$.

[Eq. PI.8]

Present Value = $FV_3 / ((1 + r_3) * (1 + r_3) * (1 + r_3)) = CF_3 / ((1 + r_3) * (1 + r_3) * (1 + r_3))$
Present Value = $\$112.16 / ((1 + 3.9\%) * (1 + 3.9\%) * (1 + 3.9\%)) = \$100.$

So the discount factor is 0.892 and the present value is $100 at the 3.9% discount rate.

Figure PI.7 graphically depicts the discounting process for cash flow received in year three.

FIGURE PI.7

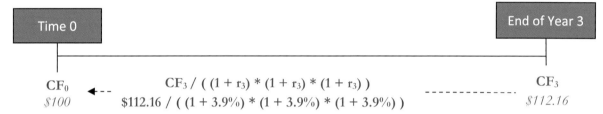

Online Companion Hands On: Select the Fig PI.7 tab in the Excel file and complete the exercise.

As with the future value equation, the present value equation can be expanded to express the present value of cash flow in the year T as:

[Eq. PI.9]

Present Value = $FV_T * ((1 + r_T) * (1 + r_T) * (1 + r_T) * ...... * (1 + r_T))^{-1}$

where there are T number of $(1 + r_T)$ factors

or

[Eq. PI.10]

Present Value = Future Value (in year T) $* (1 + r)^{-T} = CF_T * (1 + r_1)^{-T} = CF_T / (1 + r_T)^{T}$.

As with future value, the time unit can be quarterly, monthly, weekly, or daily as long as you are consistent in application. Therefore, if you use months to represent time, you must also use a monthly discount rate and monthly cash flows. Figure PI.8 illustrates the generic formula for present value at discount rate r_T.

FIGURE PI.8: GENERIC FORMULA FOR PRESENT VALUE

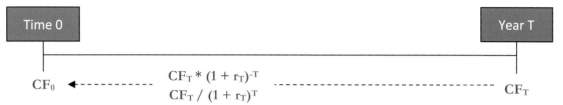

DISCOUNTED CASH FLOW (DCF)

Thus far we have only asked about the present value of the expected cash flow for a specific future year. However, most properties generate cash flows in more than one year (though not all may be positive cash flows). If you are evaluating a property, and its value is solely attributable to its ability to generate future cash flows, its value on this basis is simply the sum of the present value of all expected future cash flows.

In the following example, the present value of receiving $109.20 in two years is equal to $100, and the present value of receiving $104 in one year is equal to $100 as well. Hence, the total present value of these two future income receipts given their specific risks is:

Total Present Value of first Two Years = Present Value ($104 and $109.20) = $104 * 1.04 $^{-1}$ + ($109.20 * (1.045 * 1.045) $^{-1}$) = $200.

Expanding this example for a Year 3, the total present value of the first three years of expected cash flows is:

Total PV of first 3 Years = Present Value ($104, $109.20, $112.16) = $104 * 1.04 $^{-1}$ + ($109.20 * (1.045 * 1.045) $^{-1}$) + ($112.16 * (1.039 * 1.039 * 1.039) $^{-1}$) = $300.

Using Equation PI.12, and the addition of present values, the present value equation for a property generalizes:

[Eq. PI.11]   PV of the Property = The sum of the Present Value of all future years

$$= C_1 * (1 + r_1)^{-1} + C_2 * ((1 + r_2)*(1 + r_2))^{-1} + C_3 * ((1 + r_3)*(1 + r_3)*(1 + r_3))^{-1}$$
$$+ .... C_T * ((1 + r_T)*(1 + r_T)*(1 + r_T)....*(1 + r_T))^{-1}.$$

If the discount rate for each year's cash flow is roughly the same for all years, this simplifies to:

[Eq. PI.12] $$\text{Present Value of the Property} = \sum_{X=1}^{T} C_T * ((1 + r))^{-T}$$

where C_T is the cash flow expected in year T. **"Discounted"** literally means the cash flows are worth less than par value because of the time value of money (i.e., they are valued at a discount reflecting the time value of money required for the risk associated with future cash flows). For instance, the present value of the first three years of cash flows in our example, $104 in Year 1, $109.20 in Year 2, and $112.16 in Year 3, is an 8.45% total discount to the value of $325.36 had the three cash flows simply been valued at par. That is, the present value of $300 is $25.36 (8.45%) less than the $325.36 non-discounted sum of the 3 future values.

To evaluate property value, you will use the expected pre-tax cash flows before any financing or tax liabilities. These **unlevered cash flows** allow you to calculate the value irrespective of the financing structure. This provides a value based solely on the performance of the property. To derive the **equity value**, subtract the property's liabilities.

REVERSION VALUE

You can plug in expected cash flows until the property is no longer able to generate any income. But this valuation process is tedious, and at some point, pure guesswork. To avoid this arduous process, you generally calculate a **reversion value** or **terminal value** that captures the value of all future cash flows beyond this hypothetical exit date. This is your estimate of the next buyer's purchase price for the property. To estimate the reversion value, you will generally apply a **capitalization ("cap") rate** to a stabilized NOI.

Discount Rate: The discount rates (r_1, r_2,...r_T) are key inputs into any DCF analysis. Discount rates are always determined by your best assessment of risk of the cash stream you are discounting, that is, how high the annual expected return must be to make you willing to invest in an opportunity of a particular risk profile. For real estate projects, risk reflects many things, including: liquidity and exit risk; operating risk; political risk; lease-up risk; tenant credit risk; market risk; etc. Determining the appropriate discount rate requires judgment and is a disciplined, yet imprecise, exercise. There is no discountrate.com website to tell you the right answer.

The discount rate will not only vary between investments, but you may also need to apply different discount rates to the cash flows for different years. For instance, if you are considering a development project, you will apply a lower discount rate to the initial cash outflows than to the expected future cash inflows upon completion, as the development cash outflows are fairly certain to occur, while the operating cash inflows are relatively uncertain. If, on the other hand, it is a reasonable approximation that the risk of each year's cash flow is the same, utilize the simpler present valuation formula (Eq. PI.12).

To illustrate the use of discount rates, assume you could invest in a project that will stabilize by Year 5. The property offers the expected cash flow stream shown in Figure PI.9. Note that the Year 5 cash flow includes both operating and sale amounts.

FIGURE PI.9

Property Cash Flow	
Year 1	$300,000
Year 2	$335,000
Year 3	$350,000
Year 4	$400,000
Year 5	$2,100,000

Assume (unrealistically) that you believe the entire project is basically riskless and as liquid as U.S. Treasury bonds. You would use a discount rate approximating the U.S. Treasury rate on these cash flows to reflect the absence of risk in each year. Using a 4% discount rate (10-year Treasury rate) provides an estimated value of $2.98 million, as displayed in Figure PI.10.

FIGURE PI.10

Property NPV Assuming Constant Risk-free Discount Rate

	Year 1		Year 2		Year 3		Year 4		Year 5

$$NPV = \frac{CF_1}{(1+r)} + \frac{CF_2}{(1+r)^2} + \frac{CF_3}{(1+r)^3} + \frac{CF_4}{(1+r)^4} + \frac{(CF_5 + \text{Terminal Value})}{(1+r)^5}$$

$$= \frac{\$300,000}{(1+4\%)} + \frac{\$335,000}{(1+4\%)^2} + \frac{\$350,000}{(1+4\%)^3} + \frac{\$400,000}{(1+4\%)^4} + \frac{\$2,100,000}{(1+4\%)^5}$$

$$= \$2,977,305$$

Online Companion Hands On: Select the Fig PI.10 tab in the Excel file and complete the exercise. Do the same for Figure PI.11 when you are ready.

Alternatively, assume that based on your analysis you believe the first 2 years of cash flows are relatively riskless due to the presence of a U.S. government lease, warranting the 4% discount rate, but the remaining cash flows are riskier due to lease expirations, an uncertain operating environment and market, and exit illiquidity. As a result, you assess the appropriate discount rate for Year 3 at 20% and 18% for Year 4, while Year 5 and all subsequent years are a less risky 15%, as you expect normal market conditions to return. Once the property stabilizes in Year 5, you believe NOI will grow at roughly 2% a year.

Using Equation PI.11 to discount the expected cash flows by the individual annual discount rates yields an estimated value of $2.32 million. This lower value (i.e., greater discount) reflects the greater risk of the cash streams.

FIGURE PI.11

Property NPV Assuming Various Annual Discount Rates

$NPV =$

Year 1
$$\frac{CF_1}{(1+r_1)} = \frac{\$300,000}{(1+4\%)}$$

$+$

Year 2
$$\frac{CF_2}{(1+r_1)*(1+r_2)} = \frac{\$335,000}{(1+4\%)*(1+4\%)}$$

$+$

Year 3
$$\frac{CF_3}{(1+r_1)*(1+r_2)*(1+r_3)} = \frac{\$350,000}{(1+4\%)*(1+4\%)*(1+20\%)}$$

$+$

Year 4
$$\frac{CF_4}{(1+r_1)*(1+r_2)*(1+r_3)*(1+r_4)} = \frac{\$400,000}{(1+4\%)*(1+4\%)*(1+20\%)*(1+18\%)}$$

$+$

Year 5
$$\frac{(CF_5 + \text{Terminal Value})}{(1+r_1)*(1+r_2)*(1+r_3)*(1+r_4)*(1+r_5)} = \frac{\$2,100,000}{(1+4\%)*(1+4\%)*(1+20\%)*(1+18\%)*(1+15\%)}$$

$$= \$2,321,341$$

DCF EXAMPLE

Suppose you inherit $40 million and are deciding between purchasing The Anderson, a Philadelphia apartment complex, or The Oberkircher Building, a New York City office building. The Anderson costs $30 million to purchase, while The Oberkircher Building costs $40 million. However, you anticipate another $10 million in renovation expenditures for The Anderson to upgrade the property as part of a repositioning plan. You plan on selling the purchased property at the end of the Year 5. Based on your cash flow analyses, you estimate the expected cash flows from operations for the properties summarized in Figure PI.12.

FIGURE PI.12

Expected Operating Cash Flows The Anderson Apartments		Expected Operating Cash Flows Oberkircher Office Building	
Year 1	$3,000,000	Year 1	$4,000,000
Year 2	$5,000,000	Year 2	$4,300,000
Year 3	$6,500,000	Year 3	$4,600,000
Year 4	$8,750,000	Year 4	$4,900,000
Year 5	$9,000,000	Year 5	$5,200,000

Before conducting your DCF analysis, you must select appropriate discount rates for each year, for each property. The Philadelphia apartment complex is currently poorly run, but well-located in the middle of Center City, with a 40% vacancy rate despite strong local market conditions. You believe that you can significantly lower operating costs, increase occupancy, and reposition the building to attract higher rents. If the repositioning is successful, you expect to recognize significant cash flow growth.

The Oberkircher Building, on the other hand, is a well-run property in Midtown Manhattan with stabilized occupancy. The building is leased to high credit quality tenants who are locked into long-term leases. Based on your analysis, comparable properties in New York should generate roughly 10.5% annual returns. However, you believe that this building will fare somewhat better given its superior tenant base, quality location, and great return history. You believe you can maintain the quality management of this property and feel it is less risky than most comparable properties. As a result, you select a 10% discount rate for the New York office building for every year, as you see no notable annual variation in the property's risk profile.

The repositioning of The Anderson is a much riskier endeavor. First, there are very few comparable repositionings that have taken place in the area. Your cash flow projections assume that you will have limited success in the first year of operations, with the $3,000,000 in Year 1 roughly equaling the property's current performance. Therefore, you select a relatively low discount rate for the first year, as you feel these cash flows, although weak, are relatively certain when compared to future years. Given the uncertainty over releasing, you select an 11.5% discount rate for Year 1 (higher than that for the Oberkircher Building). For the remaining years, the cash flows are less certain due to repositioning risk. As a result, you select a higher 13% discount rate for cash flows in Years 2 through 5, believing the main risk – successful repositioning – is roughly the same for these years. The Anderson therefore requires a 300-bp **risk premium** when compared to the Oberkircher Building for these years (13% versus 10%).

Given these discount rates and the expected future cash flows, you calculate the terminal value for each property upon sale in Year 5. You believe that by the end of Year 5, when the Philadelphia apartment building is stabilized, cash flows will roughly grow with long-term inflation, which you estimate at 2% annually, as this is a highly competitive market, and the leases roll over every year.

To calculate the estimated terminal (sale) values for the two properties, we apply the **Gordon Growth Model** (named after Myron J. Gordon), which converts perpetuity DCF analysis for a cash stream growing at a constant rate into a simple cap rate approximation by dividing stabilized NOI by the difference between the property's discount rate (r) and the NOI growth rate (g) (Figure PI.13).

FIGURE PI.13

Gordon Growth Model for Property Valuation *
Value = NOI / (property discount rate – NOI growth rate) = NOI / Cap Rate
Value = NOI / (r – g) = NOI / Cap Rate
Therefore: Cap Rate = (r – g)
*Assumes Stabilized NOI and constant NOI growth rate for perpetuity.

Growing Year 5 cash flow to Year 6 to reflect forward NOI, you calculate the terminal value for The Anderson as $83.5 million, as shown in Figure PI.14.

FIGURE PI.14

The Anderson Terminal Value Calculation

$$\text{Forward Year NOI}_6 = \text{NOI}_5 * (1 + \text{growth rate})$$
$$= \$9,000,000 * (1 + 2\%)$$
$$= \$9,180,000$$

Gordon Model: Value = Stabilized NOI / (discount rate – growth rate)

$$\text{Terminal Value}_5 = \text{NOI}_6 / (r - g)$$
$$= \$9,180,000 / (13\% - 2\%)$$
$$= \$83,454,545$$

Online Companion Hands On: Select the Fig PI.14 tab in the Excel file and complete the exercise. Do the same for Figures PI.15, 16 and 17 when you are ready. Answers in PI.16 and PI.17 will feed into the Fig PI.18 tab.

To calculate the sale value for the Oberkircher Building, you similarly apply the Gordon Model. Your analysis indicates that its income growth should slightly outpace inflation due to the strength of the market and the long-term nature of the current leases which have favorable rental growth clauses. Therefore, you expect 3% annual long-term growth. Given this growth rate (g) and 10% discount rate (r), you will apply a 7% exit cap rate (r – g) to the Year 6 NOI, yielding a $76.5 million terminal value, as summarized in Figure PI.15.

FIGURE PI.15

Oberkircher Building Terminal Value Calculation

Forward Year NOI_6 = NOI_5 * (1 + growth rate)
= \$5,200,000 * (1 + 3%)
= \$5,356,000

Gordon Model: Value = Stabilized NOI / (discount rate – growth rate)

Terminal Value$_5$ = NOI_6 / (r – g)
= \$5,356,000 / (10% – 3%)
= \$76,514,286

Applying the selected discount rates to your expected future cash flows, and the estimated terminal values, you calculate the DCF value for both properties. You estimate that The Anderson is worth an estimated \$67.5 million, (Figure PI.16), while the Oberkircher Building is worth an estimated \$64.7 million (Figure PI.17). Of course, these valuations are based on expected cash flows and risks, and the actual outcomes will be much different. If you are wrong, you will overpay or underbid. In fact, in the grand scheme of things, these two properties have about the same estimated value. That is, in the face of the many assumptions required to estimate values for these properties, their estimated values reflect a small difference of only about 4%.

FIGURE PI.16

Discounted Cash Flow Valuation of The Anderson Apartments					
	Year 1	Year 2	Year 3	Year 4	Year 5
CF from Operations	\$3,000,000	\$5,000,000	\$6,500,000	\$8,750,000	\$9,000,000
CF from Sale					\$83,454,545
Total Cash Flow	\$3,000,000	\$5,000,000	\$6,500,000	\$8,750,000	\$92,454,545
Total Cash Flow	\$3,000,000	\$5,000,000	\$6,500,000	\$8,750,000	\$92,454,545
Discount Factor	(1+11.5%)	((1+11.5%) * (1+13%))	$((1+11.5\%) * (1+13\%)^2)$	$((1+11.5\%) * (1+13\%)^3)$	$((1+11.5\%) * (1+13\%)^4)$
Value of Property \$67,518,857					

FIGURE PI.17

Discounted Cash Flow Valuation of the Oberkircher Building					
	Year 1	Year 2	Year 3	Year 4	Year 5
CF from Operations	\$4,000,000	\$4,300,000	\$4,600,000	\$4,900,000	\$5,200,000
CF from Sale					\$76,514,286
Total Cash Flow	\$4,000,000	\$4,300,000	\$4,600,000	\$4,900,000	\$81,714,286
Discount Factor	(1+10%)	$(1+10\%)^2$	$(1+10\%)^3$	$(1+10\%)^4$	$(1+10\%)^5$
Value of Property \$64,731,039					

NET PRESENT VALUE (NPV)

Based on your informed, but imperfect, valuations of these properties, which building should you buy with your inheritance? A common tool that is used to help make such decisions is the **net present value (NPV)** metric. The net present value of a project is equal to the present value of the cash flows the investment generates minus your initial investment.

[Eq. PI.15]   NPV = Present Value – Initial Costs.

NPV tells you how much net value the investment is expected to create (i.e., how much more the property is worth than the costs of acquiring and/or building it). Other things equal (which they never are), you want to invest in the highest NPV project that is consistent with your expertise and abilities. Of course, expertise, as well as limited financial and human resources, prohibit you from investing in every positive NPV project. Therefore, you cannot invest based solely on the current investment alternatives available to you, but also must consider your expected future opportunities and limited capital.

In our case, you have $40 million to invest and, thus, you can purchase only one building. Using Equation PI.15, you can calculate which of the two projects you are considering has the higher NPV, generating the greatest expected profit over your costs, as shown in Figure PI.18.

FIGURE PI.18

Net Present Value Comparison
The Anderson
NPV = $67,518,857 – $40,000,000
= $27,518,857
Oberkircher Building
NPV = $64,731,039 – $40,000,000
= $24,731,039

Based on these NPV estimates, it appears as if you should purchase The Anderson apartment complex. However, always be humble as the financial analyst. Don't lose sight of the many simplifying, naïve, and frequently incorrect assumptions that went into the analysis. After all that, the NPVs are "only" about 11% different. Do you feel more comfortable with your expertise in one market or project type? Does one fit your expansion strategy better? Do you feel more comfortable with the vagaries of assumptions for one than the other? Does one have a safer downside if things go wrong? As long as project NPVs are relatively close, these factors will always dominate the numbers in your decision-making process.

Prerequisite II
Internal Rate of Return

The **internal rate of return (IRR)** is one of the most common metrics used to evaluate the performance of a real estate investment. It is most certainly the most misused performance metric. It is important to understand what IRR is, and what it is not. It is also critical understand its severe limitations. When you do, you will see that it is just one more "brick in the wall" that goes into making a sound real estate investment decision.

WHAT IS IT?

The internal rate of return (IRR) is classically defined as the annual rate of return that generates a NPV of zero for a stream of expected (or actual) cash flows. That is, the present value of the expected income exactly equals the present value of the Time 0 investment costs, where the investment costs are negative. As such, it is a break-even rate of return. You solve for the IRR of a project lasting T periods using the NPV equation from Prerequisite I, where C_T is the expected cash flow for the period and r_T is the required rate of return for the corresponding period.

NPV = Initial Costs + Present Value of future net cash streams
NPV = Initial Costs + $C_1 / (1 + r) + C_2 / (1 + r)^2 + C_3 / (1 + r)^3 + C_4 / (1 + r)^4 + ...$

So by definition: $0 = \text{Initial Costs} + \sum C_T / (1 + IRR)^T$.

What does this rate of return tell you? Only that if you were to discount your cash flows with the IRR, the project would have an NPV equal to zero. That is, the present value of the future expected net cash flows would exactly equal the initial cash investment if the IRR is the correct discount rate for every year. If this is the case, you are financially indifferent between investing in the project **only if** the IRR is the "right" discount rate (i.e., risk-equivalent rate) for all future cash flows.

Never forget that the IRR does not purport to be the correct discount rate. If you believe the appropriate discount rate for the project is lower than the IRR, the IRR math will return a positive NPV (an indication of value creation). On the other hand, if the discount rate is higher than the IRR, the math will return a negative NPV (an indication of value destruction). As such, the IRR provides a metric that can be used in conjunction with your assessment of project risk to evaluate the financial performance of an investment. Returning to the two buildings discussed in Prerequisite I, we can calculate the IRR of the alternative investments. The total net before-tax cash flows for both projects are shown in Figure PII.1.

 Online Companion Hands On: After you review Figure PII.1 on the next page, go to Textbook.GetREFM.com/toc/ and select the link for Prerequisite II. Download the Excel file and open it. Complete the exercises given on the Fig PII.1 part 1 tab and Fig PII.1 part 2 tab. Answers on these tabs feed into the Fig PII.2 tab.

FIGURE PII.1

The Anderson Apartments Cash Flows						
	Time 0	Year 1	Year 2	Year 3	Year 4	Year 5
(Before Tax)						
Investment	($40,000,000)					
CF from Operations		$3,000,000	$5,000,000	$6,500,000	$8,750,000	$9,000,000
CF from Sale						$83,454,545
Total Cash Flow	($40,000,000)	$3,000,000	$5,000,000	$6,500,000	$8,750,000	$92,454,545
Net Cash Flow	$75,704,545					

The Oberkircher Building Cash Flows						
	Time 0	Year 1	Year 2	Year 3	Year 4	Year 5
(Before Tax)						
Investment	($40,000,000)					
CF from Operations		$4,000,000	$4,300,000	$4,600,000	$4,900,000	$5,200,000
CF from Sale						$75,771,429
Total Cash Flow	($40,000,000)	$4,000,000	$4,300,000	$4,600,000	$4,900,000	$80,971,429
Net Cash Flow	$58,771,429					

Using calculators and computer packages that incorporate the highly non-linear IRR formula, you can quickly solve for the rate of return that generates a zero expected NPV for each project on an unlevered (exclusive of debt financing) basis. The **unlevered IRR** (also referred to as the **property-level IRR**) for The Anderson investment is 27%, while that for the Oberkircher Building investment is 23%, as seen below in Figure PII.2.

FIGURE PII.2

The Anderson IRR Calculation						

$$0 = (\$40,000,000) + \frac{\$3,000,000}{(1+IRR)} + \frac{\$5,000,000}{(1+IRR)^2} + \frac{\$6,500,000}{(1+IRR)^3} + \frac{\$8,750,000}{(1+IRR)^4} + \frac{\$92,454,545}{(1+IRR)^5}$$

$$IRR = 27\%$$

Oberkircher Building IRR Calculation						

$$0 = (\$40,000,000) + \frac{\$4,000,000}{(1+IRR)} + \frac{\$4,300,000}{(1+IRR)^2} + \frac{\$4,600,000}{(1+IRR)^3} + \frac{\$4,900,000}{(1+IRR)^4} + \frac{\$80,971,429}{(1+IRR)^5}$$

$$IRR = 23\%$$

379

All too often users jump to the conclusion that The Anderson is the better investment, as it has a higher IRR than the Oberkircher Building. However, this is a seriously flawed usage of the IRR, as the IRR tells you nothing about the risk of these projects, the timing of the expected cash flows, your expertise in managing the properties, or any of the many other factors that go into making an investment decision.

WHAT IT IS NOT

The IRR is simply an algebraic calculation. Since it reflects no judgment, common sense suggests that it must be limited in its analytic insight. It is nothing more than an algebraic solution to the simple math question, "What discount rate generates an expected NPV of zero?"

The 27% IRR for The Anderson does not tell you if the property is well-designed and well-located, about tenant risk, the risks inherent in an uncertain repositioning effort, leasing risk, cost overrun risk, or exit risk. The 23% IRR for the Oberkircher Building says nothing about the stability of the cash flows, the credit quality of the tenants, the liquidity of the New York office market, or the building's design or location. No formula can assess such risks. That is your job!

Note that an IRR also tells you nothing about the size or timing of the expected cash flows. And no IRR tells you if the numbers used in the analysis are sensible, much less correct. Consider the expected cash flows below.

FIGURE PII.3

23% IRR Investment of $4,000				
	Time 0	Year 1	Year 2	Year 3
Cash Flows	($4,000)	$400	$650	$6,000
IRR =	23%			

Online Companion Hands On: Select the Fig PII.3 tab in the Excel file and complete the exercise.

The IRR for this $4,000 investment is the same as the IRR of the $40 million Oberkircher Building investment. Which one should you take? Based upon your resources and assessment of risk, you may not want, or be able, to invest $40 million. Or you may find a $4,000 investment to be too small to warrant your attention. In the real world, the size of the investment is an important factor in the investment decision. Since IRR completely ignores this factor, it is clear that it is not some all-powerful investment tool.

In addition to the size of the project, IRR does not comment on the length of the investment period. For example, the Oberkircher Building project lasts 2 years longer than the alternative project shown in Figure PII.3. Whether you want your money tied up for 5 years is often a critical matter when making an investment decision. In fact, if you generate a 1% return on a one-day investment, your (extrapolated) equivalent annual IRR is astronomical even though your cash multiple is miniscule as of the end of that one day.

IRR does not distinguish between annual cash flows from operations and cash proceeds associated with exit. These sources of cash inflows have different timing and uncertainty. While cash flows from next year's operations are rarely guaranteed, even in the presence of long-term leases, they are relatively predictable compared to the exit price upon sale, which depends on factors that are years into the future. Therefore, it is generally much easier for investors to get comfortable with cash flows one to two years from now compared to proceeds from sale. Whether you prefer an investment with most of its cash flow generated from the property's sale depends on your risk aversion, opinion about the future, your need for ongoing cash inflows, etc. Again, the IRR says nothing in this regard.

While the IRR result is impacted by the timing and size of cash flows (early large positive cash flows drive it up, and repeated negative cash flows weigh it down), it does not comment on early or late cash flows. You can generate the same 15% IRR with two very different cash flow stream profiles: one with steady operating cash flows and a reasonable sale value, and another with far weaker and erratic operating cash flows, but a very high sale value. For most investors, the earlier the cash flow, the better, as a dollar received today is one less to worry about receiving in the future. Other things equal, investors generally prefer to get their money back sooner than later, as it allows them to "take their money off of the table." But the single IRR metric does not describe timing of cash flows per se.

The IRR also assumes that the appropriate risk-adjusted rate of return is the same for every year. But for many investments this assumption is inaccurate. Returning to the two buildings in Prerequisite I, the early operating cash flows from The Anderson repositioning are relatively certain compared to the cash flow upon repositioning and the sales proceeds. As a result, a higher discount rate was used to value the later operating cash flows. But IRR is calculated assuming these cash flows were equally risky. It also assumes reinvestment of cash flows at the IRR, which is not typically true for real estate investment, where distributions of cash flows are made periodically to investors instead of free cash flow being retained and reinvested in the property.

IRR fails to tell you anything about debt financing (leverage) risk. This is particularly troubling as investors (and particularly students) often only calculate the IRR on their equity. The **equity IRR** (also referred to as the **levered IRR**) is the single discount rate that sets NPV of expected future equity cash flows equal to zero. As you saw from comparing The Anderson and the Oberkircher Building, the IRR tells you nothing about property, leasing, operating, liquidity risk, etc. Now assume the $40 million total costs (purchase and improvement) for The Anderson are financed with a 75% LTV, $30 million interest-only mortgage, at a 7% interest rate, which results in an annual interest payment of $2,100,000. Further assume the $40 million purchase of the Oberkircher Building is financed with a 50% LTV, $20 million interest-only mortgage, at a 6% interest rate, which results in an annual interest payment of $1,200,000. Assume that both loans are for 10 years, with no prepayment penalties. Upon the sale of either property at the end of Year 5, the mortgage will be repaid.

Given the information above and the before-tax cash flows from Figure PII.1, the expected before-tax equity cash flows for both properties are displayed in Figure PII.4.

FIGURE PII.4

The Anderson Before-Tax Equity Cash Flow						
	Time 0	Year 1	Year 2	Year 3	Year 4	Year 5
Total Costs of Investment	(40,000,000)					
Proceeds from Mortgage	30,000,000					
Cash Flow from Operations		3,000,000	5,000,000	6,500,000	8,750,000	9,000,000
Interest Payment		(2,100,000)	(2,100,000)	(2,100,000)	(2,100,000)	(2,100,000)
Cash Flow from Sale						83,454,545
Repayment of Mortgage						(30,000,000)
Total Before-Tax Equity Cash Flow	($10,000,000)	$900,000	$2,900,000	$4,400,000	$6,650,000	$60,354,545
Net Cash Flow	$65,204,545					

The Oberkircher Building Before-Tax Equity Cash Flow						
	Time 0	Year 1	Year 2	Year 3	Year 4	Year 5
Total Costs of Investment	(40,000,000)					
Proceeds from Mortgage	20,000,000					
Cash Flow from Operations		4,000,000	4,300,000	4,600,000	4,900,000	5,200,000
Interest Payment		(1,200,000)	(1,200,000)	(1,200,000)	(1,200,000)	(1,200,000)
Cash Flow from Sale						75,771,429
Repayment of Mortgage						(20,000,000)
Total Before-Tax Equity Cash Flow	($20,000,000)	$2,800,000	$3,100,000	$3,400,000	$3,700,000	$59,771,429
Net Cash Flow	$52,771,429					

Using the IRR equation, you can solve for the equity rate of return that generates a zero NPV for the equity investor. The resulting expected equity IRR for The Anderson is 58% while the Oberkircher Building has an expected equity IRR of 35%.

Online Companion Hands On: Select the Fig PII.4 tab in the Excel file and complete the exercise. Answers on this tab feed into the Fig PII.5 tab.

FIGURE PII.5

Anderson Gardens Equity IRR Calculation						
	Time 0	Year 1	Year 2	Year 3	Year 4	Year 5

$$0 = (\$10,000,000) + \frac{\$900,000}{(1+IRR)} + \frac{\$2,900,000}{(1+IRR)^2} + \frac{\$4,400,000}{(1+IRR)^3} + \frac{\$6,650,000}{(1+IRR)^4} + \frac{\$60,354,545}{(1+IRR)^5}$$

Equity IRR = 58%

Oberkircher Building Equity IRR Calculation						
	Time 0	Year 1	Year 2	Year 3	Year 4	Year 5

$$0 = (\$20,000,000) + \frac{\$2,800,000}{(1+IRR)} + \frac{\$3,100,000}{(1+IRR)^2} + \frac{\$3,400,000}{(1+IRR)^3} + \frac{\$3,700,000}{(1+IRR)^4} + \frac{\$59,771,429}{(1+IRR)^5}$$

Equity IRR = 34%

As expected with debt-financed transactions that have **positive leverage** (where the annual property cash flow yield percentage i.e., net operating income after normal reserves / Purchase Price, is higher than the annual interest rate paid to the lender), the equity IRR for both properties is higher than the property-level IRRs (58% versus 27% for The Anderson, and 34% versus 23% for the Oberkircher Building). Also, the IRR for The Anderson is now substantially higher than the IRR for the Oberkircher Building. Whereas the difference between the two property-level IRRs was only 4% without debt, The Anderson now yields a 24% higher IRR. Based on the equity IRR alone, many students are inclined to use as much debt as possible. However, the risk of the equity cash flows is much higher than for the property due to the leverage, as the lender is entitled to the first cash flows. The more debt you use to fund the acquisition, the greater is the risk of your equity cash flows. Is the additional expected return worth the risk? Maybe 'yes' if you can afford to lose the money or the tenant base has great credit quality; maybe 'no' if your total wealth is at risk and the economy is weak.

Stated bluntly, the IRR on equity says nothing about risk (of any type). Thus, when looking at an equity IRR you need to evaluate whether the returns are being driven by strong property cash flows, extreme leverage, or extreme operating risk.

Prerequisite III
Amortization Fundamentals

Amortization refers to the repayment schedule for mortgage loan **principal** (the capital amount borrowed). To illuminate amortization, consider Kathy Crest, a residential garden apartment complex being purchased for $6.7 million, with a $5 million loan at a 5% annual interest rate, and a 7-year **loan maturity** (duration).

INTEREST-ONLY LOANS

When obtaining a loan, the borrower obligates herself to pay back the principal borrowed and the interest incurred over the **loan term** (length) on a specified schedule. Amortization specifies how the principal is repaid. In the case of an **interest-only loan** (also known as a **zero-amortization** or **bullet** loan), only interest is paid on the outstanding principal until the time of the final monthly payment, at which point the principal balance is also repaid in a lump sum. Figure PIII.1 summarizes the loan payments and the return the lender realizes on their capital for this type of mortgage.

FIGURE PIII.1

Kathy Crest First Mortgage Holder Yield for Zero-Amortization Loan								
	Time 0	Year 1	Year 2	Year 3	Year 4	Year 5	Year 6	Year 7
Loan Proceeds Disbursed	(5,000,000)	0	0	0	0	0	0	0
Debt Service Payment Received	0	250,000	250,000	250,000	250,000	250,000	250,000	250,000
Repayment of Loan Balance	0	0	0	0	0	0	0	5,000,000
Before-Tax Cash Flow	($5,000,000)	$250,000	$250,000	$250,000	$250,000	$250,000	$250,000	$5,250,000
Yield to Lender (IRR)	5.00%							

Online Companion Hands On: Go to Textbook.GetREFM.com/toc/ and select the link for Prerequisite III. Scroll down the page and download the Excel file and open it. Complete the exercise given on the Fig PIII.1 tab.

As shown in Figure PIII.2, while the payment of debt service does not affect NOI, it does impact before-tax and after-tax cash flows. This is because debt service must be deducted from cash flow, and because interest payments reduce income taxes. In the case of an interest-only loan, the borrower maximizes their income tax shelter as payments are 100% interest until the final **bullet payment** when the loan principal is repaid all at once.

While interest payments in our scenario can be paid with cash flows generated from operations, the principal will be paid off with property sale proceeds. If the property is not sold, the loan will have to be refinanced either by a new loan or an equity infusion upon maturity. Figure PIII.3 displays how the principal outstanding affects the net proceeds upon sale of Kathy Crest.

FIGURE PIII.2

Kathy Crest After-Tax Cash Flow from Operation with Zero-Amortization First Mortgage							
	Year 1	Year 2	Year 3	Year 4	Year 5	Year 6	Year 7
Net Operating Income	518,426	529,047	539,741	550,496	561,302	572,147	583,017
Loan Points	-	-	-	-	-	-	-
First Mortgage Debt Service	(250,000)	(250,000)	(250,000)	(250,000)	(250,000)	(250,000)	(250,000)
Before-Tax Levered Cash Flow	268,426	279,047	289,741	300,496	311,302	322,147	333,017
Less: Depreciation	(201,818)	(201,818)	(201,818)	(201,818)	(201,818)	(201,818)	(201,818)
Plus: Cap Ex	45,000	46,350	47,741	49,173	50,648	52,167	53,732
Plus: Principal Amortization	-	-	-	-	-	-	-
Less: Points Amortization	-	-	-	-	-	-	-
Net Taxable Income (Loss)	111,608	123,579	135,663	147,850	160,132	172,496	184,931
Less: Tax Liability	(23,438)	(25,952)	(28,489)	(31,049)	(33,628)	(36,224)	(38,836)
After-Tax Cash Flow	$244,988	$253,096	$261,251	$269,447	$277,674	$285,923	$294,182

Online Companion Hands On: Select the Fig PIII.2, .4 & .10 bottom tab in the Excel file and complete the exercise for Figure PIII.2 in row 45.

FIGURE PIII.3

Kathy Crest Net Sales Proceeds with Zero-Amortization First Mortgage	
Gross Sales Price	7,423,739
Less Selling Costs	(148,475)
Net Sales Price	7,275,264
Less Sale Income Tax Liability	(387,750)
Less Outstanding Mortgage Balance	(5,000,000)
Net Sales Proceeds	$1,887,514

Online Companion Hands On: Select the Fig PIII.3 and PIII.11 left tab in the Excel file and complete the exercise. Do the same for Figure PIII. 4 on the previous tab (Fig PIII.2, .4 & .10 bottom).

The equity IRR calculation for the use of a zero-amortization loan is presented in Figure PIII.4.

FIGURE PIII.4

Kathy Crest DCF Valuation and IRR with Zero-Amortization First Mortgage								
	Time 0	Year 1	Year 2	Year 3	Year 4	Year 5	Year 6	Year 7
Equity Investment	(1,700,000)							
After-Tax Cash Flow		244,988	253,096	261,251	269,447	277,674	285,923	294,182
After-Tax Net Sales Proceeds								1,887,514
Total After-Tax Cash Flow	($1,700,000)	$244,988	$253,096	$261,251	$269,447	$277,674	$285,923	$2,181,696
Net After-Tax Profit	$2,074,076							
NPV at 10.0%	$565,570							
IRR	16.52%							

POSITIVE AMORTIZATION LOANS

Lenders generally require you to repay part of the principal with each monthly loan payment to reduce their repayment risk. This is known as **positive amortization**, and it results in the loan balance decreasing with each payment. The length of a loan's **amortization schedule** does not have to equal the maturity of the loan (i.e., it can be longer, but not shorter than, the loan term). For instance, you can have a 30-year loan with a 30-year amortization term, or a 10-year loan with a 30-year amortization term, but not a 30-year loan with a 10-year amortization term. The latter is not possible for the simple reason that the loan is fully amortized (i.e., fully repaid) over 10 years, thus there is no principal amount that can be outstanding for another 20 years. A loan whose term and amortization schedule are equal is a **fully amortizing loan**, in which the loan is fully repaid over the course of the term through the monthly payments. If the loan matures sooner than the amortization period (e.g., a 10-year term with 30-year amortization), all remaining principal is due with the final month's payment, which is known as the **balloon payment**.

Returning to Kathy Crest, assume the same loan terms ($5 million loan at a 5% annual interest rate, and a 7-year loan maturity), except that the loan is amortized over 20 years. With this amortization schedule, the annual payment rises to $401,213 from $250,000.

The original way real estate professionals solved for the payment amount was by calculating the **annuity factor**, whose formula in shown in figure PIII.5. In the formula, R is the interest rate 5% and T is the amortization period, 20. The annuity factor for the Kathy Crest 20-year amortizing loan would be 12.462.

FIGURE PIII.5

Annuity Factor Formula
$(1 / R) - (1 / (R * (1+R)^T))$

We next take the reciprocal of the annuity factor to get the **mortgage constant**, which is the percentage of the original loan principal amount, that when multiplied by that full principal amount, produces the constant annual loan payment amount inclusive of interest and principal. Figure PIII.6 provides a summary of mortgage constants for a variety of mortgage interest rates and amortization periods. In our example, the mortgage constant percentage would be 1/12.462, which equals 8.024%. To calculate the annual payment, we multiply the loan principal by the percentage indicated for a given interest rate and amortization period. For example, if you have the $5 million loan with a 5% interest rate and a 20-year amortization schedule, you will multiply 8.024% by $5 million, for a $401,200 annual loan payment (slightly lower than the $401,213 due to rounding of the constant). Lenders used to rely on such tables to quickly determine payment schedules, but most now use Excel or web-based mortgage calculators.

FIGURE PIII.6

						Mortgage Constants for Common Interest Rate and Amortization Term Combinations					
						Amortization Schedule in Years					
	5	10	15	16	17	18	19	20	25	30
5.000%	23.097%	12.950%	9.634%	9.227%	8.870%	8.555%	8.275%	8.024%	7.095%	6.505%
5.125%	23.177%	13.029%	9.716%	9.309%	8.953%	8.638%	8.359%	8.110%	7.184%	6.598%
5.250%	23.257%	13.108%	9.798%	9.392%	9.036%	8.723%	8.444%	8.195%	7.274%	6.692%
5.375%	23.337%	13.187%	9.880%	9.475%	9.120%	8.807%	8.529%	8.281%	7.364%	6.786%
5.500%	23.418%	13.267%	9.963%	9.558%	9.204%	8.892%	8.615%	8.368%	7.455%	6.881%
5.625%	23.498%	13.346%	10.045%	9.642%	9.289%	8.977%	8.701%	8.455%	7.546%	6.976%
5.750%	23.578%	13.426%	10.129%	9.726%	9.374%	9.063%	8.788%	8.542%	7.638%	7.072%
5.875%	23.659%	13.506%	10.212%	9.810%	9.459%	9.149%	8.875%	8.630%	7.730%	7.168%
6.000%	23.740%	13.587%	10.296%	9.895%	9.544%	9.236%	8.962%	8.718%	7.823%	7.265%
6.125%	23.820%	13.667%	10.381%	9.980%	9.630%	9.323%	9.050%	8.807%	7.916%	7.362%
6.250%	23.901%	13.748%	10.465%	10.066%	9.717%	9.410%	9.138%	8.896%	8.009%	7.460%
6.375%	23.982%	13.829%	10.550%	10.152%	9.804%	9.497%	9.227%	8.986%	8.104%	7.559%
6.500%	24.063%	13.910%	10.635%	10.238%	9.891%	9.585%	9.316%	9.076%	8.198%	7.658%
6.625%	24.145%	13.992%	10.721%	10.324%	9.978%	9.674%	9.405%	9.166%	8.293%	7.757%
6.750%	24.226%	14.074%	10.807%	10.411%	10.066%	9.763%	9.495%	9.257%	8.389%	7.857%
6.875%	24.307%	14.156%	10.893%	10.498%	10.154%	9.852%	9.585%	9.348%	8.485%	7.958%
7.000%	24.389%	14.238%	10.979%	10.586%	10.243%	9.941%	9.675%	9.439%	8.581%	8.059%
7.125%	24.471%	14.320%	11.066%	10.674%	10.331%	10.031%	9.766%	9.531%	8.678%	8.160%
7.250%	24.553%	14.403%	11.153%	10.762%	10.421%	10.121%	9.857%	9.623%	8.775%	8.262%
7.375%	24.634%	14.486%	11.241%	10.850%	10.510%	10.212%	9.949%	9.716%	8.873%	8.364%
7.500%	24.716%	14.569%	11.329%	10.939%	10.600%	10.303%	10.041%	9.809%	8.971%	8.467%
7.625%	24.799%	14.652%	11.417%	11.028%	10.690%	10.394%	10.133%	9.903%	9.070%	8.570%
7.750%	24.881%	14.735%	11.505%	11.118%	10.781%	10.486%	10.226%	9.996%	9.169%	8.674%
7.875%	24.963%	14.819%	11.594%	11.208%	10.872%	10.578%	10.319%	10.091%	9.268%	8.778%
8.000%	25.046%	14.903%	11.683%	11.298%	10.963%	10.670%	10.413%	10.185%	9.368%	8.883%
8.125%	25.128%	14.987%	11.772%	11.388%	11.055%	10.763%	10.507%	10.280%	9.468%	8.988%
8.250%	25.211%	15.071%	11.862%	11.479%	11.146%	10.856%	10.601%	10.375%	9.569%	9.093%
8.375%	25.294%	15.156%	11.952%	11.570%	11.239%	10.949%	10.695%	10.471%	9.670%	9.199%
8.500%	25.377%	15.241%	12.042%	11.661%	11.331%	11.043%	10.790%	10.567%	9.771%	9.305%
8.625%	25.460%	15.326%	12.133%	11.753%	11.424%	11.137%	10.885%	10.663%	9.873%	9.412%
8.750%	25.543%	15.411%	12.223%	11.845%	11.517%	11.231%	10.981%	10.760%	9.975%	9.519%
8.875%	25.626%	15.496%	12.314%	11.937%	11.611%	11.326%	11.077%	10.857%	10.078%	9.626%
9.000%	25.709%	15.582%	12.406%	12.030%	11.705%	11.421%	11.173%	10.955%	10.181%	9.734%

As you extend the amortization period to infinity, the annual payment approaches the interest-only payment of $250,000. Thus, a bullet loan is effectively a loan with an infinite amortization period (you can use 10,000 years as the amortization term in your spreadsheets as a proxy for infinity, i.e., an interest-only loan). Figure PIII.7 displays the annual payments the lender receives for the 5%, 7-year loan with a 20-year amortization.

FIGURE PIII.7

Kathy Crest Mortgage Payment Schedule with 20-year Amortization							
Mortgage Amount $5,000,000	Year 1	Year 2	Year 3	Year 4	Year 5	Year 6	Year 7
Beginning of Year Balance	5,000,000	4,848,787	4,690,013	4,523,301	4,348,253	4,164,453	3,971,463
Interest Payment	250,000	242,439	234,501	226,165	217,413	208,223	198,573
Principal Payment	151,213	158,774	166,712	175,048	183,800	192,990	202,640
Total Payment	$401,213	$401,213	$401,213	$401,213	$401,213	$401,213	$401,213
Balloon Payment							3,768,823
Year-End Balance	4,848,787	4,690,013	4,523,301	4,348,253	4,164,453	3,971,463	0

Online Companion Hands On: Select the Fig PIII.7-8 tab in the Excel file and complete the exercise for Figure PIII.7.

Figure PIII.8 reveals that while the total payment amount is the same each year ($401,213), the interest portion decreases each successive year while the principal repayment component increases by an offsetting amount. This is because as the debt is repaid, the outstanding loan balance is reduced, and you only pay interest on the amount outstanding. Year 7 is the year in which the interest portion of the total payment amount no longer exceeds the principal payment portion.

FIGURE PIII.8

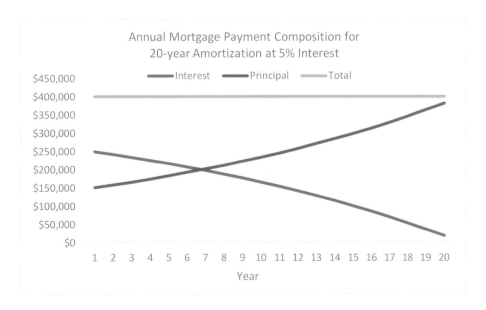

As shown in Figure PIII.9, as the amortization term increases, the interest payment amount increases for each year (excluding for Year 1).

FIGURE PIII.9

	Different Amortization Periods for a $5 MM Loan with a 5% Interest Rate and 7-Year Maturity								
	10-year Amortization			20-year Amortization			30-year Amortization		
Year	Interest Payment	Principal Payment	Mortgage Balance	Interest Payment	Principal Payment	Mortgage Balance	Interest Payment	Principal Payment	Mortgage Balance
1	250,000	397,523	4,602,477	250,000	151,213	4,848,787	250,000	75,257	4,924,743
2	230,124	417,399	4,185,078	242,439	158,774	4,690,013	246,237	79,020	4,845,723
3	209,254	438,269	3,746,809	234,501	166,712	4,523,301	242,286	82,971	4,762,752
4	187,340	460,182	3,286,627	226,165	175,048	4,348,253	238,138	87,120	4,675,632
5	164,331	483,192	2,803,435	217,413	183,800	4,164,453	233,782	91,476	4,584,157
6	140,172	507,351	2,296,084	208,223	192,990	3,971,463	229,208	96,049	4,488,107
7	114,804	532,719	1,763,365	198,573	202,640	3,768,823	224,405	100,852	4,387,255

Online Companion Hands On: Select the Fig PIII.9 tab in the Excel file and complete the exercise. Answers on this tab feed into the Plus: Principal Amortization line of Figure PIII.10 on the Fig PIII.10 top tab. Answers on this tab also feed into the Less Outstanding Mortgage Balance item on the Figure PIII.11 right tab.

Study the Figure PIII.10 top chart in the Excel to make sure you are comfortable with it.

How do different amortization periods impact the borrower? First, the shorter the amortization period, the greater are the annual payments, as you have a shorter period over which to repay the loan. In addition, the faster the amortization, the lower the total interest payments. As a result, the interest tax shield is lower for rapidly amortizing loans. On the other hand, higher amortization loans increase your equity position in the property more quickly. Figure PIII.10 shows after-tax cash flow to equity with both the 20-year and zero-amortization schedules.

FIGURE PIII.10

Kathy Crest After-Tax Cash Flow from Operation with 20-year Amortization First Mortgage							
	Year 1	Year 2	Year 3	Year 4	Year 5	Year 6	Year 7
Net Operating Income	518,426	529,047	539,741	550,496	561,302	572,147	583,017
Loan Points	-	-	-	-	-	-	-
First Mortgage Debt Service	(401,213)	(401,213)	(401,213)	(401,213)	(401,213)	(401,213)	(401,213)
Before Tax-Levered Cash Flow	117,213	127,834	138,528	149,283	160,089	170,934	181,804
Less: Depreciation	(201,818)	(201,818)	(201,818)	(201,818)	(201,818)	(201,818)	(201,818)
Plus: Cap Ex	45,000	46,350	47,741	49,173	50,648	52,167	53,732
Plus: Principal Amortization	151,213	158,774	166,712	175,048	183,800	192,990	202,640
Less: Points Amortization	-	-	-	-	-	-	-
Net Taxable Income (Loss)	111,608	131,140	151,162	171,685	192,719	214,273	236,358
Less: Tax Liability	(23,438)	(27,539)	(31,744)	(36,054)	(40,471)	(44,997)	(49,635)
After-Tax Cash Flow	$93,775	$100,295	$106,784	$113,229	$119,618	$125,936	$132,169

Kathy Crest After-Tax Cash Flow from Operation with Zero-Amortization First Mortgage (from Figure PIII.2)							
	Year 1	Year 2	Year 3	Year 4	Year 5	Year 6	Year 7
After-Tax Cash Flow	$244,988	$253,096	$261,251	$269,447	$277,674	$285,923	$294,182

Note how the after-tax cash flow is significantly lower for the 20-year amortization case (top chart) than for the zero-amortization case (bottom chart). The difference derives from the repayment of the mortgage principal in each payment period, which lowers the before-tax levered cash flow, even though NOI is the same. If the loan was fully amortized over the 7-year term, the loan payments would be $864,099 each year. With NOI of $518,426 in Year 1, the borrower would not be able to service this or future debt payments from property cash flows alone. This means fresh money would have to be injected via either equity or new debt to fund the shortfall.

While with the 20-year amortizing loan, annual cash flows are reduced for the equity holder, when the building is sold, there is less principal to retire. Figure PIII.11 illustrates the results upon the sale of the building for both cases. Higher amortization shifts the equity returns from annual cash flows to the sale of the property.

FIGURE PIII.11

Kathy Crest Net Sales Proceeds with Zero-Amortization First Mortgage	
Gross Sales Price	7,423,739
Less Selling Costs	(148,475)
Net Sales Price	7,275,264
Less Sale Income Tax Liability	(387,750)
Less Outstanding Mortgage Balance	(5,000,000)
Net Sales Proceeds	$1,887,514

Kathy Crest Net Sales Proceeds with 20-year Amortization First Mortgage	
Gross Sales Price	7,423,739
Less Selling Costs	(148,475)
Net Sales Price	7,275,264
Less Sale Income Tax Liability	(387,750)
Less Outstanding Mortgage Balance	(3,768,823)
Net Sales Proceeds	$3,118,691

All else equal among loan alternatives, a borrower generally prefers longer to shorter amortization, because they prefer to repay their loan later than earlier. Kathy Crest starts with a 75% LTV, and over time the LTV falls as the loan amortizes and property value hopefully rises. Properties that are relatively vulnerable to value declines will tend to be granted lower LTVs and restricted to shorter amortization periods by the lender, as they are concerned first and foremost with getting their capital back.

ALTERNATIVE AMORTIZATION LOANS

To cater to the different preferences of the lender and borrower, sometimes **hybrid amortization schedules** are created. For example, there may be no amortization for the first 2 years (i.e., a front-end interest-only period) and then 20-year amortization for rest of the loan term. It is also possible to have annual payments change, but the amortization dollar amount remains constant. This means you pay down your principal by a certain amount every year. Figure PIII.12 displays an example of Kathy Crest with a fully amortizing **constant amortization loan**, where $500,000 in principal, plus interest on the outstanding loan balance, is paid every year.

FIGURE PIII.12

Kathy Crest Mortgage Payment Schedule with Constant Amortization							
Mortgage Amount $5,000,000	Year 1	Year 2	Year 3	Year 4	Year 5	Year 6	Year 7
Beginning of Year Balance	5,000,000	4,500,000	4,000,000	3,500,000	3,000,000	2,500,000	2,000,000
Interest Payment	250,000	225,000	200,000	175,000	150,000	125,000	100,000
Principal Payment	500,000	500,000	500,000	500,000	500,000	500,000	500,000
Total Payment	$750,000	$725,000	$700,000	$675,000	$650,000	$625,000	$600,000
Balloon Payment							1,500,000
Year-End Balance	4,500,000	4,000,000	3,500,000	3,000,000	2,500,000	2,000,000	0

Online Companion Hands On: Select the Fig PIII.12 tab in the Excel file and study it to make sure you are comfortable with it.

CONSTRUCTION LOANS/NEGATIVE AMORTIZATION LOANS

Buildings take time to build. This means that you can go for months, even years without generating revenue, while incurring development costs. During the development phase, you will likely choose to take on a fixed amount of debt to fund project costs. You will be charged interest on all principal borrowed, but you will not be able to pay the interest from the income or sales revenue the property generates until much later after you have completed construction. Lenders understand this situation and offer **construction loans**. With these loans, principal amounts needed for each month's project costs are borrowed monthly (through a loan **draw request**), and loan interest accrues (accumulates) and is added to the loan principal balance. This uncollected interest is known as **accrued interest**, or **capitalized interest,** as opposed to the **current-pay interest** of non-accrual acquisition loans.

Because the loan principal outstanding is growing over time (rather than decreasing as with positive amortization loans), construction loans are also called **negative amortization loans**. Since interest charges that are not paid are added to the principal owed, new interest is charged on old unpaid interest plus the cumulative principal draw amount. In reality, interest is included in each month's draw of principal from the lender.

As dollars are fungible, the interest the lender lets you borrow exposes them financially to the project in the same way the drawn principal does. As such, construction loans are designed so that a portion of the overall dollar exposure is reserved for the eventual total interest amount. This is referred to as the **funded interest reserve** component of the loan.

Figure PIII.13 displays a quarterly pro forma for the conversion of a boutique office building that will become a 17-unit residential condominium building. The total project cost is $6.3 million, with $2.1 million (one-third of cost) funded by equity and $4.2 million (two-thirds of cost) funded by the construction loan. Equity funds first in full, followed by debt. The negative unlevered cash flows derive from the development and construction costs. Notice how until Q1 of Year 3, no revenue is reflected in the pro forma.

 **Online Companion Hands On:** Select the Fig PIII.13 tab in the Excel file and complete the exercise. Answers from this tab feed into the Fig PIII.14 tab.

FIGURE PIII.13

Condominium Development Pro Forma

	Time 0
Initial Investment	
Purchase of Building	(3,600,000)
Transaction Cost	(108,000)
Subtotal	(3,708,000)

	Year 1				Year 2				Year 3		
	Q1	Q2	Q3	Q4	Q1	Q2	Q3	Q4	Q1	Q2	Q3
Revenue											
Pre-sales											
2-Bedroom									946,218	946,218	
3-Bedroom									1,314,192		
Subtotal	0				0	0	0	0	2,260,410	0	0
Regular Sales											
2-Bedroom									2,365,545	946,218	
3-Bedroom									2,628,384	1,314,192	
Subtotal		0	0	0	0	0	0	0	4,993,929	2,260,410	0
Total Revenue		0	0	0	0	0	0	0	7,254,339	2,260,410	0
Expenses											
Development & Construction	(100,000)	(200,000)	(200,000)	(300,000)	(1,000,000)	(700,000)	(60,000)	(32,000)	0	0	0
Sales Costs	0	0	0	0	0	0	0	0	(217,630)	(67,812)	0
Subtotal	(100,000)	(200,000)	(200,000)	(300,000)	(1,000,000)	(700,000)	(60,000)	(32,000)	(217,630)	(67,812)	0
Unlevered Cash Flow	($3,708,000)	($100,000)	($200,000)	($200,000)	($300,000)	($1,000,000)	($700,000)	($60,000)	($32,000)	$7,036,709	$2,192,598	$0

Figure PIII.14 shows the construction loan draws and estimates the interest portion of each draw.

FIGURE PIII.14

Condominium Project Construction Loan Projection

	Total	Time 0	Year 1 Q1	Q2	Q3	Q4	Year 2 Q1	Q2	Q3	Q4	Year 3 Q1
Unlevered Cash Flows		($3,708,000)	($100,000)	($200,000)	($200,000)	($300,000)	($1,000,000)	($700,000)	($60,000)	($32,000)	$7,036,709
Debt											
Principal											
Beginning Balance			1,608,000	1,708,000	1,908,000	2,108,000	2,408,000	3,408,000	4,108,000	4,168,000	4,200,000
Draws (includes interest)	$4,200,000	1,608,000	100,000	200,000	200,000	300,000	1,000,000	700,000	60,000	32,000	0
Repayment	($3,778,060)		0	0	0	0	0	0	0	0	(3,778,060)
Ending Balance		$1,608,000	$1,708,000	$1,908,000	$2,108,000	$2,408,000	$3,408,000	$4,108,000	$4,168,000	$4,200,000	$0
Interest											
Accrual Beginning Balance			0	28,186	58,922	93,058	131,444	180,880	244,766	315,112	386,240
Interest	$421,940		28,186	30,736	34,136	38,386	49,436	63,886	70,346	71,128	35,700
Repayment	($421,940)		0	0	0	0	0	0	0	0	(421,940)
Accrual Ending Balance			$28,186	$58,922	$93,058	$131,444	$180,880	$244,766	$315,112	$386,240	$0

The debt is calculated in the following manner. At Time 0, the purchase price of the land and building, plus transaction costs, is $3.708 million. Of that amount, $2.1 million comes from equity and the remaining required $1.608 million is funded with debt. At the point of property acquisition, the entire $2.1 million of equity is invested. In Year 1 Q1, $100,000 is drawn and added to the loan principal balance, yielding a cumulative principal draw at period end of $1.708 million.

To estimate the quarterly interest amount contained in this $100,000 draw, we multiply the average of $1.608 million and $1.708 million by the quarterly interest rate, which is 6.8%/4. This calculation yields $28,186 in Year 1 Q1 interest that was borrowed in the initial $100,000 draw. The average of $1.608 million and $1.708 million is taken because we only pay interest on what we borrow. As we do not borrow the $1.708 million all at once, we average the two numbers to get a more realistic average loan balance over the 3 months of the quarter. In Q2, we multiply the average of the $1.708 million beginning principal balance and the $1.908 million principal ending balance by the quarterly interest rate. To track the total interest accrued, the $28,186 from Q1 gets carried over to the interest accrual beginning balance in Q2 and then is added to Q2 interest obligation of $30,736.

The $4.2 million in debt drawn includes $421,940 in interest. You can see this clearly in that the repayment of principal total is just $3.778 million, while the repayment of interest is $421,940. The name of the game as a construction loan borrower (all else equal) is to get the lowest interest rate possible and complete construction as fast as possible. This is for the simple reason that the higher the interest rate and the longer construction takes, the smaller the portion of the nominal loan amount that is available for project hard and soft costs, as the interest dollars consume the fixed loan size the same way that principal draws do.

When positive cash flows are generated by the property through the closing of condominium unit sales, both the loan principal and accrued interest are repaid. Once they are repaid in full, then any excess cash flows will go to the equity holders.

 **Online Companion Hands On:** Select the Fig PIII.14 tab in the Excel file and complete the exercise.

Supplemental I
The Return Characteristics of Commercial Real Estate

There are two commonly used real estate investment return benchmarks, the NCREIF Property Index and the FTSE NAREIT U.S. Real Estate Index, each of which are broken down by various sub-categories.

NCREIF

The National Council of Real Estate Investment Fiduciaries (NCREIF; pronounced nay-creef) index provides quarterly return (capital appreciation and income) data for privately-owned real estate. The index is available on the NCREIF website at www.ncreif.org. It is primarily an appraisal-based index, which means the reporting property asset managers hire an appraiser to "divine" what the property "should be" (not necessarily what it is) worth, as only a closed sale transaction can truly establish value. These non-market-based estimates can be manipulated to overstate values in order to make performance look better than reality. Furthermore, appraisals are usually conducted only once a year, or quarterly at best. This results in a "smoothed" return series relative to data series with a higher frequency of measurement, such as the NAREIT's daily data. Due to the infrequency of measurement of its comprising properties, the NCREIF Index unsurprisingly lags market valuation changes, typically by about 18 months. Additionally, the use of appraisals necessarily means that NCREIF returns will be uncorrelated with stock and bond returns, even though movements in real estate market values are moderately correlated with broader financial markets.

The index includes properties acquired and managed on behalf of large institutional managers. Properties owned by entrepreneurial investors are generally not included. The underlying assets are predominantly core properties in major U.S. markets and include the apartment, industrial, office, and retail sectors. The returns are reported on an unlevered basis, which further reduces the volatility of the return series relative to more typically leveraged real estate returns. Calculations are based on quarterly returns from these properties, indexed to the fourth quarter of 1977 (when the series began). Returns are weighted by property value, as determined by the real estate appraisals. Figure SI.1 displays the national annual total returns series. Return series are available by geographic location and property type as well as by the allocation between income and appreciation.

FIGURE SI.1

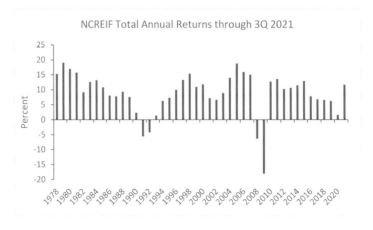

NAREIT

The National Association of Real Estate Investment Trust (NAREIT) index measures the total return (price appreciation and income) on the portfolio of publicly traded REITs, indexed to December 31, 1971. The index is available on the NAREIT website at www.nareit.com.

Unlike the NCREIF index, this is a transaction-based index of publicly traded REIT stock prices that are marked to market each trading day. The NAREIT index captures REIT share prices, not the underlying properties. Furthermore, since the NAREIT index tracks the return of publicly traded REITs, the index is moderately levered, with most companies utilizing roughly 50% leverage. This makes it more volatile than a comparable pool of unlevered properties. In addition to levered property returns, the index captures changes in the value of REIT management.

Figure SI.2 displays the historic annual total returns of the equity NAREIT index from 1978 through 3Q 2021 broken down by price appreciation and income.

FIGURE SI.2

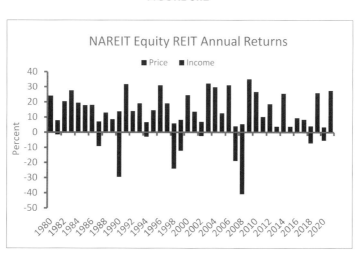

Figure SI.3 displays the annual mean return and standard deviation for the NCREIF Property Index, the NAREIT Equity Index, 1-year and 10-year Treasury yields, inflation (CPI-all goods), and the S&P 500 Index from 1978 through 3Q 2021. Using standard deviation as a proxy for volatility, CPI, which captures the broadest set of data (i.e., pricing of all consumer products) has the lowest volatility among the six metrics. This is followed by the risk-free 10-year and 1-year Treasury yields, the NCREIF Index, the S&P 500, and the NAREIT Index. Interestingly, the NCREIF and NAREIT Indices have strikingly different volatility levels despite both measuring real estate sector returns. In fact, volatility of the NCREIF Index is less than half that of the NAREIT index. While NCREIF's notably lower volatility may reflect the real residual value of real estate relative to Treasury bonds, it much more likely reflects the substantial artificial smoothing of NCREIF returns.

The NAREIT index indicates REIT stocks have modestly higher returns and return volatility versus the S&P 500 Index. This risk profile is more reflective of the volatility of modestly leveraged real estate returns than the NCREIF index.

FIGURE SI.3

Summary Statistics of NCREIF and NAREIT Index Returns (1978 - 3Q 2021)						
	NCREIF	NAREIT	1-year Treasury	10-year Treasury	S&P 500	CPI
Annual Mean Return	8.74%	12.09%	4.84%	6.05%	9.70%	3.47%
Standard Deviation	7.23%	18.91%	3.88%	3.35%	16.12%	2.77%

Figure SI.4 displays the correlation matrix for the NAREIT, 1-year Treasury, 10-year Treasury, inflation, and the S&P 500 based on quarterly returns from 1978 through 3Q 2021. These correlations are a useful metric for parameterizing the risk of an asset between the NAREIT Index and the Treasury yields, CPI, and the S&P 500. These correlations suggest a moderate relationship between real estate returns and the broader stock market. Although REITs traded inversely to the broader equity market during the late 1990s tech boom and the early stages of the 2000s tech bust, it is clear that the public REIT returns are impacted by broader market and economic fluctuations. An interesting paradox is that over short intervals real estate returns have no correlation with inflation, and thus do little to hedge inflation. However, over longer periods (say every 5 years) and for large inflation rates, real estate does provide an inflation hedge. Note any correlations with the NCREIF Index are largely meaningless due to the appraisal smoothing effect.

FIGURE SI.4

Correlation with NAREIT (1978 - 3Q 2021)			
	1-year Treasury	10-year Treasury	S&P 500	CPI
Correlation	0.06	0.11	0.53	0.09

LINKAGE BETWEEN NAREIT AND NCREIF

While the NAREIT index tracks public equity REIT returns over the long term, NCREIF returns should reflect returns on real estate. Taken alone, the standard deviation of the NCREIF Index would seem to indicate that real estate is a relatively low-risk asset, but the NAREIT Index volatility is twice as high, suggesting otherwise. So, why are the returns and standard deviations for the NAREIT and NCREIF indexes so drastically different (Figure SI.5)?

FIGURE SI.5

Comparison of Real Estate Returns (1978 - 3Q 2021)		
	NCREIF	NAREIT
Annual Mean Return	8.74%	12.09%
Standard Deviation	7.23%	18.91%

The measurement methodologies of the NCREIF and NAREIT Indices explain most of this apparent disconnect. Specifically, appraisal valuations and differential leverage are the sources. Since appraisals dictate the returns for the NCREIF index, movements in the index tend to occur only when NOI changes substantially or the cap rate fluctuates, and even then, only when the properties are appraised. Since full-blown appraisals are costly and of limited operational value, they are generally ordered only once a year (at the end of the fourth quarter). This explains the much lower volatility in the index, as value in quarters one through three remain relatively constant, only capturing the relatively minor movements in income for these stabilized assets. In comparison, the NAREIT index captures the countless transactions of publicly traded REITs. The active trading of these securities provide constant pricing based on expectations about future NOI. Therefore, the NAREIT index tends to be a leading indicator for movements in the NCREIF index. Thus, the NAREIT index is a better long-term indicator of return performance for a high-quality real estate portfolio employing moderate leverage.

BENCHMARKING

While neither the NAREIT nor the NCREIF Indices are perfect measures of real estate returns, they are frequently used to benchmark real estate performance. To quote former NYC Mayor Ed Koch, everybody wants to know, "How'm I doin'?" For real estate private equity funds, as opposed to public REITs, that question is not simply answered. Despite the proliferation of such funds, a useful return benchmark has yet to evolve. This does not mean the sector is not smart enough to create one but, rather, that these funds have diverse investment strategies, most of which are very dissimilar to traditional real estate investments. The diversity of investment strategies includes the fact that some funds invest abroad while others focus domestically. Some funds develop and redevelop, while others execute highly leveraged acquisitions of core assets. Further complications arise because some focus on distressed debt and non-performing loans, while still others acquire portfolios of corporate or government assets. And these differences only scratch the surface.

What about the applicability of common real estate benchmarks such as the NCREIF and NAREIT indices? Let us begin with the NCREIF index. Putting aside the statistical problem of the 18-month appraisal lag, ask yourself what kind of properties the NCREIF index tracks. For the most part, these are the returns of stabilized, domestic, unleveraged, institutional-grade properties. As a result, NCREIF returns will be relatively stable. The investment objective for the properties in this index is not to achieve a 20%+ IRR but, rather, to provide a relatively safe, high single-digit return.

Turning to the NAREIT index, the appraisal lag issue disappears due to its real-time pricing. Yet, returns generated by REITs are also not an appropriate benchmark for private equity funds, as REITs generally own high-quality, stabilized, domestic real estate, as opposed to the more opportunistic assets favored by private equity funds. In addition, REIT assets are leveraged 40%-60%, versus 65%-75% for private equity funds. The investment objective for firms in the NAREIT index is to provide relatively safe dividends and a low double-digit total return.

These fundamental differences between the respective NCREIF and NAREIT investment objectives and those of private equity funds render these benchmarks futile for comparison with real estate private equity funds. In fact, at almost no point during their investment horizon should private equity fund returns remotely track either the NCREIF or NAREIT indices. It is not just a matter of comparing apples to oranges but, rather, apples to screwdrivers.

To demonstrate the differences in return patterns between the NCREIF and NAREIT indices and real estate private equity funds, we simulate the expected performance of each. The first scenario is the unleveraged purchase of $100 million of stabilized properties at a going-in cap rate of 8%, with a 2% per annum NOI growth rate. A 50-basis point management fee is deducted from this return stream. This represents the typical NCREIF property. The second scenario assumes $100 million is invested in REITs, which use 50% leverage on its stabilized portfolio. The REIT properties yield 8% on NOI, with a 2% NOI growth rate and a 50-basis point management fee. The REITs pay out 70% of their cash flow in dividends and reinvest the remainder at the same 8% cap rate and the same 50% leverage. In the third scenario, a private equity fund buys unstabilized assets that will take 3 years of hard work to stabilize. By the end of the third year, these assets achieve the same stabilized performance as those owned by REITs. Assuming NOI in years 1-3 are negative $2 million, $2 million, and $6 million, respectively, and a 20% IRR is achieved over the 7-year life of the fund, we can determine the initial purchase price for these assets. In years 4-7 (the duration of our analysis), these properties are stabilized and generate exactly the same NOI as in the first 2 scenarios. The private equity fund uses 70% leverage, and management fees are also higher, at 1.5%. Figure SI.6 summarizes key information for each strategy.

FIGURE SI.6

	Simulated Return Assumptions		
	NCREIF	NAREIT	Private Equity
Purchase Price	$100,000,000	$100,000,000	$77,740,060
LTV	0.0%	50.0%	70.0%
Equity	$100,000,000	$50,000,000	$23,322,018
Interest Rate	0.0%	6.0%	6.3%
Going-in Cap Rate (Stabilized)	8.0%	8.0%	n/a
NOI Growth Rate	2.0%	2.0%	n/a
Residual Cap Rate	8.0%	8.0%	8.0%
Residual Value	$114,868,567	$136,200,746	$114,868,567
Dividend Payout	100%	70%	100%
Management Fee	0.5%	0.5%	1.5%
IRR (Mark-to-Market)	10.0%	15.2%	25.4%
IRR	9.5%	12.8%	20.0%

At the end of year 7, all assets are sold for an 8 cap by the investors, yielding about $115 million in sale proceeds, before debt, for scenarios I and III. Because of the reinvestment of retained earnings over the 7 years, the REIT generates a portfolio valued at about $136 million, including approximately $60 million of debt. In the case of the private equity fund, we assume that, at the end of year 3, when the assets are stabilized, they are refinanced at 70% of their stabilized value and excess refinancing proceeds are paid out to investors.

Each investment scenario generates its own IRR, cash payment stream, and total return stream. The cash payment stream is simply the actual cash flow generated for each year. Realized cash flows are back-end weighted, as only a liquidation event or refinancing taps value appreciation.

In the simulated NCREIF scenario, annual total returns track slightly higher than annual cash flow returns due to appreciation, but upon liquidation, the cash flow analysis will catch up with the cumulative mark-to-market return. This pattern also holds for the REIT scenario, with a larger back-end spread due to the leveraged reinvestment of retained earnings. For the private equity fund, due to the negative NOI and high leverage, negative total returns are recorded for the first 2 years of the fund. Only as the repositioning is successful in year 3 does the return become positive.

Due to its investment strategy, the real estate private equity fund returns are negative in the early years, as the properties are ramping toward stabilization. The expected cumulative private equity fund return is roughly an S-curve. As stated earlier, at no point in time should either the cash flow or mark-to-market equity returns for the private equity fund be expected to resemble those of either the NCREIF or REIT scenarios. In the first 3 years, the fund should under-perform the NCREIF and NAREIT benchmarks on a cumulative basis, but upon successful stabilization, it surpasses the performance of the other 2 investment structures (Figures SI.7 and SI.8).

FIGURE SI.7

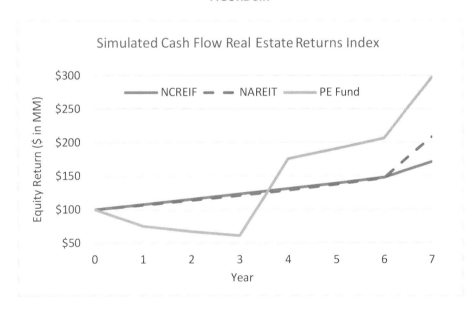

FIGURE SI.8

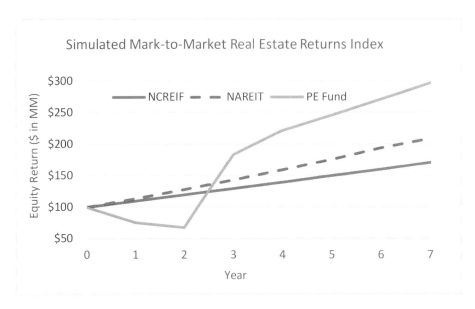

While the private equity fund achieves a higher IRR, there is the risk that they fail to achieve stabilization. Similarly, increased leverage by the REITs and the private equity investors results in a more volatile return stream than for NCREIF.

These simulations capture the fact that neither NCREIF nor NAREIT provides appropriate return benchmarks for private equity funds. With that said, there are two insights that investors can utilize to prevent their fund managers from operating in a complete return vacuum. First, private equity fund managers should regularly benchmark their actual performance against themselves. That is, how are they performing compared to their own projections? Secondly, upon fund maturity, investors can compare the actual return spread over NCREIF and NAREIT relative to expectation. This spread should be about 700 basis points above NAREIT and about 1,000 basis points above NCREIF. While these do not answer the "How'm I doin'?" question, they do provide a disciplined analytical framework.

Supplemental IA
The Return Volatility of Publicly and Privately Owned Real Estate

A comparison of historical recessions
Dr. Peter Linneman – *Wharton Real Estate Review* – Fall 2004

THE MARKETLESS VALUE OF REAL ESTATE

The debate about whether privately owned real estate has a lower return volatility than its publicly owned counterpart has been going on for a long time. It began when academics analyzed the then-newly compiled National Council of Real Estate Investment Fiduciaries (NCREIF) return series for unlevered real estate properties in the 1980s. These studies found that the returns derived from the NCREIF index had extremely low volatility, as well as very low correlations with stock and bond returns. This led some to proclaim that privately owned real estate was a "can't lose" investment, providing portfolio diversification with almost no return volatility and average returns not much different from stocks. Efficient investment frontier research seeped into investment practice, which suggested that privately owned real estate should comprise almost 100% of an "efficient" portfolio.

As the 1990s dawned, investors assumed that high-quality privately owned real estate could never fall substantially in value. But the early 1990s demonstrated that private real estate assets had substantial return volatility, with values eroding by 20% to 50% during the first half of the decade. As the chairman of Rockefeller Center, one of the nation's prime core assets in the mid-1990s, I discovered all too well the volatility of private real estate returns. Yet, the NCREIF data failed to reveal significant negative returns. Instead, the NCREIF total return in 1990 was 2.3%, with negative returns registered only in 1991 (–5.6%) and 1992 (–4.3%) (Figure SIA.1). These numbers were in stark contrast to the reality experienced by private property owners. Since the disconnect between NCREIF and the market reality was too great to be explained by differences in property or management quality, savvy observers quickly realized that the NCREIF data was at best problematic, and at worst bogus.

FIGURE SIA.1

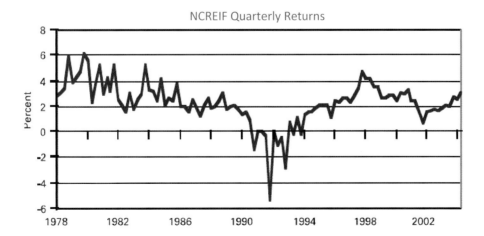

The early 1990s witnessed the emergence of major publicly owned REITs. Faced with the complete absence of debt and plummeting property values, many major private owners of real estate went public to recapitalize their properties, paying off maturing debt with IPO proceeds. Overnight, high-quality real estate was exposed to public market scrutiny and pricing, with many of the finest property portfolios trading on the NYSE. These REITs were managed by real estate professionals with expertise equal to, or better than, NCREIF asset managers. Thus, any differential return performance between the NCREIF index and REITs could not be attributed to either product or management quality.

A third investment vehicle, real estate private equity funds, evolved to help equitize real estate investments. These non-traded limited partnerships, with seven- to ten-year investment lives, use high leverage, frequently own foreign and lesser-quality properties, and often pursue development/redevelopment strategies. While the returns for these vehicles are not systematically reported, it is not surprising that the return history for these higher-risk, lower-quality, value-add investment vehicles substantially diverged from that of either NCREIF or REITs, as their returns do not generally reflect the performance of core U.S. properties.

NCREIF VERSUS NAREIT

NCREIF index properties are unlevered, while REITs are approximately 50% levered. In addition, REITs own both the company's real estate as well as the profit stream generated by management (net of executive compensation). In contrast, the NCREIF index reflects only returns on properties, with returns to managers captured by the asset management companies.

Returns to REITs, as proxied by the National Association of Real Estate Investment Trusts (NAREIT) Equity Index, and NCREIF should be highly correlated, as the key determinant of their returns is the profitability of core quality properties. REITs offer institutional investors a transparent and liquid real estate investment alternative to direct ownership. Since the mid-1990s, funds have flowed into REITs from traditional core real estate managers, causing many core managers to go out of business. Institutional investors were not only disappointed in the performance of real estate versus their expectations but also angry with managers who hid how badly their investments performed.

Yet, based upon studies of NCREIF returns, many researchers, managers, and investors continue to believe that privately owned real estate has almost no correlation with the returns of REITs, stocks, or bonds. For example, from the first quarter of 1990 through the first quarter of 2004, the correlation of NCREIF's return with that of NAREIT was -0.04, while with S&P 500 it was 0.01, and with long bonds -0.10. In addition, the standard deviation of quarterly returns for this same period was 3.4% for NCREIF, versus 10.5% for NAREIT, 11.3% for S&P 500, and 6.9% for long bonds (Figure SIA.2).

FIGURE SIA.2

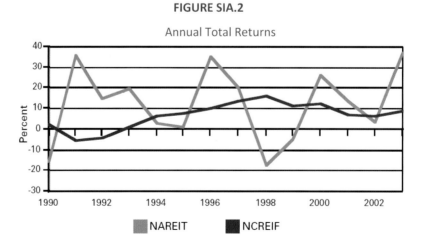

Annual Total Returns

As a result, many observers argue that institutional investors should own real estate both publicly and privately, with publicly owned real estate providing liquidity, and privately owned real estate providing return stability and diversification.

But these results cannot be correct, as buildings are inanimate objects, which do not know whether they are publicly or privately owned. Further, most core properties are managed by high-quality managers, whether the properties are publicly or privately owned. Therefore, large return discrepancies between public and private real estate ownership are not theoretically credible. Of course, minor return differences between public and private real estate can arise due to the valuation of management teams (which is a part of a REIT's valuation), or as a result of leverage, or because short-term capital movements are insufficient to arbitrage public versus private pricing. However, the return differences between NCREIF and NAREIT are not small, temporary, or occasional (Figure SIA.3). In five of the past 14 years, the annual returns for NCREIF and NAREIT are of opposite signs. Moreover, the average absolute difference in the annual returns of these series is a staggering 1,715 basis points, with this difference being fewer than 600 basis points in only two years. For example, 1998 REIT returns were shocked by the Russian ruble crisis, yielding a −17.5% return, while the NCREIF return was 16.2%, a gap of 3,370 basis points!

FIGURE SIA.3

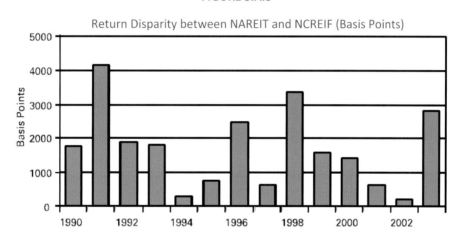

WHAT'S GOING ON?

The best research on the differences between NCREIF and NAREIT returns has been conducted by Joe Gyourko, first in a paper with Don Keim, and more recently in a paper in the *Wharton Real Estate Review*. He finds that NCREIF returns are predictable based upon historic REIT returns. Specifically, today's REIT returns foretell the NCREIF returns that will be registered roughly 18 months from now. As has been stated before, since buildings are inanimate, and since their quality of management is roughly similar, this relationship cannot be due to significant differences in property level cash flows, risk profiles, or management.

One need not be a believer in perfectly efficient markets to feel that it is inconceivable that capital markets so inefficiently value public versus private real estate cash streams. While anomalies can exist, they will be arbitraged, particularly given the large number of opportunity funds with the broad mandate to simply generate risk-adjusted real estate returns. If return differences are consistently as divergent as these series indicate, there should be no shortage of "smart money" to arbitrage the differences. In addition, REITs' property acquisitions and dispositions would arbitrage large differences in "Wall Street versus Main Street" values. Yet, during the past 14 years, despite the extraordinary differences in NCREIF and NAREIT returns, few REITs were taken private, very few major positions in REITs were taken by opportunity funds, and almost no REITs liquidated their portfolios.

The primary reason why large return discrepancies between NCREIF and NAREIT exist is simple: the data are wrong. This was vividly demonstrated during the Russian ruble crisis, when REITs fared terribly, while NCREIF registered returns well above average. Yet almost no public to private arbitrage took place, even though the return data indicate that such activity would have been highly profitable. No opportunity funds took advantage of the option suggested by the data. Nor did entrepreneurial REIT operators see an opportunity to go private. Instead, the market clearly believed that there was no significant return differential between public and private real estate. Like Sherlock Holmes' famous "dog that didn't bark," the market's silence demonstrated that the return gap is fiction rather than reality.

VALUATION ISSUES

NAREIT pricing and returns reflect market pricing by third parties investing in publicly traded securities, and thus have no notable measurement error. It is also an investable index, with several index funds readily available for investors. In contrast, the NCREIF index is neither investable nor a market-priced index. Specifically, it is impossible to create a portfolio that contains the NCREIF properties, and NCREIF property prices are very rarely set by third-party investors. Instead, they are established by appraisals.

Many have noted the so-called appraisal lag in valuing NCREIF properties. However, the NCREIF return measurement problem is much deeper, as most observers fail to appreciate how the appraisal process, even when well done, generates meaningless valuations for evaluating return volatility and correlations. In fact, the appraisal process guarantees that NCREIF's appraisal-driven returns will have very low volatility. Since the appraisal process, rather than private-market real estate pricing, creates near-zero volatility in measured returns, near-zero return correlations with REITs, stocks, and bonds are no surprise, as these assets have considerable return volatility. Specifically, if the returns for stocks, bonds, and publicly traded real estate are essentially random walks reflecting relatively efficient market pricing, NCREIF's near-zero appraisal-induced volatility will necessarily show little return correlation.

How does the use of appraised property values produce this result? The vast majority of NCREIF properties have a value appraisal only in the fourth quarter of each year. This contrasts dramatically with private property markets, where properties are constantly valued (though not appraised) by owners. Opportunity funds, entrepreneurial owners, and high-wealth families constantly evaluate their property values. Anyone who has worked with these owners knows that, over the course of a year, the values of privately owned properties rise and fall, depending on leasing, market sentiments, rumors about new developments, macroeconomic hopes and fears, and capital market animal instincts. Many private owners exploit these value movements by either selling or refinancing their properties at opportune times, or by holding their properties while waiting for better market pricing. This is the reality of private markets. Companies such as Eastdil, Secured Capital, and Goldman Sachs make their livings from the volatility of private real estate markets.

Consider what happens to a real estate return series if the value of a core property is recorded only on the last day of each year. Since a core property's Net Operating Income (NOI) generally varies relatively little throughout the year, so too will the measured return if the property price remains unchanged for four quarters. For example, if the property has a quarterly NOI growth rate of 1% (4.06% annual rate) and an 8% initial cap rate, the registered quarterly returns absent quarter-to-quarter price changes over the four quarters of the year are 2.02%, 2.04%, 2.06%, and 2.08%, respectively. Hence, for NCREIF's large pool of core assets, it is almost impossible to have much quarter-to-quarter return volatility without accurately measuring quarterly value changes. But if the preponderance of core properties is appraised only in the fourth quarter, the return registered for NCREIF is by definition basically the same in the fourth, first, second, and third quarters, as NOI does not change appreciably quarter-by-quarter. The fact that the recorded returns are basically the same over a four-quarter period provides no information about whether the actual quarterly returns were the same, and merely reflects that no attempt was made to determine whether asset prices changed quarter-to-quarter. This is the first source of NCREIF's return smoothing.

Imagine what would happen if NAREIT quarterly returns were measured simply by dividing the quarterly dividend by the fourth quarter cap rate. Since NAREIT dividends change relatively little quarter-to-quarter, this approach would record little REIT return volatility. Gyourko's research notes that during the first three quarters of the year, NCREIF returns register little volatility for private real estate. But savvy private owners know this is not the case. A point of reference is provided by (incorrectly) calculating NAREIT returns as the quarterly dividend plus appreciation, divided by the closing year-end stock price. Figure SIA.4 reveals that this exercise notably reduces the volatility of NAREIT's quarterly returns.

FIGURE SIA.4

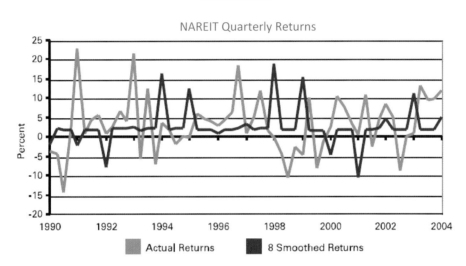

In fact, the standard deviation of NAREIT quarterly returns falls from 10.5% for actual NAREIT returns to 7.0% when this method is employed. Thus, if investors want lower REIT return volatility, and to look more like NCREIF's, they should only look at the REIT stock prices on the last day of each year!

QUADRUPLE SMOOTHING

The NCREIF measurement error story does not end here, as NCREIF's fourth quarter value generally reflects appraised—as opposed to market—property prices. To see how the appraisal process even further undercuts return measurement efforts, one must understand the appraisal process. When an "unbiased" appraiser (they may, like unicorns, exist somewhere) is engaged, their methodology for a core, stabilized property is to divide "stabilized" NOI (a second smoothing) by the cap rate of recent transactions for comparable properties. The period for which the appraiser seeks comparable sales transactions is typically 24 months. Over this 24-month period, the appraiser will generally find five to eight comparable property sales. The cap rate selected by the appraiser is usually the mean (or sometimes median) of the cap rates for these transactions. Rarely do appraisers give more weight to more recent transactions or evaluate cap rate trends. Thus, although each comparable property sold at a specific cap rate, at a specific time, the appraisal cap rate is an average (a third source of smoothing), which eliminates the high and low valuations that existed in the market; that is, it eliminates pricing volatility. The appraiser's rationale for cap rate averaging is that the market conditions that existed when those properties were sold are better or worse than those that exist "in more typical markets." Further, the appraisal for a property this year will generally re-use approximately half of the comparable sales transactions of the previous year's appraisal. Thus, this year's cap rate is mechanically linked to last year's cap rate, introducing a fourth source of NCREIF return smoothing.

Note that the appraisal methodology adopts the position that while higher and lower cap rates than average existed, they are of no relevance to a property's appraised value. In fact, every property was transacted at a cap rate higher or lower than the average, indicative of then-current market conditions. Stated bluntly, the appraisal process eliminates—not reveals—the truth about how properties are priced in private markets. In effect, the appraised value, far from being the market value, is a marketless value. That is, it is a value net of the vagaries of the market. Tellingly, no property is ever bought or sold at the appraiser's cap rate. Yet many researchers use the NCREIF return as if the cap rates used to value its properties reflect private property market prices. But by design, this is absolutely not the case.

The nature of the appraisal process means that even in the fourth quarter, the registered NCREIF value fails to reflect the prevailing market pricing, reflecting instead the average of market conditions that prevailed over the preceding two years. In fact, what NCREIF records as "today's cap rate" is actually the mean cap rate about 12 months earlier; that is, at the midpoint of the appraiser's time period. Hence, NCREIF fourth-quarter valuations effectively reflect "stabilized" NOI divided by the average cap rate a year ago. Quadruple-smoothed, with a lag.

This appraisal smoothing and lag not only reduces measured return volatility, but also almost necessarily eliminates any correlation with market return series. This is because if actual returns follow a random walk, inducing a one-year lag, the lagged series is uncorrelated with the original series, as the lag wipes out all correlation with all random series. Since stock, bond, and REIT returns have been shown to basically follow random walks, even if true private real estate returns were highly correlated with these series, the NCREIF appraisal lag would wipe out the correlation. The impact of lagging is vividly demonstrated by the fact that the correlation between quarterly S&P returns and the eight-quarter moving average of S&P returns is a mere 0.16 from 1990 through the first quarter of 2004 (Figure SIA.5). Thus, a series, which by definition is perfectly correlated with itself, is basically uncorrelated with a NCREIF-like lagged version of itself.

FIGURE SIA.5

Quarterly Return Correlation Coefficients					
Smoothed NAREIT[1]	Smoothed NAREIT[2]	Unlevered NCREIF	Levered NCREIF	S&P 500	Long Bonds
Acutal NAREIT	-.16	-.21	-.05	-.05	.40	.08
Smoothed NAREIT[1]		.55	.14	.15	-.04	-.10
Smoothed NAREIT[2]			.14	.14	.12	.24
Unlevered NCREIF				.99	.01	-.10
Levered NCREIF					.01	-.10
S&P 500						-.09

1 Based upon eight-quarter moving average NAREIT price.

2 Based upon eight-quarter moving average NAREIT price, with estimated price unchanged for four consecutive quarters.

The fact is that while NAREIT returns reflect actual returns for an investable public real estate portfolio, NCREIF returns measure nothing remotely like actual returns for a core private portfolio. The 12-month valuation lag is accentuated over the subsequent three quarters, as NCREIF's appraised values are generally not changed during these quarters. Thus, the cap rate used in the appraisals is initially four quarters out of date, falling to five, six, and seven quarters over the next three quarters. As the property values are reappraised in the fourth quarter, the lag once again reverts to four quarters, and the process repeats. It is hardly surprising that Gyourko's research consistently finds a roughly 18-month statistical relationship between REIT returns (actual market pricing) and NCREIF's lagged returns.

IT'S ONLY REAL ESTATE

To see how quadruple-smoothing-and-a-lag mechanically affects measured returns, we calculate a variety of incorrectly measured quarterly REIT returns. First, for each quarter, the quarterly return is calculated as the sum of the actual NAREIT dividend plus percentage price appreciation, where price is defined as the moving average NAREIT price for the preceding eight quarters. This smoothing and lagging reduces the standard deviation of NAREIT quarterly returns from 10.5% for actual returns, to 4.9%. Conducting the same analysis with NAREIT price calculated as the NAREIT dividend divided by the eight-quarter NAREIT moving average cap rate results in an estimated REIT quarterly return standard deviation of 5.7%.

We also recalculate quarterly NAREIT returns, where for the fourth quarter the return is the actual NAREIT dividend divided by the moving average NAREIT cap rate for the preceding eight quarters, plus the percentage increase in that price over the similarly calculated price of a year earlier, where for the first, second, and third quarters there is no price change. The standard deviation of NAREIT quarterly returns for this approach is 7.7%.

How do these results compare to NCREIF? Recall that NCREIF is unlevered, while NAREIT is roughly 50% levered. To adjust for the different leverage, we calculated quarterly returns for a 50% leveraged NCREIF, at an interest rate of the three-year Treasury plus 150 basis points. The standard deviation of this levered NCREIF series is 5.2% (versus 3.4% for unlevered NCREIF). This levered NCREIF return volatility compares to 10.5% for actual NAREIT, and 5.7% and 7.7% for the smoothed NAREIT series. Plus, one must remember that the use of actual, rather than "stabilized," NAREIT dividends in these calculations makes NAREIT returns more volatile than levered NCREIF, which uses "stabilized" NOI. Thus, when compared on an apples-to-apples basis, the return volatilities of NCREIF are NAREIT are basically the same.

The correlation coefficients of the alternative quarterly return series are displayed in Figure SIA.5. Note that smoothed and lagged NAREIT returns, like both NCREIF and unlevered NCREIF, show little correlation with the S&P 500 or long bonds. This is because the non-volatility induced by quadruple-smoothing-and-a-lag correlates to almost nothing. In contrast, the mean returns for the various NAREIT returns are only slightly altered by these smoothing calculations, because the time shifting only slightly alters the time period over which returns are effectively measured. Further, smoothed NAREIT returns have a much higher (though still low) correlation with NCREIF.

The best series to measure real estate returns is neither NCREIF nor the smoothed NAREIT series but, rather, the actual REIT return series. This is because mark-to-market, contemporaneous, arm's-length, non-smoothed pricing is the reality of both public and private real estate. The truth is that modestly leveraged core real estate has a low correlation with stocks and bonds, but displays notable return volatility, though somewhat less so than stocks.

No one involved in private real estate markets will find these results surprising. After all, real estate ownership of core assets incorporates many of the dimensions of high-quality bonds, with superior residual value protection because it is a real (rather than nominal) asset. The result is that non-residential real estate has less cash stream volatility than the equity and debt claims on its tenants, since in good times, tenants expand their space demand more slowly than their profits increase, while in bad times the reverse is true. In addition, the supply and demand fundamentals of real estate follow unique patterns, further diminishing the return correlations with other assets. Similarly, residential real estate follows its own time patterns, as even in poor economic times, population increases and absorption generally occurs, although at a slower rate. Also, supply and demand patterns for these properties move differently from other asset categories.

DAY-TO-DAY REIT VOLATILITY

As is the case with a publicly traded security of any company, one is struck by the fact that in any one-hour or one-day trading period, the price of a REIT (or any) stock can go up or down by several percentage points, for no apparent reason. It is true that privately owned real estate does not have such minute-to-minute, hour-to-hour, or day-to-day price volatility, as deals are not struck in private markets on such an instantaneous basis. The presence of such price volatility for REITs means investment opportunities are available via the public ownership of private real estate that are not present with private ownership. Specifically, this volatility allows institutional owners of REITs to take advantage of momentary mispricings of their stocks by selling or shorting when prices are "too high," and incrementally buying when prices are "too low." Such trading provides an additional margin for well-capitalized institutional investors to exploit temporary pricing anomalies. Of course, just as is the case for private real estate, if one is convinced that REIT prices are too high, one can sell one's entire position. Similarly, if one believes that prices are too low, one can hold stocks until prices rise. Publicly owned real estate allows investors to incrementally alter their investment position when they believe pricing is too low or too high. In fact, aggressive institutional investors may go so far as to short assets when they believe prices are too high. Thus, far from being a negative aspect of public real estate investment, the presence of micro price volatility can only benefit well-capitalized long-term investors. At worst, the institutional investor can simply ignore such pricing variability and simply trade out of their holdings on last day of each quarter, in which case they realize NAREIT returns.

WHAT'S IT ALL MEAN?

There is no magical potion in the private ownership of core real estate that eliminates return volatility and correlation with other assets. The fact that investors continue to believe this is the case reflects either a fundamental misunderstanding of the NCREIF data, or purposeful ignorance about the realities of real estate markets. The truth is that high-quality, stabilized real estate should be a major part of institutional investors' portfolios and that public ownership provides the same long-term return patterns as private ownership, with the enhanced advantages of exploiting temporary mispricings and liquidity.

Core real estate provides solid long-term returns, somewhat lower volatility relative to stocks, and relatively modest correlation with the returns on other assets. However, the purported advantages of private core real estate ownership are a mirage. What matters are the quality of the property and the ability of the manager to execute a viable operating strategy, whether public or private.

Private core real estate ownership for many institutions is a narcotic that creates the "comfortably numb" illusion of non-volatility in a harsh and demanding mark-to-market world. It is one of the few remaining assets where you can pretend that your assets have not changed in price, even when they have. Hopefully, such illusions will soon be a thing of the past.

Supplemental II
CMBS Case Study

Let's look a little closer at an actual CMBS issue, specifically, <u>Lehman Brothers Commercial Mortgage Trust, Series 1998-C4</u>. This particular CMBS pool originated with 286 loans, secured by 327 properties. As of May 15, 2003, two of the loans were in bankruptcy, reducing the loan pool to 284 loans. Note that the values of the CMBS issue change every day, and all of the data in this Supplemental are as of May 2003. All loans were originated prior to November 17, 1998. The CMBS package was priced on November 17, 1998 and closed on November 24, 1998. Since then, each tranche of this deal has traded separately. The pool is exemplary because of its size, mix of loans, concentration of low LTVs, low weighted-average debt service coverage ratio (DSCR), and good credit history. But remember that each CMBS pool is unique, depending on its collateral and tranche structure.

The largest loan, Omni Hotels, represented about 12% of the total loan value of the pool, with the remaining 283 loans representing 88% of the pool. The discrepancy makes the pool very sensitive to a single loan.

The pool's beginning loan balance was $2,025,590,706. As a result of amortization, the loan balance as of May 15, 2003 was $1,913,478,129. Loans begin maturing in August 2003, with the last loan maturing in September 2023. Hence, not only is each CMBS pool unique but it also changes over time as loans mature or default and as tranches expire.

The overall pool is referred to as a **fixed-rate fusion pool**, as there are both conduit loans (58% of the pool) of less than $30,000,000 and large loans (39% of the pool) of more than $30,000,000. A **conduit loan** is a relatively small loan, which was made with the objective of placing it into a CMBS offering. Net credit lease properties, which are very high LTV loans made on the basis of the high credit rating of the net lease tenant, make up 3.9% of the pool. All the loans carry fixed interest rates.

When the tranches trade, they are priced relative to the prevailing interest rate at that time. For floating rate loans and tranches, all pricing is relative to LIBOR (London Inter-bank Overnight Rate) or short-term Treasury rates at that time. The conversion from floating LIBOR to fixed Treasury can be done through a swap transaction. There are several types of LIBOR that are used: 30-day LIBOR, 90-day LIBOR, 180-day LIBOR, or 1-year LIBOR.

ORIGINATORS, SERVICERS AND ISSUERS

The originator of this CMBS pool was Lehman Brothers. They assembled the loans and constructed the pool, as well as designed the legal structure. They also marketed it for a fee. The issuer is Structured Assets Securities Corporation, a special-purpose bankruptcy-remote company whose sole assets are the loans. The pool's master servicer, which is the issuer's outsourced management, is First Union National Bank. They are in charge of servicing the loans and tranches and making sure that there are no problems with the loans. They collect the loan payments, keep the books, send disbursement checks to the tranche owners, file reports, etc. There is also a special servicer for this pool, with contractual rights and duties to deal with defaults, foreclosures, and special situations. These servicers work for fees, which are paid from the issuing entity's revenues.

GEOGRAPHY AND PROPERTY TYPES

The 327 properties are located in 35 different states and Puerto Rico, ranging from Massachusetts to Washington. The four states with the greatest loan concentration are California, New York, Florida, and Texas. There are many loans which pool properties across states (Figure SII.1).

FIGURE SII.1

Profile of Lehman Brothers Commercial Mortgage Trust, Series 1998-C4 - May 15, 2003			
Collateral Location	Loan Count	Scheduled Balance	Share Based on Balance
California	22	$385,544,509	20.15%
New York	30	162,789,424	8.51%
Florida	30	158,906,976	8.30%
Texas	30	95,819,792	5.01%
Illinois	17	76,199,735	3.98%
Pennsylvania	9	70,484,781	3.68%
Indiana	8	64,671,550	3.38%
Virginia	15	63,697,794	3.33%
Arizona	14	63,440,752	3.32%
Alabama	4	58,088,633	3.04%
Georgia	12	56,106,336	2.93%
North Carolina	15	49,821,463	2.60%
Tennessee	7	46,953,909	2.45%
Washington	7	44,297,199	2.32%
Connecticut	7	30,053,568	1.57%
Nevada	3	25,102,254	1.31%
Ohio	6	21,238,710	1.11%
Colorado	6	19,719,666	1.03%
Maryland	5	17,637,089	0.92%
Oklahoma	2	17,459,305	0.91%
Michigan	3	16,690,648	0.87%
New Jersey	5	12,580,616	0.66%
Massachusetts	4	10,706,285	0.56%
Missouri	3	9,543,099	0.50%
Oregon	2	8,909,206	0.47%
Wisconsin	2	8,451,240	0.44%
South Carolina	3	5,568,376	0.29%
Puerto Rico	1	5,337,249	0.28%
Rhode Island	2	5,023,041	0.26%
Other	10	302,634,923	15.82%
Total	284	$1,913,478,128	100.00%

Most of the loans were originated in 1998, with 2.75% of the pool maturing in 2003 and the last ones maturing on September 1, 2023. The majority of the loans (78.05%) mature in 2008, representing 10-year loan maturities.

The number of loans per property sector is shown in Figure SII.2. A weakness of the pool is the high concentration of loans in the retail sector. The problem with a large concentration of loans in one sector is that if something happens to the retail industry (e.g., the Kmart bankruptcy) during the course of the loan terms, the loan pool has a relatively concentrated potential for default.

FIGURE SII.2

Lehman Brother Commercial Mortgage Trust, Series 1998-C4 Loans by Property Sector		
Sector	Loan Count	Share Based on Balance
Retail	134	44.25%
Multi-family	63	17.84%
Lodging	16	17.43%
Office	45	15.31%
Industrial	16	3.31%
Self Storage	5	0.75%
Health Care	1	0.70%
Mobile Home	3	0.25%
Other	1	0.16%
Total	284	100.00%

The main retail loans are secured by properties such as the Bayside Mall in Miami, FL, and Mills in Ontario, Canada, which includes tenants like JC Penny, Marshall's, and Burlington Coat Factory. Of the top ten loans, six are secured by retail properties, two by lodging, one by office, and one by multifamily. The largest loan in the pool is $228,681,211 to TRT Holdings, secured by 5 hotels, an office building, and a retail component.

LTVs AND INTEREST COVERAGE

The original LTVs for the loans in the pool are displayed in Figure SII.3, which was acquired from the November 1998 Moody's rating report. Usually LTVs are only updated when the loan goes into default. The high initial LTVs are not uncommon, as the value of the properties should rise as they stabilize. The majority of the loans were in the range of 90-100%, but these loans represent only 47% of the value of the loan pool. Figure SII.3 analyzes the large loans separately, as their size may give them a larger impact on the rest of the pool. Note how the larger loans are more conservatively levered relative to the conduits, which have a 92% weighted-average LTV.

FIGURE SII.3

Lehman Brothers Commercial Mortgage Trust, Series 1998-C4 Original LTVs				
Loan-To-Value for conduit portion			Loan-To-Value for large loans	
LTV	Loan Count	Share Based on Balance	Collateral Property	LTV
Less than 80%	54	7.70%	Omni Hotels	63%
80-90%	68	28.40%	Ontario Mills	69%
90-100%	100	46.80%	Arden Portfolio	64%
100-110%	44	14.50%	Fresno Fashion Fair	71%
Greater than 110%	12	2.60%	Bayside Market Place	74%
Total		100.00%		
Conduit Weighted Average:		92% LTV		

DEBT SERVICE COVERAGE RATIO

The original DSCR (debt service coverage ratio) for the loans in this pool range from less than 1.00x, to more than 2.00x. As of May 2003, the weighted-average DSCR was a relatively strong 1.88x (Figure SII.4).

FIGURE SII.4

Lehman Brothers Commercial Mortgage Trust, Series 1998-C4 DSCRs			
Original DSCR	Loan Count	Scheduled Balance	Share Based on Balance
0.500 or less	2	$2,990,992	0.16%
0.500-0.625	0	$0	0.00%
0.625-0.750	4	$11,925,822	0.62%
0.750-0.875	4	$9,015,746	0.47%
0.875-1.000	13	$39,176,623	2.05%
1.000-1.125	22	$77,333,241	4.04%
1.125-1.125	19	$138,861,946	7.26%
1.125-1.375	21	$108,888,491	5.69%
1.375-1.500	32	$149,414,064	7.81%
1.500-1.625	33	$154,995,947	8.10%
1.625-1.750	34	$150,877,182	7.88%
1.750-1.875	27	$351,487,256	18.37%
1.875-2.000	23	$240,556,394	12.57%
2.000-2.125	15	$45,497,941	2.38%
2.125 & above	34	$429,453,774	22.44%
Unknown	1	$3,002,710	0.16%
Total	284	$1,913,478,129	100%

May 2003 weighted average DSCR: 1.88x

SALE PROCEEDS

The proceeds Lehman receives from the sale of each tranche are proprietary information. As a result, the profit from creating and selling the company is private information.

PAYMENTS IN DEFAULT

One of the benefits of a CMBS transaction is that the risk of any one loan is mitigated by diversification. As of May 2003, there were 8 loans in delinquency, 4 of which are being handled by the special servicer. If a stand-alone loan were in default, the lender would not be receiving any payment on that loan. However, since these 4 defaulting loans represent only 0.7% of the pool, the impact is small and affects only the most subordinated tranche, which incorporated the possibility for defaults into their pricing. One loan was in a foreclosure/bankruptcy state, and another was classified as "real estate owned" (REO), meaning that the property was foreclosed and the title was taken by the lender. Figure SII.5 summarizes the default status as of May 2003.

FIGURE SII.5

Lehman Brothers Commercial Mortgage Trust, Series 1998-C4 Default Status - May 2003	
Status	Loan Count
Current	277
Delinquent 30 Days	2
Delinquent 60 Days	0
Delinquent 90 Days	1
Foreclosure/Bankruptcy	1
REO (Real estate owned)	1
Special Servicer	4

It is important to note that delinquency status constantly changes. In addition, it is critical to know which loans are in default and why.

TRANCHES

A **tranche** is a specific ownership claim on the **issuer** company. Each tranche has a contractual priority claim on the cash flows of the issuer. The issuer is just a company that owns a pool of assets and sells claims on its future cash flows that have different maturities and priorities. A tranche's priority claim may be different with respect to cash flows from interest payments, amortization, or loan default proceeds versus other tranches. The contractual payment expectation of each tranche may be a fixed amount (even if the underlying loans have floating rates) or a floating amount (even if the underlying loans are fixed-rate) and may have a different maturity from other tranches and/or the underlying loans. There are 15 tranches in this particular issue, which are summarized in Figure SII.6 as of April 2003.

FIGURE SII.6

Lehman Brothers Commercial Mortgage Trust, Series 1998-C4 Tranche Detail - April 2003								
	In $000,000s							
Tranche	Opening Balance	Current Balance	Moodys Rating	S&P Rating	Coupon %	Date of Maturity	Avg. Life (years)	Original Spread
A-1A	$275.0	$198.7	Aaa	AAA	5.87	08/15/06	1.72	5 yr Treas+125
A-1B	693.6	693.6	Aaa	AAA	6.21	10/15/08	5.20	Treas Curve+135
A-2	500.0	466.7	Aaa	AAA	6.30	10/15/08	4.39	Treas Curve
B	106.3	106.3	Aa2	AA	6.36	10/15/08	5.80	10 yr Treas+160
C	106.3	106.3	A2	A	6.50	11/15/08	5.50	10 yr Treas+180
D	121.5	121.5	Baa2	BBB	6.50	12/15/08	5.59	10 yr Treas+250
E	30.4	30.4	Baa3	BBB-	6.50	12/15/08	5.65	10 yr Treas+350
F	50.6	50.6	Ba1	BB+	6.00	12/15/08	5.65	
G	45.6	45.6	Ba2	NR	5.60	04/15/13	7.38	
H	15.2	15.2	Ba3	NR	5.60	08/15/13	10.25	
J	20.3	20.3	B1	NR	5.60	08/15/14	10.52	
K	10.1	10.1	B2	NR	5.60	03/15/16	12.14	
L	15.2	15.2	Caa1	NR	5.60	10/15/17	13.59	
M	10.1	10.1	Caa3	NR	5.60	06/15/18	14.94	
N	25.3	25.3	NR	NR	5.60	09/15/23	15.68	
X (IO)			Aaa	AAA	0.77	09/15/23	NA	
Total / Weighted Avg.	$2,025.6	$1,916.0			6.18%		5.18 years	

The largest tranches received AAA ratings with par values of $275,000,000 (A-1A), $693,553,000 (A-1B), and $500,000,000 (A-2), for a total of 72.5% in AAA-rated tranches. These tranches have the highest priority claims, the highest ratings, and the tightest spreads, and are, therefore, the safest. The other 37.5% of the pool is broken into increasingly junior tranches, each with a lesser priority claim to the cash flows of the issuer (which come solely from the loan pool). Note that the pricing spreads rise in the right-most column of Figure SII.6 as the priority claim declines.

Each tranche is a detailed contract that specifies the priority claims to the issuer's cash stream. Hence, each is priced uniquely, and as the pool matures, payments are made, defaults occur, and each priority claim changes in value. For example, as amortization occurs, all tranches become safer, but especially the lower priority claims. This will often result in rating upgrades and narrower spreads as the tranches trade over time. In addition, as liquidity premiums and interest rates change, pricing changes.

As of May 2003, the spread for each tranche was narrower than on the closing date. The **pay rate** on a floating tranche floats up or down at the noted spread over whatever LIBOR is at the time. Each tranche's document will detail how the rate adjusts to the new LIBOR level. This is usually adjusted either monthly or quarterly.

One of the more significant variables that factors into the initial pricing described above is the tranches' ratings. In this CMBS issue, there are levels that range from Senior-secured fixed-rate AAA debt, to Junior fixed-rate debt that is not rated (as it was not worth paying a fee to a rating agency just to be told, "It's really risky.") Mezzanine fixed-rate debt in this pool starts with a bond rating of AA (the B through E tranches).

INFORMATIONAL PROGRAMS

While this supplement summarizes a single CMBS issue, subscription services such as Morningstar, Trepp, and Intex track all existing CMBS deals. You can access their services at www.morningstar.com, www.trepp.com, and www.intex.com, or you can call the issuer for a report. The benefit of these companies is in marketing deals and trading, allowing one to track information for every CMBS issue, including information on DSCR, pricing, LTV, loans in default, tranche size and rating, individual loan and property information, loans to watch, strengths and weaknesses, etc. The sources also provide pricing models for each tranche in order to facilitate trading.

Supplemental III
Careers in Real Estate

I am frequently asked by students, "I'm really interested in a career in real estate. So, which investment bank do you suggest I go to work for?" I always respond that while investment banking is a great career path, there are many other career options in real estate. To say you want to be in real estate is as vague as saying you want to be in medicine. Do you want to be a cardiologist, pediatrician, nurse, professor, pharmaceutical sales rep, CFO for a healthcare company, hospital administrator, technician, researcher, or dentist? The career options discussed in this chapter are in no way comprehensive but offer a glimpse of the variety of real estate career paths available. Opportunity funds and REITs are not discussed here, as they are described in detail elsewhere in the book.

Research Firms

Real estate, like any industry, constantly seeks quality information. Thus, the business has many research niches. Equity research teams at major investment houses analyze market trends and company information to evaluate publicly traded real estate companies. Other research specialists, such as Linneman Associates, Torto Wheaton, and Rosen Consulting Group provide analysis on how macro and micro events impact the real estate industry. Platforms like Reis or Costar provide market rent, building permit, vacancy, and other detailed market data. Sometimes research firms are divisions of banks or money managers.

Junior-level researchers gather and analyze data, work on surveys, and compile data in easy-to-understand formats. Writing skills are highly valued by research firms.

Brokerage Firms

Brokerage firms range from local mom and pop shops to huge public corporations including CBRE and Cushman & Wakefield. Also, major investment banks such as Goldman Sachs and Morgan Stanley perform some of these services, as does Eastdil. Brokers and leasing agents are the plankton of the industry, in that they are everywhere. These licensed real estate professionals assess local market values, market properties, and advise clients on the purchase, leasing, and sale of properties. Frequently, corporate tenants engage brokers as their representatives to identify the best office, warehouse, or retail space, or housing for their needs. They also lease space for owners. Brokers generally work for fees that are primarily based upon successful deal execution.

The advantage of working for a broker is that you learn about the demand side of real estate, as great brokers understand the type of space desired by different firms. For example, a financial services firm looking for office space in Manhattan has substantially different space needs from a major law or industrial firm. In addition, each property and each suite in a property has unique usage aspects. Good brokers seek to match these traits with customers. No two markets or properties are identical, and a good broker understands who best fits what.

A junior person in this industry works on reports, marketing materials, research, leasing and space use plans, and assists in structuring leases and property sales. In this business, writing skills are useful and knowledge of programs such as PowerPoint, Argus, and Excel are essential.

Investment Banks

This sector serves the capital needs of REITs, private equity funds, private operators, etc. They raise debt and equity, provide advisory work on mergers and acquisitions, and advise on restructuring situations. Some banks also operate real estate investment funds.

Often, when REITs and other large real estate firms float debt, they use an investment bank. This debt may be used to finance a large acquisition, the purchase of another firm, or refinance existing debt. Investment banks use their sales network to place both secured and unsecured real estate debt, frequently trading in the debt's after-market. The equity-raising process is much the same. When an investment bank is engaged to raise capital, the bank's real estate group works with the lawyers and the capital markets group to structure the offering, which is then placed through an equity syndicate that coordinates road shows with institutional investors.

Investment banks also perform advisory work, including fairness opinions, and frequently act as brokers for major property sales. For example, the bank's technology group will be advising on a merger, which creates the need to dispose of surplus office space, and the bank's real estate group may be engaged to market this property. The bank's main expertise lies in their knowledge of capital markets.

A junior person at an investment bank creates pitch books, prepares PowerPoint presentations, and constructs detailed financial models. The hours are long and the work tedious.

Institutional Investors

Insurance companies, pension funds, endowments, and investment companies have money to invest. Sometimes their assets are matched with their liabilities. For example, a pension fund has the relatively known long-term liabilities associated with current retirees and the less certain liability associated with current employees who will one day be retirees.

Institutional investors invest in real estate for both its diversification and return attributes. Some institutional investors invest a portion of their assets in higher-risk vehicles, such as private equity funds, REITs, individual properties, mortgages, and CMBS.

Junior-level people in this field work on valuation models, assist with asset and portfolio management, due diligence, financial and performance reporting, and the selection of and interaction with property managers and brokers.

Commercial Banks

Commercial banks underwrite loans, frequently acting as an intermediary between an issuer of securities and public investors. Commercial banks also engage in lending activities, sometimes holding their loans, other times, syndicating them, and sometimes packaging them into CMBS offerings. After the repeal of the Glass-Steagall Act in 1999, an integration of investment banks and major commercial banks occurred. However, local commercial banks still largely function as lenders.

Given their short-term liabilities (deposits), commercial banks are the primary source of construction loans to local property owners, typically providing 3-7-year loans. These loans frequently are provided to developers to fund the construction and stabilization of new properties.

Entry-level people at commercial banks assist in the due diligence process, credit analysis, and verification of financial projections, construction timelines, etc. Since many bank loans are secured by recourse to personal assets, they often analyze the personal balance sheets of the borrowers.

Developers

Developers range from large national firms like Prologis, Hines, and the Related Companies, to small local developers. Most specialize in a single property type, such as retail, hotel, residential, commercial, or resort, as each region and property type requires different skill sets, tenant relationships, and local connections. For example, a great condo developer knows how to create a buzz about their product and is able to quickly market the units. Some developers are experts at controlling project costs, others are great at marketing, while others are masters of design. Land developers focus on pre-selling lots and obtaining the necessary zoning approvals, while mall developers pre-lease space, using their network and relationships with retail tenants. Single-family home development is basically a manufacturing process, where land is merely production inventory.

The best developers use their core competency to get an edge on the competition and have the political and organizational savvy to get through the regulatory maze efficiently. Many developers sub-contract architects, lawyers, general contractors, brokers, and a marketing team, adding value by efficiently managing these diverse outsourced components. Others are more integrated, performing many or all of these functions in-house.

The developer's job is both about taking and eliminating risks. Developers seek out viable deals. While a development case may be assigned every couple of weeks in a real estate class, most developers will only find a viable development deal once every year or two. After finding such a deal, the developer lines up capital from both equity investors and lenders. The developer continually fine tunes building plans, as markets, tenants, regulatory, and engineering challenges evolve. Upon completion, developers must lease and/or sell space. There is often no precise timetable, and the developer must coordinate and juggle all of these moving parts.

Junior-level people at development firms create financial models and aid in the market analysis and due diligence process. They will also assist in preparing marketing materials for tenants and capital providers, as well as presentations to planning authorities.

Architecture and Planning Firms

People think of architects such as I.M. Pei, Helmut Jahn, Kohn Pederson Fox, or Frank Gehry as creators of wonderful works of art. But most architects are in the business of designing usable and profitable space. Good architects design commercial space from the "inside out," rather than the "outside in." This is because while the exterior of the building is a great advertisement for the property and architectural firms, the layout of the interior space must effectively meet the needs of space users to be successful. Layout and design vary across property types, users, and markets. It is the architect's job to make sure that a usable, flexible, and efficient structure is designed and complies with zoning codes and other local regulations. Architects often specialize in different components of a project, specializing in interiors, schematics, landscaping, mechanicals, or facades.

This field attracts many young "artists" who quickly discover that it is a highly competitive business, where one prospers by efficiently executing the creative visions of developers, rather than making grand personal artistic statements.

General Contracting Firms

General contractors coordinate construction and project logistics, creating and supervising schedules and budgets for each element of the construction process. For example, should the carpenters do their work before or after the electrical contractors? The job of general contractors is to keep the construction process on time, coordinating construction details with the developer, architect, and sub-contractors. General contractors often have a specialty in one or more aspects of the construction process. They must plan for unforeseen delays and costs and conceptualize all the details required to complete the property in a timely and cost-effective manner.

In this field, young people work on budgets, monitor project timing and costs, and facilitate negotiations with vendors and sub-contractors.

Law Firms

The real estate industry is filled with "deal people," who buy, sell, and lease properties. This requires the assistance of many lawyers who draft, finalize, and negotiate detailed documents. Sometimes lawyers have an expertise in specialties such as historic tax credits, 1031 exchanges, opportunity zones, low-income housing, environmental issues, zoning, leasing or construction.

Lawyers create the documents which will allow a developer to sell historic tax credits or purchase a property. Lawyers also draft partnership agreements so that liability, taxes, and returns are distributed among partners as agreed. For example, non-taxable entities, such as college endowments cannot use tax credits, so complex legal structures are frequently crafted which most efficiently allocate these benefits among investors.

To be on the legal side of the real estate business, a J.D. or a paralegal degree is generally required. A young lawyer or paralegal will do legal research, work on due diligence, and assist in contract drafting.

CLOSING THOUGHT

These career descriptions barely scratch the surface of the possibilities in real estate. Never forget that every building and vacant piece of land is owned by someone, and that owner (including government agencies) must operate, finance, and report on the usage of the property. Real estate is ubiquitous in our world, and career paths are literally endless. Do not limit yourself to investment banks simply because your friends are working for these firms. Also remember that while junior real estate professionals are responsible for the most minute details (e.g., data, spreadsheet proficiency, formatting, etc.) regardless of their chosen field, they must also understand the larger strategic picture to move up the corporate ladder or start their own firm.

Supplemental IV
ARGUS Enterprise by ARGUS Software

Authors:
John Lim, Sr. Dir. Global Marketing Programs, Altus Analytics
Katie Foley, Global Manager of Instructional Design, ARGUS Training
Altus Group

WHAT IS ARGUS Enterprise™?

ARGUS Enterprise® is an integrated platform for cash flow modeling, valuations, budgeting, and asset and portfolio management. For over 25 years, ARGUS® products have enabled tens of thousands of commercial real estate professionals to gain transparency into their property assets, manage risk, and optimize their portfolios. Real estate investors, asset and portfolio managers, lenders, brokers, appraisers, and other commercial real estate professionals use ARGUS to facilitate transactions and communicate value.

Serving an increasingly global community of commercial real estate investors, ARGUS Enterprise is used to model property assets from around the world. Localized to handle different area measures, currencies and leasing methods, ARGUS Enterprise models can be created for any international investor and any local property asset. These models can then be combined to provide a complete view across a global portfolio. Additionally, ARGUS Enterprise handles multiple valuation methods including Discounted Cash Flow, Traditional Valuations (UK) and Market Capitalisation (Australia). Meeting the increasing demand for cross-border investing, models from one region can be sent to investors in other regions to view and analyze in a different currency, area measure, and even valuation method.

There are multiple components of ARGUS Enterprise - cash flow modeling and valuations, property budgeting, sensitivity analysis, portfolio reporting, and investment management. In this supplement, the cash flow modeling and valuation components are showcased to provide a basic overview of the inputs and the resulting reports. ARGUS takes contract information and combines them with market assumptions to forecast cash flow projections. These results are used to calculate income-based valuations such as the present value of the cash flows or an internal rate of return from the purchase price. Results can then be changed by varying market and leasing assumptions to assess risk and make informed investment decisions.

ARGUS Enterprise is the platform of choice for transacting and managing commercial real estate investments, connecting data and business processes for acquisitions, valuations, budgeting, asset and portfolio management, and investor reporting. For commercial real estate transactions, brokers, appraisers and lenders collaborate with common data points while still allowing for their own market and investment assumptions. Using ARGUS, real estate professionals gain the visibility and the results to help make informed decisions.

EXAMPLE PROPERTY

The following simple case study of a fictitious building provides an overview of the data input into ARGUS Enterprise and the results that are generated. Each aspect of the property is accompanied by a corresponding screen shot of the ARGUS Enterprise application to show how the application accepts the data required for financial modeling. For this example, we have a user who wants to determine if an investment in this property can achieve a 15.0% IRR.

CASE STUDY – ENTERPRISE TOWER

Portfolio Creation

In ARGUS Enterprise, portfolios are collections of properties to which various scenarios can be applied. Once a portfolio has been created, properties can be added. Any changes made to a portfolio are automatically saved. Once the initial portfolio is created, it is good practice to duplicate that portfolio and make changes to the copy to test scenarios and any changes before applying them to the main portfolio.

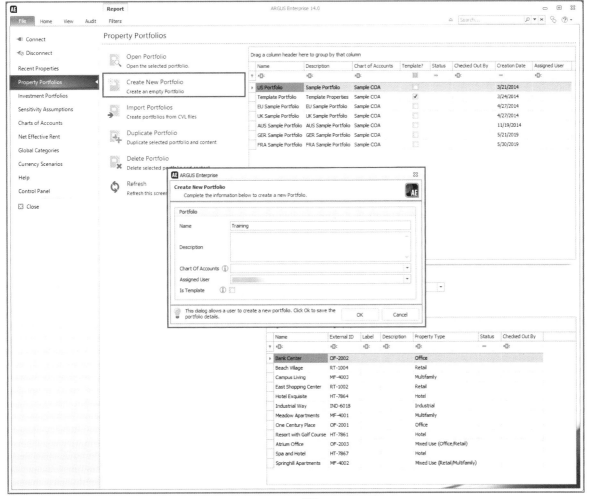

INITIAL PROPERTY ASSUMPTIONS

Enterprise Tower is a 50,000-square foot Mixed Use (Office/Retail) building located at 10 Discovery Blvd., Houston, Texas. The Analysis start date is January 1, 2024. A 5-year discounted cash flow will be used to value the property because income is expected to vary over the next few years.

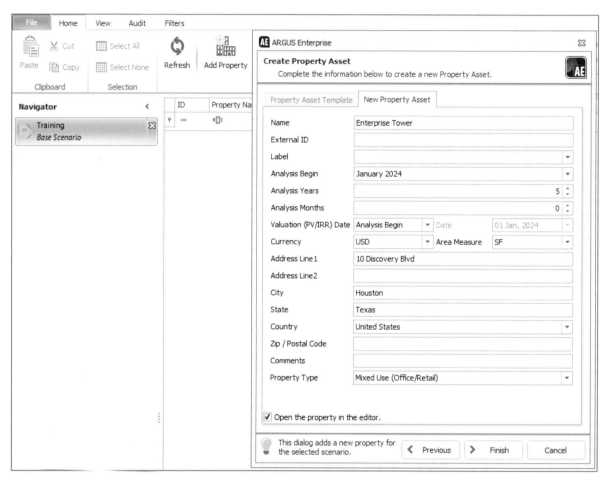

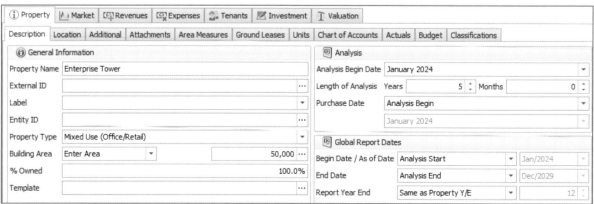

In this model, Inflation is calculated using a Calendar Recovery using Calendar Inflation. Both the General and Expense Inflations will be 3.00% for the Analysis. The rental market in the area is tightening, so Market Rent will inflate at 5.00% in 2025 and 2026, and then at 3.00% for the remainder of the projection.

MISCELLANEOUS REVENUES

In addition to base rent, revenue is also derived from leasing roof space for an antenna. This Miscellaneous Revenue is estimated initially at $15,000 per year, increasing at 3.0% per annum. The Revenues tab includes the Miscellaneous Revenue, Parking, and Storage tabs. The Miscellaneous tab is where you can enter all non-tenant related revenue.

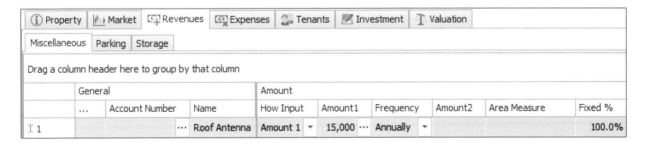

OPERATING EXPENSES

All reimbursable (recoverable) and non-reimbursable (non-recoverable) operating expenses are entered in the Expenses input screen. Reimbursable expenses are expenses that the property owner will recover from the tenants. Common reimbursable expenses include Common Area Maintenance (CAM), Taxes, Insurance, and Repairs. All entries in this window will be available for reimbursement by the tenants.

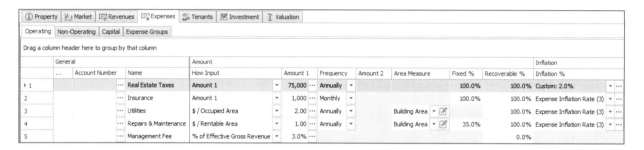

Real Estate Taxes are estimated at $75,000 per year. Thereafter, the tax liability is trended at 2.0% per year for inflationary expectations. Taxes are a 100% fixed expense and 100% recoverable.

Insurance coverage including fire insurance, extended coverage, liability, and other space coverage required by a property of the subject type is $1,000 per month. This expense is increased annually with the Expense Inflation Rate and is a 100% fixed and recoverable expense.

Utilities are estimated at $2.00 per occupied square foot per year, based on the Building Area. Since this expense is based on the Building Area, the Fixed % field becomes inactive. The expense is 100% recoverable. This expense is projected to grow at the Expense Inflation Rate.

Repairs & Maintenance is estimated at $1.00 per rentable square foot per year, based on the Building Area. This includes all interior and exterior maintenance and repairs and janitorial expenses for the building. It is estimated that the property would still incur 35.0% of this expense if the building were totally vacant. 100% of this expense is recoverable. This expense is projected to grow at the Expense Inflation Rate.

Management Fee is a non-recoverable expense and will be calculated at 3.0% of the Effective Gross Revenue.

CAPITAL EXPENDITURES

Capital Expenses are expenses that are not considered part of a property's Net Operating Income and appear below the income line on the Cash Flow. Examples of capital expenses include structural or capital reserves, building repairs, or improvements. These expenses will appear in the Capital Expenditures section of the Cash Flow Report.

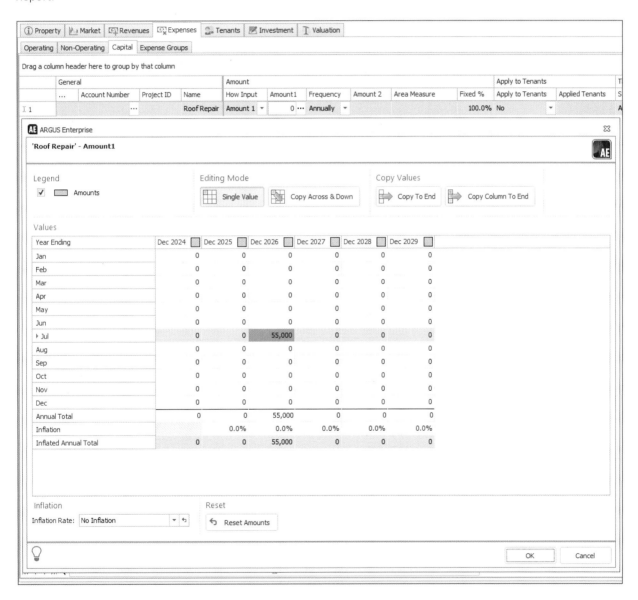

The subject's roof is partially defective, and it will need a major repair by 2026. Property management is currently projecting this repair for July of 2026. Current estimates from area contractors indicate the expense will be $55,000 at that time.

TENANTS – RENT ROLL

The Rent Roll is used to model existing tenant lease contracts, including leased area, lease start and end dates, base rent, fixed steps, CPI increases, free rent periods, percentage rents, recoveries, leasing costs, and market renewal assumptions. The Rent Roll can also be used to speculatively lease up vacant space. Alternatively, vacant space can be modeled on the Space Absorption tab. The property has four tenants listed below in the lease abstract table. Two of the leases have start dates prior to the analysis start, while the other two leases are contracted leases set to begin on or after the analysis start date.

Name Suite Area	Available Date Start Date	Term / Expire	Rental Income	Other Terms
AB Real Estate 100 3,410	Both Available and Start Dates: May 1, 2020	5 Years	$10.50/SF/Year	Recovery: Stop Amount / Area of $4.00/SF Upon Expiration: Renew
Joy Placement Center 200 6,190	Both Available and Start Dates: August 1, 2021	6 Years	$12.00/SF/Year, Base Rent Increase of 3.0% per year	Recovery: Fixed Amount of $20,000 per year increasing with the General Inflation Rate
Spring Computers 300 5,400	Available Date – Analysis Begin Start Date - February 1, 2024	5 Years	100% of Market Rent	Recovery: Base Year Stop TI: $15.00/SF LC: 5.0% - Fixed %
Richards Group 400 23,000	Both Available and Start Dates: Analysis Begin	10 Years	$10.00/SF/Year, Fixed Step Increase of $0.50/SF/Year	Recovery: Net TI: $15.00/SF LC: 5.0% - Fixed %

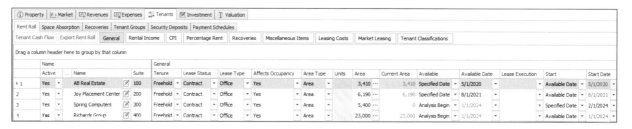

MARKET LEASING PROFILES

Market Leasing profiles in the model are used to automatically generate assumptions and calculations for new and renewal leases. In this property, the market leasing profiles are standard for space that is less than 20,000 square feet. Quoted rates and actual recent lease terms at comparable office buildings were analyzed to determine current market rent. The building has two classifications of space. One is for tenants of less than 20,000 square feet, and the other is for tenants of more than 20,000 square feet. The Less than 20,000 Market Leasing profile is shown highlighted in blue below.

For tenants that are Less Than 20,000 SF, the term is expected to be 5 years and the Renewal Probability is assumed to be 50.0%. Months Vacant is 4 months of downtime between leases. Market Base Rent is $18.00/SF/Year for new tenants and $17.00/SF/Year for renewing tenants. Recoveries are set to a Base Year Stop. Tenant Improvements are $15.00/SF for new tenants, $5.00/SF for renewing tenants. Leasing Commissions for new tenants are set to a Fixed 5.0%, while renewing tenants are set to a Fixed 3.0%.

For tenants of More Than 20,000 SF, the term is expected to be 10 years, and the Renewal Probability is assumed to be 75.0%. Months Vacant is 6 months of downtime between leases. Market Base Rent $15.00/SF/Year for new tenants and renewing tenants. Recoveries are set to Net. Tenant Improvements are $20.00/SF for new tenants and $5.00/SF for renewing tenants. Leasing Commissions for new tenants are set to a Fixed 5.0%, while renewing tenants are set to a Fixed 3.0%.

SPACE ABSORPTION

Currently, 12,000 square feet are vacant in Enterprise Tower. The Less Than 20,000 SF Market Leasing profile will be used to populate the inputs for the vacant space that remains. The 12,000 square feet of vacant space will be leased out in 2,500-square foot spaces with one lease being absorbed every month. The vacant area is available at the beginning of the analysis with absorption projected to begin July 2024.

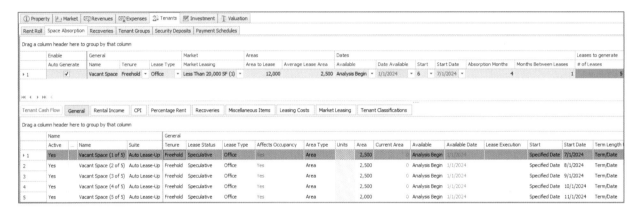

VIEWING REPORTS

ARGUS Enterprise produces a wide variety of property, tenant, comparison, and audit reports, including: Dashboard Reports, Property Reports, Valuation Reports, Tenant Reports, Audit Reports, and Review reports.

We now have enough information inputted to generate reports. The following screen capture shows the Property Reports – Cash Flow resulting from the assumptions of this property. Items to note on this report are the following: the growth of the expenses, the turnover of leases in Year 1, Year 4, and Year 6, and the calculation of the expense reimbursements based on the tenant assumptions and growing expenses.

| Dashboard Reports | Property Reports | Valuation Reports | Tenant Reports | Debt Reports | Audit Reports | Review |

| Cash Flow | Cash Flow As Of | Executive Summary | Assumptions | Market Leasing Summary | Budget Comparison | Month and Year-to-Date Variance | Sources and Uses |

Report for: Total Property Level Of Detail: Detailed Lines

Enterprise Tower (Amounts in USD)
Jan, 2024 through Dec, 2029
11/23/2021 7:57:17 AM

	Forecast	Forecast	Forecast	Forecast	Forecast	Forecast	Forecast
	Year 1	Year 2	Year 3	Year 4	Year 5	Year 6	
For the Years Ending	Dec-2024	Dec-2025	Dec-2026	Dec-2027	Dec-2028	Dec-2029	Total
Rental Revenue							
Potential Base Rent	654,610	689,396	711,716	740,054	773,080	812,428	4,381,285
Absorption & Turnover Vacancy	-146,417	0	0	-20,502	0	-61,140	-228,059
Scheduled Base Rent	508,194	689,396	711,716	719,553	773,080	751,288	4,153,226
Total Rental Revenue	508,194	689,396	711,716	719,553	773,080	751,288	4,153,226
Other Tenant Revenue							
Total Expense Recoveries	119,832	143,460	148,819	143,617	140,759	130,475	826,963
Total Other Tenant Revenue	119,832	143,460	148,819	143,617	140,759	130,475	826,963
Total Tenant Revenue	628,026	832,857	860,536	863,170	913,838	881,763	4,980,189
Other Revenue							
Roof Antenna	15,000	15,450	15,914	16,391	16,883	17,389	97,026
Total Other Revenue	15,000	15,450	15,914	16,391	16,883	17,389	97,026
Potential Gross Revenue	643,026	848,307	876,449	879,561	930,721	899,152	5,077,215
Effective Gross Revenue	643,026	848,307	876,449	879,561	930,721	899,152	5,077,215
Operating Expenses							
Real Estate Taxes	75,000	76,500	78,030	79,591	81,182	82,806	473,109
Insurance	12,000	12,360	12,731	13,113	13,506	13,911	77,621
Utilities	83,267	103,000	106,090	107,018	112,551	109,204	621,129
Repairs & Maintenance	44,562	51,500	53,045	53,904	56,275	55,778	315,064
Management Fee	19,291	25,449	26,293	26,387	27,922	26,975	152,316
Total Operating Expenses	234,119	268,809	276,189	280,012	291,436	288,674	1,639,240
Net Operating Income	408,907	579,497	600,260	599,549	639,284	610,478	3,437,976
Leasing Costs							
Tenant Improvements	606,000	17,562	0	67,640	0	178,528	869,730
Leasing Commissions	219,175	9,130	0	24,602	0	64,935	317,843
Total Leasing Costs	825,175	26,692	0	92,242	0	243,463	1,187,572
Capital Expenditures							
Roof Repair	0	0	55,000	0	0	0	55,000
Total Capital Expenditures	0	0	55,000	0	0	0	55,000
Total Leasing & Capital Costs	825,175	26,692	55,000	92,242	0	243,463	1,242,572
Cash Flow Before Debt Service	-416,268	552,806	545,260	507,307	639,284	367,015	2,195,404
Cash Flow Available for Distribution	-416,268	552,806	545,260	507,307	639,284	367,015	2,195,404

INVESTMENT AND VALUATION

ARGUS Enterprise does the intensive calculation work, allowing the analyst to look at the yields of the property based on assumptions of the potential purchase price or achieve present value results with entries of a required rate of return.

PROPERTY PURCHASE

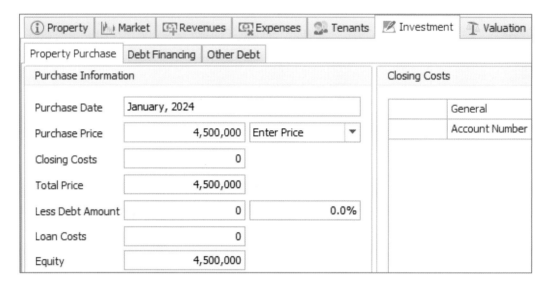

The building was purchased for $4,500,000.

DEBT FINANCING

There is a secured loan on this property. The $3,000,000 loan starts at the beginning of the analysis, amortizing over 360 months, at an 8.0% interest rate.

PROPERTY RESALE

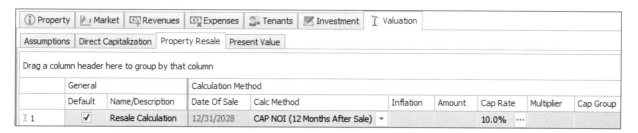

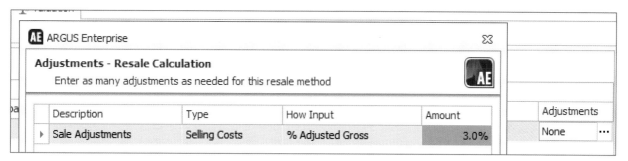

The reversion value in Year 5 is estimated by capitalizing the 6th year's Net Operating Income. The property is in a good location and is one of the better-quality office buildings in the area. Therefore, a terminal capitalization rate of 10.0% is considered appropriate. Sales adjustments, including commissions and closing costs, are estimated to be 3.0% of the gross sales proceeds.

PRESENT VALUE

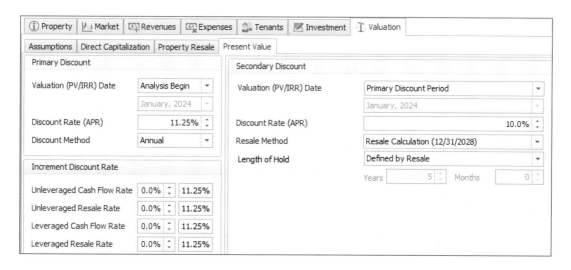

The subject is a modern office building constructed of very good quality materials and is well maintained. It is in close proximity to major roadways. This area has been experiencing high occupancies (91%+). The subject is below stabilized occupancy. Given these considerations, an annual endpoint discount rate of 11.25% is considered appropriate.

PRESENT VALUE – UNLEVERAGED AND LEVERAGED REPORTS

The Valuation – Present Value reports present a one-page summary of the property valuation, including valuation assumptions, the investment, leveraged and unleveraged cash flows, and cash-on-cash returns.

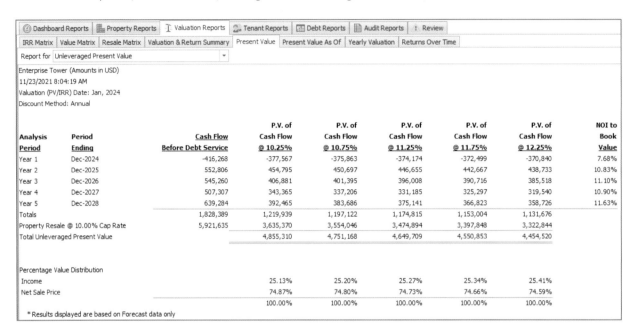

			@ Dashboard Reports	Property Reports	Valuation Reports	Tenant Reports	Debt Reports	Audit Reports	Review		

IRR Matrix | Value Matrix | Resale Matrix | Valuation & Return Summary | Present Value | Present Value As Of | Yearly Valuation | Returns Over Time

Report for: Unleveraged Present Value

Enterprise Tower (Amounts in USD)
11/23/2021 8:04:19 AM
Valuation (PV/IRR) Date: Jan, 2024
Discount Method: Annual

Analysis Period	Period Ending	Cash Flow Before Debt Service	P.V. of Cash Flow @ 10.25%	P.V. of Cash Flow @ 10.75%	P.V. of Cash Flow @ 11.25%	P.V. of Cash Flow @ 11.75%	P.V. of Cash Flow @ 12.25%	NOI to Book Value
Year 1	Dec-2024	-416,268	-377,567	-375,863	-374,174	-372,499	-370,840	7.68%
Year 2	Dec-2025	552,806	454,795	450,697	446,655	442,667	438,733	10.83%
Year 3	Dec-2026	545,260	406,881	401,395	396,008	390,716	385,518	11.10%
Year 4	Dec-2027	507,307	343,365	337,206	331,185	325,297	319,540	10.90%
Year 5	Dec-2028	639,284	392,465	383,686	375,141	366,823	358,726	11.63%
Totals		1,828,389	1,219,939	1,197,122	1,174,815	1,153,004	1,131,676	
Property Resale @ 10.00% Cap Rate		5,921,635	3,635,370	3,554,046	3,474,894	3,397,848	3,322,844	
Total Unleveraged Present Value			4,855,310	4,751,168	4,649,709	4,550,853	4,454,520	

Percentage Value Distribution

Income		25.13%	25.20%	25.27%	25.34%	25.41%	
Net Sale Price		74.87%	74.80%	74.73%	74.66%	74.59%	
		100.00%	100.00%	100.00%	100.00%	100.00%	

* Results displayed are based on Forecast data only

			@ Dashboard Reports	Property Reports	Valuation Reports	Tenant Reports	Debt Reports	Audit Reports	Review		

IRR Matrix | Value Matrix | Resale Matrix | Valuation & Return Summary | Present Value | Present Value As Of | Yearly Valuation | Returns Over Time

Report for: Leveraged Present Value

Enterprise Tower (Amounts in USD)
11/23/2021 8:04:41 AM
Valuation (PV/IRR) Date: Jan, 2024
Discount Method: Annual

Analysis Period	Period Ending	Cash Flow Available for Distribution	P.V. of Cash Flow @ 10.25%	P.V. of Cash Flow @ 10.75%	P.V. of Cash Flow @ 11.25%	P.V. of Cash Flow @ 11.75%	P.V. of Cash Flow @ 12.25%	NOI to Book Value
Year 1	Dec-2024	-680,423	-617,164	-614,378	-611,616	-608,880	-606,168	-45.36%
Year 2	Dec-2025	288,651	237,474	235,334	233,224	231,141	229,087	19.24%
Year 3	Dec-2026	281,104	209,764	206,936	204,158	201,430	198,750	18.74%
Year 4	Dec-2027	243,152	164,575	161,623	158,737	155,915	153,155	16.21%
Year 5	Dec-2028	375,129	230,297	225,145	220,131	215,250	210,499	25.01%
Totals		507,613	224,946	214,661	204,633	194,857	185,324	
Property Resale @ 10.00% Cap Rate		3,069,539	1,884,431	1,842,275	1,801,246	1,761,309	1,722,430	
Debt Balance as of Jan-2024		3,000,000	3,000,000	3,000,000	3,000,000	3,000,000	3,000,000	
Total Leveraged Present Value			5,109,377	5,056,936	5,005,880	4,956,166	4,907,753	

Percentage Value Distribution

Income		10.66%	10.44%	10.20%	9.96%	9.71%	
Net Sale Price		89.34%	89.56%	89.80%	90.04%	90.29%	
		100.00%	100.00%	100.00%	100.00%	100.00%	

* Results displayed are based on Forecast data only

VALUATION & RETURN SUMMARY

The Valuation Reports – Valuation & Return Summary presents a one-page summary of the property valuation, including valuation assumptions, the sales proceeds calculation, returns and distributions, leveraged, and unleveraged cash flows, cash-on-cash returns, and capitalization valuation assumptions.

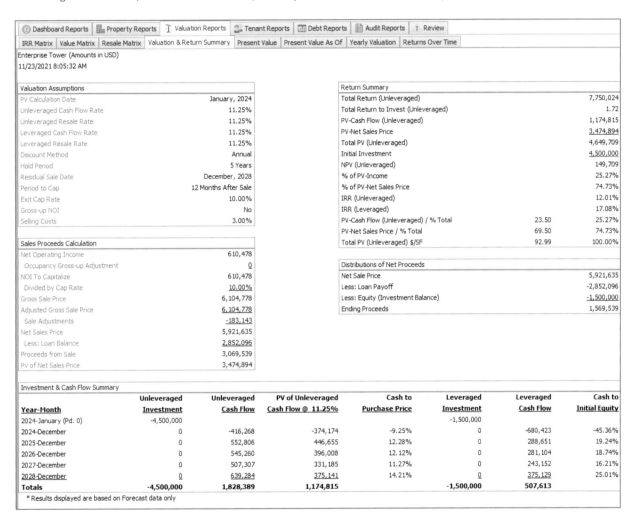

	Dashboard Reports	Property Reports	Valuation Reports	Tenant Reports	Debt Reports	Audit Reports	Review

| IRR Matrix | Value Matrix | Resale Matrix | Valuation & Return Summary | Present Value | Present Value As Of | Yearly Valuation | Returns Over Time |

Enterprise Tower (Amounts in USD)
11/23/2021 8:05:32 AM

Valuation Assumptions	
PV Calculation Date	January, 2024
Unleveraged Cash Flow Rate	11.25%
Unleveraged Resale Rate	11.25%
Leveraged Cash Flow Rate	11.25%
Leveraged Resale Rate	11.25%
Discount Method	Annual
Hold Period	5 Years
Residual Sale Date	December, 2028
Period to Cap	12 Months After Sale
Exit Cap Rate	10.00%
Gross-up NOI	No
Selling Costs	3.00%

Sales Proceeds Calculation	
Net Operating Income	610,478
Occupancy Gross-up Adjustment	0
NOI To Capitalize	610,478
Divided by Cap Rate	10.00%
Gross Sale Price	6,104,778
Adjusted Gross Sale Price	6,104,778
Sale Adjustments	-183,143
Net Sales Price	5,921,635
Less: Loan Balance	2,852,096
Proceeds from Sale	3,069,539
Pv of Net Sales Price	3,474,894

Return Summary		
Total Return (Unleveraged)		7,750,024
Total Return to Invest (Unleveraged)		1.72
PV-Cash Flow (Unleveraged)		1,174,815
PV-Net Sales Price		3,474,894
Total PV (Unleveraged)		4,649,709
Initial Investment		4,500,000
NPV (Unleveraged)		149,709
% of PV-Income		25.27%
% of PV-Net Sales Price		74.73%
IRR (Unleveraged)		12.01%
IRR (Leveraged)		17.08%
PV-Cash Flow (Unleveraged) / % Total	23.50	25.27%
PV-Net Sales Price / % Total	69.50	74.73%
Total PV (Unleveraged) $/SF	92.99	100.00%

Distributions of Net Proceeds	
Net Sale Price	5,921,635
Less: Loan Payoff	-2,852,096
Less: Equity (Investment Balance)	-1,500,000
Ending Proceeds	1,569,539

Investment & Cash Flow Summary

Year-Month	Unleveraged Investment	Unleveraged Cash Flow	PV of Unleveraged Cash Flow @ 11.25%	Cash to Purchase Price	Leveraged Investment	Leveraged Cash Flow	Cash to Initial Equity
2024-January (Pd. 0)	-4,500,000				-1,500,000		
2024-December	0	-416,268	-374,174	-9.25%	0	-680,423	-45.36%
2025-December	0	552,806	446,655	12.28%	0	288,651	19.24%
2026-December	0	545,260	396,008	12.12%	0	281,104	18.74%
2027-December	0	507,307	331,185	11.27%	0	243,152	16.21%
2028-December	0	639,284	375,141	14.21%	0	375,129	25.01%
Totals	-4,500,000	1,828,389	1,174,815		-1,500,000	507,613	

* Results displayed are based on Forecast data only

SOURCES AND USES

The Property Reports – Sources and Uses describes the inflow/outflow of funds to the property and ends in the final year of the analysis.

Dashboard Reports	Property Reports	Valuation Reports	Tenant Reports	Debt Reports	Audit Reports	Review

Cash Flow	Cash Flow As Of	Executive Summary	Assumptions	Market Leasing Summary	Budget Comparison	Month and Year-to-Date Variance	Sources and Uses

Enterprise Tower (Amounts in USD)
Jan, 2024 through Dec, 2028
11/23/2021 8:06:01 AM

	Forecast	Forecast	Forecast	Forecast	Forecast	Forecast
	Year 1	Year 2	Year 3	Year 4	Year 5	
For the Years Ending	Dec-2024	Dec-2025	Dec-2026	Dec-2027	Dec-2028	Total
Sources Of Capital						
Net Operating Gains	408,907	579,497	600,260	599,549	639,284	2,827,498
Debt Funding Proceeds	3,000,000	0	0	0	0	3,000,000
Initial Equity Contribution	1,500,000	0	0	0	0	1,500,000
Net Proceeds From Sale	0	0	0	0	5,921,635	5,921,635
Defined Sources Of Capital	4,908,907	579,497	600,260	599,549	6,560,920	13,249,133
Required Equity Contributions	680,423	0	0	0	0	680,423
Total Sources Of Capital	5,589,330	579,497	600,260	599,549	6,560,920	13,929,556
Uses Of Capital						
Property Purchase Price	4,500,000	0	0	0	0	4,500,000
Total Property Purchase Price	4,500,000	0	0	0	0	4,500,000
Total Debt Service	264,155	264,155	264,156	264,155	264,155	1,320,776
Tenant Improvements	606,000	17,562	0	67,640	0	691,201
Leasing Commissions	219,175	9,130	0	24,602	0	252,908
Capital Expenditures	0	0	55,000	0	0	55,000
Debt Retirement	0	0	0	0	2,852,096	2,852,096
Defined Uses Of Capital	5,589,330	290,847	319,156	356,397	3,116,251	9,671,981
Cash Flow Distributions	0	288,651	281,104	243,152	3,444,669	4,257,575
Total Uses Of Capital	5,589,330	579,497	600,260	599,549	6,560,920	13,929,556
Unleveraged Cash on Cash Return						
Cash to Purchase Price	9.25%	12.28%	12.12%	11.27%	14.21%	40.63%
NOI to Book Value	7.68%	10.83%	11.10%	10.90%	11.63%	51.42%
Leveraged Cash on Cash Return						
Cash to Initial Equity	-45.36%	19.24%	18.74%	16.21%	25.01%	33.84%
Running Equity Balance	2,180,423	2,180,423	2,180,423	2,180,423	2,180,423	2,180,423
Cash to Equity Balance	-31.21%	13.24%	12.89%	11.15%	157.98%	157.98%
Cumulative Total Purchase Price	4,500,000	4,500,000	4,500,000	4,500,000	4,500,000	4,500,000
Cumulative Total Book Value	5,325,175	5,351,867	5,406,867	5,499,109	5,499,109	5,499,109
Unleveraged Annual IRR					12.01%	
Leveraged Annual IRR					17.08%	

* Results displayed are based on Forecast data only

LEASE AUDIT

The Audit Reports - Lease Audit is a powerful tool for reviewing key cash flow totals, such as potential and scheduled base rent, recoveries and leasing costs, on a tenant-by-tenant basis.

Dashboard Reports	Property Reports	Valuation Reports	Tenant Reports	Debt Reports	Audit Reports	Review

| Occupancy | Lease Audit | Use Type Audit | Percentage Rent Audit | Recovery Audit | Expense Recovery | Recovery Detail by Expense | Expense Group Audit | Property Re |

Enterprise Tower (Amounts in USD, Measures in SF)
Jan, 2024 through Dec, 2029
11/23/2021 8:06:29 AM

For the Years Ending	Suite	Year 1 Dec-2024	Year 2 Dec-2025	Year 3 Dec-2026	Year 4 Dec-2027	Year 5 Dec-2028	Year 6 Dec-2029	Total
Area								
1. AB Real Estate	100	3,410	3,410	3,410	3,410	3,410	3,410	
2. Joy Placement Center	200	6,190	6,190	6,190	5,158	6,190	6,190	
3. Spring Computers	300	4,950	5,400	5,400	5,400	5,400	4,500	
4. Richards Group	400	23,000	23,000	23,000	23,000	23,000	23,000	
1. Vacant Space (1 of 5)	Auto Lease-U	1,250	2,500	2,500	2,500	2,500	2,083	
2. Vacant Space (2 of 5)	Auto Lease-U	1,042	2,500	2,500	2,500	2,500	2,083	
3. Vacant Space (3 of 5)	Auto Lease-U	833	2,500	2,500	2,500	2,500	2,083	
4. Vacant Space (4 of 5)	Auto Lease-U	625	2,500	2,500	2,500	2,500	2,083	
5. Vacant Space (5 of 5)	Auto Lease-U	333	2,000	2,000	2,000	2,000	1,667	
Total Area		41,633	50,000	50,000	48,968	50,000	47,100	
Total Occupancy %		83.27%	100.00%	100.00%	97.94%	100.00%	94.20%	
Potential Base Rent								
1. AB Real Estate	100	35,805	52,514	60,869	60,869	60,869	60,869	331,793
2. Joy Placement Center	200	79,789	82,182	84,648	101,486	123,011	123,011	594,127
3. Spring Computers	300	96,975	97,200	97,200	97,200	97,200	112,460	598,235
4. Richards Group	400	230,000	241,500	253,000	264,500	276,000	287,500	1,552,500
1. Vacant Space (1 of 5)	Auto Lease-U	44,375	45,000	45,000	45,000	45,000	48,854	273,229
2. Vacant Space (2 of 5)	Auto Lease-U	44,271	45,000	45,000	45,000	45,000	48,211	272,482
3. Vacant Space (3 of 5)	Auto Lease-U	44,167	45,000	45,000	45,000	45,000	47,569	271,736
4. Vacant Space (4 of 5)	Auto Lease-U	44,063	45,000	45,000	45,000	45,000	46,927	270,989
5. Vacant Space (5 of 5)	Auto Lease-U	35,167	36,000	36,000	36,000	36,000	37,028	216,194
Total Potential Base Rent		654,610	689,396	711,716	740,054	773,080	812,428	4,381,285
Lost Absorption / Turnover Rent								
2. Joy Placement Center	200	0	0	0	-20,502	0	0	-20,502
3. Spring Computers	300	-7,875	0	0	0	0	-18,975	-26,850
1. Vacant Space (1 of 5)	Auto Lease-U	-21,875	0	0	0	0	-8,785	-30,660
2. Vacant Space (2 of 5)	Auto Lease-U	-25,521	0	0	0	0	-8,785	-34,305
3. Vacant Space (3 of 5)	Auto Lease-U	-29,167	0	0	0	0	-8,785	-37,951
4. Vacant Space (4 of 5)	Auto Lease-U	-32,813	0	0	0	0	-8,785	-41,597
5. Vacant Space (5 of 5)	Auto Lease-U	-29,167	0	0	0	0	-7,028	-36,194
Total Lost Absorption / Turnover Rent		-146,417	0	0	-20,502	0	-61,140	-228,059
Scheduled Base Rent								
1. AB Real Estate	100	35,805	52,514	60,869	60,869	60,869	60,869	331,793
2. Joy Placement Center	200	79,789	82,182	84,648	80,984	123,011	123,011	573,625
3. Spring Computers	300	89,100	97,200	97,200	97,200	97,200	93,485	571,385
4. Richards Group	400	230,000	241,500	253,000	264,500	276,000	287,500	1,552,500
1. Vacant Space (1 of 5)	Auto Lease-U	22,500	45,000	45,000	45,000	45,000	40,069	242,569
2. Vacant Space (2 of 5)	Auto Lease-U	18,750	45,000	45,000	45,000	45,000	39,427	238,177
3. Vacant Space (3 of 5)	Auto Lease-U	15,000	45,000	45,000	45,000	45,000	38,785	233,785
4. Vacant Space (4 of 5)	Auto Lease-U	11,250	45,000	45,000	45,000	45,000	38,142	229,392
5. Vacant Space (5 of 5)	Auto Lease-U	6,000	36,000	36,000	36,000	36,000	30,000	180,000
Total Scheduled Base Rent		508,194	689,396	711,716	719,553	773,080	751,288	4,153,226

For the Years Ending	Suite	Year 1 Dec-2024	Year 2 Dec-2025	Year 3 Dec-2026	Year 4 Dec-2027	Year 5 Dec-2028	Year 6 Dec-2029	Total
Fixed Steps								
4. Richards Group	400	0	11,500	23,000	34,500	46,000	57,500	172,500
Total Fixed Steps		0	11,500	23,000	34,500	46,000	57,500	172,500
Recoveries								
1. AB Real Estate	100	1,011	986	446	700	1,375	1,251	5,768
2. Joy Placement Center	200	20,000	20,600	21,218	12,748	1,224	1,000	76,790
3. Spring Computers	300	0	3,081	3,787	4,190	5,258	422	16,739
4. Richards Group	400	98,821	111,946	114,952	116,667	121,217	120,382	683,985
1. Vacant Space (1 of 5)	Auto Lease-U	0	1,427	1,753	1,940	2,434	1,172	8,726
2. Vacant Space (2 of 5)	Auto Lease-U	0	1,427	1,753	1,940	2,434	1,367	8,921
3. Vacant Space (3 of 5)	Auto Lease-U	0	1,427	1,753	1,940	2,434	1,562	9,116
4. Vacant Space (4 of 5)	Auto Lease-U	0	1,427	1,753	1,940	2,434	1,758	9,312
5. Vacant Space (5 of 5)	Auto Lease-U	0	1,141	1,403	1,552	1,947	1,562	7,606
Total Recoveries		119,832	143,460	148,819	143,617	140,759	130,475	826,963
Tenant Income								
1. AB Real Estate	100	36,816	53,500	61,314	61,569	62,243	62,119	337,561
2. Joy Placement Center	200	99,789	102,782	105,866	93,733	124,236	124,011	650,416
3. Spring Computers	300	89,100	100,281	100,987	101,390	102,458	93,907	588,124
4. Richards Group	400	328,821	353,446	367,952	381,167	397,217	407,882	2,236,485
1. Vacant Space (1 of 5)	Auto Lease-U	22,500	46,427	46,753	46,940	47,434	41,241	251,295
2. Vacant Space (2 of 5)	Auto Lease-U	18,750	46,427	46,753	46,940	47,434	40,794	247,098
3. Vacant Space (3 of 5)	Auto Lease-U	15,000	46,427	46,753	46,940	47,434	40,347	242,901
4. Vacant Space (4 of 5)	Auto Lease-U	11,250	46,427	46,753	46,940	47,434	39,900	238,704
5. Vacant Space (5 of 5)	Auto Lease-U	6,000	37,141	37,403	37,552	37,947	31,562	187,606
Total Tenant Income		628,026	832,857	860,536	863,170	913,838	881,763	4,980,189
Tenant Improvements								
1. AB Real Estate	100	0	-17,562	0	0	0	0	-17,562
2. Joy Placement Center	200	0	0	0	-67,640	0	0	-67,640
3. Spring Computers	300	-81,000	0	0	0	0	-62,601	-143,601
4. Richards Group	400	-345,000	0	0	0	0	0	-345,000
1. Vacant Space (1 of 5)	Auto Lease-U	-37,500	0	0	0	0	-28,982	-66,482
2. Vacant Space (2 of 5)	Auto Lease-U	-37,500	0	0	0	0	-28,982	-66,482
3. Vacant Space (3 of 5)	Auto Lease-U	-37,500	0	0	0	0	-28,982	-66,482
4. Vacant Space (4 of 5)	Auto Lease-U	-37,500	0	0	0	0	-28,982	-66,482
5. Vacant Space (5 of 5)	Auto Lease-U	-30,000	0	0	0	0	0	-30,000
Total Tenant Improvements		-606,000	-17,562	0	-67,640	0	-178,528	-869,730
Leasing Commissions								
1. AB Real Estate	100	0	-9,130	0	0	0	0	-9,130
2. Joy Placement Center	200	0	0	0	-24,602	0	0	-24,602
3. Spring Computers	300	-24,300	0	0	0	0	-22,769	-47,069
4. Richards Group	400	-140,875	0	0	0	0	0	-140,875
1. Vacant Space (1 of 5)	Auto Lease-U	-11,250	0	0	0	0	-10,541	-21,791
2. Vacant Space (2 of 5)	Auto Lease-U	-11,250	0	0	0	0	-10,541	-21,791
3. Vacant Space (3 of 5)	Auto Lease-U	-11,250	0	0	0	0	-10,541	-21,791
4. Vacant Space (4 of 5)	Auto Lease-U	-11,250	0	0	0	0	-10,541	-21,791
5. Vacant Space (5 of 5)	Auto Lease-U	-9,000	0	0	0	0	0	-9,000
Total Leasing Commissions		-219,175	-9,130	0	-24,602	0	-64,935	-317,843
Market Rent								
1. AB Real Estate	100	59,675	61,465	63,912	65,829	67,804	69,838	388,524
2. Joy Placement Center	200	108,325	113,741	119,428	123,011	126,701	130,503	721,710
3. Spring Computers	300	94,500	99,225	104,186	107,312	110,531	113,847	629,601
4. Richards Group	400	345,000	362,250	380,363	391,773	403,527	415,632	2,298,545
1. Vacant Space (1 of 5)	Auto Lease-U	43,750	45,938	48,234	49,681	51,172	52,707	291,482
2. Vacant Space (2 of 5)	Auto Lease-U	43,750	45,938	48,234	49,681	51,172	52,707	291,482
3. Vacant Space (3 of 5)	Auto Lease-U	43,750	45,938	48,234	49,681	51,172	52,707	291,482
4. Vacant Space (4 of 5)	Auto Lease-U	43,750	45,938	48,234	49,681	51,172	52,707	291,482
5. Vacant Space (5 of 5)	Auto Lease-U	35,000	36,750	38,588	39,745	40,937	42,166	233,186
Total Market Rent		817,500	857,182	899,414	926,396	954,188	982,814	5,437,494

CLOSING THOUGHT

Having completed the calculations to achieve a pro forma of the property, users have a better understanding of the property. While ARGUS Enterprise provides the form and the calculations to model the property quickly and accurately, the analysis still rests squarely on the user's shoulders.

Based on the Valuation & Return Summary, a user could expect a 12.01% Unleveraged IRR and a 17.08% Leveraged IRR if they sell at the end of the 5-year analysis. If the user was looking to achieve a 15.0% return, this is doable if the debt financing is considered.

ARGUS Enterprise takes existing assumed data, base rents, reimbursement schedules, some miscellaneous income and the operating expenses of a building to generate a realistic representation of the property as it stands today. ARGUS Enterprise then takes the market assumptions and scenarios made by the user and creates a complete forecast pro forma. This consistent analytics and management tool provides data transparency for both users and investors in making informed risk and reward decisions on investment properties.

Supplemental V
Cases

CASE: WELCOME TO THE BIG LEAGUES

Introduction

You have finally arrived! Congratulations! After leaving college, you have gone on to a successful business career, and now, after 10 years of waiting, you have succeeded your mother as the head of your family's trust fund. Your grandfather and his two brothers' estates created this trust 14 years ago, when they distributed the family's assets into trusts for each branch of the family. It is now day 1 of Year 1. The current trust portfolio is shown below.

Current Trust Portfolio						
Stocks	Value	P/E	Div. Yield	Cash Flow	Bid	Ask
YPF SA ADR Oil Trading Partnership	$2,000,000	6.00x	13.62%	$272,400	$19.00	$20.00
BB&T Bank	$15,000,000	12.43x	3.35%	$502,500	$33.59	$34.00
SCS Trucking	$10,500,000	NA	0%	$0	$11.52	$11.97
Subtotal	$27,500,000		2.82%	$774,900		
Bonds	Value	Face Amount	YTM	Cash Flow	Bid	Ask
Citigroup 5-Year 5% Bonds	$9,000,000	$10,000,000	7.47%	$500,000	$90.00	$90.50
10-Year 6.5% Treasuries	$25,000,000	$24,000,000	4.48%	$1,560,000	$104.17	$104.35
5-Year Zero Coupon Treasury Strips	$5,350,000	$6,000,000	4.63%	$0	$89.17	$89.30
Subtotal	$39,350,000	$40,000,000	5.15%	$2,060,000		
Cash	$2,150,000	$2,150,000	1.25%	$26,875		
Marketable Securities Total	$69,000,000	$42,150,000	4.15%	$2,861,775		
Note Receivable	Value	Face Amount	Interest	Cash Flow	Notes	
Regency Convertible Mortgage	TBD	$70,000,000	8.00%	$5,600,000	Est. max. CF assuming no incremental participation.	

- **Marketable Securities:** The trust has a portfolio of $69 MM in stocks and bonds in primarily thinly-traded securities and cash which currently yield 4.15% per annum on a blended basis.

- **Convertible Mortgage Note:** The main asset is a $70 MM participating convertible mortgage ("Convertible Note") in a retail property by the name of Regency Mall ("Regency"), the only regional mall in Pueblecito, a metro area of 200,000 people. Twenty-three years ago, your grandfather made his name in the local real estate community developing the Regency. The subject property is a 3-anchor, 450,000-leasable square foot mall with outparcels of a tire store and three restaurants. Each anchor is 100,000 square feet and there is 150,000 square feet of in-line space. At the time the note was written, the property was valued at an 8% cap rate. Your grandfather structured a convertible participating mortgage that would give the trust a claim on 60% of the equity. As of eight years ago, the property had appreciated greatly in price and it seemed Grandpa had made a good deal. Notably, since then, a Walmart super center opened in the market and Cap rates on solid stabilized regional malls in comparable cities are 8.5-10.0%.

The details of the Convertible Note are as follows:

- o The note pays 8% per annum.
- o It is a non-amortizing mortgage due at the end of Year 6.
- o It is convertible into 60% of the equity ownership of the property at the start of Year 3.
- o If Regency's NOI (after a normal capital expenditure reserve) exceeds $10 MM, the note receives 10% of the incremental NOI over $10 MM.
- o The note is the only debt on the Regency and is a secured first mortgage which prohibits any debt or preferred equity to be placed on the property without your approval.
- o Eight years ago, the Regency was appraised at a value of $100 MM, with an NOI of $9 MM (after cap ex reserves).
- o At the end of last year, the Regency's NOI had declined to $7 MM (after cap ex reserves) and the Regency was appraised at $65 MM.
- o During Year 2, 40% of all leases will expire, with a further 20% expiring in Year 3, and 10% in Year 4.

The Trust Portfolio's Liability

When your grandfather died, your mother decided to diversify the family's portfolio into stocks and bonds. To do so, she arranged a $50 MM loan for the trust with the local bank, secured by the trust's Convertible Note on the Regency Mall. The bank loan is interest-only, matures at the end of Year 2, and bears a 9% interest rate. This bank loan contains a provision that if the appraised value of Regency Mall is less than 120% of the loan, the loan can be called at any time by the bank. In addition, the bank loan forbids any other debt being taken on by the trust so long as the loan is outstanding. The loan also has a sweep provision that allows the bank to take all trust cash inflows until the bank loan obligations are satisfied.

Market Information

- The 3-month LIBOR is 2.25%, the 5-year LIBOR is 4.5%, the 10-year LIBOR is 6.0%, and the 30-year LIBOR is 7.0%. Floating-rate mortgage spreads are between 80-125 bps.
- Short-term interest rates are expected to rise over the next few years as they are historically low.
- Having spoken with Billybob Clinton, your hometown banker, he tells you that it is unlikely that you will be able to get financing with terms similar to your $50 MM loan. He notes that currently, first mortgages require a Debt Service Coverage Ratio of at least 1.2x and a Loan-to-Value of roughly 70%, though you may be able to go beyond this.
- Two years ago, a new 220,000-square foot Walmart super center opened about 2 miles away from the subject property. The area approaching the Walmart is surrounded by several freestanding restaurants, a Best Buy, and a Bed Bath and Beyond.
- The Market occupancy rates:
  - o Class A retail is 92% occupied, with a total of 600,000 square feet of space
  - o Class B retail is 86% occupied, with a total of 1,300,000 square feet of space
  - o Class C retail is 78% occupied, with a total of 1,000,000 square feet of space.
- There are no other regional malls in Pueblecito.
- Market occupancy is expected to remain stable over the next 5 years.
- Pueblecito's residential communities will probably not grow materially in the next 5 years.

The Trustees

The principal beneficiaries of the trust are your mother (50%), your sister (25%) and yourself (25%). The beneficiaries are accustomed to total annual distributions from the trust of approximately $2-3 MM to cover their living expenses.

The Proposal

Regency's owners have approached you with concern that market conditions for Regency continue to weaken. They believe that they will be able to successfully re-lease their space as leases expire over the next few years, although at lower rents and greater concessions. The historical and their projected NOI and TIs/commissions are shown below:

Regency Mall Historical and Projected NOI, TIs and LCs		
Year	NOI *	TIs/LCs
6 Years Ago	$9,200,000	$500,000
5 Years Ago	$9,300,000	$200,000
4 Years Ago	$9,600,000	$300,000
3 Years Ago	$9,800,000	$400,000
2 Years Ago	$9,700,000	$100,000
Last Year	$7,000,000	$200,000
This Year / Year 1	**$6,800,000**	**$500,000**
Year 2	**$4,000,000**	**$3,000,000**
Year 3	**$5,000,000**	**$2,000,000**
Year 4	**$5,800,000**	**$500,000**
Year 5	**$6,000,000**	**$200,000**
Year 6	**$6,500,000**	**$200,000**

* Post-cap ex reserves, but pre-TI and LC reserves

The owners of Regency propose that they buy your note on Regency from the trust for $47 MM in cash plus a "stub" that converts into 35% equity ownership of Regency at the end of Year 6. They are willing to agree not to place more than 80% leverage on Regency prior to the end of Year 6 conversion date. The owners also would agree that prior to this conversion date they will not allow the interest coverage ratio to go beneath 1:1. You have no idea if the owners are sandbagging you, but Billybob tells you that in this market, with the new Walmart, these numbers seem to be "in the ballpark." A broker, who stands to earn a fee, says that it sounds like a great deal.

Your Task

So, are you still glad to be the head of the family trust? After leaving school you have had a successful business career but have no further real estate experience beyond having taken a real estate finance class what is now a very long time ago. You must write a business memo to your fellow trustees (the long-time family minister; the family lawyer; the President of the local bank who made the loan to the trust; your 28-year-old sister for whom the trust is her primary source of income; and your retired Mother) on how you recommend the trust proceed. The memo is not to exceed 3 pages, plus no more than 2 pages of exhibits with any charts/tables/graphs you choose to use. Welcome to the big leagues!

CASE: BUILD-TO-SUIT

Over the past 7 years you have developed 12 build-to-suit facilities for "Convenient Marts." These facilities are generally located on strip center outparcels, are roughly 11,000 SF, and completely occupied by a Convenient Marts store. These properties have all been located along the main thoroughfares of suburban Philadelphia.

The typical lease terms on these deals have been:

- A 10-year lease term
- Rent is triple net ("NNN")
- Rent has provided roughly a 350-basis point spread over the 10-year Treasury rate when the deal was signed
- A 10-year renewal option
- Convenient Marts may purchase the property (Convenient Marts has the option) at any time for "fair market value"
- Convenient Marts may purchase the property in year 10 (and year 20 if lease option is renewed) at a 10% discount to "fair market value"
- Convenient Marts has a right of first refusal ("ROFR") with respect to both lease and purchase as long as the lease is in effect.

The typical Convenient Marts store is a plain "box," and petroleum product sales are prohibited in the leases.

Over the past decade Convenient Marts has expanded in the suburban areas of the major mid-Atlantic state metropolitan areas. This publicly-traded company has been rated BBB+ (or better) for the past 7 years.

Convenient Marts has recently embarked upon an aggressive expansion campaign, targeting the suburban areas of secondary mid-Atlantic cities for new stores. As a result of this expansion effort, S&P has placed Convenient Mart's debt on a "credit watch," expressing concern that this effort may result in lower quality cash flows and an increased debt burden.

You have sold 10 of the 12 Convenient Mart stores you developed. In each case, you sold them within 18 months of completion for an average cap rate that has a spread over the 10-year Treasury of about 210 basis points. The two properties you have not sold have been completed within the past 12 months. You anticipate that these properties will each sell for a spread of about 200 basis points over the 10-year Treasury during the next year. Currently, the 10-year Treasury rate is 4.25%.

Development of a Convenient Mart requires 10-16 months to complete. Typically, it requires about 12 months to develop.

Convenient Marts has approached you and asked you to play a major development role in their expansion effort. Specifically, they have indicated that they would like you to develop stores for them in the Allentown / Bethlehem, Pennsylvania area. They plan to add about 10 stores in this region over the next 3-4 years and want you to be their developer in this effort.

Their first store site in this market is along the main suburban throughway in suburban Allentown. It is for a 10,000-SF store, with appropriate parking, ingress/egress, and signage requirements. Convenient Mart's real estate committee has approved the following non-negotiable (take it or walk) deal terms:

- 10-year lease
- 10-year renewal option
- Option to purchase at any time at "fair market value"
- Option to purchase in year 10 (and year 20 if lease in renewed) at 10% discount to "fair market value"
- Right of first refusal with respect to both lease and purchase as long as the lease is in effect
- Triple net rent lease
- Rent for the first 10 years is $50,000 annually
- Rent during the option years would be $65,000 annually
- Certificate of Occupancy must be in place within 13 months
- If the Certificate of Occupancy is not in place within 13 months, rent during the first 10 years is reduced to $40,000 annually
- If Certificate of Occupancy is not in place within 14 months, Convenient Marts is released from the lease and you must pay them a penalty of $60,000.

This project would represent your first effort outside of the Philadelphia area. You believe that you can acquire the site for $120,000. You believe that approval, planning, and design costs should run about $50,000, while hard construction costs are estimated at roughly $400,000.

You have a term sheet on a loan which provides 3-year financing of $440,000 at LIBOR plus 300 basis points. 3-Month LIBOR is currently 1.46% (a cyclical low). The loan adjusts the interest rate quarterly. The loan has no amortization and is pre-payable without penalty. You also will receive a development fee of 5% of hard costs plus approval, planning, and design soft costs.

Initial discussions with your lender and local planning officials lead you to anticipate no unusual problems with the project. The equity required for this project is available but would absorb about 30% of your equity capacity.

Should you undertake this development? You are to write a 3-page business memo to your board, with no more than 2 supplemental pages of tables/charts/graphs, explaining to them your recommendation and your rationale.

CASE: THE LONDON LOCATION CASE

You have been engaged by a large U.S. financial services firm to develop a location strategy for their new European regional headquarters. They want to locate in the London metro area. You will make a 10-minute presentation (to be followed by a question and answer period) on your location proposal to their senior managers. Questions you should address include:

- Should they choose a city or suburban location?
- Which specific location(s) do you suggest?
- Should they buy, build, or lease?
- Should they consolidate all of their facilities?
- How much space will they require?
- How should they deal with their currently leased facility?
- Are there currency exposures in your proposal, and how will they be dealt with?
- How do you propose to assign their employees within the space?
- Will your proposed strategy satisfy the technological demands of a modern financial services firm?

The client is currently in the fourth year of a 25-year lease of a 75,000-square foot building (Howell Building) in the West End of London at £65/square foot, which houses all operations, including a small trading floor. There are currently 750 employees at this site. Of these, 170 are in systems and operations, 250 are in investment and merchant banking, 300 are in sales and trading, and 30 are in the European executive office. Plans for the next several years suggest the following employment levels:

	Systems/Operations	Sales/Trading	I Banking	European Exec.
Year 1	180	300	260	32
Year 2	200	310	280	35
Year 3	250	350	325	40
Year 4	300	380	360	50

The firm wants to raise its image and visibility in Europe to a level commensurate with its presence in North America. It is also important to remember that the London office will service all of Europe, and all of its functions.

Each team should be prepared to present their recommendations, although the teams that present will be selected randomly. Each team should submit a 5-page business memo plus (up to) four supporting pages of charts/graphs/maps/tables summarizing their findings and recommendations.

CASE: THE CONDO CASE

You have slaved away for four years as an Associate in the real estate group of the prestigious investment banking group Gold in Stacks (GIS). You have been able to accumulate savings of $75,000, and your current lifestyle requires you to make a pre-tax gross income of $200,000. You have a two-year-old child and a working spouse. Secretly you have always wanted to be your own boss and to build equity with your sweat. One day while walking home you notice an old, abandoned, six-story office building that is about 30,000 gross square feet.

Intrigued by the building, you do a little homework and conclude:

- The neighborhood is solid, and is largely owner-occupied high- and mid-rise residential condominiums.
- A typical condo in the neighborhood is about 1,400 square feet and sells for $450,000-$500,000.
- You can purchase the property (inclusive of transaction costs) for $3.45 million.
- You estimate that if all goes smoothly, you can renovate the property into condos for about $3.3 million in hard and soft costs (including interest expense). The property is unlikely to support any ground-level retail.
- Construction will probably take about one year.

Based upon your knowledge of financial markets and equity joint venture deal structures, you believe that:

- You can get a combined purchase and construction loan secured by the property of 65% Loan-to-Cost, drawn down over the purchase and construction period, subject to all equity going in first.
- The loan would carry an annual interest rate of 6.8% payable monthly, accruing until cash coverage exists.
- The lender will sweep all cash inflows not required for construction and sale of units.
- The loan would be for a term of three years with no amortization.
- A private equity fund would be willing to provide the necessary equity; however, they will require you to personally invest 3% of the cash equity, which will be given a subordinated equity position.
- They will give you a 20% carried equity position on any profits the project earns in excess of an annual 11% project-level equity IRR.
- They will allow you to take a development fee of $132,000, with half paid on a pro rata basis to construction outlays, and the other half retained in a subordinated equity position. Even though half will in fact be paid out during construction, the entire $132,000 amount will be credited to you as carried equity.

Though you hate to admit it, if you undertake this project, you will have to essentially put all of your savings at risk, and also work on it full time. If you're going to take all of this risk and disrupt your predictable and stable lifestyle, you would require that the project hit a 30% gross development profit margin (sale value / total development cost − 1). This high a margin is also required to get the investor on board, as they typically do not write checks for anything less than $5 million in size.

The Assignment

- Provide a 1-page project summary (# units of each type, size, target price, when sold, total cost, etc.)
- Provide a 1-page spreadsheet showing (on a quarterly basis) the expected project cash flows
- Provide a 1-page summary of the project's unleveraged IRR, equity IRR, and your developer return
- Provide a two-page summary of what you have decided to do regarding this project (and why)
- Provide a one-page floorplan summary.

All pages should be 8.5x11 and easily readable by the investor (who wears bifocals).

CASE: THE UPZONING DECISION

Introduction

115 Arts Street (the "Artist Factory") is an existing three-story 20,000-square foot historic building located in an amenity-rich neighborhood just outside the downtown core of a major U.S. city. Under the current zoning, the property can be redeveloped another two stories into 70 residential condominiums. However, there is also a possibility of getting the parcel "upzoned" to allow for 130 units. But there are conditions for getting that extra density from the city, and it is never 100% certain that a rezoning will be successfully achieved.

Background

Donna and Terry became quick friends after meeting through a mutual acquaintance at a real estate networking event several years ago. They both worked for real estate development companies that were family businesses, but both were really entrepreneurs at heart. They eventually got fed up with working to inflate the bank accounts of these two wealthy families and decided to become business partners in a real estate development company. While it goes without saying, they named their company Modest Moguls ("MM").

After five years of successful operation, MM now has nine employees, including the two principals, and has profitably developed eight mid-size (fewer than 30 units) residential projects – all rentals, all in the close-in suburbs to the city. Each project lasted about eight to twelve months in duration and was mid-rise (6 stories or fewer) wood-frame construction.

Donna and Terry both have a keen interest in urban adaptive reuse and historic renovation projects, and crave the cachet of breathing life back into charming old buildings with the kinds of beautiful architectural details that are no longer being produced. MM had its eye on one property in particular in the city, 115 Arts Street, formerly home to an artist's workspace that produced a well-known 20th-century U.S. metals sculptor. They felt that the marketing campaign that could be tied to the history of the building could be incredibly creative and compelling, and that they could really make a splash with this as their first project in the city.

Earlier this month, MM had signed a contract to purchase the now-vacant and decrepit Artist Factory building and the land beneath it for $3.0 million (other bids also came in around that amount, but MM prevailed in the end). They put a refundable deposit down at contract signing, and are now in the 90-day due diligence period.

The Big Opportunity

Most real estate development is accomplished "by-right" or "as a matter-of-right" (also referred to as "as-of-right"). Such development projects comply with all the standards of the zoning regulations, and there is a regular permitting process managed by the jurisdiction that does not require formal public input on design or use.

An upzoning is a planning tool that can allow for developments and associated public benefits that are superior to those that would result from matter-of-right projects. The upzoning process relaxes certain limiting regulations, such as height and FAR, in return for public benefits provided by the developer. However, an upzoning involves extensive review by public bodies and neighborhood residents and other interested groups.

MM had based its $3.0 million purchase price on the property's 2.50 FAR by-right development potential of 70 residential units (which could be accomplished with wood-frame construction in conjunction with the existing structure), but recognized full well that they could possibly upzone the site in the future to the "BRD" (Bigger, Riskier Development) zoning designation, which had an FAR of 4.50. With this increased density, they could develop a total of 130 condominium units.

Based on how the land purchase and sale contract was structured, Donna and Terry knew that if they could pull off the upzoning, their land cost basis would be much lower than what it "should be" on a per-residential-unit basis for the neighborhood. The seller, a family trust, did not use a sophisticated attorney who would have structured the land cost to be a product of a per-FAR price and the ultimate density achieved on the site. With those advantageous economics, they could generate significantly higher profits than they had pitched to their investors, who had committed to providing 90% of the equity capital for the by-right project. Donna and Terry could end up becoming heroes to their investors and become pretty rich themselves, too, if they hit or exceeded pro forma returns, given the anticipated joint venture equity partnership promote structure.

The Costs

MM would have to build in concrete/steel since the building would have to be eight stories tall to accommodate the higher unit count. Additionally, they would be required to sell 7% to 9% of the residential units (they would have to negotiate) at "affordable" prices based on a government-provided pricing schedule that dealt with Area Median Incomes, or AMI (which was not negotiable). This requirement was part of the city's mandate of "inclusionary zoning," which strove to make all neighborhoods mixed-income in nature.

Inclusionary Zoning Requirements for Multi-Family Developments				
Number of Bedrooms	Occupancy Limits	Estimated Monthly Utility Allowance	Estimated Monthly Condo Fees	Maximum Purchase Price: "80% AMI" Units
Studio	1	$128	$250	$197,900
1	1-2	$175	$313	$220,800
2	2-4	$225	$425	$235,800
3	4-6	$274	$525	$285,600

And while MM initially had the sneaky idea of just making all of the Affordable-price units studios (since it was better to forfeit revenue on a smaller, lower-priced unit than on a larger, higher-priced unit), the city prevented that by requiring a ratio of Affordable unit types that was very close to the ratio of the market rate unit types in the building. The law did, however, allow for Affordable units to be 90% of the size of the corresponding market rate unit type.

From preliminary conversations with the zoning office's liaison, MM understood that they would likely also have to dedicate approximately 2,000 rentable square feet on the ground floor for a city-sponsored art exhibition space (set up legally as a commercial condominium unit within the overall building condominium regime), for which they would receive no rent. While the city would not levy real estate taxes on the commercial condominium, MM as developer, and eventually the condominium owner's association through their association fees, would have to bear the art exhibit curator's $45,000/year compensation package (which provided for 3% annual increases). MM would also be responsible for the ongoing operating expenses of the commercial condominium unit itself, which they knew would be every bit of $15 per square foot per year, naturally subject to general expense inflation.

Along these lines, Donna remembered hearing something about how condominium developers needed to also carry the costs of the individual condominium units before they were closed on by the buyers. This made sense to her, as the condo building was essentially an apartment building, and apartments have fixed operating expenses even when vacant. She thought she had it already built into the pro forma but made a note to double check the downtrending of these costs as units were closed and the per-unit costs were transferred to the new unit owners.

Additionally, if they increased the number of units in the building, they would have to build underground parking to accommodate the higher parking count requirement (they were able to get away with just surface parking otherwise). They had a nagging feeling in the back of their heads that there would be lots of "dirty dirt" from 50+ years of sculpting work, and knew that the deeper they went into the ground, the more of it they could find. While it sounded like an oxymoron, they would have to have this dirty dirt carted away at a premium cost to a "special dump."

They also would need to pre-sell significantly more units to be eligible for construction financing. Right now, they are hearing that construction lenders are requiring at least 30% of units be pre-sold (purchase and sale contracts signed, and 10% cash deposits taken and held in escrow) before the lenders would seriously consider funding a condominium project. At an assumed pre-sales rate of 7 units per month, they would be in for a much longer haul before they could break ground. A longer runway like that could potentially put them in danger of missing the hot condominium market altogether by the time they were able to deliver the larger building.

They had been over the various design and construction elements of the two scenarios with their architect and likely general contractor (with whom they would eventually negotiate a GMP, or guaranteed maximum price contract), and summarized them side-by-side, along with other key variables, for their and their investors' ease of reference.

By-Right vs. Upzoned Project Characteristics - 115 Arts Street			
		By-Right	Upzoned
Lot Square Footage		28,250 SF	28,250 SF
Maximum Allowable FAR		2.50 FAR	4.50 FAR
Allowable Above-Grade GSF		70,625 SF	127,125 SF
Stories		5 Stories	8 Stories
Art Exhibit Space Required		0 SF	2,000 SF
Building Efficiency		78.00%	81.00%
Residential Saleable SF		55,088 SF	101,351 SF
Average Residential Unit Size		787 SF	787 SF
Condominium Units		70 Units	129 Units
Affordable Units Required	7.00%	NA	10 Units
Required Parking Ratio/Unit		0.8 Spots	0.8 Spots
Surface Parking Required		56 Spots	57 Spots
Underground Parking Required		0 Spots	46 Spots
Pre-Sales Required % Total Units		30%	30%
Pre-Sales Absorption Rate		7 Per Month	7 Per Month
Regular Sales Absorption Rate		8 Per Month	8 Per Month
Pre-Construction (design/permitting) Duration		12 Months	20 Months
Construction Duration		14 Months	20 Months
Construction Type		Wood-frame	Steel/Concrete
Residential Hard Costs Per Above-Grade SF		$142 PSF	$197 PSF
Residential Construction Hard Costs		$10,000,000	$25,000,000
Construction Hard Costs - Below-Grade Parking		NA	$40,000/Spot
Land Costs		$3,000,000	$3,000,000
Soft Costs		$2,700,000	$2,700,000
Additional Upzoning Pursuit Costs		NA	$650,000
FF&E Costs		$275,000	$275,000
Financing Costs		Still Unknown	Still Unknown
Assumed Construction Loan LTC		60.00%	60.00%
Assumed Annual Interest Rate		6.00%	6.00%
Loan Front-End Fee (Funded into Reserve)		1.00%	1.00%
Loan Fees At Draws (Funded into Reserve)		0.50%	0.50%
Construction Loan Interest		Reserve funded with each draw	

The Big Risk

Pursuing the upzoning would cost Modest Moguls both time and money. There would not only be significant land use attorney's fees associated with the rezoning process, but MM would also incur various consultant's fees and additional carrying costs for property upkeep while the public hearings took place. The rezoning process would certainly delay the start of construction, likely by at least 8 months, but Donna and Terry had heard horror stories that it could drag on for as many as 14 months. On the low end, they had estimated the upzoning pursuit would cost them $650,000 in additional soft costs and carry costs, and on the high end, double that amount.

Donna and Terry knew that there was a very real chance that they could go through the entire rezoning process only to have their request for additional density rejected. At that point they would have lost time and money, and the IRR to their investors would likely drop relative to what they were pitched. It would be a lot to go through just to end up doing the 70-unit project that they already had in hand.

While they had not themselves been through the rezoning process prior to this project, MM knew it was quite detailed and could be tricky, especially when dealing with a potentially prickly community that was known to value the status quo, mid-rise nature of their neighborhood.

Blue Screen of Death

Just as Terry was making the final adjustments to the by-right scenario pro-forma for the upzone scenario, his computer crashed, giving him the dreaded Blue Screen of Death.

```
*** STOP: 0x00000404 (0x00000000,0x12345678,0x69696969,0x97f86a65)
PAGE_NOT_FOUND*** ADDRESS 09034672 has base at 09037000 - abort

CPUID:GenuineIntel  Pentium  Irql:1f    SYSVER: 0xf0096404

Dll Base DateStmp   Name                  Dll Base DateStmp   Name
80100000 336546ff - ntoskrnl.exe          80010000 331054d1 - iexplore.exe
80037386 33104f49 - atapi.sys             80070000 3341a4d9 - outlook.exe
88013faa 33107s98 - epsy.sys              8021bf09 3342ab4f - disk.sys
80037389 3310354d - CLASS2.SYS            80102848 334013fb - NTice.sys
80037390 3310098d - Siwvid.sys            f95cb000 3340101f - Ntfs.sys
800ae122 3310h896 - Floppy.sys            f1035800 336735af - Parport.sys
800bf392 33100f89 - KSecDD.sys            f031fde0 34dc3ccf - Beep.sys
801cca04 3310h854 - i8042prt.sys          f95cb000 3340101f - mouclass.sys
80037398 331034fg - kbdclass.sys          f3e3b000 33104f49 - ctrl2cap.sys
80037399 3310f987 - VIDEOPORT.SYS         f42cb000 3340101f - msfs.sys
80037400 3310g653 - vga.sys               f63cb640 3340101f - iexplore.exe
80037401 33106g89 - npfs.sys

Address    dword dump    Build [1381]                      - Name
c0948732 3340101f 8021bf09 80037391 12345678 80037401 80a0b00f - Ntfs.sys
80948732 80070000 80037386 12345678 8021bf09 1c005638 df00eabf - rnl.exe

Restart and set the recovery options in the system control panel
or the /CRASHDEBUG system start option.  If this message reappears,
Contact your system administrator or technical support group.
```

The machine then spontaneously combusted, melting instantly into a pile of smoldering noxious plastic. The timing could not have been worse! He and Donna had to present the alternatives and their decision to their investors (and potentially request more equity from their investors for the upzone scenario) on Monday, and it was Thursday night already.

To compound matters, Terry had never followed through on backing up his files to Dropbox, even though he had promised Donna that he would. He had a printout, though, of the by-right scenario.

115 Arts Street - By-Right Scenario

BUILDING INFORMATION

Project Name	115 Arts Street - By-Right Scenario	
Lot Square Footage	28,250 SF	
Allowable FAR	2.5 FAR	
Total Above-Grade Gross SF	70,625 GSF	
Stories	5 Stories	Art Exhibit Space
Residual Gross Square Feet of Residential	70,625 GSF	0 GSF

		Total
Saleable Square Feet of Residential	78.0% Efficiency	55,088 SSF
Residential Units *		70 Units
See Unit Mix and Pricing Tab		**Average SF** 787 SF
Surface Parking	0.8 spots per unit	56 Spaces
Underground Parking		0 Spaces

PROJECT TIMING AND SALES VELOCITY ASSUMPTIONS

	Value	Value	Month #	Date
Analysis/Due Diligence Start Date			Mo. 1	6/1/2018
Date of Land Contract Execution				6/1/2018
Land Deposit Date				6/1/2018
Due Diligence Find/Land Closing Date	3 Months			9/1/2018
# Months of Pre-Construction After Analysis Start	12 Months			
# of Months of Pre-sale Closings	2 Months			
Construction Duration/Construction Start	14 Months		Mo. 13	7/1/19
Pre-Sales Begin			**Mo. 7**	**12/1/18**
Pre-Sales Duration/End Month	3 Months		Mo. 9	2/1/19
Pre-Sale % Sold/Velocity/# Units **30%**	*8.00 Units/Mo.*	*24 Units*		
Market Sales Velocity/Begin	8 Units/Month		Mo. 24	
First C of O Received / First Closings	2 month lead time		Mo. 24	5/1/20
Sales Through the Month Prior to First C of O	34% Total	24 Units		
Sales Duration/Velocity	*17 Months*	*1/Month*		
Final C of O Received/End of Construction			Mo. 26	7/1/20
First Move-Ins			Mo. 24	5/1/20
Sales After First C of O	70% Total	46 Units		
Sales Duration/Velocity	*7 Months*	*6.57/Month*		
Market Sales Velocity/Completion Timing		7.67/Month	Mo. 30	11/1/20
Sell Out # Months from First C of O / Total Sell Out Period	7 Months	31 Months		

DEVELOPMENT USES OF FUNDS

		% Total	$/Unit	$/GSF	Total
Land Acquisition Costs	5.00% Deposit	16.72%	$42,857	$42.48	$3,000,000
Total Hard Costs		62.67%	$160,643	$159.22	$11,245,000
Residential Hard Costs	*$142,857/unit*		$142,857	$141.59	$10,000,000
Retail Hard Costs			$0	$0.00	$0
Owner Hard Costs	$0/Unit Premium		$0	$0.00	$0
Hard Costs Contingency	10.00%*		$14,286	$14.16	$1,000,000
FF&E			$3,500	$3.47	$245,000
Total Soft Costs and Fees	28.46% of Hard Costs	17.83%	$45,714	$45.31	$3,200,000
Soft Costs			$38,571	$38.23	$2,700,000
Developer Fee	3.00%*		$4,286	$4.25	$300,000
CM Fee (Developer)	2.00%*		$2,857	$2.83	$200,000
Financing Costs excl. any Operating Deficit		2.78%	$7,116	$7.05	$498,125
Total Uses of Funds					$17,943,125
Operating Deficit (Funded by Equity)					$0
Total Uses of Funds with Operating Def.		100.00%	$256,330	$254.06	$17,943,125
of Base Building Hard Costs					

DEVELOPMENT SOURCES OF FUNDS

		% of Total	Initial	Share of any	% of	Total Equity
		Equity	Investment	Deficits *	Cost	w/Deficits
Equity		10.00%				
Sponsor/Developer			$722,000	$13,200		$735,200
Third Party Investor		90.00%	$6,500,000	$118,840		$6,618,840
Equity Total		100.00%	$7,222,000	$132,040	40.99%	$7,354,040
Debt	7/1/2019					Total
Senior Loan **	6.0% Rate				58.87%	$10,563,194
Mortgage Recording Tax	1.25%					
Loan Fees - Front End	1.00%					
Loan Fees - At Draws	0.50%					
				Property Cash Flow	0.14%	$25,891
			Total Sources of Funds		100.00%	$17,943,126

* Operating Deficit and Financing-related Deficits

** Loan amount includes capitalized interest and capitalized points/fees

115 Arts Street - By-Right Scenario

RESIDENTIAL COMPONENT REVENUES

Residential Units	Units	Average Price		Average SF
Pre-Sales	24 Units	$344,250	$434 PSF	787 SSF
Regular Sales	46 Units	$366,743	$466 PSF	787 SSF
Total	**70 Units**			

Revenue				Amount
Residential Units Excluding Options	Deposit Amount	10.00%		$25,672,000
Options Income, net	Pre-Sales Discount	10.00%		$350,000
Parking	55 Spaces	$5,000/Unit	$40,000	$2,240,000
Gross Revenues				**$28,262,000**
Selling Costs		6.00%		($1,695,720)
Total Residential Component Revenues, Net				**$26,566,280**

RETAIL COMPONENT OPERATING EXPENSES

BUILDING OPERATING ASSUMPTIONS

Annual Inflation Rate for Operating Expenses/Deficit	3.00%
Annual Operating Expenses/Unit after First C of O	$5,000
Real Estate Taxes on Residential Units	
Average Assessed Value At Delivery	$250,000
Tax Rate	1.27%
Annual Real Estate Taxes/Unit after First C of O	$3,175

INVESTMENT RETURNS*

	Sponsor/	Third Party	Total Project
Equity Investment	$722,000	$6,500,000	$7,222,000
Net Return on Equity			$8,593,312
Multiple on Equity			2.19x
Internal Rate of Return	20.00%		59.82%
Net Present Value			$4,025,051
Profit Margin			30.41%

Calculated off of monthly cash flows.

Unit Mix and Pricing (Today's Prices)
115 Arts Street - By-Right Scenario

Market Rate Condominium Units

	Average Unit Size	Total # of Units	Share of Units	PRE-SALES UNITS				REGULAR SALES UNITS				MARKET RATE
				30% of Total Unit Count								
				10% Pre-Sales Discount								
				Pre-Sales Price/Unit	Price PSF	# of Pre-Sale Units	Gross Sales	Regular Sale Price/Unit	Price PSF	Regular Sale # of Units	Gross Sales	Gross Sales
Studio	525 SF	18.0	25.71%	$229,500	$437	6.0	$1,377,000	$255,000	$486	12.0	$3,060,000	$4,437,000
1 Bed / 1 Bath	675 SF	18.0	25.71%	$292,500	$433	6.0	$1,755,000	$325,000	$481	12.0	$3,900,000	$5,655,000
2 Bed / 2 Bath	875 SF	17.0	24.29%	$382,500	$437	6.0	$2,295,000	$425,000	$486	11.0	$4,675,000	$6,970,000
3 Bed / 2 Bath + Den	1,095 SF	17.0	24.29%	$472,500	$432	6.0	$2,835,000	$525,000	$480	11.0	$5,775,000	$8,610,000
		70.0	100.00%	Average $344,250	Average $434 PSF	24.0	$8,262,000	Average $378,478	Average $483 PSF	46.0	$17,410,000	$25,672,000
						34% of units						

Total SSF 55,088 SF
Average Unit Size 787 SF
Average Pricing $366,743
Average Pricing PSF $466 PSF

It was going to be a long weekend, but they were passionate about this deal, and were going forward with it one way or another. Plus, they reasoned, diving deep into the pro-forma analyses would allow them a final opportunity to test their convictions with respect to their assumptions. In true entrepreneurial fashion, they turned on the coffee maker, ordered some pizza, and got to work.

The Assignment

Put yourself in Donna and Terry's shoes. You need to compare and contrast the results of pursuing the two alternative densities (with appropriate sensitivity analyses for each scenario) such that you can make a decision as to which one to choose. Then write up an Investment Committee memo recommending pursuing one scenario or the other, backed up by your quantitative and qualitative analyses. **To be clear:** Donna and Terry are going forward with the development. You must take a side as to which path they should pursue, and detail why.

Assignment Deliverables

- Two-page Investment Committee Memo in a Word file, which includes the following returns metrics:
    o IRR based on the monthly cash flows
    o NPV based on the monthly cash flows
    o Multiple on Equity (how many times all equity is returned to all equity holders in aggregate)
    o Profit (Net Cash Flow)
    o Profit Margin (Net Cash Flow / Gross Sales Proceeds)
- Up to two additional pages of Exhibits pasted as images into the Word file
- A Gantt chart of the project timeline for the Upzone Scenario from Time 0 on January 1st through the closing on the final residential unit. The Gantt chart should have all of these activities, each of which has a start milestone month number, a duration in months, and an end milestone month number:
    o Pre-Construction
    o Pre-Sales
    o GMP Bidding
    o Construction
    o Market Sales

The information for the By-Right scenario is shown below:

115 Arts Street - By-Right Scenario
Total projection duration: 40 mos.

	Start Month #	Duration (months)	End Month #
Pre-Construction	1	12	12
Pre-Sales	7	3	9
GMP Bidding	10	1	10
Construction	13	14	26
Market Sales	24	17	40

Guidance

- For Parking Hard Costs, assume that the surface parking Hard Costs in the By-Right scenario are included in the "Residential Hard Costs" line item.
- For the Underground Parking Hard Costs in the Upzone scenario, you can put those into the Retail Hard Costs line (and relabel the line). Assume there is no difference in cost between 2,000 SF of lobby and the 2,000 SF of art exhibit space, so there is nothing to change on that front with respect to Hard Costs.
- For the Unit Mix for the Upzone scenario, assume that the market rate unit types, sizes and ratio of unit types to one another remain the same as is the case in the By-Right project, and also that pre-sales in the Upzone scenario occur at the same ratio as they do in the By-Right project.
- In the Upzone scenario, be sure that you are not leaving any saleable square footage on the table, i.e., that your total Saleable SF = Efficiency * GSF.

Assume that MM will contribute 10% of all equity invested.

You can run sensitivity analyses around some or all of the following variables:

- Hard Costs
- Sales Prices
- Upzoning Approvals Duration
- Upzoning Approvals Budget
- Pre-Sales Absorption Rate
- Market Sales Absorption Rate

Make sure that any sensitivity analyses you run are indeed producing valid outputs given changes made to the inputs.

THE UPZONING CASE: WORKING WITH MACROS IN MICROSOFT EXCEL

The By-Right Scenario Pro-Forma Excel file for The Upzoning Case is a "Macro-enabled file," meaning there is a "Macro," or small computer program contained in the file that automates a series of actions when you initiate the Macro. Excel files that contain Macros have the file extension ".xlsm" as opposed to ".xls" or ".xlsx".

In this case, there are actually three Macros contained in the file.

Two of the Macros simply set the Print Area on the Assumptions Input tab to either be the left-hand page or the right-hand page. We have "attached" these two Macros to their respective gray buttons on the top of the Assumptions Input tab.

The third Macro, attached to the square button near cell P43, adjusts the Senior Construction Loan size when the Uses of Funds (project costs) and Sources of Funds (project funding sources, of which the Construction loan is one) fall out of balance with one another. It does this by running the Goal Seek function to change the size of the Senior Loan in cell O34 until the check in cell P41 between Total Uses and Sources of Funds is equal to 0 (meaning total uses and sources of funds are equal to one another).

Macros are powerful and can be big time-savers, but they are inherently fragile, so you might need to "fix" the Adjust Senior Loan Macro if you make changes to the grid on the Assumptions Input tab in the course of doing the Upzoning analysis.

Instructions for launching the Excel file properly, and an example issue and solution are below.

To Launch the file properly: When you launch the file, if prompted by Excel, be sure to click "**Enable Content**" in the Security Warning ribbon that appears. This enables the Macros to run.

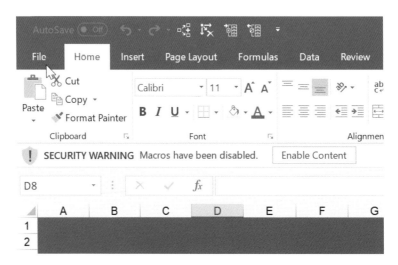

Example Problem and Solution

Problem: "I added the extra costs in the Assumptions Input tab and had to fix the errors in the S & U tab and everything checked out OK. I am now stuck at the Development Sources of Funds box on the Assumptions Input tab because I added a few extra rows - the Senior Loan Check is off/negative and the button to adjust the loan now has an error when I click it. How do I fix that?"

Solution:

FOLLOW THESE INSTRUCTIONS CAREFULLY
- Close ALL other Excel files open on your computer
- Click on the **View** tab in the Microsoft ribbon at the top
- Click on Macros > View Macros

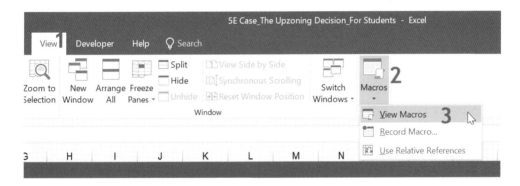

- In the dialog box that has appeared, click on SeniorLoan_Adjust and then click the Edit button on the right sidebar of the dialog box

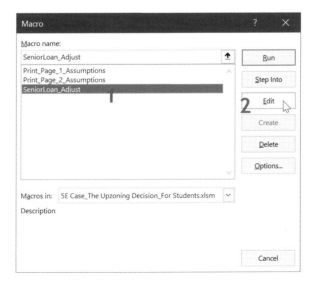

- A crazy-looking Microsoft Visual Basic for Applications screen will launch on top of your Excel file

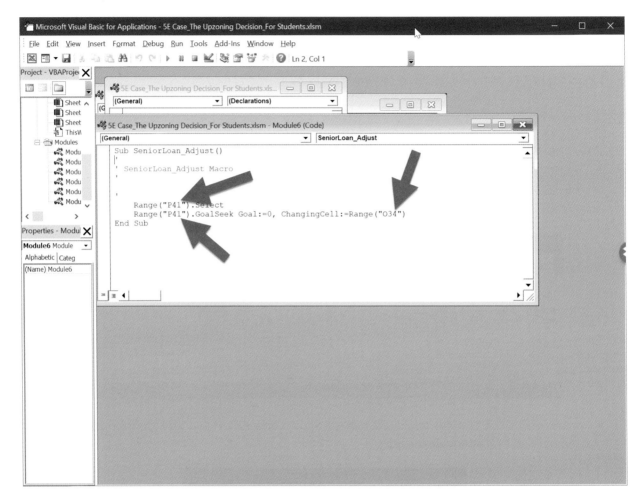

- In the floating box on that says "Sub SeniorLoan_Adjust( )", in its top line, change the cell coordinates in the quotation marks to those cells that now apply given the new set of grid coordinates on your Assumptions Input tab. For instance, if your Senior Loan check amount (cell P41 in the original version of the model) is now P42, replace P41 with P42 (in both instances where it is referenced in the Visual Basic window)

  Do the same for the Senior Loan amount (which was cell O34 in the original version of the model).

- Click the Save icon in the Visual Basic window (the little floppy disk icon), or hit Ctrl+S
- Then X out of the Visual Basic window in the top-right of the window.

Now click the Adjust Senior Loan button again and it should work fine.

INDEX

1

1980s 79, 95, 123
1990s 266, 267, 298, 307, 308

3

30/360 226

A

absolute priority rule 209
accommodation fee 360
accrual construction loan 191, 393
accrued interest...393
accumulated depreciation 258
Actual/360 226
Actual/365 226
additional rent 46
Adjusted Funds from Operations (AFFO) 200
adjusted NOI 68, 122
AEW 269
after-tax cash flow 74
agglomeration economies 106
Alfred Taubman 52
amortization 232, 384
amortization schedule 232, 239, 386
anchor..18
anchored..18
ancillary income.............................57, 60, 90, 180
Angelo Gordon...269
annuity factor 386
Apollo 269
appraisal 227
appurtenant easement 99
assessed tax value 59, 62
asset management 33
assumption of loan 102
assumptions..85

B

bad debt 61
balloon payment......................................232, 386
bankruptcy..33, 54, 101, 171, 172, 199, 207, 208, 209, 210, 412, 414, 416
base rent...46, 58
base rent escalations 46
base year 47
before-tax levered cash flow 74, 75
Black-Scholes 175
Blackstone..269
British property companies 199
brokerage commissions 95

brownfield 17
bulk warehouses 23
bullet loan 384, 387
bullet payment 384

C

CAM billings 59
CAM costs 59, 62
Canary Wharf 209
cap rate .38, 39, 40, 68, 79, 95, 97, 120, 121, 122, 123, 124, 125, 126, 127, 130, 131, 132, 134, 135, 136, 137, 138, 139, 141, 145, 146, 148, 149, 151, 163, 164, 178, 201, 202, 204, 205, 218, 219, 220, 221, 252, 253, 279, 282, 283, 286, 289, 291, 372, 375, 400, 401, 407, 408, 409, 410, 442, 445
cap rate valuation 120, 121
capital and leasing costs.............................. 67
capital appreciation. 213, 214, 215, 219, 220, 221, 222, 223
capital asset pricing model (CAPM)............................. 145
capital call 267
capital costs... 48
capital cycle 352
capital depreciation 221
capital expenditure reserves.................... 67, 102
capital expenditures (cap ex) 68, 70, 76, 194, 197
capital gains taxes .. 205, 234, 258, 260, 262, 299, 300, 301, 307
capital items 67
capital structure 212, 214, 216
capitalized interest.................................... 393
Carlyle 269
carried interest... 269
Cash Available for Distribution (CAD)............................. 200
cash flow cap rate 130
cash flow distribution waterfall 269, 285
cash flow return 213, 218, 402
cash out refinancing 176
cash sweep... 233
cash-on-cash yield 219
catch-up 278, 285
C-corporations... 302
central business district (CBD)........................ 24
Cerberus.. 269
certificate of occupancy (C of O) 169
chaebols 38
Chapter 11 bankruptcy.......................... 207, 208
Chapter 7 bankruptcy.............................. 207
chevron 24
Class A 24, 25
Class B 24, 25
Class C 24
claw-back 278
clear height 22
climate-controlled.................................. 29

CMBS 211
Colony 269
Commercial Mortgage Backed Security (CMBS) 238, 239, 240, 243, 245, 248, 412, 416, 417, 418
common area maintenance (CAM)................. 20, 47, 59, 64
common areas 47
community retail center 19
comparables (comps) 97
compound return 365
compounded annual growth rate (CAGR).....................215
compounding...365
condominiums 25, 165, 171
conduit loan..412
constant amortization loan...............................392
construction loan.................................... 191, 393
contingency reserve 190
convertible debt 222
corporate general and administrative (G&A) expense ...194
cost amortization...77
cost recoveries..45, 59
cost segregation analysis 73
co-tenancy clause 53
cram down rule...209
credit loss...61
Crow Holdings..269
cure loan delinquency 206
currency hedge 43
currency risk 38, 43
current-pay interest...393

D

debt financing...74
debt service 2, 3, 4, 55, 75, 98, 206, 207, 213, 219, 235, 384
debt service coverage ratio (DSCR)... 90, 228, 412, 415, 418
debt service expense 75, 90, 197
debt yield 227
debtor in possession (DIP) financing...............................208
defeasance...236
deficiency claim 209
demographic analysis 103
depreciable life 71
depreciable value 71
depreciation...70, 71
depreciation schedule 73, 258, 262, 266
development feasibility analysis.....................................178
development overhead 168
direct vacant space 25
discount factor...367
discount rate 123, 367
discounted 371
discounted cash flow analysis (DCF) .. 2, 120, 121, 122, 123, 125, 201, 202, 251, 252, 371, 372, 374, 375, 376
disposition (sale)... 95, 258
distressed loan investor.....................................207
distributions.. 229, 270

double taxation 302, 304
downtown shops.. 20
draw request 231, 393
dropped ceilings 22
due diligence 98

E

easement 99
EBITDA.. 197, 201
economic occupancy.. 33
effective rent per gross square foot..................... 180, 181
effective rent per leasable square foot 180
efficiency 30
eligible loan cost 227
encumbered 99
equitization 140
equity IRR 381
equity multiple 84, 164, 267, 283, 294, 314
equity REIT 298
equity value 371
estoppel certificate 98
excess loan proceeds 234
exit cap rate 95
expansion rights 51
expense caps 47
expense reimbursements.................................... 59
expense stop 47
extended stay hotel 28

F

fee simple ownership interest. 249, 250, 251, 252, 253, 254
financial modeling 84
fixed charges ratio... 228
fixed operating expenses 45, 90
fixed rate loan 226
fixed-rate fusion pool... 412
flex building 22
floating rate loan 226
floor area ratio (FAR)................................... 31, 186
floorplates 24, 25, 30
foreclosure 141, 207, 209, 210, 217, 228, 249, 250, 416
free rent 33, 48, 49, 88
FSI (Floor Space Index) 31
full service hotel 28
fully-amortizing loan 386
fund general partner 267
fund limited partner 267
funded interest reserve....................................... 393
Funds Available for Distribution (FAD) 200
Funds from Operations (FFO)................................ 134, 200
future value............................ 364, 365, 366, 367, 369, 370

G

Germany 248
going dark 50, 101
going-in cap rate 95, 173
going-out cap rate 95, 173
Goldman Sachs 268
Gordon Model 123, 125, 127, 136, 251, 375
greenfield...17
gross absorption 347
gross development profit margin 174
gross income..61
gross potential rental revenue 56, 57
gross sales price 95
gross sales proceeds 258
gross square footage (GSF)........................30
ground lease 249
guarantees.................................... 100, 173, 231, 237, 331

H

hard cost...168
heavy manufacturing 22
highrise...24
hotels 28, 132, 412
hurdle rate 269
HVAC................................... 24, 47, 48, 100, 192, 321, 322
hybrid amortization schedule 392
hybrid REIT..298

I

impairments 197
income multiple analysis 120
income tax liability......................................70
income tax shield (tax shield) 70, 71, 72, 79, 211, 222, 266, 306, 323, 326, 389
infill..17
inline store..18
installment sale...102
insurance 47, 62, 64, 232
interest accrual..168
interest coverage ratio 228
interest rate floor 226
interest-only loan 384
interim income 167
internal rate of return (IRR) 378
investment banks 177, 240, 268, 303, 305
investment commitment 267
investment vehicles 279
IPO (initial public offering)...........................265, 299, 305
issuer 412, 416, 417, 418, 420

J

Japan... 27, 123, 220, 321

K

junior creditor 207
junior debt...222
JW O'Connor 269

K

key performance indicators (KPIs) 84
Kmart..18, 414

L

labor unions 102
land cost..................................... 168, 185
land purchase option 168
landlord concessions...................................88
Latin America 39
LBO funds 269
leases 45, 230
leasing commissions (LCs) 68
Lehman Brothers.......................................412
lessee 45
lessor 45
letter of credit 54
leverage...211
levered cash flow 74
levered IRR 381
LIBOR.. 244, 412, 417
lien 99
light assembly 22
like-kind exchange......................................307
limited service hotel....................................28
liquidity 3
loan acceleration 229
loan constant 232
loan covenants 229
loan default..206
loan delinquency..206
loan draws 231
loan maturity..384
loan modification 206
loan points 74, 75, 233
loan pool 240, 243, 412, 414, 417
loan principal 384
loan restructuring.......................................206
loan term................................... 226, 384
loan terms 231
Loan-to-Cost (LTC)......................................227
Loan-to-Value (LTV).. 75, 223, 227, 228, 239, 244, 254, 260, 262, 267, 299, 381, 391, 412, 418
local partners 42
lock-out clause 229
Lonestar 269
look-back 273
loss carry-forward 78
loss factor....................................30, 178, 192, 322
Lubert-Adler 269

M

margin call 357
market research.. 7
merchant builder 176, 302
mezzanine finance 222, 223, 417
midrise 25
midrise apartments 27
millage rate.. 62
minority interest.................................... 198, 262
Morgan Stanley.................................... 177, 268
mortgage constant 386
mortgage REIT 298
multifamily..26
multiple on equity 84
multiple on invested capital 84

N

NAREIT 397, 398, 400, 401, 402, 403
natural disaster...3
NCREIF 397, 398, 400, 401, 402, 403
negative amortization loan.................... 168, 393
negative covenants.......................................229
negative leverage 218, 219
net absorption 347
Net Asset Value (NAV) 202, 203, 204, 205
net base rental revenue................................57
net effective rent 49
net leasable square footage (LSF)...................30
net lease 49
net operating income (noi) 66
net operating income (NOI)................ 57, 66, 163, 407
net present value (NPV)...................... 174, 377
net rent................................... 49, 220, 361
net sales price 95
net sales proceeds 95
new value exception.....................................209
NOI after normal reserves 68
non-climate controlled 29
noncombined affiliates 197
non-compete clause 53
non-performing loan (NPL).............................206
non-recourse 210, 212, 222, 231, 298, 323
non-reimbursable expenses 63
non-stabilized property 95
normalized reserves 122

O

Oaktree..269
occupancy..33
office..24
open plan...347
operating expenses........................... 2, 62, 102
opportunity funds...266

origination costs... 75
origination fees 233
outparcel 19
overage 46, 58

P

pari passu 269
parking 53
participating debt... 222
pass-through entity 75
pass-throughs.. 59
pay rate 417
pay requisition 232
pension funds.............. 222, 239, 240, 243, 267, 269, 298
percentage rents 46, 53, 58
perpetuity 123
physical occupancy...................................... 33
positive amortization 386
positive covenants 229, 230
positive leverage 218, 220, 383
possible maximum loss (PML).......................... 100
power center.. 20
preferred equity 222
preferred return (pref) 269
pre-lease 171
prepayment penalty..................................... 229
pre-sale 171
present value 364, 367
private equity funds 199, 222, 266, 267, 400, 401, 402, 403
pro forma 10, 13, 52, 55, 60, 70, 83, 98, 102, 103, 112, 165,
   168, 174, 193, 194, 196, 218, 219, 221, 240, 254, 324,
   347, 350, 361, 393, 450, 451
promote .. 269, 270, 280, 281, 282, 283, 285, 286, 289, 291
property design 192
property line... 17
property management 64
property market fundamentals..................... 130, 137
property tax billings 59, 62
property tax reassessment........................... 102
property taxes 47, 62
property title search.................................... 99
property-level IRR 379
purchase cap rate.. 95
put option 231

Q

qualified intermediary (QI)........................... 264
quantitative easing...................................... 352

R

radius restriction 53
rate cap 226
rating agencies 243, 244

real estate cycles 344, 347
real estate owned (REO) 207, 416
Realpoint 418
receivables 231
recourse 54, 231
recoverable expenses 59
recovered expenses 59
refinancing 234, 260
regional mall 20
reimbursable expenses 62
REIT . 256, 298, 302, 303, 304, 306, 307, 308, 398, 399, 400, 401, 402
REIT implied cap rates 126
release price 171
rent 46
rent abatement 48
rentable square footage (RSF) 30
rental growth 4
replacement cost 122, 123
replacement rent 182
replacement reserves 67, 91
residential mortgage-backed securities (RMBS) 355
residual 95
residual land valuation 185
residual split 270
residual value. 14, 43, 94, 145, 201, 214, 216, 220, 398, 410
retail 58, 171, 322
return on cost 173
reversion value 95, 372
rezoning 168
risk premium 126, 136, 169, 319, 374
risk-adjusted 364
Rockefeller Center 209, 258
run rate 191
Russian ruble crisis 132

S

S&P 243, 398, 399
secondary equity offering 302
secured lender 208, 209, 223, 227, 231, 237
securitization 243
security deposit 54, 88, 231
security interest 99
sensitivity analysis 57
September 11th 102, 219, 232
setback restriction 31
short sale 206
signage 50
single taxation 298
soft costs 168, 190
special servicer 243, 412, 416
special-purpose-bankruptcy remote entity (SPE) 240
speculative (spec) 165, 352
speculative homebuyers 355
sponsor 267

stabilized NOI . 121, 122, 123, 135, 137, 138, 139, 173, 372, 375
stabilized property 57, 95, 121, 122, 136, 163, 262, 408
stacking plan 33
stand-alone center 18
Starwood 269
strip retail center (strip center) 18
subleasing 25
sublet rights 51
subprime 354
suburban garden apartments 26, 27
suburban office buildings 25
superflat floors 22
Superfund Law 100
sweep 233
syndicate 266
synthetic lease 331

T

target return 183
tax liability 75
tax lot 17
taxable income 71, 75, 212, 222, 302, 314, 331
tenant improvements (TIs) 48, 67
tenant mix 53
tenant reimbursements 45, 59
tenant turnover 57
terminal value 2, 4, 201, 251, 252, 372, 374, 375
TI allowance 48, 67
Time 0 364
time value of money 49, 260, 364, 371
title 17
title survey 99
total annual return 219
total operating income 61
total rental income 58
total returns to equity 213
trade area analysis 103
tranche 243, 416
tranching 243
trending rents 183
Trepp 418
triple net (NNN) lease 49

U

unanchored 18
underwriting 227
unencumbered 99
unlevered cash flow 68, 75, 76, 371
unlevered IRR 379
unsecured debt 209
unsecured deficiency claim 210
UPREIT 141, 301, 307
utilities 2, 47, 64, 90

V

vacancy 2, 33, 57, 89
value engineering 189
variable operating expenses.......................45, 90
variable rate loan...226

W

Walmart...18
Walton Street 269
warehouse 22, 23, 322
wealth position 259
weighted average cost of capital (WACC)......................223
Westbrook 269

Western Europe 39, 40
work letter 232
WorldCom 130

Y

yield maintenance... 236
yield on cost 173, 181

Z

Zell-Merrill fund 267
zero-amortization loan................................. 384